WITHDRAWN

THIRD EDITION

The Modern Family

ROBERT F. WINCH
NORTHWESTERN UNIVERSITY

Holt, Rinehart and Winston, Inc.

NEW YORK · CHICAGO · SAN FRANCISCO · ATLANTA
DALLAS · MONTREAL · TORONTO · LONDON · SYDNEY

To Martie

Copyright 1952, Copyright © 1963, 1971 by Holt, Rinehart and Winston, Inc.
All rights reserved
Library of Congress Catalog Card Number: 73-148031

SBN: 03-079675-X

Printed in the United States of America
1 2 3 4   038   9 8 7 6 5 4 3 2 1

Preface

The two purposes of this book are to present a general theory of the family and to utilize this theory in an analysis of the family in the United States. The general theory of the family is both sociological and sociopsychological. The family as a social system and the determinants of its structure and functions are the foci of sociological analysis. Such considerations lead into the concepts and principles of general sociology and to a view of the family as a social system with respect to which the general theory is applied. The sociological level of analysis is explicit in Chapter 1 and is conspicuous in Parts One through Four. The interpersonal relations of family members, the effects of members on each other and the pressures they experience from extrafamilial systems necessitate analysis at the level of social psychology. This is especially evident in Parts Five and Six. Of course both levels of analysis permeate the entire book.

The sociological analysis of the family is much more thorough and more developed in the second and third editions than in the first. The point of view is structural-functional. To the writer the essence of this point of view is that the social structure of the system defines the social roles and positions of those individuals to whom the actor is related; social functions denote the content of meaningful interaction.

Personality viewed as a product of social interaction involves analysis at the level of social psychology. As compared with the first edition, the social psychology employed herein is somewhat less Freudian. It continues to make use of what the writer views as Freud's major contribution—his emphasis on unconscious motivation—but it moves away from what the writer views as an increasingly dubious premise: that adult behavior and personality are to be explained as the generalized residue of infantile experiences. The first edition, moreover, used a homeostatic model of man, that is, that the wellspring of all human activity was physicochemical imbalance and that all behavior could be viewed as merely an effort to restore the Nirvanalike condition of homeostatic balance. The writings of Gordon Allport and Robert W. White and of Ernest Schachtel and Abraham Maslow throw this premise into doubt.

In the first edition the writer gladly acknowledged his intellectual debt to his teachers at the University of Chicago: W. F. Ogburn, S. A. Stouffer, L. L. Thurstone, Ellsworth Faris, and especially Ernest W. Burgess. It is sad to note that since its publication they have died.

To a considerable degree the difference between the second and third editions and the first one is a consequence of subsequent interaction with colleagues at Northwestern University, especially with the members of the Department of Sociology. Over the years there has been a profitable traffic in ideas and criticism. Although we lack the ideational isotope tracers to give credit to individual colleagues for specific ideas, the writer expresses his sincere appreciation of their stimulation.

R. F. W.

Contents

Preface   iii

Figures   xv

Tables   xvi

PART ONE   Introduction   1

1. Family and Society: *a bit of general sociology*   3

Introduction   3
Basic Societal Functions   5
Function as a Janus-Faced Concept   13
Functions, Core Relationships, and Structures   14
Institution   16
How the Theory Works   16
Corollaries of Function and Structure   19
Derived Function of Emotional Gratification: Corollary of the structure of the nuclear family   19
Derived Function of Position-Conferring: Corollary of the nuclear family's basic function   20
The Derived Parental Functions: Corollary of the nuclear family's basic function   21
Individual-Serving Functions as Rewards   21
A Functional Analysis of the Relation between Family and Society   23
When Does the Family Exist? Our Structural-Functional View   25
The Family as Cause and as Effect   27
Summary   29

2. A Family of Great Functionality: *the peasantry of traditional China*	30
Purpose of Chapters 2 and 3	30
The Peasant Family in Traditional China	31
The economic function	34
The political function	35
The socializing-educational function	36
The religious function	36
Summary and conclusions concerning the basic societal functions	36
The familial functions and mate-selection	37
Marital relations and filial obligations	39
China and the Industrial Revolution	41
The peasant family and the Industrial Revolution	43
The Chinese Family and the Communist Revolution	45
Some Conclusions about China	49
3. A Family of Little Functionality: *a kibbutz*	51
The Family in a Kibbutz (in Israel)	51
Historical Background	51
Kibbutzim in General	53
Kiryat Yedidim	54
The economic function	58
The political function	58
The socializing-educational function	59
The religious function	60
Mate-selection	61
The Kibbutz Family and Social Change	62
The Product of the Socializing-Educational and Parental Functions	64
Summary and Conclusions of Chapters 2 and 3	67
PART TWO The Family in America and Its Functional Matrix	71
4. The Economic and Political Functions	77
Purpose of This Chapter	77
Points of Emphasis	77
The Family as an Economic Unit	78
Economic organization of the early American farm family	79
Economic self-sufficiency and interdependence of family members	80
The coming of the machine age	81
Employment of children and women	83
The economic contribution of the modern housewife	86
Categorical employability	88
Dependence, independence, and interdependence	91
Recent trends in the maintenance of dependents	92
Relation of welfare programs to family stability	93
The Political Function and Family Type	94

Contents vii

    Power in the nuclear family   98
    Summary and Conclusions   99

5. **The Socializing-Educational and Religious Functions**   101

    Purpose of This Chapter   101
    Points of Emphasis   102
    The Nature of Socialization   104
    The Nature of Education   104
        The school   106
        Shifts in educational emphasis   108
        The "whole child" and the school   109
        The school in the status system   114
        Socialization and the media of mass communication   116
    The Religious Function   119
        The constant and the variable in the folk-urban transition   120
        Stress and theology   121
        Religion in America   122
        Secularization and functional equivalents   125
        The religious function and the family   128
    Functions and Societal Complexity   129

6. **Suburbia:** *the family's response to the loss of functions*   132

    Introduction   132
    The Suburb: New classes in an old pattern   135
    Points of Emphasis   137
    The Economic Function   138
    The Political Function   142
    The Socializing-Educational Function   146
    The Religious Function   148
    Summary and Conclusions   149

PART THREE   Basic and Derived Functions of the Family   151

7. **The Function of Replacement:** *urbanization, industrialization and the birth rate*   153

    Reproduction and the Family   153
    Points of Emphasis   154
    American Fertility from the Latter Part of the Eighteenth Century to the Present   156
        Description   156
        Analysis of the American scene in the seventeenth and eighteenth centuries   159
        The downward trend in fertility: 1800–1936   162
        The cycle in fertility since 1936   167
        Urban-rural differentials in fertility   169
        Socioeconomic status and differential fertility   171

Race and differential fertility	172
Religion and differential fertility	173
Some Additional Remarks on Societal Organization and Culture	178
Societal and Familial Organization	179
Culture	181
Instrumental Factors	182
Avoidance of intercourse	183
Avoidance of conception	184
Avoidance of complete gestation	185
Infanticide	187
Artificial insemination	187
Summary	188

8. Position Conferring: *functional corollary of the family's basic societal function* — 191

Introduction	191
Points of Emphasis	192
Social Position at Birth: Legitimacy and illegitimacy	193
Adoption	198
Inheritance	200
The Ascription of Race, Ethnicity, and Religion	203
The Concept of Stratification	205
Subcultures of Social Classes	208
The subculture of the level below the common man	209
The subculture of the class of the common man	210
Subcultures of strata above the common man	211
Some class differences in criteria of status	213
Qualifications regarding the subcultures of social classes	213
How the Family Confers Positions and Provides Status-Orientation	215
Stability and mobility: permanence and impermanence of statuses conferred by the family of orientation	223
Status-Conferring by Other Structures in Adulthood	227
Society-Oriented and Family-Oriented Statuses: Age and sex categories	228
The status of the child	229
The statuses of women	230
Statuses of the aged	232
Summary	233

9. Emotional Gratification: *functional corollary of the family's structure* — 236

Introduction	236
Purpose of This Chapter	239
Security and Insecurity	239
Physical security	240
Psychic security	240
Status-security and status-insecurity	242
Interpersonal security	244
Ways of alleviating psychic insecurity outside the family	245

Gratification and the Third View of Man	246
Parenthood	246
Rewards of parenthood	247
Penalties of parenthood	249
Personality and parenthood	250
Relative gratifications of childless and parental marriages	254
Summary of This Chapter	256
Summary of Parts Two and Three	257

PART FOUR Elements in the Structure of American Family Forms — 259

10. Mate-Selection and the Field of Eligibles — 261

Purpose of This Chapter	261
Principle of Incest Avoidance	262
Principle of Ethnocentric Preference	262
Field of Eligibles Resulting from the Two Principles	263
Two Types of Mate-Selection	264
Familial Functionality and the Type of Mate-Selection	264
Field of Eligibles and Method of Choice	266
Mate-Selection in America	266
Residential Propinquity as a Factor in Mate-Selection	269
Dimensions of Ethnocentric Preference	270
Race	270
Religioethnic identity	272
Socioeconomic status	280
Age	282
Previous marital status	284
Residential Segregation, Ethnocentric Preference, and the Field of Eligibles	285
Age at Marriage Related to Other Variables	289
Mate-Finding	293
Summary	294

11. Familial Structure and the Composition of American Families — 296

Purpose of This Chapter	296
The Range of Familial Structure	296
Determinants of Familial Structure	297
Structure of the American Domestic Family (or Familial Household)	298
Recent Confusion about the Structure of the American Family	298
Some Findings about the Structure of the American Family	299
Some Types of American Family Structure	302
Is This Typology Exhaustive?	304
Conclusions and Summary	305

12. Role-Differentiation and Role-Strain — 307

Introduction — 307
Points of Emphasis — 307
Position, Status, Role, and the Differentiation of Roles — 308
The Division of Labor and the Differentiation of Roles — 309
Conditions Affecting the Differentiation of Roles — 310
The Differentiation of Sex and Age Roles in Primitive Societies — 311
Activities Affecting Role-Differentiation in the Family — 312
The Parental Function and the Content of the Paternal and Maternal Roles — 312
Familial Role-Differentiation Associated with Sex Differences in Ability — 314
Tasks, Abilities, and Sex-Role Differentiation — 315
Women in the Labor Force — 317
Positions and Role-Differentiation in the American Family — 319
The Woman's Dilemma — 326
Housework and Child Rearing — 333
Marital Roles and Domestic Power — 334
Familial Roles and Role-Strain — 336
Conformity or Hypocrisy? Role versus Personality — 338
Summary and Conclusions — 340

PART FIVE Parental Functions and Intergenerational Relations: the first phase of the affectional cycle — 345

13. The Nurturant Function and the Infant — 351

Introduction — 351
Parenthood and Culture — 352
The Biophysical Basis of Activity — 354
What Is Nurturance? — 355
  Some studies bearing on the narrow conception of nurturance — 356
  Some studies bearing on the broad conception of nurturance — 357
  Some negative views — 359
Reactive Outrage — 360
Where Do We Stand? Agnosticism or Synthesis? — 361
The Maternal Role as the Biosocial Basis of Infantile Love — 361
Summary — 363

14. Rearing by the Book — 364

Introduction — 364
Examples of Advice Giving — 364
Breakdown of Tradition and Demand for Advice — 366
Advice Giving — 367
  Sunley on the nineteenth century — 367
  Stendler on "Sixty Years of Child Training Practices" — 367
  Wolfenstein on "Infant-Care" — 369
Child Rearing and Original Nature: The Puritan and more recent views — 372

	The Traditional and the New Developmental Points of View	375
	The New-New View	376
	The Present Status of Family-Life Education	378
	Attempts to Assess Effectiveness of Education for Family Life	379
	How Scientific Have Been the Advice Givers?	380
	Summary	384
15.	**Nurturance, Control, and Parent-Child Relations**	385
	Purpose of This Chapter	385
	Points of Emphasis	385
	The Key Skills of Childhood	386
	Changing Needs and Parental Functions	386
	Internalization of Discipline: Development of conscience	388
	Development of Goals: The ideal self	391
	Lasting Effects of Parental Control: Identification	391
	Culture, Subculture, and the Content of Learning	393
	Subculture, the Position-Conferring Function, and the Child's Test of "Reality"	398
	Social Class and Child Rearing	400
	Correlates in Children's Responses of Some Variations in Familial Structure and Functions	404
	Parents' Experiences	411
	Parenthood as a Value	413
	The Individual Child	414
	Summary	415
16.	**The Adolescent and the Fusion of the Parental Functions**	418
	Purpose of This Chapter	418
	Points of Emphasis	418
	Ambiguity of Adolescence in American Society	419
	Some Problems of the Adolescent as an Individual	422
	Developmental Tasks of Adolescence in the Middle Class	423
	The "success" imperative	423
	The sex-type imperative	424
	Some Sources of and Reactions to Adolescent Conflict in the Middle Class	428
	The Parent of the Adolescent	430
	Conflict between Adolescent and Parents	432
	Is Adolescence Necessarily a Period of "Storm and Stress"?	434
	Orienting the Adolescent to the Adult System	436
	Resources and the Relative Influence of Parents and Other Adults on Adolescents	437
	Summary	438
17.	**The Adult and His Parents**	440
	Purpose of This Chapter	440
	Adulthood, Independence, and the Parental Functions	440
	Rewards and Penalties	441

Social class	441
The period of young adulthood	443
The middle years	444
The aged	445
The Adult Offspring and the Family Cycle	446
The offspring's feelings about the parents	447
The view from the parents' side	450
Grandparenthood	451
Retirement	452
Disengagement	455
Nurturance and three stages of grandparenthood	455
Is the grandparental generation isolated?	456
Contact between the parental and grandparental generations	457
Dependency in the older generation and filial responsibility	462
The mother-daughter dyad in intergenerational contacts	465
Aged without Offspring: Improvisations of child-surrogates	466
Familism, Extraversion, and Anomia	466
Summary	468

PART SIX Love, Mate-Selection, and the Marital Relationship: the second phase of the affectional cycle   471

18. A Need-Based Theory of Love and a Theory of Mate-Selection Based on Complementary Needs   473

Introduction: The old mystery—the new problem	473
Points of Emphasis	473
A Theory of Love	474
Previous discussions relevant to the present chapter	475
Behavior arises from needs	475
Motivation may be unconscious	478
Love is based on needs	479
Socialization and the need for acceptance	479
Love defined	482
Ambivalent love and "infatuation"	484
Differences among groups and among individuals in the concept of love	485
Identification and the organization of needs	485
Needs, cultures, and congeniality groups	486
Homogamy and the field of eligibles	486
The theory of complementary needs in mate-selection	487
The status of the theory	489
The case of Bill and Mary Carter	496
Some implications of the theory of complementary needs	502
Supplementary Agencies of Mate-Selection: Lonely hearts clubs	505
Summary	507

Contents　xiii

19. Sex, Romance, and Love　508

    The Confusing Relation between Love and Sex　508
    Points of Emphasis　508
    Love and Sex in Some Non-Western Societies　509
    Sex in Western History　511
    Sex in Sweden　513
    Sex in American Society　513
    Socialization in Attitudes toward Sex in the American Middle Class　518
    Some Principles concerning the Fusion of Love and Sex　521
    Sex Practices under the Assumption of Completely Effective and Harmless Contraception: The basis of a sexual revolution　525
    Summary　527

20. Dating, Courtship, and Engagement　528

    Introduction　528
    Points of Emphasis　528
    What Is Dating?　529
    The Functions of Dating　530
    Cultural and Psychic Definitions of the Ideal Mate　532
    Cultural Definition Not Necessarily a Lifelong Ideal　536
    The Increasing Commitments of the Dating-Engagement Continuum　538
    A Few Data on Incidence of Broken Relationships and Reactions Thereto　539
    Engagement and Its Functions　539
    Summary and Conclusions　540

21. Marriage　544

    Introduction　544
    The Nature and Structure of Marriage　544
    The Married and the Unmarried　546
    The Functions of Marriage　547
    Adjustment in Marriage　550
        Role-adjustment and psychic adjustment　551
        Subroles as criteria of marital performance　551
        Sources of difficulty in role-adjustment　552
        Psychic (or emotional) adjustment　556
        Changing roles and need-patterns and the marital relationship　560
        Measuring and predicting marital adjustment　565
    Summary　569

PART SEVEN　Familial Disorganization and Reorganization: concluding observations　571

22. Marital Dissolution: *types, trends, and causes*　573

    Introduction　573
    Types of Marital Dissolution　574

The Legal Concept of Divorce in the United States	575
Trends in Marital Dissolution in the United States	580
Causes of Marital Dissolution	583
Other Correlates of Divorce in the United States: Early Marriages	599
Summary	603

23. Consequences of, and Responses to, Marital Dissolution: *remarriage* — 605

Introduction	605
Points of Emphasis	605
The Nuclear Family and Marital Dissolution	606
American Family Structure and Marital Dissolution	607
The economic function	609
The socializing-educational function	611
Other basic societal functions	612
The position-conferring function and role-adjustment to marital dissolution	612
The function of emotional gratification and the emotional response to marital dissolution	615
Remarriage	618
Summary	620

24. Concluding Observations: *value positions and familial organization* — 622

Introduction	622
Purpose of This Chapter	623
What is Familial Disorganization?	624
Familial disorganization as moral evaluation	624
Familial disorganization as loss of consensus about roles	627
Familial disorganization as reduction in the number of familial positions	628
Familial disorganization as loss of functionality	631
Societies without Families?	632
And So?	634
Name Index	637
Subject Index	646

Figures

7.1	Birth Rates by Live-Birth Orders of Native White Women, United States: 1920 to 1965	160
7.2	Fertility Rate and Percent of Rural and Urban Population by Censal Years, United States: 1800–1960	169
12.1	Percent of Labor Force Participation by Married Persons Whose Spouses Are Present, by Sex and by Age: March 1958	320
12.2	Percent of Labor Force Participation by Persons Who Are Single and of "Other" Marital Status, by Sex and by Age: March 1958	321
V.1	Percent Distribution of the Age Composition of the Population of the United States, for Selected Age Categories: 1890–1968	348
14.1	The Watsonian View	383
14.2	The Ribble-Spitz View	383
14.3	The "Reconciliation"	383
22.1	Divorces per 1000 Population by Five-Year Intervals: United States, 1860–1864 to 1950–1954, and Selected European Countries, 1900–1904 to 1950–1954	581
22.2	Marital Dissolutions by Death (1860–1963) and Divorce (Including Annulments) (1860–1965) per 1000 Existing Marriages, United States	583
22.3	Percent of Ever-Married Males 25–34 Years of Age Who Were Separated, Divorced, or Had Been Married More Than Once at the Time of the 1960 Census, by Income and Race	594
22.4	Percentage of Those Ever Married Who Were Divorced, Separated, or Had Been Married More Than Once at the Time of the 1960 Census, by Education (Age 14 and Over)	595
22.5	Percentage of Those Ever Married Who Were Divorced, Separated, or Had Been Married More Than Once at the Time of the 1960 Census, by Occupation (Ages 25–34)	596

Tables

1.1	Basic Concepts and Their Definitions	6–12
1.2	Proposed List of Basic Societal Structures: Defined in Terms of Associated Basic Societal Functions and Core Relationships and Presented with Inferred Individual-Oriented Functions	16–17
4.1	Distribution of the U.S. Labor Force by Sex: 1890, 1900, 1920, 1930, 1940, 1950, 1960, and 1970	86
4.2	(A) Number and (B) Percent Distribution of Females (14 Years of Age and Over) in Labor Force by Marital Status and (C) Percent of Each Marital Status in Labor Force: 1890, 1940, 1950, 1960, and 1969	87
5.1	Mean Annual Income for Males 25 Years Old and Over and Total Lifetime Income for Males from Age 18 to Death, by Years of School Completed: 1968	115
5.2	Use of Media of Mass Communication by Children of Selected Grades in School: San Francisco, 1958–1960	117
6.1	Some Characteristics of the Populations of Central Cities and of Suburban Rings of Standard Metropolitan Statistical Areas of the United States, 1968	136
7.1	Percent Childless among Women Ever Married, by Age of Woman: United States, 1910 to 1969	159
7.2	Number of Children Ever Born per 1000 Women Aged 15–44 Ever Married, by Selected Characteristics: 1969	170
7.3	Number of Children Ever Born per 1000 Married Women Aged 40–44, by Family Income: 1960	172
7.4	Crude Rates of Birth, Death, and Natural Increase and Net Reproduction Rates for Whites and Nonwhites, 1905–1910, 1930–1935, 1935–1940, 1940, 1945, 1947, 1950, 1952, 1960, 1966; and Proportion Childless among Women Ever Married, White and Nonwhite, 1910, 1940, 1950, 1960, 1966	174
7.5	Number of Children Ever Born per 1000 Women by Age Category and Religious Affiliation: 1957	176
8.1	Percent Distribution by Educational Level of Persons 16–24 Years Old, by Family Income and by Father's Education, for the United States: October 1960	217
8.2	Median Level of School Completed by Employed Males 25–64 Years Old, by Major Occupational Group, 1969; and Median Earnings of Year-Round Full-Time Workers, by Occupational Group and by Sex, 1968: United States	218
10.1	Permutations of Preferential Mating and Arrangement of Marriage	267
10.2	Percent Distribution of Persons 14 Years Old and Over, by Marital Status and Sex, Standardized for Age and Unstandardized, for the United States, 1960 to 1969, and for Coterminous United States, 1890 to 1955	268

xvi

10.3	Number of Total Marriages and Interracial Marriages in Selected States of the Marriage-Registration Area, and Percentage Distribution of Interracial Marriages by Race of Bride and Groom, 1963	271
10.4	Percentage Distribution of Religion Reported for Persons 14 Years Old and Over, by Sex, for the United States: Civilian Population, March 1957	273
10.5	Theoretical Percentages of Religious Intermarriage, Assuming Random Mate-Selections, with Marginal Totals Based on Columns 2 and 4 of Table 10.4	274
10.6	Comparison of Theoretical (Random) Mating (Diagonals from Table 10.5) with Actual Mating (from Table 10.7)	275
10.7	Percentage Distribution of Married Couples by Religion Reported for the United States: Civilian Population, March 1957	276
10.8	Percent Catholic of the Total Population and Percent Mixed Marriages, by Regions of the United States, 1955	278
10.9	Rental Areas and Percentage of Catholic Marriages That Are Mixed	279
10.10	Percentage Distribution of Marriages Classified by Occupational Category of Husband's Father and Wife's Father: United States, 1962	282
10.11	Percent Distribution of Couples with First Marriages between January 1947 and June 1954, by Years of School Completed by Husband and by Wife	283
10.12	Percentage Distribution of Marriages by Age of Bride, by Age of Groom: Marriage-Registration Area of the United States, 1961	284
10.13	Specified Age of Husband or of Wife by Median Age of Spouse at First Marriage of Both, for Couples Who Married between January 1947 and June 1954	285
10.14	Percent Distribution of Difference between Ages of Husband and Wife, for Couples with Marriages between January 1947 and June 1954	286
10.15	Percent Distribution of Marriages by Previous Marital Status of Bride and Groom, for the Marriage-Registration Area: 1961	286
10.16	Median Age at First Marriage, by Sex, for the United States, 1890 to 1969	289
10.17	Percent of American Population 15–19 and 20–24 Years of Age Ever Married, by Color and Sex: 1890–1966	291
11.1	Percentage Distribution of Familial Status, by Sex, for the United States, 1966	300
11.2	Percentage Distribution of the Composition of American Households, March 1967	301
12.1	Labor-Force Participation Rates of Wives (16 Years of Age and Over with Husband Present), by Income of Husband in 1966 and Presence and Ages of Children, March 1967	317
12.2	Labor-Force Participation Rates of Mothers, by Marital Status and Age of Children, March 1967	318
12.3	Labor-Force Participation Rates of Women (18 Years of Age and Over), by Educational Attainment and Marital Status, March 1968	319
12.4	Familial Positions Resulting from Generation and Sex Categories in (a) Stem Family of the Traditional Chinese Peasantry, (b) American Middle-Class Family, and (c) Kibbutz Family	322
12.5	Percentage Distribution of Arrangements of Working Mothers for the Care of Their Children under 14 Years of Age, by Ages of Children, 1965	332
V.1	Median Age of Women at Selected Stages of the Family Life Cycle, for Women Born from 1880 to 1939, by Year of Birth	347

15.1	Kohlberg's Formulation of Levels and Types of Moral Judgment and of Corresponding Motivations	389
17.1	Median Ages of Ego's Parents at Time of Their Marriage, at Time of Ego's Birth, and at Various Points in the Establishment and Development of Ego's Family of Procreation: by Sex and Birth Order of Ego, Based on Rates Prevailing around 1965–1970	448–449
17.2	Labor-Force Status, Males 65 and Over, by Type of Community, April 1952	453
17.3	Percentage Distribution of Males 65 and Over in Labor Force and Voluntarily and Involuntarily Retired, by Occupation Engaged in for Longest Time, April 1952	454
17.4	Percent Distribution of the U.S. Population by Marital Status, by Age and Sex: March 1968	458–459
18.1	Percentage Distribution of Characteristics Requested in Prospective Mates by Members of a Lonely Hearts Club, by Sex	506
19.1	Technological, Social Structural, and Psychocultural Factors Believed to Enter into a Disposition to Fuse or to Dissociate Love and Sex: for the American Middle Class in the Victorian and Post–World War II Periods and Projected Two Generations into the Future	526
22.1	Number of Males 14 Years of Age and Older Who Were Ever Married and Who Were Divorced, by Occupational Categories of the United States Civilian Labor Force: 1950	590
22.2	Number of Males 14 Years of Age and Over Divorced and Separated per 1000 Ever Married, by Race and by Income Received in 1949: United States, 1950	591
22.3	Number of Persons 25 Years of Age and Over Divorced and Separated per 1000 Ever Married, by Sex and Race and by Level of Education: United States, 1950	593
22.4	Percentage Distribution of Ever-Married Persons Aged 14 Years and Older, by Present Marital Status, Presence or Absence of Spouse, Single or Multiple Marriages, Sex, Area of Residence, and Color: United States, 1960	597
23.1	Hypotheses about the Remaining Person's Emotional Reaction to the Other's Departure as a Consequence of the Circumstances of the Departure	617
24.1	Composition of "Approximate Households" in the United States: 1800, 1940, and 1967	629

PART ONE

Introduction

Since the purpose of this book is the sociological analysis of a pattern of human association known as the family, we begin in Chapter 1 with some concepts from general sociology and then show their application to the family. Structure and function are the two key concepts, and of these we shall make greater use of function and of its cognate, functionality.

Someone has spoken of anthropology as the zoo of mankind. The educational value of a zoo is that it acquaints us with the range of variation in the forms of animal life. If he has never visited the zoo, the contemporary urban child may well grow up thinking that man and the creatures visible in animated cartoons constitute the gamut of the animal kingdom. Similarly there is a likelihood that the student who has lived in just one society and knows just one culture—indeed has lived in just one stratum of that society and knows just one subculture—will presume that the form of the family with which he is acquainted is *the* family, wherever found. The literature of anthropology, or more properly of ethnography, is the specific treatment for this parochialism.

Family forms may vary in numerous ways—the size and location of households, the methods of selecting mates, the transfer of property that occurs at marriage and at death, the ways in which kinship is reckoned and names are given, and so on and so on. To keep our consideration of the ethnographic literature from degenerating into a mere preoccupation with curiosa we shall focus on our two key concepts: social structure and social function. In Chapter 2 we shall take up the traditional family of the Chinese peasantry, which was largely self-sufficient and multifunctional, and whose structure included three generations. In the following chapter we shall view an Israeli kibbutz wherein the household contains only one generation and the family is so reduced in function that by some definitions it doesn't even exist. These two descriptions will anchor our conceptions of the observable range of functionality of the family.

1

Family and Society:
a bit of general sociology

Introduction

The family, we are often told, is breaking down. Those who propagate this view usually look for evidence to one of two familial relationships: the *marital*, where the divorce rate is presented as evidence of familial disintegration; or the *parent-child*, where the exuberance, excesses, delinquencies, and crimes of the child are interpreted as indicating either the parent's avoidance of his responsibility or the deterioration of the parent's authority.

The writer of such excited prose seems usually to have in the back of his mind a family standard by which the modern type is judged to be riding to hell in a basket if it doesn't undergo centrifugal disintegration first. Virtually never explicit, this idealized standard appears to be the Victorian family on its best behavior and exuding solidarity as it rides the belled sleigh to grandmother's house for Thanksgiving dinner.

There are important sociologists who view the modern family in a manner that is roughly similar to that just noted. This kind of writing seeks normally to provide explanation rather than to assign blame, and hence the prose may seem to substitute the objective monotone for the indignant cadence. This similarity is "rough" because about the only point of convergence is the conclusion that the modern family is less completely organized than were certain earlier forms of the family. Over a generation ago William F. Ogburn took a look at certain services that the family provided for its members. Distinguishing six such family functions, Ogburn found that five were being largely transferred from the family to outside agencies. These, he said, were the economic, protective, recreational, educational, and religious functions. Examples of the states of affairs to which Ogburn was pointing were these: (1) an increasing proportion of the meals of family members was being eaten in restaurants rather than at home; (2) an increasing proportion of their laundry was being done commercially; (3) responsibility was being transferred from home to school for increasing portions of the child's education; and (4) from home to church for the child's religious instruction. The sixth family function distinguished by Ogburn was the affectional. This function, he said, was still centered in the family, and the "future stability of the family will depend . . . [largely] . . . on the strength of the affectional bonds."[1]

E. W. Burgess and H. J. Locke have used the phrase "from institution to companionship" to denote the trend in the loss of functions other than the affectional.[2] Carle Zimmerman has taken somewhat the same theme, has placed it in the context of Western history, and has emerged with a cyclical interpretation of civilizations. He has distinguished three kinds of family organization on the basis of their influence over the behavior of individual members. From the most highly influential (and organized) to the least his rubrics are the trustee, the domestic, and the atomistic forms of the family. According to Zimmerman, the atomistic form, which has little influence and function, characterizes the late or decadent phase of such civilizations as the Athenian, the Roman and our own.[3]

Where Ogburn speaks of the transfer of all the family's functions except the affectional, Talcott Parsons expresses a similar idea by asserting that "the family, on the 'macroscopic' levels, [has become] almost completely functionless." Accordingly, "the functions of the family in a highly differentiated society are not to be interpreted as functions directly on behalf of the society, but on behalf of personality." Then Parsons goes on to break down the remaining function, which Ogburn called affectional, into one aspect involving the parent-child relationship and another aspect concerning the marital relationship. In his phrasing these relate respectively to (1) "the primary socialization of children so that they can truly become members of the society into which they have been born" and (2) "the stabilization of the adult personalities of the population of the society."[4]

From the standpoint of the sociologist the family is a *social system* located in the larger, more comprehensive, and more complex organization that he calls *society*.[5] Because of this and because the sociologist talks about the

---

[1] William F. Ogburn, "The Changing Family," *Publications of the American Sociological Society*, 23: 124–133 (1929); "The Changing Functions of the Family," in Robert F. Winch and Louis Wolf Goodman (eds.), *Selected Studies in Marriage and the Family* (3d ed.; New York: Holt, Rinehart and Winston, Inc., 1968), pp. 58–63; the quotation is from "The Family and Its Functions," in President's Research Committee on Social Trends, *Recent Social Trends* (New York: McGraw-Hill, 1933), p. 708.

[2] E. W. Burgess and H. J. Locke, *The Family: From Institution to Companionship* (New York: American Book, 1945, 1953, and 1963). Other writers object to the phrase since they dispute the implication that the family has ceased to be institutionalized. See, e.g., Talcott Parsons and Robert F. Bales, *Family, Socialization and Interaction Process* (New York: Free Press, 1955), p. 17.

[3] Carle C. Zimmerman, *Family and Civilization* (New York: Harper & Row, 1947).

[4] Parsons and Bales, *op. cit.*, pp. 16–17.

[5] In the formulation of Talcott Parsons a social system consists of "two or more actors

passing of functions from the family to other systems or structures of society, it seems advisable to begin our study of the family by presenting a conceptual scheme that will enable us to analyze societies in general. This will involve a consideration of such concepts as *function, structure,* and *institution* and such related terms as *position, status,* and *role.* Since these terms will constitute the working vocabulary of the book, it is crucially important that the writer and the reader use them with a common meaning. To this end Table 1.1 is presented for the reader's reference. It is believed that the definitions in Table 1.1 conform quite closely to other sociologists' views of the concepts defined, but as the reader moves from one writer to another, it is advisable that he check definitions in order to avoid confusion. Figuratively speaking, these concepts will constitute spectacles through which we shall be able to peer intelligently into any given societal context and to see the family in relation to the rest of that society.

(In explaining, illustrating, and elaborating principles we shall speak of persons and individuals as actors, as occupants of positions, as incumbents of roles, and so on. Moreover, we shall occasionally make use of such hypothetical actors as Mr. Smith *et al.*, as A and B, and as ego and alter. Concerning the last pair, please note that the reader is asked to view himself as the occupant of the place [whether position, status, office, station, or role] of ego and to regard alter as the incumbent of the position, status, office, station, or role to whom ego's action is directed.)

Basic Societal Functions

Various writers have begun their theorizing about the nature of society by asserting that certain things must be done in order for the society to continue in being.[6] These "things" have been called "functional prerequisites of

occupying differentiated statuses or positions and performing differentiated roles, some organized pattern governing the relationships of the members and describing their rights and obligations with respect to one another, and some set of common norms or values, together with various types of shared cultural objects and symbols. Parsons postulates [that social systems] are boundary-maintaining, in the sense that there tends to be a tighter, more integrated organization among the components of the system, while it is operating as such, than there is between these components and elements outside the system. And . . . he also postulates an equilibrium tendency: indeed, unless the system has built-in mechanisms which function to hold it in some sort of steady state over a period of time, it is hardly worth designating as a system at all. . . . The defining properties of social systems are thus conceived [by Parsons] as differentiation, organization, boundary maintenance, and equilibrium tendency."—Edward C. Devereux, Jr., "Parsons' Sociological Theory," in Max Black (ed.), *The Social Theories of Talcott Parsons: A Critical Examination* (Englewood Cliffs, N.J.: Prentice-Hall, 1961), pp. 1–63. Quotation is from pp. 26–27. Cf. also Talcott Parsons, *The Social System* (New York: Free Press, 1951), esp. chap. 1; and "An Outline of the Social System," in Talcott Parsons *et al.* (eds.), *Theories of Society: Foundations of Modern Sociological Theory* (New York: Free Press, 1961), I, 30–79.

[6] W. G. Sumner and A. G. Keller, *The Science of Society* (4 vols.; New Haven, Conn.:

TABLE 1.1 Basic Concepts and Their Definitions

CONCEPT	DEFINITION	COMMENT
Group (or *social group*) and *relationship*	Two or more persons who interact with each other in terms of a set of shared symbols and with respect to some common activity which may or may not be task-oriented and who interact with each other long enough to recognize each other and to react to each other in a patterned (i.e., repetitive) fashion *are* a *group* (or *social group*) and are *in* a *relationship*.	*Group* emphasizes the view of the actors as a collectivity. *Relationship* emphasizes the interaction and its patterning, as well as each actor's expectations concerning his own behavior and the behavior of the other actors in the group (orientation to future behavior) and the evaluative assessment of such behavior (orientation to present and past behavior).
System (or *social system*)	A social group with two or more differentiated social positions.	Some systems contain others and/or are contained by other systems. Thus we speak of the familial system as containing the mother-daughter subsystem. A recurring problem in conceptualizing interaction in terms of a system concerns the location of the system's boundaries. Another recurring question is whether to regard the system as "open" or "closed." If the changes in the state of the system can be accounted for without reference to extrasystemic influences, it is feasible to regard the system as "closed"; otherwise, not. Of course a familial system is routinely regarded as a subsystem within the societal system. "Social position" is defined below.
Society (or *societal system*)	A social system which survives its original members, replaces them through biological reproduction, and is relatively self-sufficient.	
Role (or *social role*)	"A part of a social position consisting of a more or less integrated or related sub-set of social norms which is distinguishable from other [subsets] of norms forming the same position."—Frederick L.	Within the structure of the family Mr. Smith's *position* includes the *roles* of husband and of father; within the business firm his *position* includes the *roles* of supervisor and of employee. A position may be

TABLE 1.1 (Continued)

CONCEPT	DEFINITION	COMMENT
	Bates, "Position, Role, and Status: A Reformulation of Concepts," *Social Forces,* 34: 313–321 (1956), at p. 314.	viewed as a role-set, which is defined by Robert K. Merton as "that complement of role-relationships in which persons are involved by virtue of occupying a particular social status."—"The Role-Set: Problems in Sociological Theory," *British Journal of Sociology,* 8: 106–120 (1957), at p. 110. A role may be *active* or *latent.* It is active when it is "being played by an actor at any given moment." Otherwise it is latent.—Bates, "Position, Role and Status," *loc. cit.,* p. 320.
Subset of norms (or of *social norms* or of *role-expectations*)	An evaluative standard concerning the performance associated with a role, i.e., without regard to the individual who may be occupying the role at any given time.	Related is the discussion of sanctions and role sectors in Neal Gross, Ward S. Mason, and Alexander W. McEarchern, *Explorations in Role Analysis* (New York: Wiley, 1958), pp. 62–67. "What are sanctions to ego are role-expectations to alter and vice versa."—Talcott Parsons, *The Social System* (New York: Free Press, 1951), p. 38.
Role-performance	The behavior that an actor manifests while acting out a role, whether or not this behavior conforms to the norms.	See the above comment on "role."
Position (or *social position*)	"A location in a social structure which is associated with a set of social norms."—Bates, "Position, Role, and Status," *loc. cit.,* p. 314.	*Social structure* is more inclusive than *institutional structure.* Mr. Smith's positions in the social structure include one in his poker club. As the definition of the latter of these terms implies, Mr. Smith's positions in the institutional structure include his place in his family, business firm, and church. (*Social structure* and *institutional structure* are defined below.)

TABLE 1.1 (Continued)

CONCEPT	DEFINITION	COMMENT
Status (or *social status*)	*Position* plus the connotation of invidious evaluation, differential prestige, and hierarchy.	To facilitate communication the writer will use *status* rather than *position* when it is desired to emphasize considerations of prestige, hierarchy, and the like.
Office	"A position in a deliberately created organization, governed by specific and limited rules in a limited group, more generally achieved than ascribed."—Kingsley Davis, *Human Society* (New York: Macmillan, 1948), pp 88–89.	Simply stated, we use a common noun to denote a *position* and a proper noun to denote an *office*. Mr. Smith's *position* is in the middle echelon of management in a business firm; his *office* is Purchasing Officer of the XYZ Corp. On the achieved-ascribed distinction see page 21 below.
Station	A cluster of positions combined in a single individual.	Mr. Smith is a husband and father, a middle-level executive, a member of a poker club, and so on. Let us speak of Mr. Smith's situation with respect to all these relationships, viewed simultaneously, as a station. The term is borrowed from Kingsley Davis and defined with similar intent but different phrasing.—Davis, *op. cit.*, p. 92.
Social structure	A social system viewed as a network of social roles and positions.	
Core relationship	Two or more differentiated social roles, the occupants of which interact with each other with respect to one of the five basic societal functions.	With the following exceptions, *core relationship* is roughly equivalent to Bates's conceptions of *reciprocal roles:* (1) a core relationship must center about one of the basic functions, whereas Bates does not stipulate this; (2) a core relationship may involve more than two roles, whereas Bates's concepts involve just two roles. A relationship without the qualifying adjective "core" involves two or more persons whose interaction does not necessarily relate to any of the basic societal functions

Family and Society

TABLE 1.1 (Continued)

CONCEPT	DEFINITION	COMMENT
		and/or whose roles are not necessarily differentiated. In general, the interaction in a core relationship tends to be highly patterned; a relatively low level of patterning in a core relationship would suggest that the corresponding institution and structure are unstable.
Function	(1) "A condition, or state of affairs, resultant from the operation (including in the term operation mere persistence) of a structure through time." —M. J. Levy, Jr., *The Structure of Society* (Princeton, N.J.: Princeton University Press, 1952), p. 56; and (2) the task-oriented (and usually cooperative) activity resulting in the state of affairs denoted in (1). Where qualification is not used, both denotations are intended.	When consequences "are intended and recognized by participants in the system," R. K. Merton suggests that we speak of them as *manifest;* if "neither intended nor recognized," they are called *latent.* —*Social Theory and Social Structure* (New York: Free Press, 1949), p. 51. Levy suggests that it may be useful to break down Merton's terms and to consider intention and recognition separately.—Levy, *op. cit.*, p. 87. Levy distinguishes between *eufunction,* which "increases or maintains adaptation or adjustment . . . to the . . . setting," and *dysfunction,* which "lessens the adaptation or adjustment."—*Ibid.*, p. 77. W. J. Goode's *positive* and *negative* functions have substantially the same meanings respectively, but he proposes a third category, *irrelevant,* which is neither conducive to nor against adaptation and adjustment.—W. J. Goode, *Religion among the Primitives* (New York: Free Press, 1951), p. 33. Functions may be *individual-serving* as well as *society-serving* (see text below).
Basic societal function	A function that must be fulfilled in any society in order for that society to continue in being.	Five such basic societal functions are postulated in the accompanying text: reproduction, provision of goods and

TABLE 1.1 (Continued)

CONCEPT	DEFINITION	COMMENT
		services, maintenance of order, socialization-education, and maintenance of a sense of purpose. Levy conceives of a function as basic (his term is "requisite") if its absence leads to any one of the following four conditions: "(a) the biological extinction or dispersion of the members [of the society], (b) the apathy of the members, (c) the war of all against all, and (d) the absorption of the society into another society." —Levy, *op. cit.*, p. 137.
Basic societal institution (or *institution*)	A set of folkways, mores, and laws pertaining to a basic societal function. Adapted from Davis, *op. cit.*, p. 71.	In this context the most important folkways and mores are those that constitute role-expectations with respect to core relationships.
Basic societal structure (or *institutional structure*, or *functional structure*)	A social structure whose principal activity is oriented to carrying out one or more of the basic societal functions.	We may distinguish between *analytic* and *concrete* structures. *Analytic* structures never exist except in our theorizing, wherein they are simple, idealized, usually single-functional structures. In the "real world," however, there are only *concrete* structures, which are inescapably multifunctional. Still a concrete institutional structure, such as a parish church, does specialize in carrying out a single function. The most important differentiation of roles in a basic societal structure is that involved in the corresponding core relationship.
Household	A set of persons occupying a common dwelling unit.	*Household* refers to people who live together, whether related to each other or not.
Family	A set of persons related to each other by blood, marriage,	Members of a family may or may not live together.

Family and Society

TABLE 1.1 (Continued)

CONCEPT	DEFINITION	COMMENT
	or adoption, and constituting a social system whose structure is specified by familial positions and whose basic societal function is replacement.	
Domestic family	Those related persons who occupy a common dwelling unit.	This is what the U.S. Bureau of the Census regards as a "family." Our denotation differs from that of Zimmerman, which appears on p. 98 below.
Nuclear family (or *conjugal family*)	A nuclear family is a social system having the following three positions: husband-father, wife-mother, and offspring-sibling.	"It should be noted that there may be more than one incumbent of each position, that is, there may be a polyandrous nuclear family (more than one incumbent in the position of husband-father), a polygynous nuclear family (more than one incumbent in the position of wife-mother), and of course a nuclear family including two or more children."—Robert F. Winch and Rae Lesser Blumberg, "Societal Complexity and Familial Organization," in Robert F. Winch and Louis Goodman (eds.), *Selected Studies in Marriage and the Family* (3d ed.; New York: Holt, Rinehart and Winston, Inc., 1968), pp. 70–92. Quotation is from p. 75.
Nuclear dyad	A relationship between occupants of two different nuclear positions	When the positions of the nuclear family are considered two at a time and with respect to the connecting relationship (e.g., the marital relationship of husband and wife), we speak of a dyad of the nuclear family. There are exactly three dyads in the nuclear family—husband-wife, mother-offspring, and father-offspring. Of course we could mention more if we were to distinguish more positions, such as brother, sister, older brother, younger sister, senior wife, and so forth. Richard Adams makes a forceful and persuasive argument that it is most useful to conceptualize the dyad (rather than the nuclear family) as the basic structural building block of human kin

TABLE 1.1 (Continued)

CONCEPT	DEFINITION	COMMENT
		organization. Therefore, dyadic families, such as the one consisting of the mother and her child(ren), are not viewed as abnormal by this structural approach.—Cf. Richard N. Adams, "An Inquiry into the Nature of the Family," in Gertrude Dole and Robert L. Carniero (eds.), *Essays in the Science of Culture in Honor of Leslie A. White* (New York: Crowell, 1960), pp. 30–49.
Incomplete nuclear family	A social system including incumbents in only one or two of the three nuclear positions.	"Among the types of incomplete nuclear family are: (a) a mother and her child(ren), (b) a marital couple with no children, and (c) a set of siblings."—Winch and Blumberg in Winch and Goodman (eds.), *op. cit.*
Extended family	A social system consisting of two or more familial positions, at least one dyad of which is *not* a nuclear dyad.	"An example would be a complete nuclear family plus the paternal uncle of the husband-father . . . It should be noted that: (a) unlike the nuclear family, the extended family does not have a fixed number of specifiable positions; (b) the extended family must include at least one non-nuclear dyad; and (c) of course a system involving two or more related nuclear families is an extended family."—*Ibid.*, p. 76.
Extended-familism-isolation	A conceptual variable one pole of which represents the maximum degree of involvement of a nuclear family or individual with kinsmen outside the nuclear family; the other pole, representing minimum involvement, typifies the nuclear family having no contact with kinsmen outside the nuclear family.	The adjective characterizing a nuclear family or individual at or near the maximum pole is "familistic"; the adjective for the minimum pole is "isolated."
Family of orientation	A nuclear family viewed from the standpoint of one of the children.	For this and the following term the writer is indebted to W. Lloyd Warner.
Family of procreation	A nuclear family viewed from the standpoint of one of the parents.	

societal survival and continuity"[7] and "functional requisites."[8] On the ground that it seems to communicate more easily, this writer prefers the term *basic societal functions*, or *basic functions* for short.

It seems as though each sociologist who has thought about basic societal functions has come up with his own list. The anarchy is more apparent than real, however, since the diversity is more in phrasing than in meaning. In the writer's list, which follows, no claim is made for originality of content; rather, the effort has been to capture the essence of the basic functions about which there seems to be general consensus and to phrase these functions as simply as possible. Thus it seems to the writer that the following functions must be carried out in order for a society to remain in being:

1. Replacements for dying members of the society must be provided.
2. Goods and services must be produced and distributed for the support of the members of the society.
3. There must be provision for accommodating conflicts and maintaining order, internally and externally.
4. Human replacements must be trained to become participating members of the society.
5. There must be procedures for dealing with emotional crises, for harmonizing the goals of individuals with the values of the society, and for maintaining a sense of purpose.

In other words, every known human society has some organized way of carrying out the above functions. For this reason we think of these functions as universal, as being basic societal functions.

Function as a Janus-faced Concept[9]

On page 5 it was remarked that functions were activities which had to be carried on if the society was to survive. A somewhat different meaning of the term *function* was suggested earlier on page 4, however, where functions denoted services that the family or other agency provided for individuals. This points up an ambiguity in the literature to which Homans has referred: that on the one hand function refers to consequences of activities that contribute to the survival of the society, and on the other to outcomes of activities that meet the needs of individuals. (It is hardly necessary to emphasize that not all activities will promote *both* societal survival *and* individual welfare.

Yale University Press, 1927); J. W. Bennett and M. M. Tumin, *Social Life* (New York: Knopf, 1948); M. J. Levy, Jr., *The Structure of Society* (Princeton, N.J.: Princeton University Press, 1952).

[7] Bennett and Tumin, *op. cit.*, p. 42.

[8] Levy, *op. cit.*, p. 62.

[9] *Janus:* A Roman deity thought to preside "over doors and gates and over beginnings and endings, commonly represented with two faces in opposite directions."—*The American College Dictionary.* In the present context the emphasis is not on the connotation of deceit but on the two points of view with respect to function—that of society and that of the individual.

Thus defensive war may be necessary for the society's survival while still being fatal to numerous individuals.) Homans observed that two eminent anthropologists have taken opposite sides in their emphasis on this question: Radcliffe-Brown has emphasized function as related to group survival, whereas Malinowski has emphasized the gratification of the needs of individuals.[10]

In the writer's judgment it is fruitless to debate whether Malinowski or Radcliffe-Brown was right. Both asked cogent questions, and it would be folly not to continue asking these questions. It seems useful to incorporate both views and to propose that the analysis of functions be consistently Januslike in that an effort should be made to describe and to explain their two distinguishable aspects: the individual-oriented and the society-oriented. This seems the obvious locus in which to observe the interlocking of the theories of social psychology and of sociology, respectively.[11]

Functions, Core Relationships, and Structures

If we can agree that any ongoing society must provide for what we have called the five basic societal functions and if we can visualize these functions as the consequences of social interaction (of what else could they be consequences?), then it makes sense to assume that for each function there will be in all societies some characteristic interaction between two or more individuals whose roles are differentiated with respect to the function under consideration. When there is a characteristic relationship between two or more differentiated roles in the carrying out of a basic societal function, let us speak of it as a *core relationship*. Then it is useful to think of *basic societal structures* (or *institutional structures*) as elaborations of core relationships. (See Table 1.1.)

Now let us apply our concepts of core relationship and basic societal structure to the five basic societal functions postulated above. Let us begin with the first function. The replacement of members can occur through birth or through recruitment from some other society. It seems obvious that throughout history most replacements have been of the former kind. Virtually without exception the only institutionalized setting for human reproduction is the marital relationship. Thus the *core relationship* for the *function of replacement* is husband-wife-offspring, or, stating the relationship from the viewpoint of the last-mentioned, *father-mother-child*.[12] Irrespective of the phrasing,

---

[10] George C. Homans, *The Human Group* (New York: Harcourt, 1950), p. 268. The reader may have noticed that this distinction was implied in the quotation from Parsons on page 4.

[11] Related to the individual- and society-oriented aspects of function is Pareto's conception of utility to the individual and utility to the community. Cf. Vilfredo Pareto, *The Mind and Society* (New York: Harcourt, 1935) Vol. IV, chap. 12, esp. p. 1461.

[12] It is obvious that both of these phrasings refer to the same triad of positions. The difference in phrasing points up the fact that we lack terms to denote familial positions and must refer to them in terms of composites of roles (or role-sets), e.g., husband-father and wife-mother.

this triad of positions constitutes the nuclear family. Then we may view the extended family as an elaboration of the nuclear family, and family (or *familial structure*), which refers to both nuclear and extended forms, is the basic societal structure corresponding to the basic societal function of replacement.

With respect to goods and services it seems useful to try to capture the relevant variation by positing one core relationship with respect to *production* —*worker-manager*—and a second bearing on the *distributive* aspect— *producer-consumer*. Of course in modern mass societies the *economic function* is elaborated into a commercial-industrial complex (or *economic structure*) with thousands of occupations.

Let us speak of the maintenance of order and the accommodation of conflicts as the *political function*. A corresponding core relationship of *official-constituent* could include both the policeman on the beat with his concern for the footpad and the latter's quarry, and also the judge listening to two disputants. The corresponding *political structure* includes not only elected and appointed public officials and civil servants, but party workers and members, lobbyists and "influence-peddlers," and members of the general public viewed as actual or potential voters.

Let us refer to the training of replacements as the *function of socialization-education*, and let us use that phrase with a wide denotation so that it includes not only what the infant learns from his mother about the emotional content of the mother-child relationship[13] and what the army recruit learns from the rifle instructor on the firing range but also what the older worker learns from *his* elders about how to occupy his time after retirement. Here the core relationship seems without question to be *teacher-pupil*. The *educational structure* includes schools (both public and private) from the prenursery to the postdoctoral levels, the in-service training of trade unions and of corporations, the formal instruction of the lecture hall, and the informal tuition of a boy teaching his younger brother to spit through his teeth.

Every society needs some procedure whereby individually conceived goals are brought into some sort of harmony, or accommodation at least, with the goals the group must subscribe to if the group is to persist. It is usual for such goals of the group to be embedded in the society's theology. Furthermore, there must be some patterned ways of explaining and responding to recurring crises—flood, drought, pestilence, death. Frequently explanations for the inexplicable appear in theology, and patterned responses for recurring crises appear in religious ritual. Let us use the term *religious function* to denote the consequences we have just noted. The core relationship is *priest-parishioner*. The *religious structure* may be conceived of as including not only religious functionaries and devout believers but also those who perform the religious function in what we customarily think of as nonreligious settings. In other words, aspects of the religious function, as it has been specified above, may

---

[13] Here we distinguish between the content of what is learned and the emotional gratification or reward that may accompany learning. Emotional gratification and reward will be considered later in this chapter.

be carried out in secular occupational roles. Examples are the producers of consumers' goods, their advertising agencies and television networks, all of which contribute to the integration of goals; the scientists who push back the frontier of the unexplained; the social agencies and psychiatrists who deal with crises of various kinds.

Institution

Frequently the family is spoken of as an institution, as are the church and the state. Let us consider what we shall mean by the word "institution." From the total normative order of any society, segments may be distinguished that pertain to the carrying out of functions—not only the five basic societal functions referred to above but others as well, e.g., the recreational function. We shall use "institution" to refer to a set of interrelated norms (folkways, mores, laws) pertaining to the carrying out of a function.

How the Theory Works

To this point we have presented the elements of our theory—basic societal functions, societal structures, core relationships, and individual-oriented functions. Now let us try to weave those elements into a theory.

TABLE 1.2

Proposed List of Basic Societal Structures: Defined in Terms of Associated Basic Societal Functions and Core Relationships and Presented with Inferred Individual-Oriented Functions

---

I. Familial

    A. Core functions
       1. Society-oriented: to provide replacements for dying members
       2. Individual-oriented: to provide a sense of "immortality," or temporal continuity, with ongoing society
    B. Core relationship: father-mother-child
      (An alternate and more restricted view is that the one "essential" enduring core relationship is the mother-child.)

II. Economic

    A. Core functions
       1. Society-oriented: to produce and to distribute the goods and services required for the maintenance of the members
       2. Individual-oriented: to provide the material means of maintenance and pleasure and perhaps of status-improvement
    B. Core relationships
       1. With respect to production: worker-manager
       2. With respect to distribution: producer-consumer

TABLE 1.2 (Continued)

III. Political

A. Core functions
 1. Society-oriented: to accommodate conflicting interests and to maintain internal and external order
 2. Individual-oriented: to provide protection and to resolve conflicting claims without recourse to violence

B. Core relationship: official-constituent

IV. Socializing-educational[a]

A. Core functions
 1. Society-oriented: to train replacements for social roles and social positions
 2. Individual-oriented: to provide the individual with the skills required for participation in society

B. Core relationship: teacher-pupil

V. Religious

A. Core functions
 1. Society-oriented: to achieve and to maintain solidarity and consensus about general goals, values, and norms and to prevent a state of normlessness; to maintain a state of purposefulness
 2. Individual-oriented: to provide procedures for meeting crises and explanations for otherwise unexplainable occurrences and thus to assuage anxiety; to prevent feelings of alienation

B. Core relationship: priest-parishioner

[a] In thinking about the process whereby an infant becomes an adult qualified to participate in his society it is customary to conceptualize that process as consisting of two aspects: socialization and education. There is precedent for using the term *socialization* to refer to the process of personality development and for using *education* to refer to the acquisition of values and of skills—both intellectual and motor. But sometimes *socialization* is used with the connotation of education (as when we speak of XYZ Corporation socializing college graduates into "organization men"), and sometimes *socialization* is used in a broader sense to include both personality development and education.

The broad sense is intended here. To communicate this as clearly as possible the hyphenated form *socialization-education* is introduced. The adjectival form is *socializing-educational*. At times one or the other of these pairs may be dropped when there is occasion to emphasize the connotation of the remaining term.

Socialization-education is not to be confused with emotional gratification. To be sure, emotional gratification enters into learning, but so does food. Our conceptual formulation, then, draws a distinction with the result that we shall regard socialization-education as referring both to a basic societal structure and its core function, while we shall think of emotional gratification as a function fulfilled largely through primary relationships, including those in the nuclear family.

As we begin to examine some of the implications of Table 1.2, it will be seen at once that by axiom every society must carry out all five basic societal functions, and we conceptualize for every society a corresponding set of five *analytic* structures. (See comment on basic societal structure in Table 1.1) Another way of phrasing the same thing is to say that our conception of the term *society* involves the *assumptions* (1) that the five basic societal functions must be carried on for any society to survive, (2) that every society has some set of differentiated positions and roles related to these functions, and (3) that there are individual-serving functions associated with the society-serving functions. From these assumptions, however, it does *not* follow that in every society there will be five recognizably separate *concrete* structures corresponding to the five basic societal functions. An example is provided by pietistic frontier families in America of the eighteenth and nineteenth centuries. In this setting not only was it frequent that the adult male held the position of husband-father in the familial structure, but since the family was also a unit of religious worship, he served as priest in the religious structure (and the other members of the family held the role of parishioners). In the peasantry of traditional China a part of the religious function was carried out within the family; here the family was also the major economic unit, both productively and distributively, the agency for resolving conflicts and controlling individual behavior, and for educating the young into fully participating adults. It is possible, then, for the five basic societal functions to be largely fulfilled within the family, and accordingly it is possible—*analytically* speaking—for the five basic societal structures to be located for the most part within the single *concrete* structure of the family.

The qualifying phrase "for the most part" implies that although most of the socializing, economic, and other basic activities may be centered in the family, still we shall almost inevitably find some socializing, economic, and other basic activities being carried on outside the family. In contrast to these societies in which the family seems to be nearly self-sufficient and almost a "pseudo society" Spiro describes a community in Israel where the family operates with only its basic function of replacement plus the corollary function of emotional gratification.[14] Stated more generally, functions are distributed among concrete organizations in various ways. Therefore, we conclude that whereas all societies have five basic functions, the number of types of corresponding concrete structures may vary. Accordingly the number of types of concrete structures becomes an index of structural differentiation.[15]

It should be concluded from the preceding paragraph that not only *may* concrete structures fulfill functions other than the one about which they are explicitly organized but it is *inevitable* that such will occur. As an example, we find a church organization integrating the goals of its members with the values of the society, providing sanctions for approved and disapproved behavior, and handling the anxieties of parishioners, and also concerned with recruiting and training new functionaries and accommodating conflicts. Not

---

[14] Melford E. Spiro, *Kibbutz: Venture in Utopia* (Cambridge, Mass.: Harvard University Press, 1956). On functional corollaries cf. pages 22–25.

[15] The *folk* type of society and the *urban* type represent extremes of such differentiation. Cf. Linton C. Freeman and Robert F. Winch, "Societal Complexity: An Empirical Test of a Typology of Societies," *American Journal of Sociology*, 62: 461–466 (1957).

only does a business firm produce goods and/or services and distribute them; it also recruits and trains personnel, integrates their goals, adjudicates conflicts, and so on. More generally, a concrete organization will probably be called upon at one time or another to carry out all the functions listed in Table 1.2.

This conclusion does not mean that we are about to abandon the conceptual scheme outlined in Table 1.2 just as we finish explaining it. Rather, what we have offered is a distinction between analytical and concrete structures. Analytical structures are high-level abstractions (the economy, the polity, the family, and so on) which by postulate universally discharge the postulated basic societal functions. Concrete structures are particular organizations, such as the XYZ Corporation, the village of Jonesville, and the Smith family. With the analytical perspective, we view societies as being alike in having political structures and functions, economic structures and functions, and so on. With the concrete perspective, on the other hand, we become sensitive to the idiosyncrasies of each structure. Although concrete structures tend to specialize in one function or another, they also tend to some degree to carry out all of the basic societal functions.

Corollaries of Function and Structure

The presentation of basic societal functions and structures leads to a view of the family in terms of the societal function of replacement, the individual-serving function of the sense of continuity with the generations, and the nuclear structure involving relationships among father, mother, and children. Of course this is only the barest skeleton of the family as each of us experiences it. From this beginning we proceed by tracing implications of this analysis. We know that families do many different things and take many different forms. The task of building a systematic conception of the family involves a specification of why or, more precisely, under what conditions, variations in form and function appear. To the extent that this effort is successful we build a sociological theory of the family. We begin by examining corollaries of the structure and function of the nuclear family.

Derived Function of Emotional Gratification:
Corollary of the structure of the nuclear family

Usually the members of a nuclear family have a common residence.[16] Moreover, we think of the nuclear family as a small group within which interaction is intimate and face to face; these are the characteristics of a primary group. We routinely think of "love" as being involved in the relationship of husband and wife, of parent and child, of brother and sister; or

[16] Cf. Table 1.1 for the definition of nuclear family. An example of a setting wherein the members of the nuclear family, as defined for this book, do not have a common residence is the kibbutz described in Chapter 3.

perhaps it is more accurate to say that in middle-class America, we tend to think of these relationships as "right" when characterized by love. Now it has been proposed that we think of love—marital, filial, fraternal, and other—as the emotional response of a person in a dyadic relationship in which the emotional needs of that person are being met—to some extent at least—by the behavior of the other.[17] It appears that most people, young and old, in most societies have need of some such intimate relationship in which to share hopes and fears, triumphs and anxieties. In the present context *emotional gratification* is used to denote the response—primarily in its more positive aspects—to the friendly interaction of intimate companions. In American society, especially in the middle class, it seems generally to be believed that the nuclear family is the setting *par excellence* in which to obtain this sort of gratification, particularly within the marital relationship.

It must be appreciated that although emotional gratification requires some sort of primary relationship, this function may be, and frequently is, carried on outside the family. A familiar example in middle-class America is the adolescent who seems no longer to be in emotional communication with his family and whose emotional gratification derives from some extrafamilial relationship: perhaps with a gang or perhaps with an individual—a peer-age boy or girl or a coach or other model. The cartoonists have made us aware that the customer-bartender is another relationship for the (largely unidirectional?) sharing of hopes and frustrations. In many societies around the world men derive the emotional gratification of intimate and congenial companionship not so much from interaction with their wives as with other men.

Derived Function of Position-Conferring: Corollary of the nuclear family's basic function

The production (or to use the usual word, "reproduction") of human beings has been presented as the society-serving function of the family. This points to the cross-cultural generalization that the routine way for a neonate to enter the society is as the recognized offspring of a married couple.[18] This state of affairs provides him with (1) legitimacy that (2) arises from a family connection, and that (3) is frequently symbolized by a family name. Viewed from the standpoint of the individual (in this case the newborn child) this function (in its individual-serving aspect) provides him with a place in society, with a social position. From the society-serving standpoint this function may be expressed as the relating of each individual to all others, the integration of society.

Although nothing like a perfect correlation exists, there is widespread

---

[17] Robert F. Winch, *Mate-Selection: A Study of Complementary Needs* (New York: Harper & Row, 1958), esp. p. 88.

[18] Or of a couple about to be married since in some societies the wedding rite is deferred until after the first child is born.

recognition cross culturally of a tendency for those with high social status to be rich in material possessions and, conversely, for the lowborn to live in poverty. In American society we can observe the working of a rather general rule that a rise in social status is preceded by the acquisition of wealth. For example, Commodore Vanderbilt, who amassed the family fortune, was not as acceptable in the upper reaches of New York society as have been his descendants. Time, it seems, ripens the fortune and imparts to it the aroma of respectability. When property is privately owned, there is the question of inheritance, and quite generally the family constitutes the structure within which property is passed from one generation to the next. Thus the transmission of property through inheritance is intimately related to the position-conferring function of the family.

In the two foregoing paragraphs we have been talking about *ascribed* position, which is accorded to the individual because of the family into which he was born. (As Davis observes, customary bases for ascribing position other than family or kinship are sex, age, and race.[19] Ascribed position is to be contrasted with *achieved* position, which is accorded to an individual as a reward for his accomplishments or personal characteristics.) The family may also confer an ascribed position on members brought in by methods other than birth, i.e., through marriage and adoption. This is especially true when the newcomer is from outside the society and thus is known to the society only through the family which he or she joins. For example, when an American soldier brings back to his home town a bride from England, say, or from Germany, it would be expected that her status in the community would be determined, at least initially, by the status of the soldier and of his family of orientation.

The Derived Parental Functions:
Corollary of the nuclear family's basic function

The helplessness of the newborn infant results in the necessity for someone to nurture him if he is to survive. The lack of understanding of the very young child means that someone must control him if he is to avoid the hazards of his environment. Accordingly, the function of replacement, which brings children into the family, calls for the *parental functions of nurturance and control*.

Individual-Serving Functions as Rewards

Now let us bear in mind that in any society each of the concrete social systems that specialize in one or another of the basic societal functions tends to fulfill not only its own basic function but also—to some extent, at least—

---

[19] Kingsley Davis, *Human Society* (New York: Macmillan, 1948), pp. 97–98, 112–113.

each of the other basic functions. (There is one exception: the familial institution has a monopoly on its basic function of providing legitimate replacements through sexual reproduction.) Since the individual-serving functions were formulated as the individual-oriented counterparts of society-serving functions, it seems reasonable that this interchange of fragments of functions should apply to individual-serving functions as well as to those that serve societies. As illustrations we can call to mind instances when the state has distributed goods and services to relief clients, especially during and since the depression of the 1930's; when the extended family has provided protection against violence (the feuding Hatfields and McCoys of the Kentucky hills); when the business firm has provided release from anxiety and attunement of the individual's goals with those of the group (recently a dominant theme in personnel administration); and so on.

We can now rephrase the concept of the individual-serving function so as to say that a societal structure can provide the individual with gratification or rewards. In this context *reward* refers to the achievement of a *goal*, and a *goal* is the state of affairs for which a person seeks when he has a need or drive. For example, the hungry man seeks for the agreeable feeling of being well-fed. Implied in this formulation is the view of Dollard and Miller that, pragmatically speaking, a reward (or, in their phrasing, reinforcement) does not and cannot exist if the person does not have the corresponding drive or need. In other words, comfortable postprandial satiety is not a goal or a reward state to a man who is not hungry.[20]

A reward is something an actor wants. It may be tangible, like a piece of candy; it may be intangible, like a smile of approval. In psychology it is conventional to think of something as constituting a reward for an actor under consideration if and only if the actor modifies his behavior in order to acquire it. If a child abandons a toy and approaches an adult to get the candy, if a boy plays harder to get his coach's smile of approval, then these are rewards in the psychological sense. To state the matter a bit more operationally, a reward may be defined as an event that strengthens "the connection between a given response and a particular cue."[21] As this implies, reward is a key concept in many theories of learning. Reward is regarded as important in determining what is learned and at what rate. To the extent that this is true it follows that the ability to manipulate rewards (i.e., to proffer and to withhold gratifications) implies the power to influence the behavior of others. From the viewpoint of the adult holding the candy or of the coach about to smile at

---

[20] John Dollard and Neal E. Miller, *Personality and Psychotherapy: An Analysis in Terms of Learning, Thinking, and Culture* (New York: McGraw-Hill, 1950), p. 40. The anticipation of such pleasure may be so appealing, however, that a person will exercise strenuously in order to "work up an appetite."

[21] Calvin S. Hall and Gardner Lindzey, *Theories of Personality* (New York: Wiley, 1957), p. 432. For a discussion of the concept of need, drive, goal, and reward in learning theory see Ernest R. Hilgard, *Theories of Learning* (2d ed.; New York: Appleton, 1956), pp. 422–433.

the athletic aspirant, the candy or the smile is a resource the control of which is instrumental in influencing the behavior of an alter. Thus control of the resource and the knowledge of how to use it constitute the means whereby one person can influence the behavior of another.

We may summarize this argument in the following two points: (a) that the individual-serving functions may be viewed as rewards, and (b) that the power to control rewards implies the power to control the behavior of others. These points enable us to see the process through which the overt behavior and, indeed, the attitudes of individuals may be influenced by the institutional structures of their society.

A Functional Analysis of the Relation between Family and Society

To become quite specific, one recurring problem in contemporary society concerns the degree to which parents should be held accountable for the transgressions of their children. Thus within a single month it was reported that measures were being taken both in New York City and in the Soviet Union to punish parents for their children's delinquencies.[22] One might expect a sociologist to make some sort of response to two questions: Is such a move sound, and is it moral? What light can our analysis throw on this issue?

Let us begin by applying the mode of analysis of the foregoing section to the consideration of influence in institutional structures. Influence may be defined as "the effect that the behavior of one party (individual or group) has upon the thinking or action of some other party (individual or group)."[23] A business executive may exert influence over his subordinates not only through stimulating them to be productive but also by exhorting them to "dress right" and to "talk right" politically. An example of a lack of influence would be a father who fails in his effort to persuade his son to leave a delinquent gang.

What causes influence and differences in influence? In our homely examples why is the businessman influential and why is the father without influence? To some extent a person's influence depends on his carriage, mien, and other personal characteristics; to some extent it depends on his position or office. Here we are interested mainly in the latter source of influence, which Davis calls "structural or positional power,"[24] and with differences in influence associated with differences in position or office.

It is not an uncommon experience of parents that, as a boy passes through

[22] "Fine for Parents of Vandals Voted: Council Adopts Plan Wagner Opposed in '52—Action on Gangs Also Approved," *The New York Times,* October 14, 1959, pp. 1, 36; "Soviet to Set Up Youth Tribunals: Panels Will Get Wide Power on Children and Parents —'Comrades' Courts' Due," *The New York Times,* October 25, 1959, p. 24.

[23] Bernard Barber, *Social Stratification* (New York: Harcourt, 1957), p. 234.

[24] Davis, *op. cit.,* p. 95.

various ages, his scoutmaster or his football coach or, still later, his boss in a business firm can elicit exertions of the most exhausting sort whereas the same boy's parents can discover no formula to stir him from foot-dragging lethargy. The foregoing analysis suggests the interpretation that the coach and the boss have under their control—and the father lacks—rewards that motivate the boy (the coach's shout of praise within the hearing of the rest of the squad, the boss's promise of higher pay and of promotion). We may regard the number and attractiveness of such rewards as a measure of the power of the position and of the influence of the officeholder. If, then, the coach or the boss has a much more attractive set of rewards to offer the young man than have his parents, it should not astonish us to discover that the former has greater influence over him than the latter. It should be emphasized that this argument has nothing to do with the personalities involved; there is no assumption that the personality of the coach or that of the boss is a bit more attractive than that of the father. The argument was made entirely on the basis of variation in "structural or positional power."

Let us return to the question, Should parents be held responsible for the delinquencies of their children? Presumably the justification for doing so is the belief that the parents can control their offspring and prevent the latters' delinquencies. Our analysis raises a doubt. At least it leads us first to remark that urban parents of low income and belonging to ethnic minorities (a category of parents from which delinquent offspring are likely to come) have fewer resources, tangible and intangible, at their command than have parents with other social characteristics, and then to infer that for this reason they are probably less able to control their children. (Whether or not parents of the former category make as effective use of the resources they have in influencing the behavior of their children is problematic.) To be sure, we have not made a clear-cut case, but to the extent that parents lack control over rewards, it is both futile and immoral to punish them for the transgressions of their children.

With these points in mind let us recall the studies of Ogburn and of Zimmerman (pages 3–4). Ogburn found that the family in America had been losing functions. Zimmerman reported that the contemporary American family—like that of the late periods of classical Athens and Rome—had become weak or, to use his term, "atomistic." One example Ogburn offered of the family's loss of functions was that it had virtually ceased being a unit of economic production. We might rephrase this by saying that business firms and other organizations subsumable under the economic institution were taking from the family more and more of the economic function. Now we can see the implication of this statement: whereas at one time the father had economic power over his son, to a considerable degree this form of control has passed to the occupational system, and the boss has superseded the father in a position of influence. Thus when we construe function in its individual-serving aspect as reward, Ogburn's finding regarding the loss of functions becomes an explanation of Zimmerman's finding of the family's loss of power.[25]

This line of discussion leads us to a major theoretical conclusion that is an implication of the entire chapter to this point, especially of our three basic assumptions (cf. page 18): *that the power of a societal structure is positively correlated with the number of functions it carries out and with the degree of monopoly it has (among the various societal structures) in the fulfillment of these functions.*

When Does the Family Exist?
Our Structural-Functional View

Occasionally one encounters the question as to whether the family is universal, i.e., whether there have ever been any societies without families. Two examples of family-less societies are frequently proposed: the Nayar on the Malabar Coast of India in the eighteenth century, and the Israeli kibbutz described by Spiro as of 1951.

The basis for regarding the Nayar as exceptional is that although there was a clear pattern of marriage, the sexual partners who procreated were not the couples who were ritually married to each other. The question, then, is whether the socially recognized father of a child tended also to be the socially recognized husband of that child's mother. "At a convenient time every few years," according to Gough, "a lineage held a grand ceremony at which all of its girls who had not attained puberty, aged about seven to twelve, were on one day ritually married by men drawn from their linked lineages."[26] After four days of ceremonies the ritual husbands left their brides and had no further obligations to them. One way of phrasing what happened thereafter was that the girl would subsequently have a series of affairs with other men whom she tried to get to contribute to the support of the resulting children, but the children were reared by her matrilineage[27] and were largely supported by it. The social and legal rights and obligations between the father of the child and its mother were so slight as to throw Gough into uncertainty as to whether it was appropriate to think of the procreating couple as husband and wife;

---

[25] We still need a theory that will account for the conditions under which functions flow from one concrete structure to another. Some remarks on this topic appear in Robert F. Winch and Rae Lesser Blumberg, "Societal Complexity and Familial Organization," in Robert F. Winch and Louis Wolf Goodman (eds.), *Selected Studies in Marriage and the Family* (3d ed.; New York: Holt, Rinehart and Winston, Inc., 1968), pp. 70–92.

[26] E. Kathleen Gough, "Is the Family Universal? The Nayar Case," in Norman W. Bell and Ezra F. Vogel (eds.), *A Modern Introduction to the Family* (New York: Free Press, 1960), pp. 76–92. Quotation is from p. 79.

[27] The domestic family typically consisted of a group of brothers and sisters together with the sisters' children and the sisters' daughters' children.

she finally resolved the question in the affirmative by ignoring the strength of the legal tie and focusing on the legitimizing function of the relationship. Here the nub of the argument is that if the basic societal function is reproduction and if there is doubt that the procreating couple is married, is there a family in our structural-functional (more particularly, our functional) sense?

In the case of the kibbutz the marital couple is the functional unit with respect to reproduction, but the child resides from birth in communal quarters and is socialized, educated, nurtured, and controlled by teachers and nurses. Those who define the family in terms of a nurturing function, then, are entitled to be in doubt as to whether this kibbutz has a familial system.[28]

What should be our stance in this matter? Since the question is definitional, it seems clear that the first step is to settle on a definition and then to determine whether there are any known societies whose familial patterns would fall outside the accepted definition. A definition has been proposed on page 11 above. It may be recalled that our definition of the family involves a structural criterion and a functional criterion. Our definition reads as follows: a family is (1) a set of persons related to each other by blood, marriage, or adoption, and constituting a social system whose structure is specified by familial positions (*structural criterion*), and (2) whose basic societal function is replacement (*functional criterion*).

It seems clear that the Nayar societal system contained a familial structure. They had a familial pattern that was matrilineal and matrilocal. With the Nayar the critical question is functional, or, more precisely, the locus of the function. Was the procreating man to be regarded as the woman's husband? If yes, the replacement function was within the family, and the Nayar pattern satisfied the definition functionally as well as structurally. If no, then the first brief, yet necessary, step of the reproductive function—impregnation —took place outside the family, and perhaps this suffices to raise a doubt as to whether the family should be regarded as having fulfilled the replacement function. As noted above, Gough ultimately decided "yes."

What about Spiro's kibbutz? Here there is no question about reproduction; it is a marital function. In this setting, however, a structural question can be raised. Since the family is defined in part as a social system based on familial positions and since a social system is defined as having differentiated social positions, might the lack of differentiation among the kibbutzniks disqualify their familial system from full standing as a family? (It will be seen in Chapter 3 that they tried vigorously to eliminate sex differences, especially those pertaining to occupations.) It appears that although their egalitarian ideology resulted in the abandonment of the terms for "husband," "wife," and

---

[28] Such is the dilemma of Reiss, who resolves his doubt by concluding that the marital couple in this setting did more nurturing than did the teacher-nurse, the crèche, and the school. Cf. Ira L. Reiss, "The Universality of the Family: A Conceptual Analysis," *Journal of Marriage and the Family*, 27: 443–453 (1965).

"marriage," they could not abolish the physiological differentiation whereby only women conceive, go through pregnancy, and bear children. In this kibbutz, then, the question as to whether there was a familial system within the terms of our definition rests upon whether we think they differentiated sufficiently between the social position of husband-father and that of wife-mother. If we give emphasis to and accept literally their abandonment of the terms of differentiation—e.g., "husband" and "wife"—the answer must be no; if we emphasize the facts of pregnancy, childbirth, and breast-feeding of infants that must have forced them to acknowledge sex-linked differentiation with respect to the function of replacement, the answer is yes.

We come now to two final questions: (1) What is the position of this writer with respect to the universality of the family? (2) Is question (1) important? The answers are (1) that this writer chooses to leave the Nayar and the kibbutz as doubtful cases and (2) to regard the universality of the family as a somewhat unimportant theoretical question. The reason is that the writer is committed to structural-functional definitions; it seems desirable to define phenomena with respect to their elements and the relations among their elements as well as with respect to what the phenomena do. But functions can be fulfilled in diverse structures; hence it seems futile to seek universality in a structural-functional sense. In other words, no matter how ingenious we may be in our definition to make it all-inclusive, there is always the possibility that an assiduous archivist or an enterprising ethnographer may turn up some society with a social pattern falling outside our definition. It is quite possible, moreover, that societal systems now well known to us as having families will evolve in such a fashion as to cease to have families as we define them. Such possibilities have been foreseen by Hitler and Aldous Huxley, as well as by Barrington Moore.[29]

The Family as Cause and as Effect

Let us consider two kinds of questions about the family. One line of questioning takes the direction of asking what is happening to the family: Why is it that parents do not control their children as much as parents used to in the old days? Why is it that children are so wild today? Why are there so many divorces? Why are divorces so much more frequent than in the old days? The other line of questioning asks what the family does: Is it true that

---

[29] On Hitler and Huxley see notes 3–4, p. 154, below. Asserting that "motherhood is frequently a degrading experience," Moore believes that child rearing (and childbearing?) may become mechanized and bureaucratized. Cf. Barrington Moore, Jr., "Thoughts on the Future of the Family," in Maurice R. Stein, Arthur J. Vidich, and David Manning White (eds.), *Identity and Anxiety: Survival of the Person in Mass Society* (New York: Free Press, 1960), pp. 391–401.

parents mold the personalities of their children? To what extent is this so? How is it done?

What is the difference between these two lines of questioning? In the first kind the question concerns the family as result, as consequent state of affairs, or as the dependent variable; the second kind of question concerns the family as cause, as antecedent state of affairs, or as independent variable.[30] In our study of the familial institution it is appropriate that we should consider both kinds of questions, but it is useful to distinguish between the two kinds.

Implicit in this distinction is a strategy for answering the two kinds of questions. If our interest lies in what is happening *to* the family, then let us look at its societal context: at the relations among the five analytic structures in the society under consideration; let us note which concrete structures are fulfilling which functions, which functions are passing from one structure to another, and so on. The answers to such questions will inform us concerning the power of the familial structure of a society relative to the power of the other structures of the same society, and they will enlighten us concerning the power of the familial structure in one society as compared with its power in a society with a different distribution of society-oriented and individual-oriented functions. Such answers will enable us to understand the observed structure and functions of the family in a given society and perhaps the direction in which they seem to be moving. In particular this line of analysis will lead us to conclusions on such questions as: Why is it that parents do not control their children as much as parents used to in the old days? When the family is the dependent variable, then, we look outside the family at other institutions for our explanation—for the independent variables.

If our interest lies in personality development as a consequence of parent-child interaction, then let us look for our explanation within the family. Let us note the nicety of the balance between the structure of the family and its functions. Let us examine the functions that, as we have seen from our deductive argument, constitute the power of the institution. Let us scrutinize the nature of the influence of the family's members resulting from these functions and how this influence is exerted. When the family is the independent variable, we look to it to explain variation in such presumably consequent phenomena as personality development in children.

It is the belief of the writer that this mode of analysis constitutes a useful way of thinking about the family, a promising strategy for the formulation of research on the family, and a convenient way to organize a book about the family.

---

[30] In this context no distinction is made among "result," "consequent state of affairs," and "dependent variable." Similarly "cause," "antecedent state of affairs," and "independent variable" are viewed as mutually equivalent in this context. That is, we shall not be concerned here with the difference between necessary and sufficient conditions.

Summary

To keep going, any society must fulfill certain basic functions. These basic societal functions have individual-serving as well as society-oriented aspects. In carrying out these functions individuals in differentiated roles interact in core relationships. A basic societal structure is founded upon one or several interrelated core relationships.

The basic function fulfilled by the family in all societies is the replacement of dying members. Because of this basic function the family usually has the corollary function of conferring ascribed position on its members. Consequent on the structure of the nuclear family is the fact that it can fulfill the function of providing all members with the emotional gratification derivable from primary relationships and of providing its children with nurturance and control.

Is this as arid and sterile as it sounds, one may ask, or does it lead to any interesting conclusions? At the beginning of the chapter we noted some of the ways in which the layman looks at the family, such as viewing the divorce rate as evidence of familial disorganization. Why has the divorce rate risen over the past century? An answer on the basis of common sense is that formerly people were more moral, whereas nowadays divorce is more acceptable. Perhaps so. It seems true that there has been an increase in the proportion of the population looking upon divorce as acceptable, and according to some views this is immoral. But if we have a more serious interest than to make dinner-table conversation, such a reply is inadequate. Why has there been this change in attitude toward divorce? The concepts and postulates of the present chapter provide a means for answering this question. The reader is invited to try constructing his own answer. The writer's analysis will be presented in a later chapter.

2

A Family of Great Functionality:
the peasantry of traditional China

Purpose of Chapters 2 and 3

In Chapter 1 we argued that to the degree the family carries out basic societal functions it has power to influence the behavior of its members.[1] Let us now develop this point by conceiving of a continuum of "functionality." This refers to the relatively simple idea that in some settings the family is more functional than it is in other settings. It will improve our understanding if we become acquainted with a specific type of family near each end of the continuum. Then having examined the functionality of each of these two types of family, we shall push on to see how familial structure is consonant with function and how norms, especially those specifying the content of familial relationship, fit function and structure.

When we speak of a highly functional family, we mean that the social group we designate as the family is the grouping that carries out a high proportion of the activities denoted in the basic societal functions.[2] Then in order to chart the potential range of types of familial functionality, let us imagine the two limiting cases: a type of maximum functionality and one of minimum. The maximally functional type would be coterminous with the society and would fulfill the economic, political, socializing-educational, and religious as well as the familial functions. The type of minimum functionality would perform no societal function except the familial one.

Actually such extreme cases as we have been imagining are hard to find, but there are two well-documented familial patterns that come satisfactorily close to portraying these ideal-types. An empirical type of family that comes

[1] Cf. pages 21–23.
[2] Therefore, unless otherwise qualified, "functional" should be understood to mean "basically functional."

30

close to having been maximally functional is the traditional family of the Chinese peasantry. This is the subject of the present chapter. A type of virtually minimum functionality has appeared in a kind of local community in Israel known as a *kibbutz*. This is the subject of Chapter 3. After an examination of these two types of family it will be instructive in later chapters to locate somewhere between these extremes various types of American family.

It should be emphasized that the purpose of Chapters 2 and 3 is to anchor the two ends of the continuum of functionality. This is best accomplished by presenting somewhat historical forms of the family. The Chinese form began to go out of existence by the end of the last century; the Israeli may have begun to go out of existence as it was being born. In each case there will be an indication of the direction in which the historical type has changed, or at least is believed to have changed.

Finally, there is no intention that the term *functional* is to be interpreted as either equivalent with, or connoting, the evaluative adjective "good"; the intention is to make distinctions between degrees of functionality but not to judge them invidiously.

The Peasant Family in Traditional China

Love, we are told, should prevail between a man and a woman before they marry each other. Then what should we think of a society wherein we have substantial reason to conclude that it is usual for no love to exist prior to marriage? Would there be something immoral about such a state of affairs?

What about a young couple getting married and wanting to live with the parents of the bridegroom rather than to set up a home of their own? Doesn't this seem like regrettable dependency on the part of the younger generation? But if a majority of the members of the younger generation and of the parental generation as well regard it as a misfortune bordering on tragedy for the young couple to live elsewhere, what should we think?

What should we think of a young man who would obey a mother's order to divorce a wife he loves? What should we think of a society that would praise the son for this show of obedience?

Old age, we are told, is not only a category for classifying people but a social problem in our own country. Where are the aged to turn for emotional and financial security? Is there something topsy-turvy, then, about a society that gives preferential treatment and maximum security to the aged?

To learn how such seemingly bizarre practices make sense let us turn to a consideration of the Chinese family.

For perhaps twenty centuries there existed among the peasants of China a familial form that was just about as completely functional as is theoretically possible. All members of the family contributed their energies to the production of a common pool of wealth. The wealth was dispensed by the family head, who acted not as an individual with arbitrary power but as the responsible executive charged with the duty of looking out for the family as a whole and for all its individual members. It was taken for granted that the young would be indoctrinated by the family in the ways of the world, that the aged and the ailing would be cared for, and that the conduct of all members would be controlled by the overriding consideration of family welfare rather than individual gratification. The patriarch, being closest to the world of the ancestors, served as a sort of family priest in honoring and worshiping those who had departed. Let us examine the elements of this family, which was almost a little society in itself.[3]

Ideally this traditional family included within a single household a father and a mother, all their sons and unmarried daughters, the wives of their sons, all of the sons' children except married daughters, and so on through the complete roster of the living generations. This is spoken of as a joint family. It is probable, however, that this idealized household was seldom achieved even in the gentry and virtually never in the peasantry. Lang explains that the death rate was higher among the peasants than among the gentry and served to keep peasant families smaller.[4] Another important factor, according to Hsu, is the fact that the landholding of the average peasant family was too small to support a joint family.[5] Levy believes that the average peasant family tended to be a stem family, which consists of the parents and one married son with his wife and children.[6]

[3] It is in order to explain why we are using a historical rather than a contemporary family and a family of the peasantry rather than one of the gentry. Over the past century the impact of Western culture and industrialization has resulted in considerable breakdown, disintegration, and abandonment of traditional familial practices. Since the resulting family has been shrinking in structure and functions, it is less suited to our analysis than is the traditional. The traditional family of the gentry was larger in size and more complex in structure than that of the peasantry. Because it was less self-sufficient than the peasant family (cf. n. page 34), however, the latter is a better approximation of the ideal type of the maximally functional family. Cf. Marion J. Levy, Jr., *The Family Revolution in Modern China* (Cambridge, Mass.: Harvard University Press, 1949), esp. pp. 42–48.

[4] Olga Lang, *Chinese Family and Society* (New Haven, Conn.: Yale University Press, 1946), p. 16. Among the gentry, second wives and concubines would be included in the size of domestic family and size of household.—*Ibid.*, pp. 50–52.

[5] Francis L. K. Hsu, "The Myth of Chinese Family Size," *American Journal of Sociology*, 48: 555–562 (1943). For economic reasons concubinage was not common among the peasants.—Levy, *op. cit.*, p. 98.

[6] Levy, *op. cit.*, p. 52. The stem family is also known as the *famille souche*, a term introduced in Frederic LePlay, *Les Ouvriers européens* (Tours: 1879). Social scientists have been greatly handicapped in studying China by the lack of comprehensive and reliable social statistics. There is evidence, however, from the first third of the present century, of a lower proportion of large families among the poorer than among the richer classes of China. In a study done just prior to World War II Lang found that landlords in villages had a higher proportion of extended family households (joint and stem) than did farm laborers (88 percent of 51 families and 46 percent of 61 families, respectively). The average size of the domestic family of the landlords was 8.9 persons; that of the farm laborers was 4.3.—Lang, *op. cit.*, pp. 136, 148. Buck classified 16,786 farms into eight sizes and found that larger farms had larger households. For example, households of very

Within the family age and sex were attributes that determined prestige. The elders and the males were accorded prestige. There was consensus that the old were wise and that they should have power and be given deference. In accordance with the concept of filial piety they were highly valued. The Chinese did not encourage their children to act in a childish fashion; they made it "clear to the young that it [was] not very desirable and comfortable to be young, but that it [was] advantageous and dignified to be old."[7]

The key relationship was that between father and son. The family was carried on through the male line. To the son the father represented the immediate link in the chain of venerated ancestors. To the father the son represented the immediate link with posterity. The mother was merely a necessary accessory for the perpetuation of the line; the daughter would leave the house one day and would be the means of perpetuating the line of some other family. The Chinese family was patrilineal and patronymic. Ideally, it was also patrilocal and patriarchal,[8] but the latter two features could only be achieved where the conditions of subsistence permitted the existence of a sufficiently large familial system.

Whereas the son represented familial continuity between successive generations, the daughter more nearly occupied the status of a visitor who would depart on reaching a marriageable age. As between a son who would carry on the family line and a daughter who would assist another family in doing so, there is little question as to which was the more important in the parents' eyes. When times were good, all children were welcome; when food was short, female infants were sometimes allowed to die. According to the formal structure females had little influence in the family; informally, however, women, especially grandmothers, generally exercised considerable influence.

small farms contained an average of 4.2 persons; those of medium farms contained 5.5; large farms, 8.3; and very, very large farms, 10.7.—J. L. Buck, *Land Utilization in China: Statistics* (Nanking: University of Nanking, 1937), p. 300. A study of the census of Kunyang County, Yunnan Province, as of 1942 shows a median size of domestic family to be 5.5; for 26 families of the gentry, however, the median was 11.—Yung-Teh Chow, *Social Mobility in China: Status Careers among the Gentry in a Chinese Community* (New York: Atherton, 1966), pp. 108–109. It is of some interest to compare the foregoing figures with national averages obtained by Burch from fourteen countries over the two decades following World War II. (His data do not include China.) With respect to average size of domestic family he found a range of 3.3 (United States) to 5.8 (Honduras and Nicaragua), and the domestic *nuclear* family ranged from 3.1 (United States) to 5.1 (Honduras).—Thomas K. Burch, "The Size and Structure of Families: A Comparative Analysis of Census Data," *American Sociological Review,* 32: 347–363 (1967), esp. Table 7, p. 359.

[7] Francis L. K. Hsu, *Under the Ancestors' Shadow: Chinese Culture and Personality* (New York: Columbia University Press, 1948), p. 239.

[8] *Patrilineal:* descent is traced through the male line; *patronymic:* the child takes the name of the father's family or sibling; *patrilocal:* the bride takes up residence near or with the parental family of the groom; *patriarchal:* pertaining to an extended-family system ruled by the oldest male of the oldest generation.

THE ECONOMIC FUNCTION

Now let us look at the traditional family of the Chinese peasantry as an economic unit. The peasant family was highly self-sufficient. It produced virtually everything it consumed—clothing and household furnishings as well as food—and needless to say, it consumed nearly everything it produced. The chief goods that it could not produce and therefore had to purchase were salt, ceremonial objects, and iron for tools.[9] This meant that virtually no contacts of family members with outsiders were required for economic purposes. Another implication of economic self-sufficiency is that each member of the family was called upon to perform many different tasks. The multiplicity of task-oriented activities required all to be jacks-of-all-trades.[10]

Let us examine the implications of the preceding description of productive activity in the Chinese family. Economic production must be carried out in every society. In some societies, such as the one we are now considering, the family is the most important unit of productive organization, and hence most production takes place within the family. Where the economic function is differently organized, e.g., in contemporary America and in the Israeli kibbutz, the important productive units are outside the family (e.g., the corporation and the collective farm), and consequently there is little productive activity within the family. In settings such as traditional China, where production is carried on within the family, the members are related to each other through interlocking economic roles as well as through the bonds of kinship. Man and boy are manager and worker as well as father and son. Their joint participation in production binds them into economic interdependence irrespective of other aspects of their total relationship. Phrased in other words, the core relationship of productive activity creates a powerful incentive for father and son to work together no matter how much each may "get on the nerves" of the other. In suburban America and the Israeli kibbutz, on the other hand, this economic core relationship is absent and thus cannot serve to counterbalance the strains of interpersonal irritation. This exemplifies the significance of the family's functions for family life and family solidarity.

What about the distribution and consumption of goods and services within the family? From the very few purchases listed above (salt, and so on) it follows that family members were unable to obtain for their individual use goods and services outside the family. This is the consequence for the in-

---

[9] Levy, op. cit., pp. 211–212.

[10] Members of gentry families, whether child or adult, did not usually engage in physical labor, and the families did not generally produce goods or services directly for the consumption of their members. Family income derived in cash and in kind from the renting of land. Individual members also had income from occupations, especially civil service. Because the family of the gentry was not economically self-sufficient in the sense of producing directly for consumption, it is not being presented here to exemplify a family of high "functionality."

dividual of economic self-sufficiency and interdependence. Family income, consisting of the goods and services produced by the family plus those few that were purchased, was pooled.[11] The father (more strictly, the oldest male of the oldest generation in the household) was responsible for the distribution of income. He might delegate this responsibility to the mother, but it was clearly understood that her responsibility had come to her through delegation. Distribution would normally be effected to provide the basic necessities for everyone in the household. The opportunity for differential treatment arose as the margin increased between the total family income and the minimum required for subsistence. We might offer a maxim regarding their differential expectations: from each according to the abilities associated with his sex- and age-roles; to each according to the prestige accorded to those roles. High prestige was accorded to age; the old were the closest of the living to the venerable ancestors. Thus the aged were given preferential treatment with respect to the goods of life: the rarest delicacy, the choicest garment.[12]

THE POLITICAL FUNCTION

Next let us consider the traditional family as a social grouping that carried out the political function. There was, of course, the central government of the empire. In the towns (corresponding to American county seats) the law of the emperor was enforced by his prefect, whose duties included the collection of taxes as well as the maintenance of order. The prefect relied on a council of heads of families to control their members. In this way the father (or oldest family member) was responsible to other families for the good conduct of members of his family. Within the family he had power to command obedience and the right, if necessary, to use force to implement his orders. Although the father did not have the absolute power over life and death as was held by the Roman *paterfamilias,* his power was very great, and the punishment of a father for killing his son was relatively mild. Should such a killing occur while the father was chastising the son "in a lawful and customary manner," the father was to be exonerated.[13] The Chinese view of

---

[11] In a gentry family not all of the income would be pooled. The principal family income, e.g., rent from family-owned lands, would be treated collectively, but adult males might also have income from positions in the civil service or elsewhere, and such income would be regarded as individual rather than family income.

[12] Some feeling for the attitude of the continuity of generations, especially of the aged as the link between the active participants in this world and those who have already gone to the other world, comes from Levy's observation that to present a coffin to an aged parent was regarded as "a highly filial gift, not a brutally aggressive hint of impatience."—Levy, *op. cit.,* p. 133.

[13] Lang, *op. cit.,* p. 27. The clan was another organization that maintained order and protected its members. A clan is "a consanguineal kin group . . . based on a rule of descent rather than of residence."—G. P. Murdock, *Social Structure* (New York, Macmillan, 1949), p. 65. Membership in a powerful clan contributed to one's feeling of personal safety on travels about the countryside.

violence directed from son toward father was as harsh as it was lenient when the hostility was directed from the older generation to the younger. Being the most flagrant violation of filial piety, "patricide was, perhaps, the worst possible crime in the society and was punishable by death or torture or both."[14]

THE SOCIALIZING-EDUCATIONAL FUNCTION

Let us consider the socializing-educational function. Some boys of the gentry were sent away to school; others in that class received instruction at home from tutors. For children of the peasantry there were neither schools nor tutors. In the peasant family it was taken for granted that a child would and should grow up to be much like the parent of the same sex and to carry on the same activities. In particular there was no great question as to "what" the child "would be" when an adult: if a boy, a peasant; if a girl, a peasant's wife. Since this was so, no one was in a better position than the parent of the same sex to train the child for his adult roles. And outside the family no one was available to teach him at all. As might be expected, children were inducted into useful (economic) sex-differentiated activities as soon as their participation was helpful. By the time they were five or six years old, boys of the peasantry were accompanying their fathers to the fields and were assigned tasks appropriate to their strength: fetching tools and weeding, and presently planting and harvesting. Girls learned the corresponding feminine activities: washing and cleaning, preparing food, making garments, and weaving baskets.

THE RELIGIOUS FUNCTION

Buddhism and Taoism have been the major organized religions in China. In general a family would be Buddhist or Taoist or perhaps both (since Western religious exclusiveness is alien to Oriental practice), but in addition the family would engage in the worship of its ancestors. In imperial times the family worshiped those ascendants who had recently passed to their rewards, and the clan worshiped more remote ancestors. It was believed that ancestors continued to live as long as they were worshiped. Without this service, as was the fate of those without descendants, they would have had to wander in the world as ghosts. The rites of ancestor worship were performed by the oldest male of the oldest generation.

SUMMARY AND CONCLUSIONS CONCERNING THE BASIC SOCIETAL FUNCTIONS

Now we can summarize the import of our remarks about the highly functional traditional family of the Chinese peasantry. All societies recognize some sort of kinship relationship that we speak of as father-son. But let us note

[14] Levy, *op. cit.*, p. 242.

how much more is involved between two such individuals in this highly functional family. Not only does the man enact the role of father with respect to the boy's role of son, but the man and the boy are also related as manager and worker, producer and consumer, official and constituent, teacher and pupil, and priest and parishioner. Here the total relationship between man and boy involves all the core relationships involved in the five basic societal functions. Man and boy are functionally interdependent in five different ways.

When so many of the individual's needs are institutionally provided for within the family, it may be expected that there will be correspondingly less provision for meeting them outside the family. With respect to productive activities this society did not have an active job market. Especially was this true for women. If a girl should have felt "fed up" with life at home, it would not have occurred to her to run away. There was no place to go. She could expect to leave her family of orientation in due course in one of two ways: probably by marriage, but possibly by being sold into prostitution or concubinage. Similarly with the family functioning as a distributive organization, it follows that there would not be supermarkets or even much in the way of small shops or peddlers. With the family functioning as a political organization, it follows that the individual would be looking to the family for protection of his rights, and if he were to leave the family, he would become quite defenseless. With the family functioning as a socializing-educational organization, it follows that a child would have no way to learn adult roles outside the family. With the family functioning as a religious organization, the child would be dependent upon his father to communicate the appropriate sentiments to the ancestors. In a society such as this anyone who would try to live outside the family would not only be regarded as without ancestors but he would immediately find himself defenseless and unemployed, without food, shelter, or clothing, and without friends or associates. In a society such as this almost all of life goes on within the family.

THE FAMILIAL FUNCTIONS AND MATE-SELECTION

We began this section with a discussion of the structure of the traditional family of the Chinese peasantry, and we have commented at length on its functional aspects. We have also mentioned the valuation placed upon roles differentiated by age and sex. Let us proceed to other values and to norms and expectations, the sorts of phenomena we subsume under the term *culture*. Since the family was almost the total source of all blessings, it should follow that there would have been a great interest in seeing that it was maintained and in particular that replacements were provided for those who died. This surmise is readily substantiated. The primary orientation of the married couple was toward procreation; the primary purpose of the bride was to bear children. As Levy puts it, the failure to have children or at least to adopt some implied the negation of one's own life and of the lives of all one's ancestors. Each person had a lively and practical interest in having one or more sons, since this was the one direct way of providing for one's old age. Mencius, the ancient Chinese philosopher, had said, "Of the three unfilial acts the greatest is to lack posterity."[15]

The Chinese attitudes toward childbirth and toward women and the concept of filial piety will be illuminated by a consideration of the process of mate-selection. The young Chinese boy or girl was expected to accept without question a spouse chosen by the family. Because the family was patriarchal, the ultimate responsibility for getting the son a wife rested with the father. In practice, however, the mother might assume the more active role. This procedure made good sense because the choice of the son's bride was of greater practical interest to the mother than to anyone else in the household. The reason for this was that most of the hours of the incoming bride would be spent in assisting the mother with domestic chores. Hence the mother was selecting an assistant, and it was clear that to some degree the efficiency of the housekeeping would depend on her making a sound decision. It was true that the son was getting a mother for his children, but the woman, as we have noted, was regarded as a mere implement for maintaining the continuity from father to son.

Although it was not usual to do so, the marriage could be arranged while the principals were still children or even before either was born. The mate thus selected might well be a person whom the son or daughter did not know. In most areas of China premarital meetings between the betrothed were not approved. Romantic love was condemned, and elopement might be punished.

The process of mate-selection began when the family appointed a go-between. It was the task of the go-between to locate suitable young women for the family to consider as wife-candidates for its son. That the marriage of the son was clearly a matter of familial rather than individual concern was symbolized by the fact that the marriage was made in the names of the parents who took the daughter-in-law rather than in the name of the son who took the wife. Levy remarks that in the actual selection of a spouse the go-between was more important than either set of parents, and the parents in turn were more important than the bride and groom themselves. The go-between served two important purposes. In the first place he enabled all parties to the negotiation to save face. If one family wished to avoid a liaison with another, the fact that negotiations were being carried on by the go-between allowed them to be terminated without embarrassment to anyone. Second, the go-between could be more objective than those more closely involved in the negotiations.[16]

Since marriages were arranged by the families, the considerations taken into account were primarily those of relevance to the families. Among the gentry marriage was conceived as an alliance of houses. The wealth, influence, and status of the prospective bride's family were naturally subjected to careful scrutiny. Among the peasants the girl's strength and working ability were the

---

[15] Levy, *op. cit.*, pp. 94, 127, 168, 175.
[16] *Ibid.*, n., pp. 100–101.

main consideration.[17] While investigating a prospective spouse for a son, a parent might give consideration, secondary though it was, to such personal characteristics as the appearance and health, disposition, and horoscope of the candidate in order to assure as good a match as possible.

MARITAL RELATIONS AND FILIAL OBLIGATIONS

Since the marriage partners could well be total strangers, it was not assumed that marriage was based on love.[18] Overt expressions of affection between husband and wife were disapproved. Hsu reports the case of a young man who walked down the street holding hands with his bride. Human excrement was thrown over their heads because of this violation of the mores.[19] It was expected and hoped, however, that in due course affection would develop in the marital relationship.

According to the principle of filial piety the primary obligations of both the son and his wife were to *his* parents. Hsu states that praise was bestowed upon a man who neglected his wife in order that he might better serve his father or mother, and upon a woman who neglected her husband in order to serve her parents-in-law.[20] The death of a parent was expected to evoke much greater manifestations of sorrow than the death of a wife. If the son's parents were displeased with his wife, they could force him to divorce her irrespective of his feelings in the matter.[21] Indeed, the greater his affection for her and hence the greater his loss, the greater would be his honor for such a demonstration of filial piety.

In her new home the bride was definitely subordinated to the groom's mother. Although in practice wives and mothers-in-law occasionally got along well together, this relationship was one of traditional hostility. Because the son had been the means of improving her position in the family, the mother's affection for the son seems to have been characteristically quite strong, and thus a ready basis existed for the mother to resent the intrusion of another woman into her son's life. The lot of the daughter-in-law was to relieve the mother of menial and undesirable tasks, to provide the most accessible target for the latter's aggression, and to produce children, particularly sons. One study even reports that the obtaining of a daughter-in-law was similar to the

---

[17] H. Fei, "Peasantry and Gentry: An Interpretation of Chinese Social Structure and Its Changes," *American Journal of Sociology*, 52: 1–17 (1946).

[18] One authority asserts that the word "love" as used by Americans would appear from the Chinese point of view to be indistinguishable from licentiousness. Cf. Francis L. K. Hsu, *Americans and Chinese: Two Ways of Life* (New York: Abelard-Schuman, 1953), p. 37.

[19] Hsu, *Under the Ancestors' Shadow*, pp. 27, 225.

[20] Francis L. K. Hsu, "The Family in China: The Classical Form," in Ruth Anshen (ed.), *The Family: Its Function and Destiny* (rev. ed.; New York: Harper & Row, 1959), p. 126.

[21] Hsu, *Under the Ancestors' Shadow*, pp. 59, 61, 246.

acquisition of a long-term laborer.[22] The status of women was symbolized in the practice of patrilineal inheritance, whereby women were excluded from owning land.

> Women never bring land to their husbands' families, and inheritance by the sons from the father is so absolute that a widow who holds custody for a young son is prohibited from making any disposition of the property. Even the woman who contracts a matrilocal marriage is considered only a temporary link in the chain of patrilineal inheritance.[23]

Other indications of the status of women in traditional China are the observations that "a woman should obey her father before marriage, obey her husband after marriage, and obey her son when her husband has deceased" and that "perhaps the most miserable and unbearable life is that of the young, childless widow (even worse than a spinster). . . ."[24]

The positive attitude of the Chinese toward having children was suggested by the phrase that characterized a pregnant woman as "having happiness in her body."[25] On bearing a child her standing in the family was improved; if she bore a son, it was greatly improved. If she bore no child, she was thought to be at fault, and this provided her husband with one of the seven grounds for divorcing her.

We may summarize some of the foregoing paragraphs with the observation that for the Chinese girl marriage represented not a gateway to happiness but the initiation into her most trying role. The low prestige generally accorded feminine roles, the absence of a relationship of affection with any member of her new family, and the traditional hostility of her mother-in-law were the outstanding features of her unhappy lot.

There were three principal conditions that served to mitigate the bride's difficult plight: time, poverty, and, occasionally, matrilocal marriage. With the passage of time a woman would progress from the relatively low status of bride to the successively higher statuses of mother and grandmother. Since the culture emphasized that the prime function of traditional Chinese marriage was procreation, the wife with "happiness in her body" was demonstrating that she was performing her most important task. She added a considerable increment to her status if the child was a son. Her standing in the family was further improved and her influence was increased on the marriage of a son, for she then acquired a daughter-in-law, who was clearly her inferior in status and whom she could order about.

In the poorer classes the wife's work constituted a real contribution to the family's income, whereas in the gentry, wives had little economic sig-

---

[22] Hsiao-Tung Fei and Chih-I Chang, *Earthbound China: A Study of Rural Economy in Yunnan* (Chicago: University of Chicago Press, 1945), p. 66.

[23] *Loc. cit.* The practice of matrilocal marriage is explained on page 41.

[24] Shu-Ching Lee, "China's Traditional Family. Its Characteristics and Disintegration," *American Sociological Review*, 18: 272–280 (1953), at p. 275 and 275–276.

[25] Levy, *op. cit.*, pp. 66, 114.

nificance. Moreover, since remarriage might prove prohibitively costly for the laborer and poor peasant, in these poorer classes the departure of a wife could represent a very considerable loss.[26]

Matrilocal marriage occurred in a family having one or more daughters but no son. This was a device whereby the family line could be carried on even though there was no son. According to this practice the son-in-law changed his name to that of his wife's family and in a sense became an adopted son. It was understood that this was a purely temporary device (in terms of the family's genealogy) and that with the birth of a son to the matrilocally married couple, the conventional patrilineal and patrilocal pattern was to be resumed. Matrilocal marriage was degrading to the man; in general his family was poorer than that of the woman. Since, in this situation, the bride continued to live in the home of her parents and it was the groom who was added to the family, the treatment of the bride was much better and that of the groom somewhat worse than was customary.[27]

China and the Industrial Revolution

We began the discussion of the traditional Chinese family by remarking that it was historical rather than contemporary. More recently the Industrial Revolution has come to China. Its coming has exerted profound pressures on the family and is continuing to do so. Industrialization arrived later in China than in Western Europe and its conquest in China has been less complete. Although it may actually have begun as far back as a century ago, by the 1920's, as Latourette observes, it was still "only incipient."[28] Because industrialization has come only recently to China, we can see, in the recent developments of the family there, a better-documented history than is available in the West of a change from a preindustrial to an industrial family form. Let us note some of the features of the Industrial Revolution and then turn to the Chinese family of the more recent period.

The Industrial Revolution has meant a profound change in all the basic societal institutions. We are accustomed to thinking of it as a revolution in the economic institution characterized by the introduction of nonhuman power and large-scale organizations. Some writers believe that developments came first in the economic institution and that these caused changes in other basic

---

[26] It may appear paradoxical that the status of women tended to be relatively high when the socioeconomic status of the family as a whole was low. The apparent paradox results from the fact that we are talking about two kinds of status. When we speak of the status of women, we are thinking of status within the family, and the standard is the status of men. When we speak of socioeconomic status, on the other hand, we are thinking of a position shared by the members of a family that is relative to the positions of other families in the hierarchy of socioeconomic statuses.

[27] Hsu, "The Family in China" in Anshen, *op. cit.*, pp. 130–131.

[28] Kenneth Scott Latourette, *A Short History of the Far East* (3d ed.; New York: Macmillan, 1957), p. 496.

institutions (religious, political, and so on). Such a theme has animated the writings of Marx and numerous others. Other writers have looked elsewhere for a "prime mover" to explain social change. An example is Max Weber, who regarded the Reformation—a revolution in the religious institution—as an antecedent condition without which the Industrial Revolution could hardly have occurred. There are still others, moreover, who look upon the family itself as occasionally a prime mover initiating change in other institutional structures.[29] At this point it is not our purpose to engage in this dispute over which so much ink has been spilled. For our purpose the important point is that a great revolution in man's way of life has occurred, and we are interested in understanding the implications of this revolution for the familial institution.

The revolution can be seen in each of the five basic institutions. In the *economic* institution we can see that industrialization requires sizable accumulations of capital and, at least in its early stage, of labor. Among the most remarkable consequences are corporations with assets in the millions of dollars and metropolitan areas with populations in the millions of human beings. In the *political* institution we note a revolution in the rise of nationalism and nation-states. In Europe this took place mostly in the last century; in Asia and Africa it is a phenomenon of the present century. There is a stage in which industrialization creates a demand for masses of skilled personnel, and the revolution appears in the *socializing-educational* institution with the rise of organizations for the purpose of public education. Prerevolutionary Europeans made their peace with their God through intermediaries, both living and canonized. The debits of sin and guilt could regularly be balanced by the prescribed units of penance. In the West the most conspicuous manifestation of the revolution in the *religious* institution was the Reformation, which brought man face to face with an inscrutable God. Now an adaptive anxiety arose from the understanding that accounts could not be settled until the Day of Judgment. Hard work, thrift, and the accumulation of capital, which happened to be values consistent with incipient industrialization, became the virtues of the new Protestant ethic.[30] And now to get some understanding of the implications of the Industrial Revolution for the *familial* institution let us see what has been happening to the Chinese family since the turn of the century. Our discussion will be divided into two phases: the first, about which

[29] E.g., William J. Goode, *World Revolution and Family Patterns* (New York: Free Press, 1963).

[30] Max Weber, *The Protestant Ethic and the Spirit of Capitalism* (trans. by Talcott Parsons; New York: Scribner, 1930); Abram Kardiner, *The Psychological Frontiers of Society* (New York: Columbia University Press, 1945), esp. chap. 14. That these virtues of Puritanism and of Ben Franklin and *Poor Richard's Almanac* may be consistent only with an early stage of industrialization is suggested by the fact that although they are incorporated into the ideology of the U.S.S.R., they have been represented as un-American, or at least un-Madison Avenue, by the strident voice of American advertising, which would have us believe that thrift and saving would eventuate in national ruin, whereas heavy spending and rapid obsolescence lead to salvation.

our information is generally adequate, concerns the period up through World War II; our information is still very sketchy about the second phase—the period during and since the Communist Revolution.

THE PEASANT FAMILY AND THE INDUSTRIAL REVOLUTION

The most readily visible changes bearing on the familial institution are those that have been formalized into legal codes. Shortly after the Boxer Rebellion at the beginning of the twentieth century the pressure for change became so importunate that a committee was appointed to formulate a new legal code. In 1930 and 1931 (well before the Communist Revolution in China) new codes were finally promulgated that reflected a quite Westernized conception of the family. The code reduced male authority, eliminated the idea that it was the families of the principals who were primarily concerned in a marriage, and required the consent of both parties to betrothal. The new code did not mention concubines and thus outlawed them; it listed penalties for bigamy, but such penalties had existed in the previous law. In the theme of filial piety, however, there was a significant difference from Western conceptions: in the new code the responsibility for the welfare of parents continued to take precedence over the concern for the welfare of children.[31]

Now let us note some of the changes reported by observers. In traditional China marriage had come early. Although formal statistical evidence is impossible to obtain, it appears that during the first half of the present century the average age at marriage increased among the more "modernized" Chinese —the intellectuals and the urban workers. Lang observed that female workers were unconcerned if still unmarried in their middle twenties or as late as twenty-seven, "an age at which village girls are considered old maids and are unable to obtain good matches."[32] In traditional China everyone married except those afflicted with gross abnormalities; in the present century bachelors and spinsters have been appearing in greater numbers.[33]

In the traditional conception man's emotional life was divided into three relationships: a wife for home and children, a concubine or prostitute for sexual gratification, and a male companion with whom to share ideals, dreams, and hopes.[34] In the modern family the wife became more than merely the woman with whom the husband had sexual relations for procreative purposes; she was also called upon to provide sexual gratification and companionship.

The cleavage between traditional and modern attitudes toward marriage resulted in considerable disorganization and tragedy. Two particularly obvious types of difficulty resulted. One of these was an intensified conflict of

---

[31] Lang, *Chinese Family and Society*, pp. 115–119.

[32] *Ibid.*, p. 129. It seems plausible that such an increase in age at marriage occurred in the United States during the nineteenth century. See Chapter 10.

[33] *Ibid.*, p. 129; Levy, *op. cit.*, p. 301.

[34] Lang, *op. cit.*, p. 202. Cf. also Levy, *op. cit.*, pp. 260–261 and note 4, page 32, above.

generations. The parents expected the young man or woman to behave in traditional fashion and to accept unquestioningly the mate selected by them. The resistance of the "modern" son or daughter was interpreted as inexcusable disobedience and lack of filial piety.

The other form of difficulty occurred between the sexes. It took place where a young man was betrothed and perhaps married in the traditional fashion at a relatively early age. He then went to the city or perhaps to America, where he learned to accept Western ideas, and upon returning to China proceeded to fall in love with someone of his own choosing. Various expedients were employed to resolve the difficulty. The husband might try to educate his wife to be a companion and hostess; he might take a second wife in the city and leave the first in the country; or he might divorce the first.[35] The consequence was usually unhappiness for all concerned.

As we have noted before, arranged marriages put mate-selection on a familistic basis, whereas love marriages put mate-selection on an individualistic basis. Another indication of the decline of familism and the rise of individualism was the apparent increase in the number of households consisting only of nuclear families, i.e., households consisting only of parents and their unmarried children. And as this implies, there appeared a kind of family new for China—old parents whose children had married and had moved away from them.[36]

Running through these new developments in the family has been the theme of change in the relations between the generations. Unlike the old days, the more recent situation provided the young with an opportunity to find jobs and support themselves if they left home.[37] The opportunity to leave home was especially relevant to father-son relations in that it afforded the son a means of escape from the traditionally harsh discipline of the father. As a result of these conditions parents appeared to become somewhat restrained in the degree in which they enforced discipline by beating.[38]

There were intimations that among some of the more "modern" parents an atmosphere of parent-child relations was developing in a direction familiar to Americans—one emphasizing companionship and de-emphasizing status relationships, phrasing parental wishes as requests rather than as commands, and verbalizing some benefit for the child upon his carrying out the desired behavior.[39] (The shift from responding in terms of age- and sex-roles to responding in terms of companionship is symbolized in some middle-class American families by the preference of the parents to have their children address them by their given names rather than as "father" or "mother.")

The innovation of neolocal residence (i.e., the practice whereby the son

[35] Lang, *op. cit.*, pp. 202–203.
[36] *Ibid.*, pp. 141–143.
[37] Levy, *op. cit.*, p. 303.
[38] Lang, *op. cit.*, pp. 243–244.
[39] Levy, *op. cit.*, p. 338.

sets up a separate household for his family of procreation when he marries) is fraught with implications, of which we shall note four: (1) Filial piety was mitigated and filial responsibility was relaxed. (2) The son assumed the full power and authority of adulthood at the time of marriage rather than at the (usually later) death of the father. (3) The immediate and practical interest of the parents, especially of the mother, in the characteristics of the son's wife was reduced. (4) Chinese society began to face what was for it a new social problem—how to care for the aged.

One of the major themes of this book is that what has been happening in the Chinese family illustrates the major social forces that determine familial structures, functions, and norms. The traditional Chinese family of the peasantry was very different from the family best known to us—that of the urban and suburban American middle class. The family that was resulting from industrialization in pre-Communist China was coming to look very much like the American middle-class family. Shortly we shall try to sketch in some of the Communist innovations, but first let us look at three descriptive remarks about differences between Chinese and American family life that appear in a book[40] comparing these two cultures. Although the author of that book might not agree with our point of view and certainly is not responsible for it, it is suggested that we might read his remarks about the Chinese family as pertaining to the traditional Chinese family we have discussed and his remarks about the American family as referring to the modern Chinese family we have just been presenting as the pre-Communist concomitant of industrialization.

(1) In the Chinese family, says Hsu, the child is trained to rely on the family and his kinsmen; in the American, he is taught to be self-reliant. (2) In the Chinese family the parents and children accept their relations with each other as permanent and given; in the American, it is recognized that parents and children may come one day to reject each other, and their relations may be ruptured. (3) In the Chinese family the child has no urge to seek alliances outside the family; in the American, he has, and we might add that American parents frequently show overt concern over children who are, in their judgment, insufficiently "extraverted" and not able to integrate with their peer groups.

The Chinese Family and the Communist Revolution

After World War II the Communists conquered the forces of the Kuomintang party under Chiang Kai-shek and by 1950 took over all the Chinese mainland. For our information as to the societal consequences of the Communist Revolution we are dependent largely upon the reports of journalists

[40] Hsu, *Americans and Chinese.*

of other nationalities than American and upon analyses made of the press of Communist China. We are dependent upon journalists because Communist governments do not show enthusiasm about having their institutions studied—at least by scholars from the West. We are dependent upon non-American journalists because of the negative policies of both the United States and the Chinese governments on travel in Communist China by American nationals. Noting, then, the qualifications arising from the fact that we must depend heavily upon journalistic accounts, let us see what the visible trends may be.

Because China has been and remains largely an agricultural country, probably the most important single change has been in the organization of the agricultural sector of the economy. By the latter part of 1958 the government had not only taken ownership of almost all heavy industries, but it had established 26,500 rural people's communes, each averaging 5000 households and about 6000 mow of land (about 2400 acres). The commune, which has become the standard form of rural community organization, seeks to become economically self-sufficient by manufacturing tools, fertilizer, and clothing, as well as food. Its multifunctional nature is seen in services it provides: "communal dining-rooms, nurseries, kindergartens, schools, 'happy homes for the aged,' hospitals . . . laundries, sewing shops, barber shops, public baths, etc."[41]

In the light of this radical change in societal organization, let us look at three features of familial structure: familial form, mate-selection, and the pattern of authority. We recall that in the traditional period the ideal familial form (apparently realized only by some of the families of the gentry) was the joint family and that most families, both of gentry and of peasantry, were of the stem type. Yang points out that the traditional society consisting of "numerous semiautonomous local units . . . structured around the kinship system" with their "generational continuity . . . rigid organization [and] multiplicity of socio-economic functions" was suited neither to the rise of economic organization, industrial and commercial, nor to the emergence of a centralized national polity. The same author says it is unclear what form of the family will emerge from the Communist Revolution, but that from early in the twentieth century (well before the Communist Revolution) there has seemed to be a drift away from traditional familial forms and toward the two-generation conjugal (or nuclear) family.[42]

The trend away from selecting a spouse on familial grounds and toward selecting one for personal reasons was evident before the Communists were in power. Under the Communists there was promulgated in 1950 the Marriage Law of the People's Republic, which makes voluntary mate-selection the law of the land and forbids interference of any third party.[43] Deploring Western

---

[41] Inger Hellström, "The Chinese Family in the Communist Revolution: Aspects of the Changes Brought about by the Communist Government," *Acta Sociologica*, 6: 256–277 (1963). Quotation is from p. 269.

[42] C. K. Yang, *The Chinese Family in the Communist Revolution* (Cambridge, Mass.: Technology Press, 1959), pp. 20, 44. Quotation is from p. 20.

[43] *Ibid.*, p. 221. The Marriage Law of 1950 also contained nine articles concerning

bourgeois marriage as demeaning to women and as "little more than legalized and monolithic prostitution,"[44] the Communists assert that spouses have a duty to love each other, that "true feeling should be built on mutual labor"[45] and to regard marriage as a "spiritual union of two comrades of different sexes [the important purpose of which] is to strengthen and cherish their commonly shared belief of communism, and then to engage in production to build a new society."[46]

According to another writer it is Communist doctrine that the decision to marry should be based upon the conviction that the marriage will "result in greater contributions to revolutionary work," and he continues: "It is written into the marriage law that husband and wife should love and respect each other, 'engage in production,' and work 'for the building of a new society.'"[47]

A British journalist quotes a Chinese housewife on "the five goods of a housewife and mother of the new China": "It is good to encourage the husband in his work. The housewife must be good to her husband. It is good to attend literacy classes. It is good to have friendly relations with neighbors and mutually assist them. It is essential to make a good budget and adhere to it."[48]

The foregoing paragraphs have emphasized the new look in Communist China. One who has ever observed resistance to change among the traditionally oriented may surmise that there would be less than total conformity to the new policies of the Communists. Hellstrom states that a study was undertaken in 1953 to investigate enforcement of the Marriage Law of 1950:

> . . . the law was only partially effective in Central-South and East China, and hardly at all observed in Northwest and Southern China, where parents still arranged marriages, reared daughters-in-law for their sons, and married off their children too young; even female slavery and concubinage were still practices.

In two rural counties, he adds, 90 percent of all marriages were arranged.[49]

---

divorce. Immediately there followed a marked increase in divorce cases. Cf. Hellström, *op. cit.*, pp. 266–267.

[44] Morton H. Fried, "The Family in China: The People's Republic," in Anshen, *op. cit.*, pp. 146–166. Quotation is from p. 157.

[45] "True Love Story: Chinese Version—The tale of Pang Yu-lan, a city girl, and Chang Tien-hsi, a peasant, illustrates the ways of romance down on the Communist farm," *The New York Times Magazine*, June 8, 1958, pp. 12, 16. This is an excerpt in translation of an article that appeared in the *Shansi Daily News*.

[46] Shu-Ching Lee, "China's Traditional Family," *loc. cit.*, p. 280. An analysis of letters to a publication for Chinese women has led to the conclusion that compatibility of political ideology has become a criterion of importance in mate-selection. Cf. Lucy Jen Huang, "Attitude of the Communist Chinese toward Inter-class Marriage," *Marriage and Family Living*, 24: 389–392 (1962).

[47] T. H. Chen, "The Marxist Remolding of Chinese Society," *American Journal of Sociology*, 58: 340–346 (1953), at p. 343.

[48] Walton A. Cole, "Austere Housing Pleases Chinese," *The New York Times*, February 26, 1958, p. 6.

[49] Hellström, *op. cit.*, p. 272.

Traditional China had a lively sense of familial authority: the old gave orders to the young, and males gave orders to females. Trends to equalize authority were evident early in this century. The Communist Revolution has continued and intensified these two equalitarian trends—the rise in the relative authority of the young and of women. By assessing ancestor worship as superstitious and by discouraging family rituals, the Communists have done much to secularize the family.[50] Fried says that the Communists are not trying to destroy the concept of filial piety nor to terminate the practice whereby young adults provide support as well as respect for their aged parents; rather, they are changing the basis for such respect and support. "Where the old beliefs exalted complete and unquestioning obedience, the new belief requires that the parent be correct and worthy of respect." One implication is that if the parent harbors "reactionary" sentiments, it is the offspring's duty because of higher loyalty to the state to denounce the parent.[51]

Yang summarizes the conditions that resulted in the subordination of women in the traditional family:

> Forced seclusion and imposed ignorance, lack of occupational opportunities, general discrimination against working women, and repressive marriage customs inevitably resulted also in women's economic dependency in traditional society. And, since that dependency was accompanied by the lack of family property rights for women, the simple threat of hunger forced them to submit to the inferior status assigned them by the male-dominant family institution.[52]

Since 1950 women, both married and unmarried, have been engaged in all sorts of occupations "ranging from railroad engineers to ministerial posts in the Government."[53] The invasion of women into the traditionally masculine occupations has occurred in rural areas as well as in the city. In some rural communes husbands eat in community dining rooms because their wives are too busy in the fields to cook at home.[54]

Although it appears that at first women may not have wanted their new freedom and rights,[55] an Australian journalist reports that more recently women have accepted their new status with such a vengeance that they have become "the backbone of Chinese communism" and "Mao Tse-tung's most fanatical supporters."[56]

---

[50] Yang, *op. cit.*, chap. 10.

[51] Fried, "The Family in China," in Anshen, *op. cit.*, p. 158; Yang, *op. cit.*, pp. 173 ff.

[52] Yang, *op. cit.*, p. 112.

[53] "Attlee and Party Rest in Hangchow: Girl Car Conductor on Train Exemplifies Widening Role of China's Women Workers," *The New York Times*, August 30, 1954, p. 3.

[54] Gerald Clark, "Rural Red China Changes Sharply: Communes Offer 'Security' to Peasants, but Deprive Them of Individuality," *The New York Times*, November 30, 1958, p. 37.

[55] "New Marriage Law Is Opposed in China," *The New York Times*, October 16, 1951, p. 5.

[56] Reg Leonard, "'Liberated' Women in Red China Constitute Backbone of Regime: Emancipation Decree after Civil War Won Millions of Fanatic Supporters—Feminine Influence Now Widespread," *The New York Times*, August 25, 1956, p. 2.

As women have acquired their freedom, they have begun to wear the blue jackets and trousers that are the uniform of Chinese men. The women neglect their hair and their grooming generally. It is reported that "some venturesome girls who think clothing should be brightened up become so shy when they wear brightly colored blouses that they hide them beneath their drab, shapeless jackets."[57] As they become visually indistinguishable from their men, Chinese women appear to the journalists as among the drabbest and most inelegant in the world.

Although the Communist philosophy proclaims the equality of the sexes, Communist administrators have found that women employees represent higher costs than do men because of the necessity of setting up nurseries to care for their children as well as of providing leaves with pay to pregnant women. By 1955, therefore, women were being advised to take note of their contribution as "family women" and to await the state's call for them to take part in production.[58] Here we see the primary sex characteristics of women and their immediate social implications overriding the Communist doctrine that there should be no role-differentiation along sex lines.

Under the Communists there has been a continuation of the flight of the basic societal functions from the family. Indeed, the Communists have intensified and accelerated this shift by insisting that the political structure—state and party—is the proper locus for many functions. Most obvious is the transfer of the clan's and the extended family's political function to party and state. It seems certain that this transfer of power has been the major objective of the Communists in advocating the dismantling of the larger familial and kin structures. Scarcely less obvious has been the presentation of the party as the functional equivalent of, and successor to, the family with respect to the religious function. We have noted the party's disparagement of ancestor worship. Yang presents anecdotes from Hong Kong and Peking papers of Chinese who, because of boredom or misery, had become very religious but who subsequently discovered that it was the party rather than religion that could bring them the desired relief.[59] What is left to the family after the loss of these functions, according to one writer, is that "the family has become an institution for producing babies and enjoying the leisure time left over from the major pursuits of everyday life."[60]

Some Conclusions about China

The traditional family controlled most, if not all, of the goods and services upon which the individual depended for his maintenance and sense of well-being. This is implied in the conception of the multifunctional family. Since

---

[57] *Ibid.*
[58] Yang, *op. cit.*, p. 210.
[59] *Ibid.*, pp. 125–126, 203.
[60] Maurice Freedman, "The Family in China, Past and Present," *Pacific Affairs*, 34: 323–336 (1961–1962). Quotation is from p. 333.

the traditional family held a monopolistic position, it could impose stern sanctions to enforce conformity. As the family loses functions, as it loses its monopoly, it also loses control over the behavior of its members.

In the traditional family, because many functions were involved, members responded to each other in terms of their respective roles and core relationships. In the modern family because the functions and the respective roles and core relationships are few in number and reduced in importance, responses are made in terms of affection, intimacy, and personality. Thus it appears that the Chinese are moving toward a family system more like that of the American middle class. Hsu offers a relevant observation with respect to the difference between American and traditional Chinese painting. American painting, he says, portrays the man or woman as an individual. Conflict and the emotional state of the subject are depicted in facial and other expressions. In Chinese painting the faces are blank, and "The viewer obtains a much better idea of the status, rank, prestige and other characteristics of the subjects portrayed than he does of their personalities or any intimation of what they are about to do."[61]

The gradual erosion of the Chinese large-family system apparently began in the early years of the twentieth century. The Communists are happy for this process to continue. They do not want the family to be multifunctional and strong, but, like totalitarians generally, they assert that the political structure is and should be multifunctional. Thus they are pushing the political structure as the successor to the elaborate familial and kin structure of traditional China.

The policies of Communist China, especially the collectivization of agriculture, have deprived the large-family system of resources and of the means of exerting its influence. Indeed this is the first government in Chinese history not to endorse the clan and not to rely on it for local administrative tasks.[62] To balance the evidence of radical and rapid change, however, we noted one study reporting considerable degree of traditional practice in mate-selection. Moreover, it should be noted that the Chinese government is not trying to weaken the nuclear family but rather to have it survive and even flourish as an instrument for achieving the orderly working of a Communist society.[63]

[61] *Americans and Chinese*, p. 20.
[62] Hellström, *op. cit.*, p. 273.
[63] Freedman, "The Family in China," *loc. cit.*, p. 333.

3

A Family of Little Functionality:
a kibbutz

The Family in a Kibbutz (in Israel)

From a kind of family that has been experienced back to the dawn of the Christian era by hundreds of millions of persons in one of the largest countries in the world we turn to a kind that was developed recently in one of the world's smallest countries. If we count those—both living and dead—who have known its variations from one settlement to another, it has probably embraced no more than one or two hundred thousand members. Indeed this familial type is so young that the observations to which we shall refer most extensively were made while the founding generation of the little communal society was still active. Since it is not our purpose to describe the most popular kinds of families in history but rather to anchor the two ends of the continuum of functionality, it is not critical that the total population of the settlement we shall describe was no more than approximately five hundred.[1]

Historical Background

In the 1880's some idealistic Russians of Jewish faith established the first Jewish agricultural colonies of modern times in the territory which was then under Turkish rule and called Palestine and which is now the State of Israel. In 1882, before the migrations began, there were some 24,000 Jews in Palestine. This migration brought approximately 25,000 additional Jews to Palestine be-

---

[1] Melford E. Spiro, *Kibbutz: Venture in Utopia* (Cambridge, Mass.: Harvard University Press, 1956), p. 60.

tween 1882 and 1903.[2] A second wave of Jewish migration from Eastern Europe to Palestine was sparked by pogroms that swept Russia in 1903–1904.[3] The second wave brought 40,000 more Jewish migrants between 1904 and the outbreak of World War I.[4] In November 1917, the British government issued the Balfour Declaration, which committed Britain to support the establishing in Palestine of a national home for Jewish people. In 1922 the League of Nations conferred upon Britain a mandate over Palestine. During the years 1919–1931 the third and fourth waves of immigration brought 116,000 more Jewish immigrants.[5] By the latter date the Jewish population of Palestine was about 175,000 of whom 136,000 lived in nineteen urban settlements and the remainder in more than a hundred rural settlements.[6] A fifth wave (1932–1939) was stimulated by the rise of Hitler and brought some 225,000 more Jews. There was little migration during World War II (1939–1945). In 1948 the Jewish State of Israel was proclaimed.

The land to which these hundreds of thousands of Jews migrated was "desolate and barren after hundreds of years of neglect . . . the hills were denuded and rocky, the valleys covered with swamps, and the plains were sand-blown waste-land."[7]

Those who turned to farming developed three basic kinds of settlements —the *moshava*, the *moshav*,[8] and the *kibbutz* (plural *kibbutzim*). The moshava is a settlement based upon an aggregate of individually owned and operated farms and plantations. In the moshav each family is allotted a plot of land, which as a rule is owned by the Jewish National Fund. The family works its plot of land and retains the income from the produce. As in America, children live in the home, and the wife-mother has the usual duties of housewifery plus some of the chores associated with farming. Marketing is a collective operation, and consumers' goods are purchased collectively. The type of community with which we shall be concerned is the kibbutz, a highly collectivized settlement. With few exceptions all the property in a kibbutz is collectively owned, and all work is collectively organized. Housing, eating, and the rearing of children, and all of the other essentials of life are organized for the most part in a collective manner.[9]

---

[2] Raphael Patai, *Israel between East and West: A Study in Human Relations* (Philadelphia: Jewish Publication Society of America, 1953), p. 57.

[3] Efraim Orni, *Forms of Settlement* (2d ed.; Jerusalem: World Zionist Organisation, 1955), p. 16.

[4] Patai, *op. cit.*, p. 58.

[5] *Ibid.*, p. 66.

[6] *Ibid.*, pp. 61–62.

[7] Orni, *op. cit.*, p. 5.

[8] A distinction is sometimes drawn between the *moshav* and the *moshav ovdim*, the latter generally connoting greater emphasis on economic cooperatives. The present discussion will follow the widespread usage of regarding the terms as interchangeable and of using *moshav* to refer to both.

[9] The writer's former colleague, Richard D. Schwartz, has been very helpful in clarify-

While immigration was at a low ebb during and immediately after World War II, the only type of rural settlement to show sizable growth was the kibbutz. In 1936 there were 47 kibbutzim in Palestine; in 1941, 87; in 1948, 149; and in 1954 there were 227 kibbutzim with 76,000 members.[10] Despite these impressive gains since the State of Israel was established in 1948, the increase in kibbutzim has been exceeded by the development of the moshav type of settlement. Of some 300 new settlements established in the four and a half years beginning January 1947, less than one third were kibbutzim. Patai attributes this to two considerations: (1) Because many of the recent migrants from Europe had spent years in concentration camps and camps for displaced persons, they yearned for a home that would provide privacy. (2) A sizable proportion of the recent immigration is made up of Oriental Jews, who as a rule are "too tradition-bound to understand the ideological basis of communal *kibbutz* life."[11]

Kibbutzim in General

A kibbutz is a legally constituted cooperative society. Children are not members; to become a member one must be elected in a vote of the membership. A general assembly or town meeting is the governing body of the kibbutz. It elects officers and members of committees to deal with such aspects of kibbutz life as education, cultural activities, and the allocation of labor for the different branches of agriculture. Each member is obliged to perform not only the regular job to which he is assigned but also any extra duties, such as committee work. In theory at least, kibbutzim have tended to subscribe to the principle of making annual reassignments of offices, committee posts, and duties in general in order to avoid establishing an entrenched bureaucracy and to prevent overburdening some members unduly.

In general every kibbutz has a communal dining hall, shower house, laundry, and clothes depot. The dining hall is the center of social life in the kibbutz. Meetings, ceremonies, and cultural functions take place there. Soiled clothes are taken to the laundry and are received, cleaned and repaired, from the clothes depot.

ing the distinctions among the types of settlement. Cf. also Orni, *op. cit.*; Patai, *op. cit.*; and Spiro, *op. cit.*

[10] Patai, *op. cit.*, p. 71; Spiro, *op. cit.*, p. 5.

[11] Patai, *op. cit.*, p. 72. Orni states that although the kibbutzim account for only about 5 percent of Israel's Jewish population, "the influence of the kibbutz movement on national and social developments has been far out of proportion to its numbers."—*op. cit.*, p. 54. Professor Richard Schwartz has suggested to the writer a third reason for the apparent decline in the appeal of the kibbutz type of settlement. During the period of the mandate the kibbutzim provided an opportunity to serve nationalistic aims through participation in secret military organizations, and numerous kibbutzim served as strong points against Arab attacks. After the mandate was terminated in 1948 an Israeli who was animated by nationalism could serve in the army and in various civil agencies that have arisen since independence.

Kiryat Yedidim

Kiryat Yedidim is a pseudonym for a particular kibbutz in which we are interested because it has been described in detail.[12] Because the observer on whom we are relying for our information did his field work in 1951 and because there is evidence of significant change since then, the account of Kiryat Yedidim will appear in the past tense. Since there is considerable variation among kibbutzim, it is important to note in which ways Kiryat Yedidim differed from the majority of them. These are reported to have been as follows: (1) Kiryat Yedidim was Marxist in ideology and pro-U.S.S.R. in the East-West struggle. (2) Its collective rearing of children was of longer duration—from infancy through high school. (3) It was anticlerical and hostile to any kind of religious expression. (4) There was strong pressure for ideological and political conformity. (5) There was especially strong adherence to such of its traditional values as industry and the avoidance of luxuries and of hired labor. Aside from these five points Kiryat Yedidim is reported to have been a fairly typical kibbutz.

Kiryat Yedidim was founded in 1921 by some ninety young Jews from Poland. Like most travelers, they carried their culture with them, but unlike most they regarded it as decadent and degenerate and were determined to avoid reproducing certain of its features. These migrants were anticapitalistic and antibourgeois, vigorously socialistic and vehemently egalitarian; they were anticlerical and atheistic, and they were antifamilistic. They were convinced that many of the ills of mankind were generated by the system of private property, enterprise for individual profit, and the exploitation of the worker by the owner. Accordingly the means of production—the trucks and tractors as well as the cattle—were collectively owned. There was no need for money. The distributive system of the kibbutz provided each individual with housing, and he ate in the communal dining room. The anticapitalistic convictions of the founders led them to abolish virtually all categories of personal property. At the outset all clothing was communally owned; but when it was discovered that this arrangement resulted in outrageous misfits as well as some laxity in the care of clothing, it was decided to give effective title to the individual once he had drawn a garment from the clothes depot. Medical and hospital bills and even the costs of combs and toothbrushes were borne by the kibbutz.[13]

With certain exceptions presently to be noted, Kiryat Yedidim stood

---

[12] This account is based principally upon the following two books: Melford E. Spiro, *Kibbutz: Venture in Utopia* (Cambridge, Mass.: Harvard University Press, 1956); and Melford E. Spiro, with the assistance of Audrey G. Spiro, *Children of the Kibbutz* (Cambridge, Mass.: Harvard University Press, 1958). Throughout the balance of the present chapter there will be numerous citations to both books. To facilitate these citations the former book will be referred to simply as *Kibbutz* and the latter volume as *Children*.

[13] *Kibbutz*, pp. 19–20.

emphatically on the principle of economic and social equality, especially with respect to the following features: that all should receive the same material goods; that none should be accorded special rewards, tangible or otherwise, because of occupation; and that the sexes should have equal access to the various occupations.

In accordance with this principle, each man, irrespective of age or occupation, got one pair of trousers and four shirts a year, and each woman received one dress a year. Clothing, food, and housing were distributed with approximate equality, i.e., without regard to the recipient's prestige or power, skill or industry. Absolute equality, however, was sometimes disturbed by the individual's opportunity to obtain goods outside the settlement (through receiving a gift package, for example, or through working in another settlement while on vacation) or through need, as might arise because of a medical condition.[14] Moreover, two categories of persons—old settlers and children—received special treatment, thus constituting exceptions to the principle of equality. Old settlers were favored in being assigned newer and more attractive housing. Children were favored by having a more varied diet than the adults; furthermore, although from the seventh grade on they were given regular work assignments, they worked no more than three hours a day and had a three-month vacation each year, whereas adults had only brief annual vacations.[15]

With respect to the principle of occupational equality, Spiro states that there was no class structure in Kiryat Yedidim, that although some jobs were more highly regarded than others, their occupants were not more highly rewarded, and that "the general manager—the highest elective officer in the kibbutz—[was] not the social superior of the cleaner of the latrines."[16] He does indicate, however, that contrary to the prestige pattern in the *shtetl* (village) from which the Polish Jews migrated, this kibbutz accorded more esteem to the person who did physical labor than to the individual who concentrated on intellectual activities.

Since most sociologists would probably agree with Davis and Moore that some stratification is necessary within a society in order to motivate and to place qualified people in important positions,[17] they would expect that sooner or later the value of efficiency would importune an unstratified society to endow its more important positions with greater rewards than its less important. To a sociologist, therefore, it would seem that Kiryat Yedidim was in a state of unstable equilibrium, that given enough economic pressure, the rotation of jobs would be dropped in the interest of efficiency, and that some jobs would be evaluated as having more influence, as being more important, and as involving more attractive work than others. At this point it would seem

[14] *Ibid.*, pp. 21–23.
[15] *Kibbutz*, p. 124; *Children*, pp. 301–302.
[16] *Kibbutz*, p. 24.
[17] Kingsley Davis and Wilbert E. Moore, "Some Principles of Stratification," *American Sociological Review*, 10: 242–249 (1945).

virtually impossible to avert a state of affairs whereby the holders of the more influential and more attractive jobs would be given increments of prestige. Studies made at about the same time in other kibbutzim suggest that the sociologist's expectation is being borne out. One observer who has studied three of the oldest kibbutzim reports the emergence in those settlements of two social strata—leaders-managers and the rank and file.[18] Another writer reports that in the kibbutz he studied in 1949–1950 the rotation of jobs, especially for men, had already been found to be uneconomical and had become somewhat symbolic.[19]

An important application of the principle of equality was with respect to the sexes. The European culture out of which these migrants came accorded high prestige to males and low prestige to females. In the shtetl the proper area of woman's activity was in the nursery and the kitchen; she was not expected to be able to read Hebrew nor to have intellectual ambitions: "The husband needs the wife for her domestic and economic services and for aid in fulfilling the mitsvos [divine commandments]. The wife needs the husband for guidance, for performance of domestic ritual, and for final admission to Olam Habo, the world to come."[20]

By contrast the founders of Kiryat Yedidim sought "to abrogate the traditional dependence of the female on the male, of the wife on her husband . . . to abolish the consequences of . . . 'the biological tragedy of woman.' "[21] They reasoned that if women could be liberated from the tasks involved in rearing children and in keeping house, they could and would become the intellectual and cultural equals of men. They adopted a number of measures to achieve this end.

To eliminate the legal dependence of women on men they eliminated the traditional wedding ceremony. No longer would marriage entail the woman's loss of her own name and the taking of her husband's. Indeed, the only significance of the married state that was explicitly recognized by the community was a change in housing arrangements: the man and woman involved applied for a common room. The words for husband and wife were avoided and the avoidance was justified on the ground that such terms smacked of the bourgeoisie. A more visible implementation of the equality of the sexes resulted from the establishing of a communal dining room. With all meals centrally prepared and all dishes centrally washed, a substantial reduction in the household chores was effected. Still the founders of the kibbutz

---

[18] Eva Rosenfeld, "Social Stratification in a 'Classless' Society," *American Sociological Review*, 16: 766–774 (1951). Rosenfeld does not specify which kibbutzim she observed. Degania, the first kibbutz, was established in 1909. For a personal account of its history see Joseph Baratz, *A Village by the Jordan: The Story of Degania* (London: Harvill, 1954).

[19] Richard D. Schwartz, "Functional Alternatives to Inequality," *American Sociological Review*, 20: 424–430 (1955). Cf. esp. p. 427.

[20] Mark Zborowski and Elizabeth Herzog, *Life Is with People: The Jewish Little-Town of Eastern Europe* (New York: International Universities Press, 1952), pp. 228–229.

[21] *Kibbutz*, p. 122.

could not eliminate the biological differentiation of the sexes, and so in Kiryat Yedidim, as elsewhere, it was the women who became pregnant, bore children, and breast-fed them. Aside from these immediate consequences of physiological differentiation, however, the kibbutz sought to eliminate sex-role differentiation.

Each mother brought her newborn infant from the hospital, not to the quarters she shared with her husband, but to a communal Infants' House. At the outset the practice of breast-feeding required the mother to go to the Infants' House every four hours. Breast-feedings tapered off as the weeks went by, and weaning was usually completed in about eight months. Aside from bearing and breast-feeding the infant, however, the mother had no responsibilities to him, and after conception the father had none. In another kibbutz, however, Schwartz found that parents and children were expected to demonstrate solidarity toward, and emotional support of, each other, but that the expectation was not backed up by any sanction.[22]

The kibbutz provided around-the-clock care for all the physical needs of the child. Thus at an average age of four days the newborn began their communally oriented lives. From that time until they finished high school and two years of military service they continued to live in communal quarters. Since the kibbutz wanted every individual to make an explicit decision whether or not to join before becoming a member and since the kibbutz wanted that decision to be based upon experience that included life outside the kibbutz, young men and women were expected to live away from Kiryat Yedidim for approximately a year before joining the kibbutz.[23] After high school and military service one became eligible for membership in the kibbutz. As of 1951 no child born in Kiryat Yedidim had chosen to live outside, and none had been denied membership in the kibbutz.[24]

At the outset an effort was made to eliminate the differentiation of the sexes in occupations. Members of both sexes toiled on the roads, drove tractors, and worked in the communal kitchen. At the time of Spiro's study it appears that there was an effective policy of preventing the development of a division of labor along sex lines among children and adolescents,[25] but some sex differentiation in occupations had appeared among adults with the result that most men were in "productive" jobs and most women were performing "service" work.[26] Unfortunately Spiro did not report whether efficiency or preferences of individuals (for "masculine" or "feminine" types of work) were the more responsible for this shift.

[22] From a personal conversation.
[23] *Children*, p. 10.
[24] *Kibbutz*, p. 139.
[25] *Children*, pp. 301–302.
[26] *Kibbutz*, p. 81. Cf. also Ivan Vallier, "Structural Differentiation, Production Imperatives and Communal Norms: The Kibbutz in Crisis," *Social Forces*, 40: 233–242 (1962).

THE ECONOMIC FUNCTION

There was a conscious effort to keep individuals and cliques from developing a hold on any segment of the economy. This was inspired by the egalitarian desire to disperse economic influence and to avoid creating any opportunity for one person or group to exploit another. With respect to the labor force the basic technique used to implement this goal was the concept of the complete interchangeability (or complete absence of specialization) of personnel. Two noteworthy features of this technique were the rotation of personnel through various jobs, and the abolition of sex differentiation of labor. It seems probable that the complete absence of specialization was somewhat inefficient in the sense that more goods and services could probably have been produced with the same amount of labor and resources if workers and managers had been allowed to stay on the same jobs for longer periods and to develop specialized skills. The observations of Rosenfeld and Schwartz support this speculation and indicate that there was a growing reluctance to sacrifice economic goods for ideological goals. On the other hand, it might be argued that efficiency was irrelevant as a criterion for policy: one informant told Spiro that since life was so difficult in this kibbutz, no one would stay if he thought only of his physical pleasure.[27] With respect to consumption all members were supposed to be treated equally. However, children received a bit more than their share, and a small increment above absolute equality went to veteran workers.

In Kiryat Yedidim the level of consumption of an adult did not depend upon the family to which he or she belonged (either by birth or marriage) but only on his or her being a member of the kibbutz. (This stands in sharp contrast to American society, where a woman typically determines her future level of consumption by her choice of husband.) For the child, eligibility to share in the consumers' goods depended only on his being the recognized offspring of some adult who was a member of the kibbutz, while the size or quality of his share was determined by the principle of equal apportionment among children and was thus independent of the status of his parents or other kinsmen. Thus all economic roles, productive and consumptive, were carried on outside the family and without relation to the family.

THE POLITICAL FUNCTION

Politically the kibbutz operated as a primary group. If a member became reluctant to accept a work assignment, or if some group was not performing up to standard, the community found informal ways of expressing criticism, and usually this brought the derelict members into line. There were formal procedures that included bringing an offense to the official attention of the

---

[27] *Kibbutz,* pp. 178–179.

members at a weekly meeting, and ostracism was the ultimate sanction. These formal procedures were virtually never used. If informal procedures failed to produce the desired result, usually the intimation of formal action sufficed. As for children, they spent almost all their time under the control of their teachers (or nurses, when quite young), and it was the persons carrying out these roles who enforced discipline on the young. It follows that the family was not involved in the political process.

THE SOCIALIZING-EDUCATIONAL FUNCTION

Let us turn to the socializing-educational function and begin by noting the conception of the ideal member, i.e., the goal toward which the socializing-educational function was oriented. In the European shtetl intellectual values were prized. On the other hand, the ideology of Kiryat Yedidim defined physical labor as a virtually sacred task because its product bore not on the gain of the individual but on the welfare of the group.[28] Friedmann has summarized the values of the pioneer kibbutzniks as "asceticism, collectivism, redemption by tilling the soil."[29]

As is true of all utopian societies Kiryat Yedidim looked back on "bad old times" and forward to the promise of a golden future. A future-oriented society must count heavily on its children and value them. In Spiro's phrasing, Kiryat Yedidim was "a child-centered society, par excellence."[30] Adults who worked in the fields did not take siestas but worked through the heat of summer days in order to devote the late afternoons to their children, and, as we have noted, adults accepted monotonous fare in order to provide a varied and nutritious diet for their children.

We have noted that the mother took her newborn child to the Infants' House. Since regulations did not permit infants to be taken to parents' rooms until the babies were six months old, mothers went to the Infants' House to nurse their young ones. At one year children were moved to the Toddlers' House, where they were toilet-trained and taught to feed themselves. As they entered kindergarten, they moved into another building for a year or two. At five or six the children went into a new dormitory for the first six grades of school. Then another shift was made into high school. Concerning the schools Spiro makes the following points: The curriculum was similar to that of a progressive school in America. The project method was used. There were no examinations, no grades, and no failing students. The atmosphere was egalitarian, and students addressed teachers by their first names.

From the age of four days through high school the child of Kiryat Yedidim lived in what we might call a boarding school, which is located in the settle-

---

[28] *Ibid.,* p. 89.
[29] Georges Friedmann, *The End of the Jewish People?* (New York: Doubleday, 1967), p. 122.
[30] *Kibbutz,* p. 124.

ment. In the care of children there was an exception to the general lack of sex-role differentiation. During the early years women served as nurses and teachers to the children. Because of the rotation of duties and the emphasis upon nonspecialization each child could usually count on having a succession of nurse-teachers as he progressed from the Infants' House through the grades. When he entered the combined junior-senior high school, the child encountered male teachers for the first time. From the child's point of view the functionally significant role was fulfilled by the nurse-teacher who fed and taught, bathed and clothed, rewarded and punished him. By contrast, the parents had little functional significance for the child: they expressed love and affection, and they provided companionship. According to Spiro's account, the parents were effusively doting in their expression of love, seemed anxious lest the child reject them, and allowed the child's wishes to govern their interaction with the child during the child's daily visits to the parents' quarters: "If the child wishes to take a walk, the parents take a walk; if the child wishes to visit a friend, they visit a friend, if the child wishes to hear a story, they tell him a story. . . . Parents not only allow their children to control the visiting situation, but they rarely scold them at these times, and they deliberately refrain from arguing or disagreeing between themselves."[31]

THE RELIGIOUS FUNCTION

We have discussed at some length the ways in which three basic societal functions were carried out in Kiryat Yedidim: the economic, the political, and the socializing-educational. What observations can we make about the religious function in this avowedly antireligious society? In Chapter 1 we have asserted as an axiom that the religious is one of the basic societal functions, and hence we have stated that it must be carried out in all societies. Does the existence of an antireligious, atheistic society nullify this view?

Let us recall the definition of the religious institution in terms of its core functions: to integrate goals, to provide sanctions, and to alleviate anxieties. Note that there is nothing in these words about a belief in a supernatural being although it is probably true that in most societies some sort of theology is involved in the institutionalized ways of fulfilling these core functions. It follows, then, that there may be organizations and activities fulfilling the religious function—as "religion" is conceived in this context—that are nonreligious or even antireligious in the more general usage of "religion." The

---

[31] *Children*, p. 58. Spiro reports that the few parents who had been born in Kiryat Yedidim and had grown up under this regimen seemed less effusive than the others.—*Ibid.*, p. 355. Viewing a similar kibbutz about a decade later (1964), Bettelheim commented that the interaction of parents and their children, i.e., during "the children's hour," seemed seldom to be relaxed. Rather, it was a time when both parent and child seemed to be on best behavior, and since only positive emotions were appropriate, the interaction tended to be emotionally shallow.—Bruno Bettelheim, *The Children of the Dream* (New York: Macmillan, 1969), pp. 133–138.

conclusion is that, given our definitions, the religious function is carried out even in antireligious societies.

One conspicuous feature of the culture of Kiryat Yedidim was its sense of mission, its vision of utopia, its conviction that when socialism was achieved, life would be happy and man would be good. This ideology appeared to motivate the members of the kibbutz to tolerate privation and to work energetically rather than to withdraw to a physically more pleasant life outside Kiryat Yedidim. This ideology emphasized the priority of the group's welfare over the individual's pleasure and the priority of the vision of the future utopia over present gratification. This ideology integrated the goals of the members of Kiryat Yedidim and provided the basis for sanctions against sloppy work or selfish behavior.

The society, moreover, was organized to allay a number of anxieties. In an economic sense this was the consequence of the fact that the society operated the distribution of goods and services on the principle of equality. Thus a person who was ill or too old to work could take comfort in the thought that he would be as well supplied with the community's goods as when he was able-bodied, and that he would have a job to return to if he recovered his health. Psychological security is enhanced by a strong sense of belonging and a relative absence of many kinds of competition. This was a community in which one was elected to membership. Furthermore, the frequent meetings and committee responsibilities must have imparted a strong sense of participation. Indeed, at one time the sense of tie to the community was so highly developed that it was regarded as bad form for couples in love to appear in public together, and married couples would not go off on trips together. Here we encounter the sort of reaction familiar in an adolescent group of boys when the first one or two threaten the integrity of the gang by showing interest in girls.

MATE-SELECTION

It is customary in the kibbutzim for a young man to marry a young woman from outside the settlement in which he was reared. Mate-selection is carried out by the individuals seeking spouses rather than by their families, as in traditional China. Because of the absence of private property economic factors are of no importance in the choice of mate, and of course there is neither bride price nor dowry. "All that is of importance is the personal relationship, and the desire of the couple to live their lives together."[32]

In Kiryat Yedidim if a man and a woman agreed that they loved each other, they needed the consent of no third party in order to marry. The

---

[32] Esther Lucas, "Family Life in the Kibbutz," in Gideon Baratz et al., *A New Way of Life: The Collective Settlements of Israel* (London: Shindler & Golomb, 1949), pp. 54–66. Quotation is from p. 62. Cf. also Yonina Talmon, "Mate Selection in Collective Settlements," *American Sociological Review*, 29: 491–508 (1964).

kibbutz conceived of marriage as "a union between a man and a woman to be entered into on the basis of love and to be broken at the termination of love."[33] Thus the norms made marriage a concern only of the couple involved and not of their respective families of orientation (as in traditional China) or of the society as a whole (as is implied by the licensing procedure in the United States). Spiro points out that consequently this kibbutz was not of course an autonomous society but an Israeli settlement and subject to Israeli laws; when a woman became pregnant in the kibbutz, a couple became legally married.[34] Apparently the mores of Kiryat Yedidim did not require a pregnant woman to be married, and the functional organization of the kibbutz society was such that the physical care and the formal education of the child were not affected by whether he had a father. Moreover, since a woman obtained the goods and services she needed as a member in her own right, she was not economically dependent on her husband. Hence divorce did not involve any loss of support. Since this community reared children outside the family and since virtually no property was owned by it or by individuals, there was little functional necessity for a concept of legitimacy. The functionalist might predict that if the entire country had been organized like the kibbutzim, the concept of legitimacy would have disappeared.

The Kibbutz Family and Social Change

In Chapter 2 we saw that the Communist revolution of the latter 1940's had continued a gradual change in familial organization that had begun around the beginning of the twentieth century. What can we say about societal and familial change in Kiryat Yedidim? A decade after his original field work, Spiro returned to this kibbutz for a short stay. His impressions as of 1962 were as follows:

1. There is a new factory; agriculture is no longer the sole occupational interest.
2. The settlement is more prosperous.
3. The growth of the kibbutz movement has practically ceased, and the kibbutznik has ceased to be a culture hero.
4. Asceticism is no longer a major tenet in the ideology of the kibbutz.
5. Sabras[35] have taken primary responsibility for most facets of kibbutz life.
6. Although the kibbutz continues its socialistic ideology, it no longer regards the Soviet Union as a model.
7. There is more division of labor along sex lines.

[33] *Kibbutz*, pp. 112–113.
[34] *Ibid.*, p. 112.
[35] *Sabra:* Here the term denotes a person born in Kiryat Yedidim; it is also used to refer to a native Israeli born into the Jewish tradition.

8. More attention is given—and without guilt—to women's dress and grooming.
9. The emphasis on group living has receded; "the demand for privacy seems to have been recognized as legitimate."[36]

How shall we interpret these changes? Perhaps the place to begin is to recall that the founders of Kiryat Yedidim were zealots, that they were filled to the overflowing with protest against many features of shtetl life and were determined to create a society divested of its evils. The task of creating the new society, especially under conditions of such hardship, drained off much of the energy generated from the frustrations and resentments of the generation of pioneers. As they have aged, they have been replaced with sabras, who have not experienced the same set of frustrations. Thus the zealous energy and ascetic ideology of the pioneers have given way to routine and increasing emphasis on present gratification.

Another writer, the very talented late Yonina Talmon, has made observations about social change in the kibbutzim. After the achievement of the goals of the pioneers, relaxation was in order. Antifamilism, which had been more of a drive toward emancipation of women and liberation from patriarchy than toward negation and the elimination of the family, became more subdued. Couples ceased being embarrassed about being seen together. Indeed they began spending their leisure with each other. The kibbutzim ceased relying primarily upon the recruitment of outside adults for replacements and began to reproduce; whereas in the pioneering period women had constituted 20 to 35 percent of the population, the sex ratio came more nearly into balance, and the birth rate shot up. As the number of children increased, parents began to show more interest in the socialization of their children, and gradually there developed a sense of intergenerational ties.

Weddings began to be important events, and wives began adopting their husbands' names. Extramarital relations and divorce came under condemnation as the kibbutzim came to affirm the lifelong companionship, trust, and understanding between spouses. The child's experience of constantly sharing in his peer group often created "a craving for a complete monopoly over the parents and persistent demands for individual attention." One of the consequences of divorce that caused it to be condemned was that usually one of the divorced spouses withdrew from the kibbutz and left the child with only one parent; the loss of a parent was thought to be harmful to the child.[37]

Further developments included an increase in the amount of housekeeping: in the proportion of families having evening meals at home, in wash-

---

[36] Melford E. Spiro, *Kibbutz: Venture in Utopia* (New York: Schocken, 1963), "Preface to New Edition," pp. ix–xix. Quotation is from p. xiii.

[37] Although he was thinking of marital dissolution resulting from death rather than from divorce, Bettelheim implies a contrary view by arguing that "the omnipresence of caretakers (including all kibbutzniks) and the peer group" goes a long way to compensate the child for the loss of a parent.—*Op. cit.*, p. 170.

ing, mending, and ironing their clothes. Such duties have become defined as part of the female sex role, and a differentiation of sex roles with respect to occupation has emerged. One other change in the family has been the gradual emergence of wider kinship ties, which seemed to come along with the continuity of the generations.[38]

The Product of the Socializing-Educational and Parental Functions

From the viewpoint of social psychology perhaps the most fascinating question to ask about the kibbutzim is, What sort of adults do the children become? In *Children of the Kibbutz* Spiro makes three especially interesting observations about children reared in Kiryat Yedidim: (1) Parents are the children's most important love-objects.[39] The other social role that might seem an obvious competitor for the child's love is that of nurse-teacher. Three considerations seem to reduce the importance of the nurse-teacher: She is called upon to punish as well as to reward, whereas the parent is only indulgent, seldom punitive. Each child shares his nurse-teacher with seven other children of the same age, whereas each set of parents usually has one or two or possibly three children. The role of nurse-teacher is filled by a succession of women, and this renders it more difficult for the child to form an emotional attachment to an individual woman enacting this role. (2) As a rule girls identify with the nurse-teacher as "a well-defined, socially sanctioned social role."[40] This is not astonishing since the social role of nurse-teacher is functionally of overwhelming importance to the children, and women fulfilling this role are constantly before the children. (3) On the other hand, the identifications of boys are "with a vague, inchoate masculinity which is not translated into any identifiable social role."[41] Boys have little opportunity to observe adult male occupational or other differentiated social roles.

In another publication Spiro reports that the sabras of Kiryat Yedidim do not share the sense of mission so evident among the generation of settlers, and, furthermore, that the sabras are bored by and reject "Jewish" culture, which they assess as inferior.[42] Another observer comments generically on the

---

[38] Yonina Talmon, "The Family in a Revolutionary Movement—The Case of the Kibbutz in Israel," in M. F. Nimkoff (ed.), *Comparative Family Systems* (Boston: Houghton Mifflin, 1965), chap. 13. Quotation is from p. 278.

[39] *Children*, p. 80. Our earlier presentation of Spiro's material was put into the past tense because it was followed by more recent information that pointed to changing features. The above presentation on children of the kibbutzim is in the present tense because no analysis of change is being made.

[40] *Ibid.*, p. 241.

[41] *Ibid.*

[42] Melford E. Spiro, "The Sabras and Zionism: A Study in Personality and Ideology," *Social Problems*, 5: 100–110 (1957). The entire issue in which this article appears is devoted to the kibbutz.

sabras of the kibbutzim. He finds that the modal sabra is not only different from, but the very antithesis of, the modal personality in the parental generation. From the viewpoint of the parental generation of settlers the typical offspring appears to be "physically competent, physically courageous, rather cold, insensitive, simple-minded . . . a person to be feared, envied, and contemned . . . a goy [gentile] . . . 'normal' . . . as opposed to the 'abnormal,' 'alienated' Jew. . . ."[43] The same writer continues: "the parents . . . feel estranged from them. It is pertinent that the sabras themselves prefer to be called Israelis, rather than Jews, and their image of the Jew is a highly stereotyped one, negatively toned."[44]

Impressionistic corroboration of these remarks comes from Friedmann, who, remarking that the term *sabra* denotes "prickly pear," continues with the observation that therefore the term means "good inside although the inside [is] difficult to get at."[45] The abruptness of the sabra, according to Friedmann, is part of his liking for prompt decision and effective action.

> They are much less extroverted than their parents and grandparents and are as simple in their speech as in their clothing; they are reacting against the subtleties of the traditional Jewish mind and (as one of them told me) are opposed to "socialist pathos and Talmudic quibbles." Their ambition seems to be to do their jobs properly and without fuss . . . [their] apparent guiding principle is "action without ideology."[46]

Noting that Spiro and Diamond are anthropologists and that Friedmann is a sociologist, let us turn now to other accounts coming from more psychiatrically, psychoanalytically, and psychologically oriented observers. We find that the latter writers do not portray the sabras as so dramatically different.

Rabin's study compares four age-groups (infants, 10-year-olds, 17-year-olds, and soldiers) from several kibbutzim with comparable subjects from other types of Israeli villages. Generally the differences between the offspring of the kibbutzim and those from other settlements were few and of small magnitude. He concluded that under the age of ten there seemed to be a lag in the development of basic trust in other human beings, but that this lag disappeared by age ten, and was not visible in adolescence or young adulthood. He thinks this difference probably results from the arrangement whereby at a very tender age the child of the kibbutz must learn to live with several mother-substitutes and a number of peers.[47] One phenomenon that

---

[43] Stanley Diamond, "Kibbutz and Shtetl: The History of an Idea," *Social Problems*, 5: 71–99 (1957), at p. 92.

[44] *Ibid.*

[45] Friedmann, *op. cit.*, p. 123.

[46] *Ibid.*, p. 117.

[47] "By the time the Kibbutz child has reached kindergarten or school age he has been through many of the battles which the non-Kibbutz child has yet to face."—A. I. Rabin, *Growing Up in the Kibbutz* (New York: Springer, 1965), p. 203.

does seem to persist into the later years is phrased by Rabin as "lower Oedipal intensity,"[48] which is perhaps a part of the generally low level of expressiveness and affect remarked by the previous observers.

Salomon Rettig has noted that whereas children of the kibbutzim spend most of their time with their peers, children of the moshavoth[49] spend relatively more time interacting with their parents. For this reason Rettig hypothesized that there would be more intergenerational difference in moral attitudes among people from the kibbutzim than among those from the moshavoth; his data provided some support for the hypothesis.[50]

Bettelheim says that the founding generation complains about the indifference and rudeness of their preteen and adolescent children. His own assessment seems to be that although collectively they are rudely assertive, individually they are shy. Some interpretation of their behavior comes from his statement that these sabras seem to show some of the psychological features of twins:

> ... the deep dependence and reliance on each other, the feeling that no one but their twin can ever fully understand them or share their innermost being. Only instead of one twin they have several, and of both sexes.[51]

What conclusions can we draw about the sabra? It seems agreed that the shtetl family in Eastern Europe was united in religion, in ritual, and in encouragement of the expression of emotion. Affection and anger were not incompatible; it was dangerous to retain feelings that should be expressed. In accordance with the Jewish religion "the father was formally and conventionally revered by wife and children."[52] Typically overprotecting her children, the mother equated rejection of her food with rejection of her love. The shtetl Jew tended to examine, analyze, and seek for meanings behind meanings. The migrants to Israel who founded the kibbutzim rejected shtetl life and set about with the zeal of missionaries to found communities that would be socialistic, atheistic, and antifamilistic. The conditions of life that confronted the settlers involved wresting a living from an inhospitable, nearly barren countryside.

It seems reasonable to infer that the settlers probably communicated to their children much of their own rejection of shtetl culture. For this reason it does not seem surprising that the sabras reject "Jewish" culture. Because of the long hours of fatiguing labor demanded by the environment, it seems

---

[48] Or a "less intense attachment to the parent of opposite and [a] less ambivalent relationship and attitude to the parent of the same sex."—*Ibid.*, p. 203; see also p. 199.

[49] Moshavoth is the plural of moshava. As stated on page 52 above, a moshava is a settlement of individually owned and operated farms or plantations.

[50] Salomon Rettig, "Relation of Social Systems to Intergenerational Changes in Moral Attitudes," *Journal of Personality and Social Psychology*, 4: 409–414 (1966). Differences pertained to such matters as: "married persons using birth-control devices" and "living beyond one's means in order to possess luxuries enjoyed by friends and associates."

[51] Bettelheim, *op. cit.*, p. 87. Cf. also pp. 92, 144, 262, 281.

[52] Diamond, "Kibbutz and Shtetl," *loc. cit.*, p. 79. A widely cited source on shtetl life is Zborowski and Herzog, *Life Is with People*.

quite possible that both the sabras and their parents have less time and energy for the pursuit and development of cultural and intellectual interests than did the members of the shtetl. Furthermore, there seems to be consensus that the sabras from the kibbutzim differ from their parents, the pioneers, by being less ascetic, less ideological, less intellectual, less verbal, less expressive, and more action-oriented.

Summary and Conclusions of Chapters 2 and 3

We have examined a maximally functional family—that of the peasantry in traditional China—and a minimally functional family—from the Israeli kibbutz of 1951 whose pseudonym is Kiryat Yedidim. For each of our five basic societal functions let us note how these two societies anchor the dimension of familial functionality, and we may note in passing where between these termini the middle-class American urban (or suburban) family seems to lie.

With respect to the *economic* function the Chinese family was the unit both of production and of consumption. In the kibbutz the unit of production is (not the family but) the community, and the unit of consumption is (not the family but) the individual. With respect to the economic function, then, the ends of our dimension are well represented by these two societies. For the most part, in America the corporation and not the family is the unit of economic production, but the family is a widely recognized unit of consumption.

The Chinese family served as a unit of *political* function in that it maintained order within the family and assumed at least part of the responsibility for protecting its members from the aggression and depradation of outsiders. The adjudication of disputes, both within the family and between family members and outsiders, was a responsibility of the elders. No such arrangement prevails in the kibbutz, where the kibbutz as a whole enforces sanctions and provides for such protection as may be needed. In America we have known of families functioning as political units—e.g., the feuding Hatfields and McCoys of Kentucky—but we are generally much closer to the kibbutz in placing political functioning in extrafamilial institutions.

The entire *socializing-educational* process for a peasant child was performed within the Chinese family—to a large degree by the parent of the same sex. In sharp contrast, the kibbutz baby is taken from the mother at the age of four days and is reared to adulthood by the community. All responsibility for instruction resides with the teachers. With the development in America of kindergartens, prekindergartens, and nursery schools there has been an increasing disposition to turn over children to the schools at younger age levels. Since the average age at which children leave school has been increasing, moreover, the family has been relinquishing and the school absorbing more and more of the total responsibility for socializing and educating American children.

For the Chinese, the *religious* function of integrating goals was performed, in past at least, by the formal religions (Taoism and Buddhism); the expression and reinforcement of the group's solidarity—another aspect of the religious function—was centered in ancestor worship, a family ritual that was a kind of religious observance. For the members of the anticlerical and antitheological kibbutz the integration of goals was addressed largely through a sociopoliticoeconomic utopianism. Probably the central arena for the interpretation, implementation, and reinforcement of this ideology was the general assembly (or town meeting). All members participated in parties and ceremonies (e.g., secularized versions of Passover and Hannukah), which were the principal way of expressing the solidarity of the group. Once again the kibbutz family was not a relevant unit. In America it seems that the integration of goals is carried out mostly by the four extrafamilial institutions. Such economic organizations as corporations, trade associations, advertising media, and occupational groups define goals. Occasionally the national government assumes leadership, especially in times of crisis, such as war or depression. The school and the church are quite self-conscious in trying to define the "good" and moral life and to specify a way to achieve it. It does not appear that the American family is involved systematically in goal integration although it is clear that individual parents are very active in this area. In America solidarity is expressed in a variety of ways and settings. With respect to the family, it occurs in the celebration of birthdays, anniversaries, and holidays. The church does it too, especially through ceremonies at *rites de passage*—christenings, confirmations, weddings, and funerals. But there are many other settings—school rallies, fraternity meetings, service clubs, baseball games, and national elections, to cite only a few. Again in America the family is not as inconsequential as is conceivable, nor is it as influential as it can be.

Although we have not sought to address formally the matter of the derived functions (cf. pages 19–21) in the Chinese or the kibbutz family, we shall comment on them briefly before concluding this chapter. For the Chinese peasant, *position-conferring* was carried out almost entirely by the family. To be sure, there was some social mobility. A man might obtain an appointment in the civil service, rise in the hierarchy, and achieve a social status above that of his family, but this would be exceptional. In the Kiryat Yedidim of 1951 we have noted Spiro's assertion that status differentials were absent (cf. pages 55–56). The critical position-conferring was that of granting or withholding membership in the kibbutz, and this was done by a vote of the members. In America the family provides the child was an initial ascribed social status, and the occupational system provides him with an opportunity to alter that ascribed status either upward or downward.

The *parental functions of nurturance and control* are, of course, carried out within the Chinese family. In the kibbutz a good deal of the "parentifying," especially with respect to control, is carried out in the children's residences by nurses and teachers. Parents of the kibbutz tend to be indulgently nurturant but not controlling. In America parental functioning is graded with the age of the child. Until he enters the school system, the parental function is typically discharged by the family. Thereafter the family shares it with the school and gradually with other social structures. For the young child, then, the exercise of the parental function by the American family resembles that of the Chinese family, but as the child ages, extrafamilial structures become more important, and the situation becomes more like that in the kibbutz.

In the matter of *emotional gratification* it appears that intrafamilial relationships were seen as important sources of affection and gratification in China. Although the marital relationship was not expected to be highly gratifying nor was that between father and son, intimacy and affection were regarded as usual in the relations between brothers, between father and daughter, and between mother and son.[53] Spiro reports that in the kibbutz of Kiryat Yedidim the marital relationship is based on love and that parents and children usually treat each other with a considerable show of affection.

Now let us note how familial function can affect the role of love in mate-selection. We have noted that in the maximally functional Chinese family love is regarded as irrelevant to mate-selection. The incoming bride should represent a liaison with an important family; she should possess skills relevant to her role, and she should show industry in carrying out that role. In middle-class America there is a cultural expectation that mates should select each other on the basis of mutual love. Occasionally third parties express snide doubts about the sincerity (or mutuality) of that love. It appears that such doubts are especially likely if the bride is the daughter of the groom's boss or if a poor girl is marrying a rich man, i.e., if one party appears to be improving his or her situation appreciably through the marriage. This can be translated into our functional language to the effect that the degree of doubt about the sincerity of the love underlying a person's marriage seems positively correlated with the degree to which that person will get a higher level of consumption (economic function) and/or a higher social status (position-conferring function).

Note that our description of Kiryat Yedidim renders it improbable that a person could select a mate for any of the reasons just enumerated because the kibbutz family carries out none of those functions. If the level of one's consumption is set on a principle of equality by the collective, there is no way of marrying to improve one's level of consumption. If there are no status differentials (or if they exist but are unrelated to the family organization), there is no way to marry upward. If there is no private property, there is nothing to inherit. It seems to follow then that the fewer and less important the functions that are carried out by the family, the less incentive there is to select a mate on any other basis than compatibility and congeniality, affection and love. Or to phrase it more baldly, the less important the family becomes, the more probable are love-marriages.[54]

---

[53] Levy, *op. cit.*, chaps. 3 and 4.
[54] Further discussion of some of these points appears in Robert F. Winch, *Mate-*

This same principle can be observed in the case of parent-child relationships. In the Chinese family the father-son relationship had great functional strength. In their mutual core relationships the man served as foreman, teacher, priest, and so on, to the boy's roles of worker, pupil, parishioner, and so on. In the kibbutz, on the other hand, it would be sheer coincidence if the boy's father should also be his foreman or his teacher or be related to him in any other extrafamilial functional capacity. The Chinese boy's percept of his father was typically one of awe and respect; his behavior toward the father was typically avoidant and deferent. The boy of the kibbutz relates to his father with easy but demanding camaraderie. It appears that although functional activities are likely to have individual-oriented payoffs, they are also likely to eventuate in frustration and feelings of hostility, especially on the part of the person in the subordinate role. Consistent with the latter part of this observation is Levy's report that the Chinese did not expect such highly functional relationships as that between father and son to be affectionate; rather, they "were accustomed to find emotional warmth and affectionate response of a high degree of intensity in precisely those relationships of weakest strength in the kinship structure."[55] Moreover, it seems as though the founders of Kiryat Yedidim had come to somewhat the same conclusion, had lamented the intrafamilial hostility of the shtetl—especially that directed toward the father—and accordingly designed a new type of family in which the level of hostility would be lower because of the absence of functions.

From these observations it follows that functions constitute bonds that tie family members to each other, irrespective of the feelings they may have for each other. For this reason the highly functional family tends to be a highly stable family. The absence of function (in the relatively functionless family) leaves feelings as the basis for interpersonal relationships. Thus the cohesiveness of the relatively nonfunctional family depends on mutual love. For this reason the relatively nonfunctional family tends to be an unstable family. We shall return to this thesis later in the book.

Last and certainly not least is the observation that these two polar types of family are receding from their extremities of function and structure and are moving toward an intermediate position, i.e., they are becoming more like each other and more like the middle-class family of urban and suburban America. This topic will engage our interest in Part Four after we have had an opportunity to consider systematically the functions and structures of the family in the United States.

Selection: A Study of Complementary Needs (New York: Harper & Row, 1958), chaps. 1–4, 14, 15.

[55] Marion J. Levy, Jr., *The Family Revolution in Modern China* (Cambridge, Mass.: Harvard University Press, 1949, p. 196. See also Shu-Ching Lee, "China's Traditional Family, Its Characteristics and Disintegration," *American Sociological Review*, 18: 272–280 (1953), esp. p. 275.

PART TWO

*The Family
in America
and
Its Functional Matrix*

It is difficult to summarize in a single statement what the family is, in terms of whom it includes (structure), or of what it does (function), or of the kinds of expectations people entertain about it (institution). The nature of its structure varies from one society to another. Let us conceive of a scale of inclusiveness of the number of kin relationships and/or of persons. At the high end of the scale would be the traditional Chinese family. Ideally, as we have seen, the traditional Chinese household embraced three or more generations and had numerous collateral kinsmen located nearby. The Chinese recognizes as at least nominal kinsmen all the thousands who bear his surname. At the lower end of the scale would be the childless married couple living in a kibbutz or in an apartment area of a large American city. The two may be thousands of miles from their place of birth, may have lost contact with such kinsmen as they have known, and may have come to regard themselves as virtually without relatives. For them the family includes only themselves. The last two chapters have illustrated the range of functions, and wide variation in expectations is easily seen in ethnographies of the family.[1]

If we look at the history of the territory that is now the United States since the first permanent white settlement in the seventeenth century, we see that America has had a multitude of familial forms. Although some forms are subject to both kinds of variation, we may classify the origins of differences as (a) *imported,* or the variation resulting from the cultural diversity among those who migrated to this country; and (b) *indigenous,* or the variation resulting from differences in ways of life within this country.

It is a commonplace that our country was settled by people from many lands with divergent ways of life. From 1820, when the United States began a continuous record of immigration, through 1969, it is estimated that more than 44 million immigrants entered this country.[2] They came from Europe, Africa, and the Orient, and, more recently, from Latin America. Represented in this massive migration was a multitude of cultures, each with its own conception of the family.

It is commonly thought that, on reaching American shores, these immigrants proceeded to learn American ways, and that their children or at least their grandchildren became indistinguishable from other Americans except perhaps for name, religion, or color. If this "melting-pot" idea were totally accurate, we should not expect to find such diversity in conceptions of the family, or, more generally, in ways of life. The notion that assimilation occurs in American society with such ease is a bit romanticized. In the seventeenth and eighteenth centuries settlements were quite isolated so that, for example,

---

[1] See, for example, Stuart A. Queen, and Robert W. Habenstein, *The Family in Various Cultures* (3d ed.; Philadelphia: Lippincott, 1967).

[2] U.S. Bureau of the Census, *Statistical Abstract of the United States: 1970* (Washington, D.C.: GPO, 1970), Table 128, p. 91.

the Germans of Pennsylvania had little opportunity to acquire the family concepts of the Puritans of Massachusetts. Since all the original colonies were settled at roughly the same time, moreover, there was no single culture that could be held up as *the* American way of life, and accordingly there was no reason why one group should seek to imitate the ways of another. Gradually, however, because of developing communication and the common problems involved in making a living in a new land, acculturation began to take place and cultural differences began to diminish. Such differences did not disappear, however, and later immigrants were confronted with various cultural patterns. Whether the immigrant met the modes of life of the Pennsylvania farm, the Carolinian plantation, or the New England village, he saw it as *the* American way. Although some immigrants were speedily assimilated in the communities where they arrived, others sought refuge in ethnic enclaves and clung tenaciously to the people and customs of their own group.

Ethnic islands in our cities and countryside give evidence concerning the degree to which assimilation is incomplete. Characteristic of the large city are the Little Italy, the Little Poland, Chinatown, Harlem, and, in recent years, the enclave of Puerto Ricans. Not only do such ethnic islands indicate the incompleteness of assimilation but they serve to maintain the minority culture and thus to foster cultural separatism. Although the rural counterpart is less conspicuous, it is exemplified in rather extreme form by the German-speaking Amish of Pennsylvania.[3]

Heterogeneity in ways of life indigenous to the American setting is of numerous kinds. We shall note those associated with (1) race and religion, (2) differences in socioeconomic status or social class, and (3) early rural versus modern urban living. The last two of these will receive considerable elaboration, especially in Parts Two and Three.

One would ordinarily think of racial and religious differences as being imported rather than indigenous to the American scene. But there is one racial group—the blacks—and one religious group—the Mormons—whose distinctive family organizations developed in this country.

Among urban blacks there exists a familial pattern that departs markedly from the more general one by being matriarchal, or mother-dominated, frequently having no man in the household to occupy the position of husband-father. Under slavery it was a common practice to keep mother and children together, but no such concern was exercised to keep the father in the slave family. In itself this would seem adequate to account for the development among the blacks of a matriarchal form of family, which placed great emphasis on the mother-child relation and attached little importance to the husband-father. Conditions favorable for the continuation of the matriarchal family have inhered in the economic marginality of blacks in American society and the fact that black women can frequently find employment, especially as

---

[3] One of the best indexes to the assimilation of a group is the proportion of its members who marry outside that group. This topic is taken up in Chapter 10.

domestic servants in urban and suburban areas, when black men cannot. (According to another school of thought, the matriarchal tone of the black family is rooted in the more remote past when earlier generations lived in polygynous tribes in Africa.[4])

A familial pattern consisting of a woman and her children is a *mother-child incomplete nuclear family*. A frequently remarked pattern, especially among urban blacks, is one wherein the maternal grandmother raises the children while the mother goes out to work. This is a *matrilineally extended mother-child family*. There is no information on just how frequent this pattern is since the Bureau of the Census enumerates it as such only when the grandmother shares the household with the others, and not when she lives in the next apartment or down the block. It is important to realize, moreover, that whereas these two familial patterns—mother-child nuclear, and matrilineally extended mother-child—are apparently more characteristic of blacks than of whites in the United States, they do also occur among whites, and indeed mother-child families are not the prevalent pattern among blacks; in 1969, 27 percent of all nonwhite families and 9 percent of white families were reported as having female heads.[5]

Although the Mormon family is of more historical than contemporary interest, it received much notice in the nineteenth century because it was polygynous. Because of internal religious unity and external persecution the Mormons constituted a closely knit, highly organized society. Although their religion sanctioned polygyny and numerous children, it demanded abstemiousness from alcohol, nicotine, and coffee. Polygyny has long been outlawed, but Mormons continue to deviate from non-Mormons (or "gentiles") by having a high fertility rate and a low divorce rate.

Although status differentials were apparent in colonial society, the range of socioeconomic statuses has increased tremendously since then. The development of a highly differentiated status system has been accompanied by a differentiation in ways of life, or *subcultures*.[6] In the upper class, for example, there is considerable recognition of remote degrees of kinship and corresponding control over the behavior of children by kinsmen outside the immediate or nuclear family. In the middle class the parents are the locus of ultimate authority, and the withholding of affection is a common technique of parental

---

[4] *Polygyny:* the marriage of one man to two or more women. According to E. F. Frazier, "In America there was no social organization to sustain whatever ideas and conceptions of life the Negro slave might have retained of his African heritage."—*The Negro Family in the United States* (Chicago: University of Chicago Press, 1939), p. 23, also pp. 41, 61, 107. M. J. Herskovits, on the other hand, sees the looseness of the father-child tie as an outgrowth of the polygynous origins of the African Negro.—*The Myth of the Negro Past* (New York: Harper & Row, 1941), pp. 167–186, esp. p. 181.

[5] U.S. Bureau of the Census, *op. cit.*, Table 42, p. 36.

[6] *Subculture:* the cultural traits characteristic of a social class or other reasonably homogeneous group or aggregate within a society. For a discussion of subcultures, see Chapter 8.

control. In the lower class discipline involves physical punishment rather than the withholding of affection. (See Part Five.)

It is clear that the family has been changing. The family of today operates in a setting very different from that of 1800 or even from that of 1900. It is one of the basic theses of this book that the changes in the family have been necessitated by alterations in our ways of life.

In the seventeenth and eighteenth centuries our population was overwhelmingly rural. As late as 1800 over 90 percent of the population of the United States lived in rural areas. The relatively isolated farm family and the antebellum slaveowning plantation household tended toward self-sufficiency with respect to the economic and socializing-educational functions, and the plantation household plus its extended kin group tended toward political self-sufficiency.

Today about two thirds of the population are urban.[7] Whether in a squalid tenement, a workingmen's area of single detached dwellings, a suburb of split-level homes, or a luxurious penthouse, an urban family cannot produce all that it consumes. One or more members are expected to participate in the specialized occupational system, and the children are expected to go to school. The family is forced to yield numerous aspects of its functions, especially with respect to the production of goods, and for some families the level of functionality is so diminished that the family represents little more than a common mailing address and dormitory.

Where such materials are available and illuminating, we shall present trend data to show the various ways in which the family is changing. To interpret the significance of these data we shall make repeated use of two polar or contrasting types of family: the "early American rural family" and the "modern American urban family." Although there is little evidence of change in the structure of the American family,[8] we shall be able to document considerable change in function. In this formulation the "early American rural family" lived on an isolated farm and produced practically all it consumed while selling or trading very little of its produce. Such families were numerous a century or two ago. The term "modern urban American family" will denote a middle-class nuclear family living in a large city or its suburbs. Thus it should be emphasized that, except where otherwise noted, "urban" includes "suburban."

[7] In 1960, 63 percent of the population was urban by the "old" definition and 70 percent by the new.—U.S. Bureau of the Census, *op. cit.*, Table 14, p. 16. By "urban" is generally meant incorporated places of 2500 or more inhabitants plus the densely settled urban fringe or urbanized areas. The new definition classifies more areas as urban than did the old.—*Ibid.*, p. 2. By 1960 the proportion of the American population classified as farm population had declined to 9 percent and by 1968 to 5 percent.—U.S. Bureau of the Census, *Current Population Reports—Farm Population*, Series P-27, No. 40, July 31, 1969, Table A, p. 1.

[8] The only relevant data available concern the domestic family and show little change in the structure of the domestic family since 1800. See p. 629 below.

In Part Two we begin a functional analysis of the American family. It is the thesis that as basic societal functions migrated from the family to other structures in the society, the family became less important. Our purpose is not so much to concentrate on American society—although an understanding of American family and society is useful and valuable—but rather to use American society as a much-studied specimen from which we can learn a great deal about the sociology of the family in general. To the degree that we succeed in developing a general sociology of the family we should be able to specify correctly not only the conditions that have resulted in the modern American family[9] but also the conditions that would produce the same general type of family—whether in China or in the kibbutzim, whether in Nigeria or in the Netherlands.

---

[9] We shall use this term as a convenient designation for the variety of American familial forms just alluded to above even though it be understood that the term subsumes enough variation to justify the plural of "family." See also Chapter 11.

4

The Economic
and Political Functions

Purpose of This Chapter

It is one of the major theses of this book that, other things being equal, the greater the family's control over the resources made available to each member and desired by him, the stronger and more stable will be the family structure. It was postulated in Chapter 1 that functional activities eventuate in such resources, and hence it is reasoned that the more activities the members of the family engage in jointly and the more functional these activities, the greater will be the interdependence of the members of the family; and the greater their interdependence, the stronger and more stable will be the familial structure. In this chapter we shall compare the economic and political activities of the modern American family with those of earlier American family forms and note the implications of this comparison for an understanding of familial solidarity.[1]

Points of Emphasis

The production of the family is intimately bound up with a division of labor among family members. Where the social organization is simpler than that of an urban-industrial society, the family tends to be much more of an economic unit than is the case with us. Where technology is crude, as in nonindustrial societies, the immediate objective of economic activity is survival. Except for the poorest classes, on the other hand, we in America tend to take

---

[1] There will be further consideration of the roles of producer and consumer in the familial context in Chapter 12.

for granted the availability of sufficient goods for survival and to strive for a level of consumption that represents an increase in level of living and, coincidentally, an elevation in status. When large-scale enterprise becomes the basis of economic activity, family members are integrated into productive organizations as individuals with the result that for their occupational activity their family membership becomes quite irrelevant. This is another way of saying that as a society becomes more differentiated, the familial and the productive systems no longer have the same persons in their respective structures: a young man's father and his foreman are not the same person; it will be a coincidence if the foreman's work gang includes his son.

The extent to which an economy makes use of money is an index of the separateness of the roles of retailer and consumer from the familial system. When, as in large-scale enterprise, production is for sale rather than for use, the effect of the money economy is to create a large class of economic dependents. This in turn creates a problem concerning the maintenance of the economically unproductive.

To function effectively as a unit of political organization a human group must have greater size than the nuclear family, and it must have more control over rewards than is true of the contemporary American family. The familial form that Zimmerman calls "trustee" is the prototype of maximum political functionality. The traditional Chinese family, especially the family of the gentry, and the Appalachian-Ozark family of our own country are better examples than the early American farm family of great political functionality.[2]

The Family as an Economic Unit

Every family engages to some degree in activities that we may think of as economic. Economics is the study of the relation of scarce goods to unlimited and competing uses; it is concerned with the production, distribution, and consumption of goods and services in the satisfaction of wants. The economic function includes determining the composition of output, organizing production, distributing income, and providing for the future. Each of us must be a consumer, and what we consume must be produced by someone; hence, each of us enters into the economic process at some point.

We shall examine the family at various times and places and note the degree to which it functions as a *self-sufficient economic system* or *unit*. This phrase refers to the degree to which the family produces all the goods and services it consumes, and consumes all the goods and services it produces. It is doubtful that there has ever been a family that was a complete economic unit, but there have been some family forms that have produced all but a few of the goods consumed. At the other extreme it is difficult to conceive of

[2] Carle C. Zimmerman, *Family and Civilization* (New York: Harper & Row, 1947), esp. chap. 27.

a family engaging in any interaction without some production of goods and services. A mother who drives her youngster to school is creating a service; a boy who brings in the laundry from the back porch is adding what the economist speaks of as "place utility."

In Chapter 12 we shall develop the point that because of primary sex differences there are certain types of activity that can be handled better by men than by women. Although they are less categorical than sex differences, age differences present all societies with another ready-made basis for a division of labor. To the very old and the very young are generally allocated tasks requiring minimum strength and skill, while vigorous adults assume the heavier work of the society.

ECONOMIC ORGANIZATION OF THE EARLY AMERICAN FARM FAMILY

As we cite some of the historical facts, we shall note that the modern urban American family is in general much less an economic unit than was the American family of one to three centuries ago, which was typically rural. Although the early American family was not a "Robinson Crusoe" type in the sense that it created from the beginning all goods it consumed, nevertheless it approximated that type of economy much more closely than many contemporary urban dwellers might think possible. There was, of course, some variation associated with such factors as time, region, and class, but most of the commodities of the eighteenth century were produced by means of the productive activities of family members within the household. An example of the self-sufficiency of the farm home of the eighteenth century is the following statement made by a farmer in the *American Museum* in 1787:

> At this time my farm gave me and my whole family a good living on the produce of it, and left me one year with another one hundred and fifty silver dollars, for I never spent more than ten dollars a year, which was for salt, nails, and the like. Nothing to eat, drink, or wear was bought, as my farm provided all.[3]

This degree of economic self-sufficiency was particularly evident in the South and on the frontier as the pioneers began the move to the West following the Revolutionary War. The Southern plantation, which should be regarded as a household rather than as a family,[4] was very self-sufficient economically.

---

[3] Quoted in Carl Holliday, *Woman's Life in Colonial Days* (Boston: Cornhill, 1922), p. 108.

[4] The term "household" has been defined by the Bureau of the Census as including "the person or the entire group of persons who occupy a house, an apartment or other group of rooms, or a room that constitutes a dwelling unit. It includes the related family members and also the unrelated persons, if any, such as lodgers, maids or hired hands who share the dwelling unit."—U.S. Bureau of the Census, *Current Population Reports—Population Characteristics*, P-20, No. 92, March 5, 1959, p. 5. As applied to the plantation, therefore, the term includes the master's family and his slaves, who sometimes numbered several hundred.

Goodsell points out[5] that the plantation carried out a wide variety of productive activities, such as the raising of crops and livestock, milling, the production and storage of food, the spinning and weaving of cloth, and the tailoring of garments. By means of such diversified production practically all maintenance requirements of the members of the families of master and slaves were provided for.

ECONOMIC SELF-SUFFICIENCY AND INTERDEPENDENCE OF FAMILY MEMBERS

In the case of the family farm the local unit of economic organization was practically coterminous with the family. In the case of the plantation the unit of economic organization was the household, which, as we have seen, included the family of the master plus his slaves, whether or not the latter were organized in families. That these conditions were typical of early America can be seen from the fact that in 1790 only about 5 percent of the population lived in cities; in 1960 the proportion living in urban areas was about two thirds.

The high degree of economic self-sufficiency in the early American rural family was apparently reflected in and supported by the character of interpersonal attitudes and relationships. In mate-selection, for example, there was the obvious consideration of the actual or potential wealth to which each prospective spouse might lay claim. Beyond this consideration, to which the present generation has not proved totally indifferent, was the fact that the selection of a mate was also the selection of a business partner. Thus both man and woman had a lively interest in the aptitude and energy of the other. This consideration has become one-sided in recent years with the decline in the economic function of the wife. In the middle-class subculture[6] of most college students it appears that intelligence and education are regarded as resources giving promise of upward mobility. The one-sidedness of the interest in the possession of these attributes by a prospective spouse was indicated some years ago by a study of university students wherein 76 percent of the men, but only 18 percent of the women, answered "yes" to the question: "All other things being satisfactory, would you marry a person of less intelligence and (or) education than your own?"[7] Whereas the earlier conception of the economic roles of husband and wife made the strength and skills of each real considerations in mate-selection, the sentiment expressed by these college

---

[5] Willystine Goodsell, *A History of Marriage and the Family* (New York: Macmillan, 1934), p. 423.

[6] As used here, the term *subculture* designates cultural traits characteristic of a social class.

[7] R. E. Baber, *Marriage and the Family* (New York: McGraw-Hill, 1939), p. 149. A more recent study employing the same question on a college group reported exactly the same proportion of affirmative responses (18 percent) among the women, but a reduced proportion (56 percent) among the men.—Mirra Komarovsky, "What Do Young People Want in a Marriage Partner? Results of a Questionnaire Study of 550 Young Men and Women," *Journal of Social Hygiene*, 32: 440–444 (1946).

students reflected the perception of the husband as the "breadwinner" and of the wife as his "dependent." Findings of a more recent study are consistent with this view.[8]

The multitude and variety of tasks on the family farm provided almost every individual, irrespective of sex, age, and vitality, with an opportunity—indeed, an obligation—to contribute to the family's production. In the case of the healthy adult the contribution was present and obvious. In the case of the child, the contribution might be small but was expected to increase proportionately with the child's strength and skill. Later, moreover, we shall see that in the eyes of the Puritans work was conceived as having a virtue-inducing quality and was thought to toughen children against the Devil's wiles.[9] Each member was viewed, therefore, as having a justified claim on a portion of the family's production. To be sure, the share received might be far from an equal portion, but it was sufficient for the preservation of life.

Where the consumed goods are immediately produced by the family, it is clear that the work of each contributes to the welfare of all. It seems in general that the economically self-sufficient farm family has operated on the Marxian dictum "from each according to his ability" and, to a considerable degree, "to each according to his needs."

THE COMING OF THE MACHINE AGE

Early in the nineteenth century, machine industry began to spread and to displace domestic production. Its advent involved also the demand for larger concentrations of population to provide the labor to tend the machines. It required an increase in the division of labor, and resulted in a greater volume of production, which in turn created the basis for more capital equipment and further division of labor. The story of the Industrial Revolution has often been told. We shall note only such of its consequences as are of importance in understanding the modern American family.

1. The relation between the hour-to-hour labor and individual and family welfare became much less apparent. If one is making a dress for a daughter or tilling beans for the dinner table, the relation of toil to result will be quite evident. If, however, a man toils hour after hour and year after year, tending a machine whose product is shipped to someone he never sees, the relation of this operation to his own welfare and that of his family is somewhat more difficult to grasp. Here we see how the advent of the money economy diluted the emotional satisfaction a man got from his work. His rewards are no longer tangible and self-evident but take the impersonal form of money that will be exchanged for goods.

2. With the shift of locus of economic activity from home to factory, the

---

[8] John W. Hudson and Lura F. Henze, "Campus Values in Mate Selection: A Replication," *Journal of Marriage and the Family*, 31: 772–775 (1969). See table 2, p. 774.

[9] Cf. pages 372–375.

family as a whole lost the sense of participation in the productive process. For those who remained in the home such labor took on the aura of mystery and remained outside their body of experience. For those family members who went to the factory there was created a new body of experiences, shared not with the other members of the family, but with the other workers at the factory. Perhaps the significance of this change can be suggested by the remark that in the days of the self-sufficient family the most important question to ask about a person in order to place him in the social system was the identity of his family; in the modern urban-industrial society, the question is the nature of his occupation.

3. Industry's demand for large concentrations of labor meant that the workers and their families had to live for the most part in towns and cities. It appears that in our country a migration of population from farm to city has been going on for at least a century and a half, but it has been especially well documented for the period since World War I. In thirty-eight of the forty-one years from 1920 through 1960 inclusive the farm population decreased not only in proportion to the total population, which was growing, but also in absolute numbers. The decrease was of the order of 21.5 million people over a period during which the general population was increasing by about 94 millions. In the forty-nine years from 1920 through 1968 the total population of the United States nearly doubled; during the same interval the number of people on farms shrank by two thirds with the consequence that the farm population diminished proportionally from 30 percent of the total in 1920 to 5 percent in 1968.[10] The move from rural to urban areas frequently involved the reduction of productive facilities in the home. There was little or no space for gardens, livestock, churns, looms, and all the other implements of domestic production.

4. The development of manufacturing made much domestic production uneconomic even for home consumption. Accordingly more and more commodities were bought from commercial sources.[11] Ogburn and Nimkoff point out that over the past two centuries American families have largely given up not only the tanning of leather and the building of furniture but also spinning and weaving, have given up not only much of the making of clothes but also

---

[10] U.S. Bureau of the Census, *Statistical Abstract of the United States: 1968* (Washington, D.C.: GPO, 1968), Tables 2 and 894, pp. 5 and 594, respectively.

[11] One of the more recent examples of the change from a largely self-sufficient economic system to participation in the larger economy concerns the Old Order Amish of Pennsylvania. They constituted a highly sacred society organized on a basis of agricultural self-sufficiency. A study done around 1940 showed that they were coming to rely more and more on the money economy to purchase such commodities as bread, apples, peaches, canned vegetables, underclothes, and linoleum. Because of its self-imposed segregation, consciously preserved ethnic features, and highly traditional value system, this subsociety showed great resistance to social change; but even here "self-sufficiency is in retreat."
—Walter M. Kollmorgen, *Culture of a Contemporary Community: The Old Order Amish of Lancaster County, Pennsylvania* (Washington, D.C.: U.S. Department of Agriculture, Rural Life Studies, No. 4, 1942), pp. 46–48.

a good deal of the cleaning of clothes, and have reduced not only the proportion of meals eaten at home but also the amount of processing going into the food consumed at home.[12] For every $100 spent in retail sales of food and liquor in 1935, $25 was spent in eating and drinking places; by 1945, this figure had risen to $47.[13] For years much of the bread consumed in this country has been produced by commercial bakeries; frozen pies and TV dinners are examples of relatively new food products purchased at a very advanced stage of processing for home consumption. Commercial laundries, dry cleaners, and exterminators are examples of services that have passed out of domestic production. Although Ogburn and Nimkoff are convinced that "the removal of economic production from the home and the household has not ceased,"[14] it does appear that power, which constitutes the base of industrial technology, may at least slow the trend. The widespread distribution of electricity and the consequent diffusion of diverse electrical appliances (sewing machines, washers, dryers, drills, and so on) are bringing some productive activities back into the home.[15] Apparently one consequence has been a slowing down in the growth of commercial laundries.[16] Until a precise analysis is made, however, it is impossible to assess the significance of the "do-it-yourself" movement for the economic functioning of the American family.

5. When numerous productive activities were carried on in the home, it was generally obvious that the wife and mother was a productive worker and usually this would be true to some extent of children and of the aged and handicapped as well. As economic production moved out of the home, the wife and mother, the young and the aged became increasingly unproductive in an economic sense, and hence, in the money economy, more and more of a burden.

EMPLOYMENT OF CHILDREN AND WOMEN

As the machine age developed, there were numerous jobs that required neither much skill nor great strength. For such jobs it was deemed profitable to obtain the very cheapest labor. Employers turned to children and to women to fill these jobs.

It was not uncommon for boys and girls to be employed in textile mills at the age of six. In itself, the mere fact of employment of children and women was certainly no innovation, but the conditions of employment meant a radical change in the way of life, with oftentimes profound implications for the de-

---

[12] W. F. Ogburn and M. F. Nimkoff, *Technology and the Changing Family* (Boston: Houghton Mifflin, 1955), p. 127.

[13] Margaret Reid, "The Economic Contribution of Homemakers," in *Annals of the American Academy of Political and Social Science*, 251: 61–69 (1947).

[14] *Op. cit.*, p. 126.

[15] Howard F. Bigelow, *Family Finance: A Study in the Economics of Consumption* (rev. ed., Philadelphia: Lippincott, 1953), chap. 6.

[16] Ogburn and Nimkoff, *op. cit.*, p. 128.

velopment of the child and for his family. The working day was customarily long, so long that the juvenile workers would spend all the daylight hours at their labors. In 1866, a committee of the Massachusetts legislature reported that overseers in need of "small help" went about canvassing for children at any age "if they are old enough to stand."[17] The conditions under which children worked are described in testimony given by a textile worker before a Pennsylvania Senate Committee in 1838:

> ... I have known work to commence as early as twenty minutes past four o'clock, in the summer season, and to work as long as they can see. I have known children of nine years of age to be employed at spinning—at carding, as young as ten years. . . . The children are tired when they leave the factory; [have] known them to sleep in corners and other places, before leaving the factory from fatigue. The younger children are generally very much fatigued, particularly those under twelve years of age; [have] known children to go to sleep on arriving home, before taking supper; [have] known great difficulty in keeping children awake at their work; [have] known them to be struck, to keep them awake. . . . I have known some [children] to get no more than fifty cents per week; I have known some to get as much as $1.25; the common rate is $1.00.[18]

To the present generation of urban middle-class Americans, the attitudes of the parents who permitted their children to enter the labor force under the conditions just described or who pushed them into it must seem to have been grasping and callous. The harshness of this judgment may be mitigated if not pardoned by recalling that, in terms of their agrarian background, parents were accustomed to think of children as economic assets soon after they were able to walk. In addition to the then prevalent view that work had character-building values, the impoverished condition of the newly created proletariat was such as to make child labor an economic necessity. By the shift from agriculture to industry whole families suddenly became dependent upon money for their livelihood. Wages were low[19] and it was necessary to put as many family members as possible into the labor force. It seems safe to suspect, moreover, that the relatively uneducated parents could hardly have been sensitive to whatever effects the conditions in the factory had on the child's health, personality, and skills.

[17] Grace Abbott, *The Child and the State* (Chicago: University of Chicago Press, 1938), I, 275.

[18] *Ibid.*, pp. 280–281.

[19] In 1850 the average American worked 70 hours per week and produced 34 cents' worth of goods per hour. In 1952 the average American worked 40½ hours per week and produced $2.03 worth in dollars of the same (1950) purchasing power.—J. Frederic Dewhurst and associates, *America's Needs and Resources: A New Survey* (New York: Twentieth Century Fund, 1955), p. 40. Output per man-hour rose by about 60 percent from 1952 to 1967, and by the latter year the hourly output averaged nearly ten times that of 1850. —U.S. Bureau of the Census, *Statistical Abstract of the United States: 1968*, Table 329, p. 229.

Dewhurst has shown that child labor in the United States increased from 1870 to 1900 and has decreased since 1900. Of boys in the 10–15 age group 19 percent were employed in 1870. By 1900 the percentage was 26, and by 1930 it had dropped to 6; the corresponding percentages for girls were 7 in 1870, 10 in 1900, and 3 in 1930.[20] The demand for child labor took a very considerable proportion of the juvenile workers into mines, factories, and tenement sweatshops—frequently under shocking conditions. As such facts became known, a movement gathered impetus to improve the conditions of working children and to establish minimum ages for working—at least in certain occupations. Child labor laws and compulsory school laws began to take hold shortly after the turn of the century. The full-time employment of children under 14 has become so rare that the Bureau of the Census defines the labor force in terms of persons of 14 years of age and above. (In July, 1957, the Bureau of the Census made a special inquiry of summer employment of children 10 to 13 years old and found that 1.8 million, or 15 percent, were doing some kind of work—more than half in agriculture and most of the rest as newsboys, laborers, and private household workers, including baby-sitters.[21])

The entrance of women into the labor market, according to Calhoun, was met with the charge that this was an "unsexing" activity. The same author remarks, however, that such criticism overlooked the fact that women had always been productively engaged. By 1860 the census reported that a million women were gainfully employed.[22] By 1890 the number of women in the labor force had risen above the 3 million mark; it was 14 million by 1940 and over 31 million in 1970. (See Table 4.1.) Even more remarkable than the increase in numbers is the increase in the proportion of females in the total labor force. From 17 percent in 1890 this proportion had risen to 37 percent by 1970.[23]

Two other trends in the composition of the labor force may be noted at this point. First, since 1890 the proportion of married women in the labor force has increased much faster than has the proportion of single or of widowed and

---

[20] Dewhurst *et al., op. cit.*, p. 727.

[21] U.S. Bureau of the Census, *Current Population Reports—Labor Force*, Series P-50, No. 83, April 1958, p. 5.

[22] A. W. Calhoun, *A Social History of the American Family*, Vol. III, *Since the Civil War* (New York: Barnes & Noble, 1945), p. 86. See "Tasks, Abilities, and Sex Role-Differentiation in the Family" and "Women in the Labor Force" in Chapter 12 below.

[23] It has been argued, however, that there have been many changes in the conditions attending the enumeration of the female labor force—"the broadening of census definitions, improvement of census organization and procedure, growing awareness on the part of enumerators that many women do work, increasing willingness of respondents to report women's work, and the shift of working women from self-employment and homework to wage and salary employment outside the home"—with the result that the actual growth of the female labor force may have been considerably less than reported in Tables 4.1 and 4.2.—Robert W. Smuts, "The Female Labor Force: A Case Study in the Interpretation of Historical Statistics," *Journal of the American Statistical Association*, 55: 71–79 (1960), at p. 78.

TABLE 4.1

Distribution of the U.S. Labor Force by Sex: 1890, 1900, 1920, 1930, 1940, 1950, 1960, and 1970 (numbers in thousands.)

YEAR	TOTAL Number	Percent	MALES Number	Percent	FEMALES Number	Percent
1890	21,833	100	18,129	83	3,704	17
1900	27,640	100	22,641	82	4,999	18
1920	40,282	100	32,053	80	8,229	20
1930	47,404	100	37,008	78	10,396	22
1940	56,180	100	42,020	75	14,160	25
1950	64,749	100	46,069	71	18,680	29
1960	72,142	100	48,870	68	23,272	32
1970	85,231	100	53,899	63	31,332	37

SOURCE: Data for 1890–1950 are from U.S. Bureau of the Census, *Historical Statistics of the United States, Colonial Times to 1957* (Washington, D.C.: GPO, 1960), Series D 13–25, p. 71. Data for 1960 and 1970 are from U.S. Bureau of the Census, *Statistical Abstract of the United States: 1970* (Washington, D.C.: GPO, 1970), Table 316, p. 213.

divorced women. (See Table 4.2.) Between 1890 and 1969 the proportion of married women who were in the labor force increased nearly ninefold—from 4.5 to 40.4 percent. In 1890 there were five times as many single women in the labor force as married women; in 1969 there were nearly three times as many married women as single women in the labor force. In part B of Table 4.2 it can be seen that the proportion of the female labor force that is married increased from about one eighth in 1890 to about five eighths in 1969. Second, there has recently been a marked increase in the proportion of women past the childbearing years who are in the labor force—the percentage of women in the 45–64 year age category went from 12 in 1890 to 48 in 1969—and in the proportion of the total labor force represented by these women—from 2 percent in 1890 to 12 percent in 1969.[24] Additional material concerning women in the labor force will be presented in Chapter 12.

THE ECONOMIC CONTRIBUTION OF THE MODERN HOUSEWIFE

If we think of utility in the economic sense as the capacity of a good or a service to satisfy a human want, then we may speak of the economic activities carried on within a household as "consumer production," which Kyrk asserts is largely represented by "the utilities provided by the unpaid activities of the

---

[24] *Historical Statistics of the United States, Colonial Times to 1957*, Series D 13–25, p. 71; *Statistical Abstract of the United States: 1970*, Table 317, p. 214.

TABLE 4.2

(A) Number and (B) Percent Distribution of Females (14 Years of Age and Over) in Labor Force by Marital Status and (C) Percent of Each Marital Status in Labor Force: 1890, 1940, 1950, 1960, and 1969

MARITAL STATUS	1890	1940	1950	1960	1969
	\multicolumn{5}{c}{Number (in thousands)}				
A. Single	2,565	6,710	5,621	5,401	6,501
Married	500	5,040	9,273	13,485	19,100
Husband present	(NA)[a]	(4,200)	(8,550)	(12,253)	(17,595)
Husband absent	(NA)	(840)	(723)	(1,232)	(1,505)
Other marital status	638	2,090	2,901	3,629	4,297
Total	3,703	13,840	17,795	22,516	29,898
	\multicolumn{5}{c}{Percent of Female Labor Force}				
B. Single	69.3	48.5	31.6	24.0	21.7
Married	13.5	36.4	52.1	59.9	63.9
Husband present	(NA)	(30.3)	(48.0)	(54.4)	(58.9)
Husband absent	(NA)	(6.1)	(4.1)	(5.5)	(5.0)
Other marital status	17.2	15.1	16.3	16.1	14.4
Total	100.0	100.0	100.0	100.0	100.0
	\multicolumn{5}{c}{Percent of Each Marital Status}				
C. Single	36.9	48.1	50.5	44.1	51.2
Married	4.5	16.7	24.8	31.7	40.4
Husband present	(NA)	(14.7)	(23.8)	(30.5)	(39.6)
Husband absent	(NA)	(NA)	(NA)	(NA)	(NA)
Other marital status	28.6	32.0	36.0	37.1	35.8
Total	18.2	27.4	31.4	34.8	41.6

[a] NA = not available

SOURCE: Data for 1890 are from J. D. Durand, *The Labor Force in the United States, 1890–1960* (New York: Social Science Research Council, 1948), pp. 216–217. Data for 1940–1969 are from U.S. Bureau of the Census, *Statistical Abstract of the United States: 1970*, Table 330, p. 223.

family members for the family members."[25] Having noted that much economic activity has moved outside the home, we are entitled to inquire what is left. Ogburn and Nimkoff offer the answer: "cooking and preparing meals, housecleaning and decorating, some laundering, a little sewing and marketing."[26]

By now the reader may have gained the impression that in the old days the housewife had an economic function, that the "working" wife has an

[25] Hazel Kyrk, *The Family in the American Economy* (Chicago: University of Chicago Press, 1953), p. 47.
[26] *Op. cit.*, p. 129.

economic role, but that the contemporary housewife has no economic significance. Such an observation is not justified. In the early American farm family there was a division of labor both in production and in consumption. In the modern urban family a new division of labor has arisen. The husband and father now has the major role of producer. He produces, however, not directly for the consumption of the family members but for the market. The wife and mother, on the other hand, now assumes charge of consumption. Through the activity of shopping she adds to the commodities purchased what the economists call "place utility" and "time utility." In other words, she sees that goods are available in the home when needed. Her day-to-day shopping, therefore, brings home food for the family table, supplies for household maintenance, and clothing for family members.

Besides shopping, other productive activities of the housewife include the exacting job of child care, the final processing and serving of foods, and the maintenance of clothing and home furnishings. To summarize, then, the bulk of the economic contribution of the modern housewife is in housekeeping, marketing, and child care. It is not possible to make a very accurate estimate of the monetary value of the contribution of the average housewife. Yet her contribution can be appreciated when one tries to hire a competent worker to manage a home.

CATEGORICAL EMPLOYABILITY

In contemporary American life we are accustomed to think of people as "employable" or "unemployable," i.e., as "normal" or as "handicapped." This conception seems to be a consequence of the large-scale, impersonal organization of our business life. "Sound" business policy, which means maximization of efficiency and of profits, is construed as implying that managers and proprietors should seek to hire the most vigorous, alert, intelligent workers available at rates they can afford to pay. Thus, in an economy where some degree of unemployment is regarded as "normal" there are very few jobs available to the aged and the otherwise handicapped.

This situation may be contrasted with life on an American family farm, where there is ordinarily plenty of work for everyone, where the standards of work are not as rigid as in the commercial field, and where, therefore, tasks may be tailored to meet individual capabilities. In the farm situation, for example, an old man may find work whose demands in terms of duration and exertion can be suited to his declining strength. At the other end of the life span the child can be set about useful pursuits soon after he learns to walk, and his duties can be expanded as he grows in size and strength. Moreover, tasks can be found for the feeble-minded, and frequently, to some degree at least, for persons with other types of handicap. Thus this type of socioeconomic organization does not imply as rigid a distinction between the categories of "employability" and "unemployability."

By "categorical employability" we mean a situation in which certain criteria—especially age, and the presence or absence of physical and/or mental handicap—are the bases for classifying job aspirants as "employable" or "unemployable." The commercial-industrial situation is characterized by categorical employability. By contrast, on the family farm no such sharp distinction is drawn. Since in the latter situation the job can be suited to the individual's ability, it is not a situation of categorical employability. Categorical employability is implied in the very concept of the labor force with people moving into it as they seek and take paid jobs and moving out of it as they become housewives, retire, or become unsuitable for paid employment.

If this analysis is correct, we should expect to find certain relationships: (1) The proportion of elderly males in the labor force should have been declining as we have been converting from an agricultural to a primarily urban-industrial society. The data support this expectation: with the exception of the years during World War II there is virtually an unbroken decline in the rate of labor force participation by males over the age of 64 from 68 percent in 1890 to 26 percent in 1969.[27] (2) We should expect a higher proportion of workers in agriculture than in other major industry groups to be outside the categorically employable age group. We find that of all males who worked for salaries or wages during 1958, 90.3 percent were in the 18–64 age group, and 9.7 percent were of other ages; in agriculture the respective percentages were 67.6 and 32.4.[28] (3) We should expect a higher percentage of the farmers to be over 65 than in other occupations. Of all employed males in 1958, 3.5 percent were 65 years of age or older; of the farmers and farm managers, 15.8 percent were in this age group.[29]

The conception of categorical employability has special import for the child in our culture. Because of a number of considerations, including the harsh working conditions of children in the nineteenth century, the view has come to prevail in our society that childhood is a time for play and carefree development. Many of our states have child labor laws whose major function is to proscribe most occupations as unsuitable for the employment of children. This facet of categorical employability results, therefore, in large numbers of middle- and upper-class children growing to maturity with no work experience, and with little conception of the real nature of the work they will undertake in their careers.

Here we have an opportunity to note the impact of culture on our perspective. The Puritans believed that the Devil would find mischief for idle hands, but that a child kept busy at productive activities would acquire such

---

[27] *Historical Statistics of the United States, Colonial Times to 1957*, Series D 13–25, p. 71; *Statistical Abstract of the United States: 1970*, Table 317, p. 214.

[28] U.S. Bureau of the Census, *Current Population Reports—Labor Force*, Series P-50, No. 91, June 30, 1959, Table 6, p. 16.

[29] *Current Population Reports—Labor Force*, Series P-50, No. 89, June 1959, Table 16, p. 39.

...and antithetical opinions ...personality, undermines his health, and ...may be regarded as a breach of morality and of parental ...responsibility to put a child at productive activities; the appropriate activity of childhood is play. As we shall see in Chapter 14, however, the tireless pendulum of doctrine on child care is now moving in a direction that may produce new rationalizations in favor of child labor.

Like the child, the aged and the handicapped have come to be regarded as almost useless in an economic sense. And increasingly the time at which one becomes economically "aged" is a matter of the achievement of a particular age, irrespective of the person's physical and mental vitality. The consequence is that persons who fall into the "unemployable" category—children, the aged, the handicapped—are deprived to a great degree of the opportunity to contribute according to their abilities to the family's production. Unless they have independent income, they become "burdens" and "dependents."

To these remarks we must add certain qualifications. One qualification has to do with the part-time employment of housewives; this will be considered in Chapter 12. Another qualification concerns the time at which one becomes economically "aged." It is generally understood that a professional man, a business executive, or a politician may be regarded as "just in his prime" at 65, whereas the prime of life for a professional athlete is probably around 25, and he is generally "old" at 35. There is evidence that perceptions of such differences may be generalized in the sense that upper-status people regard various age grades as happening later in life than do lower-status people. Thus to "upper-middle class" respondents the prime of life for a man is at the age of 40 and a "good-looking woman" is 35 years old on the average. To respondents of the "upper-lower class," on the other hand, both these terms refer to ages five years younger.[30] Such differences make some sense in the light of (1) the greater formal schooling and occupational training required in the upper strata, (2) the consequent lateness in beginning their careers and in marrying, and (3) the less demand on their bodies to perform their jobs adequately.

Irrespective of the age at retirement it appears that those who are forced to retire do so largely against their own wishes. According to the Commissioner of the Bureau of Labor Statistics, "Most older workers, whether they are above or below 65 years of age, want to continue working as long as they can. They will not voluntarily retire from the labor force, but will withdraw only when they are forced out."[31] In recent years there have been movements to counteract such categorical attitudes as they concern the handicapped and, to some extent, as they concern the aged.

---

[30] Warren Peterson, "The Game of Life: Sex and Class Perspectives on the Stages of Adulthood," *Human Development Bulletin,* 1956, pp. 1–7.

[31] Ewan Clague, "Employment Problems of the Older Worker," *Monthly Labor Review,* 65: 662–663 (1947).

DEPENDENCE, INDEPENDENCE, AND INTERDEPENDENCE

We have noted that in the early self-sufficient farm family each member had an obligation to contribute to family production, and had a claim on this production. On the other hand, the concept of categorical employability involves the concept of categorical dependence. In our commercial-industrial economy anyone who has a job for which he receives money has a limited claim (in terms of money) on the fruits of production of the entire economy. Obviously, the size of this claim depends upon the amount of his income. But if he is categorically unemployable and without independent income, he has no direct claim on the production of the economy. Since there is relatively little production in the family of the urban industrial society, he is without direct claim on any goods. He may exercise an indirect claim through the family, as in the case of a dependent child, or through some other institution, as in the case of a person on relief.

In the farm family the economic relation among family members was one of interdependence. All contributed, all received. The activities of each affected the welfare of all. In the modern urban family the nonworking members are dependent on the "breadwinner." The working member or members stand to lose economically rather than to gain by sharing the product of their labor with nonworking family members. Economically, they are independent. By virtue of the fact that so much of the production of consumers' goods has gone out of the home into the market, those with incomes can satisfy most of their purely physical needs outside the home. Economically, they have little need of a family. Conversely, the nonworkers, or more precisely, those without income, are economically dependent on the working members. If the sentiments of loyalty, love, and so on, of the latter are sustained, the family remains intact, and the dependents are taken care of.

Although the argument in the preceding paragraph is correct in direction, it needs some qualification in degree. The discussion of the contribution of the housewife reveals that she does make a positive contribution. In the urban community, however, her contribution is more of a convenience than a necessity to the employed husband. Thus the employed person can take his coat to a tailor to have a button sewed on, can eat his meals in a restaurant, and so on. Similarly with other dependent family members: by cutting the grass Junior can save his father some labor; Grandmother can help out by "sitting" with the children while the parents go out. But if Father has the money, he can also buy these services. More generally stated, the economically independent family member can buy the services performed for him in the home; the dependent cannot survive without the "gainfully employed."

The moral of this story is that in the modern urban family it is no longer to the obvious economic advantage of all to stay together and to work together. In this transition from the early American farm family, which was a self-sufficient economy, to the modern urban family the mutual economic bond has been lost. This appears to be one of the most conspicuous conditions associated with the instability of the modern family.

This raises the question as to how we should regard a family in which two or more members are employed and pool their incomes.[32] With respect to each other, are the working members dependent, independent, or interdependent? Let us take an example in which both members of a childless couple are employed in different organizations. Let us assume, further, that they have agreed to continue this arrangement until certain major purchases have been made (home, car, refrigerator, television). Presumably each would be capable of maintaining himself by means of his own job. Yet by pooling their resources for such purchases as those noted above, they are able jointly to achieve a level of living above that which each could achieve singly. They can be regarded as independent from the standpoint of production, but interdependent from the standpoint of consumption. They are productively independent in the sense that they are not co-workers engaged in a common productive enterprise. (Even if both should be employed by the same corporation, the common productive bond between them would be no greater than that shared with all the other employees in the same work situation.) On the other hand, they are interdependent with respect to consumption in that they achieve by cooperation what neither could accomplish alone.

RECENT TRENDS IN THE MAINTENANCE OF DEPENDENTS

It is in order to consider how dependents are maintained when they have no "breadwinner" on whom to exercise a claim or are unwilling to press their claim, i.e., when the family no longer fulfills its function of maintaining its members. In the organization of the care of economically dependent persons in this country, we can discern a trend that has been characteristic of the development of many of our institutions. When a situation comes to be defined as a social problem (the care of orphans, say, or the care of the aged), some voluntary organization takes over the problem or a new voluntary organization is created to handle it. Thus churches and fraternal organizations have established homes for the orphans and the aged of their memberships. Presently it is recognized that the problem concerns not only the membership of a particular church or fraternal organization but the people of an entire area. At this juncture the problem is turned over to the government for three reasons: (1) the need is being felt throughout the population (and not just within the membership of some voluntary organization), (2) consensus develops that the burden should be spread over all members of the society, and (3) the govern-

---

[32] In 1967 of those families headed by year-round full-time workers 60 percent had more than one earner, 17 percent having three or more earners. Median income for families with one earner was $7,883; for those with two earners, $9,740; for those with three earners, $11,793; and for those with four or more earners, $13,894. U.S. Bureau of the Census, *Current Population Reports—Consumer Income*, Series P-60, No. 64, October 6, 1969, Table 12, p. 37. The median income of husband-wife families with no wage earners was $3,425.—*Ibid.*, Table 3, p. 21.

ment is the only organization commanding sufficient resources to handle the problem.

Public agencies have been established to care for various categories of dependents. Frequently these programs are administered by states with funds contributed jointly by the state and the federal government. Such programs have been set up to provide for children who are in need because a parent is dead, disabled, unemployed, or absent from the home (Aid to Families with Dependent Children), the aged (Old-Age Assistance and Medical Assistance for the Aged), the blind (Aid to the Blind), and adults with other serious handicaps (Aid to the Permanently and Totally Disabled); and programs of aid are extended to disabled war veterans and their families. These programs generally provide three kinds of help: cash to buy food, clothing, shelter, and other necessities; payments to hospitals, physicians, and others for medical care; and social services to help the recipients of such aid to achieve as much personal and economic independence as possible. In many communities, though not all, there is also a general relief program that provides subsistence to families that do not come within the above classifications or categories. This is administered and financed either by the local community alone or with state help. In addition, there are insurance programs, notably Workmen's Compensation, providing against the risk of industrial accident, and Old-Age and Survivors Insurance which, among other provisions, makes possible an income after retirement for those who have come under its program. The physically and mentally ill and children who are full orphans are cared for in various ways through state and local programs.

This trend toward ever-increasing assumption of responsibility on the part of the state for the welfare of its citizens has been opposed at every step by countless persons, groups, and organizations who see any offer of help from the government as a threat to the economic system and as stultification of individual initiative. The history of each of these programs is replete with drama, the cast being drawn from the ranks of social workers, legislators, fraternal, labor, religious, and business organizations—now opposing, now proposing, solutions to these various problems.[33]

RELATION OF WELFARE PROGRAMS TO FAMILY STABILITY

Many of the programs were founded on the principle that the family, extended as well as nuclear, should take care of its own and that public assistance should become available only after it had been established that there was no kinsman who would or could provide the assistance required by the person or persons in need. Of course if the family, especially the extended family, had been functioning adequately to maintain its members, there would have been little or no demand for the development of welfare programs. It

---

[33] For an interesting account of the extreme opposition to a federal program for meeting mass relief needs during the early depression years of the thirties see Harry Hopkins, *Spending to Save* (New York: Norton, 1936). Cf. also "The Adult Offspring and the Family Cycle" in Chapter 17.

appears that maintenance has traditionally been a function of the nuclear family in the United States but that this function was not widely fulfilled by extended families. In other words, people did feel responsible for seeing that their parents and siblings were cared for, as well as their own children, but were less willing to assume responsibility for nonnuclear relatives. Hence the efforts of legislators to force kinsmen to support the needy generally foundered on the fact that the kinsmen did not have a lively sense of responsibility (another way of saying that the extended family in America did not have the function of maintenance), as well as the fact that the relatives of the needy tend to be poor.

The long-range trend in social security is in the direction of releasing persons from responsibility for their parents and siblings (nuclear relatives) as well as for nonnuclear collateral relatives (extended kinsmen). As Old-Age and Survivors Insurance, unemployment insurance, and other programs extend their coverage, more dependents will be entitled to make claims on the state. (One way of conceiving of the objective of the so-called welfare state is that by making contributions during periods of productivity one may make claims on the state—rather than on relatives—during periods of need.) On the other hand, the basic tenet of the Aid to Families with Dependent Children (AFDC) and other child programs is that, wherever possible, children and mothers should be kept together as family units. To achieve this objective, private and public social agencies have developed such techniques as the homemaker service and the day nursery.

The policies underlying these welfare programs seem to be in harmony with the realities of the American familial system. Where the dependent adult has only extended kin on whom he might make a claim, there has not been a highly developed sense of responsibility and hence there has been little for welfare to erode; where there is a nuclear relative, the evidence seems to indicate that such relatives will continue to provide other kinds of service (e.g., shopping, bringing in prepared food) and hence that functionality is not eroded. Taking into account also the statement in the preceding paragraph that the AFDC program reinforces the parents' efforts to care for their minor children, we can now conclude that the effect of present welfare policy is to reduce somewhat one's responsibility toward parents, grandparents, and collateral relatives but, if anything, to increase responsibility to one's own children. This is the reverse of the hierarchy of loyalties in the traditional Chinese family (where one's responsibility to one's parents outranked the responsibility to one's children) and serves to strengthen the nuclear family while not greatly affecting the extended family.

The Political Function and Family Type

In Chapter 1 we defined the political function in terms of the accommodating of conflicting interests, the maintenance of internal and external order, and the providing of protection. As these consequences imply, the essence of the political function is the acquisition and exercise of power, and from the scholar's standpoint the essence of the political problem is to ascertain the locus of power. Before pushing on we may note that because of its age and sex composition the nuclear family is probably too small and too weak to function effectively by itself. No doubt it usually functions as an organizational unit subordinate to some larger and more powerful unit, e.g., the extended family, or the clan, or the state.

The prime student of the political science of the family has been Carle C. Zimmerman.[34] For him these are key questions: Of the total power in any society, how much belongs to the family? And if one is in need, violates a law, or wants to marry, who has the power to handle the situation? As noted in Chapter 1, Zimmerman has constructed a threefold typology of families along a dimension of power. In descending order of their power they are trustee, domestic, and atomistic.

Where the family is powerful, it follows that the gravest of crimes are those against the family—its persons and its property. In the *trustee* family, accordingly, parricide and matricide are especially horrendous crimes. The trustee family, "being the punishing power and the main local manifestation of *total* power, can put the individual to death, sell him into slavery, or banish him as an outcast to make his living, if he can, as a pirate or a robber."[35] Another evidence of the political power of the trustee family is "passive solidarity," the responsibility of one family to a second if the second should suffer an injury because of some crime committed by a member of the first family. This collective responsibility might well involve contributions from all members of the criminal's family to compensate the injured family. "Active solidarity" is another characteristic of the trustee family whereby members are expected to be ready to assist in securing revenge for wrongs done to a kinsman by an outsider. When the trustee family is ascendant, then, there prevails what Zimmerman calls "active and passive solidarity for blood vengeance."[36] The trustee family represents the maximum degree of familism. According to Zimmerman familism involves self-sacrificing loyalty.[37] Burgess and Locke define familism in terms of five characteristics:

> (1) the feeling on the part of all members that they belong preeminently to the family group and that all other persons are outsiders; (2) complete integration of individual activities for the achievement of family objectives; (3) the assumption that land, money, and other material goods are family property, involving the obligation to support individual members and give them assistance when they are in need; (4) willingness of all other members to rally to the support of another member if attacked by outsiders; and (5) concern for the perpetuation of the family

[34] Carle C. Zimmerman and Merle E. Framptom, *Family and Society: A Study of the Sociology of Reconstruction* (Princeton, N.J.: Van Nostrand, 1935); and especially, Carle C. Zimmerman, *Family and Civilization* (New York: Harper & Row, 1947).
[35] *Family and Civilization*, p. 128. Italics in original.
[36] *Ibid.*, p. 129.
[37] *Ibid.*, p. 778.

as evidenced by helping an adult child in beginning and continuing an economic activity in line with family expectations, and in setting up a new household.[38]

At the opposite end of the power continuum is the *atomistic* family. Here individualism prevails over familism; the rights of the individual are sacred, just as the rights of the family are sacred in the trustee family. The individual is responsible for himself and not for kinsmen of the extended family. Zimmerman lists the following characteristics as symptomatic of the atomistic family: "widespread popularity of divorces, feministic movements, great development of social life outside the family, youth problems, revolt of children against the parents, childlessness, great expansion of positive law about the family, increasing rights of men, women, and children to have and control their own incomes and property. . . ."[39]

The *domestic* family has intermediate power. In times of change it stands as a transitional form between the trustee and the atomistic. Zimmerman's exposition stands largely on three historical cases, each beginning with the trustee type, having a transition into the domestic type, and passing into the atomistic type. For the first two—the Greeks and the Romans—the atomistic family heralded the final stage in the decay of their civilizations. Contemporary Euro-American societies constitute Zimmerman's third major case. Convinced of the plausibility of his analysis and anticipating evil times, Zimmerman sees the modern urban family of the United States, chiefly Protestant, as atomistic; our farm and rural families are largely of the domestic type, he declares; and the mountains of the southern and southeastern states are the habitat of our trustee family.[40]

Zimmerman asserts that the nuclear family has had three types of ruling bodies. (The opinion was expressed above that the nuclear family is probably not usually strong enough to stand alone, but must operate in a relation subordinate to some stronger organization.) The three types of ruling bodies that he postulates are the extended family, the church, and the state. Although Zimmerman is not explicit on the following point, it seems safe to infer that he perceives these three ruling bodies as corresponding respectively to the three types of family: trustee, domestic, and atomistic. If we turn our attention momentarily to the implication of this observation for the nature of the deities that would be consistent with each of the three family types, the implication

---

[38] Ernest W. Burgess and Harvey J. Locke, *The Family: From Institution to Companionship* (2d ed., New York: American Book, 1953), p. 60. In a later part of this book we shall examine the degree to which nuclear families in the United States are enmeshed in networks of kinsmen, and we shall conceptualize a bipolar variable called isolation-extended-familism. When the five properties mentioned above by Burgess and Locke are applied to the extended kin network, we have a good characterization of the extended-familistic end of this variable. Cf. pp. 298–299 below.

[39] *Family and Civilization*, p. 161.

[40] *Ibid.*, p. 131.

would seem to be that in the trustee period household gods (e.g., the Roman *lares* and *penates*) should be ascendant, that in the domestic period there should be a central and societally accepted deity, and that in the atomistic period there should be some deterioration in religious belief.

Zimmerman makes some observations about the relationships between the three types of family and four order of phenomena: adultery, bastardy, quarreling, and will making. Adultery and bastardy both imply behavior contrary to familistic values. In the ascendancy of the trustee family, adultery and bastardy are regarded with extreme gravity, says Zimmerman, whereas in the atomistic period they are regarded with casual tolerance.[41] In the trustee family, quarrels within the family are settled by family councils or courts; when family members use the civil courts and litigate with each other, Zimmerman says this is an indication that the trustee family has weakened.[42] In the trustee family, he asserts, it is the custom to die intestate because there will be strong family customs for the disposition of property. Moreover, property is regarded within the trustee family as being held in trust. After the passing of the trustee family, on the other hand, property comes to be regarded as a personal possession. Will making implies the freedom to dispose of property as the testator sees fit. This in turn implies that family customs for the disposition of property either have broken down or do not exist.[43]

Zimmerman speaks of the trustee type of family as the simplest form of organized society.[44] To some it may seem astonishing, then, to read Zimmerman's statement to the effect that the trustee family has existed among white people in this country. He cites as examples the people who lived in the Appalachian and the Ozark mountains and especially in the Kentucky hill country in the nineteenth century and earlier. The feuding families, he asserts, were largely of the trustee type. Of these perhaps the most famous were the Hatfields and the McCoys. In areas where these extended families held sway law was largely a private matter. That is to say that the *de facto* legal authority of these areas resided in the families. These families had their own rules, which they enforced on their members, and these rules would at times call for family members to violate public law. The families were generally able to deal with public officials in such a fashion that family members were free to carry out the private laws of the families and yet remain more or less immune to the sanctions of public law.[45] In this context Zimmerman interprets the feuds as "the breaking-out into actual war of jurisdictions of families which have always placed themselves above public agencies as law-making and regulating organisms for their members."[46]

[41] *Ibid.*, pp. 135, 151.
[42] *Ibid.*, p. 258.
[43] *Ibid.*, p. 179.
[44] *Ibid.*, p. 721.
[45] *Ibid.*, p. 718.
[46] *Ibid.*, p. 715.

POWER IN THE NUCLEAR FAMILY

Running through this book is the theme that the functional family has control over resources, and control over resources implies the power to control the behavior of members of the family. It would seem plausible to suppose that within the nuclear family power would accrue to a position in proportion to the resources its occupant brings into the family. Thus a nonworking wife should have less power than a working wife, and a lower-class husband should have less power than a husband in the middle or upper class. The latter point is based on the fact that where the nuclear family is relatively independent and detached from the extended family, its social status tends to be determined by the occupational performance of the husband-father.

Directly relevant is a study based on interviews with housewives in Detroit. On the basis of the wives' answers to questions as to who makes family decisions the families were classified into "husband dominant," "wife dominant," and two other categories. It was found that the "husband dominant" type of family was generally higher in income and had a lower proportion of working wives than the "wife dominant." It was also found that more wives in the "husband dominant" type than in the "wife dominant" reported a high need for love and affection.[47]

Further support for this general point comes from a study of lower-class black families in British Guiana, where the position of husband-father is so attenuated that it scarcely exists. There the family is primarily a child-rearing unit in which the children are fed and clothed by their mothers. If they know their fathers, they receive practically nothing of importance from them, and many children are reported to grow up without ever seeing their fathers. The three-generation family headed by the maternal grandmother is prominent in this setting. The author of this study asserts that there is a correlation between the familial status of the adult male and his position "in the economic system and in the system of social stratification in the total Guianese society."[48]

---

[47] Donald M. Wolfe, "Power and Authority in the Family," in Dorwin Cartwright (ed.), *Studies in Social Power* (Ann Arbor: University of Michigan Press, 1959), pp. 99–117; reprinted in Robert F. Winch, Robert McGinnis, and Herbert R. Barringer (eds.), *Studies in Marriage and the Family* (rev. ed.; New York: Holt, Rinehart and Winston, Inc., 1962), pp. 582–600. For theoretical interpretation of the correlation between socioeconomic status and domestic power, see: David M. Heer, "The Measurement and Bases of Family Power: An Overview," Robert O. Blood, Jr., "The Measurement and Bases of Family Power: A Rejoinder," and David M. Heer, "Reply," *Marriage and Family Living,* 25: 133–139, 475–477, and 477–478 (1963).

[48] Raymond T. Smith, *The Negro Family in British Guiana: Family Structure and Social Status in the Villages* (London: Routledge, 1956), esp. pp. 135, 147, 221. Quotation is from p. 221.

Summary and Conclusions

Viewed from the standpoint of the economic function, the family in the United States has undergone a marked transformation. In our early history the nation was heavily rural and agricultural. At that time the family came close to being a self-sufficient economic unit. By superseding family farms as major productive units, giant corporations have dissolved the economic unity of the family. Production for use, which was an integral aspect of the self-sufficient family, has given way to production for sale and the consequent emphasis upon working for money rather than working for immediate consumption. The following passage was written about the consequences of these processes in England, but it applies with equal force to our own history:

> A man's life was profoundly altered in its reach, its habits, its outlook, its setting, when, from being some kind of a craftsman or a peasant with various tasks and interests, he became a unit in a series of standardized processes. The lives of women were not less intimately affected. In the economy by which the family was provided with food and clothing before the Industrial Revolution, woman's share was definite and visible. Women spun and wove in their homes, brewed the ale, looked after the pigs and fowls; their functions, if different from those of their husbands, were not less important. Specialization extinguished this life, and the women who helped to spin and weave the nation's clothes under the new system left their homes for the factory, where they found themselves involved in competition with men, working under disadvantages so easily exploited by their masters that the law treated them as young persons in order to protect them. Thus for men and women alike the Industrial Revolution destroyed a great body of significant custom.[49]

This has resulted in a shift from a family in which the members were economically interdependent to one in which one or more are economically independent while the others are classified as dependents. Thus the economic bond, which has been regarded as central to marriage and the family, has been greatly weakened. This loosening of the economic bond is interpreted as one of the significant factors associated with the instability of the modern American family.

The shift in the form of the economic organization and the development of a money economy serve to make the problem of maintaining economic dependents considerably more difficult. In consequence, the care of certain categories of dependents, particularly at the lower income levels, has been passing from the family to private and public social agencies. As is usual in such a transition, there is uncertainty as to rights and obligations with the

---

[49] J. L. Hammond and Barbara Hammond. *The Rise of Modern Industry* (5th ed.; New York: Harcourt, 1937), pp. 241–242.

consequent feelings of rejection and animosity, of guilt and misgiving. Public programs of social security seem calculated to strengthen the nuclear family but not the extended family.

A thesis of this book has been that functionality results in resources that provide the incentive for family members to conform to each other's expectations. It would seem that the more monopolistic the family's position with respect to the resources sought by its members, the more the family can control the behavior of its members. Of course it should be emphasized that in this context "resource" is conceived to include the nonmaterial as well as the material—a loving and nurturant spouse or parent need not be rich in money or lollipops to command resources.

5

The Socializing-Educational and Religious Functions

Purpose of This Chapter

In the present chapter we consider the contribution of the family in carrying out two other basic societal functions: the socializing-educational and the religious. The writer does not propose to continue using the awkward expression "socializing-educational" as a routine adjective. As noted in Chapter 1, the two adjectives used together are intended to make explicit the breadth of the concept in its totality. "Socialization" will be used to refer to the general process of training people to enact the roles that constitute the social positions they occupy, are about to enter, or aspire to. "Education" will routinely refer to more or less formalized socialization, especially to instruction in the classroom.

Although childhood is the period of life with maximum emphasis on socialization, it is obvious that learning about one's roles can be, and probably usually is, a lifelong activity. Especially is this likely in societies undergoing rapid change. It has been remarked that the contemporary middle-aged American finds himself in a world of work wherein half the occupations did not exist during his childhood. Even in the occupations of long standing, moreover, the skills are in such flux that refresher courses and other procedures are useful in obviating or deterring occupational obsolescence. Not only in the world of work but also in the context of the family are there adult roles to be learned—those of spouse, parent, grandparent—and these roles too can be in flux.

The treatment in this chapter of the socializing-educational function focuses on the child and his experiences outside the family. The socialization of the child within the family, as well as the little we know about the socialization of the parent, are considered in Part Five. Some remarks concerning preparation for marital roles appear in Part Six. Accordingly, the length of the treatment here accorded to the function of socialization does not imply that this is a trivial function of the family generally or even of the modern American family. On the contrary, a considerable amount of the socializing process has been regarded in most societies, including our own, as a familial responsibility. Only a very few societies, such as the Israeli kibbutz described in Chapter 3, do not have this expectation.

We shall distinguish four aspects of the function of socialization: the acquisition of intellectual and motor skills, the development of moral character, the preparation for assuming adult roles, and the development of personality. Actually these four aspects of socialization represent differences in emphasis rather than easily distinguishable categories of a developmental process; hence some overlap in their discussion is inevitable.

The latter part of this chapter will take up the religious function. We shall be interested to see what aspects of this function may be carried out by the family and under what conditions. Also we shall take note of the phenomenon of secularization, which involves a change in the belief system, and attendant changes in the locus of the religious function.

Points of Emphasis

In Chapter 2 we have seen a highly socializing family, the Chinese, and in Chapter 3 a minimally socializing one from an Israeli kibbutz. Because of the helplessness and immobility of the infant the family almost always has responsibility for the earliest stages of socialization. (This topic will be developed in Chapter 13.) Since, however, it is not usual for families to be isolated from their societies, the process of socialization normally goes on to some extent outside the family as well.

In contemporary America the child is socialized in a number of settings: the family; schools of numerous varieties; play groups; "character building" and recreational agencies, e.g., the church, Boy Scouts, YMCA, playgrounds; and media of mass communication, including radio, movies, television. As we look back over American history, it appears that, except for the mass media, each of these types of agencies of socialization has generally contributed to the development of the urban child. In Puritan New England the church was an especially vigorous institution, and schooling was available in the towns although boys were given preferential treatment in the amount and kind of schooling. The more isolated the residence of the family or (as on the plantation) the household, however, the less available were these extrafamilial agencies of socialization. We have seen that under conditions of isolation the family became the unit of economic organization and developed a virtually self-sufficient economy. The same conditions serve, of course, to make the family (or household) the sole means of carrying out such other socially necessary functions as socialization.

In the present chapter we shall consider the degree to which and the conditions under which the family shares with other institutions the responsibility for socializing the young. We shall see that under modern urban conditions there seems to be a trend in the function of socialization that is in some respects similar to but less demonstrable than that which we noted in the case of the economic function. In other words, when we use the early rural family as a standard of comparison for the contemporary urban family, it seems clear that the former carried much more nearly complete responsibility for socializing its young than does the latter. This generalization is quite evident in the skill-training and role-development aspects of socialization. With respect to character formation and personality development there are counteracting influences, as we shall see, and consequently the situation is somewhat more complex.

No matter what the level of man's sophistication, he is always able to ask large questions that he cannot answer. What is life? What is death? What constitutes an unanswerable question shifts with time, culture, and especially the state of science. One of the aspects of the religious function is to provide answers for unanswerable questions and thereby to enable man to achieve poise and serenity in the face of tragedy and suffering. Faith is required to provide answers for unanswerable questions, and as Davis observes, "faith feeds on subjective need."[1] The designation and integration of values also enter into the religious function.

From these remarks it follows that the content of religious belief is subject to great variation but that the religious function, sociologically defined, is everywhere fulfilled. It appears that, to some extent at least, the state of belief (or faith) has bearing on what structures are to carry out the religious function. In a period of secularization a good part of the religious function may be fulfilled in nonreligious structures. The rise of a counseling-psychiatric series of occupational specialties is one of the more obvious instances. The designation and integration of values in the economic structure (giving rise to an ideology of bourgeois materialism) is another. A third instance is seen in the noninstitutional neosacralism that appeared on some college campuses in the latter 1960's and early 1970's.

We shall conclude this chapter by trying to bring together our remarks about trends in the four nonfamilial functions—the economic, political, socializing-educational, and the religious. As a society develops from an undifferentiated to a highly complex condition, there evolves a series of societal structures with specialized functions. The transition from simplicity to complexity then takes important functions out of the familial setting, thereby reducing familial interdependence, and resulting in a weakened familial structure.

[1] Kingsley Davis, *Human Society* (New York: Macmillan, 1948), p. 532. For a fascinating study of the fate of a belief system that ran afoul of reality see Leon Festinger, Henry W. Riecken, and Stanley Schachter, *When Prophecy Fails* (Minneapolis: University of Minnesota Press, 1956).

The Nature of Socialization

All societies must have some patterned ways for making participating adults out of the protoplasm that is the human infant. Along the route from infancy to adulthood the individual must learn how to live and work with others and to cooperate to the degree required by his society. More particularly he must learn

1. *Skills*

Each culture contains expectations that, at all ages beyond infancy, the members of the society will exhibit a variety of skills, ranging from walking, and talking in the right language, to those that are involved in earning a living and making love.

2. *Moral character and generally acceptable attitudes*

The problem of creating a moral adult out of an amoral infant is roughly, but not entirely, comparable to the task of "character development." In common usage the emphasis in the term *morality* is on conformity with the values and mores of one's culture. Character does not necessarily connote conformity; in character development attention is given not only to morality but also "to volitional factors and to individual creativeness in the realm of goals to be achieved. . . ."[2] Generally speaking, the individual's behavior should suggest attitudes of acceptance of the values of his culture.

3. *Roles*

The individual must learn to combine his skills and attitudes, morality and character into behaviors appropriate to situations in which he repeatedly finds himself. To the extent that he succeeds he is learning to enact roles ascribed to him and achieved by him.

4. *Personality*

It is expected that he will learn to combine his skills and attitudes, his strivings and his aversions, his self-indulgences and his self-denials into an individual style that is both acceptable and distinctive.

The Nature of Education

Notions as to what education is and ought to be vary from time to time and from place to place. A theme to be developed in Chapter 14 is that one of the determinants of the content of education is the conception of original

---

[2] Vernon Jones, "Character Development in Children—an Objective Approach," in Leonard Carmichael (ed.), *Manual of Child Psychology* (2d ed.; New York, Wiley, 1954), p. 781.

nature. With respect to our four aspects of socialization, we in American society are most familiar with the idea that education is a process of instruction in mental skills. An example of this is the ability to recite the Twenty-Third Psalm from memory or to solve a quadratic equation. A second conception is that of instruction in motor skills, such as learning to swim or to make a dress. A third conception centers on the process of moralization. The form that was especially prevalent in Puritan New England assumed an originally "depraved" child who learned through inhibiting his sinful impulses to become a moral member of society. In contemporary America there are two topics that command attention in moralizing instruction—the curbing of violent and predatory behavior, largely with respect to boys, and sexual behavior, chiefly with respect to girls. Schools have difficulty providing moral instruction in these areas for a variety of reasons—partly because there is little knowledge as to how to indoctrinate the students to produce the desired behavior and indeed, given counterinfluences from peers and others, whether it lies within the power of schools to do so, and partly because of a lack of consensus as to the objectives to be pursued.[3]

A fourth conception of education concerns the presentation of self, i.e., the acquisition of behavioral skills such that one's interaction elicits responses of approval from others. In some social circles such skills cause a person to be regarded as "well-mannered," which includes such traits as politeness, deference, and self-restraint, knowing not only how to use a knife and fork but which knife and which fork, how to dress for various social occasions, and having sufficient knowledge of a variety of "cultural" topics (music, literature, sports, and so on) to be able to engage in "small talk" about them. Given the difference between the masculine and feminine sex roles with the former's emphasis on social position, achievement, and prospect for social mobility and given the latter's emphasis on personal attractiveness and beauty, it is not surprising that there are special courses and schools (e.g., charm courses and finishing schools) designed to instruct girls in self-presentation.[4] A fifth conception, sometimes called "general education," involves acquainting oneself with the "essence" of one's cultural heritage, intellectual and moral, scientific and humanistic. Sixth and last is a conception more inclusive than any of the others. Sometimes known as "progressive education," it involves the education of "the whole child." By this is apparently meant education in all four aspects of socialization with special emphasis on personality development. It includes the development of mental skills, motor skills, and socially

---

[3] Some comments on these aspects of education appear in the following two articles: William Simon and John H. Gagnon, "The Pedagogy of Sex," and Edgar Z. Friedenberg, "Requiem for the Urban School," *Saturday Review of Literature,* November 18, 1967, pp. 74–76 and 77–79, 92–94 respectively.

[4] One of America's largest merchandising chains advertises an eight-week course for four- to ten-year old girls to learn "setting the table and good manners; how to act with company; personal grooming and wardrobe care; sitting, standing and walking like a model" for ten dollars.—*Chicago Sun-Times,* May 1, 1967, p. 39.

approved attitudes and sentiments. With one important qualification it is a summation of the first five conceptions of education plus a concern for personality development. The qualification is that it proceeds to stand the third conception (moralization) on its head. In other words, the theory of progressive education seems to proceed from the Rousseauan premise of the goodness of original nature rather than from the Puritan premise of the depravity of original nature.

The reader may be interested in comparing the sixfold classification of educational objectives set forth in the preceding paragraph with the fourfold classification of categories of socialization in the preceding section.

THE SCHOOL

Formal schooling becomes a functional necessity when parents generally are unable to transmit to their children the skills they believe the children must learn. Conditions are favorable for establishing a system of formal education: (1) when the sheer volume of culture to be transmitted becomes great; (2) when there is enough surplus production to support the professional group of teachers; (3) when the occupational organization is complex, containing a variety of specialties; and (4) when occupations are not hereditary. The early rural family, as we saw in Chapter 4, contained little specialization except that associated with age and sex categories. The way of life demanded that each adult be master of a wide variety of skills (for men: hunting, fishing, clearing land, farming, and the like; for women: milking, churning, spinning, weaving, cooking, and so on). Since there was little interest in transmitting the heritage of Western culture and little surplus to support teachers, each adult was presumed to have the background necessary to train children for the requirements of adult life.

Puritan children generally learned to "read, write, and calculate," and also acquired the skills of husbandry and housewifery. The law of Massachusetts Colony required every father to have his children instructed in "some honest lawful calling." It was expected, moreover, that each family would provide these facets of education not only for its own children but, in addition, for any apprentices in its household. Probably most children were set to some kind of work by the age of seven. Records of the Governor and Company of the Massachusetts Bay in New England for the period 1642–1649 reveal the following in this connection:

> This court, taking into consideration the great neglect in many parents and masters in training up their children in learning, and labor, and other imployments which may bee profitable to the common wealth, do hearupon order and decree, that in every towne the chosen men appointed for managing the prudencial affaires of the same shall henceforth stand charged with the care of the redresse of this evill, so as they shalbee liable to bee punished or fined for the neglect thereof . . . and they shall have power to take accompt from time to time of their parents and masters,

and of their children, concerning their calling and impliment of their children, especially of their ability to read and understand the principles of religion and the capital lawes of the country.[5]

There was a provision whereby children might be removed from the home and put under more capable care if the parents neglected their duty to the point that children and servants became "rude, stubborn and unruly." In Plymouth, fines might be imposed upon the parents, and the children might be removed from the home.[6]

Formal schooling was provided for Puritan boys. Since woman was regarded as being distinctly inferior to man, there was little disposition to "squander" the resources of school or home on the education of girls.[7] Calhoun notes the case of one girl who took her seat daily on the schoolhouse steps in order to learn what she could from the lessons,[8] a situation remarkably parallel to that of the Untouchables of India. In general, where school facilities were made available for the instruction of girls this was done so as not to interfere with the instruction of boys. Classes for girls might be held very early in the morning, late in the afternoon, or during vacation periods. Calhoun holds that the only significant tutelage of the Puritan girl lay in what she could learn from her mother. It has been estimated that over half of the propertied class

---

[5] Grace Abbott, *The Child and The State* (Chicago: University of Chicago Press, 1938), I, 199.

[6] A. W. Calhoun, *A Social History of the American Family* (New York: Barnes & Noble, 1945), I, 72.

[7] In his *History of New England*, Governor John Winthrop wrote in 1640 about

. . . a godly young woman, and of special parts, who was fallen into a sad infirmity, the loss of her understanding and reason, which had been growing upon her divers years by occasion of her giving herself wholly to reading and writing, and had written many books. Her husband, being very loving and tender of her, was loath to grieve her; but he saw his error, when it was too late. For if she had attended her household affairs, and such things as belong to women, and not gone out of her way and calling to meddle in such things as are proper for men, whose minds are stronger, etc., she had kept her wits, and might have improved them usefully and honorably in the place God had set her.—John Winthrop, *The History of New England from 1630 to 1649* (rev. ed.; Boston: Little, Brown, 1853), II, 265–266.

A sampler worked by a young girl in colonial Virginia gave voice to a similar sentiment:

> One did commend me to a wife both fair and young
> That had French, Spanish and Italian tongue.
> I thanked him kindly and told him I loved none such,
> For I thought one tongue for a wife too much.
> What! love ye not the learned?
> Yes, as my life.
> A learned scholar, but not a learned wife.

From A. H. Wharton, *Colonial Days and Dames* (Philadelphia: Lippincott, 1895), p. 195.

[8] Calhoun, *op. cit.*, I, 84.

of women in Massachusetts and Virginia during the latter half of the seventeenth century was illiterate.[9]

Where there are specialized trades, there are limitations to the range of instruction that a father is competent to provide for his sons. On the other hand, if occupations are hereditary, as in the caste system of India or in the guild system of medieval Europe, vocational training can take place in the home or in the father's shop. Where social mobility, both horizontal and vertical, are culturally approved, however, there arises a need for vocational instruction outside the home. In urban America this applied to sons but rarely to daughters. Accordingly, in Puritan New England, boys who learned trades usually began a seven-year apprenticeship between the ages of 10 and 14. The work of women was much less differentiated than that of men. There was virtually no other career for a girl than that of housewife. Therefore, the training that a mother could give her daughters was expected to prove adequate to later demands, and daughters could begin preparing for their calling at an early age. It was not unknown, however, for daughters as well as sons to be bound out.[10]

From these observations it seems quite evident that the degree to which, and the areas wherein, the family retains the responsibility for training its children have varied from society to society, contingent, in part, upon the way in which the training in vocational skills has been administered. In general, as the practice of formal education grows, the function of the family shifts from that of providing education to one of providing the opportunity to be educated. For example, the practice of employing tutors in upper-class families of the Old South signified that the family had yielded to the tutors primary responsibility for the task of instructing the children in mental skills, manners, and "culture." To the degree that the tutor, or private or public schoolmaster, took over educational responsibilities, the participation of the family became indirect, i.e., through providing the economic basis in terms of instructors' salaries. Another way in which the family participated was through providing the children with the necessary leisure to receive formal instruction.

SHIFTS IN EDUCATIONAL EMPHASIS

The ethos of Puritan culture can be stated largely in terms of the dominance and pervasiveness of religious attitudes.[11] The deity was of the Old Testament variety and demanded total compliance with a rigid moral code.

---

[9] This estimate was made by the U.S. Department of Education as a result of checking deeds and other legal documents. It was found that over half of the women entering into contracts were obliged to sign with marks because they could not write their names. —Carl Holliday, *Woman's Life in Colonial Days* (Boston: Cornhill, 1922), p. 71.

[10] "The Pennsylvania Germans thought it no disgrace for a daughter to work in another family, where she might add to her knowledge of good housekeeping."—Calhoun, *op. cit.*, I, 203.

[11] The *New England Primer* communicated religious and moral lessons. This book

To comply with the code called for a great exercise of self-restraint. To produce restrained and literate children was the purpose of socialization in the school.

As we turn our attention southward, we may note that in the Middle Colonies parochial schools were prevalent.[12] In the South many of the rich planters tried to establish their class as a facsimile of the landed gentry of England. They employed tutors and governesses for the early training of their children and then sent their sons to be educated in English universities. In the post-Revolutionary period the economic base necessary for the foreign education of sons began to dwindle because of soil exhaustion and the repeated division of estates. Hence many of the sons who might otherwise have gone abroad for instruction were sent instead for a period of training in the counting houses of the major trading cities.[13]

The concept of our public school system was achieved during the decades 1830–1860. Because in many places (notably Pennsylvania, New Jersey, Delaware, and generally throughout the South) it was regarded as proper for the children of gentlemen to be given private instruction, publicly supported schools were originally conceived as institutions of charity for the education of the children of paupers. With the growth of public schools it is not surprising, then, that the emphasis in education shifted from the content of theology and the classics and the method of memorization to one of general education and manual training, and a method of useful experiences and activities.[14] Prior to this time the apprenticeship system had been the primary technique of vocational education.

THE "WHOLE CHILD" AND THE SCHOOL

Under Francis Parker and John Dewey there began a rebellion against highly formalized educational practices. The movement they launched around the beginning of the present century became organized in the Progressive Education Association. The novel aspect of the "progressive" formulation lies in its emphasis that it is the task of the school to educate the "whole child." As noted above, this perspective embraces virtually all the aspects of socializa-

---

was widely used after the establishing, around 1650, of schools for towns of fifty or more in Massachusetts and Connecticut. Included in the *Primer* was the colorfully titled "Spiritual Milk for American Babes Drawn out of the Breasts of Both Testaments."—James Mulhern, *A History of Education* (New York: Ronald, 1946), p. 280.

[12] *Ibid.*, p. 468.

[13] Calhoun, *op. cit.*, I, 290; II, 333.

[14] Mulhern, *op. cit.*, pp. 489, 494. It is estimated that at the beginning of the nineteenth century well over half the pages in children's textbooks emphasized moral teaching (loyalty, generosity, and so on); since then this stress had declined steadily and by 1950 any emphasis on morality had virtually disappeared. Emphases on achievement and affiliation peaked during that century and a half, the former around 1870 and the latter around 1930. Cf. Richard deCharms and Gerald H. Moeller, "Values Expressed in American Children's Readers: 1800–1950," *Journal of Abnormal and Social Psychology*, 64: 136–142 (1962).

tion and of education that have been distinguished in this chapter. Its emphases have been on "useful" knowledge and skills, on the stimulation of the child to creativity or allowing him spontaneously to achieve an appreciable level of creativity, on his integration with his peer group, and on the development of his personality. Through the practice of progressive education has run a strain of permissiveness and a de-emphasis on the competitive feature of the grading system. It has been reasoned that if a relatively conflictless personality is developed, the child will learn both skills and self-restraint more easily and efficiently, and he will not be "blocked" in spontaneous and creative expression.[15]

One obvious way to make schooling "useful" is to train children directly and explicitly for adult roles. Although occupational training has been available for a long time (as, for example, through apprenticeship in the trades and through "reading" law in an attorney's office), no doubt progressive education has had some influence in the expansion of the number of training programs in the schools. Since the turn of the century there has burgeoned at both the college and secondary levels a new line of training that concerns socialization into adult familial roles through courses in marriage, parenthood, and family life. In view of the fact that familial roles embrace much more of the life of the average woman than of the average man, it is not surprising that such courses appeal primarily to girls.[16] Some indication of the degree to

[15] In 1951 a committee of educators and laymen made a report to the Governor of Illinois on the subject of education. In a section of this report entitled "Healthy Personality through the Schools" the committee wrote approvingly of "helping students come to grips with real life problems in home, school, and community," and of the progress being made in curricular orientation toward "the total personality development of boys and girls." They noted a trend, moreover, not to rate each pupil in terms of the standards of his grade or class but rather on "whether [he] has done the best he is capable of, taking due account of his emotional and physical as well as mental ability." They note: "It is becoming increasingly the custom not to hold a child far back of his social group in grade placement because of his inability to meet scholastic requirements."—Governor's Committee for Illinois on the Midcentury White House Conference for Children and Youth, *Children and Youth in Illinois,* pp. 40, 45. (No place or date of publication is shown; the letter of transmittal is signed on August 15, 1951.)

[16] For a criticism of courses on preparation for marriage, see Harriet Mowrer, "Getting Along in Marriage," in Howard Becker and Reuben Hill (eds.), *Family, Marriage and Parenthood* (2d ed.; Boston: Heath, 1955), pp. 363–364. Father Schmiedeler, writing from a Catholic point of view, denounces the practice of giving sex instruction in the schools, holding this to be the responsibility of the family. His denunciation is equally vehement on the subject of nursery schools, which he regards as a device for the parent to avoid responsibility. Interpreting papal authority to support his position, Schmiedeler regards both of these practices as weakening the family.—Edgar Schmiedeler, *An Introductory Study of the Family* (rev. ed.; New York: Appleton, 1947), pp. 359–364. Another priest asserts that Catholic families (he doesn't qualify with "some" or "many") are "either incapable or unwilling" to give their children adequate instruction concerning sex. He notes that although the Church resisted such a move with "the traditional Catholic objection that this was primarily and properly the obligation of parents," the widespread de-

which this emphasis on adjustment has influenced the curriculum of the public schools comes from a study of 190 school systems throughout the country. According to this study about one half the high schools studied offered courses bearing such titles as "family living," "family problems," and the like.[17]

An interesting variation of this trend has been an occasional course designed to train the modern version of mother-substitute known as "babysitter."[18] Other aspects of homemaking such as cooking and sewing have become integral parts of both high school and college curricula.

It is consistent with the newer, expanded view of education that schools should have developed a wide variety of services. Such ancillary activities, which are unevenly distributed, include counseling, psychiatric and other medical service (although frequently limited to diagnosis), and job placement service. Some schools have established counseling services that employ specially trained persons in ways that may be viewed as functionally equivalent to the role of parents. Their duties may include the handling of emotional as well as social and occupational problems of the student. Apart from their duties in advising students concerning curricular and occupational choices, counselors identify those cases of serious maladjustment to be referred for more extensive therapy. Some school systems have their own psychological divisions, employing psychiatrists, social workers, and psychologists to take care of these referrals; others utilize established clinics. Visiting teachers are another aspect of this psychiatric service. It is their function to investigate the home situation and its relation to the maladjustment of the child in school. Although medical care remains largely the responsibility of the parents, schools do provide some health service. The matter of finding a job after high school is facilitated in many schools by the establishment of placement bureaus, which thus give the child his initial contact with the occupational system. To some extent, then, the school is taking over the position-conferring function of integrating the young person into the occupational system, whereas in bygone days he would have tended to rely more on his family to put him in touch with prospective employers.

A view prominent in the psychology of recent decades has been that the

---

mand for sex information has resulted in the introduction by the Church of a number of courses, forums, lectures, and the like.—John L. Thomas, *The American Catholic Family* (Englewood Cliffs, N.J.: Prentice-Hall, 1956), p. 335.

[17] Douglas E. Scates, "Education for Personal and Family Living in Public Schools: A Sample Survey," *Social Hygiene Papers*, December, 1955, pp. 18–26.

[18] At least one book on this subject was published as early as 1949: Marion Lowndes, *A Manual for Baby Sitters* (Boston: Little, Brown, 1949). By 1958 it was reported that 40 percent of all YWCA's in the country had courses in baby-sitting. The National Board of the YWCA has suggested a basic outline for such a course. It contains the following six units: importance of baby-sitting as a real job, necessity of getting to know the family and routine of the household, safety, health, child development, and child care.—Dorothy Barclay, "Proposing a B.S. for Baby Sitters," *The New York Times Magazine*, April 6, 1958, p. 49.

individual's behavior is largely determined by his history of social interaction and in particular that "problem children are the children of problem parents."[19] Educators have pursued the implications of this proposition by seeking to induce parents to participate in school programs with a view to modifying the attitudes and behavior of problem parents toward their children. At this juncture we see that the organismic view of education results not only in the school's invading the area of personality formation as regards children, but in making gestures in the direction of socializing parents as well.[20]

As would be expected in the light of the expanding functions of the school, formal education is taking up more years in the life of the child and more days per year than heretofore.[21] The school program, moreover, frequently includes programs of activities to be undertaken "after hours" and during vacation periods. It is quite clear that this concept of education involves the school in a much larger proportion of the total process of socialization than heretofore and that, correspondingly, the role of the family has been reduced.

Even when the progressive movement was enjoying its greatest vogue, it had many critics among educators and laymen as well. Teachers who have

---

[19] A. L. Baldwin, J. Kalhorn, and F. H. Breese, "Patterns of Parent Behavior," *Psychological Monographs,* 58: 72–74 (1945).

[20] The authors of the study cited in the last footnote express the opinion that it is futile to instruct parents in "approved" techniques of child rearing if their personalities are not compatible with their parental roles.

[21] Between 1870 and 1956 the proportion of the U.S. population 17 years old who were high school graduates rose from 2.0 percent to 62.3 percent. As recently as 1930 it was only 29.0 percent.—U.S. Bureau of the Census, *Historical Statistics of the United States, Colonial Times to 1957* (Washington, D.C.: GPO, 1960), Series H, 223–233, p. 207. By 1967 the median number of years of formal schooling for all persons 25 years of age and over was 12.0, i.e., just half the population over 25 had had four years of high school, and 10.0 percent of the population over 25 had had four or more years of college. The race-sex-age category having the highest percentage of college graduates was white males 30–34 years old with 20.6.—U.S. Bureau of the Census, *Current Population Reports—Population Characteristics,* Series P-20, No. 169, February 9, 1968, Table 1, pp. 8–9. It was predicted that by 1985 the median number of years of school for those 25 and over would have risen to about 12.5. U.S. Bureau of the Census, *Current Population Reports—Population Estimates,* Series P-25, No. 390, March 29, 1968, Table 1, p. 10. Men who were 20 to 64 years of age in 1962 had median schooling of 12.2 years, whereas the median of their fathers was 9.2; that is, in one generation the median rose by exactly 3 years.—U.S. Bureau of the Census, *Current Population Reports—Population Characteristics,* Series P-20, No. 132, September 22, 1964, Table A, p. 1. A further increase in the number of years involved in schooling has been predicted by H. C. Hunt, who foresees a new type of program that will enroll the 3-year-old in kindergarten and graduate the 20-year-old from a community junior college.—"'School of Tomorrow' Plan for Pupils from 3 to 20," *The New York Times,* July 2, 1950, p. 9E. In the three quarters of a century after 1870 the average length of the school year for elementary and secondary public schools increased from 132 to 176 days.—H. J. Otto, "Elementary Education—III. Organization and Administration," in W. S. Monroe (ed.), *Encyclopedia of Educational Research* (rev. ed.; New York: Macmillan, 1950), p. 369.

the traditional view of their function in terms of the transmission of skills and, to some degree at least, of character development, tend to view the success of their efforts in terms of grades competitively achieved and in terms of politeness, deference, and the other marks of manners. In their eyes progressive teachers fail to give systematic instruction and produce pupils lacking discipline in behavior as well as in intellect. In the view of those who see "the whole child," the traditional teacher tends to rate "the children in terms of their learning accomplishment, the problem of controlling their behavior in the group, their family background and status, or their personal appeal to the teacher," while the traditional teacher's grades describe "the children less than they described the reaction of the persons making the entries."[22]

The battle between the traditionalists and the progressives has been going on for decades.[23] Depending upon where one looks, one can see reactions against permissiveness and against rigidity.[24] The technological achievements of the U.S.S.R. and the ascent of the first Russian sputnik convinced many that America might be losing to the Soviet Union the struggle for pre-eminence in world influence because of "soft" educational practices that emphasize the pupil's personal and social adjustment over the development of his intellectual skills. On the other hand, reaction against the participation of the United States in the war in Viet Nam and more generally against middle-class values led to rejection of the emphasis on discipline and deferred gratification, on competition and achievement; affirmatively, this reaction led to emphasis on self-expression and self-fulfillment, and on spontaneity and intimacy in interpersonal relations.

If the trend outlined in the present section were to continue, it would appear that the family was destined to become merely the child's caretaker during the fragments of after-school hours left over from extracurricular activities and of summer weeks before and after camp. As is emphasized in Chapter 14, however, both popular and "expert" thinking on child rearing are extremely

---

[22] D. A. Prescott et al., *Helping Teachers Understand Children* (Washington, D.C.: American Council on Education, 1945), p. 6. Since grading in the progressive system is so individualized, since making out cards takes considerable time, and since such cards are sometimes difficult for parents to comprehend, there has been some disposition to substitute parent-teacher conferences for grade reports in elementary schools.—Benjamin Fine, "A-B-C of Grading Puzzles Parents: Report Cards Now Stress Capacity to Learn and Non-Academic Traits," *The New York Times*, November 18, 1957, pp. 33–34.

[23] In 1951 the superintendent of schools of New York City addressed a group of psychologists and asked them to provide educators with an answer to the question whether progressive education was as good as its advocates claimed or as bad as its critics contended.—"Jansen Bids Psychologists Assay New and Old Systems of Teaching," *The New York Times*, January 27, 1951, p. 15. In Bertrand Russell's opinion, "Conventional schools sacrifice individuality, and progressive schools, however unintentionally, tend to sacrifice citizenship."—"As School Opens—The Educators Examined," *The New York Times Magazine*, September 7, 1952, pp. 9, 44–45. Quotation is from p. 45.

[24] Cf. Chapter 14 below.

variable. A century or more of analyzed history offers evidence that no trend will last very long but that some sort of countertrend will set in and give the beliefs about child rearing a cyclical appearance somewhat akin to the hemlines of women's dresses.

THE SCHOOL IN THE STATUS SYSTEM

Since social classes have their own subcultures (a topic taken up in Chapter 8), the parents of a vertically mobile child are usually not equipped to indoctrinate him in the subculture of his class of destination. Warner, Havighurst, and Loeb develop the widely held belief that one of the functions of the American educational system is to select and train children for vertical social mobility.[25] Since the values taught by the schools are usually those of the middle class and since upward mobility is a dominant, perhaps *the* dominant, theme in the ethos of the middle class, it would not be surprising to find that the schools do impart to the children both the will and the means to move upward in the status system. An anthropologist has proposed that the most direct technique for the achievement of upward social mobility lies in the acquisition of the overt behaviors (or manners) of the next superior class.[26] These observations render meaningful the great importance attached to the nonacademic pursuits of the college student. They also help to explain the popularity and, indeed, the very existence of books on etiquette.

If the school is the ladder of upward mobility, it should follow that income correlates positively with schooling. Such is clearly the case, as can be seen in Table 5.1. What is sometimes overlooked, however, is that the children of wealthy people receive more education on the average than do the children of poor people, and thus the correlation so obvious in Table 5.1 *could* exist with no mobility at all. With respect to this point, American, English, and Swedish data indicate that with father's social status held constant, there is some positive correlation between amount of schooling and son's upward mobility. The author of the study concludes that whereas education does influence mobility, it is only one of numerous factors that do, and its influence is probably less than is usually thought.[27]

The prolongation and diversification of education tend to reduce the cul-

[25] W. L. Warner, R. J. Havighurst, and M. B. Loeb, *Who Shall Be Educated?* (New York: Harper & Row, 1944), pp. 56–57.

[26] Ralph Linton, *The Cultural Background of Personality* (New York: Appleton, 1945), p. 61. An intriguing example of the correlation between behavior and mobility is the report that by the age of sixteen the sexual patterns of those males who will move upward in the American status system are already different from those of the nonmobile boys.—Alfred C. Kinsey, Wardell B. Pomeroy, and Clyde E. Martin, *Sexual Behavior in the Human Male* (Philadelphia: Saunders, 1948), p. 419.

[27] C. Arnold Anderson, "A Skeptical Note on the Relation of Vertical Mobility to Education," *American Journal of Sociology*, 66: 560–570 (1961). Empirical confirmation of Anderson's view appears in Peter M. Blau and Otis Dudley Duncan, *The American Occupational Structure* (New York: Wiley, 1967), p. 196.

TABLE 5.1

Mean Annual Income for Males 25 Years Old and Over and Total Lifetime Income for Males from Age 18 to Death, by Years of School Completed: 1968 (in 1968 Dollars.)

YEARS OF SCHOOL COMPLETED	EARNINGS	
	Annual	Lifetime
Elementary		
Less than 8 years	$4,093	$201,888
8 years	5,624	265,198
High school		
1 to 3 years	6,983	303,663
4 years	8,430	361,082
College		
1 to 3 years	9,692	422,156
4 years	12,236	543,308
5 years or more	13,672	621,906
Average	7,889	347,859

SOURCE: U.S. Bureau of the Census, *Current Population Reports—Consumer Income*, Series P-60, No. 74, October 30, 1970, Tables A and F, pp. 2 and 14, respectively. Men in the bottom educational category have this highest median income in the 35-44-year age group ($5,344); those in the top educational category have their maximum in the 50-64 age group ($17,590).

ture shared by parents and children. So far as the intellectual content of education is concerned, the subject matter undergoes such radical revision from generation to generation as to make it difficult for even a college-educated parent to follow the direction of his child's training. When we add indoctrination in the subculture of a higher class, interests common to parent and child are further reduced.

In espousing the value system of the middle class the American public school system has frequently assumed values and motivations that have little meaning for lower-class children. This observation accounts, in part, for the special difficulties between teachers and pupils in lower-class areas, for the relatively low achievement levels in these areas, and for the high mortality rates in school enrollment.[28] Warner and his associates have summarized the relation between school, family, and social mobility:

[28] In 1960 over half (53.9 percent) of the persons 16 to 24 years old whose fathers did not graduate from high school and whose families had incomes under $5,000 had not themselves graduated from high school; roughly one fifth of this category (19.1 percent) had had some college training. Among those whose fathers had attended college and who had families with incomes in excess of $10,000 the proportion who failed to graduate from high school was less than one twenty-fifth (3.7 percent) and the proportion having attended college was nearly nine tenths (88.6 percent).—U.S. Bureau of Census, *Current*

Most children are trained by home and neighborhood to occupy the social positions to which they are born. The school offers some opposition to home and neighborhood training in the case of the lower-class children, but usually fights a losing battle over them. It supports and supplements the home and neighborhood training of middle-class children. It tends to democratize the training of upper-class children, but loses many of these children to private schools which give them a class education.[29]

SOCIALIZATION AND THE MEDIA OF MASS COMMUNICATION

The family and the school have been socializing children for centuries, but the media of mass communication had to await the necessary technological developments before they could make their contribution. Mass communication entertains and transmits information rapidly, transiently, and publicly to relatively large, heterogeneous, and anonymous audiences.[30] The media are printed (newspapers, magazines, books), auditory (radio), and audio-visual (motion pictures, slides, and television). More than any other medium television furnishes a common body of information for the early socialization of children.[31] For this reason there has been much concern about and inquiry into the impact of television on children.

According to the studies of Schramm and his associates, the typical American child has had direct experience with television by the time he is two and by the age of three is able to shout for his favorite programs. In the years between three and six he is becoming acquainted with radio, learns about printed media through pictures and having stories read and cartoons interpreted to him, and by six he has built up a strong set of preferences for certain television programs.[32]

It is difficult to calculate the amount of time children spend in viewing television, but it is estimated that the average American child of five spends about two hours each weekday (Monday through Friday) before the screen, that the amount of time peaks at three hours in the five-to-eight-year-olds and tapers off by from a half hour to an hour during high school. On Sundays it is reported that the typical child devotes an additional half hour to an hour above the daily average.[33] (See Table 5.2.)

In the younger years (under 10 to 13 years) it is the brighter children who surpass the less bright in hours spent before the television; by the age of

Population Reports—Population Characteristics, Series P-20, No. 110, July 24, 1961, Table 10, p. 15.

[29] Warner, Havighurst, and Loeb, *op. cit.*, pp. 56–57.

[30] Charles R. Wright, *Mass Communication: A Sociological Perspective* (New York: Random House, 1959), chap. 1.

[31] Wilbur Schramm, Jack Lyle, and Edwin B. Parker, *Television in the Lives of Our Children* (Stanford, Calif.: Stanford University Press, 1961), p. 27.

[32] *Ibid.*, pp. 24–25.

[33] *Ibid.*, p. 34.

TABLE 5.2

Use of Media of Mass Communication by Children of Selected Grades in School: San Francisco, 1958–1960

MEDIUM AND MEASURE OF USE	GRADE 2	GRADE 6	GRADE 12
Television: average number of hours of viewing per weekday	2.2	2.9	2.3
Radio: average number of hours of listening per weekday	1.1	1.2	1.9
Movies: number attended last month	1.0	1.6	1.2
Books: number read outside school during last month	1.1	2.1	1.0
Magazines: number read last month	0.8	2.6	2.8
Comic books: number read per month	0.6	2.3	0.7
Newspapers: percentage reading every day	3.0%	57.0%	66.2%

SOURCE: Adapted from Wilbur Schramm, Jack Lyle, and Edwin B. Parker, *Television in the Lives of Our Children* (Stanford, Calif.: Stanford University Press, 1961), p. 36, with permission of the publishers. © 1961 by the Board of Trustees of the Leland Stanford Junior University.

15 it is the less bright who are engaging in more viewing. The example of the child's family appears to be very influential with respect to the amount of the child's viewing. Where parents are highly educated, both they and their children view less than do members of both generations in families where the families are less well educated; families in which the parents read little and view a great deal tend to have children who do likewise. A relatively low rate of viewing is reported among families having middle-class norms of work, activity, and self-betterment.[34]

The diffusion during the 1950's of television receivers in American society was so widespread that it may seem to younger readers always to have been a salient element in American culture. By 1969 it was estimated that 95 percent of the households in the United States had one or more television sets, and that 29 percent had two or more.[35] Consistent with the preceding paragraph is a finding from a study done in 1950 around Harvard University that categories of families having the lowest proportions of sets were those in which

---

[34] *Ibid.*, pp. 34–35. An English study reports that parental example and parental control are important in determining the amount of children's viewing. In this study social class seemed to affect the amount of children's viewing only through the earlier bedtimes imposed on younger children by middle-class parents.—Hilde T. Himmelweit *et al.*, *Television and the Child: An Empirical Study of the Effect of Television on the Young* (London: Oxford University Press, 1958), p. 12.

[35] U.S. Bureau of the Census, *Statistical Abstract of the United States: 1970* (Washington: GPO, 1970), Table 760, p. 496.

the heads were professionals and where the family income was high.[36] Comparisons of families having and not having receivers make it possible to draw inferences as to what children did before television with the two to three hours per day they now devote to it. It appears that part of the time the child now spends before the television was previously devoted to play (a half hour) and to sleep (about a quarter of an hour). There is also evidence that he now devotes less time to other mass media (radio, movies, reading), to helping around the house, to practicing musical instruments, and to such other forms of activity as are thought to be "creative" or "productive."[37]

The evidence that television is ubiquitous and so much attended to by children (as well as by parents) has precipitated the questions, What is television doing to children? What is it doing to family life? Those who study the content of television programs, especially if they come with the values and attitudes of intellectuals, tend to view the content of the programs either with alarm (as inciting children to mayhem, murder, and other aggressive antisocial behaviors) or with regret that children spend so much time as passive spectators of television's bland fare that they will become human vegetables. The fact that television viewing is done in the home has been construed by some writers as fostering family unity. Less optimistic writers insist that family unity cannot be built on a semilit room full of family members staring silently at the same screen or perhaps engaged in noisy conflict as to whose preference will control the channel selector switch.

Hilde Himmelweit and her associates have carried out a study in five English cities based upon the written responses of 1854 television viewers 10–11 and 13–14 years old and a like number of nonviewers (children in families without receivers). With respect to aggression she found that children were more disturbed by a display of anger than by one of shooting, more by danger to animals such as Lassie and Rin-Tin-Tin than by a battle scene; more disturbed, in other words, by what to them are situations with which they can make identifications than by historical or fictional scenes. They did not find that viewers showed signs of being more or less aggressive or maladjusted than the nonviewers. They did conclude, however, that programs of violence could precipitate aggressive behavior in those few children who were already emotionally disturbed.[38]

---

[36] Eleanor E. Maccoby, "Television: Its Impact on School Children," *Public Opinion Quarterly*, 15: 421–444 (1951), Table 1, p. 422.

[37] Schramm *et al., op. cit.*, pp. 71–73; Maccoby, "Television," *loc. cit.*, p. 439.

[38] Himmelweit *et al., op. cit.*, pp. 19–20, 210. A study of American children reports that those who were well integrated with their peer groups manifested less interest in violent programs on radio and television than did the less well integrated.—Matilda Riley and John Riley, "A Sociological Approach to Communications Research," *Public Opinion Quarterly*, 15: 445–460 (1951). In another American study it was found that among upper-middle-class families more highly frustrated children spent more time viewing television than did less frustrated children. The relationship did not appear among upper-lower-class families, and the interpretation was offered that the subculture of the latter class gives more

In the same study it was found that the viewers seemed to be no more passive than the nonviewers, nor did they appear to be more enterprising. Television seemed to be neither an aid nor a deterrent in the development of general knowledge; the only difference seemed to be a slight advantage for viewers if they were young or dull. Television seemed to stimulate no increased interest in any school subjects. The increase in demand on the viewers' time did have the consequence that less time was spent in casual companionship with other children: there was less time to do "nothing in particular," "to stand and stare."[39]

And what about the family? Although television keeps members of the family at home more, it is doubtful whether it fosters any family unity. It does assist parents in keeping an eye on the children; although it does not appear to create conflicts, it does precipitate them.[40]

The Religious Function

The fact that sociology is a social science results in our viewing religion naturalistically. The nature of the sociology here employed results in our viewing religion functionally. In Chapter 1 it was stated that the society-oriented function of religion was to achieve and to maintain solidarity and consensus about general goals, values, and norms, and to maintain a state of purposefulness; and that the individual-oriented function was to explain the unexplainable, to allay man's fears, anxieties, sorrows, and to prevent feelings of alienation.

Derivative from these specifications of religion's basic societal function is its capacity for social control, i.e., to induce the members of a society to act in ways consistent with societal welfare and to refrain from behaving antisocially through (1) the integration of individual goals with institutionalized values, (2) the threat of punishment by extrahuman agencies, and (3) reinforcing the solidarity of the group (i.e., the individual's sense of "belonging"). Religion also provides, says Kingsley Davis, "release from the very thing it instils, guilt."[41]

With respect to the individual-oriented properties of the religious function—especially the allaying of fears, anxieties, and sorrows—it can be seen that there is some common ground between the religious function and the

---

unqualified approval to viewing.—Eleanor E. Maccoby, "Why Do Children Watch Television?" *Public Opinion Quarterly*, 18: 239–244 (1954).

[39] Himmelweit et al., *op. cit.*, pp. 21, 24, 26–27.

[40] *Ibid.*, pp. 25–26.

[41] Davis, *Human Society*, p. 532. A religion may be defined in Lenski's terms: "a system of beliefs about the nature of the force(s) ultimately shaping man's destiny, and the practices associated therewith, shared by the members of a group."—Gerhard Lenski, *The Religious Factor: A Sociological Study of Religion's Impact on Politics, Economics, and Family Life* (New York: Doubleday, 1961), pp. 298–299.

function of emotional gratification (to be taken up in Chapter 9) when the latter is conceived in its negative aspect of assuaging feelings of insecurity.

Two of the most conspicuous and articulate atheists in the history of Western man have been Karl Marx and Sigmund Freud. They were concerned respectively with making explicit the society-oriented and the individual-serving functions of religion. They felt, moreover, that to demonstrate its function was to dispose of religion.

To Marx religion was the opiate of the masses.[42] By this Marx meant that by holding up the illusion of post-mortem spiritual rewards and by representing them as superior to here-and-now material rewards the bourgeoisie was able to appease the proletariat, which would otherwise have been aroused to revolt against the unjust and inhuman oppression of the bourgeoisie. Thus Marx saw religion as the means used by the bourgeoisie to keep the proletariat working submissively toward the goals of the bourgeoisie—profits.[43]

To Freud the father-son relationship was laden with conflict. In his analysis religion was the re-creation of this relationship in fantasy but with the conflict much reduced: "Now that God was a single person, man's relations could recover the intimacy and intensity of the child's relation to the father."[44] Thus he interpreted religion as a manifestation of the adult's need for protection analogous to "the child's defensive reaction to his helplessness."[45] Furthermore, he saw religion as a device by which man protected himself against the "dangers of nature and fate, and against the evils of human society."[46]

THE CONSTANT AND THE VARIABLE IN THE FOLK-URBAN TRANSITION

It appears that as society changes from a simple, undifferentiated structure to one that is complex and has specialized subsystems, religion tends to change in more or less predictable ways. According to Kingsley Davis, (1) the

---

[42] Karl Marx, *A Criticism of the Hegelian Philosophy of Law* (1844). Another student has explained religion as a way of trying to obtain "those blessings which are commonly supposed to be beyond the reach of mortals . . . to give rain and sunshine in due season, to make the crops grow, and so on."—Sir James George Frazer, *The Golden Bough: A Study in Magic and Religion* (abr. ed.; New York: Macmillan, 1958), p. 11.

[43] Yinger's functional analysis of the sect has a similar ring: "The sect may have a latent function for the high status groups, because of its ability to funnel the attention and energy of the lower classes away from this world's problems onto the problems of the hereafter. Better to hate the devil than the boss—certainly from the point of view of the boss, who can sometimes be found among the financial supporters of revival services . . . ." —J. Milton Yinger, *Religion, Society and the Individual: An Introduction to the Sociology of Religion* (New York: Macmillan, 1957), p. 172. Another writer adds the suggestion that the sect may function to socialize lower-class groups with respect to the values and usages of middle-class American society.—Benton Johnson, "A Critical Appraisal of the Church-Sect Typology," *American Sociological Review*, 22: 88–92 (1957).

[44] Sigmund Freud, *The Future of an Illusion* (New York: Doubleday Anchor Books, 1957), p. 31.

[45] *Ibid.*, p. 40.

[46] *Ibid.*, p. 29.

gods cease to be localized, (2) the gods are conceived less anthropomorphically and more abstractly, (3) areas of everyday affairs become separated from religion, (4) homogeneity of belief diminishes and sects appear, with the result (5) that the religious system becomes fragmented. This process, says Davis, is secularization.[47]

From these remarks it follows (1) that the religious function is universal, but that (2) the content of religious belief is highly variable, and (3) that where belief becomes so secularized as scarcely to seem religious, more and more of the religious function will be fulfilled within societal structures that are not explicitly religious and may even be explicitly antireligious. Sociologists speak of such a structure as being the "functional equivalent" of religion. Since science and various forms of nationalism (e.g., Nazism and Communism) offer belief systems that in certain settings meet the same needs that religion meets, it follows that the educational structure and the polity can become functional equivalents of religion.[48]

STRESS AND THEOLOGY

To Max Weber, the eminent sociologist, religion was a source of social change.[49] Some other sociologists, e.g., Mills, have seen religion as epiphenomenal, i.e., as reflecting rather than causing changes in other societal structures.[50] In the latter vein is the writing of Abram Kardiner, a psychoanalyst, who has studied the religions of a number of peoples and who believes that the nature of the anxieties and insecurities common to the members of a society can be inferred from the form and content of the society's religion. Among the Alorese, for example, the nature of social relationships is accurately reflected in the fact that "the individual acts toward the deity as if [the deity] were an insistent creditor whom [the individual] would rather not pay off."[51] This conception of the deity is a reflection of the very important creditor-debtor relationship among the Alorese. Kardiner believes that the degree and manner of elaboration of a religion is related to the degree and nature of the stresses experienced in the society, especially during childhood. It would seem to be part of this reasoning that if the culture encourages or even tolerates expressive reactions to frustration, there will be less disposition to weave the source of that frustration into the theology than in situations where such ex-

[47] *Op. cit.*, p. 543.
[48] Elizabeth K. Nottingham, *Religion and Society* (New York: Random House, 1954).
[49] Max Weber, *The Protestant Ethic and the Spirit of Capitalism* (New York: Scribner, 1930; first edition published in German in 1904–1905) and *The Sociology of Religion* (Boston: Beacon, 1963; first edition published in German in 1922).
[50] "Families and churches and schools adapt to modern life; governments and armies and corporations shape it. . . ."—C. Wright Mills, *The Power Elite* (New York: Oxford, 1956), p. 6.
[51] Abram Kardiner, *The Psychological Frontiers of Society* (New York: Columbia University Press, 1945), p. 429; cf. also the rest of chap. 14.

pressive reaction is discouraged or prohibited or, by the nature of the case, is impossible. In societies where life is relatively easy and psychological stress is minimal, according to this formulation, the theology will be relatively undeveloped; and if a relatively long period of good (easy) times follows a considerable period of rigorous times, some of the sharpness of the dogma will be lost with the consequence that the religion will appear simpler and less compelling.

RELIGION IN AMERICA

In early colonial times Puritanism emphasized man's innate sinfulness. From this sorry condition salvation lay only in the grace of God. Toward the time of the American Revolution, however, "the sense of this world as a vale of tears and the acceptance of the doctrines of grace and election were speedily losing ground before the conviction . . . that man saves himself by his own effort and that he accomplishes his salvation in the world of here and now."[52] From the theory of Kardiner it would follow that there would be a reduced interest in theological issues if life became less stressful and that there would be a renewed interest in creed if conditions should become more anxiety-producing. In the eighteenth and nineteenth centuries and during the first quarter of the twentieth century, economic conditions generally improved; concomitantly there developed the doctrine of self-reliance and the related faith that through organization men can control their natural environment and also to some degree their destiny.

This line of reasoning leads to the question as to what has been happening in recent years with respect to religious commitment in the United States. Have living conditions in America caused a greater proportion of the people than in bygone generations to feel more anxious and to express it in religion? The complexity of our culture makes it possible to draw opposite conclusions, depending upon the features one considers. If one concentrates on the possibilities of the cold war's turning into an atomic holocaust, or if one regards the increase in interpersonal and intergroup tensions and violence, there is much room to conclude that this is indeed an age of anxiety. With this emphasis in mind it seems appropriate to anticipate an upswing in religious interest.

On the other hand, there is the general picture of marked economic improvement, the gradual reduction of poverty, and progress toward an "affluent society." And one may interpret the violence of the age as providing such catharsis as to remove any need to reflect unexpended emotional stress in the "projective screen," under which Kardiner subsumes theology. These latter considerations imply a reduction in the proportion of church activities that are

---

[52] Harold J. Laski, *The American Democracy* (New York: Viking, 1948), p. 729. Weber felt that although the assumption was widespread that one's suffering would mollify the deity and improve one's chances for a felicitous existence after death, still such concepts as humility and salvation have generally seemed "remote from all elite political classes." —*Sociology of Religion* (Boston: Beacon, 1963), pp. 114, 85.

purely religious and imply a progressive blandness in theology. There is some evidence to support this point of view.

After reviewing a number of best-selling books of inspirational religious literature published since 1880, Schneider and Dornbusch conclude that in the books reviewed, a concern with the hereafter has diminished, that an instrumental conception of religion has arisen (i.e., salvation, which is being conceived more in the here-and-now, is seen as involving "release from poverty or handicapping inhibition in personal relations or from ill health or emotional disequilibrium"), and finally that the validity of the Judeo-Christian tradition is being assumed "with significant vagueness."[53]

According to the Gallup Poll there has been in recent years a slight decrease in the proportion of Americans who go to church every week—in 1955, 49 percent reported that they attended church weekly; in 1969 the percentage was 42.[54] A more dramatic shift is reported with respect to expressed belief in a decrease in the influence of religion. Over the period 1957–1970 the Gallup organization has taken seven polls on the question " . . . do you think religion as a whole is increasing its influence on American life, or losing its influence?" In 1957, 69 percent responded "increasing" and 14 percent "losing"; by 1968 the percentages were reversed with 14 percent responding "increasing" and 75 percent "losing."[55]

Further evidence comes from interviews with 845 parents belonging to 63 Presbyterian churches throughout the United States. The authors of the study point out that theologians have one conception of the church and the parents in this study quite another. The theologians think of the church "as a redeeming and redemptive community of faith [of those] who are called by God in Christ to a priesthood of all believers."[56] In other words, the theologians emphasize creed. The parents, however, conceive of the church as a "bundle of organizations, a mass of activities, and a crew of willing workers . . . who are engaged in about the same basic business as 'other character-

---

[53] Louis Schneider and Sanford M. Dornbusch, "Inspirational Religious Literature: From Latent to Manifest Functions of Religion," *American Journal of Sociology*, 62: 476–481 (1957) at p. 477. It is difficult to measure religious trends and even to be sure of the direction in which they are going. There is no way to determine, e.g., whether the proportion of devout believers in this country is higher or lower than it was in colonial times. The sort of information available is illustrated by the fact that over 96 percent of the Americans over the age of fourteen who are included in a survey were recorded as "religious" by their responses to the question: "What is your religion?" Needless to say, the interviewers did not probe the sincerity or intensity of religious belief.—U.S. Bureau of the Census, *Current Population Reports—Population Characteristics*, Series P-20, No. 79, Feburary 2, 1958, Table 1, p. 6.

[54] "Gallup Poll: 75 pct. say religion is losing grip," *Chicago Sun-Times*, March 7, 1970, p. 36.

[55] *Gallup Opinion Index*, Report No. 35, May 1968, p. 23.

[56] Roy W. Fairchild and John Charles Wynn, *Families in the Church: A Protestant Survey* (New York: Association Press, 1961), p. 174.

building agencies,'" as contributing to family unity and to mental health, as helping to improve the neighborhood and their own social status.[57]

(Here we see a difference between the view of the professionals and that of the laity with respect to a basic societal structure. The former have a professional conception of the structure's essential function with respect to which all else is, or should be, derivative. To the clergy creed is basic, and mental health and church suppers are derivative. The professional conception of function tends to be closely related to such specialized knowledge and skills as justify the functionaries in conceiving of themselves as professionals. To preside over church suppers does not require professional talent, and the clergymen recognize that they are not uniformly qualified for practice in the field of mental health. Parishioners, on the other hand, are responding to the ongoing society in a more total sense; they can see an opportunity for "building character" in the community's children and perhaps latitude for improving the neighborhood. The disgust of the clergy at the layman's point of view is captured in the following: "Thus . . . the church appears to many to be a good thing for a town to have, like substantial banks, swim clubs, or a city dump."[58] A similar difference between the professionals and the laity exists in the educational structure. Professors validate their academic positions on the basis of their scholarship; they tend to be outraged at undergraduates who major in fraternities and dating and show little interest in Sophocles or calculus. The students can argue that for them college has the function of preparation for adult roles and that "making contacts" and getting engaged are relevant to this conception of the function.)

The results of the survey of inspirational literature by Schneider and Dornbusch and of the interviews with Presbyterian parents by Fairchild and Wynn seem consistent with the following observations:

> It is easier to pass as a religiously identified person today than it was a century ago when a more sacred pattern of conduct very definitely marked the church member off from the unchurched. . . . Increased identification with formal religion is explainable not so much that the American people are becoming more religious as that religion is becoming more like American culture.[59]

Yinger concurs by observing that the Protestant tradition "has been so secularized that to join many middle class churches is not sharply different from joining Kiwanis."[60]

[57] *Ibid.*, p. 175.

[58] *Ibid.* A corresponding difference on the Catholic side between the professional and the lay point of view seems implied in Bishop Sheen's remark that anxiety is to be valued. Cf. n. 68 below.

[59] W. Seward Salisbury, "Religion and Secularization," *Social Forces*, 36: 197–205 (1958), at p. 204.

[60] *Op. cit.*, p. 280.

SECULARIZATION AND FUNCTIONAL EQUIVALENTS

The process of secularization that has just been noted has been characterized by one writer with the felicitous phrase "deterioration in belief."[61] In an earlier paragraph it was noted that the function of religion was universal, but the content of religious beliefs was quite variable. If belief "deteriorates" markedly, this implies that at least for a considerable segment—if not for all members—of a society the religious function can no longer be adequately fulfilled by the traditional religious structure, the church. At this point we invoke the concept of functional equivalence. That is, we look about to discover what other relationships and institutional structures take over some part of the religious function. To see what functional equivalents there may be, it is necessary to recall the elements going into the religious function.

The over-all religious function was defined in terms of the society-oriented function of the designation and integration of values and the individual-oriented function of providing a sense of belonging and the handling of anxiety.

Let us begin by looking at some values in American culture and try to discover how they are manifested. Kluckhohn and Strodtbeck have proposed that there are five questions every society must try to answer. The answers a society gives, they assert, give orientation to the society's basic values. Following is their list of orientations, questions, and possible answers:

ORIENTATION	QUESTION	ANSWER
Human nature	What is the character of human nature?	Good, mixture of good and evil, neutral, or evil; mutable or immutable
Man-nature	What is the relation of man to nature?	Mastery over nature, harmony with nature, or subjugation to nature
Time	What is the temporal focus of life?	Future, present, or past
Activity	What is the modality of human activity?	Doing, being in becoming, or being
Interpersonal relationships	What is the modality of man's relationship to other men?	Individualistic, collateral, or lineal

SOURCE: Florence Rockwood Kluckhohn and Fred L. Strodtbeck, *Variations in Value Orientations*, Evanston, Illinois, Row, Peterson, 1961, pp. 10–20.

[61] Sebastian De Grazia, *The Political Community: A Study of Anomie* (Chicago: University of Chicago Press, 1948). Cf. n. 3, p. 133. This book relates fear, anxiety, and insecurity to the breakdown of systems of values and beliefs. Cf. also Erich Fromm, *Escape from Freedom* (New York: Holt, Rinehart and Winston, Inc., 1941).

It seems that the dominant value-orientations of American society have been that man can be trained and educated to perform competently and morally, that man should use nature toward man's ends, that there is reason to have faith in progress, that through his own effort man is able to make progress a reality, and that it is the responsibility of each man to provide for himself. In other words, to the extent that there has been an American ethos ever since the founding of the colonies on the Atlantic Seaboard in the seventeenth century it seems statable in the categories of Kluckhohn and Strodtbeck as follows: man is *mutable* and should *master nature*, he should live for the *future*, and he should be *doing* constructive things in an *individualistic* way.

Such a set of value-orientations seems to have been characteristic of the industrious task-oriented upwardly mobile middle class for several centuries. As Weber has pointed out, these values have been imbedded in Protestant theology, and it is quite clear that they are highly consistent with the objectives of the economy and tend to be given strong support by the occupational structure.[62] Morse and Weiss report that for the man in a typical middle-class occupation "working means having a purpose, gaining a sense of accomplishment, expressing himself." They explain that "even if there were no economic necessity . . . to work, most men would work anyway. It is through the producing role that most men tie into society. . . ."[63]

The integration of the value-system with the ideology of business has been very marked. As recently as the 1950's such phrases as the "gray flannel suit" and the "organization man" connoted that hordes of young men with a middle-class background and an orientation toward white-collar occupations learned and accepted the business ideology. Nonadherents to this value-system, however, have been conspicuous for more than fifty years—from the days of Greenwich Village and its bohemians early this century through the zoot-suiters of the 1940's, the beatniks of the 1950's, and the more recent categories of dissenting youth: the hippies, the alienated, the activists, the new left, and of course the black nationalists. Many of the dissenters have come from prosperous families and have experienced the benefits of an unprecedentedly affluent society. They seem, however, to have come to see this society as "unnecessarily oppressive, inhuman, machinelike, unresponsive and out of control."[64] The values that they apparently wish to substitute are: self-expression; knowing and experiencing everything; antipathy to large organizations, to authority, and to self-interested behavior (and to its corollary, hypocrisy); participatory democracy; and interpersonal relationships with free expression of emotions.[65]

---

[62] Max Weber, *The Protestant Ethic and the Spirit of Capitalism* (New York: Scribner, 1930).

[63] Nancy C. Morse and Robert S. Weiss, "The Function and Meaning of Work and the Job," *American Sociological Review*, 20: 191–198 (1955), at p. 198.

[64] Mary Harrington Hall, "A Conversation with Kenneth Kenniston, or The Psychology of Student Activists," *Psychology Today*, 2: 16–20, 22–23, 59 (November 1968), at p. 19.

[65] Richard Flacks, "Student Activists," *Chicago Today*, 5: 44–47 (Summer 1968).

The handling of anxiety is an individual-oriented function of religion. In the United States and elsewhere in the Western world anxiety and psychic insecurity occur in an exaggerated form in a considerable, though unknown, number of persons so that they develop emotional disorders of various degrees of seriousness. The handling of such emotional problems in bygone days seems to have been a normal part of the clergyman's pastoral duties.[66] Through its practice of confession the Roman Catholic Church has long provided an opportunity for its parishioners to experience emotional catharsis.[67] Within the past couple of generations, however, there has grown up a coterie of specialists to give help to the troubled. Psychiatrists and psychoanalysts, clinical and counseling psychologists, and social case workers are all engaged in the endeavor to try to re-establish the security of their troubled patients and clients.[68] In the more recent years there has been evidence of an attempt to recapture this function for religious structures through qualifying clergymen in the psychiatric and psychological procedures of the specialists. Protestant denominations especially have been showing increasing interest in utilizing contemporary psychological viewpoints and skills in the pastoral work of clergymen. For example, the point that with psychological training the theological student (presumably Protestant) can achieve a less moralistic attitude toward others is made in an article entitled "Set Thyself First in a Psychology Class."[69] Relevant to these considerations is the rejection by some youth of bourgeois values (see page 126 above) and of organized religion and their forming of religious communes. Sociologically speaking, these young people seem to be forming quasi-families for the purpose of fulfilling the religious function.

[66] Yinger sees Dr. Norman Vincent Peale and Bishop Fulton J. Sheen as appealing respectively to the "standard" Protestants and Roman Catholics of the urban middle class who are afflicted with fear, inferiority, tension, and kindred troubles.—*Op. cit.*, pp. 99, 101.

[67] The role of the Christian Science practitioner has been likened to that of the psychiatrist or psychiatric social worker in that "the practitioner becomes an object of affection, a rock of security, a confessor, and a source of hope, as well as a technical healer" to an aggregate that appears to consist largely of "urban, middle-class, married females who are suffering from bodily disorders of physical or emotional origin."—R. W. England, "Some Aspects of Christian Science as Reflected in Letters of Testimony," *American Journal of Sociology*, 49: 448–453 (1954), at p. 453.

[68] The Roman Catholic practice of confession differs from contemporary conceptions of psychotherapy in a number of important respects, one of which is the moralistic position of the priest. This is contrary to the nonnormative, permissive attitude frequently deemed appropriate among contemporary psychotherapists. While reduction of anxiety is one of the usual objectives of psychotherapy and one of the purposes of the therapist's permissive attitude, Bishop Fulton J. Sheen, arguing from the Catholic viewpoint, contends that feelings of guilt and anxiety are valuable in making people repentant and desirous of forgiveness. Those who are free from feelings of guilt and anxiety are castigated by Bishop Sheen, who regards them as complacent and unregenerate. Cf. *Peace of Soul* (New York: McGraw-Hill, 1949), chaps. 2, 3, 5–7, and 10, esp. p. 84). Ever since Bishop (then Monsignor) Sheen denounced psychoanalysis in 1947, the official Catholic view on this topic has been somewhat unclear. Cf. "Sheen Denounces Psychoanalysis: He Recommends Confession of Sin as 'Key to Happiness of the Modern World,'" *The New York Times*, March 10, 1947, p. 18.

[69] Frank Auld, "Set Thyself First in a Psychology Class," *Motive*, 8: 16 (1948).

THE RELIGIOUS FUNCTION AND THE FAMILY

It will be recalled that Zimmerman speaks of the trustee family as a simple society. As this implies, it appears that in some places the trustee family may have carried out the religious function more or less in its entirety. Frequently the large family has had household gods; we may think of ancestor-worship as a special case. Probably the practice of ancestor-worship provides the clearest picture of the family carrying out the religious function. Ancestor-worship generally involves the belief that the dead ancestors have control over some resources—power to alter conditions of the living that the living can do nothing about, such as to bring rain, warm weather, and protection from pestilence. As we saw in the case of China, not only does ancestor-worship give "the individual a sense of identity with the distant past and the limitless future,"[70] but tends to make the older among the living generations value the younger because of the former's dependence on the latter for burial and worship.

By the time the domestic family comes along, there tends to be a specialized priesthood and a differentiated religious structure, or church. At this point it is desirable to distinguish between two kinds of activity that we may call religious and that the family may carry out. The first pertains to religious forms, e.g., saying grace at meals. Here the family is carrying out an activity developed in the religious structure, the church, and is reinforcing the religious structure. The second kind of activity pertains to alternate ways of performing the religious function—alternate, that is, to the ways offered by the church. To the extent that the family assuages the anxieties of its members or provides its own explanations for mysterious events it is carrying out religious activities of the second kind. To the degree that the family does this it becomes the functional equivalent of the church. Thereby it becomes competitive with the religious structure and weakens it.

Although it seems likely that the nuclear family has never carried out totally the religious function and is incapable of being religiously self-sufficient, it has carried on worship and the religious instruction of the young, especially under conditions of isolation. With the reduction in isolation and the rise of specialties that accompany urbanism, worship and religious instruction appear to become less frequent activities of family life.

From its first white settlement our country has had its religious forms grounded in the monotheistic Judeo-Christian tradition. Therefore the family-supporting practice of ancestor-worship has not been possible. The chief forms of religious activity that have been carried on by the American family (referred to in the second paragraph above as being of the "first kind") are instruction of the young and worship services. As early as 1642 there was a law in Massachusetts requiring heads of families to "catechize their children and servants in the grounds and principles of Religion" at least once a week.[71]

[70] Davis, *op. cit.*, p. 533.
[71] Quoted in Edmund S. Morgan, *The Puritan Family: Essays on Religion and Domestic*

Except for a few denominations and sects, religion in America has had a specialized clergy. This means that from the beginning the religious function had its own differentiated structure outside the family. Accordingly, although some early farm families went so far as to have a family altar,[72] the conduct of religious services by the family has tended to take place not as an institutionalized practice but rather as a substitute procedure to be followed when a professional clergyman is not available.

Not much is known about trends in the exercise of the religious function in the American family. We have noted some evidence of increased secularization in American culture. It is reasonable to suppose that a general trend toward secularism would be accompanied by a decrease within the family in the amount of religious activity of the "first kind," e.g., family prayers, family Bible-reading, grace at meals, and so on. Secularization results in "deterioration in belief." This means that the church loses its appeal to and power over some of the population. As this happens, the demand arises for other structures in the society to carry out aspects of the religious function, i.e., to become functionally equivalent to the church. It is impossible to say what the trend has been with respect to the family's carrying out of religious activities of the "second kind," such as the assuaging of anxiety. It does seem clear, however, that people look in increasing proportions to both the polity and the economy to serve as functional equivalents—to give various forms of security, to designate and to integrate values, to provide impersonal sanctions, and the like.

Functions and Societal Complexity

To a considerable extent the nuclear family can function and has done so as a self-sufficient and self-contained economic unit with each member acting both as producer and as consumer and with members thus being interdependent in both roles. Since the nuclear family is necessarily a very small social system, it seems to follow that when operating in isolation, it would have to operate at a low technologic level. It is conceivable that a family could supply its food and other economic needs from gathering, fishing, hunting, or agriculture, or some combination of these. In American history the condition under which the economically self-sufficient nuclear family would have been most likely to occur was the isolated farm family, and it is in this situation that the nuclear family would be most likely to take complete responsibility for the socializing-educational function.

The political and religious functions, on the other hand, have probably seldom if ever been *totally* carried on by the nuclear family. For this reason it seems probable that the early American farm family was less self-sufficient

Relations in Seventeenth-Century New England (Boston: Trustees of the Public Library, 1944), p. 45.
[72] Calhoun, *A Social History of the American Family*, II, 331.

politically and religiously than economically and educationally. With respect to all four of these basic societal functions, however, it seems clear that the early American farm family did much more than does the contemporary urban family. To state the matter more generally, as a society becomes urbanized there arise specialized structures that take over one or another of the basic societal functions, with the result that such activities occur less and less frequently within the family. Up to this point the evidence in support of this theme has been fragmentary.

Freeman and Winch have integrated several orders of evidence in support of the proposition that it is fruitful to postulate an ordering of societies along a dimension of simplicity-complexity or folkism-urbanism. For many years sociologists have conceived of societies along a dimension of societal complexity. Usually this dimension has been stated as a dichotomy. Sometimes the dichotomies are stated in nouns, sometimes in adjectives. Some of the opposites (or polar concepts) in which the idea has been stated (with the pairs in the order "simple-complex") are: *Gemeinschaft-Gesellschaft* (Tönnies),[73] *solidarité mécanique* and *solidarité organique* (Durkheim),[74] sacred-secular (Park and Becker),[75] culture-civilization (Small),[76] kinship-territory (Maine),[77] folk-urban (Redfield),[78] and in terms of personality, tradition-directed and other-directed (Riesman).[79] Freeman and Winch have shown that it is fruitful to postulate such a dimension of societal complexity with a minimum of seven differentiable phases of stages (scale types). Five of these are based upon the establishment of a distinct societal structure for one or another of the basic societal functions. In order from the simple or folk end to the complex or urban end they are:

Scale Type	Distinguishing Characteristic and Function
0	Simple undifferentiated folk society
1	Money supersedes barter and exchange: economic function
2	Government (rather than self, kin, or gods) punishes crimes against person or property: one phase of political function
3	Full-time specialized priest: religious function

[73] Ferdinand Tönnies, *Fundamental Concepts in Society* (trans. and ed. by Charles P. Loomis; New York: American Book, 1940).

[74] Émile Durkheim, *The Division of Labor in Society* (trans. by George Simpson; New York: Macmillan, 1933).

[75] Robert E. Park in lectures at the University of Chicago during the 1920's. Harry Elmer Barnes and Howard Becker, *Social Thought from Lore to Science* (Boston: Heath, 1938), Vol. I; Howard Becker, "Current Sacred-Secular Theory and Its Development," in Howard Becker and Alvin Boskoff (eds.), *Modern Sociological Theory in Continuity and Change* (New York: Holt, Rinehart and Winston, Inc., 1957), pp. 133–185.

[76] Albion W. Small, *General Sociology* (Chicago: University of Chicago Press, 1905).

[77] Henry Sumner Maine, *Ancient Law* (London: J. Murray, 1861).

[78] Robert Redfield, "The Folk Society," *American Journal of Sociology*, 52: 293–308 (1947).

[79] David Riesman, *The Lonely Crowd* (New Haven, Conn.: Yale University Press, 1950).

4		Full-time specialized teacher: socializing-educational function
5		Full-time bureaucrats: another phase of the political function
6		Written language present[80]

The evidence in the article showed that the above sequence was not absolute although there was a very strong tendency for societies to follow it.[81]

Contemporary American society as a whole stands at scale type 6, and presumably it would be at any higher scale position that might be differentiated. Moreover, it appears that American society has stood at a high scale value throughout virtually all its history. And what about the early American farm family and the modern urban family? This scale is for societies and not for institutional structures within societies; nor is it intended even for subsocieties.[82] If, however, we were to take liberties with the scheme and to try to locate the subsocietal setting of the isolated early American farm family and the modern urban family, we should probably place the former at type 0 (although to the degree that the people in those families could write, we should have an inconsistency or "error"), and certainly we should place the subsociety of the latter family in type 6.

For our purpose, then, the relevance of the Freeman-Winch analysis is (1) to bring some general evidence to bear in favor of the simple-complex or folk-urban concept and (2) to show that as a society proceeds in the direction of complexity or urbanism, it develops a differentiation of societal structures with the attendant specialties, with the result (3) that the rise of the priest and the teacher represents part of the whole transition that has removed functions from the family, thereby reducing the interdependence of its members.

---

[80] Linton C. Freeman and Robert F. Winch, "Societal Complexity: An Empirical Test of a Typology of Societies," *American Journal of Sociology,* 62: 461–466 (1957). Cf. also Raoul Naroll, "A Preliminary Index of Social Development," *American Anthropologist,* 58: 687–713 (1956).

[81] The coefficient of reproducibility was .97. It is possible that some of Becker's distinctions may help to account for the few exceptions. Cf. Howard Becker, "Current Sacred-Secular Theory and Its Development," in Becker and Boskoff, *op. cit.* If the reader is disposed to reject the foregoing analysis on the ground that it is a restatement of a discredited doctrine of societal evolution whereby it is maintained that *all* societies evolve through the *identical* sequence of stages, he is urged to take a second look. Not all societies fell into the pattern. To the question as to whether or not the Freeman-Winch analysis lends support to an evolutionary hypothesis, the answer is this: The data show a clear-cut pattern; if the evolutionary hypothesis is stated in terms of a *tendency* rather than an *inevitable* sequence, the data are consistent with the hypothesis.

[82] Subsequently, however, this type of analysis has been applied to Mexican villages for the purpose of differentiating levels of structural differentiation. Cf. Frank W. Young and Ruth C. Young, "Social Integration and Change in Twenty-four Mexican Villages," *Economic Development and Cultural Change,* 8: 366–377 (1960).

6

Suburbia:
the family's response to the loss of functions

Introduction

It will be recalled that Zimmerman has postulated three types of family structures along a dimension of power—trustee, domestic, and atomistic, of which the weakest is the atomistic. As Zimmerman sees it, when the family is atomistic, the birth rate is low and the people have no religious faith, the atomistic family provides a respectable cover for the "Hollywood type of marriage" (temporary sex liaison), and "is carried by its own momentum to its extinction."[1] This dour conception is seen as the ultimate working out of the process of urbanization with the concomitant loss of familial functions. This trend, which is seen as a most lamentable state of affairs in itself, is interpreted as having presaged the collapse of Greek and Roman civilizations and perhaps of our own as well. The tone of Zimmerman's analysis is that the American family is afflicted with the cancer of atomism and that since the family is a vital organ of the society and civilization, extreme unction is in order.

One of the most popular themes in the literature of sociology over the past century has concerned the meaning of urbanism and hence the end product of the process of urbanization. In line with Zimmerman's concept of the atomistic family and with our presentation regarding the loss of functions from the familial structure, urbanism has generally been represented as involving the loss of importance of kinship and neighborhood groups to formal secondary groups that organize work, religion, and politics.[2] The essence of

---

[1] Carle C. Zimmerman, *Family and Civilization* (New York: Harper & Row, 1947), pp. 762–765.

[2] Scott Greer, "Individual Participation in Mass Society," in Ronald Young (ed.), *Approaches to the Study of Politics* (Evanston, Ill.: Northwestern University Press, 1958), pp. 329–342, esp. p. 330.

urbanism has been presented as the heterogeneity of urban populations, the impersonality of interaction, the anonymity of urban life, and the more or less chronic anomia of urban citizens as a result of their not being integrated into a society.[3] And among the more obvious correlates in familial organization are (1) a decline in the birth rate, (2) a consequent decrease in the size of family, and (3) an increase in the proportion of married women in the labor force.[4]

Within recent years, however, the foregoing view of urbanism has been called into question. The most important point of the revisionists is that the interaction of urban residents with their kinsmen is not at all trivial, but, rather, constitutes "the most important social relations for all types of urban populations."[5] A relevant set of data on this point comes from the Detroit Area Study of the University of Michigan. According to this survey, only 11 percent of Detroit families have no relatives living in that metropolitan area. The most numerous category of relatives in the area was sibling and sibling-in-law, reported by three quarters of the respondents. Two thirds of the respondents see one or more relatives outside the nuclear family as often as once a week. A considerable amount of mutual aid is reported, especially between parents and offspring and between siblings. About two thirds reported receiving help from parents, slightly more than one half said they received help from siblings, and one sixth indicated they had received help from other relatives. The visiting pattern tends to be one of "dropping in" rather than of arranged visits, and slightly over half the respondents reported attending "large family gatherings" as often as once a year. The study draws this conclusion: "The 'typical' Detroiter is very much a member of an extended family group. . . . There is little doubt that the kin group is continuing to play an important part in the life of the metropolitan family."[6]

Two comments are in order. First, although the earlier theorists of urbanism did not make the point clear, it seems unlikely that they intended their remarks about the segmentalism, impersonality, anonymity, and so on, of urban life to be understood as categorically true in an empirical sense. It seems more credible that Louis Wirth intended to create a heuristic (or ideal-typical) version of urbanism than to describe life in the city with photographic realism. (After all, Wirth had a brother in the Chicago metropolitan area.)

---

[3] Louis Wirth, "Urbanism as a Way of Life," *American Journal of Sociology*, 44: 1–24 (1938). "Anomia" is roughly equivalent to "alienation" and refers to the attitudinal state of an individual; "anomie" refers to the normlessness of a group or a society. See Leo Srole, "Social Integration and Certain Corollaries: An Exploratory Study," *American Sociological Review*, 21: 709–716 (1956); Dorothy L. Meier and Wendell Bell, "Anomia and Differential Access to the Achievement of Life Goals," *American Sociological Review*, 24: 189–202 (1959).

[4] Ernest W. Burgess and Harvey J. Locke, *The Family: From Institution to Companionship* (2d ed.; New York: American Book, 1953), p. 685.

[5] Greer, "Individual Participation," in Young, *op. cit.*

[6] Survey Research Center, *A Social Profile of Detroit: 1955* (Ann Arbor, Mich.: Institute for Social Research, 1956), chaps. 4–5. Quotation is from p. 26.

Rather than intending to represent the empirical reality of the city as *totally* impersonal, for example, the early theorists undoubtedly meant that on the average it was *more* impersonal, say, than was true of rural or small-town life. As reported in Chapter 11, Winch and Greer have found slight but statistically significant evidence that rural domestic families do show more extended familism than is shown by urban families: on the average rural families interact with more categories of kin and exchange more goods and services with them than do families in metropolitan areas.[7]

The second comment is that we could usefully distinguish between interaction within the individual's and the spouse's families of orientation and interaction with other relatives. By failing to draw this distinction, those who have been characterized as "revisionists" of the concept of urbanism seem to be saying that there is much interaction throughout the system of extended kinship. The data on mutual aid cited above suggest that the meaningful interaction is more or less confined to parent-child and sibling-sibling relationships, i.e., within the individual's and his or her spouse's families of orientation. For the understanding of the impact of urbanism on the family it is necessary not only to determine how the social interaction of urbanites with various categories of persons compares with that of residents in nonurban areas but also to discover, for the various types of residential areas, to what extent the social interaction consists of mere sociability and to what extent it involves the carrying out of basic societal functions.[8]

Irrespective of the merits of the foregoing argument, it does seem that many people believe that urban living conditions are inhospitable to families with children. Urban dwellings frequently lack any sort of play area—protected or otherwise. Especially in a time of housing shortage, moreover, large numbers of urban rental units have been available only on a "no children and no pets" basis. Childless couples can be flexible in housing requirements. They may not like dirt and noise, cramped quarters, poorly heated rooms, bath facilities shared with others, and an unreliable supply of hot water, but such conditions become considerably less tolerable with the arrival of children. As might be expected, then, the most mobile part of the population in a residential sense seems to be the young couple with children. During the stage of expansion the family "typically moves from smaller to larger dwellings, from mobile, family-less areas to areas where family living is the typical pattern of household existence."[9]

---

[7] Cf. p. 298 below; cf. also references to studies by Key and Straus at that point. There is one study that shows that interaction with relatives decreases after families move from an urban area, where they and their kinsmen have lived for generations, to new housing in a suburban development where no kinsmen live nearby. Cf. Michael Young and Peter Willmott, *Family and Kinship in East London* (New York: Free Press, 1957). Another study that reports a reduction of contact with kinsmen after the move to the suburb is Herbert J. Gans, *The Levittowners: How People Live and Politic in Suburbia* (New York: Pantheon, 1967), p. 233.

[8] Cf. Marvin B. Sussman, "The Help Pattern in the Middle Class Family," *American Sociological Review*, 18: 22–28 (1953).

[9] Peter H. Rossi, *Why Families Move: A Study in the Social Psychology of Urban*

Studying one hundred families in newly developed areas of suburbs of Chicago, Bell found that over two thirds had moved from Chicago, and four fifths said they had moved to their new housing because of a wish to have desirable conditions for their children. Among the considerations mentioned were more space, less traffic, cleaner areas, fresh air, and sunshine. Bell concludes:

> . . . the data support the hypothesis that the new suburbanites are largely persons who have chosen familism as an important element in their life styles, and [perhaps also] . . . the desire for community participation or sense of belonging . . . if anonymity, impersonality, defilement of air and land by industry, apartment living, crowding, and constant nervous stimulation are inherent in "urbanism as a way of life," . . . then the findings of this study necessitate the conclusion that the suburbanite *is* seeking an escape from many traditional aspects of city living . . . a way of life in which family, community, and immediate enjoyment through living the "good life" are dominant and interdependent ends.[10]

The Suburb: New classes in an old pattern

Mumford points out that the attraction of living outside central cities—"to withdraw like a monk and live like a prince"—has been appreciated throughout most of the annals of Western history. The suburb is at least as old as ancient Greece. At the close of the Middle Ages one Leone Batista Alberti listed desiderata for gracious suburban living—including what sounds like the ranch-type house with picture windows.[11] Several generations ago well-to-do families in major cities in the eastern part of the United States established their homes along railroad lines leading into the cities from which they migrated, and where some of the wealthier continued to maintain city homes. Thus the idea of suburban living is far from new.

But there is a very important feature that *is* new. Just as the railroad established one new pattern for suburban living whereby an upper-middle or upper-class head of house could work in the city and live away from it, so the development since World War I of highway systems and the wide distribution of automobiles extended to lower social strata the possibility of commuting. Since commuting is the essence of suburbanism, this development made possible the mass migrations of lower-middle and working-class people to sub-

---

Residential Mobility (New York: Free Press, 1955), p. 178. In a predominantly lower-middle-class suburb the two most popular reasons for moving in were the need for space (26 percent) and the wish to own a single-detached house (18 percent). Cf. Gans, *op. cit.*, pp. 27, 33.

[10] Wendell Bell, "Familism and Suburbanization: One Test of the Social Choice Hypothesis," *Rural Sociology*, 21: 276–283 (1956), at pp. 282–283.

[11] Lewis Mumford, *The City in History: Its Origins, Its Transformation, and Its Prospects* (New York: Harcourt, 1961), pp. 482–487.

urbs. To illustrate, during the decade from 1950 to 1960 suburban areas were growing at about five times the rate of central cities.[12]

The preceding paragraph implies that there is considerable variation in the wealth and social position of suburban dwellers. It could also be said that since suburbs tend to be internally homogeneous, there is considerable variation among suburbs, some containing stately old mansions and families listed in the social register and others consisting of mass-produced crackerboxes and lower white-collar or blue-collar workers. Keeping this variation in mind, however, we find that the total aggregate of suburbanites differs in social characteristics from the total aggregate of dwellers in central cities. In comparison with suburbanites, populations in central cities tend to have (1) higher proportions of blacks, (2) fewer young and more older dependents, (3) a lower proportion of domestic families headed by men whose wives are present, and (4) lower median income. Some pertinent data appear in Table 6.1. An interesting pattern of income differentials has been reported by Schnore, who

TABLE 6.1

Some Characteristics of the Populations of Central Cities and of Suburban Rings of Standard Metropolitan Statistical Areas of the United States, 1968

	PERCENT IN	
	Central Cities	Suburban Rings
Blacks	20	5
Dependents	48	48
Under 20	(37)	(40)
65 and over	(11)	(8)
Domestic Families	100	100
Husband-wife	(82)	(90)
Female head	(15)	(8)
Other male head	(3)	(2)
Median family income in 1967	$7,813	$9,367

SOURCE: U.S. Bureau of the Census, *Current Population Reports—Special Studies*, Series P-23, No. 27, February 7, 1969, pp. 5, 8, 12, 36.

[12] A more precise statement is as follows. A Standard Metropolitan Statistical Area is "an area which includes at least one central city of at least 50,000 persons together with the county or counties which are economically and otherwise oriented to the central city." Between 1950 and 1960 the population of the central cities in SMSA's increased by 10.7 percent while the population in the outlying areas of SMSA's increased by 48.6 percent.—Metropolitan Life Insurance Company, *Statistical Bulletin*, 42: 1–3 (July 1961), at footnote to Table 2, p. 3. Between 1960 and 1968 the population of central cities increased by 1 percent; the population of suburban rings, by 28 percent. U.S. Bureau of the Census, *Current Population Reports—Special Studies*, Series P-23, No. 27, February 7, 1969, p. 2.

has discovered a tendency for the average incomes of the largest and oldest cities to be surpassed by those of their suburbs, whereas smaller and younger cities tend to have income levels greater than those in their surrounding areas.[13]

Having noted this sort of development, one pair of writers has asked whether or not a new form of family is emerging.[14] By the close of this chapter we should be better able than at present to answer this question, but for the present the question seems at least partly definitional, i.e., how "new" the emerging form may be is to some extent determined by how narrowly one defines the old.

Points of Emphasis

The move to the suburbs and the urban fringe can be interpreted as a defensive maneuver on the part of the family to avoid being "atomized," as Zimmerman has been foreseeing. To analyze this matter we shall use our formulation of basic societal functions. As we have done before, we shall consider each of the four extrafamilial functions—economic, political, socializing-educational, and religious—to note the level of the family's participation in fulfilling them.

From the economic standpoint, the cultural exhortation to "do-it-yourself" returns a bit of the productive function to the household. The shopping center's dominance over the suburban countryside reflects the primacy of the nuclear family as the unit of consumption, especially through its purchasing agent—the wife-mother. In some communities—especially some of the newer and smaller ones—there is grass-roots political activity. "Do-it-yourself-ism" in organizing the community for purposes of mutual protection and the administration of services imparts an aura of political amateurism. A strong emphasis on communal life in some of the new suburbs may be seen as affording to nuclear families with commuting fathers protection and mutual aid that in other settings would be provided by the extended family. Families are highly active in the socializing-educational function, both indirectly through participation in the PTA, "den mother," and kindred activities; through the providing of lessons in dancing, tennis, golf, and the like; and also through direct instruction of their children. There is considerable participation in religious organizations, but theological considerations appear to receive little emphasis, nor is there evidence of any return of the religious function to the family.

To a considerable degree the foregoing remarks seem generally applicable

[13] Leo F. Schnore, "City-Suburban Income Differentials in Metropolitan Areas," *American Sociological Review*, 27: 252–255 (1962), and "The Socio-Economic Status of Cities and Suburbs," *American Sociological Review*, 28: 76–85 (1963).

[14] E. Gartly Jaco and Ivan Belknap, "Is a New Family Form Emerging in the Urban Fringe?" *American Sociological Review*, 18: 551–557 (1953).

to the entire range of American suburbs. One must be careful, however, about remarks intended to characterize all suburbs, for they differ in a variety of ways, some of which are indexed by (1) the age of the suburb, (2) the modal socioeconomic status of its residents, and (3) the age and size of the central city to which the suburb is related.[15] As Gans observes, when a suburb is new, there seems to be a good deal of socializing on the basis of propinquity, i.e., people interact with immediate neighbors concerning matters of mutual concern in getting settled. After a time the pattern of interaction shifts to one tending to follow the planes of social stratification; especially does this seem to hold for the women who seek female companions with interests at their own cultural levels.[16] It was reported on page 137 above that Schnore found the urban-suburban differentials in socioeconomic status to vary with the age and size of the central city.

Taking into account the considerable variation among suburbs, still we may interpret suburbanism as an effort to realize the advantages of both ends of the folk-urban or simple-complex continuum (see "Functions and Societal Complexity" at the end of the preceding chapter) by keeping the productive activities of the husband-father in the specialized, differentiated, and economically advantageous city while locating consumption and other familial activities in the more folklike suburb. Indications of the outcome of this effort with respect to the family are the high birth rate of the suburbs, the large size of suburban families, and the low proportion of suburban married women in the labor force.

The Economic Function

The suburbs discussed in this chapter are the so-called "dormitory" suburbs and not those of the industrial type. It is of the essence of the dormitory suburb, hereafter called simply "suburb," that productive activities are not cen-

---

[15] The reader who is interested in exploring diversity among suburbs may wish to consult:
1. A study of a blue-collar suburb: Bennett A. Berger, *Working-Class Suburb: A Study of Auto Workers in Suburbia* (Berkeley and Los Angeles: University of California Press, 1960).
2. A study of a suburb whose workers are mostly in "lower-white-collar" occupations: Herbert J. Gans, *The Levittowners: How People Live and Politic in Suburbia* (New York: Pantheon, 1967).
3. A study of an upper-middle-class suburb of Toronto: John R. Seeley, R. Alexander Sim, and Elizabeth W. Loosley, *Crestwood Heights: A Study of the Culture of Suburban Life* (New York: Basic Books, 1956).
4. A journalistic account of upper-income suburbanites in the myriad specialties of communications and living "in a fan-shaped area twenty-five miles deep" from northwest to northeast of New York City: A. C. Spectorsky, *The Exurbanites* (New York: Berkley, 1955). Cf. also Thomas Ktsanes and Leonard Reissman, "Suburbia —New Homes for Old Values," *Social Problems,* 7: 187–195 (Winter 1959–1960).

[16] Herbert J. Gans, *op. cit.,* chap. 3.

tered there. Accordingly the work of most adult males (husbands and fathers) is located elsewhere—principally in "the city." As Frederick Lewis Allen phrases it, the commuter's "heart and his treasure are twenty miles apart."[17] This fact has several important consequences:

1. The men of working age who are in the suburb on an ordinary working day are usually those engaged in the production of services and the distribution of goods for local consumption: local professional men, service personnel, and shopkeepers. The men who work in the suburb differ from the commuters in that the former tend on the average to be older, to have less income, to have resided longer in the community, and to have less education.[18] No doubt Wolcott Gibbs had an impression that these generalizations were true when he wrote with characteristic hyperbole that "by Connecticut standards there is little to choose between a non-commuting adult male and a lunatic in the attic."[19]

2. Accordingly the sex ratio of the suburb typically shifts markedly between the daylight and the evening hours of working days; during the day the sex ratio on the streets suggests an implausible sort of world where adults are almost all female and yet children abound. As David Riesman describes it, "only the women live in Crestwood Heights, along with the young people and the professionals servicing both, while the men are, so to speak, visiting husbands from the bush—from the 'real world' of [the] booming economy."[20]

With the family's productive activity carried on typically by the husband-father in his office in the city and consumption being supervised by the wife-mother at home, suburbanism virtually maximizes the distance separating these two aspects of the economic function. The widespread understanding of this point by merchants is evidenced by the mushrooming of shopping centers and the decentralization of department stores. Thus the wife-mother is in a role that necessitates her becoming a specialist in consumption—the family's chief purchasing agent. Since merchandisers of consumers' goods are well versed in this fact of family sociology, housewives are targets for a prodigious amount of advertising and promotion. Both because of her role and because of the incredible volume of advertising and promotion, the wife-mother is in position to become the family's arbiter in questions of taste with respect to most items of consumers' goods. Because the children grow up in the suburb (the capital of consumership) with the mother (the parent in charge of purchasing), the children become specialists in consumption and its significance.

[17] Frederick Lewis Allen, "The Big Change in Suburbia, Part I," *Harper's Magazine*, 208: 21–28 (1954), at p. 22.

[18] These studies are summarized in Walter T. Martin, "The Structuring of Social Relationships Engendered by Suburban Residence," in William M. Dobriner (ed.), *The Suburban Community* (New York: Putnam, 1958), pp. 95–108.

[19] In a review of the play "Cloud 7," in *The New Yorker*, February 22, 1958, p. 62.

[20] In the introduction to John R. Seeley, R. Alexander Sim, and Elizabeth W. Loosley, *Crestwood Heights: A Study of the Culture of Suburban Life* (New York: Basic Books, 1956), p. xiii.

Suburbs vary considerably in the degree to which they offer either full- or part-time employment to women. This variation is seen as of prime importance in accounting for differences among three suburbs of Seattle, Washington, in the rate of participation in the labor force by mothers of high school students.[21] To the degree that there is an absence of opportunities for the employment of women, there is a tendency to crystallize the categorical distinction between the gainfully employed husband the dependent wife. Some jobs are available for children. Generally these are more or less outside the main sweep of business and industry (e.g., mowing lawns for boys and baby-sitting for girls), and generally it is thought that any employment should be of this sort in order to be suitable for minors. The earnings of the child tend to be more symbolic ("teaching the child the value of money") than significant economically, and so the child's earnings are not regarded as altering his categorical dependency.[22]

The categorical employability of suburbia results, of course, in relatively little income from the wife-mother and children. In this sense the suburban way of life has a built-in source of economic strain. Another source of strain comes from the cost of commuting. It seems that in most metropolitan areas public transportation available to commuters continually becomes more expensive while the service deteriorates. Housing, too, is a source of economic strain. Some years ago *The Wall Street Journal* published a study by the National Housing Conference which concluded that many families could not afford the houses they bought and were saved from foreclosure only by the continuing inflation that enabled them to amortize their mortgages with devalued dollars.[23]

Spectorsky offers some impressionistic evidence about a selected group of high-income suburbs in the metropolitan area of New York City. He calls the residents of these suburbs "exurbanites." To show how money is spent in "exurbia" Spectorsky presents an informal financial analysis of "good old, poor old" Freddy Barber, a presumably mythical advertising manager of a trade magazine on a salary of $33,000 a year.[24] This resident of Westport, Connecti-

---

[21] George C. Myers, "Labor Force Participation of Suburban Mothers," *Journal of Marriage and the Family*, 26: 306–311 (1964). The rates for the three suburbs varied from 27 to 40 percent. Noting that the rates of participation in the labor force were higher for working-class mothers than for those of the white-collar category, the author sees economic necessity as a second major factor. According to a study by the Women's Bureau, psychic rewards constitute another important factor, especially among more educated women. Cf. U.S. Department of Labor, *1965 Handbook on Women Workers* (Washington: GPO, 1965), p. 5.

[22] Seeley *et al., op. cit.*, p. 186.

[23] "Most Middle-Income Families Can't Afford Even Cheapest Homes Today, Survey Shows," *The Wall Street Journal*, July 8, 1957, p. 9.

[24] To make the example more contemporary, the present writer has updated Spectorsky's figures. The first edition of *The Exurbanites* was published in 1955. If it is assumed the manuscript was written in the preceding year, 1954, then we find that the purchasing power of the dollar with respect to consumer prices was in 1969 about three fourths of what

cut, says Spectorsky, "is in the top one half of one percent for the country as a whole: nevertheless, for the exurbs, [his income] is by no means atypical."²⁵ After Barber pays taxes, the maid, mortgage and interest, insurance, and other items related to the house, charities, and expenses in connection with his two not-so-new automobiles, he has spent $20,000. Food, liquor, and medical expenses take another $7,300. Clothes amount to $2,850. By the time vacation, baby-sitters, telephone, entertainment, gifts, books, and magazines are considered, he has spent more than his $33,000 salary (which is presumably his total income). When one adds Barber's laundry bills, the cost of his hobbies, and his alimony, Barber has overspent his $33,000 by something in excess of $9,300. "What each [exurbanite] does believe firmly about the other," says Spectorsky, "is that the truth of his own financial situation would appall his neighbor."²⁶ Suggesting that it requires about $80,000 per year to break even in exurbia, Spectorsky says that Barber and the thousands like him "operate on the necessity to earn more each year . . . it is typically exurban to really believe that everyone else is doing better than oneself, or that those who appear not to be are intelligently budgeted, so that they live, if not well, at least in solvency."²⁷ Spectorsky discusses extra work that the highly skilled exurbanites do to balance their budgets. Another writer says that for the lower-income "mass-produced suburbs" many people are "running on their nerve" financially speaking, and that a "sizable" number of men have second jobs.²⁸

Before leaving the economic function of the family in the suburban setting, let us note that the widespread emphasis on "doing it yourself" is an exhortation to increase economic production in the home. According to Spectorsky, this movement has great vigor among the exurbanites, whose purchases of all kinds of equipment for house and grounds exceeds the purchasers' competence to use it.²⁹ The "do-it-yourself" phenomenon may be regarded either

---

it had been in 1954, or that the price level had risen to about four thirds of the 1954 level.—*Statistical Abstract of the United States: 1970*, Table 516, p. 338. Accordingly, the figures used by Spectorsky have been adjusted upward by a third.

²⁵ A. C. Spectorsky, *The Exurbanites* (New York: Berkley, 1955), p. 155.

²⁶ *Ibid.*, p. 152.

²⁷ *Ibid.*, pp. 153, 163. *Life* has published a comparable essay whose message concerns the impossibility of getting along on $12,000 per year. In the budget of their problem case a key set of items consists of payments to instalment collectors at the rate of $3700 per year.—Ernest Havemann, "Why Nobody Can Save Any Money: Everyone Frets Over Where It All Goes, but It Isn't Moral Collapse—Just That Spending Often Makes More Sense Than Thrift," *Life*, June 15, 1959, pp. 120–122, 125–126, 128, 131–132.

²⁸ Harry Henderson, "The Mass-Produced Suburbs. I. How People Live in America's Newest Towns," *Harper's Magazine*, 207: 25–32 (November 1953). In 1966 about 5 percent of all employed persons held two jobs or more. The typical multiple-job-holder was a young married man with children who was experiencing a financial squeeze. Among the occupations whose members were most likely to "moonlight" were policemen, firemen, postal workers, and farmers. Cf. Harvey R. Hamel, "Moonlighting—An Economic Phenomenon," *Monthly Labor Review*, 90: 17–22 (1967).

²⁹ *Op. cit.*, p. 236.

from the viewpoint of its significance for familial interaction or from that of its economic significance. With respect to the former, it seems probable that "do-it-yourself" creates new opportunities for members of families to interact in the accomplishment of some usually useful task. And if the interaction proves amicable and productive, quite possibly there results a strengthening of an affectional bond; of course the outcome may also be infelicitous. Moreover, there may be a feeling in this setting that such enterprise is not necessary but is "made work," created for the purpose of stimulating familial interaction. Such a perception may lead the actors not to regard themselves even as amateur carpenters, electronic technicians, or tuckpointers but as *playing* at one or another of these crafts.

From the economic standpoint it is problematic to what degree "do-it-yourself" is efficient. Numerous factors enter into the answer: the availability of the relevant goods and/or services in the community, the worth of the time of the family members involved, the size and make-up of the family, the abilities of family members, and the physical equipment of the household.[30] In many cases it seems clear that families pay more to "do-it-themselves" than it would cost to purchase the goods or services. However, if returning some production to the household solidifies the family (for which the writer is aware of no evidence) or if, as Spectorsky suggests, it fulfills a dream,[31] then to some extent economic efficiency is a subordinate consideration.

The Political Function

Under the political function we may consider three questions. (1) What about suburbanism and the political function within the nuclear family? That is, does the family in the suburb exercise more control over its members than does the family in the city? At present the answer seems to be that although many people believe that the suburban family controls its children better than does the urban family, we still await definitive studies in this whole area. (2) Is there any difference between the suburban and the urban family with respect to the locus of domestic power? (3) What about the community's control? That is, does the community exercise more control over the behavior of family members in the suburb than in the city?

On the second question evidence based on interviews with urban and suburban housewives in the Detroit metropolitan area indicates that suburban families are more "husband-dominant" than urban families at every status level. The authors go on to report that this result is not a matter of racial difference.[32] This conclusion runs counter to the usual view that because of the

---

[30] See a discussion of some of these points in Howard F. Bigelow, *Family Finance* (rev. ed.; Philadelphia: Lippincott, 1953), chap. 6.

[31] *Op. cit.*, chap. 10, "The Limited Dream."

[32] Robert O. Blood, Jr., and Donald M. Wolfe, *Husbands and Wives: The Dynamics of Married Living* (New York: Free Press, 1960), p. 36.

absence of the husband-father the suburban housewife exercises greater domestic power than her urban counterpart. The authors venture the interpretation that perhaps the suburban wives are content to have their husbands make decisions on account of feeling "indebted to their husbands for providing them with a place to live which is more attractive than the industrial city of Detroit."

What about the community's control? In Chapter 4 it was noted that the small and politically ineffectual nuclear family was characteristically influenced by more politically effective societal structures. This observation calls to mind the frequently heard remark that a distinctive characteristic of suburban life is conformity or, in Henderson's phrase, "a kind of amiable, thoughtless conformity."[33] Since conformity involves some form of control over someone's behavior, let us ask what is the story on conformity in suburbia?

One of the most eloquent writers on this topic is William H. Whyte, Jr., a former editor of *Fortune* who has studied Park Forest, Illinois, which was developed after World War II in an area southwest of Chicago. By 1953 the developers had sold some two thousand ranch-type houses built on lots 60 feet by 125 feet. The lots are grouped into courts. Since social interaction among the residents tends to be organized around these courts, says Whyte, the back door is the functional door. In this setting Whyte reports that there is little privacy, knocking on the door before entering is not customary, and people feel that they are being reserved and feel somewhat guilty about it if they try to create privacy for themselves.[34] This leads to such characterizations of suburbia as a "projection of dormitory life into adulthood," "a sorority house with kids,"[35] and "being like a fraternity house at a small college, in which like-mindedness reverberates upon itself as the potentially various selves within each of us do not get evoked or recognized."[36]

What values does this gregarious mode of life enforce? The most talked of answer is gregariousness itself. "Group activity is fervently believed to be good for all," says Henderson.[37] "One is made *out-going*," adds Whyte.[38] "Such communities are paradises for the well-adjusted," concludes Allen.[39] The pressure is reported to be on adults and children alike; the child who wishes to play with only one or two friends is regarded as withdrawn and unadjusted, while the lone adult is seen as psychically disordered.[40] That the

---

[33] Harry Henderson, "Rugged American Collectivism: The Mass-Produced Suburbs, Part II," *Harper's Magazine*, 207: 80–86 (1953), at p. 80.

[34] William H. Whyte, Jr., *The Organization Man* (New York: Simon and Schuster, 1956), p. 352.

[35] *Ibid.*, p. 280.

[36] David Riesman, "The Suburban Sadness," in Dobriner, *op. cit.*, pp. 375–408. Quotation is from p. 386.

[37] "Rugged American Collectivism," *loc. cit.*, p. 81.

[38] *Op. cit.*, p. 350.

[39] Allen, "The Big Change in Suburbia, Part I," *loc. cit.*, p. 26.

[40] Whyte, *op. cit.*, pp. 384, 394.

courts and their lack of privacy result in conformity is indicated by Whyte, who speaks of the court as "the greatest invention [for enforcing sexual morality] since the chastity belt."[41]

Henderson speaks of the wives' *Kaffeeklatsch* as "a kind of floating, daylong talkfest, shifting from house to house . . . to help fill their need for adult conversation and companionship."[42] There are diverse kinds of mutual aid: baby-sitting pools (mothers tend each other's children), assistance in transportation and in repairing automobiles, erecting television antennas, and helping out in sudden emergencies. Communal living also imparts a sense of protection and security when the husband-father is away overnight. Such mutual aid and mutual protection make the court into a kind of surrogate for the absent extended families.

From the foregoing analysis it appears that conformity may well be a result of the high level of interaction, or at least that the conformity would be difficult to enforce without the high level of interaction. Should we conclude that all suburbs are like Park Forest in being so frenetically gregarious and in imposing conformity? It appears not, for two reasons: the ecology of Park Forest, and the kind of people.

The fact that each court (or group of several houses) had a common backyard made a high level of interaction not only easy to achieve but really difficult to avoid. Several studies have shown how the ecology of a housing development determines which families develop friendly relationships with each other.[43] If the residents of Park Forest wished to live less interactively, they could do so more easily in a different type of housing.

And what about the kind of people? When Whyte was studying Park Forest, it was newly settled; i.e., the couples were all newcomers to the development. They were unusually homogeneous with respect to age (being young couples), family status (already possessing children or beginning to have them soon after arrival), and with respect to occupation (professional and white-collar). For the most part they did not have kinsmen nearby. In this setting they experienced a need for friends and tended to develop friendships with neighbors who lived in the same court.[44]

There are theoretical and empirical reasons to believe that after a community ages a bit, a system of stratification develops.[45] In turn, the developing

---

[41] *Ibid.*, p. 356.

[42] Henderson, "The Mass-Produced Suburbs," *loc. cit.*, p. 28.

[43] Robert K. Merton, "The Social Psychology of Housing," in Wayne Dennis (ed.), *Current Trends in Social Psychology* (Pittsburgh: University of Pittsburgh Press, 1948), pp. 163–217; Leon Festinger, Stanley Schachter, and Kurt W. Back, *Social Pressures in Informal Groups* (New York: Harper & Row, 1950).

[44] Whyte, *op. cit.*, p. 346.

[45] Form speaks of this as a "strain toward stratification." Cf. William H. Form, "Status Stratification in a Planned Community," *American Sociological Review*, 10: 605–613

system of stratification alters patterns of interaction. As Gans sees it, "Voluntary associations are formed on the basis of religious, ethnic, class, 'brow' level, as well as urban–small-town differences."[46] In other words, in a new community there is a disposition to form friendships on the basis of residential propinquity, but in established communities friendships tend to follow similarities in education, occupation, income, and the like. In his study of a new housing development with three distinguishable social classes, moreover, Gans found "no pressure to be sociable," and he concluded, "Levittowners have not become outgoing, mindless conformers; they remain individuals. . . ."[47]

Let us summarize the factors conducive to a high level of interaction: (1) a young community consisting of (2) young couples with children (3) belonging to the same social class and "brow" level and (4) living in a housing development that maximizes residential propinquity. The young community implies that all residents have recently arrived after having been uprooted from earlier homes, and the characteristic of having been uprooted implies a heightened need for mutual aid, for a sense of belonging, and for companionship. All of these conditions appear to have been present in Park Forest. Where these conditions are absent, our analysis would lead us not to expect a high level of interaction or of conformity.

From Spectorsky's account it would seem that the exurban communities, especially in Rockland County, New York, are much less interactive and conforming than Park Forest. In Rockland County, he says, "the fetish is nonconformity, individuality, originality," and joining and communal enterprises are virtually unknown.[48] Of course, as among the beatniks, hippies, or whatever contemporary bohemians may be called, there may be great pressure to conform to a standard of nonconformity, but the low level of social interaction reported for Rockland County would suggest that this is one of the more individualistic suburban communities.

Berger reports on a new suburb with a high degree of economic homogeneity. Many of the heads of families in the suburb and all of those interviewed were blue-collar workers in a Ford factory. Unlike the residents of Park Forest, these people had a relatively low rate of interaction with their neighbors. Berger interprets the low rate of neighboring as a consequence of a high rate of interaction with the extended family, and he quotes one informant: "I don't think it pays to have a lot of friends—maybe because we have so many relatives."[49]

(1945); also Eva Rosenfeld, "Social Stratification in a 'Classless' Society," *American Sociological Review*, 16: 766–774 (1951).

[46] Herbert J. Gans, "The Sociology of New Towns: Opportunities for Research," *Sociology and Social Research*, 40: 231–239 (1956), at p. 236.

[47] Herbert J. Gans, *The Levittowners*, pp. 156, 154.

[48] *Op. cit.*, p. 64.

[49] Bennett M. Berger, *Working-Class Suburb: A Study of Auto Workers in Suburbia* (Berkeley: University of California Press, 1960), p. 68.

The Socializing-Educational Function

Through our discussion of suburbia to this point has run the theme that in the orientation of the middle class the suburbs are a much better location than the central cities in which to raise children to be healthy, adjusted, moral, and upwardly mobile. In part the superiority of the suburbs is seen in the space, lawns, trees, and good air, and in part in the public schools. As the towns of Europe have been dominated by the spires of churches, so the landscapes of our suburbs are dominated by two types of secular structure —schools and shopping centers. These two types of structure symbolize two activities basic to suburbia—child rearing, and an aspect of the economic function we have already considered, consumption.[50]

In 1957 *The New York Times* published a comprehensive series of articles on suburbs and their problems. One of the articles, written by the educational expert of *The Times*, analyzed public schools and concluded that, generally speaking, in metropolitan areas the city schools were deteriorating, whereas in the suburbs the schools were improving. Having pointed to suburban schools as a major reason for the move by many families to the suburbs, the writer proceeded to point out that by comparison with suburban schools, those of the city tended (1) to be overcrowded, with classes in shifts in some cases; (2) to provide little opportunity for the participation of parents; and (3) to be geared to mass education with little or no provision for superior children or for children with problems and handicaps. The educational expert of *The Times* went on to observe that some urban parents are motivated to move to the suburbs because of the presence in the city schools of children of minority groups. (Currently in New York the Puerto Ricans and the blacks are the minorities most usually cited in this connection.) No doubt many of these parents fear that their children might become involved in violence and delinquency and/or dating and courtship if they were to associate with children of minority groups. In addition to having the advantages noted above, according to *The Times*'s writer, the suburban schools pay better salaries and get better teachers, have newer and more modern buildings, use newer methods, and have higher standards. One feature of suburban public schools that is an attraction to some parents and their children but a difficulty for others is the emphasis given to preparation for college and corresponding lack of provision for children who are not oriented to college.[51] Insofar as this is a class-linked

---

[50] Wood says that school systems represent the greatest proportion of the budgets of suburban governments and in that sense constitute the most important function suburban governments perform.—Robert C. Wood, *Suburbia: Its People and Their Politics* (Boston: Houghton Mifflin, 1958), p. 187.

[51] Benjamin Fine, "Some Problems Follow City Dwellers to Suburbs: New Vexations, Like Some Old Ones, Include Soaring Costs and Taxes and Overcrowded Facilities," *The New York Times,* January 30, 1957, pp. 1, 18.

phenomenon, this would seem to be a conflict resulting from the invasion of an upper-middle-class community by families of lower-middle-class orientation.

More recently the efforts of black residents in central cities to have the schools reflect their interests and to improve the instruction of their children have resulted in turmoil and conflict in the school systems affected. Contributing have been such factors as drives to increase the number of black teachers and administrators, to replace white teachers and administrators with blacks, to introduce studies of Afro-American history and culture, and such episodes as teachers' strikes, parents' sit-ins, and students' boycotts. In the long run, of course, there is a hope and some prospect that improvement will emerge from the disorder and that the objectives of the black parents will be achieved.

The authors of *Crestwood Heights* point out that success in modern society is in part dependent upon the acquisition of certain social skills—especially the ability to compete without seeming to or, in another phrasing, to compete while seeming to be cooperative.[52] They assert that the social structure of the small nuclear family is not adequate to provide training for this kind of "requisite delicate balance." Only in school can the necessary number of children of the same age be trained in this sort of skill.[53] Noting that while he is still little more than a toddler the child moves out of the family into nursery school and then kindergarten, that the schools are assuming increasing responsibility for his social adjustment, and that to implement this adjustment they create an expectation that the child will become a "joiner," these authors say that secondary groups (especially the school) are claiming more and more of the "whole child" as within their jurisdiction.[54]

In the suburbs, as was suggested above, it is usual for parents to participate in the functioning of the school system. This is done chiefly through conferences with the teachers of their children and through meetings of the Parent-Teacher Association. No doubt the nature of parental participation varies considerably from one setting to another. In Crestwood Heights "the parents are *educated* by the school for their cultural obligations towards the child." In bygone times the parents of Crestwood Heights were seen as agents of the church (the only structure that could provide salvation),[55] but now they are viewed as agents of the school (which has control of the means of training children for a materially successful life).[56] Riesman has commented tellingly on the involvement of the parents of Crestwood Heights in the activities, development, and adjustment of their children:

> Their parents want to know how they have fared at school: they are constantly comparing them, judging them in school aptitude, popularity,

[52] *Op. cit.*, p. 229.
[53] *Ibid.*, n. 14, p. 461.
[54] *Ibid.*, pp. 100–101, 116, 245.
[55] Cf. Zimmerman's formulation of the domestic family, presented in Chapter 4 above.
[56] *Crestwood Heights*, p. 284. Italics in original.

what part they have in the school play; are the boys sissies? the girls too fat? . . . After school there are music lessons, skating lessons, riding lessons, with mother as chauffeur and scheduler. In the evening, the children go to a dance at school for which the parents have groomed them, while the parents go to a PTA meeting for which the children, directly or indirectly have groomed *them,* where they are addressed by a psychiatrist who advises them to be warm and relaxed in handling their children! They go home and eagerly and warmly ask their returning children to tell them everything that happened at the dance, making it clear by their manner that they are sophisticated and cannot easily be shocked. As Professor Seeley describes matters, the school in this community operates a gigantic factory for the production of relationships.[57]

Parents look to camps, scouting, and other activities, as well as to the schools, to carry out the dual purposes of giving their children social skills, maturity, and a sense of responsibility, and giving the parents a respite from the children. Moreover, these other organizations, as well as the schools, can "educate" parents. Under the headline "3,000 Den Mothers Trained in Nassau" *The New York Times* has reported that mothers have been taught "such diverse subjects as the making of Indian headdresses and baskets, the technique of etching glass and the building of campfires . . . knot-tying, how to perform Indian tribal dances and how to make tom-toms out of metal cans."[58] Once in a while there is a reaction against the strenuously active life of suburban children. One day in 1959 some parents in the Chicago suburb of Winnetka decided "to save their children from the treadmill of overorganization" and to dissolve Cub Scout Pack 21. The story was carried in one newspaper under the headline, "Winnetkans Unpack Their Cub Scouts." The reaction was apparently immediate and vigorous, for the next day's paper carried a story under the headline, "Cub Scouts Together Again: Winnetkans Decide to Go with the Pack."[59]

The Religious Function

Whether despite, or because of, any deterioration in religious belief, the studies of Park Forest and of Crestwood Heights agree that in the first instance organized religion serves the children. Whyte says that in Park Forest it is customary for a family to approach church through its children, with the parents waiting about a year before they become regular parishioners.[60] In Crestwood Heights it is thought that the child should be exposed to *some* religious training, that on reaching adulthood the offspring can decide whether to continue in the original religious tradition, to shift to a new one, or to

[57] David Riesman, "Some Observations on Changes in Leisure Attitudes," in *Selected Essays from Individualism Reconsidered* (New York: Doubleday, 1955), pp. 127–147. Quotation is from pp. 136–137. Italics in the original.
[58] February 3, 1952, p. 55.
[59] *Chicago Sun-Times,* June 11, 1959, p. 3; June 12, 1959, p. 29.
[60] *Op. cit.*, p. 380.

abandon religion entirely.⁶¹ In the process the parents may or may not hold themselves aloof from religious participation.⁶²

In Park Forest, says Whyte, the residents, because of their transiency, developed the habit of "shopping" with respect to churches. "Their mobility," he says, "weakened denominational barriers."⁶³ A query as to the considerations entering into the choice of church on the part of Protestants showed that denomination was fourth—after minister, Sunday school, and location. In view of the small importance attached to creed it is not surprising that they developed a United Protestant Church, with the cooperation of twenty-two denominations. Organized religion in Park Forest, says Whyte, tends to be social, pragmatic, and instrumental. Even among the Catholics, he says, "there is a ferment for a more socially useful church."⁶⁴ Where the population is transient, the temptation is irresistible to make friendship, the sense of belonging, the chief appeal of religion.⁶⁵ Henderson corroborates this view with the observation that to most people in the mass-produced suburbs the church is the most important organization, not because of its theological content, but because it provides for so many needs: "social activity, group identification, family counseling, spiritual security."⁶⁶ Similarly in Crestwood Heights, religion per se is represented as "emotionally cool." It is viewed as a means to other important ends: peace of mind or mental health, and in the language of the people the terms of mental health (e.g., responsibility, immaturity) tend to supersede those of religion (e.g., grace, sin).⁶⁷

Summary and Conclusions

Previous chapters have discussed the functioning of the urban family. The suburban family does not differ profoundly from it with respect to the *economic function*. Categorical employability and categorical dependence are present in both forms. More goods and services are probably produced in the suburban family. If it does exist, however, such an increment is probably of little significance for either the family's economy or its solidarity. What is significant is the maximum spatial separation of production and consumption with the consequent increase in absence of the husband-father and specialization of the wife-mother in the role of familial purchasing agent.

With respect to the *political function* a study in Detroit reports that with socioeconomic status and race controlled, suburban wives indicate a greater proportion of "husband-dominant" families than do urban wives. A study of Park Forest shows a high degree of control of behavior by the per-

---

⁶¹ Seeley *et al., op. cit.,* p. 214.
⁶² *Ibid.*
⁶³ *Op. cit.,* p. 367.
⁶⁴ *Ibid.,* p. 373.
⁶⁵ *Ibid.,* chap. 27.
⁶⁶ Henderson, "Rugged American Collectivism," *loc. cit.,* p. 82.
⁶⁷ Seeley *et al., op. cit.,* pp. 239–240, 355.

ceived expectations of neighbors (conformity). Conditions that seem to bear on the degree of conformity through affecting the amount of interaction appear to include propinquity and ecology of the housing units and homogeneity of the residents. The study of auto workers shows that homogeneity by itself is not a sufficient condition for a high degree of interaction with neighbors.

With respect to the *socializing-educational function* there seems to be a considerable difference in the relations of urban and suburban families to the school system. It has been suggested that parental participation in the school system is greater in the suburbs than in the central city and that the public schools support the family through utilizing parents as their agents, just as the church did in the Middle Ages.

It was stated in Chapter 5 that urbanization leads to secularization, and this in turn means that nonreligious structures and occupational roles (counselors, psychiatrists, and so on) are used to fulfill the *religious function*. The suburb resembles the city in creating a demand for what the clergy calls an "institutional" church rather than for a purely creedal function.

The reasons people give for moving from central cities to suburbs indicate that there is a widespread conviction that rearing children is more difficult in cities than in suburbs, that cities are not hospitable to children whereas suburbs are generally viewed as being geared primarily to the needs of children. Such declarations can be rephrased to say that there is a widespread wish on the part of Americans to discharge their parental roles well and that they see the city as making difficult the fulfillment of the parental functions of nurturance and especially of control and, of course, the function of socialization-education. In view of our formulation that replacement is the basic societal function of the family, it follows that the flight to the suburbs is a mass effort to improve the quality of the family's functioning and to render false the predictions of Zimmerman and others of his persuasion that for the family atomism is the wave of the future.

Early in this chapter we noted the question of Jaco and Belknap—is a new family form emerging? In considering the question let us recall that we have looked upon the transition from a folk society to an urban society, or from a simple to a complex society, as a recurring event in the history of man. One of the features of this transition is the proliferation of specialized societal structures for carrying out basic societal functions. This proliferation involves the replacement of the man of many skills by a host of occupational specialists. In this context it is possible to view suburbanism as in a sense a reversal, or at least as an attempt at a reversal, of this evolutionary sequence, i.e., an effort to simplify rather than to proliferate societal structures, to make of oneself a jack-of-all-trades insofar as one is serious in responding to the "do-it-yourself" emphasis, and thus to create, among other things, an amateur politics (e.g., as one participates in discussions whether or not to enlarge the high school) and an amateur culture (e.g., community theater). The suburban family seems to be a defensive reaction against urbanization, but it looks new only if we place it in a short historical perspective.

PART THREE

Basic and Derived Functions of the Family

Five basic societal functions were postulated in Chapter 1. With respect to any given society it was noted that the degree to which there was a specialized societal structure for each of the five functions was an indication of the complexity (or urbanization) of that society. Where the society is simple, the one all-purpose societal structure tends to be the family (cf. Zimmerman's trustee type of family). In this sense we may view societal complexity as a measure of the degree to which in any society the family is *not* the all-purpose structure.

In the present part we consider the basic societal function of the family —replacement—and derived functions. As explained in Chapter 1, derived functions are functions that the family carries out as consequences of its basic societal function or of its structure. Since the family is not the only structure to carry out these functions, it is *not* correct to conclude that the basic societal function of replacement *necessarily* implies that any one of the derived functions will be fulfilled within the structure of the family.

7

The Function of Replacement: urbanization, industrialization and the birth rate

Reproduction and the Family

Reproduction replaces members of a society through the creation of new lives. In this chapter we shall not be concerned with other kinds of replacement, e.g., through adoption, capture, or voluntary immigration.

Although births do occur outside the family, the usual and approved (i.e., the institutionalized) locus of reproduction is within the family. With very few exceptions, two of which are noted below, societies condemn reproduction outside the family. A society that disapproves of extramarital reproduction does not necessarily condemn premarital intercourse or conception. In some societies it is conventional to defer the wedding until the bride-to-be has become pregnant.

There are two examples of somewhat institutionalized reproduction outside marriage. Prior to British control of India, two centuries ago, there was among India's numerous peoples one that had marriage in symbolic form only. The Nayars, a large group living on the Malabar Coast, were warlike, and they regimented their young men into military organizations. Promiscuous sexual relations were permitted. When a young woman became pregnant, it was customary for one or more men of the appropriate subcaste to acknowledge paternity. Such acknowledgment obligated the man to pay the expenses of delivering the baby, but thereafter mother and child were maintained by her kinsmen.[1] While the Nazis were in power in Germany (1933–1945), they developed the concept of the *Kriegsvater*. This meant that an unmarried girl

---

[1] The most accessible account of the Nayars is E. Kathleen Gough, "Is the Family Universal? The Nayar Case," in Norman W. Bell and Ezra F. Vogel (eds.), *A Modern Introduction to the Family* (New York: Free Press, 1968), pp. 80–96.

who bore a child by a German soldier would be honored rather than stigmatized.[2] Both the Nayar and the Nazi societies were oriented to war, and the arrangement for extramarital reproduction freed the young men from obligations that might have interfered with their military effectiveness.[3]

In his satirical fantasy concerning the future of mankind Aldous Huxley foresaw the day when children would be produced without any social father or mother, but would be incubated and hatched oviparously (outside the mother's body) and reared communally according to their predetermined stations.[4] Despite these few instances of real, attempted, or fantasied societal approval of extrafamilial reproduction and despite the large numbers of babies actually born out of wedlock, it seems clear that the original proposition is true—that it is universally in the mores that reproduction should take place within the structure of the family. One writer has neatly phrased the relation of reproduction to the family by asserting that the family consists of a woman with a child, and a man to look after her.

Points of Emphasis

This analysis starts from a very obvious fact—that people die, and hence for a society to maintain its numbers, provision must be made for replacements. Most societies, ours included, acquire some replacements through migration. (In the last century and a half well over forty million people have migrated to this country.[5] Of course some countries experience a net loss of population through migration; Eire is an example.) The important part of the function of replacement, however, takes place through reproduction. The

[2] Moreover, a memorandum discovered in the Reich Ministry of Justice revealed that Hitler planned to increase the German population by a postwar program of free love and polygamy.—"Polygamy Slated by Hitler and Aide: Campaign Mapped to Offset Declining German Births as the Asiatic Rate Rose," *The New York Times*, August 18, 1946, p. 9.

[3] The rearing of the children of *Kriegsväter* would have required some structural innovation in German society. The structure of Nayar society, on the other hand, was matrilineal and matrilocal, and therefore there was no structural problem in rearing children with fathers absent.

[4] Aldous Huxley, *Brave New World* (New York: Doubleday, 1931). Occasionally some writer has expressed the view that the genetically superior members of populations should have many children, whereas the genetically inferior should be discouraged from reproducing—perhaps should be sterilized. (Usually such a writer makes the assumption that high social status is the hallmark of genetic superiority.) The freezing of the genes of great men and the subsequent use of these genes through artificial insemination over a period as long as twenty years after such men have died has been proposed by biologist Herman J. Muller.—"Man and His Future: The Road to Genetic Progress," *Medical World News*, February 28, 1964, pp. 68–69, 72, 74. For another exhortation of this general type see William H. Sheldon, *Varieties of Delinquent Youth: An Introduction to Constitutional Psychiatry* (New York: Harper & Row, 1949), pp. 836–837.

[5] It is estimated that from 1820 through 1969 44,789,000 immigrants entered the United States.—U.S. Bureau of the Census, *Statistical Abstract of the United States: 1970* (Washington, D.C.: GPO, 1970), Table 131, p. 93.

amount of reproduction required to replace the losses over any period is, of course, the number of deaths plus the number of out-migrants minus the number of in-migrants.

Since it has been postulated that replacement through reproduction is the basic societal function of the family, it seems plausible that the pressures of the rest of the social order on the family might be reflected in variations in the birth rate. Of course the impact of the family on the rest of society through the replacement function is also to be noted. In the 1930's evidence of this impact took the form of concern over the declining birth rates in Western countries; more recently it has been over high birth rates in developing countries. The major phenomena that we shall note and endeavor to explain are the marked reduction in the American birth rate and differential fertility associated with urban versus rural residence, socioeconomic status, race, and religious affiliation.

In a sense the birth rate is one of the best-documented series of social data. Our information about it, however, is largely on the descriptive level. That is, we have a quite good idea of what has been happening to the birth rate over our national history, but we have a less adequate understanding of why, or just what the determinants of variation in the birth rate have been.

There are at least four levels on which the explanation of variation in birth rates may be undertaken:

1. *Societal organization,* or the way in which extrafamilial structures and functions affect the birth rate. A key example concerns the way in which economic production is organized.
2. *Culture,* or the value attached to procreation.
3. *Familial organization:* (a) whether the system is extended or nuclear, (b) the primacy of filial or marital solidarity (i.e., whether there is customarily a stronger sense of obligation and attachment between parent and child or between husband and wife), and (c) whether residence is patrilocal, matrilocal, or neolocal.
4. *Instrumental factors:* circumstances that affect directly (a) the frequency of sexual intercourse (especially age at marriage and proportion of adults married), (b) the proportion of acts of intercourse that eventuate in conception (especially the use of contraceptive techniques), and (c) the proportion of conceptions that eventuate in live births (especially the practice of abortion). Davis and Blake call these "intermediate variables."[6]

Not all these four levels will be used in the analysis of all the data to be presented. In particular, slight use will be made of the third point because there is little recorded information relating fertility to variation in structural-functional variables in the American family. Moreover, lack of data will deter us from employing the other three levels with complete consistency.

[6] Kingsley Davis and Judith Blake, "Social Structure and Fertility: An Analytic Framework," *Economic Development and Cultural Change,* 4: 211–235 (1956).

American Fertility from the Latter Part of the Eighteenth Century to the Present

DESCRIPTION

Over much of the past three centuries the death rate has been declining among Euro-American peoples. In these countries the birth rate has also declined, but the decline in the birth rate has generally lagged behind the decrease in the death rate. A very considerable increase in population has resulted. The population of the world has undergone a fivefold expansion during the past three and a half centuries; indeed, an increase of 50 percent is estimated to have taken place in the thirty-five years following 1920,[7] and of nearly 20 percent—from 2.5 billions to 3.0 billions—in the 1950–1960 decade.[8]

Although it is difficult to develop any precise data on birth rates in our early history, the informed consensus is that the birth rates in the colonial and early national periods were remarkably high. According to Lotka, "Each fertile married woman in the Revolutionary Period . . . bore on the average eight children (the exact estimate for the year 1790 is 7.76, with an inference that at an earlier date the figure may have been even higher)."[9] The corresponding figure for native-born white women in 1940 was 3.53,[10] and in 1950 for fertile women of all races whose period of fertility was completed the average number of children ever born was 3.13.[11]

Calhoun cites considerable evidence of an impressionistic nature to support the view that the populace of the colonial and early national periods was extraordinarily fertile. Concerning the colonial period he observes that families with 10 children were common and those with 20 were not unusual.[12] Although

---

[7] Donald J. Bogue, *The Population of the United States* (New York: Free Press, 1959), Table 1–1, p. 2.

[8] John V. Grauman, "Population Growth," in David L. Sills (ed.), *International Encyclopedia of the Social Sciences* (New York: Macmillan and Free Press, 1968), vol. 12, pp. 376–381, at Table 1, p. 377.

[9] National Resources Committee, *Problems of a Changing Population* (Washington, D.C.: GPO, 1938), p. 18.

[10] Inter-Agency Committee for the National Conference on Family Life, *The American Family: A Factual Background* (Washington, D.C.: GPO, 1948), p. 48.

[11] Conrad Taeuber and Irene B. Taeuber, *The Changing Population of the United States* (New York: Wiley, 1958), p. 255. As of 1950 the average married American woman aged 45–49 had born 2.49 children; by 1969 this average had risen to 2.79. For all women, irrespective of marital status, the corresponding figures are: 1950, 2.29, and 1969, 2.66. In 1969 it was estimated that replacement of the generation called for 2.13 children per women for all women.—U.S. Bureau of the Census, *Current Population Reports—Population Characteristics*, Series P-20, No. 178, February 27, 1969.

[12] A. W. Calhoun, *A Social History of the American Family* (New York: Barnes & Noble, 1945), I, 87.

The Function of Replacement 157

Lotka did hold that the average number of children per fertile married woman in the colonial period might well have exceeded 8, it is doubtful that the number was higher than 9.[13] It should be borne in mind, however, that the death rate at this period was also very high. According to the death rates of 1789, the average newborn baby boy would live 34.5 years.[14] By contrast, in 1967 the figures for white males and females were 67.8 and 75.1, respectively, and for both sexes, 71.3; for nonwhite[15] males and females, 61.1 and 68.2, and for both sexes, 64.6.[16] In 178 years, then, the dramatic drop in the death rate resulted in doubling life expectancy at birth.

Concerning mortality in the colonial period Calhoun remarks: "In the seventeenth century, in spite of early marriage and a very high birth rate, increase was offset by frightful mortality of children; so that the slaughter of womanhood in incessant child-bearing was relatively vain. Significant is the inscription on a Plymouth grave-stone: 'Here lies —— —— with twenty small children.'"[17]

The very high birth rates of the seventeenth and eighteenth centuries were not to prove permanent. In France the birth rate began to decline around 1770.[18] The earliest data on trends in the birth rate in this country, going back to the early years of the nineteenth century, show a practically unbroken decline from that time to a low point in the depression immediately preceding World War II.[19]

In 1820 there were 55.2 live births per 1000 population. By 1860 this figure, the crude birth rate, was down to 44.3 and by 1900, to 32.3. In 1920 it was 27.7, and in 1930, 21.3. The American birth rate hit its depression low in 1936 at 18.4—exactly one third of the crude birth rate of 1820. By 1940 it had risen slightly to 19.4. In the last year of World War II, 1945, the crude birth rate was 20.4. In 1946, the first year of peace, it rose by nearly 4 per 1000 to 24.1, and in the following year by another 2.5 to its recent high of 26.6. (This is the highest birth rate the country has recorded since 1921 but is somewhat below those of the first quarter of the century, which were in the range 27–30.)[20] During the fourteen years 1946–1959 the crude birth rate did not fall

---

[13] On the basis of the Pearl-Reed law of population growth Lotka has estimated this value to be 8.33.—A. J. Lotka, "The Size of American Families in the Eighteenth Century," *Journal of the American Statistical Association*, 22: 167 (1927).

[14] National Resources Committee, *op. cit.*, p. 22.

[15] For the period 1941–1950 the expectation of life at birth in India was 32.5 years for males and 31.7 years for females.—Metropolitan Life Insurance Company, *Statistical Bulletin*, April 1958, p. 2.

[16] *Statistical Abstract of the United States: 1970*, Table 65, p. 53.

[17] Calhoun, *op. cit.*, I, 89.

[18] Frank Lorimer, *Culture and Human Fertility: A Study of the Relation of Cultural Conditions to Fertility in Non-Industrial and Transitional Societies* (Paris: UNESCO, 1954), p. 207.

[19] In England and Wales the birth rate started down around 1870.—*Ibid.*

[20] U.S. Bureau of the Census, *Historical Statistics of the United States, Colonial Times to 1957* (Washington, D.C.: GPO, 1960), Series B 19–30, p. 23.

below 24,[21] but thereafter a decline set in and by 1968 it had fallen to an all-time low of 17.5.[22]

The decline of the birth rate in the latter 1960's may be a short-run deviation—if, say, it is the temporary result of a shift in age at first marriage and/or of the interval between marriage and the birth of the first child—or it may presage a long-run trend. Data on unwanted births, cited on page 181 below, provide some basis for the latter interpretation.

The net reproduction rate is a more satisfactory index than the crude birth rate of the degree to which the replacement function is being carried out. The crude birth rate is affected by temporary peculiarities in the composition of the population, whereas the net reproduction rate is not. The latter rate is based upon the birth and death rates of a population and answers the question of how many female children the average female in a hypothetical cohort of females will bear. If the number is 1,00, the cohort is just replacing itself; if the number is below or above 1.00, the vital rates are resulting, respectively, in a deficit or a surplus. For example, if the rate is 1.50, this means that over a generation at the prevailing vital rates, the population is reproducing itself with a 50 percent surplus.

What happened to the net reproduction rate as birth rates were hitting bottom? By the 1930's it had become doubtful whether or not the countries of Western Europe and North America would eventually be able to replace themselves. Between 1930 and 1940 the net reproduction rate of the United States was running about 0.98. By 1940 our vital rates had risen above the replacement level (1.03). In 1947 the net reproduction rate hit 1.51, and by 1959 it was 1.72. Thus in roughly a generation, i.e., from 1935 to 1959, the birth rate rose from below the level of replacement to a point where there was nearly a three-fourths surplus per generation. By 1968 the net reproduction rate of the United States was back down to 1.17.[23]

A dramatic rise in the proportion of childless wives and an even more dramatic reduction have taken place in about two thirds of a century. (We may assume that American women are in the middle of their childbearing period when they are around 25 to 28 years old. The precise median age of childbearing shifts as successive cohorts of women delay or advance their childbearing.) Table 7.1 shows that wives who were in the midst of their childbearing period in 1890 had a low proportion of childlessness of less than one in ten. Among the depression generation of wives, however, one in every five was childless. By World War II this proportion was declining to one in seven, and by the late 1950's only one wife in thirteen was childless.[24]

---

[21] National Center for Health Statistics, *Natality Statistics Analysis: United States—1964* (Washington, D.C.: GPO, 1967), Table 1, p. 2.

[22] *Statistical Abstract of the United States: 1970*, Table 53, p. 47.

[23] Taeuber and Taeuber, *op. cit.*, Table 92, p. 297; *Statistical Abstract of the United States: 1970*, Table 61, p. 51.

[24] The precise tabulated values used in this statement are: 9.5 percent of the cohort that was 45–49 in 1910; 20.4 percent of the cohort that was 45–49 in 1950; 14.1 percent

TABLE 7.1

Percent Childless among Women Ever Married, by Age of Woman: United States, 1910 to 1969

AGE OF WOMAN (IN YEARS)	PERCENTAGE CHILDLESS AMONG WOMEN EVER MARRIED				
	1910	1940	1950	1960	1969
30 to 34	13.7	23.3	17.3	10.4	7.1
35 to 39	11.6	19.9	19.1	11.1	7.2
40 to 44	10.4	17.4	20.0	14.1	8.0
45 to 49	9.5	16.8	20.4	18.1	10.5

SOURCE: *Statistical Abstract of the United States: 1970*, Table 62, p. 51.

In an earlier section of the present chapter we noted Lotka's estimate that toward the close of the eighteenth century the average fertile American married woman was bearing eight children. An impression of the reduction in the higher birth orders can be derived from Figure 7.1. In 1920 there were 109 births per 1000 native white women of age 15–44, and of these 23 were of fifth or higher birth order. By the time of the lowest birth rate of the depression, 1936, there were 74 births per 1000 native white women, and of these just 13 were of fifth or higher order. In the 1950's the birth rate rose appreciably—hitting 116 per 1000 in 1956—but the number of births of fifth or higher order was barely above the 1936 level—15 per 1000 women.

ANALYSIS OF THE AMERICAN SCENE IN THE SEVENTEENTH AND EIGHTEENTH CENTURIES

To facilitate our analysis of reproductive trends in America let us examine the scene in three historical blocks: the period of high fertility and high mortality up to 1800, the period of declining vital rates from 1800 to 1936, and the period since 1936.

On page 155 reference was made to four levels of explanation with respect to variation in fertility: (1) societal organization, (2) culture, (3) familial organization, and (4) such instrumental factors as proportion of adults married, age at marriage, and availability of contraceptive devices. We shall summarize each of these three eras in terms of these four levels of analysis.

With respect to societal organization we may note that both in the New England towns of the seventeenth and eighteenth centuries and later, on the frontier, the conditions of life were such as to encourage early marriage and the raising of a family.

---

of the cohort that was 40–44 in 1960; and 8.0 percent of the cohort that was 40–44 in 1969. Although the 40–44 cohorts have not completely passed through their childbearing years and hence their percentages of childlessness can rise or fall, it is unlikely that the percentages when they become 45–49 will vary more than 2 or 3 percent from the values shown.

FIGURE 7.1

Birth Rates by Live-Birth Orders for Native White Women,
United States: 1920 to 1965

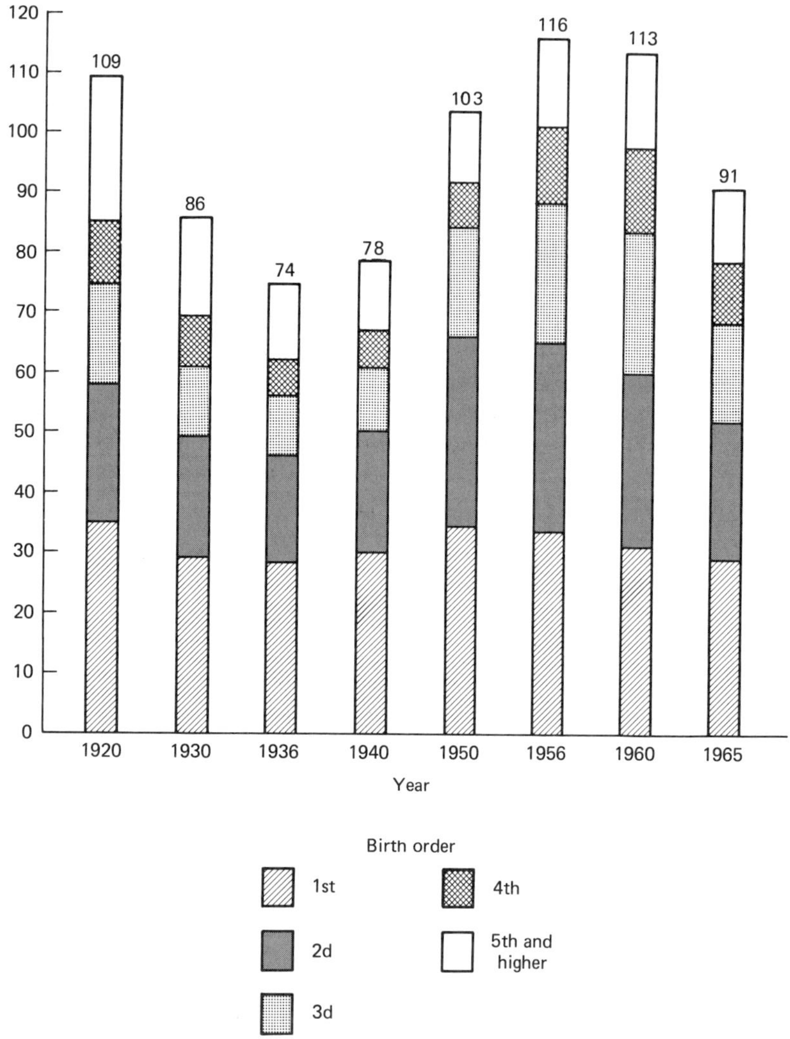

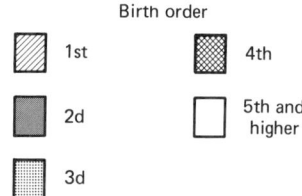

SOURCE: For 1920 through 1956, *Historical Statistics of the United States: Colonial Times to 1957*, Table B 10–18, p. 22; for 1960 and 1965, *Statistical Abstract of the United States: 1968*, Table 59, p. 50.

In Puritan New England early marriages were regarded as "right" and "normal," while bachelors were regarded with suspicion. Large numbers of women were wedded at 16, and if a girl remained at home until her 18th birthday the Puritan parents began to lose hope.[25] The unmarried woman became a "stale maid" at 20; if she was married, she might well be a grand-

[25] Carl Holliday, *Woman's Life in Colonial Days* (Boston: Cornhill, 1922), p. 262.

The Function of Replacement   161

mother at 27.²⁶ There were comparatively few unmarried people, and the lot of these was far from bright in the Puritan society. Bachelors were carefully watched and were not allowed to live alone. Each one was assigned to a family with whom he lived and who was responsible for his keeping proper hours.²⁷ Unmarried women lived with relatives, assuming responsibility for household tasks, or perhaps they managed to achieve a bare living by keeping a dame's school. Early marriage and the rearing of a large family constituted the usual pattern of the times.

In the life of the pioneer, settling, building and protecting the home, and growing crops constituted a set of activities necessary for survival. The frontier had an abundance of land and a low density of population; accordingly, labor was scarce. From the discussion of the domestic division of labor in Chapter 4, we can see that a wife and children provided opportunity for a considerably more adequate life than was possible for a man alone. While life for the single man was difficult on the frontier, it was practically impossible for the single woman. Her alternative to matrimony was that of menial service in the household of a kinsman. Given these conditions of life, it is not difficult to understand why early marriages and numerous children were the order of the day, and why, as Calhoun points out, the family was "the one substantial social institution in a nation that had discarded hierarchical religion and that had reduced government to a minimum, while business corporations had not yet attained notable development."²⁸

Commenting in 1776 on the relation between the conditions of life in the New World and the economic value of children, Adam Smith observed:

> Those who live to old age, it is said, frequently see there from fifty to a hundred, and sometimes many more descendants from their own body. Labor is there so well rewarded that a numerous family of children, instead of being a burden, is a source of opulence and prosperity to the parents. The labor of each child before it can leave their house, is computed to be worth a hundred pounds clear gain to them. A young widow with four or five young children, who, among the middling or inferior ranks of people in Europe would have so little chance for a second husband, is there frequently counted as a sort of fortune. The value of children is the greatest of all encouragement to marriage. We cannot, therefore, wonder that the people in North America should generally marry very young. Notwithstanding the great increase occasioned by such early marriages, there is a continual complaint of the scarcity of hands in North America.²⁹

Thus in the seventeenth and eighteenth centuries conditions at all four levels of explanation were favoring high fertility. We may summarize the argument:

---

[26] Calhoun, *op. cit.*, I, 245; II, 13.
[27] S. G. Fisher, *Men, Women and Manners in Colonial Times* (Philadelphia: Lippincott, 1898), p. 175.
[28] Calhoun, *op. cit.*, II, 11.
[29] Adam Smith, *The Wealth of Nations* (Edinburgh: Oliphant, Waugh and Innes, 1814), I, 114–115.

1. Societal organization

That, as Calhoun says, the family was "the one substantial social institution" indicates that the family was a structure of many functions and that other societal structures were not applying pressure on the family.

2. Culture

As Adam Smith noted, conditions made children valuable in an economic sense. Since the country was young and expanding, it is natural that there should have been an emphasis on and hope and confidence in the future, with a consequently high valuation on the individual's link to the future —his children.

3. Familial organization

The family was neolocal with the consequence that the household was based on the nuclear family. See Table 24.1 for data pertaining to the year 1800.

4. Instrumental factors

Age at marriage was apparently quite low. There was little in the way of contraceptive technology.

THE DOWNWARD TREND IN FERTILITY: 1800–1936

Our frontier crossed the continent and disappeared by the end of the last century. Behind the frontier developed settled farm life, towns, and cities. With the advent of sanitation and power machinery, cities began to grow in number and in size. The development of power equipment brought the demand for labor to operate the machines. In Chapter 4 we surveyed the consequences of the Industrial Revolution for the organization of the family. We noted that, as the economy became more complex and specialized, a progressively larger proportion of the population was engaged in production for the market rather than for its own consumption. The separation of work and home, which is characteristic of urban and suburban living, meant that the family ceased to be an important unit of production, that the laboring unit became the individual worker rather than the family, that the population became categorized into gainfully employed and dependents, and that children became "mouths" rather than "hands." As we also saw in Chapter 4, the proportion of married women employed outside the home has increased greatly in recent years. This fact undoubtedly bears a close, albeit complex, relationship to the birth rate.

> The causal relationship is not simple. Having a child evidently reduces very greatly the probability that the mother will be in the labor force. At the same time, being in the labor force reduces the probability that a woman will bear a child within a given period of time. Having children involves an economic sacrifice to the parents in any case, but the sacrifice is doubly great when the wife must give up her job to become a mother.

The Function of Replacement

Furthermore, trends in fertility and in the employment of married women are jointly related to other factors. Gainful employment and family limitation may both be means of attaining the same objectives: a higher level of living or more independence and a broader sphere of interests for the wife. In many cases, also, women work in order to save money so that they can afford to have children.

Therefore, no one can say exactly how much of the increase in employment of married women has been caused by the decline of the birth rate or how much of the decrease in fertility has been due to increased employment of potential mothers.[30]

However, the same writer goes on to say that "Increasing gainful employment of married women is not necessarily incompatible with a rising birth rate, as shown by our experience during the war when the number of wives in the labor force rose to an unprecedented figure while the birth rate shot upward."[31]

Irrespective of how ill defined may be the nature of the relationship between paid employment and fertility, it is clear that married women in the labor force have fewer children than those who are married but are not in the labor force. In 1960 it was estimated that the married women aged 15–44 in the labor force had 343 children under age 5 per 1000 women; for those not in the labor force the ratio was 884 children under age 5 per 1000 married women.[32]

Several other factors should be taken into account as we seek to understand the decline in fertility: the development of contraceptive techniques, the decline in the death rate, and the apparent rise in age at first marriage. First, it seems clear that during the period under consideration reliable and relatively inexpensive means of contraception were introduced and information about them was rather widely disseminated.

Second, concerning the death rate, data for Massachusetts show life expectation at birth for males to have been 38.3 years in 1850, 41.7 in 1878–1882, 42.5 in 1890, and 46.1 in 1900–1902.[33] We have noted above that in 1965 it was 67.6 for white males. This dramatic improvement in life expectation at birth was largely the consequence of a reduction of death rates for the years of infancy and childhood.[34] Lorimer remarks that prior to the rise of modern technology half or more of the females did not survive until they reached the middle of the childbearing period. By contrast, female mortality to the same period of life is less than 10 percent with the rise of technology, and in par-

---

[30] J. D. Durand, "Married Women in the Labor Force," *American Journal of Sociology*, 52: 219 (1946). Published by the University of Chicago Press.

[31] *Ibid.*, p. 223.

[32] Calculated from U.S. Bureau of the Census, *U.S. Census of Population: 1960, Subject Reports, Women by Children under 5 Years Old*, Final Report PC(2)-3C (Washington, D.C.: GPO, 1968), Table 45, pp. 90–91.

[33] Taeuber and Taeuber, *op. cit.*, p. 270.

[34] *Ibid.*, p. 272.

ticular with the development of sanitary, medical, and food-producing techniques. In the period of high mortality, he says, it was necessary for the average woman who lived through the childbearing period to bear from four to six children just to maintain a stable population. In other words, mere replacement required "the actual realization of some 50 to 75 percent or more of the total procreative capacity of the population."[35] Thus the decline in the death rate, especially since it was most marked in the years of infancy and childhood, reduced the number of children needed to achieve replacement, and it has been estimated that under the present low mortality rates for infancy and childhood "the three-child family would lead to a population [for the United States] of 312 million by [the year] 2000 and of 600 million by 2050."[36]

The third observation concerns the trend in age at first marriage. We have noted impressionistic evidence that people married at youthful ages in the early days. In Chapter 10 we shall present evidence that age at first marriage has been falling slowly from 1890 to 1960, but it does not seem generally to be believed that age at first marriage in 1960 was as low on the average as it was in the early days. For these observations to be correct the average age at first marriage must have risen appreciably between some time in the eighteenth and the end of the nineteenth century. Direct evidence on this point is lacking. There is no systematic study of factors affecting age at marriage. Some clues, however, are offered by Tawney, who in a study of sixteenth-century England found that marriages were deferred if the young man had to await the permission of a guild in order to set up a shop or if the young couple had to await the death of a parent in order to succeed to land. He concluded that the average age at marriage is likely to be higher in a society composed largely of small property owners than in one composed largely of a propertyless proletariat.[37]

A sterling example of Tawney's point comes from a study in rural County Clare, Ireland. The property system and the way in which land is transmitted from one generation to the next are the key to understanding marriage and the family in County Clare. The farms are not subdivided. Accordingly, the father selects from his sons the one whom he wishes to succeed him on the property. The father's retirement from active farming usually occurs at about the age of seventy. The son who is to succeed the father as a rule does not

---

[35] Lorimer, *Culture and Human Fertility*, p. 204.

[36] Ronald Freedman, Pascal K. Whelpton, and Arthur A. Campbell, *Family Planning, Sterility, and Population Growth* (New York: McGraw-Hill, 1959), pp. 404–405. A more recent estimate based on an assumed average of 3.1 children per woman gave projections of 336 millions by the year 2000 and 430 millions by 2015.—U.S. Bureau of the Census, *Current Population Reports—Population Estimates*, Series P-25, No. 388, March 14, 1968, pp. 2, 4.

[37] R. H. Tawney, *The Agrarian Problem in the Sixteenth Century* (London: Longmans, 1912), n. 3, pp. 104–106.

marry until the father is about to retire. The son, therefore, may well be thirty-five or forty years of age, or even older at the time of marriage.

Obviously, then, the father's retirement has great significance for the son who succeeds him. It means that the son is to become the master of the farm, that he can now marry, and, as a consequence of these two developments, that he can at long last pass into the status of a full-fledged adult. Until they are married, men and women, irrespective of age, are still called "boys" and "girls." This lack of fully adult status was dramatized by an Irish legislator who pleaded "for the special treatment in land division for 'boys of forty-five and older.'"[38] Sean O'Faolain relates a story of two "boys" haled into court for having their first venture into liberty and liquor. The occasion was the death of their 92-year-old father; the "boys" were 60 and 65 years old.[39] As a result of all this the average age at marriage and the proportion of unmarried in rural Ireland have been very high. In 1926, according to Arensberg and Kimball, the proportion of unmarried males between the ages of 35 and 40 in the Irish Free State was 62 percent. In the United States the corresponding proportion was 24 percent.[40]

The downward trend in the American birth rate from 1800 to, say, 1920 or 1925 may be interpreted as largely the result of the conversion of our society during that period from a rural-agricultural social order to an urban-industrial form of societal organization. It was noted above that the most rapid decline in fertility in American history apparently occurred from 1925–1929 to 1930–1934. Thus the birth rate, which was already declining in response to urbanization and industrialization, was given a further downward shove by the greatest economic depression in American history, which resulted in later marriages and in the deferment, and sometimes complete avoidance, of conception.[41]

We have noted the convergence of a number of factors apparently related to a decline in the birth rate and size of family and to an increase in the incidence of childlessness. We have yet to show by more than circumstantial evidence that the decrease in fertility has been in any way planned and controlled. In 1941 a study was made in Indianapolis of native white Protestant couples who had been married from 12 to 15 years. Of this group it was found that 89 percent reported having used methods to prevent conception.[42] Although this study does not inform us about the rural, the nonwhite, or the non-Protestant segments of the population, still it seems plausible that if such

---

[38] Based on C. M. Arensberg and S. T. Kimball, *Family and Community in Ireland* (Cambridge, Mass.: Harvard University Press, 1940). Quotation is from p. 56.

[39] "Love among the Irish," *Life*, March 16, 1953, pp. 140–142, 144, 146, 149–150, 152, 154, 157.

[40] *Op. cit.*, pp. 103–104, 155.

[41] Grabill, Kiser, and Whelpton, *op. cit.*, pp. 33–36, 293.

[42] P. K. Whelpton and Clyde V. Kiser (eds.), *Social and Psychological Factors Affecting Fertility* (New York: Milbank Memorial Fund, 1950), II, 212.

an overwhelming majority of the Indianapolis sample was controlling fertility, probably a sizable proportion was doing so in the unstudied segments of the population. This surmise is partially corroborated by later studies, which we shall consider presently, based on national samples of white wives.

Now let us summarize our analysis of the drop from a very high birth rate in 1800 to one below the level of replacement in 1936:

1. *Societal organization*

By comparison with other societal structures, especially with economic structures, the family had become weak and had become responsive to the level of activity in other structures. This was markedly evident in the depression of the 1930's, when the family responded to the low level of economic activity.

2. *Culture*

The trend over the whole period involved a shift in the economic value of the child from plus to minus, from asset to liability, from "hand" to "mouth." Moreover, the reduction in the mortality rates of infancy and childhood lowered sharply the number of children needed to provide replacements, and no doubt this reduction decreased the "scarcity" value of the individual child. The period following the stock market crash in 1929 was a depression not only in the economic sense but in a sociopsychological sense as well. Young people entering the occupational system tended to abandon thought of "careers" and to congratulate themselves on getting "jobs." When the future looks as bleak as it did in the early 1930's, there is little incentive to procreate and thus, in the phrasing of Francis Bacon, to give a hostage to fortune. A parallel in some African societies has been noted by Lorimer, who says that there "the disorganization of traditional social structures and related value systems . . . has resulted . . . in behaviour leading to frequent avoidance of childbearing, or sterility, or both. . . ."[43]

3. *Familial organization*

A progressively larger proportion of wives was entering the labor force, i.e., was working away from home. The proportion was 5 percent in 1890 and 17 percent in 1940. (See Table 4.2.)

4. *Instrumental factors*

(a) Relatively convenient and inexpensive contraceptive techniques had been developed and were being used. (b) It seems likely that average age at first marriage rose appreciably prior to 1890, fell from then to the depression, and then increased temporarily as a result of the depression. It is well known that among those who marry early there are fewer childless wives and the wives bear more children on the average than do those who marry late in life.

[43] Lorimer, *op. cit.*, p. 133.

THE CYCLE IN FERTILITY SINCE 1936

Virtually by the time the demographers had begun to toll the knell of a vanishing population the birth rate had begun to rise—slowly to 1940, more rapidly through World War II, and spurting up after the war to a level it had not achieved in a generation. From its low in 1936 of 18.4 births per 1000 population, as we have seen, the crude birth rate rose to 26.6 in 1947. Thereafter it began to decline and by 1968 had fallen to 17.4.

What produces these shifts? Freedman cites some evidence to show that rates of fertility correlate strongly in the positive direction with the business cycle. He believes the correlation results from more marriages in more prosperous times.[44] Easterlin has presented data to show that fertility is related to the conditions of the labor market as it affects young people in the labor force. With low supply of labor and high demand, fertility is relatively high. Easterlin points out that as children born during the baby boom become old enough and enter the labor force, the demand-supply balance of labor becomes less favorable for young workers.[45] This might well have been the state of affairs at the close of the 1960's, and we have seen a sharp reduction in the crude birth rate after the high of 1957. These studies seem to lead to a view that the having or not having of children may be seen as governed in part by factors that influence other aspects of human behavior, such as getting married or buying a new house or automobile.

In reviewing trends in American fertility over the last half century Arthur Campbell distinguishes two components in the fluctuation of the birth rate: the timing of births, and the number of children couples ultimately have. So far as timing is concerned, the baby boom of the 1950's resulted from births deferred from the years of depression and war by older women and also from the "early" deliveries of women marrying young and starting their families quickly.[46] Campbell makes the point that "a major portion of the upward and downward swings in fertility have been due to changes in the ages at which women bear children."[47]

Both Table 7.1 and Figure 7.1 bear on the second of Campbell's components—the number of children born into the average family. Comparison of these two sets of data shows that they covary in a way to make their impact cumulative: the proportion of childless women was low at the ends of the period and high in the middle; the combined birth rates for third and higher birth orders were highest in 1920 and 1956, lowest in 1936 and 1940.

[44] Ronald Freedman, "American Studies of Family Planning and Fertility: A Review of Major Trends and Issues," in Clyde V. Kiser (ed.), *Research in Family Planning* (Princeton, N.J.: Princeton University Press, 1962), pp. 211–227, esp. pp. 221–223.

[45] Richard A. Easterlin, "On the Relation of Economic Factors to Recent and Projected Fertility Changes," *Demography*, 3: 131–153 (1966).

[46] Arthur A. Campbell, "Population Dynamics and Family Planning," *Journal of Marriage and the Family*, 30: 202–206 (1968).

[47] *Ibid.*, p. 203.

The changes in timing that produced the baby boom of the 1950's have about run their course, and the decline in the birth rate during the 1960's did not astonish the demographers. They are less sure as to whether there is also a change in the direction of smaller families. In terms of our four levels:

1. *Societal organization*

As the depression receded, millions of unemployed individuals began to find jobs. The period from 1936 to the 1960's begins in unprecedented depression and ends in unprecedented prosperity. Although poverty was not eliminated and, indeed, became a more pressing social problem as the general economic level of the society rose, still for the society as a whole economic conditions became more favorable to having children than they had been during the depression.

2. *Culture*

The emotional tone of the society was given a lift, first, by the economic recovery of the latter 1930's, then by the solidifying experience of being at war, and after 1945, by an era of high employment and productivity. (It is difficult or perhaps impossible to document the point, but it is conceivable that the gloomy predictions of the demographers in the 1930's heightened for some individuals the value of children.) During the Johnson administration (1963–1969), however, the unpopular war in Viet Nam and the increasingly bitter struggle of blacks for equality resulted in the alienation of sizable segments of the American population and in some breakdown of societal norms.

3. *Familial organization*

The proportion of working wives continued to increase—from 17 percent in 1940 to 25 percent in 1950, 32 percent in 1960, and 40 percent in 1969. (See Table 4.2.) In itself this fact would seem to portend a decrease rather than an increase in the birth rate. The great increase in the proportion of working wives, however, came in the age group over 35, i.e., in a category that has largely completed bearing children.

4. *Instrumental factors*

(a) For about two decades after 1936 there was a gradual lowering of the median age at first marriage. In 1930, 1940, 1950, and 1956 it was 24.3, 24.3, 22.8, and 22.5 respectively for males, and 21.3, 21.5, 20.3, and 20.1 respectively for females. Since 1956 there has been a slight increase: 23.2 for males and 20.8 for females in 1969.[48] (b) The proportion of adults who are married has increased. The proportion of males over 14 who were married in 1890, 1940, and 1969 were 52, 60, and 67 percent respectively. Of more direct relevance are the corresponding proportions for females: 55, 60, and 62 percent respectively. (See Table 10.2.) (c) An increasing proportion of married women are bearing children. (See Table 7.1, which shows a reduction in childlessness among all cohorts since 1950.) (d) Between 1965 and 1970 there was an increase in the size of the child-

---

[48] Cf. Table 10.16.

The Function of Replacement 169

bearing population. In particular, the number of women in the 20–24 age bracket increased by about one quarter. (e) The most widely remarked instrumental factor to develop in the period under consideration has been the development of new contraceptive techniques, especially the intrauterine devices (IUD) that are widely used in other countries and "the pill" that is reported to be used by a quarter of the married women under 45 in this country.[49]

URBAN-RURAL DIFFERENTIALS IN FERTILITY

We have noted that the purpose of this chapter is to learn from American experience something of the conditions under which the family carries out the replacement function at various levels. To further our understanding it is relevant to examine segments of our population that differ in levels of fertility.

We have interpreted the decline of the birth rate from 1800 to 1936 as a response by the family to the urbanization and industrialization of the society. In Figure 7.2 it can be seen that from 1800 to 1940 there was a remarkably

FIGURE 7.2

Fertility Rate and Percent of Rural and Urban Population by Censal Years, United States: 1800–1960

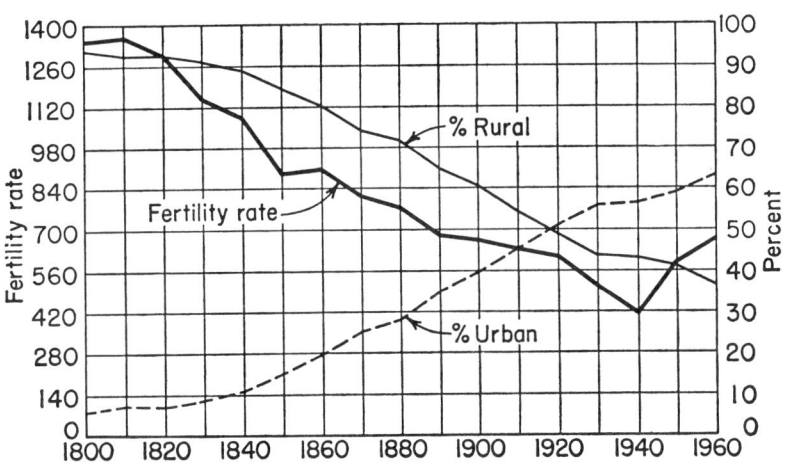

SOURCE: For 1800–1950, Conrad Taeuber and Irene B. Taeuber, *The Changing Population of the United States* (New York: John Wiley & Sons, Inc., 1958), Table 34, p. 118, Table 82, p. 211. For 1960, personal communication from Dr. Paul C. Glick of the U.S. Bureau of the Census. The fertility rate used here is the number of children under 5 years old per 1000 white women, 20–44 years old. The 1940 or old definition of "urban" is followed.

[49] Arthur A. Campbell, *op. cit.*

close relation between the proportion rural (or urban) and the birth rate. In 1800 the proportions rural and urban were 94 and 6 percent respectively, and the fertility rate[50] was 1342; in 1940 the rural-urban proportions were 44 and 56 percent respectively,[51] and the fertility rate was 419. As the preceding section emphasizes and as the portions of the curves after 1940 demonstrate, a new era of fertility trends started just prior to World War II.

As these data and the foregoing interpretation have suggested, the birth rate in rural areas has been consistently higher than that in the cities. The urban-rural appears to be the oldest and most clearly established of the various differentials in fertility. (Others we shall consider are those relating to socioeconomic status, race, and religion.)

Table 7.2 provides evidence of the continuing relationship between fer-

TABLE 7.2

Number of Children Ever Born per 1000 Women Aged 15–44 Ever Married, by Selected Characteristics: 1969

Total	2466
Residence	
Farm	2919
Nonfarm	2445
Standard metropolitan statistical areas	2394
Central cities	2408
Outside central cities	2381
Nonmetropolitan areas	2608
Color	
White	2390
Nonwhite	3046
Black	3118
Years of school completed	
Elementary: Less than 8 years	3398
8 years	3206
High school: 1 to 3 years	2944
4 years	2286
College: 1 to 3 years	2116
4 years or more	1790
Labor force status	
In labor force	2123
Not in labor force	2737

SOURCE: *Statistical Abstract of the United States: 1970*, Table 63, p. 52.

[50] Number of children under the age of 5 per 1000 white women aged 20–44.
[51] By the "old" or "1940" definition of the Bureau of the Census. In 1950 a more inclusive definition of "urban" was adopted.

tility and the nature of the area of residence. It can be seen that the number of children ever born to each 1000 farm women ever married (2919) is 19 percent greater than the number born per 1000 nonfarm women (2445) and 22 percent greater than the number born per 1000 urban (SMSA) women ever married (2394). In bygone years the suburbs showed a higher rate of fertility than did the central cities. Table 7.2 shows, however, that the rate for the central cities (2408) is virtually the same as for the contiguous areas outside the central cities (2381). This appears to reflect the extensive migration to central cities of blacks with their high rates of fertility. (We shall comment presently on other data in Table 7.2.)

SOCIOECONOMIC STATUS AND DIFFERENTIAL FERTILITY

The adage that the rich get richer and the poor get children appears to have been generally true over much of our history—at least as early as the beginning of the nineteenth century and as late as the middle of the twentieth century. There are no nation-wide data categorizing people by social class, nor is there any single variable regarded as *the* index of socioeconomic status. Therefore students have relied on several indirect measures, such as educational level, occupation, value of housing occupied, and the like. Jaffe has shown that at the beginning of the nineteenth century—before the diffusion of modern techniques of contraception—the birth rates in the lower economic classes were higher than those in the middle and upper classes.[52]

The part of Table 7.2 that pertains to the level of education shows a monotonic inverse relationship[53] between number of years of schooling and fertility rate. In the total columns for both whites and nonwhites of Table 7.3 there is evidence of the familiar negative correlation between family income and number of children, and the evidence is even more impressive for the nonwhites than for the whites. When only urbanized areas are considered, however, the relationship is less marked in the case of whites and even shows some tendency toward reversal in the case of nonwhites. A similar finding has been reported from a national sample of white married women in the childbearing years (18–39) in the United States. When the nonfarm respondents were divided into those who had ever lived on farms (whom they called "farm migrants") and those who had not (designated "indigenous nonfarm" respondents), it was found that the negative correlation between income and fertility disappeared completely for the indigenous nonfarm couples.[54]

---

[52] A. J. Jaffe, "Differential Fertility in the White Population in Early America," *Journal of Heredity*, 31: 407–411 (1940).

[53] If as one variable increases (or decreases), the other does also, the relationship is said to be *positive* or *direct;* on the other hand, if they covary in opposite directions, i.e., as one increases the other decreases, they are said to have a *negative* or *inverse* relationship. A *monotonic* relationship is one that is *consistently* either direct or inverse.

[54] Ronald Freedman and Doris P. Slesinger, "Fertility Differentials for the Indigenous Non-Farm Population of the United States," *Population Studies*, 15: 161–173 (1961).

TABLE 7.3

Number of Children Ever Born per 1000 Married Women Aged 40–44, by Family Income: 1960

	COLOR			
	WHITE		NONWHITE	
FAMILY INCOME	TOTAL	URBANIZED AREAS	TOTAL	URBANIZED AREAS
Total	2557	2317	3177	2458
Under $3000	3072	2447	3883	2402
$3000 to $4999	2738	2317	2973	2451
$5000 to $6999	2549	2336	2828	2503
$7000 to $9999	2433	2301	2637	2418
$10,000 and over	2404	2303	2666	2549

SOURCE: U.S. Bureau of the Census, *U.S. Census of Population: 1960. Subject Reports. Women by Children Under 5 Years Old,* Final Report PC(2)–3C (Washington, D.C.: GPO, 1968), Tables 60 and 61, pp. 120–123.

Further corroboration of the disappearance of the correlation between fertility and socioeconomic status comes from an analysis of a national sample from which it was concluded that either of two conditions sufficed to remove the correlation: if both spouses were two generations away from farm residence, and/or if both spouses had attained a high level of schooling.[55] Still another report asserts that within a sample of urban women current family income was not related to family size, but satisfaction with current income and/or the expectation of a considerable increase in income was related to having larger families.[56]

RACE AND DIFFERENTIAL FERTILITY

Blacks constitute the largest racial minority in the United States (11 percent in 1966[57]). Blacks exceed whites in birth rates, death rates, rate of natural increase, and—somewhat inconsistently—the proportion of married women who are childless. In the pre-World War II years of 1935–1940, when the crude birth rate for the country as a whole was 18.8 births per 1000 population, the rates for whites and nonwhites were 18.0 and 26.0, respectively. When the national birth rate reached its peak for recent times in 1947 at 26.6, the rates for whites and nonwhites were 26.1 and 31.2, respectively. And by 1966 the

[55] Otis Dudley Duncan, "Farm Background and Differential Fertility," *Demography,* 2: 240–249 (1965).

[56] Ronald Freedman and Lolagene Coombs, "Economic Considerations in Family Growth Decisions," *Population Studies,* 20: 197–222 (1966).

[57] U.S. Bureau of the Census, *Current Population Reports—Social and Economic Conditions of Negroes in the United States,* Series P-23, No. 24, October 1967, p. 3.

two aggregates had respective rates of 17.4 and 26.1 to make up a national composite of 18.4.[58] (See Table 7.4.)

With respect to death rates it has been noted above that from birth the average white American lives about seven years longer than the average nonwhite. This represents a marked shrinkage since the turn of the century, when the difference in life expectancies was twice as great.[59]

The high birth rate of the nonwhite portion of the population might lead to the expectation that relatively few of the married nonwhite women would be childless. From Table 7.4 we see that in 1910 the two races were quite similar in this characteristic. This same table shows that the proportion of childless married women has been increasing much faster among nonwhites than among whites. Whereas the childless proportion of nonwhites was slightly lower in 1910, by 1964 the nonwhite rate was more than 50 percent larger than that of whites. Over those five decades nonwhites were becoming urbanized at a faster rate than whites. In 1910, 48 percent of the whites but only 27 percent of the nonwhites were classified as urban; by 1960 the proportion urban (by the "new" definition) was 69 percent for whites and 72 percent for nonwhites.[60] Perhaps the dramatic rise in childlessness among nonwhites is a response to the city, especially to being relegated to poorly paid and menial urban jobs.

RELIGION AND DIFFERENTIAL FERTILITY

With rare exceptions, such as the Shakers, organized religions in America have typically espoused values that are congenial to family life and to the bearing of children. Some religions put a high valuation on having many children. As is well known, the doctrines of the Roman Catholic Church forbid the use of chemical and mechanical means of avoiding conception. The one method of birth control of which the Church approves is periodic continence, or the use of the so-called safe period during the woman's menstrual cycle when it appears that she is unable to conceive. Father Thomas interprets the Church's position to the effect that human beings are believed to be agents of God. Since God is thought to have given man sex organs for the purpose of procreation, it is, according to the Catholic view, "gravely sinful" to seek the pleasure of intercourse while avoiding conception—the "natural" consequence of the sex function.[61] Pope Pius XII is quoted to the effect that God ordained that the bearing of children was the price of sexual gratification: "The mar-

---

[58] The blacks make up well over 90 percent of the nonwhites. Accordingly, statements regarding the nonwhite group apply very largely to blacks.

[59] For 1900–1902 the Metropolitan Life Insurance Company estimates life expectancy at birth for blacks as 33.8 years and for whites as 49.7, a difference of 15.9 years.—Metropolitan Life Insurance Company, *Statistical Bulletin*, Vol. 31, No. 2, March 1950, p. 2.

[60] *Statistical Abstract of the United States: 1961*, Table 21, p. 30.

[61] John L. Thomas, *The American Catholic Family* (Englewood Cliffs, N.J.: Prentice-Hall, 1956), p. 59.

TABLE 7.4

Crude Rates of Birth, Death, and Natural Increase and Net Reproduction Rates for Whites and Nonwhites, 1905–1910, 1930–1935, 1935–1940, 1940, 1945, 1947, 1950, 1952, 1960, 1966; and Proportion Childless among Women Ever Married, White and Nonwhite, 1910, 1940, 1950, 1960, 1966

RATE	1966	1960	1952	1950	1947	1945	1940	1935–40	1930–35	1905–10	1910
Crude birth rate											
Total	18.4	23.7	25.1	24.1	26.6	20.4	19.4	18.8	19.6	29.9[a]	
White	17.4	22.7	24.1	23.0	26.1	19.9	18.6	18.0	18.8	28.8[a]	
Nonwhite	26.1	32.1	33.6	33.3	31.2	26.5	26.7	26.0	26.5	38.1[a]	
Crude death rate											
Total	9.5	9.5	9.6	9.6	10.1	10.6	10.8	11.0	11.0	15.2[b]	
White	9.5	9.5	9.4	9.5	9.9	10.4	10.4	10.6	10.6	15.0[b]	
Nonwhite	9.7	10.1	11.0	11.2	11.4	11.9	13.8	14.4	14.9	23.4[b]	
Crude natural increase											
Total	8.9	14.2	15.5	14.5	16.5	9.8	8.6	7.8	8.6	14.7[a]	
White	7.9	13.2	14.7	13.5	16.2	9.5	8.2	7.4	8.2	13.8[a]	
Nonwhite	16.4	22.0	22.6	22.1	19.8	14.6	12.9	11.6	11.6	14.7[a]	
Net reproduction rate											
Total	1.29	1.72	1.56	1.44	1.51	1.14	1.02	0.98	0.98	1.34	
White	1.23	1.66	1.51	1.39	1.49	1.11	1.00	0.96	0.97	1.34	
Nonwhite	1.68	2.09	1.89	1.78	1.59	1.38	1.20	1.14	1.07	1.33	
Percent childless among women ever married 45–49											
Total	15.2[c]	18.1		19.5			16.1				
White	14.0[c]	17.1									9.6
Nonwhite	25.5[c]	26.7		28.1			23.4				8.7

[a] Estimated.   [b] Death Registration Area.   [c] These rates are as of June 1964.

SOURCE: For percent childless in 1964 and 1960, U.S. Bureau of the Census, *Current Population Reports—Population Characteristics*, Series P-20, No. 147, January 5, 1966, Table 1, p. 12 and U.S. Bureau of the Census, *U.S. Census of Population: 1960. U.S. Summary Detailed Characteristics*, PC(1)–1D, Table 19e: other data for 1966 and 1960, *Statistical Abstract of the United States: 1968*,

riage contract which confers upon husband and wife the right to satisfy the inclinations of nature, sets them up in a certain state of life, the married state. But upon couples who perform the act peculiar to their state, nature and the Creator impose the function of helping the conservation of the human race."[62] To use the method of the "safe period" continuously, he added, "would be a sin against the very meaning of conjugal life."[63] In July 1968 Pope Paul VI published the encyclical "Of Human Life" in which he upheld the Church's traditional prohibition of all artificial means of contraception. Ensuing debate, both in this country and abroad, reflected considerable dissent among clergy and laity from the Pope's position, and there was evidence that in the United States a majority of Catholics disagreed with the Pope in this matter.[64]

Other religious groups in this country vary in the degree to which they advocate large families as well as in their views on the use of contraceptives, but for the most part Protestant and Jewish religions in the United States have condoned the use of such devices.

Since Catholics constitute the largest non-Protestant group, and since they have an official policy in opposition to contraception, most of what little research is extant on religious differentials in fertility has been concerned with Catholic-non-Catholic or Catholic-Protestant comparisons. Over the period 1919–1933 Stouffer found that the Catholic fertility in Wisconsin was higher than that of non-Catholics, but that the fertility of Catholics was declining at a faster rate than the fertility of non-Catholics.[65] A study in Indianapolis in 1941 showed that Catholics had higher fertility than Protestants by nearly 20 percent, but that in mixed Protestant-Catholic marriages fertility was 10 percent lower than among Protestant couples.[66]

As was foreshadowed by Stouffer's study, there is some evidence of a narrowing of the gap between Catholic and Protestant fertility. Table 7.5 shows the number of children ever born per 1000 ever married women who in 1957 were either over 45 years of age or 15–44 years of age. Relevant to Stouffer's finding is the fact that whereas among the older women Catholics bore 11 percent more children than did Protestants (3056 and 2753, respectively), among the younger the difference is virtually invisible—2210 for Catholics and 2206 for Protestants. It seems likely that part of the elimination of the Catholic-Protestant differential is attributable to blacks, since most blacks are Protestants and since Table 7.4 shows the nonwhite (mostly black)

---

[62] Pius XII, "To the Italian Catholic Union of Midwives, October 29, 1951," quoted in Lorimer, *Culture and Human Fertility*, p. 195.

[63] *Ibid.*, p. 196.

[64] According to a Gallup Poll 54 percent of the Catholics interviewed (and 62 percent of the Protestants) opposed the Pope's position.—"U.S. Catholics Critical of Birth Control Ban," *Chicago Sun-Times*, September 1, 1968, p. 20.

[65] S. A. Stouffer, "Trends in the Fertility of Catholics and Non-Catholics," *American Journal of Sociology*, 41: 143–166 (1935).

[66] P. K. Whelpton and C. V. Kiser, "Social and Psychological Factors Affecting Fertility, I: Differential Fertility among 41,498 Native-White Couples in Indianapolis," *Milbank Memorial Fund Quarterly*, 21: 221–280 (1943).

TABLE 7.5

Number of Children Ever Born per 1000 Women by Age Category and Religious Affiliation: 1957

RELIGION	WOMEN 45 YEARS OLD AND OVER	WOMEN 15–44 YEARS OLD STANDARDIZED FOR AGE
Total	2798	2188
Protestant	2753	2206
Baptist	3275	2381
Lutheran	2382	1967
Methodist	2638	2115
Presbyterian	2188	1922
Other Protestant	2702	2234
Roman Catholic	3056	2210
Jewish	2218	a
Other, none, and not reported	2674	2075

[a] Rate not shown where base is less than 150,000.
SOURCE: *Statistical Abstract of the United States: 1961,* Table 51, p. 53.

fertility to have risen more than the white during the 1940's and 1950's (see especially the net reproduction rates).

A very similar result is reported in a study based on a national sample of 2713 white married women: the Protestants and the Catholics had an identical average number of births—2.1 per woman. The authors of the latter study assert the expectation, however, that the Catholic women interviewed will ultimately outproduce the Protestants by an average of 3.4 children to 2.9. Several factors entered into the expectation: (1) the Catholic women were married at a later average age than were the Protestant women, but (2) began bearing children sooner after marriage (23 months on the average before the first Catholic birth, 27 months for the Protestants), (3) were reproducing at a faster rate (33 months on the average between the first and second births for Catholics, and 36 months for Protestants), (4) on the average expected to have more children than did the Protestants, and (5) it is probable that a higher proportion of the Catholic women will continue in unbroken marriages because of the lower divorce rate of the Catholics.[67]

---

[67] Freedman, Whelpton, and Campbell, *op. cit.,* pp. 277–280. When couples of the three religious categories were matched on duration of marriage and five socioeconomic variables, the Catholics were highest both on average number of children born (2.0 for Catholics, 1.7 for Jews, and 1.4 for Protestants) and also on average number expected when the family would be completed (3.4 for Catholics, and 2.4 for both Jews and Protestants). Cf. Ronald Freedman, Pascal K. Whelpton, and John W. Smit, "Socio-Economic Factors in Religious Differentials in Fertility," *American Sociological Review,* 26: 608–614 (1961).

The narrowing of the spread between Catholic and non-Catholic birth rates suggests that the Catholics have been limiting family size and perhaps adopting Protestant attitudes toward family limitation. From a study in the middle 1950's we learn that 62 percent of a national sample of white wives gave unqualified approval to the general principle of spacing children and thus of preventing excessively large families. It may surprise no one to read that 72 percent of the Protestant and 88 percent of the Jewish wives approved unqualifiedly of limiting family size, but it may astonish some to learn that as many as 33 percent of the Catholic wives gave unqualified approval. That a favorable attitude toward family limitation represents an attenuated loyalty or submission to the Catholic Church is intimated by the negative correlation of this attitude with frequency of attending church: only 25 percent of the Catholic wives who report attending church "regularly" gave unqualified approval to family limitation as contrasted with 56 percent of the Catholic wives who report attending church "seldom or never."[68]

In the same study it is reported that a majority of the couples in each religious group had used some method of avoiding conception. Fifty-seven percent of the Catholic women reported using some contraceptive method: 27 percent reported using rhythm only, and 30 percent reported the use of some method unacceptable to the Church. (By contrast, 75 percent of the Protestant wives and 87 percent of the Jewish wives reported the use of some contraceptive method, but only 6 percent and 1 percent, respectively, reported the use of rhythm only.[69] It appears that Catholics typically start avoiding conception longer after marriage than do Protestants, i.e., when they are confronted with a rapidly growing family.[70] At the time of marriage Catholic women favor distinctly larger families than do Protestant women, but with the passage of time the Catholic women seem to revise their wishes downward. Catholic women who were interviewed in the middle 1950's and who were married in the years just before World War II said that at the time of marriage they wanted an average of 3.5 children. Protestant women of the same generation reported that at the time of marriage they had wanted an average of 2.9 children. Some fifteen to twenty years later the average Catholic wife's wish was down to 3.1 children, but the average Protestant wife was holding steady at 2.9 children.[71] From these considerations the authors of the study note that (a) a smaller percentage of Catholic than of Protestant wives reported their families to have been completely planned, and (b) as the sample of Catholics passes into the later stages of the childbearing period, it seems clear that more than the 57 percent reported above will use some method of

---

[68] *Ibid.*, pp. 156, 161. In a survey of the religious affiliations of clients of Planned Parenthood Clinics in seven cities it was found that Catholics were overrepresented in four of the cities.—Eugene J. Kanin, "Value Conflicts in Catholic Device-Contraceptive Usage," *Social Forces*, 35: 238–243 (1957).
[69] Freedman, Whelpton, and Campbell, *op. cit.*, pp. 104, 181.
[70] *Ibid.*, pp. 106–107.
[71] *Ibid.*, p. 280.

contraception, and more than the above noted 30 percent will turn to appliance methods "after trying rhythm and having accidental conceptions."[72] Finally, this study shows that the employment of the wife virtually eliminates the difference in the proportion of users of contraceptive techniques between Catholics and non-Catholics.[73]

Some Additional Remarks on Societal Organization and Culture

Before concluding our discussion of the function of replacement there are a few further observations to be made under each of the four levels of analysis referred to on page 155 and used throughout this chapter.

Over the past generation or so some countries have wanted more children and others less. Countries that look upon war as an acceptable technique for carrying out their (usually expansionist) national policies tend to favor maximizing their birth rates. Countries that had completed the demographic transition by the 1930's and that seemed to be faced at the time with the prospect of ultimately declining populations were interested in preventing any further drop in their birth rates. The former condition has prevailed in Fascist Italy, in the U.S.S.R., and in Communist China. Sweden and Canada are examples of the latter. Both conditions obtained in Nazi Germany. Under both conditions countries have sought to reward the bearing of children. In the authoritarian countries it has been usual to give both material and honorific rewards. In the democratic type of country the phrasing of the positive sanctions for having children has not emphasized heroic service to the fatherland so much as the equitable distribution of the cost of bearing and rearing the next generation.

On the other hand, some contemporary governments have been concerned about overpopulation. India has allocated resources to research and education on birth control and has initiated a program of sterilization.[74] India tried out in the city of Madras a policy of paying 30 rupees (about 6 dollars) to every poor person with three living children who "got himself or herself sterilized in a government hospital" there. The plan proved so "successful" that it was extended to several thousand villages. Since 1963 over 100,000 sterilizations have been performed each year. It is reported that by 1965 there were over 15,000 family-planning clinics, mostly in rural areas, and there were over 3000

---

[72] *Ibid.*, pp. 111, 182–183.

[73] *Ibid.*, p. 141. According to another report, 71 percent of the Catholics polled in a national survey approved the use of contraception, and 65 percent said they had used contraceptives.—"Catholics Found Easing Sex and Birth Curb Views: Survey by Jesuit School," *The New York Times,* October 1, 1968, pp. 1, 51.

[74] R. A. Gopalaswami, "Family Planning: Outlook for Government Action in India," in Clyde V. Kiser (ed.), *Research in Family Planning* (Princeton, N.J.: Princeton University Press, 1962), pp. 67–81.

surgical sterilization units. Contraceptives were being manufactured in both private and public sectors.[75] Closer to home there has been an active program in highly fertile Puerto Rico despite the vigorous protests of the Roman Catholic Church.[76]

In 1948 Japan adopted a law that was overtly not a measure to reduce population growth but to modify the National Eugenics Law of 1940. It had three provisions pertaining to fertility. These permitted "an extension of contraceptive facilities, the performance of abortions by private physicians for reasons of maternal health, and sterilization for reasons of excessive childbearing as measured by health criteria."[77] From 1949 through 1953 the number of induced abortions increased fourfold. In the latter year the number exceeded a million and was estimated to have terminated more than a third of all conceptions.[78] Between 1952 and 1954 the rates of use of contraceptive practice almost doubled among married women with children.[79] In the decade following enactment of the law Japan's crude birth rate dropped nearly 50 percent—from 33.7 per 1000 population in 1948 to 18.0 in 1958[80] and it averaged about 17 during the decade thereafter.[81]

Societal and Familial Organization

It has been the argument of this book that the familial system is important to its members to the degree that it is functional, i.e., to the extent that it provides goods and services, protection and security, care for the ill and for the aged, and so on. These are circumstances that make it desirable to have offspring. If a condition of high mortality be added, then there is an incentive to have many offspring in order to increase the probability that some will survive into adulthood. Conversely, where the society is organized so that

---

[75] B. L. Raina, "India," in Bernard Berelson *et al.* (eds.), *Family Planning and Population Programs* (Chicago: University of Chicago Press, 1966), pp. 111–121.

[76] José Nine Curt, "Puerto Rico," in Bernard Berelson *et al.* (eds.), *op. cit.*, pp. 227–233.

[77] Irene B. Taeuber, *The Population of Japan* (Princeton, N.J.: Princeton University Press, 1958), p. 269.

[78] *Ibid.*, p. 276. The high incidence of abortion in Japan has been interpreted as reflecting the acceptance of the small family concept but also "the lack of experience and skill in the use of other techniques for achieving this goal." The same writer concludes that under these conditions "if women cannot avoid pregnancy they will resort to induced abortion."—Yoshio Koya, "Why Induced Abortions in Japan Remain High," in Kiser, *op. cit.*, pp. 103–110. Quotation is from p. 109.

[79] *Ibid.*, p. 275.

[80] To place the problem in better perspective we may note that during that decade the crude birth rate of Guatemala, a highly fertile country, dropped from 52 to 48; the birth rate of East Germany, an area of low fertility, rose from 13 to 16; and the birth rate of the United States dropped from 27 to a fraction over 24.—Metropolitan Life Insurance Company, *Statistical Bulletin*, *loc. cit.*

[81] Minoru Muramatsu, "Japan," in Berelson *et al.* (eds.), *op. cit.*, pp. 7–19, at p. 13.

specialized economic structures, welfare structures, political, religious, and educational structures are so important that the individual's life goals are largely defined and attained outside the familial system, the importance of offspring diminishes.

A previous section of the present chapter ("The Downward Trend in Fertility: 1800–1936") made the point that the familial or other societal subsystem might be so organized as to delay the attainment of adult standing with the consequence of delaying marriage and parenthood. The property system of the rural Irish and the plight of the "boys" over 45 constituted an example. In 1941, 34 percent of Eire's men in the 45–49 age group and 26 percent of the women of those ages were still single.[82] A contrasting datum concerns the same year in Ceylon, where the proportion of women who had not married by the end of their reproductive period was 3.3 percent; the corresponding percentage in India a decade earlier hit the dramatically low figure of 0.8 percent.[83] The proportion of women who are childless is directly related to their age at marriage.[84]

Earlier passages have noted that the extended family system emphasizes filial solidarity, mutual assistance, early marriage, and childbearing. In the nuclear family system, by contrast, there is emphasis on privacy and individualism (i.e., freedom from the control of parents and other kinsmen) and upon marital solidarity. Under the latter system the assistance of relatives is viewed as more of an emergency measure. Since the man is immediately responsible for the support of his own wife and children, the age at which he marries (and whether or not he can marry at all) is, under the nuclear family system, especially responsive to the economic position of the potential bridegroom.

It has been asserted that traditional China had the extended family system, whereas America has the nuclear (or as it is sometimes called, the conjugal) family system. Some feeling for the consequences of this remark can be achieved by noting what happens to living arrangements under the two familial systems when economic conditions are favorable and when they are not. In Chapter 2 it was noted that among the traditional Chinese the size of household was directly correlated with socioeconomic status. That is, the ideal of having under one roof all living male members of a lineage plus their wives and unmarried daughters tended to be achieved only among the rich. In the United States, where the nuclear system is followed, the living arrangement that the traditional Chinese regarded as ideal would be spoken of as "doubling up," and would in general be avoided except under unfavorable economic conditions, e.g., the great depression, when the lack of financial means to support separate households forced the formation of households of extended

[82] Lorimer, *op. cit.*, p. 175.
[83] Davis and Blake, "Social Structure and Fertility," *loc. cit.*, p. 219.
[84] Wilson H. Grabill, Clyde V. Kiser, and Pascal K. Whelpton, *The Fertility of American Women* (New York: Wiley, 1958), Table 99, p. 291.

families, and World War II, when the shortage of housing had the same consequence. As economic conditions improve in the United States, the number of households increases faster than the number of families. In the United States, in other words, prosperity leads families to "undouble."[85]

Culture

It has been observed that the ideal number of children in our country seems to fluctuate "perhaps in response to economic conditions, perhaps in response to such intangibles as fashion."[86] Polls conducted in 1941, 1945, 1955, and 1960 reported on the number of children desired. Over this period the size of family generally preferred was in the range of two to four children, but the modal number desired moved up from two in 1941 to three in 1951 and to four in 1955 and 1960.[87] At the same time there has been a decrease both in the number of childless wives and in the number of wives having six or more children. Thus in America performance is converging onto the cultural ideal.[88]

There is evidence, however, that a sizable proportion of children born, even to married women, is unwanted. On the basis of interviews with married women under the age of forty-five Bumpass and Westoff have found that one fifth of all births and two fifths of black births were reported as unwanted by at least one spouse. From this finding it would appear that the diffusion and availability of contraceptive materials would result in a substantial reduction in the birth rate.[89]

---

[85] The percentage of married couples in the United States living with relatives was 5.1 in 1900; it rose to 6.1 in the depression year of 1933; it fell to 5.4 just before the country entered World War II in 1940; it was 8.6 in 1947 just after World War II; and it had fallen to 2.8 in 1957 after a considerable period of prosperity.—Paul C. Glick, David M. Heer, and John C. Beresford, "Social Change and Family Structure: Trends and Prospects," paper presented before the American Association for the Advancement of Science, Chicago, December 29, 1959.

[86] Freedman, Whelpton, and Campbell, op. cit., p. 223.

[87] Ibid., pp. 223–224; and Pascal K. Whelpton, Arthur A. Campbell, and John E. Patterson, Fertility and Family Planning in the United States (Princeton, N.J.: Princeton University Press, 1966), p. 37.

[88] Freedman, Whelpton, and Campbell, op. cit., p. 229. In a study of 145 couples at the time of their engagement and in marriage twenty years later it was found that the number of children they said they wanted at the time of engagement did not correlate very highly with the number they actually had at the later date, but the aggregate number wanted by all the couples at the earlier time corresponded reasonably well with the actual aggregate number two decades later. Cf. Charles F. Westoff, Elliot G. Mishler, and E. Lowell Kelly, "Preferences in Size of Family and Eventual Fertility Twenty Years After," American Journal of Sociology, 62: 491–497 (1957).

[89] Larry Bumpass and Charles F. Westoff, "The 'Perfect Contraceptive' Population," Science 169: 1177–1182 (1970).

Instrumental Factors

We have considered societal organization, culture, and familial organization, and we have observed that at each of these levels there are some factors that are favorable toward, and others that are inimical to, a high birth rate. With respect to the function of replacement, a final level of analysis involves the consideration of instrumental factors. These are procedures or practices that are means of facilitating or inhibiting the creation of new human beings; i.e., they militate for or against intercourse, conception, gestation, and the survival of the neonate.

Occasionally one hears a person "explain" a reduction in a birth rate as having been "caused" by the introduction of a contraceptive technique. It is the point of view of this writer that the use or nonuse of a contraceptive technique does not in itself constitute an adequate explanation of a variation in a birth rate; in addition it is necessary to note the societal, cultural, and familial conditions that result in the use or nonuse of the technique. For example, in a society having a scarcity of labor, a high rate of infant mortality, a high valuation of children, and a matrilineal and matrilocal system facilitating care of the young, there would be little reason to expect very effective use of contraception. On the other hand, contemporary Americans live in a world alive to the hazards of overpopulation and the misery of hungry millions, in a world where steam and electric power have rendered man's muscle obsolete and where the computer appears to many to offer the prospect of rendering man's brain obsolescent. If we add the further conditions of low infant mortality, unstable marriages in a small-family system, and the child's being an economic liability, we can see that the coming of a child—or of an additional child—may not be highly valued and indeed may appear calamitous. Under such conditions the development of efficient contraception can be expected to make possible the realization of a desired low birth rate. In this setting, moreover, it can be expected that efficient and inexpensive contraception makes possible the distinction between sexual expression for procreational and recreational purposes.[90]

As noted above, a factor is instrumental if its presence enables or facilitates the carrying out of the views, attitudes, policy, and implications for fertility of the societal and familial organization and of the culture. For the most part instrumental factors have to do with the avoidance of live births. They may be considered under the following headings:

> 1. Avoidance of intercourse: prohibitions and sanctions against intercourse among the unmarried and periods of sexual avoidance among the married, e.g., during lactation, periods of religious observance, and so-

---

[90] The author has developed this point at greater length in "Permanence and Change in the History of the American Family and Some Speculations as to its Future," *Journal of Marriage and the Family* 32: 6–15 (1970).

called unsafe periods. (We have considered above some factors tending toward late marriage and celibacy. Below we shall distinguish between the instrumental and cultural levels of analysis.)

2. Avoidance of conception: incomplete intercourse, sterilization, and contraception.

3. Avoidance of complete gestation: abortion.

4. Preventing neonate from becoming participating member of society: infanticide.

The one instrumental factor conducing *toward* live births is artificial insemination. (Of course in an obvious sense the negatives of the factors tabulated above are also conducive to live births.)

AVOIDANCE OF INTERCOURSE

Many societies proclaim that there should be no sexual intercourse between persons not married to each other. In American society an effort has been made to implement the sexual avoidance of the unmarried both through indoctrinating the young with avoidance attitudes and through institutionalized procedures, such as segregating the sexes in dormitories. With respect to the former it has been usual to impress upon the child that extramarital sex relations are morally wrong and that they might well lead to undesirable consequences—punishment and/or ridicule on being discovered, venereal disease, and pregnancy for the girl.[91]

Some societies rely more on building avoidance into the personalities of the young; some more on institutional arrangements. Levi cites southern Italy of the 1930's as an example of the latter since the peasants are reported as having regarded love or sexual attraction as "so powerful a force of nature that no amount of will-power can resist it." If a man and a woman were to meet in a sheltered place, he continues, it was expected that intercourse would inevitably occur.[92]

This brings us to our distinction between a cultural factor and an instrumental factor that is in the culture. The distinction hinges upon whether or not there appears to be an openly recognized direct connection between the practice and the desirability of children. The positive valuation of children in a unilineal extended family system is a cultural factor in the sense that it leads to high fertility because children are desired. We have noted that some countries are becoming very conscious of the hazards of overpopulation, and it

[91] For the pragmatic moralist the undesired consequence *is* what makes the behavior morally wrong. In a sample reportedly corresponding to the upper 20 percent of the United States socioeconomically, the Kinsey group finds that 6 percent of the girls who had premarital coitus at or before the age of 15 had become premaritally pregnant; by the ages of 20 and 30 the percentages were 13 and 21, respectively.—Paul H. Gebhard, Wardell B. Pomeroy, Clyde E. Martin, and Cornelia V. Christenson, *Pregnancy, Birth and Abortion* (New York: Harper & Row, 1958), pp. 39, 65.

[92] Carlo Levi, *Christ Stopped at Eboli* (New York: Farrar, Straus, 1947), pp. 99–100.

seems possible that in these countries children may come—for a time—to be regarded as undesirable. This would be a cultural factor. On the other hand, the practice in our country of segregating adolescent boys and girls in separate dormitories has not been animated by an aversion toward children or a wish to depress the birth rate but by a wish to avoid the act of intercourse itself. For this reason such a practice of segregation is treated here as an instrumental factor.

Instrumental factors among married couples include such a cultural prohibition, reported to be widespread among African tribes, as that against inducing pregnancy in a nursing mother.[93] In India there is a practice whereby a wife goes to her parental home for a visit of a few months after the birth of each of her first two or three children. With respect to India, furthermore, it has been estimated that because of religious observances husbands and wives avoid each other sexually on an average of twenty-four days a year.[94] On Tikopia, a small island in the southwestern Pacific, there is a sanction against a woman's becoming pregnant if she is the mother of a married man, and a somewhat similar avoidance has been reported for Japan.[95] In our own society military service and even business trips must reduce the frequency of marital intercourse although the effect has no doubt been mitigated by the development of rapid transportation. Finally, there is the avoidance of the woman's period of ovulation by those who follow the so-called safe-period method of avoiding conception.

AVOIDANCE OF CONCEPTION

Here we consider methods of avoiding conception although intercourse does take place. One of the most widespread methods is *coitus interruptus* or incomplete intercourse. Another technique is the sterilization of one of the mates. (We have noted above that Japan and Puerto Rico are making considerable use of this technique.) Finally there are the various mechanical and chemical means for preventing conception—condom, diaphragm, IUD, jelly, and "the pill." In societies that are not industrialized such devices tend to be prohibitively expensive,[96] and the people lack the information to use them effectively. As Davis and Blake observe, these peoples have little understanding of the physiology of reproduction and tend therefore not only to be inefficient but also inept to the point of being unhealthful and unesthetic in their use. As examples of unpleasant and unhygienic contraception they cite an Egyptian practice of inserting dung into the vagina and a Central African practice of inserting rags or finely chopped grass.[97]

[93] Lorimer, *Culture and Human Fertility*, p. 86.
[94] Davis and Blake, "Social Structure and Fertility," loc. cit., p. 232.
[95] Lorimer, *op. cit.*, pp. 108, 162.
[96] It has been reported that the price of an abortion in Japan is five dollars, and since this is less than the cost of a year's supply of contraceptives, more than half of the pregnancies in Japan terminate in induced abortions.—Gebhard *et al.*, *op. cit.*, p. 219.
[97] Davis and Blake, "Social Structure and Fertility," loc. cit., p. 223.

AVOIDANCE OF COMPLETE GESTATION

An abortion is the expulsion of the human fetus from the uterus before it is capable of living outside. An abortion is spontaneous if it is not the consequence of an intentional act on the part of the mother or some other person. Otherwise it is spoken of as an induced abortion. As Gebhard *et al.* observe, induced abortion is an ancient method of trying to control fertility. Not only have historic and primitive peoples used magic and externally applied physical treatment (massaging, pounding, or compressing the abdomen of the pregnant woman) but they have employed their versions of currently utilized techniques of surgery and drugs.[98] Induced abortion has been completely accepted in some modern states, e.g., Japan and the U.S.S.R. Countries with a Christian tradition vary from a qualified acceptance (in Scandinavia) to no provision for legal therapeutic abortion (in Bolivia and Colombia).[99]

There seems to be an impression that induced abortion is engaged in exclusively by unmarried women who "get caught" with a pregnancy. Although it is probably true that a greater proportion of the pregnancies of unmarried than of married women terminate in induced abortion,[100] yet the number of induced abortions performed on married women seems to be considerably greater than the number performed on unmarried women. It has been estimated that as many as 90 percent are performed on married women.[101] In interpreting this observation it is important to recall that of course married women have vastly more pregnancies than do single women. Between one fifth and one quarter of the married women in the Kinsey study had had an induced abortion. Although the text is not explicit, this appears to include abortions occurring before these women were married.[102]

The gathering of data on sexual behavior in general is a difficult task; the fact that many abortions are illegally performed makes data on this topic especially inaccessible. Some conception of the magnitude of ignorance concerning the statistics of induced abortion in the United States is suggested by the fact that after reviewing the available evidence a committee of experts concluded that the number of abortions induced annually in this country probably fell somewhere between 200,000 and 1,200,000.[103]

---

[98] *Op. cit.*, pp. 189–191.

[99] Gebhard *et al., op. cit.,* pp. 215–247. There is information on the practice of and the law concerning abortion in Scandinavia, Japan, Germany, the U.S.S.R. and Finland in Mary Steichen Calderone, *Abortion in the United States: A Conference Sponsored by the Planned Parenthood Federation of America, Inc., at Arden House and The New York Academy of Medicine* (New York: Hoeber, 1958), sec. 3 and Appendix C. On legal aspects of abortion in the United States, see sec. 4 and Appendix A.

[100] Gebhard *et al., op. cit.,* pp. 56, 74.

[101] Norman Himes and Abraham Stone, *Practical Birth Control Methods* (New York: Modern Age, Inc., 1938), p. 157.

[102] Gebhard *et al., op. cit.,* pp. 93–94.

[103] Calderone, *op. cit.,* sec. 10.

Although the Kinsey study has been criticized on various grounds, it is probably the best source of data on induced abortions in the United States. The committee referred to in the preceding paragraph reported that because the more educated, the more urban, and probably those of higher socioeconomic status were overrepresented in the study, Kinsey's female subjects were not representative of the female population of the United States.[104] It seems preferable, however, to keep these points in mind as we look at Kinsey's data rather than to reject the Kinsey study and remain in complete darkness on the topic.

Of the women in the Kinsey study who were past thirty-six years of age 8 percent had had induced abortions.[105] Nearly half the women in their sample had had premarital coitus.[106] The women in the sample had had 355 pregnancies that terminated prior to marriage. Of these, 6 percent terminated in live births, 5 percent in spontaneous abortions, and 89 percent in induced abortions. Of the women in this study who married while they were pregnant 75 percent terminated pregnancies in live births (as opposed to 6 percent of those who were not married). As the authors observe, the fact that "the vast majority of pre-marital pregnancies terminate in induced abortion" reflects the force of the sanctions against pregnancy outside the marital relationship.[107] But there is ample evidence of a shift in the American norms concerning abortion: some states (e.g., California, Colorado, Georgia, Hawaii, Maryland, New York, and North Carolina) have liberalized the grounds for legal induced abortions, a hospital insurance association has included abortion as a coverable illness (and simultaneously provided maternity benefits for single women), at least one mutual aid fund has been established to help college girls pay for abortions, the American Civil Liberties Union has asked for an end to abortion bans, a group of clergymen has announced a "Clergymen's Consultation Service on Abortion," the American College of Obstetricians and Gynecologists has endorsed abortion on broadly stated medical grounds, and a referral service has been established to assist out-of-state women in obtaining abortions under the liberalized laws of New York.[108]

Sweden, Denmark, and the United Kingdom have more liberal laws concerning abortion than have most of the states in this country and most countries with a Christian tradition. In both of these countries the law recognizes "medical indications, extended medical indications, eugenic indications, and

[104] *Ibid.* Among the signers of the report was Paul K. Gebhard, who had been a member of Kinsey's staff and who succeeded to the direction of the project after Kinsey's death.

[105] Gebhard *et al., op. cit.,* p. 56.

[106] Alfred C. Kinsey, Wardell B. Pomeroy, Clyde E. Martin, and Paul H. Gebhard, *Sexual Behavior in the Human Female* (Philadelphia: Saunders, 1953), p. 286.

[107] Gebhard *et al., op. cit.,* p. 59.

[108] "Coeds Here Tell of 'Slush Funds' To Help Girls Pay for Abortions," *The New York Times,* January 19, 1968, p. 22; "A.C.L.U. Asks End to Abortion Bans," *The New York Times,* March 25, 1968, p. 35; "Clergymen Offer Abortion Advice," *The New York Times,* May 22, 1967, p. 1; "Ob-Gyn College Takes a Bold Stand on Abortion," *Medical World News,* May 24, 1968, pp. 22–23.

humanitarian indications."[109] Such laws fall considerably short, however, of making abortion available upon the woman's request. On the other hand, Japan and the countries of Eastern Europe have virtually voluntary abortion. In Eastern Europe, abortions are typically performed gratis for medical reasons but for a fee otherwise. In 1963 Hungary had 13.1 live births and 0.2 stillbirths per 1000 population and 17.2 legal and 3.4 other abortions. Thus all abortions outnumbered live births by more than three to two. In Czechoslovakia there were 7.1 abortions and 16.9 live births per 1000 in 1963, and here live births were more than twice as numerous as abortions.[110]

INFANTICIDE

Kingsley Davis asserts that primitive cultures generally permit or encourage infanticide under such conditions as the wish to limit size of family, the occurrence of a plural birth, the occurrence of deformity or illness in the child, or the appearance of an unwanted female.[111] Remarking that numerous societies have practiced infanticide, Sir James Frazer makes such observations as "the Polynesians seem regularly to have killed two-thirds of their children."[112] Lorimer notes that infanticide was common among Japanese peasants of the Tokugawa period and that female infanticide was a widely recognized practice in China.[113] Thompson asserts that infanticide, especially with respect to females, has been widely practiced in India and that in Shanghai "many thousands of infants [have been] annually gathered from the streets by the free burial societies," and he concludes that in the pre-World War II years something like a third to a half of the babies born there were killed or allowed to die immediately after birth.[114]

ARTIFICIAL INSEMINATION

Artificial insemination is a procedure whereby the seminal fluid is taken from a man, placed into a tube, perhaps frozen for a time, and is subsequently injected into the vagina of a woman. As we saw above, Professor Muller has suggested that the seminal fluid of outstanding men should be used in this fashion for the improvement of the human race. Presumably the demand for

---

[109] Christopher Tietze, "Induced Abortion and Sterilization as Methods of Fertility Control," in Mindel C. Sheps and Jeanne Clare Ridley (eds.), *Public Health and Population Change: Current Research Issues* (Pittsburgh: University of Pittsburgh Press, 1966), pp. 400–416, at p. 402; "Legal Abortion Upsurge—Is the U.S. Ready," *Medical World News*, December 26, 1969, p. 4.

[110] Tietze, *op. cit.*, p. 408.

[111] Kingsley Davis, *Human Society* (New York: Macmillan, 1948), p. 560.

[112] Sir James George Frazer, *The Golden Bough: A Study in Magic and Religion* (abr. ed.; New York: Macmillan, 1958), p. 341.

[113] Lorimer, *op. cit.*, pp. 161–162.

[114] Warren S. Thompson, *Population Problems* (3d ed.; New York: McGraw-Hill, 1942), p. 8.

this arrangement arises only when sexual intercourse fails to result in a desired pregnancy.

A medical society in this country, the American Society for the Study of Sterility, has approved artificial insemination if the following conditions are met:

1. Urgent desire of the couple to have such therapy applied to the solution of their infertility problems.
2. Careful selection by the physician of a biologically and genetically satisfactory donor.
3. The opinion of the physician, after thorough study, that the couple will make desirable parents.[115]

As might be expected, this procedure has been condemned by the Roman Catholic Church.[116]

Artificial insemination poses some fascinating legal problems: Is the wife guilty of adultery? Is the child illegitimate? Is the child entitled to inherit property from his mother's husband?[117] A court in New York has held in the affirmative on the question of legitimacy.[118]

Summary

The replacement of members of a society who are lost through death, out-migration, or capture can be made up in part through in-migration or the capture of members of other societies. Every society, however, looks upon sexual reproduction as the principal means of replacing human losses.

When there is no set of social or cultural conditions that tend to lower fertility among relatively stable populations, Lorimer believes that the average number of live births tends to be in the range of six to eight.[119] The degree to which reproduction actually does take place is the consequence of factors that may be analyzed at four levels: societal organization, culture, familial organization, and instrumental factors. Under societal organization we consider such structures and functions outside the family as the manner in which

---

[115] "Doctors Endorse Test-Tube Births: Artificial Insemination Gets Approval in Sterility Study as 'Ethical and Moral,'" *The New York Times,* June 5, 1955, p. 53.

[116] "Pontiff Repeats Condemnation of Test Tube Births," *Chicago Sun-Times,* September 16, 1958, p. 7. Similarly, the Church is reputed to have condemned a report of a successful fertilization of human egg cells with spermatozoa in a test tube; i.e., the Church leaders branded as a violation of natural law an effort by British scientists to achieve Aldous Huxley's proposal of oviparous reproduction.—"First Test-Tube Fertilization?" *Medical World News,* March 7, 1969, p. 17.

[117] Clifton Daniel, "British Peers Grapple with Legal Problem Posed by Use of Artificial Insemination," *The New York Times,* March 17, 1949.

[118] "Paternity Rights Upheld by Court: Justice Rules in Case of Child Brought into Being through Artificial Insemination," *The New York Times,* January 14, 1948.

[119] Lorimer, *op. cit.,* p. 57.

economic production is organized. For our purposes the key cultural factor is the value placed upon parenthood and children; it appears that urbanization without industrialization is not sufficient to bring about a change in the traditional value-system. In familial organization we are interested in such matters as the nature of the kinship system, with its pattern of claims and obligations; the rules and practices concerning residence; the relative emphasis upon filial solidarity as compared with marital solidarity; and the degree to which the activities of husband and wife are located in or away from the home. By instrumental factors we refer to considerations affecting the frequency of sexual intercourse, conception, gestation, and whether a neonate is allowed to survive.

The birth rates and death rates that prevailed in this country during the colonial and early national period were much higher than those that have prevailed in the present century. The decline in the birth rate from 1800 to the great depression of the 1930's is interpreted societally in terms of the superseding of the family as a productive unit by larger-scale economic units. Culturally the sharp drop in the death rate removed the desirability of a large progeny to assure the survival of a few while the shifting locus of production changed the valuation of children from an asset to a liability at a time when many people were unable to afford necessities. With respect to familial organization it is noted not only that the urban-industrial social order was taking the husband out of the home to his employment but also that many wives were leaving the household to seek gainful employment. At the instrumental level we have noted the development of efficient and relatively inexpensive contraception.

That these factors have continued to operate is suggested by the fact that although for a decade following the depression the birth rate rose (it crested in 1947 at a level more than 40 percent above the depression low), the latter part of the period since the depression has seen a resumption of a low birth rate. In this interpretation the depression and World War II represent short-run influences on a downward trend that has been apparent for the greater part of two centuries.

Certain clear-cut reproductive differentials have been associated with social characteristics. In line with the theme of this book we should expect rural regions to have higher birth rates than urban. This seems to have been true over the period for which data exist, i.e., since 1800. The relation of socioeconomic status to fertility is somewhat complex. Historically the most obvious feature of this correlation is a negative relation between the two series; i.e., the people of low status and poverty have had burgeoning birth rates, whereas those of (at least relative) wealth and high status have at times failed to reproduce themselves. Tentatively it would seem that there has been little effort below the status of the middle class to restrict fertility. (The meaning of middle class is presented in the next chapter.) The writer speculates that a pattern may be emerging whereby from the lower fringe of the middle class on through the higher socioeconomic strata there is considerable consensus that families should have about four children—if they can afford them. Concern over the providing of food, clothing, shelter, education, medical care, and other goods and services then is coming to allocate children, like other commodities, on the basis of ability to pay. It should be emphasized, however, that the data on the correlation between fertility and socioeconomic status are not conclusive and hence that the foregoing interpretation remains for the present a hypothesis rather than a conclusion.

For the most part, when we speak of nonwhite people in the United States, we are talking about blacks. Nonwhites have a higher birth rate than whites and also a markedly higher rate of marital, and presumably of familial, disorganization.

With respect to religious affiliation the best documented reproductive differential is between Catholics and non-Catholics. With their official condemnation of "artificial" means of contraception, Catholics have a higher birth rate than non-Catholics. In the United States the Catholics appear to have a high rate of violation of their official norms about birth control.

Conditions with respect to all four levels of analysis appear to call for a relatively small number of children—in the range of two to four per ever married woman. Given the low death rate, however, variation within this range can mean either a relatively stable population or one growing at a quite rapid rate. With only 2.13 children per married woman required to replace a stable population, we have seen that the three-child family will bring about a very sizable increase in the American population.

In a developed country like the United States societal conditions that affect the birth rate appear to include wars and economic conditions, and there is some reason to believe that the latter work through job opportunities for young workers and the prospect for assured and increasing income.

8

Position Conferring: *functional corollary of the family's basic societal function*

Introduction

In Chapter 1 it was noted that a (social) position was a location in a social structure defined by a set of social norms and that a (social) status was a position plus the connotation of invidious evaluation, differential prestige, and hierarchy. From the postulate that one has as many social positions as there are social systems in which one has membership—in other words, that membership implies position—it follows that at birth one acquires as many social positions as there are social systems into which one is born. A distinction is made between positions that are inherited, i.e., *ascribed,* and those that are earned or won, i.e., *achieved*.

The proposition that the familial is the social system that is universally legitimated to carry out the replacement function means that it is customary everywhere for the newborn to have membership in a family and therefore an ascribed familial position. That it is customary does not imply, however, that every neonate acquires such membership; the lack of such membership is the condition known as illegitimacy.

With the passage of time the growing child is admitted to other (extrafamilial) social systems—the peer group, the work group, and so on. To varying degrees the particular systems he joins and his positions in them are influenced by the particular family from which he emerges. In Great Britain, for example, it has been traditional for the son of a noble family to enter the army at commissioned rank and for a boy from a modest family to become an enlisted man. The *position-conferring function* refers to this process of launching new members into social systems and thus integrating them into the total society.

As with other functions, we are interested in the degree to which position-conferring function is carried out by the family, to what degree by other structures, and the conditions associated with such variation. For example, to what degree is a brokerage house interested in knowing the family from which a prospective employe comes and to what extent from which college? More generally, under what conditions are the recruiting officials of the receiving social system more interested in the candidate's family and the social characteristics his family implies, and under what conditions in his other memberships and social characteristics? In any given case the answer signifies the relative importance of the family and other social structures with respect to the position-conferring function.

The family confers on the newborn ascribed positions that orient him in his relations with other members of the family (as designated by such kinship terms as brother, father, niece, and so on), and that the newborn shares with the other members of the family and orient him in relation to members of the society outside the family (in terms of citizenship, religious affiliation, and membership in a community). We shall speak of the former as "family-oriented" and the latter as "society-oriented" positions. We may further distinguish between the society-oriented positions conferred by the family that originate in the particular family, e.g., being known as a Medici or a Kallikak, and those that the family transmits to its members from societal categories to which the family belongs, e.g., being urban, Protestant, middle-class. An analysis of family-oriented positions appears in Chapter 12. Part Five takes the individual through a life cycle of relationships with other family members. Accordingly, the nature of family-oriented positions is treated extensively (although somewhat implicitly) in that section. The present chapter is concerned primarily with the positions (and statuses) that relate persons to members of the society outside the family (i.e., with society-oriented positions) and with the degree to which such positions are conferred by the family or by other societal structures.

Structures other than the family confer positions, especially achieved positions, e.g., a corporation's president, a religious order's novitiate. Societies vary greatly in the latitude provided for achieved positions. The presence of achieved positions implies social mobility and an open-class society. The purpose of the present chapter is to develop some general principles concerning the position-conferring function of the family and to illustrate these principles with data from the United States.

Points of Emphasis

When a child is born into a family he acquires legitimacy. This means that the family confers upon the neonate a society-oriented position that defines his relationships to other members of the society. Simultaneously the family confers another ascribed position (or set of roles) which defines his relationships to other family members in terms of age, sex, and kinship. The illegitimately born child does not receive either of these two kinds of ascribed position. Conceptually it makes sense to regard bastardy not as a peculiar social position but as a lack of a social position. The illegitimately born child has no family, and his position vis-à-vis society is undefined.

Since the ethnic background, religious affiliation, and social class by which the neonate will be characterized are determined—initially, at least—by the family into which he is born, the neonate's initial position forecasts with which categories of people he will associate, what kinds of experiences he will have, and what characteristics he will develop as an adult. Habits of dress and speech are familiar as cues to a person's statuses. Less obvious but equally differentiating are habits of thought and of aspiration. To some degree interaction within the family sets these habits for the individual and thus stamps on him the marks of statuses conferred by the family. In addition, through placing the child in a particular community, in a particular school, or the like, the family foreordains his subcultural characteristics.

A society with an open-class system provides a man with an opportunity to alter some of his statuses. As he approaches adulthood—when vertical mobility usually takes place—he finds that his starting point in the hierarchy of socioeconomic statuses is determined to a large degree by the socioeconomic status of his family of orientation.

Social Position at Birth:
Legitimacy and illegitimacy

A child born outside the family is spoken of as illegitimate, a bastard, as a *nullius filius* or son of nobody. Human reproduction being what it is, a society usually can link a child to a mother; the question of the child's paternity is the nub of the doubt that may exist. In describing what he calls the "principle of legitimacy," Malinowski asserts that in all societies the father has been regarded to be indispensable to the child, that everywhere it is thought necessary to have a masculine link between the child and the rest of the society.[1] A necessary condition for legitimacy is that an offspring should have a social father, i.e., an adult male who assumes paternal rights and duties with respect to the offspring although the adult male may not be the biological father (or genitor) of the offspring. Although in some societies "father" means "mother's husband," with no necessary reference to biological paternity, the principle of legitimacy, like the incest taboo, is universally recognized.

It is somewhat hazardous to impute rational bases to the mores, but it is reasonably clear that the principle of legitimacy tends to enforce a certain functional efficiency. This efficiency results from the fact that the family is the only societal structure that is almost universally organized to provide care for

---

[1] Bronislaw Malinowski, "Marriage," *Encyclopaedia Britannica* (1929), XIV, 940–950.

and to socialize the very young child. (The Israeli kibbutz described in Chapter 3 is one of the very rare exceptions.) In most societies it would be inefficient to have procreation take place outside the family because of the absence of any institutionalized ways of taking care of the infant and young child outside the family. Penalties attached to illegitimacy, therefore, function to keep reproduction within the family, the one structure usually equipped to care for and to socialize the young child.[2] As Goode observes, however, Malinowski's principle of legitimacy rests upon the function of position conferring, and not of protection: "the bastard daughter of a count is still illegitimate even if he 'protects' her."[3]

In most parts of the world, including the United States, it is difficult to estimate the number of illegitimate births. Stockholm and Copenhagen[4] are reported as having had illegitimacy rates in the range of one out of seven to one out of eight in the 1950's. In Latin America, which reports generally higher rates of illegitimacy than do the countries of Europe and North America, the rates in the late 1950's were from one out of four to three out of four.[5] Such data as are available concerning illegitimacy in the United States indicate that over the years 1938–1955 about 4 percent of all live births were illegitimate; since 1955 the reported rate has increased considerably, being a bit over 8 percent in 1966. The proportion is much higher for nonwhites (28 percent of all live births in 1966) than for whites (4 percent).[6] Goode asserts that in the United States and Western Europe the illegitimacy rates seem to range from 4 or 5 percent to about 11 percent.[7]

To read such data as rates of illegitimacy without some cultural context, however, is to risk arriving at false conclusions. In some societies it is approved that marriage should occur after the birth of the first child, whereas in others the custom of common-law marriage may cause children to be reported as illegitimate. Some scholars believe that there is ground for distinguishing between legal illegitimacy and social illegitimacy. In Latin America, for example, there is a form of association known as "consensual union."[8] This form of association differs from common-law marriage of Anglo-Saxon coun-

---

[2] Kingsley Davis, "Illegitimacy and the Social Structure," *American Journal of Sociology*, 45: 215–233 (1939), and "The Forms of Illegitimacy," *Social Forces*, 18: 77–89 (1939).

[3] William J. Goode, "Illegitimacy in the Caribbean Social Structure," *American Sociological Review*, 25: 21–30 (1960), at p. 27.

[4] Harold T. Christensen, "Cultural Relativism and Premarital Sex Norms," *American Sociological Review*, 25: 31–39 (1960). Cf. Table 1, p. 33.

[5] M. F. Nimkoff, "Illegitimacy," *Encyclopaedia Britannica* (1963), vol. 12, p. 83.

[6] For the period 1938–1950 see Conrad Taeuber and Irene B. Taeuber, *Changing Population of the United States* (New York: Wiley, 1958), p. 266. More recent data appear in: U.S. Department of Health, Education, and Welfare, *Vital Statistics of the United States: 1966, Vol. I—Natality* (Washington, D.C.: GPO, 1968), Table 1-25, p. 1-23.

[7] Goode, "Illegitimacy in the Caribbean," *loc. cit.*, p. 22.

[8] In Spanish the term *concubinato* is used to designate consensual union and concubinage.

tries in that the former is not a legally recognized marriage. These scholars assert that whereas children born of a consensual union carry no stigma and are therefore socially legitimate, they are regarded as legally illegitimate and therefore cause the rates of illegitimacy in Latin-American countries to be spuriously high. On the other hand, Goode believes that the consensual union is not completely legitimate in a social sense, and from this belief it follows that the children of such a union would not be regarded as entirely legitimate in either a social or a legal sense.[9] From her study of fertility and family structure among lower-class Jamaicans Blake concludes that in that setting a common-law union is a relationship into which a woman is typically forced after illegitimate childbearing and consequent loss of status, that such unions last about two years on the average, that the proportion in such unions hits a peak for men in the late thirties (32 percent of those 35–39 years old) and for women in the latter twenties (30 percent of those 25–29), and that by the ages 45–49 over half of both sexes enter into the preferred relationship of legal marriage.[10]

Three questions follow in the wake of an illegitimate birth. (1) Who will assume responsibility for the child? (2) How will the child acquire his social positions? (3) Can the child inherit and from whom?

What are the conditions that make it relatively easy for the mother to keep the illegitimate child with her, to support the child, and to confer some sort of social position upon the child? As Goode has observed, circumstances favor the child's remaining with the mother (1) where the mother or mother's mother is dominant in the household (because no father is present), and (2) in lower strata of society where the commitment to the norm of legal marriage is relatively weak and the punishment for deviation and the reward for conformity are relatively low.[11] (In the United States the "matrifocal" pattern denoted in [a] is especially common among blacks of the lower social strata. We have observed that in 1966 the rate of reported illegitimacy among nonwhites was a little over six times that of the whites.) In a patrilineal and patriarchal society, on the other hand, an illegitimate child remaining with his mother is in a more conspicuously anomalous position.

Direct care and supervision of children lacking parents who can care for them has been handled in a variety of settings in this country: indenture,

---

[9] Goode, "Illegitimacy in the Caribbean," loc. cit., esp. p. 26.

[10] Judith Blake, *Family Structure in Jamaica: The Social Context of Reproduction* (New York: Free Press, 1961), pp. 111, 168, 178. Cf. also Fernando Henriques, *Family and Colour in Jamaica* (London: MacGibbon & Kee, 1953); Raymond T. Smith, *The Negro Family in British Guina: Family Structure and Social Status in the Villages* (London: Routledge, 1956); William J. Goode, "Illegitimacy, Anomie, and Cultural Penetration," *American Sociological Review*, 26: 910–925 (1961); M. G. Smith, *West Indian Family Structure* (Seattle: University of Washington Press, 1962); and Nancie L. Solien Gonzalez, *Black Carib Household Structure: A Study of Migration and Modernization* (Seattle: University of Washington Press; 1969).

[11] Goode, "Illegitimacy in the Caribbean," p. 30.

almshouses, public and private orphanages, and boarding home placements.[12] The widspread conviction that a child needs love in order to be properly socialized and the belief that the mother is more likely than anyone else to give love to the child lend force to the conclusion that the child should stay with the mother and that, if necessary, the state should lend financial assistance to make this possible. Sentiments about motherhood and the rights of a parent give further weight to this view. On the other hand, doubts as to the fitness for parenthood of an unwed mother plus the ever-present desire to avoid higher taxes bring pressures for the contrary conclusion. Thus the question as to who should assume responsibility for the illegitimate child is one that elicits conflicting responses of humanitarianism and indignation—both moral and economic.

In 1909 the first White House Conference on Children stated that children should not be removed from their homes because of poverty alone. In 1935 the Congress of the United States established a national policy of providing financial aid to a mother and her children when they did not have the support of a breadwinner. This program, subsequently called Aid to Families with Dependent Children (AFDC), enabled a mother to keep her children with her. Initially more than 40 percent of the beneficiaries of the program had suffered the loss of a husband-father through death. Because of social insurance benefits (and probably also because of a drop in the death rates) the proportion of beneficiaries who are eligible through death of the husband-father has dropped to between 10 and 15 percent. More recently the great majority of the families who receive aid under this program have undergone "family breakup and unmarried parenthood."[13]

The high cost of welfare programs results in cries of outrage from taxpayers and legislators who complain that the state is coddling miscreants and subsidizing sin. Woven through this complex of sentiments is the fact that blacks are heavily overrepresented among the poor and hence among those on welfare rolls. The suggestion to give information about contraception to unmarried mothers is one of the milder reactions.[14] It has been proposed that

[12] Elizabeth G. Meier, "Foster Care for Children," in Russell H. Kurtz (ed.), *Social Work Year Book: 1960* (New York: National Association of Social Workers, 1960), pp. 277–285.

[13] Maurice O. Hunt, "Child Welfare," in Kurtz, *op. cit.*, pp. 141–157. Quotation is from p. 144. Cf. also Bureau of Public Assistance, *Illegitimacy and Its Impact on the Aid to Dependent Children Program* (Washington, D.C.: GPO, 1960), Chart III, p. 32.

[14] "Birth-Control Role Urged for ADC," *Chicago Sun-Times*, December 11, 1959, p. 36. And since the respectable elders of the community cannot decide whether the sexual pleasure of the women or the illegitimate children they bear constitute the greater affront, the suggestion to give contraceptive information and devices to unmarried women, whether mothers or not, elicits opposition on the ground that to do so is to encourage sin. But while some of the elders of the establishment resist the providing of contraceptive devices and instruction on the ground that it facilitates and rewards sin, some black nationalists agree vehemently with the conclusion for the very different reason that it is an alleged establishmentarian plot to commit black genocide. An earlier version of the AFDC program was called Aid to Dependent Children, and hence ADC.

the amount of relief payments be reduced for mothers who have more than one illegitimate child and that women "who stray too often from the paths of orthodoxy" be sterilized.[15] In Philadelphia a judge recommended that unwed mothers of three or more children be sent to jail for terms from three to six months.[16] In California two women who had been getting support for their illegitimate children were convicted of having fraudulently accepted aid for dependent children. They were given probation on the condition that they not get pregnant and were later ordered back to jail for having violated this condition.[17] The results of a study of ADC cases in Chicago will be summarized in Chapter 23.

Illegitimate children are sometimes placed in foster homes until they can be located in adoptive homes. Placement of a child in a foster home leaves two problems unsettled: how the child is to be supported financially and how the child is to acquire social positions. On the former point foster parents are usually paid for their services, and not infrequently the payer is a social agency, either public or private.[18]

Vincent has studied a series of unmarried mothers and has found that, in contrast to those who placed their babies for adoption, those who kept their babies had less education, lower socioeconomic status, a higher proportion of broken parental homes, a greater number of siblings, and more unhappy and mother-dominated homes.[19] This finding is consistent with the proposition that the strength of support for marital and familial norms is positively correlated with socioeconomic status.

The American middle-class view has been that every child needs a social father, partly to give the child a position in the society and partly to provide an adult male model from whom to learn about the differentiation of sex- (or gender-) roles. With this view as a premise it appears that in bygone years the profession of social work has taken a more or less tacit position that although the unwed mother should decide for herself whether or not to keep her child with her, yet for the foregoing reasons her decision should be to give up the child. More recently it appears that several considerations have contributed doubts to the proposition that a husband-father is indispensable for the rearing of a child: (1) An increasing tolerance regarding extra-marital sex relations seems to have led to a reduced condemnation of the illegitimate sexual relationship and its issue. (2) An increasing proportion of mothers in the labor force correspondingly increases the proportion of children whom mothers can maintain and to whom they can confer societal positions. (3) The studies on father-absent families have led to no clear conclusion that fathers are

---

[15] "Illegitimacy Rise Alarms Agencies," *The New York Times,* August 9, 1959, p. 62.

[16] "Judge Suggests Jail for Unwed Mothers," *The New York Times,* March 4, 1958, p. 31.

[17] "Unwed Mothers Sent to Jail for Getting Pregnant," *Chicago Sun-Times,* December 6, 1959, p. 56.

[18] Meier, "Foster Care," in Kurtz, *op. cit.,* p. 281.

[19] Clarke E. Vincent, *Unmarried Mothers* (New York: Free Press, 1961).

needed for the adequate socialization of children.[20] (4) Increasingly militant advocates of women's rights have denounced sex-role differentiation as enslaving women and hence as immoral.

Adoption

Adoption is a procedure by which a minor assumes the legal status of an offspring of an adult person or a couple who are not his natural parents. Reciprocally, adoption is a procedure that enables childless adults to assume parental roles. Through adoption the illegitimate child can find a family to accord him positions in societal structures. It should be noted, however, that not all adoptions involve illegitimate children.

Legal provisions for adoption existed in ancient Rome and in France as early as 1792, but in most Western countries legal codes concerning adoption have appeared since 1920.[21] Although adoption has been practiced from time immemorial, its incidence appears to have been increasing in relatively recent times, especially since World War I. It is estimated that in 1945 there were 54,000 adoptions in the United States[22] and that by 1960 the number had risen to 107,000. In the latter year approximately 55 percent of the children adopted were adopted by unrelated persons, and about 70 percent of the children were less than a month old when adopted.[23] In 1968, 166,000 children were adopted, 52 percent of them by unrelated persons.[24]

In the typical situation the adopter is childless and desires an heir whereas the natural parent or parents (if the natural father is known) are not in position to give the child a normal upbringing. According to a publication of the United Nations, the emphasis in recent years has shifted from providing the adopters with direct heirs to providing a permanent parental relationship for children deprived of their natural parents. In other words, the point of view of persons involved in child-placing procedures has shifted from that of the adopting parents to that of the adopted child.

No doubt this shift is in line with the humanitarian viewpoint of the

---

[20] See "Correlates in Children's Responses of Some Variations in Familial Structure and Functions," in Chapter 15. There is impressionistic evidence that a larger proportion of unmarried mothers are keeping their babies as is implied by the four points in the above paragraph. This plus a presumed increase in the proportion of pregnancies terminated by abortion seems to be intensifying the shortage of white babies available for adoption. "Adoption Agencies Report Shortage of White Infants," *New York Times*, December 7, 1970, pp. 1, 35.

[21] Department of Economic and Social Affairs, *Comparative Analysis of Adoption Laws* (New York: United Nations, 1956), pp. 2–3.

[22] U.S. Children's Bureau, *Trends* (U.S. Department of Health, Education, and Welfare; Washington, D.C.: GPO, 1958), p. 2.

[23] Bernice R. Boehm, "Adoption," in *Encyclopedia of Social Work* (New York: National Association of Social Workers, 1965), pp. 63–68.

[24] *Statistical Abstract of the United States: 1970*, Table 460, p. 303.

times and an awareness of past exploitation by individuals who used this device to acquire cheap labor.[25] It might also be observed, however, that the new viewpoint is in line with the economics of the adoption market: each year there are in the United States about ten times as many families applying for adoptive children as are placed for adoption.[26] Such an imbalance between supply and demand leads quite expectedly to a black market in children whereby a child may cost the adopting parents several thousand dollars, most of which goes to the lawyer or other intermediary.[27] Further imbalances in the adoption market result from the following considerations. There is a strong sentiment—in some cases embodied in the law—that the adoptive parents should be of the same religious affiliation as the adoptee, even though the adoptee may be only a few days old. In the state of New York, moreover, atheists and agnostics have been ineligible to become adopters, and even couples wherein husband and wife are of different faith have had little chance of getting a child through routine channels.[28] Presumably such regulations serve to expand the black market. Since public and private social agencies handle about 39 percent of the adoptions and about 48 percent are made by relatives,[29] however, the black market can account for no more than 13 percent of the adoptions. (But if the black market accounted for no more than 1 percent of all adoptions, it would still be an operation involving millions of dollars.)

Race is another factor that contributes to the imbalance of the adoption market. There are fewer blacks applying for children than there are black children available for adoption. In response, social workers in some large Northern cities have inaugurated black adoption projects.[30]

[25] That the exploitation of children for their labor is not exclusively a Dickensian phenomenon of the nineteenth century is suggested by a report of a few years ago that in a semiannual "child market" in Benevento, Italy, boys of from 12 to 16 years of age were "sold" for a year to perform such tasks as stable cleaning and goatherding for prices of $8.50 to $10.00.—"Boys Sold for a Year in Italy for Up to $10," *The New York Times*, September 10, 1952, p. 9.

[26] Florence G. Brown, "Adoption," in Kurtz, *op. cit.*, pp. 85–90, esp. p. 85.

[27] For a journalistic account see Marybeth Weinstein, "The Markets—Black and Gray —in Babies," *The New York Times Magazine*, November 27, 1955, pp. 12, 16, 18, 20. The fact that in less than a year in 1957–1958 some 1200 children from other countries were imported for adoption is another manifestation of the "tight" adoption market. Half of these 1200 were adopted "by proxy," i.e., under an arrangement whereby the adoptive parents gave power of attorney to another person who adopted the child for them, with the implication that adopter and adoptee had not seen each other.—Bess Furman, "Flemming Urges Adoption Change," *The New York Times*, May 19, 1959, p. 19.

[28] John Wicklein, "Religious Rule on Adoption Bars Many Couples in State," *The New York Times*, October 11, 1959, pp. 1, 82.

[29] *Statistical Abstract of the United States: 1970*, Table 460, p. 303.

[30] Cf. Brown, "Adoption," in Kurtz, *op. cit.* Another factor that might contribute to the imbalance of the adoption market under some circumstances is the alleged practice of some social agencies of regarding as unadoptable babies having mixed racial backgrounds. —Warren Weaver, Jr., "Mixed Racial Stock Decried as Barrier to State Adoptions," *The New York Times*, December 6, 1958, p. 24.

Of the roughly 170,000 adoptions made annually in the United States nearly half are of legitimate children whose homes have been broken by divorce, desertion, separation, or death, or whose natural parents were unable to take care of them for other reasons. Slightly more than half are reported to have been illegitimate and therefore in need not only of the care of parents but of status as well.[31] About 38 percent of the adoptions are made by stepparents and about 10 percent by other relatives.

Finally, it has been reiterated that adoption provides the child with a new set of positions and statuses. By bringing him into a community, selecting a school for him, and so on, the adoptive couple is providing the adoptee with positions in structures. Perhaps an anecdote will make the point clearer. Following a gangland type of murder in Chicago it was revealed that the victim, a twenty-six-year-old man, had been adopted from "a world-famous institution" by a man who was assassinated in the same fashion shortly after the adoption. At the time of the adoption the baby who was to become the second murder victim was also wanted by a couple nationally known and respected in the world of entertainment. If the "world-famous institution" had decided the other way . . . .

Inheritance

Since it is generally true that an individual's initial societally oriented positions are determined by his family of orientation, and since the possession and appropriate use of property are instrumental in enabling an individual and a family to achieve and to maintain favored statuses, it is of interest to examine the topic of inheritance.

Property exists in all societies. Systems of ownership vary. In some societies most property, including that upon which production is based, is privately owned. Even here there is some property that is not private, e.g., public parks and buildings. In some societies most property, including the means of production, is publicly or communally owned. Even under socialism, however, there is always a small amount of property, such as personal effects, that is privately owned.

Since communal property is not inherited at all, the existence of inheritance implies that the title to whatever property is under consideration resides in an individual. To the extent that there is privately owned property there exists a question as to its disposition when the owner dies. Such disposition may be carried out either by custom or by observing the idiosyncratic wishes of the owner. The prospect that the owner may draft a will implies testamentary freedom, i.e., that the owner's heirs are not fixed by custom but can be designated—to some extent, at least—on the basis of the owner's preference.

Usually inheritance has involved the male line only. Indeed, in some

---

[31] U.S. Children's Bureau, *Child Welfare Statistics*, extrapolated from Table 33, p. 40.

societies women are not even permitted to own property.³² Among the customary patterns of inheritance are those that specify a particular kinsman as the recipient-designate of the entire or virtually entire estate. Such a procedure is spoken of as impartible (as contrasted with partible inheritance, where the estate is divided more or less equally among one or more categories of heirs). First or, sometimes, last sons are the usually designated heirs in impartible inheritance.³³ These practices are known, respectively, as primogeniture and ultimogeniture.

A society's system of inheritance, and, indeed, whether or not it has a system of inheritance are related to two considerations: the nature of the society's kinship system and the nature of its economic order. As Sumner and Keller suggest, systems of descent might well have been developed solely to take care of property interests: "property follows the blood."³⁴ Among the Mundugumor of New Guinea descent is traced through "ropes" from parent to offspring of the opposite sex. Here, according to Mead, "All property, with the exception of land, which is plentiful and not highly valued, passes down the rope; even weapons descend from father to daughter."³⁵

It is probably correct to assert that the greater the emphasis upon filial (rather than marital) solidarity and upon the extended, especially the stem, family rather than upon the nuclear, the more likely it is that property will tend to be communally rather than privately owned, and that where it is privately owned, there will tend to be customary designation of heirs rather than testamentary freedom.³⁶ In traditional China the family owned the land, buildings, and animals. The patriarch of the family functioned as a steward and an administrative head. There was a clear norm that his handling of the property was to be not for his personal gain but for the welfare of the family. When he died, there was no doubt that the family retained the property; his death merely necessitated the designation of a new steward.³⁷ Mandelbaum reports that in the joint family of India all property is held in common and there is a common purse, that every male is a co-owner of the family property, and that the senior male is the manager of the family funds.³⁸

---

³² William Graham Sumner and Albert Galloway Keller, *The Science of Society* (New Haven, Conn.: Yale University Press, 1927), I, 341.

³³ Richard A. Schermerhorn, "Family Carry-Overs of Western Christendom," in Howard Becker and Reuben Hill (eds.), *Family, Marriage and Parenthood* (2d ed.; Boston: Heath, 1955), chap 5, esp. p. 109.

³⁴ *Op. cit.*, pp. 341–342.

³⁵ Margaret Mead, *Sex and Temperament in Three Primitive Societies*, p. 176, reprinted in *From the South Seas* (New York: Morrow, 1939).

³⁶ According to Zimmerman, members of trustee families largely die intestate (without having made a will); will-making arises with the domestic family and becomes an individual right in the atomistic family. Cf. *Family and Civilization* (New York: Harper & Row, 1947), pp. 378–379 and "wills and will-making" on p. 829.

³⁷ Cf. Chapter 2 above.

³⁸ David G. Mandelbaum, "The Family in India," in Ruth Nanda Anshen (ed.), *The Family: Its Function and Destiny* (rev. ed.; New York: Harper & Row, 1959), chap. 10,

Ireland's famines in the first half of the nineteenth century led to a conviction that the successive partitioning of farms was economically unsound. Impartible inheritance was Ireland's response. A similar pattern of inheritance has been reported in Cumberland in northwestern England. Here also the father designates an heir—more usually the eldest son than any other kinsman—who awaits the father's retirement before marrying and assuming direction of the farm.[39] Both here and in rural Ireland the nature of the economic order has affected the system of inheritance and has brought about a high average age at marriage and a low birth rate.

In the seventeenth century the Comanche, as described by Linton, changed their economic base. Prior to that time they lived on the plateaus of Montana. They were a migratory people whose livelihood came largely from hunting game animals and from the gathering of berries and roots. At this time each man's property consisted of his clothing, a few weapons, and utensils. When a man died, his property was destroyed. By 1700 the Comanche had moved south and were established on the plains of the Texas Panhandle and southwestern Oklahoma. Here they began to acquire sizable heards of horses; one herd was reported to run to 2000 animals. As they began their new economy, they continued their custom of destroying a man's property when he died. Then they apparently began to realize that to slaughter an entire herd of animals was deleterious to the welfare of the tribe. Finally, they developed a new custom of killing only a man's favorite horses and distributing the rest among surviving relatives. Linton adds that since the Comanche did not develop rules governing the distribution of horses, "there was usually hard feeling among the heirs."[40] As economic conditions have changed in India so that an individual can accumulate property by his own efforts without drawing on family funds, there have been legal changes enabling him to keep such property rather than to have it regarded as communal family property.

Where the family—either communally or through individual members—owns property, such property represents potential influence over individual family members. Where the societally important property—the means of production—is owned communally by the family, as in traditional China, the family is frequently the important unit of production. In this situation the individual has multiple role-relationships within the family, the family has much to do with determining his positions and statuses in other societal structures, and thus strong controls over the individual's behavior are placed within the family.

Presumably people are more aware of the concept of property where

esp. p. 168. The joint family described by Mandelbaum is characteristic of rural, upper-caste, wealthy, orthodox, Hindu families, Cf. *ibid.*, p. 167.

[39] W. M. Williams, *Gosforth: The Sociology of an English Village* (New York: Free Press, 1956), pp. 49–53.

[40] Ralph Linton, *The Study of Man* (New York: Appleton, 1936), p. 298. Cf. also Abram Kardiner, *The Psychological Frontiers of Society* (New York: Columbia University Press, 1945), ch. 3.

ownership is individual rather than communal. We have noted that it is only under individual ownership that the topic of inheritance arises. Where heirs are designated by custom as in the transmission of titles and estates by primogeniture in the British peerage, there is no incentive for one's descendants to try to outmaneuver each other and there is little occasion for them to develop hard feelings. Where the practice of will making is observed, however, and where the testator is free to designate his heirs, he presumably has maximum latitude for influencing the behavior of all whom he wishes to consider as potential heirs. As Simmons observes, this state of affairs is of special significance in determining the status of the aged, for the ownership of property "is among the most flexible, impersonal, and effective means of influencing others with a minimum of physical effort."[41]

The Ascription of Race, Ethnicity, and Religion

We have already noted that the fact of being born into one family rather than into another determines a set of ascribed characteristics in terms of which members of the society will respond to a person. Race, ethnicity, and religion are such characteristics. Along with one's sex, one's race is about as permanent an ascribed characteristic as there is in American society. Until the latter 1960's in American society one was born into the white race or into a nonwhite race and virtually every phase of one's life—associations, career, and so on—were greatly influenced by that fact. Biologically one's racial constitution is as fixed at birth as one's sex. However, since the sociological significance of race lies in its social definition rather than in its genetic determinants, one's race is not necessarily fixed for life. Until the latter 1960's, then, there was an economic advantage for a black to be accepted as a white in the occupational system, and it is generally believed that every year a considerable number of blacks (i.e., of people who have been regarded as blacks from birth) were crossing the color "line" and were "becoming" socially white. More recently, however, most sectors of the economy have been recruiting talented blacks. It would appear that the result has been that for a person who is able to be accepted as either black or white, the advantage may now generally be in the opposite direction. For example, a young woman of modest skills as typist or clerk may have a better chance for acceptable employment if socially classified as black rather than as white.

Since it is rare for a child to grow up in an ethnic-religious tradition different from that of his parents, we may regard ethnicity and religion as other statuses that are ascribed. As in the case of race, there are some who upon reaching adulthood do alter the ethnicity and/or religion ascribed to them.

---

[41] Leo W. Simmons, "Aging in Pre-Industrial Cultures," in Clark Tibbitts and Wilma Donahue (eds.), *Aging in Today's Society* (Englewood Cliffs, N.J.: Prentice-Hall, 1960), pp. 65–74. Quotation is from p. 70.

Name changing is a familiar device for altering one's ethnic identification. One group of authors believes that the desire to protect children from "name prejudice" motivates a substantial number of petitioners for change of name. They hypothesize that the function of status conferring causes some parents to seek to alter the status they are conferring on their children by removing its indication of identification with a minority group.[42]

The specific religious identification conferred by parents usually involves acts of validation by the child—attendance at Sunday school and church, confirmation, and so on. For this reason it is awkward if not impossible for a child to accept the ascription to two different religions that are potentially his when his father and mother are of different religious faiths. It is precisely at this point of conferring religious identification upon the children that the strain from religious exogamy becomes most severe. And it is at this point where the Roman Catholic church seeks to protect its members, as well as to increase its numbers, through prenuptial agreements to rear children of mixed marriages in the Catholic faith.

Liston Pope has documented the proposition that Protestant churches tend to be "class churches,"[43] a point that Vance Packard captured in his phrase "the long road from Pentecostal to Episcopal."[44] As blacks move up the social ladder within their community, some hold membership in two churches. Such a person might maintain his old membership in the relatively low-status Baptist or Methodist Church because it is the church of his black clients, and concurrently he might take up membership in the relatively high-status Episcopal, Congregational, or Presbyterian Church, since the latter would be more consonant with his newly achieved status.[45] A popular joke of some years ago captured the same general idea with respect to the Jews. It concerned the rabbi who was alleged to have lamented, "Some of my best Jews are Friends."

As with the weather or other conditions of life, one becomes aware of status when exposed to variation in it. If all the children are rich, neither riches nor poverty is a meaningful concept to the children. Since the play group is ordinarily confined to the neighborhood, and since neighborhoods tend to be homogeneous with respect to socioeconomic status, the young child is not generally exposed to gross differences in socioeconomic status. As the child comes into daily contact with children of another social class or of different ethnic and religious origin, however, he will become more conscious of his

---

[42] Leonard Broom, Helen P. Beem, and Virginia Harris, "Characteristics of 1,107 Petitioners for Change of Name," *American Sociological Review*, 20: 33–39 (1955).

[43] Liston Pope, "Religion and the Class Structure," *Annals of the American Academy of Political and Social Science*, 256: 84–91 (1948).

[44] Vance Packard, *The Status Seekers: An Exploration of Class Behavior in America and the Hidden Barriers That Affect You, Your Community, Your Future* (New York: McKay, 1959), chap 14.

[45] E. Franklin Frazier, *Black Bourgeoisie: The Rise of a New Middle-Class in the United States* (New York: Free Press, 1957), pp. 89–90.

own origins. The average child will observe that such children differ from himself in behavior, but it is doubtful that he will comprehend that the differences include habits of thought and aspiration as well as habits of speech and dress.

When he will first encounter such differences depends in considerable measure upon the conditions under which he grows up, goes to school, and so on. A child who lives in a homogeneous residential suburb has vastly less occasion to become aware of gross differences in socioeconomic status than a child brought up around "the gold coast and the slum." Some encounter such differences upon beginning school. Because the high schools serve larger areas than do grade schools, there is a good probability that the child who has not previously encountered such differences will meet them there. For still others this discovery may await their arrival at college or in the work situation.

The Concept of Stratification

One of the propositions that sociologists are most sure of is that societies of any degree of complexity and age are stratified, i.e., that there are positions of high and of low status in each such society.[46] There is less consensus, however, on some of the theoretical refinements. One of the points of theoretical contention is whether a society can exist without stratification and whether stratification is a good thing in the long run.[47] Another point that has engaged scholarly attention is whether social classes exist in the United States and elsewhere.

Warner asserts that an American community with a fully developed class system has six social classes: upper-upper, lower-upper, upper-middle, lower-middle, upper-lower, and lower-lower. The proportions of the population in the various social classes in a medium-sized New England city are reported to be in the following percentages:[48]

---

[46] In Chapter 3 it was remarked that the efforts of the members of kibbutzim to avoid social stratification might prove unavailing, and the studies of Rosenfeld and Schwartz provided some support for this opinion. Status differentials have been quite visible, moreover, in the Soviet Union, which has been ideologically committed to the "classless society."

[47] Those who are interested in divergent views on the functional significance of social strata may wish to consult Kingsley Davis and Wilbert E. Moore, "Some Principles of Stratification," *American Sociological Review*, 10: 242–249 (1945); Melvin M. Tumin, "Some Principles of Stratification: A Critical Analysis," *American Sociological Review*, 18: 387–394 (1953); a reply by Kingsley Davis and a comment by Wilbert E. Moore appear on pp. 394–397 and p. 397, respectively, just following Tumin's article cited above. Cf. also Richard D. Schwartz, "Functional Alternatives to Inequality," *American Sociological Review*, 20: 424–430 (1955); Richard L. Simpson, "A Modification of the Functional Theory of Social Stratification," *Social Forces*, 35: 132–137 (1956); and Walter Buckley, "Social Stratification and the Functional Theory of Social Differentiation," *American Sociological Review*, 23: 369–375 (1958).

[48] W. Lloyd Warner, *American Life: Dream and Reality* (Chicago: University of Chicago Press, 1953), p. 58. Cf. also the series of volumes on Yankee City, of which the

Level above the Common Man	Upper-upper	1.4
	Lower-upper	1.6
	Upper-middle	10
Level of the Common Man	Lower-middle	28
	Upper-lower	33
Level below the Common Man	Lower-lower	25

The Warner group holds, however, that not all the six classes are present in all communities. Since the upper-upper class is conceived as consisting of "old families," this class may not show up in relatively new communities, such as "Jonesville" or "Elmtown," in the Midwest. The size of the community also has bearing upon the degree of elaboration of the class system, the smaller communities tending to have fewer than six social classes. In Warner's view of social class, the basic criterion that reveals to which social class any individual belongs is his reputation in the local community.

Warner's method has been criticized on various grounds, including the charges that it fails to take into account the history of the community[49] and that the conception of social class cannot be generalized to communities larger than the small cities to which it has been applied.[50] Warner's representation of empirical reality has been criticized on such grounds as that there are not clear-cut divisions between social classes, and that the social classes he dis-

---

first is W. Lloyd Warner and P. S. Lunt, *The Social Life of a Modern Community* (New Haven, Conn.: Yale University Press, 1941); A. B. Hollingshead, *Elmtown's Youth: The Impact of Social Classes on Adolescents* (New York: Wiley, 1949); R. J. Havighurst and Hilda Taba, *Adolescent Character and Personality* (New York: Wiley, 1949); Allison Davis, B. B. Gardner, and M. R. Gardner, *Deep South* (Chicago: University of Chicago Press, 1941); and W. Lloyd Warner, Marchia Meeker, and Kenneth Eells, *Social Class in America* (Chicago: Science Research Associates, 1949).

[49] Stephan Thernstrom, "'Yankee City' Revisited: The Perils of Historical Naivete," *American Sociological Review*, 30: 234–242 (1965).

[50] The communities most completely studied in terms of the class system have not been metropolitan areas. The most complete studies of class are those of Yankee City, population 17,000 (cf. Warner and Lunt, *op. cit.*) and of Elmtown or Prairie City, population 6,200 (cf. Hollingshead, *op. cit.*, and Havighurst and Taba, *op. cit.*). A corresponding type of analysis was executed in a small Southern city in *Deep South*, population "over 10,000" (cf. Davis, Gardner, and Gardner, *op. cit.*). Less complete analyses have been made of the class structure of Middletown, population 36,500 in 1925 and 47,000 in 1935 (cf. R. S. and H. M. Lynd, *Middletown* and *Middletown in Transition* [New York: Harcourt, 1929 and 1937]), and of the Negro population of Chicago (cf. St. Clair Drake and Horace Cayton, *Black Metropolis* [New York: Harcourt, 1945]). Such studies as exist, however, reinforce the contention that social classes in metropolitan areas do have subcultures. See Martha C. Ericson, "Social Status and Child-Rearing Practices," in T. M. Newcomb and E. L. Hartley (eds.), *Readings in Social Psychology* (New York: Holt, Rinehart and Winston, Inc., 1947), pp. 494–501; E. M. Duvall, "Conceptions of Parenthood," *American Journal of Sociology*, 52: 193–203 (1946).

tinguishes lack complete, integrated, and distinctive subcultural systems.[51] Even more critical has been the allegation that Warner "blurs the distinction between matters of basic and those of secondary importance" and that he "confuses classes with status groups." Mayer, who makes this charge, indicates that there are three key dimensions of social stratification in modern mass societies—class, status, and power—and that each of these constitutes a separate rank order. Class, to Mayer, is an economic dimension based upon the amount and source of income. Status refers to differentiation of prestige and deference. Power is the ability to control the behavior of others.[52] Since the various dimensions of American stratification seem to be highly correlated with each other, it seems satisfactory for our purposes to proceed as though there were but a single dimension.[53] Ignoring for the moment two of the elements of social stratification—class and power—and considering only status, we find that there are three commonly used indexes: occupation, income, and level of formal education. Fortunately, high positive correlations have been

---

[51] Paul K. Hatt, "Stratification in the Mass Society," *American Sociological Review*, 15: 216–222 (1950), and "Occupation and Social Stratification," *American Journal of Sociology*, 55: 533–543 (1950) and a review of *Democracy in Jonesville* by W. Lloyd Warner and associates, *American Sociological Review*, 14: 811–812 (1949); Harold W. Pfautz and Otis Dudley Duncan, "A Critical Evaluation of Warner's Work in Community Stratification," *American Sociological Review*, 15: 205–215 (1950); Milton M. Gordon, "Social Class in American Sociology," *American Journal of Sociology*, 55: 262–268 (1949); Llewellyn Gross, "The Use of Class Concepts in Sociological Research," *American Journal of Sociology*, 54: 409–421 (1949); Ruth Rosner Kornhauser, "The Warner Approach to Social Stratification," in Reinhard Bendix and Seymour Martin Lipset, *Class, Status and Power* (New York: Free Press, 1953), pp. 224–255.

[52] Kurt B. Mayer, *Class and Society* (New York: Doubleday, 1955), chaps. 3–5. Quotation is from p. 45. Mayer says that the economic ranking and that based on prestige are closely related but not identical.—*Ibid.*, p. 25. The conception of class as the aggregate of persons sharing a "specific causal component of their life chances" and status as "determined by a specific, positive or negative, social estimation of honor" was presented by Max Weber. Cf. *From Max Weber: Essays in Sociology* (trans. by H. H. Gerth and C. Wright Mills; New York: Oxford, 1946), pp. 181, 187.

[53] To the degree that the dimensions are not perfectly correlated there exists *status inconsistency*, a term that applies to a person who has high standing with respect to certain status variables and low standing with respect to others. Status consistency-inconsistency has been found to be correlated with political behavior. Cf. Gerhard E. Lenski, "Status Crystallization: A Non-Vertical Dimension of Social Status," *American Sociological Review*, 19: 405–413 (1954), "Social Participation and Status Crystallization," *American Sociological Review*, 21: 458–464 (1956), "Status Inconsistency and the Vote: A Four Nation Test," *American Sociological Review*, 32: 298–301 (1967), and *Power and Privilege: A Theory of Social Stratification* (New York: McGraw-Hill, 1966), pp. 86–88. Cf. also the following articles in the *American Sociological Review*: William F. Kenkel, "The Relationship between Status Consistency and Politico-Economic Attitudes," 21: 365–368 (1956); Irwin W. Goffman, "Status Consistency and Preference for Change in Power Distribution," 22: 275–281 (1957); Werner S. Landecker, "Class Crystallization and Class Consciousness," 28: 219–229 (1963); Charles B. Nam and Mary G. Powers, "Variations in Socioeconomic Structure by Race, Residence, and the Life Cycle," 30: 97–103 (1965); and Gary B. Rush, "Status Consistency and Right-Wing Extremism," 32: 86–92 (1967).

reported among these and other more or less derivative indexes of socioeconomic status (frequently abbreviated SES).[54]

We shall assume that American society and each community within it has a continuous distribution of socioeconomic statuses and that a slice excised from this distribution is a social stratum and a social class. That is, we shall use "social stratum" and "social class" as interchangeable terms to denote a collectivity of positions in a community or a society having roughly equal amounts of prestige, power, and material resources, and sharing a somewhat homogeneous style of life.

Subcultures of Social Classes

The Warner studies have emphasized two points that bear directly on the position-conferring function of the family: (1) The associations and experiences of the members of a family are closely correlated with its status (or in Warner's usage, its social class). (2) Correlated with gross differences in status are differences in culture and style of life.

From the Warner studies there emerges the conclusion that people tend to fraternize (i.e., to have "clique" relations) only with others in their own class. Parents, moreover, tend to foster the same pattern in their children, and

---

[54] Joseph A. Kahl and James A. Davis, "A Comparison of Indexes of Socioeconomic Status," *American Sociological Review*, 20: 317–325 (1955). Kahl and Davis studied a representative group of white urban men with respect to 19 indexes of stratification. After intercorrelating and factor analyzing the 19 indexes these authors found two factors that were identified as (1) occupational prestige and closely related variables, such as education, and (2) ecological variables plus the social status of the respondents' parents and of the parents of the respondents' wives. Warner reports that he has found his conception of social class (based on reputation and prestige) to correlate .91 with occupation and .89 with income.—W. Lloyd Warner et al., *Social Class in America* (Chicago: Science Research Associates, 1949), p. 168. Lenski, however, cites studies showing lower correlations. Cf. his *Power and Privilege*, p. 408. Income is one of the favorite indexes of socioeconomic status. When income data are not available, rental value of the home is regarded as an acceptable substitute. Occupation is frequently used as an index of socioeconomic status either in terms of the categories employed by the U.S. Bureau of the Census (cf., e.g., entries under "occupation group" in Table 8.2) or in terms of the North-Hatt scale of occupational prestige. (Cf. National Opinion Research Center, "Jobs and Occupations: A Popular Evaluation," in Bendix and Lipset, *Class, Status and Power*, pp. 411–426.) Cf. Albert J. Riess, Jr., et al., *Occupations and Social Status* (New York: Free Press, 1962). According to one report, other countries having marked cultural differences accord prestige in approximately the same rank order to occupations as does this country; the principal variations from this generalization pertain to agricultural and service occupations. Cf. Alex Inkeles and Peter H. Rossi, "National Comparisons of Occupational Prestige," *American Journal of Sociology*, 61: 329–339 (1956). Cf. also Edward A. Tiryakian, "The Prestige Evaluation of Occupations in an Under-Developed Country: The Philippines," *American Journal of Sociology* 63: 390–399 (1958); and J. Michael Armer, "Intersociety and Intrasociety Correlations of Occupational Prestige," *American Journal of Sociology*, 74: 28–36 (1968). But for a cautionary view cf. Archibald O. Haller and David M. Lewis, "The Hypothesis of Intersocietal Similarity in Occupational Prestige," *American Journal of Sociology*, 72: 210–216 (1966).

especially to discourage their own children from playing with children from families of distinctly lower status. This kind of parental mandate is apparently easy to enforce in suburbs and other areas of homogeneous status, but quite difficult to maintain in certain urban areas where great heterogeneity prevails.

The Warner group emphasizes that differences in manners constitute only a fraction of the cultural distinctions among classes. Vastly more subtle and significant are the differences in ideology, value systems, and sources of anxiety and frustration.

We shall use the term *subculture* to designate the set of cultural traits characteristic of each of the social classes. We shall now proceed to consider some aspects of subcultures that are relevant to the position-conferring, and especially the status-conferring, function of the family.[55]

THE SUBCULTURE OF THE LEVEL BELOW THE COMMON MAN

There is some disagreement about whether the impoverished are sufficiently homogeneous to be treated as a single social class having its distinctive subculture. S. M. Miller is among those arguing the negative side of the issue.[56] On the other hand, the "culture of poverty" is a phrase that has been intended to refer to beliefs, understandings, and expectations common to the poor, and one widely remarked ethnographic account has used the phrase in its subtitle.[57] Although there are undoubtedly numerous ways to be poor, the following will be an attempt to deal with elements common to these diverse ways.

The key fact about the level below the common man, or the lower-lower class, according to Allison Davis, is its poverty and consequent proximity to the threshold of survival. Warner emphasizes the attitudes held toward members of this class by those in higher classes—attitudes of disapproval for their being unrespectable and of pity for their being so unfortunate. Matza documents Warner's point by remarking that lower-lower people have also been spoken of as paupers, the disreputable poor, the dregs, the lumpenproletariat, and the spurious leisure class.[58]

Davis traces the poverty of lower-lower people to irregularity of employment. Irregularity of employment, he says, means irregularity of income, and from the latter flows a host of consequences. Because of irregularity of income

[55] We may have occasion also to refer to the subcultures of such ethnic minorities in the United States as the Chinese, Puerto Ricans, Italians, and Eastern European Jews.

[56] S. M. Miller, "The American Lower Class: A Typological Approach," *Social Research*, 31: 1–22 (1964).

[57] Oscar Lewis, *La Vida: A Puerto Rican Family in the Culture of Poverty—San Juan and New York* (New York: Vintage, 1968).

[58] David Matza, "The Disreputable Poor," in Reinhard Bendix and Seymour Martin Lipset (eds.), *Class, Status, and Power: Social Stratification in Comparative Perspective* (2d ed.; New York: Free Press, 1966), pp. 289–302.

the lower-lower class is insecure with respect to food, clothing, and shelter. For these reasons, Davis holds, persons at this level tend to gorge themselves when food is available, look favorably upon obesity as a form of reassurance against future hunger, like to overheat their homes when they have money for a bucket of coal, and so on.[59] Because they rotate between employment and the relief rolls, and because they must establish "need" to be eligible for relief, there is little incentive to save. Since planning and thrift are usually not rewarded, they seldom become habits. In this context the spree on payday and heavy installment buying become intelligible. Since their parents need their financial help, the children cannot count on staying in school beyond the minimum legal age. Hence there is no reason for them to regard seriously school subjects that lead to professional and white-collar jobs.

Warner points out that lower-lower people are frequently migrants from other parts of this country (as, for example, from the rural South) or from a foreign land. They are frequently "greenhorns" or recently arrived "ethnic" peoples moving into the bottom to "begin their slow ascent in our status system." Matza adds that the lower-lower class includes not only migrants but also the infirm and the skidders, the latter including alcoholics, addicts, perverts and otherwise disturbed who have fallen from higher social standing.[60] They tend to live "on the riverbanks, in the foggy bottoms, in the regions back of the tanneries or near the stockyards, and generally in those places that are not desired by anyone else."[61]

Allison Davis sees the morality system of the lower-lower class as diverging from those of the middle and upper classes. The principal differences center about the freer expression of sexual and aggressive impulses. As we shall see in Chapter 19, the Kinsey study reports—at least for males—greater frequency as well as distinctive modes of sexual expression in the lower-lower class. The subculture of this class carries little penalty for the overt expression of aggression. Physical violence is an accepted way of settling disputes. Warner tends to believe that a characteristic of the lower-lower level is an absence of ambition and of desire to "get ahead."[62]

THE SUBCULTURE OF THE CLASS OF THE COMMON MAN

Warner describes the common man as respectable, thrifty, moral, and eager to be regarded favorably by his neighbors. With respect to Warner's scheme of social classes, a small business man or a white-collar worker is likely to be classified as lower-middle, whereas a semiskilled worker or a tradesman is probably classified as in the upper-lower class, a category that corresponds

---

[59] Allison Davis, "Child Rearing in the Class Structure of American Society," in *The Family in a Democratic Society: Anniversary Papers of the Community Service Society of New York* (New York: Columbia University Press, 1949), pp. 56–69.

[60] *Op. cit.*, pp. 295–296.

[61] W. Lloyd Warner, *American Life* (Chicago: University of Chicago Press, 1953), p. 57.

[62] *Ibid.*, pp. 57–58.

generally to what some other writers call the "working class." The subculture of the working class has been described as containing six prominent themes: a striving for stability and security; an emphasis on traditional values; intensity of belief and of emotional involvement; a "person-centered" theme that causes the individual to relate to people rather than to roles; a disposition to distrust abstractions in favor of the concrete and to assess behavior in the light of consequences rather than of intent; and the desire for excitement.[63]

Middle-class persons are far enough removed from the level of subsistence, says Allison Davis, to be spared anxiety about the immediate necessities of life.[64] Where the economy permits a level of consumption that is comfortably above the level of subsistence, there is a disposition to view economic activity as a means of improving status. Because of their proximity to the subsistence level, Davis holds that people below the level of the common man tend not to develop status aspirations. A conspicuous characteristic of the middle class, on the other hand, is the striving for upward mobility and the conception of occupation as a means of fulfilling this aspiration.

Chapters 15 and 16 present a more complete interpretation of the process by which the middle-class child acquires the pattern of striving behavior. For the present it is enough to note that the family seems to start this process, and that, as the child's social horizons widen, other societal structures reinforce it. Correlated with the middle-class emphasis on striving are various other phenomena distinctive of this class. Davis argues that the goal of mobility and the means employed in the family to implement it result in a form of anxiety that further stimulates the striving motivation.[65] In contrast to the situation in the lower class, middle-class children are taught to refrain from the overt expressions of aggression and to direct this energy into competitive goal-directed behavior. Sexual impulses also are more controlled, with considerable pressure to refrain from complete expression in heterosexual intercourse. (Again Kinsey provides a measure of corroboration.)[66]

SUBCULTURES OF STRATA ABOVE THE COMMON MAN

In a community with a fully developed system of social classes there are, according to Warner, three strata above the common man. Of these the lowest consists of civic leaders, i.e., people who belong to service clubs and kindred

[63] S. M. Miller and Frank Riessman, "The Working Class Subculture: A New View," *Social Problems*, 9: 86–97 (1961).

[64] Writers in the field of primitive economics have introduced the distinction between subsistence economics and prestige economics. This is a useful distinction for the present analysis because it points not only to variation in levels of living, but also to a fundamental difference in attitude concerning the purpose of general economic activity and of individual productive effort. Cf. M. J. Herskovits, *The Economic Life of Primitive Peoples* (New York: Knopf, 1940), esp. chap. 18.

[65] Allison Davis, "Socialization and Adolescent Personality," in Theodore M. Newcomb and Eugene L. Hartley, *Readings in Social Psychology* (New York: Holt, Rinehart and Winston, Inc., 1947), pp. 139–150.

[66] Cf. Chapter 19 below.

organizations but are not sufficiently "in" to mingle socially with the elite. Occupationally they are in the professions and hold substantial positions in business. In Warner's scheme they belong to the upper-middle class.

Above the category just noted, Warner's analysis asserts, there are the two upper classes. In some ways members of these two classes are indistinguishable from each other. They live in exclusive residential areas. Occupationally they are found in the upper reaches of finance, industry, and the professions. The key difference between the two classes—where such a difference exists—is that some do not belong to "old" families whereas others do. The former are *arrivistes:* their money is too "new" or, more explicitly, the financial basis for their social standing was developed too recently. In Warner's terms, these people belong to the lower-upper class.

The others are people from "old" families. This is shorthand for the proposition that the family has had its money long enough for the money to become respectable (even though the fortune may have originated under circumstances thought to be questionable at the time), for the lineage to acquire legitimation as a "pillar of society," and for the bearers of the line to acquire genteel manners and patrician tastes. If they happen to live in one of the dozen "social" cities, their families are undoubtedly listed in the *Social Register*.[67] Warner's term for the latter category of persons is the upper-upper class.

The subculture of the upper-upper class has been sketched with less completeness than is true of the subcultures of other strata. This probably indicates that upper-class persons are better able to maintain barriers of privacy against inquiring social scientists. Perhaps the best evidence derives from literary sources.[68] Therefore, we should proceed with some reservation in accepting the following description, whose major emphasis centers about what might be called a dynastic tradition: a reverence for the history of the family; avoidance of behavior that would bring disgrace on the family (as opposed to a relatively greater emphasis on the avoidance of self-disgrace in the middle class); control of individual behavior by deceased as well as living members of the extended family. A repugnance toward the striving behavior of the middle class and its symbols of conspicuous consumption also distinguishes this subculture. This is exemplified by conservatism in taste and by a conspicuous emphasis upon inconspicuous consumption: the woman who wears a ten-year-old tweed suit rather than the latest mode from a fashion magazine; the man who not only

---

[67] ". . . the Social Register Association of American cities only considers candidates for membership after three or more individuals already belonging to the Social Register certify that they accept the candidate as a person with whom they associate regularly and intimately."—Seymour Martin Lipset and Hans L. Zetterberg, "A Theory of Social Mobility," in Bendix and Lipset, *Class, Status, and Power,* pp. 561–573, at p. 563.

[68] J. P. Marquand, *Point of No Return* (Boston: Little, Brown, 1949); Christopher Morley, *Kitty Foyle* (New York: Grosset & Dunlap, 1939); Cleveland Amory, *The Proper Bostonians* (New York: Dutton, 1947). Cf. also Davis, Gardner, and Gardner, *op. cit.;* Lynd and Lynd, *op. cit.;* Warner and Lunt, *op. cit.*

eschews Hollywood "casuals" but feels uncomfortable in a suit until it has lost any air of "newness"; the family that prefers its fifteen-year-old Rolls Royce to a new Cadillac.

SOME CLASS DIFFERENCES IN CRITERIA OF STATUS

What is the most important fact to know about a person in order to place him in the structure of a society? Another phrasing is to ask how we answer the question, "Who is that?" Various settings come to mind as one contemplates some of the possible answers—son of Ugo, a Lee, a Catholic, a black, a plumber, an old man. These answers suggest respectively that the most important thing to know about a person are the identity of his father, the name of his family, his religious affiliation, his race, his occupation, his age and sex.

To illuminate this problem Form and Stone asked respondents of three widely different social strata the following question:

> If your daughter came home one night and told you she was in love with a young man you didn't know, what would be the first questions you would ask her about him?

Respondents from the lower stratum were primarily concerned with whether or not the young man had a job and would be a good provider. (Recall Allison Davis's assertion that the key fact about the lower class was its proximity to the threshold of survival.) In the middle stratum, occupation, religion, and prospects for mobility were the immediate foci of concern. (This is reminiscent of Davis's interpretation of the middle class as "being on the make.") Additional points of interest in the middle stratum had to do with the young man's "background" and morality. In the upper stratum respondents concentrated on the education, religion, and financial position of the young man and were concerned about the young man's family.[69]

QUALIFICATIONS REGARDING THE SUBCULTURES OF SOCIAL CLASSES

In introducing the related concepts of social class and subculture, we began by making certain reservations about these concepts, and by noting a lack of consensus among sociologists. To reinforce these reservations let us note that the descriptions of the class subcultures are undoubtedly oversimplified.

If the only important kind of variation in family forms were that associated with difference in social class, the foregoing discussion would require no qualification. There are, however, numerous sources of variation. Aside from social class, the most important of these are associated with ethnic (including religious and racial) and rural-urban differences. If all Americans were white, Protestant, and native-born of native parentage, if they all lived in large cities,

---

[69] William H. Form and Gregory P. Stone, "Urbanism, Anonymity, and Status Symbolism," *American Journal of Sociology*, 62: 504–514 (1957), at p. 511.

and if they were all several generations removed from ancestors who had come to America from Northwestern Europe, we could regard our discussion as essentially adequate. But of course such conditions do not square with the facts.

The most generally remarked difference between urban middle-class families of the ethnic majority (i.e., white, Protestant, and so on) and those of other ethnic and of rural origin concerns the greater extended familism of the latter. Thus, for example, a rural person or an Italian Catholic or a Polish Jew will generally be somewhat more conscious of kinship obligations than is suggested in the foregoing sketch. (Evidence on this point will be presented in Chapter 11.)

Concerning some of these differences in family form, however, there are writers who hold that they are more apparent than real; and concerning others, we have evidence that they may be disappearing. With respect to race, for example, it is frequently held that the subculture of the black middle class resembles more greatly that of the white middle class than it does that of the black lower class. According to this view, moreover, the traits of the stereotype of the black (indolence, sexual freedom, and so on) are phenomena of class rather than of race, i.e., they are elements in the subculture of the lower-class rather than of the blacks.[70]

The assimilation of ethnic groups involves their acceptance of American institutions and abandonment of their own. A theme running through the literature on ethnic groups is that native-born children of foreign-born parents tend to repudiate the distinctive cultural traits of their ethnic ancestors and seek to become "Americans," i.e., they work at becoming assimilated. (It can be appreciated that the usually strong familism in these groups combined with a disposition of their younger members to reject the culture and to repudiate the authority of their parents constitutes a basis for interpersonal and emotional conflict.) It seems improbable, however, that ethnic variation will disappear in the foreseeable future. Color and religion serve to some extent as axes of association and hence as dimensions of continuing ethnic variation. Glazer and Moynihan state that in large American cities four major ethnic categories are visible: whites classified by the three major religious traditions—Protestant, Catholic, and Jewish—and blacks.[70a] Chapter 11 will consider familial variation among these four ethnic categories.

We may summarize our qualifications regarding the subcultures of the three social classes as follows: (1) The descriptions are most applicable to the

---

[70] Cf. R. L. Sutherland, *Color, Class, and Personality* (Washington, D.C.: American Council on Education, 1942), chap. 9; Allison Davis and John Dollard, *Children of Bondage: The Personality Development of Negro Youth in the Urban South* (Washington, D.C.: American Council on Education, 1942); and a follow-up twenty years later of the study of Davis and Dollard: John R. Rohrer *et al.*, *The Eighth Generation: Cultures and Personalities of New Orleans Negroes* (New York: Harper & Row, 1960).

[70a] Nathan Glazer and Daniel Patrick Moynihan, *Beyond the Melting Pot* (Cambridge, Mass.: M.I.T. Press, 1963), p. 314.

urban majority; rural families and families of ethnic minorities do not fit the descriptions as well. (2) Probably the major point on which rural and minority families differ from urban middle-class families of the majority group is in the greater familism of the former and of the greater individualism of the latter.

How the Family Confers Positions and Provides Status-Orientation

After a disquisition of this length one is entitled to question its relevance to the position-conferring function of the family, i.e., to the process whereby the family integrates its members into other social systems and into the total society. It should be emphasized that whereas the more conspicuous and societally more important part of this function concerns the conferring of positions on children, still the function concerns, and is important for, other members of the family as well. With respect to the child the response to the question has already been foreshadowed and will be developed in the rest of the present chapter—through its location in the society the family confers a set of society-oriented positions on the child, and through transmitting a particular subculture it provides status-orientation. Of course each spouse integrates the other into a new family of orientation and a new extended family. The degree to which a person integrates the spouse into other systems depends upon the organization of the community and of the society and upon the couple's location in both. In American society the husband typically confers upon his wife a socioeconomic status and membership in at least one new category ("married woman"); the wife confers upon her husband at least membership in the category "married man."

The categories of persons with whom the child comes in contact affect the positions he comes to assume. Such differential association is, in turn, influenced by the family's spatial and social positions in the society. Whether a family is urban or rural, white or nonwhite, of the working or of the professional class, and so on, determines not only what categories of persons the child meets and what schools he attends but, as we shall see with special reference to social class, how he is received. In this way the family integrates the child into extrafamilial social systems. To varying degrees, however, *all* members of the family (including at times the family dog) are engaged in integrating the rest of the family with the society outside the home. The range over which the activity is practiced is a function of age and sex categories. In general, the young children integrate their parents with other families in the immediate neighborhood (and the family dog may make its contribution along this line). Integration into the wider but still local community is typically an activity of the older children and especially of the suburban wife. She is in touch with the school, the church, the neighbors, and serves as the family's social secretary. At some social levels and with some families integration of family members with the spatially and institutionally dispersed segments of society is typically the function of the father. Through his business or professional connections he may be in a position to help his son enter a business or a profession in a remote part of the country or to help his daughter enter the college of her choice.

Relevant to the child's status-orientation is the observation that the family is the chief medium through which culture is transmitted to the young child. The version of the total culture that is transmitted depends upon the experiences of those who do the transmitting. Since it is largely the parents and other members of the household who are in immediate contact with the child, it is their version of the culture that is transmitted. Since their beliefs and values tend to be consistent with their positions in the total society, the family becomes the conduit through which is transmitted a version of the culture that is characteristic of the family's social class, ethnoreligious affiliation, and so on—i.e., of the subculture inherent in the family's society-oriented positions and social categories.

Some idea as to how the family confers upon its sons society-oriented positions can be derived from an examination of data on the relation of family income and father's education to the educational level of offspring, the relation of education and occupation, and the relation between occupation and income.

From Table 8.1 it is evident that the chance of a young person's progressing through the educational system is highly associated with the income of his family and with the education of his father. About two of every ten children from families under the $5000 level had any college experience, whereas six of every ten did at the $10,000 level. An even greater spread of proportions is associated with the levels of education of fathers. From Table 8.2 it is evident that the higher-paying and more prestigeful occupations are those with the higher levels of education.[71]

How does it happen that among the lower social strata the proportion of children who pursue their studies to any given level is appreciably less than the proportion among the upper strata? There are four sets of causes, any one of which is probably potent enough to account for this correlation. (1) At any grade level it probably costs the family more to have the child in school than not to; the increment of cost seems to increase with the age of the child, rising sharply as he enters college, even if the college is publicly financed. (2) There is some evidence that teachers expect the offspring of families in the lower strata to have relatively little academic competence at all grade levels; the "Rosenthal-effect" reported in psychological studies[72]

---

[71] The Spearman rank correlations between median level of education and median earnings in Table 8.2 are +.96 for men and +.66 for women. See also Table 5.1.

[72] Rosenthal reports a series of studies in which the psychologist's hypothesis was shown to influence the experimental results. These studies involved both human and animal subjects. For example, experimenters who believed they had maze-bright rats reported consistently fewer errors for their animals than did experimenters who believed they had maze-dull rats; the animals were actually undifferentiated.—Robert Rosenthal, "On the Social Psychology of the Psychological Experiment," *American Scientist*, 51: 268–283 (1963).

TABLE 8.1

Percent Distribution by Educational Level of Persons 16–24 Years Old, by Family Income and by Father's Education, for the United States: October 1960

FAMILY INCOME AND EDUCATIONAL LEVEL OF THE FATHER	PERSONS 16 TO 24 YEARS OLD	EDUCATIONAL LEVEL OF THE PERSON					
		Did Not Graduate from High School	Graduated from High School, Did Not Attend College	Total with College Attendance (sum of columns to right)	Attended College, Did Not Graduate	Currently Enrolled in College	Graduated from College
All educational and income levels	100.0	32.4	36.4	31.2	8.6	18.3	4.3
Father did not graduate from high school	100.0	42.9	38.0	19.1	5.9	11.0	2.3
Father a high school graduate, did not attend college	100.0	14.4	39.4	46.2	14.5	25.2	6.5
Father attended college	100.0	6.1	18.6	75.3	13.4	51.2	10.7
Father's education not reported	100.0	36.1	46.7	17.2	8.6	4.8	3.8
Less than $5000	100.0	45.3	35.8	19.0	7.0	9.2	2.7
$5000 to $7499	100.0	25.8	41.2	33.0	10.8	17.3	5.0
$7500 to $9999	100.0	13.9	37.6	48.6	11.5	32.0	5.1
$10,000 or more	100.0	13.2	26.5	60.3	8.0	44.1	8.2

SOURCE: U.S. Bureau of the Census, *Current Population Reports—Population Characteristics*, Series P-20, No. 110, July 24, 1961, Table 10, p. 15.

TABLE 8.2

Median Level of School Completed by Employed Males 25–64 Years Old, by Major Occupational Group, 1969; and Median Earnings of Year-Round Full-Time Workers, by Occupational Group and by Sex, 1968: United States

OCCUPATIONAL GROUP	MEDIAN SCHOOL YEARS COMPLETED	MEDIAN EARNINGS	
		Male	*Female*
Professional, technical, and kindred workers	16.5	$10,542	$6,610
Managers, officials, and proprietors, except farm	12.8	9,794	5,101
Sales workers	12.8	8,292	3,388
Clerical and kindred workers	12.5	7,324	4,778
Craftsmen, foremen, and kindred workers	12.0	7,958	4,315
Service workers	11.7	5,898[a]	3,159[a]
Operatives and kindred workers	10.9	6,773	3,956
Farmers and farm managers	10.8	3,353	1,095
Laborers, except farm and mine	9.0	5,606	$3,490
Farm laborers and foremen	7.8	$ 2,870	[b]

[a] Private household service workers are excluded from the data on earnings.
[b] Base less than 75,000.
SOURCE: For years of school, U.S. Bureau of the Census, *Current Population Reports—Population Characteristics,* Series P-20, No. 194, February 19, 1970, Table 6, p. 25; for earnings, U.S. Bureau of the Census, *Current Population Reports—Consumer Income,* Series P-60, No. 66, December 23, 1969, Table 43, pp. 103–105.

would lead us to anticipate that teachers would get empirical confirmation of these expectations. (3) The subcultures of the lower social strata do not accord the high valuation to education that is characteristic of subcultures of higher strata. (4) It is consistent with point (3) that lower-status families give less emphasis to academic achievement than do upper-status families. The first of these four points seems quite obvious; the other three warrant some discussion.

According to Hollingshead, it was widely believed among the high school students of Elmtown that in giving out grades the teachers placed greater weight on the social status of the student's parents than upon the performance of the student. With respect to the child from the upper- or upper-middle class family the teacher was disposed to expect a competent performance and, if necessary, to assist the child to "make good," reports Hollingshead. As might be expected from such a classroom climate, the failures in the lower strata exceeded the number that might be expected on differences in intelligence—the proportion decreased monotonically from 23 percent in the lower-lower stratum to 3 percent in the upper class. There were three curricula in the high school: college preparatory, general, and commercial. Consonant with the foregoing observations was the finding that the children of upper-class and upper-middle parents concentrated in the college preparatory curriculum, while children from lower strata concentrated in the other two curricula. None of the parents of lower-lower students had finished high school, and few of the offspring from this stratum expected to do so.[73]

The differences among children of the various social classes in expectations of achievement, quality of performance, and amount of recognition received are probably not, however, a consequence solely of the school system. Hyman has shown that whatever measure of stratification is employed, lower-status people place less value on education than do those in higher strata. Since entry into some occupations requires considerable education, it is relevant to consider status-linked attitudes about work. Hyman found that people of lower status favored the following reasons for selecting an occupation: wages, fringe benefits, and especially the security of employment. By contrast, upper-status people were reported to be attracted to a job because of the "congeniality of the career pattern to the individual's personality, interests, and individual qualifications."[74] Similarly Lyman reports a tendency for blue-collar workers to emphasize monetary rewards and the easy nature of the job, whereas white-collar workers emphasize gratifications deriving from the nature of the work itself.[75]

It appears that the generally superior school performance of middle-class children is in part a consequence of their having internalized a drive to achieve to a greater degree than is characteristic of lower-class children. Empey has

[73] A. B. Hollingshead, *Elmtown's Youth* (New York: Wiley, 1949), pp. 168–181. It has been claimed that both intelligence tests and personality tests contain biases that favor the children of the middle class and represent the children from lower strata in an unfavorable light. Cf. Allison Davis, *Social-Class Influences upon Learning*, Inglis Lecture (Cambridge, Mass.: Harvard University Press, 1948); Martin L. Hoffman and Carlos Albizu-Miranda, "Middle Class Bias in Personality Testing," *Journal of Abnormal and Social Psychology*, 51: 150–152 (1955); James S. Coleman *et al.*, *Equality of Educational Opportunity* (Washington, D.C.: GPO, 1966).

[74] Herbert H. Hyman, "The Value Systems of Different Classes: A Social Psychological Contribution to the Analysis of Stratification," in Bendix and Lipset, *Class, Status, and Power*, pp. 488–499, at p. 492.

[75] Elizabeth L. Lyman, "Occupational Differences in the Value Attached to Work," *American Journal of Sociology*, 61: 138–144 (1955). Douvan placed a task—the taking of a psychological test—before high school seniors of both sexes and of middle- and working-class families. In some performances she offered monetary reward; in others, abstract reward. The middle-class subjects responded under both conditions, but the average effort of working-class subjects dropped significantly when the reward was abstract. One can see a strand of consistency between Douvan's results and the reports of Hyman and Lyman above: that working-class people tended to be attracted toward jobs on the basis of extrinsic rewards whereas middle-class people were motivated by intrinsic considerations as well. Elizabeth Douvan, "Social Status and Success Strivings," in John W. Atkinson (ed.), *Motives in Fantasy, Action, and Society: A Method of Assessment and Study* (Princeton, N.J.: Van Nostrand, 1958), chap. 36, pp. 509–517.

found that middle- and upper-class male high school seniors aspire to higher occupational positions than do lower-class seniors.[76] Sewell and associates found that both educational and occupational aspirations of male and female high school seniors in Wisconsin correlated positively with the social status of their families when level of intelligence was controlled.[77] From a sample of high school sophomores Rosen reports that both the drive to achieve and the value placed upon achievement are positively correlated with socioeconomic status.[78] On the other hand, a suggestion that the relation between socioeconomic status and the drive to achieve may not be monotonically positive throughout the entire range of socioeconomic statuses comes from a study of Harvard students. McArthur used the kind of secondary school attended as an index of social class: preparatory school denoted upper class, and public high school denoted middle class. He discovered that the achievement drive was significantly higher on the average in the middle-class students than in the upper-class.[79] It is consistent with this finding that the hippies, who generally reject established values, are from upper-middle class families and reject occupational achievement and material possessions.[80]

Toby summarizes his views concerning the ways in which the average middle-class child is advantaged with respect to performance in school in comparison with the lower-class child:

(1) [the middle-class child's] parents are probably better educated and are therefore more capable of helping him with his school work if this should be necessary; (2) his parents are more eager to make his school work seem meaningful to him by indicating, implicitly or explicitly, the

---

[76] LaMar T. Empey, "Social Class and Occupational Aspiration: A Comparison of Absolute and Relative Measurement," *American Sociological Review*, 21: 703–709 (1956).

[77] William H. Sewell, Archie O. Haller, and Murray A. Straus, "Social Status and Educational and Occupational Aspiration," *American Sociological Review*, 22: 67–73 (1957). In another article on the same study it is reported that urban high school boys aspire to more education than do rural high school boys when intelligence is controlled. —Archie O. Haller and William H. Sewell, "Farm Residence and Levels of Educational and Occupational Aspiration," *American Journal of Sociology*, 62: 407–411 (1957).

[78] Bernard C. Rosen, "The Achievement Syndrome: A Psychocultural Dimension of Social Stratification," *American Sociological Review*, 21: 203–211 (1956).

[79] Charles McArthur, "Personality Differences between Middle and Upper Classes," *Journal of Abnormal and Social Psychology*, 50: 247–254 (1955). A somewhat comparable finding is reported concerning students at Beloit College: that striving for upper-class position could not be detected among students from upper middle-class families. The author of the study suggested that his results might indicate contentment with the upper-middle way of life and some aversion to the concept of the upper class on the grounds of democratic ideology.—E. E. LeMasters, "Social Class Mobility and Family Integration," *Marriage and Family Living*, 16: 226–232 (1954).

[80] Kenneth Keniston, *The Uncommitted: Alienated Youth in American Society* (New York: Delta, 1965); David L. Westby and Richard G. Braungart, "Class and Politics in the Family Backgrounds of Student Political Activists," *American Sociological Review*, 31: 690–692 (1966).

occupational applications of long division or history; (3) the verbal skills which he acquires as part of child training on the middle-class status level prepare him for the type of training that goes on in school and give him an initial (and cumulating) advantage over the lower-class child in the classroom learning situation; and (4) the coordinated pressure of parents, friends, and neighbors reinforce his motivation for scholastic success and increase the probability of good school adjustment.[81]

From a study in which they find that Americans with a high school education or less spend most of their work-lives in manual occupations, Lipset and Bendix conclude that "educational attainment is a major determinant of career patterns, a fact which provides the strongest and most direct statistical link between family background and the assets and liabilities with which individuals enter the labor market."[82]

From our interest in the significance of statuses conferred by the family we have been considering the differences in aspiration and the drive to achieve that have been found to be correlated with levels of social status. Ethnoreligious differences are frequently seen as related to levels of aspiration and the drive to achieve. Warner and Srole note that in Yankee City the Russian Jews rose faster through the status system than did any other ethnic minority and that they telescoped into thirty years a rise through strata that took the French Canadians forty years and the Irish seventy years.[83] Hurvitz believes that from four sociohistorical sources—the Jewish religious tradition, the "business ethic" of the Jews, their having lived in cities, and their having been a minority group—there has resulted an outlook especially conducive to upward mobility. This outlook includes an individualistic democratic philosophy and a this-worldly, utilitarian, rationalistic, empirical attitude toward life with an emphasis on moderation.[84]

---

[81] Jackson Toby, "Orientation to Education as a Factor in the School Maladjustment of Lower-Class Children," *Social Forces*, 35: 259–266 (1957).

[82] Seymour Martin Lipset and Reinhard Bendix, *Social Mobility in Industrial Society* (Berkeley: University of California Press, 1960), p. 197. That status-orientation operates in addition to position-conferring is suggested by their finding that with educational level held constant, sons of manual workers go into manual occupations in considerably greater proportion than do sons of nonmanual workers.—*Ibid.* The topic of occupational inheritance is taken up in the next section.

[83] W. Lloyd Warner and Leo Srole, *The Social Systems of American Ethnic Groups* (New Haven, Conn.: Yale University Press, 1945), pp. 203, 309.

[84] Nathan Hurvitz, "Sources of Middle-Class Values of American Jews," *Social Forces*, 37: 117–123 (1958). Strodtbeck's finding that differences between Italians and Jews in values related to social mobility disappear when social status is controlled might be interpreted as negating the proposition that the ethnoreligious variable has any explanatory value in the matter. Such an interpretation would be plausible if it had been possible to use a truly experimental method in his study, i.e., to assign subjects randomly to ethnoreligious categories and to social classes, but it leaves unexplained the fact that most of the Jews were in the highest of three socioeconomic statuses, whereas over five sixths of the Italians were in the lower two statuses.—Fred L. Strodtbeck, "Family Interaction, Values,

We have been dwelling at some length on the consequences of having one status rather than another ascribed to an infant, and we have seen these statuses as transmitted by, or at least through, the family. We have not begun to exhaust the range of possibilities, but in order to get back to our main theme, we shall run somewhat quickly over some of the other consequences of status conferring.

Upper-status adults tend to vote more in elections, to participate in more formal associations, and to hold more offices in organizations than do middle-status adults, and the latter tend to exceed lower-status adults in these respects.[85] Other phenomena correlated with socioeconomic status are types of imagery, capacity to conceptualize, and modes of communication;[86] the kinds of organizations one joins;[87] how one spends his leisure time, e.g., by attending a concert or a baseball game;[88] whether or not one reads for pleasure, and if so, what he reads, e.g., *Atlantic* or *True Confessions;*[89] the probability that one

and Achievement," in David C. McClelland *et al., Talent and Society: New Perspectives in the Identification of Talent* (Princeton, N.J.: Van Nostrand, 1958), chap. 4, pp. 135–194.

[85] W. A. Anderson, "Family Social Participation and Social Status Self-Ratings," *American Sociological Review*, 11: 253–258 (1946); Wendell Bell and Maryanne T. Force, "Urban Neighborhood Types and Participation in Formal Associations," *American Sociological Review*, 21: 25–34 (1956); Floyd Dotson, "Patterns of Voluntary Association among Urban Working-Class Families," *American Sociological Review*, 16: 687–693 (1951); Floyd Dotson, "A Note on Participation in Voluntary Associations in a Mexican City," *American Sociological Review*, 18: 380–386 (1953); John M. Foskett, "Social Structure and Social Participation," *American Sociological Review*, 20: 431–438 (1955); Mirra Komarovsky, "The Voluntary Associations of Urban Dwellers," *American Sociological Review*, 11: 686–698 (1946); Leonard Reissman, "Class, Leisure, and Social Participation," *American Sociological Review*, 19: 76–84 (1954); Charles R. Wright and Herbert H. Hyman, "Voluntary Association Memberships of American Adults: Evidence from National Sample Surveys," *American Sociological Review*, 23: 284–294 (1958); and Basil G. Zimmer, "Farm Background and Urban Participation," *American Journal of Sociology*, 61: 470–475 (1956).

[86] Leonard Schatzman and Anselm Strauss, "Social Class and Modes of Communication," *American Journal of Sociology*, 60: 329–338 (1955).

[87] Wendell Bell and Maryanne T. Force, "Social Structure and Participation in Different Types of Formal Associations," *Social Forces*, 34: 345–350 (1956); C. Wayne Gordon and Nicholas Babchuk, "A Typology of Voluntary Associations," *American Sociological Review*, 24: 22–29 (1959); Joseph R. Gusfield, "Social Structure and Moral Reform: A Study of the Woman's Christian Temperance Union," *American Journal of Sociology*, 61: 221–232 (1955).

[88] Alfred C. Clarke, "The Use of Leisure and Its Relation to Levels of Occupational Prestige," *American Sociological Review*, 21: 301–307 (1956); R. Clyde White, "Social Class Differences in the Uses of Leisure," *American Journal of Sociology*, 61: 145–150 (1955).

[89] Milton C. Albrecht, "Does Literature Reflect Common Values?" *American Sociological Review*, 21: 722–729 (1956); George Gerbner, "The Social Role of the Confession Magazine," *Social Problems*, 6: 29–40 (1958).

will become a mental patient, and the kind of treatment one will receive if one does;[90] the probability of surviving if one is in military combat;[91] and if one succumbs, the probability of being cremated.[92]

STABILITY AND MOBILITY: PERMANENCE AND IMPERMANENCE OF STATUSES CONFERRED BY THE FAMILY OF ORIENTATION

There are no really adequate data to indicate the permanence of ascribed statuses in American society. Many people in America are vertically mobile. Just what proportion a study finds to be mobile seems to depend on an array of factors, some of which are

1. The period studied—more mobility takes place during a period of prosperity and economic expansion than during a depression and economic stagnation.
2. The location studied—there is more mobility in urban areas than in rural, in large cities than in small.
3. The number of strata differentiated by the researcher—this is a purely artifactual source of variation, for it is obvious that the more strata one postulates, the thinner the strata will be, and the greater will be the apparent mobility.

With respect to the proportion mobile or immobile, Young and Mack state: "Most of the research on occupational mobility indicates that approximately two-thirds of the sons have been vertically mobile, either upward or downward, from the class strata of their fathers."[93] Without revealing much of his procedure, McGuire tentatively concludes that in a fivefold system of social classes about 20 percent of each generation moves upward and about 5 percent moves downward.[94] An over-all trend toward upward mobility can be seen in the shift in the American occupational structure, noted in Chapters 4 and 12, consisting of an increasing proportion of the labor force in white-collar, especially professional, occupations and a decreasing proportion in blue-collar and farming occupations.[95]

---

[90] Robert E. Clark, "Psychoses, Income, and Occupational Prestige," in Bendix and Lipset, *Class, Status, and Power*, pp. 333–340; August B. Hollingshead and Frederick C. Redlich, *Social Class and Mental Illness: A Community Study* (New York: Wiley, 1958); Jerome K. Myers and Bertram H. Roberts, *Family and Class Dynamics in Mental Illness* (New York: Wiley, 1959).

[91] Albert J. Mayer and Thomas Ford Hoult, "Social Stratification and Combat Survival," *Social Forces*, 34: 155–159 (1955).

[92] William M. Kephart, "Status after Death," *American Sociological Review*, 15: 635–643 (1950).

[93] Kimball Young and Raymond W. Mack, *Sociology and Social Life* (New York: American Book, 1959), p. 222.

[94] Carson McGuire, "Social Stratification and Mobility Patterns," *American Sociological Review*, 15: 195–204 (1950).

[95] On this point see Gerhard E. Lenski, "Trends in Inter-Generational Occupational Mobility in the United States," *American Sociological Review*, 23: 514–523 (1958).

Two factors make the larger city and the metropolis more favorable for vertical mobility than are the smaller city and the village. One has to do with the greater opportunities in the metropolitan occupational system; the other with the greater anonymity of urban relationships. On the former point Lipset and Bendix point out that large cities differ from small ones in having a greater degree of occupational specialization and therefore a wider variety of positions, a higher ratio of nonmanual to manual positions, and a higher rate of community growth resulting in (as well as from) more new and higher level positions.[96]

With respect to the anonymity or nonanonymity of relationships, we are told that in Elmtown (population 6200)

> the family sets the stage upon which the adolescent is expected, if not compelled by subtle processes and techniques, to play out his roles in the developmental tasks he faces in the transition from child to adult. As he moves into the community, he carries his family's station in the prestige structure with him. He is identified by his family name, and the heritage of the family is his heritage. To be sure, he is a personality separate from his family; however, sociologically, he is an inseparable part of it since he has not had an opportunity to emancipate himself from it and establish a station of his own in the community's prestige structure. Consequently, when an adolescent leaves his home and goes into the community, his family goes with him in a very real sense. Elmtowners know the history and reputations of families, as well as their mannerisms and traits. The boy or girl who has matured in a family learns these things from his ancestors for better or for worse, since the type of behavior that has marked his family is expected from him. A successful business man epitomized this process when he said, "My dad used to tell me, 'Get out of town; you can't cross the railroad tracks here.' But I showed him. Sometimes, though, I think Dad was right."[97]

Where a person's history is known, his efforts at upward mobility are impeded by a sort of friction factor in terms of the conceptions of his initial status that

---

[96] Lipset and Bendix, *Social Mobility in Industrial Society*, pp. 216-219.

[97] Reprinted by permission from *Elmtown's Youth* by A. B. Hollingshead, published by John Wiley & Sons, Inc., 1949, p. 159. Cf. also Albert Blumenthal, *Small Town Stuff* (Chicago: University of Chicago Press, 1932), chap. 11. Merton reports that in "Rovere" (an eastern city of 11,000) locally oriented people tend to succeed on the basis of whom they know rather than what they know; personal ties outweigh professional talents.— Robert K. Merton, "Patterns of Influence," in P. F. Lazarsfeld and F. N. Stanton (eds.), *Communications Research: 1948–1949* (New York: Harper & Row, 1949), pp. 180–219, esp. pp. 197–200. When colleges are ranked with respect to the "average aptitude of entering freshmen," it is found that average annual earnings are higher for male graduates of the higher than for the lower-ranking colleges. With the resulting distribution of colleges trichotomized, the average income of the male graduates of the middle-ranking colleges is 22 percent above, and of those in the top-ranking colleges 45 percent above, the average of those in the bottom rank. *Current Population Reports—Population Characteristics*, Series P-20, No. 180, March 24, 1969, Table 4, p. 3.

are carried around in the attitudes of other members of the community. In other words, it appears that achieved status is more characteristic of a secondary community; and ascribed status, of a primary community.

In the contemporary urban setting the individual, especially the young adult, may enter into a social situation relatively devoid of his history. That is to say, the nature of one's associations in an urban (secondary) community tends to be segmental, of relatively brief duration, and hence with persons who are unacquainted with his origins and history. This means that in the city one is treated more as an individual and less as a member or representative of a family. Except in the upper strata of society, where the status of one's family of orientation is of primary concern in the problem of gaining acceptance, facts about one's origins and initial status seem to be of the order of "incidental intelligence." When a man applies for a job in the office of a large corporation, he may expect the personnel officer to be interested in his history and his family and to investigate his references. It is likely, however, that the personnel officer will register less interest in the young man's family than in the schools he has attended, his record there (areas of specialization, honors, activities), the kind of record he may have established for himself in the military, and the like. To the extent that this is so, the important question in placing the young man in the occupational system is not what family did he come from, but what kind of record has he made for himself in school, and what kind of school was it? To the extent that this also is so, the educational system is more important than the family in placing the young man in the occupational system, but as we have seen, the family is important in placing the young man, while still a boy, in the educational system.

Both because of the low valuation placed on formal education by people in the lower social strata and because families at the lower levels are less able than those in higher levels to finance their children through college (and quite possibly also because performance tests discriminate in favor of children from upper strata) the probability of a child's going to college, as we have seen, is positively correlated with the socioeconomic status of his family. Since people who attend college subsequently earn more than those who do not attend (as we saw in Table 5.1 above), this situation tends to create some rigidity in the system of stratification. Moreover, the offspring of rich families tend to go to expensive colleges, and the graduates of these colleges average more income than do graduates of less expensive schools. From this observation one might be in doubt as to whether the educational system is contributing to rigidity of the stratification system, or is reflecting such rigidity, or is perhaps doing both. The answer would appear to depend on the degree to which attendance at the more expensive schools seems to "cause" the higher income. There is evidence that students from rich families earn more after college than do students from poor families, and that students from poor families who work their way through expensive schools earn more after college than do students from poor families who work their way through less expensive colleges.[98]

Because of the anonymity of the metropolis, people in that setting seek to read each other's appearance and overt behavior for clues as to their ascribed statuses. After allowance is made for the urban-rural difference in per capita income, it is still clear that—consistent with the urban emphasis on appearance—urban residents spend more on such items as clothing. At the lowest income levels urban-rural differences in expenditures for clothing are small. As income increases, however, the proportion spent for clothing by urban families becomes much greater than the proportion spent by rural families. "Where the individual lives—in a large city, a small city, a village, or on a farm—has an effect on the amount spent for clothing; the greater the urbanization, the greater the outlay."[99]

This general point of view seems to be expressed in the characteristically urban notion of "selling oneself." By this is apparently meant that one of the techniques available for the achievement of upward mobility is that of creating the "best possible impression" upon those whom one meets. "It is not the genuine self that is put on the market in the race for success," says Riesman, ". . . but the 'cosmetic' self, which is free of any aroma of personal, non-marketable idiosyncracy."[100] To "sell oneself" seems generally to mean that one should strive to appear more "able," more "successful," of "higher class," and so on, than one actually is. Because so many of a person's contacts are of brief duration, it is assumed or hoped that strangers will accept him at a falsely high value and correspondingly grant him jobs, sales, promotions, and other favors. It seems clear that such an idea would be relatively meaningless in a society made up of persons one had known all one's life. In *Small Town Stuff* Blumenthal reports, "One must be 'common' in Mineville."[101]

Although one's origins and history tend to be less widely known in cities than in small towns and rural communities, one's background is not completely ignored even in the metropolis. It has been said that in England a man's social class is stamped on his tongue. It is difficult to lose all the marks of one's origins in terms of modes of speech, dress, and the like. Moreover, racial, ethnic, and religious continuities are frequently ineradicable—to some degree at least.

---

[98] Ernest Havemann and Patricia Salter West, *They Went to College* (New York: Harcourt, 1952), esp. pp. 178–185.

[99] U.S. Department of Agriculture, *How Families Use Their Income* (Washington, D.C.: GPO, 1948), pp. 29, 60. Cf. also J. Frederic Dewhurst, *America's Needs and Resources* (New York: Twentieth Century, 1947), p. 128; National Resources Planning Board, *Family Expenditures in the United States: Statistical Tables and Appendices* (Washington, D.C.: GPO, 1941), p. 13.

[100] David Riesman, *Selected Essays from Individualism Reconsidered* (New York: Doubleday Anchor Books, 1955), p. 54.

[101] *Op. cit.,* p. 105.

Status-Conferring by Other Structures in Adulthood

Where the society is of the open-class type, adulthood is the time of greatest opportunity to alter one's status. Stated in other terms, an open-class society creates opportunities for adults to acquire achieved statuses. The structures that confer new statuses vary from one society to another, contingent upon the major activities in the society. Where there is considerable emphasis on military activities, as with the Comanche and Nazi Germany, warfare is an obvious activity in which to achieve recognition, and thereby higher status. Since the industrial-commercial emphasis in the United States has made the occupational system an important locus of opportunity to achieve higher status, we find that status-conscious persons, especially in the middle class, take their occupations particularly seriously, prepare for them in trade and professional schools and colleges, and evaluate jobs as good or bad in terms of the prospect they hold for "promotion."[102]

It should be noted that implied in the concept of status is the idea that it is the payoff in a zero-sum game. That is, assuming a constant population, for each individual who moves up there must be a compensating downward move by someone else. It appears, however, that many people are disposed to use another criterion of their own mobility: the opportunity to acquire and to consume more, and more expensive, goods. It is an economic commonplace that the general level of living has been rising in this country for better than a hundred years and especially since the great depression of the 1930's.[103] Because of the general upward trend in the level of living many can elevate their level of consumption greatly over the course of their adult lives, i.e., they can buy more, bigger, and more expensive automobiles, boats, television sets, electric refrigerators, clothing, vacations, and so on, and also they can increase the rate of obsolescence. Thus the allocation to consumers' goods of a large part of the gross national product means that many can interpret their rising level of consumption as evidence that they are "arriving."

Since in adulthood the opportunity arises for people to achieve new statuses and in America this is done to a considerable extent in the occupa-

---

[102] There is no dearth, however, of fantasies regarding upward mobility that involve less labor than the rung-by-rung occupational conception. Of special relevance to the study of marriage and the family is the Cinderella fantasy. This fantasy involves being elevated to vastly higher status through being loved by someone of exalted status. The Cinderella fantasy, which is perpetuated in our media of mass communication, seems to appeal to persons of both sexes.

[103] Herman P. Miller, *Income of the American People* (New York: Wiley, 1955), chap. 8. In 1933 expenditures for personal consumption averaged $897 per capita in 1958 dollars; by 1967 the corresponding figure was $2160.—*Statistical Abstract of the United States: 1968,* Table 466, p. 319.

tional system, it follows that for such persons the status-conferring function no longer resides in the structure of the family but in the economic structure. This has implications for the family. Typically the (society-oriented) socioeconomic status of the wife and children, who are economic dependents, is determined by the socioeconomic status of the husband-father, and hence by the degree of his occupational success.

The fact that the status of wife and children depends upon the occupational performance of the father points up the paramount importance of his role in the family. In contrast with certain other family forms, this type of organization places great emphasis upon the economic productivity of the father. His performance determines whether his dependents wear rags or sables, whether they fall or rise in the status hierarchy. This kind of family organization has implications for feelings of responsibility and anxiety on the part of the father, and for ambivalent feelings of resentment and of gratitude on the part of other family members. It is he who is vulnerable to censure when wife and children are unable to occupy the status to which they aspire, and to possess the overt marks of such status in terms of expensive cars, clothes, entertainment, and memberships. We shall explore some of these implications in later chapters.

Society-Oriented and Family-Oriented Statuses: Age and sex categories

Early in this chapter a distinction was drawn between a society-oriented status, which is an evaluated position with respect to the society as a whole, and a family-oriented status, which refers to the value placed upon the individual because of the position he occupies within the family. Up to this point we have been preoccupied with the society-oriented statuses a person acquires by virtue of being born into one family rather than into another. Now it is in order to consider children, women, and the aged in connection with both society-oriented and family-oriented statuses. In part this discussion is an introduction to a more thorough consideration of familial positions and roles in Chapter 12.

A convenient way to think about family-oriented statuses is to take some familial position such as husband-father as a standard and to examine the prestige of other positions relative to this standard. We shall be looking upon the rights and privileges normatively associated with these positions as indicative of their statuses. From our functional orientation, moreover, we shall be sensitive to the prospect that when the occupant of a position is generally able to make large contributions to the well-being of the family, that position will carry high status, and we might anticipate the converse proposition to obtain also.

THE STATUS OF THE CHILD

In the peasant family of traditional China the child was put to useful labor virtually as soon as he was physically capable of it. In view of the child's ability to make a progressively greater contribution to the welfare of the family as the capacity of the grandparents was waning, we should expect the child of the Chinese family to enjoy high family-oriented status. We have seen, however, that the contrary was true. Both within and outside the family prestige was positively correlated with age, with the consequence that the aged were revered and the children were told it was not dignified to be young.

In Kiryat Yedidim children were expected to make some contribution to the economy of the community, but their chief responsibility was the currently unproductive one of going to school. There was little expectation of an immediate important economic contribution from the children of the kibbutz. Our functional analysis would lead us to the expectation that the children would have low status. But, as we have seen, it was customary to save for the children the most succulent and nutritious bits of food; their status was very high. Accordingly it seems either that status is not to be explained on functional grounds or that the functional grounds must be revised.

Let us try the latter course. Let us assume that status is not to be explained, or not necessarily, on the ground of direct economic contribution but on other and perhaps more symbolic grounds. Old China was a highly traditional society in the full sense of that adjective. The ways of the ancestors were good, and the living aged were revered in part because of the imminence of their crossing into the hereafter and becoming objects of worship.

The orientation of Kiryat Yedidim, on the other hand, was decidedly to the future. The immediate past was one of travail and frequently of persecution, and the present was a period of hardship. As in all utopian societies the golden period lay in the future, and the children represented the nexus to the golden period. Since the children represented the means of achieving the golden age, sacrifice for them was regarded as no more than expected. Even though food, clothing, and labor were scarce, the children were so highly valued that they were given the best food and clothing and leisure to attend school and go on holidays.

And what about American middle-class society? There can be little doubt that economically the American child is a liability. Each year the magnitude of the liability seems to increase. But there can also be no doubt that the status of the American child is high. Foreign travelers in our land are aware of and sometimes distressed by the freedom given to children, the privileges extended to them, the lack of demands of deference from them, and the absence of any expectation that they are, or should be, capable of useful work.

In traditional China and the kibbutz we observed a correlation between the high or low status of the child on the one hand and the future or past orientation of the culture on the other. On the basis of this tentative generalization the observation that the American child enjoys high status would lead us to the expectation that American culture is forward-looking rather than backward-looking. This seems generally to be true. To move through one's own efforts from poverty and squalor to social respectability and high status is the American dream. This is the essence of the concept of America as the land of opportunity. Of course to value upward mobility is to be future-oriented. Not only does the concept of mobility involve the future of one's own career but a frequently appearing form of the dream is that one's children will continue the climb and arrive at what would be for the parent a very dizzy perch on the status ladder.

The foregoing analysis suggests that, other things being equal, the family-oriented status of the child should be highest in those strata of American society wherein there is the greatest emphasis on mobility, i.e., in the middle strata. Some tangential evidence can be adduced to support this point. There has been much discussion in recent years to the effect that the middle-class family has become child-centered, i.e., that the wishes and the welfare of children loom relatively large in the family life of these strata. The writer is aware of no such characterization of families in the upper or lower strata. The literature on social class and child rearing[104] seems to be converging on the conclusion that families in the middle strata tend to be warmer and less punitive toward their children than is true of lower-class families. Little study has been given to socialization in the upper strata, but the extensive employment of governesses and of boarding schools implies that the relations of upper-class children to their parents probably tend to be less warm and close than is usual in the middle class.[105]

THE STATUSES OF WOMEN

In connection with the statuses of women there are two major considerations that we may put into the form of questions: (1) How are a woman's socioeconomic, ethnic, religious, and other statuses determined? (2) What sort of status does a person have by virtue of the fact that the person is a woman? With respect to the former question it is generally the case in Western societies that a woman maintains the statuses conferred upon her by her family of orientation until she marries, when she assumes the socioeconomic status and frequently the ethnoreligious identification of her husband. The recognition that the woman takes her socioeconomic status from her husband is of course

[104] To be considered in Part Five.

[105] At first thought it might seem absurd to regard the status of the middle-class child as higher than that of the upper-class child. It should be recalled, however, that we are considering family-oriented status. In a royal family (to take a family of top society-oriented status) it is true that there is much deference accorded to the crown prince, for some day he will be king, but the crown prince must show deference to his father for the latter *is* king.

the crux of the interest of single girls, and their parents, in the "prospects" of their young men. Popenoe has telescoped much discussion into the remark that a man marries a wife but a woman marries a standard of living.[106]

In Western societies there are two conspicuous exceptions to the proposition that the status of the wife is determined by the status of the husband: the statuses of Britain's Queen Elizabeth and of the Netherlands' Queen Juliana determine the statuses of their husbands rather than vice versa. In American upper-class society a married woman does not entirely lose the ascribed status conferred upon her by her family of orientation. Family lines are known and remembered. At this class level Miss Smith is remembered as being of *the* Smith family long after she becomes Mrs. Jones. An example from Oriental societies comes from the exceptional practice of matrilocal marriage, noted in Chapter 2.

More generally speaking, it appears that anything that obscures the woman's premarital status facilitates her taking status from her husband. In American society four conditions tend to produce this consequence: (1) the practice whereby the bribe drops her surname and adopts her husband's, (2) the practice of neolocal residence (i.e., the bride and groom set up a new residence apart from the home of either set of parents), (3) living in the relative anonymity of the secondary community, and (4) an open-class society with emphasis on achieved statuses (since the achievement of status is generally determined by the course of the career of the husband-father).

Now let us take up the question as to the status of a person by virtue of the fact that the person is a woman.

Puritan culture had many emphases in common with that of the ancient Hebrews. Among these was the conception of woman as being of limited competence and rights and of questionable moral worth. Women's activities centered in housekeeping and the rearing of children, and it was believed that this was their divinely ordained sphere. They were believed to be incapable of dealing with larger issues of a nondomestic order, or with the abstractions found in such spheres as law and philosophy.

A number of considerations have entered into the change in the status of women from one of inferiority and subservience to their husbands in the seventeenth century, to one of increasing but less than absolute equality in the twentieth century. Among the factors relevant to the change in the status of women have been the scarcity of women on the frontier, the demand of industry and commerce for the labor of women, and the resulting release of women from total dependence upon marriage as a carrer and a livelihood. These factors have enabled women to improve their bargaining positions vis-à-vis their husbands. Moreover, in the later eighteenth and early nineteenth centuries the romanticism of Rousseau began to provide an ideological justification for the altered position of woman in our society. Perhaps the simplest

---

[106] Paul Popenoe, *Modern Marriage: A Handbook for Men* (New York: Macmillan, 1946), p. 22.

way to characterize this change might be to remark that whereas, for the Puritan, Eve was the symbol of womanhood, this symbol has come to be displaced by the Madonna.[107]

Chapter 12, on the differentiation of roles within the family, will have some observations concerning the family-oriented status of the woman. For the moment let us merely note that the separation of home and work for the husband-father leaves the wife-mother during each working day where she is called upon to supervise the children and administer the home. The nature of this role exerts a pressure for a high family-oriented status of the wife-mother.

STATUSES OF THE AGED

With respect to the aged we may rephrase our two questions about the statuses of women: How are an aged person's statuses determined? What sort of status does a person have by virtue of the fact that the person is aged?

Since in modern societies occupation, income, and prestige are the bases of socioeconomic status, a crucial condition affecting the socioeconomic status of the aged person is whether or not he (or her husband, if the person is a wife) is retired. If the husband-father is still working at his usual occupation and is maintaining his level of income, presumably his socioeconomic status is unaffected. If he has retired from his usual occupation but is working, it is probable that he is employed at a job offering less prestige and income than he derived from his usual occupation. Of course this implies some reduction in socioeconomic status. If he is completely retired, his income is probably substantially reduced, with the probable consequence of a loss in status. A study of old people in a working-class section of east London reports: "Retirement from work is a tragedy for most men. It alters their lives, lowers their prestige, thrusts them into poverty or near poverty, cuts them off from the friendships and associations formed at work and leaves them with few opportunities of occupying their time."[108] As we shall see in Chapter 17, however, the upper class again constitutes an exception. At this level socioeconomic status tends to be more ascribed than achieved and more grounded in property than in occupation. For these reasons and since there is no demand for continuing validation of one's status by occupational performance, age contributes only further respectability to the upper-class person.

[107] Parsons suggests that a disposition to associate "goodness" with "femininity" lies at the root of much ambivalence in Western culture. (Cf. Talcott Parsons, "Certain Primary Sources and Patterns of Aggression in the Social Structure of the Western World," in Lyman Bryson, Louis Finkelstein, and Robert M. MacIver [eds.], *Conflicts of Power in Modern Culture* [New York: Harper & Row, 1947], pp. 29–48, esp. p. 36.) Cf. also Simone de Beauvoir, *The Second Sex* (New York: Knopf, 1953); and Morton M. Hunt, *The Natural History of Love* (New York: Knopf, 1959).

[108] Peter Townsend, *The Family Life of Old People: An Inquiry in East London* (London: Routledge, 1957), p. xii.

In America the aged person tends to be more an object of pity than a recipient of deference. In line with our analysis of the status of the child, it seems consistent that a future-oriented society with an emphasis on upward mobility should honor its children but not its elders. As Townsend observes, the economic dependence of elders on their offspring "weakens the family, for the family is partly built on reciprocal services."[109] Once again the upper class stands in contrast, for here the emphasis is not on mobility. Here property and power are in the hands of the elders, who become patriarchs and matriarchs rather than "burdens."

Summary

Position-conferring refers to the assigning to an individual of a (social) position in some social structure. To call the function "status-conferring" is to emphasize the social evaluation of the position conferred. A person is said to have as many social positions as there are social systems in which he holds membership. A "family-oriented" position locates a person in the familial system, i.e., in his relations with occupants of other positions in the family. "Society-oriented" positions relate him through his memberships in other social systems to occupants of other positions in those systems. For example, when a given man, who is "husband-father" in his familial system, leaves home for the factory, he becomes a "worker" in relation to his "foreman." At school the boy, who is "son-brother" in his familial system, becomes "pupil" in relation to the "teacher." "Ascribed" positions and statuses are inherited; "achieved" positions and statuses are won.

Illegitimacy is a lack of a social position. A legitimate child is born into a family, and in all societies the family confers social positions upon its young. In American society, race, ethnoreligious identification, and socioeconomic status are involved in such ascription.

There are two aspects of the process by which the family confers social positions upon its young: providing locations for them in extrafamilial social systems, and transmitting the appropriate subculture.

By being located in a particular kind of community and at a particular level in the status system a family influences the probability that its sons will finish high school, attend and finish college, enter a manual or nonmanual occupation, and the rate at which they will move upward in the status system. (And since we shall see in Chapter 10 that women tend to marry at around their parents' status levels, families influence their daughters' social statuses as well.) Of course the outcome for any given young man is the resultant of a large number of influences, including his own intelligence, energy, and special aptitudes. The focus of interest here is on what generally happens, what is the tendency, what is the outcome for the average person in such and such a

[109] *Ibid.*, p. xiii.

situation. The theme is forcefully summarized in the formulation that a person's life chances are critically influenced by the social position ascribed to him by his family, and that his life chances include "everything from the chance to stay alive during the first year after birth to the chance to view fine arts, the chance to remain healthy and grow tall, and if sick to get well again quickly, the chance to avoid becoming a juvenile delinquent—and very crucially, the chance to complete an intermediary or higher educational grade."[110]

Through exposing the child to a set of experiences both within and outside the home, the family creates a situation in which the child learns behaviors and attitudes and acquires the values and modes of perception more or less appropriate to the social positions the family confers upon him.

The more permanent the positions and statuses conferred by the family in any given society, the less is the opportunity that society provides for achieving positions and statuses. In this country the socioeconomic is one of the most emphasized of the achievable statuses. With certain exceptions, most particularly at the higher socioeconomic levels, the ultimate determinant of this kind of status in American society is the occupational system (and thus the economic structure). And of course marriage provides another avenue of vertical mobility, especially for women.

As young people leave school to get jobs, the educational system helps to find jobs, provides references to employers, and in such ways integrates those young people into the economic system. As young people leave the educational system to marry, the school provides not only a congenial locale for their meeting and interacting with eligible spouse-candidates but also provides them with school pedigrees (i.e., school-linked social positions and statuses) and in this way integrates those young people into the familial system.

With respect to the position-conferring function in America it seems correct to conclude that the usual sequence is as follows: The child acquires from the family an ascribed socioeconomic status, one aspect of which is that the family determines the schools the child attends and to some degree the kind of reception the child gets at these schools. When the child emerges some years later as an adolescent or young adult, the school places its assessment on him as an applicant in the labor market (and in a sense in the marriage market as well). Both the reputation of the school and of the individual within the school influences the position (and status) at which the young person enters the occupational system and the familial system. Thus at first the family and later the school and finally the occupational system are largely responsible for fulfilling the position-conferring function.

With certain exceptions a woman loses many of her statuses on marrying, and for those she loses she takes over the corresponding statuses of her husband. The status-bearing link between the occupational structure and the

---

[110] Hans Gerth and C. Wright Mills, *Character and Social Structure* (New York: Harcourt, 1953), p. 313.

family is the person or persons who are employed. Usually this is the husband-father, and therefore in the American family it is usual for the husband-father to confer statuses, including socioeconomic, on the wife-mother and the children.

The relative family-oriented status of children and of the aged appear to depend in part at least upon the degree to which the society is oriented to the future or to the past. Having upward mobility as a major theme, middle-class America is oriented to the future and gives a favored place to children. Deprived of occupation and faced with a reduction in income, the aged have difficulty in holding onto the symbols of the socioeconomic status achieved during their productive years.

9

Emotional Gratification: *functional corollary of the family's structure*

Introduction

We derive emotional gratification from a variety of sources—food, drink, and esthetic experiences, among others. Interaction with our fellow human beings is a very important source of gratification. We use the terms *friendship* and *companionship* to denote relationships that are primary in Cooley's sense —intimate and face to face—and in which we may know the joy and comfort of sharing our hopes and fears, our accomplishments and our failures. In the present chapter we are interested in looking at the family as a societal structure in which we experience such emotional gratification and, conversely, the degree to which other categories of social relationships compete with the familial in offering emotional gratification. The function of emotional gratification deals with man's responses to and demands upon his fellows.[1] As we begin

---

[1] As used in this book, the function of providing emotional gratification pertains to much the same set of phenomena as are denoted by Parsons, Bales, and Zelditch in their phrase "expressive roles." Cf. p. 235 above.

There is a bit of overlap between the function of emotional gratification and the individual-oriented aspect of the religious function in that both embrace the objective of reducing negative affect—through consoling the defeated, the afflicted, and the bereaved. There is, however, a distinction as to the means employed. In the function of emotional gratification the means is the intimate relationship. In religion the means may involve ritual (e.g., the comfort derived from the funeral service) and/or theology (e.g., the idea that pre-mortem sufferers will be favored when post-mortem rewards are distributed) although the social relationship too may appear (as in the work of the pastor).

The function of emotional gratification also overlaps slightly the individual-oriented aspect of the political function in that both include protecting the individual (here our concern is especially with the young child) against physical threat and thereby providing physical security.

the analysis of this function, then, it becomes necessary to make some assumptions concerning the nature of man.

Among the ways of viewing man there are three especially worthy of our notice. The first of these conceives of man as a responding machine. John Locke thought of the human mind as being at birth a *tabula rasa*. Gordon Allport has described Locke's view of the human intellect as "a passive thing acquiring content and structure only through the impact of sensation and the crisscross of associations, much as a pan of sweet dough acquires tracings through the impress of a cookie cutter."[2]

The view of man as a responding machine has the following implications: Since by postulate nothing of psychological interest has been built into the organism, everything of psychological interest happens where it is external and visible. By this criterion thoughts, fantasy, imagery, and so on, are dismissed as not psychologically relevant. The same postulate, moreover, suggests that subhuman species are capable of behavior similar to human behavior in its psychological essentials. This tends to focus attention on behavior that both rats and men can perform. And since rats are capable of only somewhat simple behaviors, the emphasis is on simple, or molecular, behaviors. This view of man has been dominant in Anglo-American laboratory psychology, according to Allport.[3]

Whereas in the first view the organism is reactive when stimulated, in the second and third views man is self-propelling. According to the second view, man is born with a source of energy, an *id*, a built-in system of impulses that put his organism into a state of tension. The course of man's life then becomes a series of efforts to gratify impulses, and gratification, or pleasure, is stated in terms of the relaxation of tension. But since the impulses are basically sexual and aggressive in nature, there is in the culture a moral code that denies the individual his gratification. First from his parents, and later from society, man encounters obstacles to, and prohibitions against, the expression of his impulses. Some of these prohibitions—especially those met in childhood—are internalized as inhibitions, whence the individual learns fears and avoidances and acquires anxiety and neurosis. Man is destined to fight a futile lifelong battle with society for pleasure and for self-realization. Accordingly, impulses bring only travail, pain, and sorrow. Man is best off in a state of quiet, of relaxation, of sleep, of Nirvana, of death. And life is a struggle to achieve unconsciousness, to regain the womb.

The third view of man shares with the second the postulate that man has a built-in source of motive power. The third view differs from the second, however, in two important respects: (a) not all behavior is seen as tension-reducing, and (b) the third view is less pessimistic. As Schachtel phrases it, the human infant seeks encounters with the environing reality "not in order to

[2] Gordon W. Allport, *Becoming: Basic Considerations for a Psychology of Personality* (New Haven, Conn.: Yale University Press, 1955), p. 7.
[3] *Ibid.*, p. 8.

still hunger or thirst or as a detour on the way to return to the comfort of sleep, but out of a growing urge to get in touch with and explore the world around...."

As Schachtel says in connection with dining, each of us has felt a zest— not to remove the discomfort of hunger and thirst—but to experience "the positive tension feeling of eagerness and the enjoyment in eating when hungry [and] drinking when thirsty."[4] Thus man, according to this view, not only seeks at times to relieve his tensions but at other times takes positive action to increase certain tensions for the purpose of heightening his pleasure, being creative, and realizing his possibilities. In this view, moreover, the culture is seen as less forbidding and the parents as less punitive.

For our purposes the first of our three points of view has generally been concerned with behaviors too molecular, or small, for our consideration. The principal reason for mentioning the Lockean view is to answer the possible question as to the relevance of much of laboratory psychology to the problems of this chapter. The molar behaviors connoted in the second and third views are at the heart of our interest. The second, or Freudian, view points to a host of relevant considerations—especially to anxieties, insecurities, and other consequences of negatively toned experiences. These considerations lead us to consider the family as an emotional haven, as a security-giving structure. But the literature suggests that when the family becomes dysfunctional in this regard, it can become a cesspool of hostility, a fertile culture for neuroses. The third view leads us to look upon the family as a setting for the expression of eagerness, interest, and zest for living.

Our treatment will reflect the fact that whereas the literature on the second view is large and the concepts are numerous, the literature on the third is small and the concepts are few and not very adequate. Apparently the main reason for this state of affairs is that most of the thinking, research, and writing on molar behaviors in psychology has been in connection with the problems of the emotionally disturbed and the mentally ill. Freud concentrated on anxiety as central to the explanation of the kinds of psychoneuroses he observed in his patients. In view of his monumental contribution, the magnitude of the subsequent interest in psychopathology, and the large numbers of psychiatrists and psychologists who have worked in the field, the literature relating to negative affect (unpleasure) is rich in ideas and in concepts. (Because of the difficulty of designing effective experiments on molar behaviors, however, the field is woefully short on corroborated propositions.) On the other hand, literature relating to positive affect (pleasure) and to the more optimistic emphasis in the third view is virtually nonexistent. This lack

---

[4] Ernest G. Schachtel, *Metamorphosis: On the Development of Affect, Perception, Attention, and Memory* (New York: Basic Books, 1959), pp. 9, 25. Another writer in this tradition is Goldstein, who has emphasized that man has a motive for "self-actualization." Cf. Kurt Goldstein, *The Organism* (New York: American Book, 1939). Cf. also Robert W White, "Motivation Reconsidered: The Concept of Competence," *Psychological Review* 66: 297–333 (1959).

may result in part from a "tenderness taboo"⁵ in Western cultures and an avoidance of "corniness" associated with positively gratifying experiences. The poverty of the literature is suggested by the fact that one of the best-known concepts comes not from the laboratories nor from the pen of a famous clinician. Rather it is a cliché that bears the stigma of having come from Madison Avenue; the concept is togetherness. Perhaps the best summary is still a statement made in 1939 by Kardiner: "Psychoanalytic technique is at the present time capable of evaluating personality only from the line of sight established by repression and frustration; it does not yet have reliable criteria for pursuing the joyful and creative aspects of personality."⁶

Purpose of This Chapter

In accordance with the second view of man noted in the introduction to this chapter we shall consider feelings of insecurity. Among the topics to come under scrutiny are the kinds and sources of insecurity, and some of the settings—both familial and extrafamilial—in which feelings of insecurity are assuaged. The latter part of the chapter will consider the third view of man as well as the second. It will take up parenthood from the standpoint of its potential for emotional gratification—both for the assuaging of feelings of insecurity and for the prospect of positive gratification.

Security and Insecurity

The concept of security implies the concept of threat, for without threat one would not be conscious of security. We become conscious of the air we breathe only when its supply is short. Life is filled with a number of threats of various kinds. Threats may be real or imaginary, sensed or not sensed. In imagination, e.g., through superstitions, some may conceive of hazards that cannot be objectively demonstrated. Young children may fail to perceive threats that are evident to their elders. We may conceive of two broad classes of threats. There are physical threats against one's body and psychic threats against one's self. The former are a threat against one as an organism; the latter are against one as a social being.

Let us conceive of one part of the function of providing emotional gratification—a subfunction perhaps—as that of providing security, i.e., of pro-

⁵ Cf. Ian Suttie, *The Origins of Love and Hate* (London: Routledge, 1935), chap. 6.
⁶ Abram Kardiner, *The Individual and His Society: The Psychodynamics of Primitive Social Organization* (New York: Columbia University Press, 1939), p. xxiv. The present writer would disagree, however, with Kardiner's next sentence: "This is a limitation of the method and not, as may appear, a conception of the human personality." Psychoanalysis, particularly in the writings of Freud, does seem to offer a conception of personality in terms of repression and frustration and not in terms of joy and creativity.

tecting an individual against threats, whether real or imaginary, and whether or not the person is aware of them. It is the purpose of the next few sections to examine the nature of these threats, and hence of the various types of insecurity. We shall seek to understand the degree and the manner in which the family functions to provide security against these threats.

PHYSICAL SECURITY

Threats against the organism come from war and other forms of violence, from disease, and from famine. In a mass society the principal basis of protection against such threats resides not in the family but in the state (with its monopoly on the use of force through the military and police establishments), in the various branches of medical practice, and in the economy as a whole. It is true that in childhood and adolescence siblings may provide protection for each other, but at subadult ages the gang is probably more important than the family as an organization for mutual protection against violence.

In illness the family plays some part in providing protection. Because of the development of medical knowledge and the consequent professionalization of physical care, the family's responsibility is, on the one hand, to provide care and attention in such a way as to improve or keep up the patient's morale, and, on the other, to provide the resources to buy the required medical services. At the lower economic levels the latter function is to varying degrees passed on to public assistance and to private charity. Probably the most conspicuous example of the family's providing physical security is with respect to the young child who has yet to learn responses appropriate to various kinds of physical threat.

In the so-called civilized societies death from starvation appears to be rare. In general, such societies have relief organizations to prevent starvation. As we have seen, however, Allison Davis regards anxiety about food and shelter as characteristic of the lower class.[7] This remark does not imply an absence of widespread anxiety in American society over money, but this, as we shall see, is more related to psychic security and especially to status-security rather than to fear of starvation.

PSYCHIC SECURITY

The nature and condition of psychic security is a topic of too great scope to be given systematic treatment here. It will be our purpose merely to try to point out some of the salient factors. For most middle-class persons it appears that job and family are the major sources of gratification and security; but job and family can also be major sources of frustration and insecurity. The job is the source of income, the determiner of socioeconomic status for the hus-

---

[7] Cf. pages 209–210 above.

band-father (and hence for the entire nuclear family), and accordingly the job is the source of one kind of security or insecurity. Our culture defines the lover, marital, and filial relationships as the most appropriate sources of affection and love, of reassurance and response, and hence of another kind of security. The security arising from the job situation comes from competition and achievement. The security arising from the family comes from love and acceptance. On the job, as well as on the playground, in the school and gang, recognition tends to go to the able competitor. This is a central implication of the concept of achieved status. In some families, perhaps most, recognition and affection are given to each member simply because he belongs to the family—ascribed, in other words, because of kinship. In other families affection is granted or withheld, depending perhaps on the quality of the offspring's grades or the size of the husband's commissions, and here family-oriented status is achieved rather than ascribed.

To facilitate the discussion let us designate security based on achievement as *status-security* and security based on affection and response as *interpersonal security*. There is a cultural expectation that a well-balanced person will seek both kinds. Some persons, however, emphasize one more than the other; some seek to exploit one as a compensation for failure in the other. No doubt it is the compulsively striving person who, disliking and distrusting people, aspires to gratification and security solely from his job—status-security; and it is the passive-dependent person who seeks to derive gratification solely from family relationships—interpersonal security. (Our cultural expectations concerning sex roles are that men will deviate in the former direction and women in the latter.)

In a sense, although the emphasis in this distinction is correct, the foregoing interpretation is overdrawn. The family situation frequently manifests competition, especially among siblings, and the work situation frequently provides the counterpart of the parent-child and sibling relationships (between superior and subordinate, and among workers at the same level, respectively). There is an emphasis in many types of work situations on having a "pleasing personality" and "selling oneself." For example, in certain types of sales work the salesman's achievement seems to depend upon the degree to which his "prospects like" him. The familial sort of relationship is evident in McGregor's statement: "Security for subordinates is possible only when they know they have the genuine approval of their superior."[8]

It has been noted that status-security and interpersonal security are somewhat independent, but that one may be used as a compensation for a deficiency in the other. When a family member meets rebuff on the job or the playground, therefore, the opportunity arises for other members of the family

---

[8] Douglas McGregor, "Conditions of Effective Leadership in the Industrial Organization," in T. M. Newcomb and E. L. Hartley (eds.), *Readings in Social Psychology* (New York: Holt, Rinehart and Winston, Inc., 1947), p. 430.

to restore security through expressions of affection, reassurance, and recognition. This is a point at which the family can do much in buttressing psychic security and generally make the home seem a haven from the cruel practices of the outside world.

STATUS-SECURITY AND STATUS-INSECURITY

Sociologists are fond of saying—and at present there is no compelling reason to think otherwise—that a society in which a maximum of one's statuses are ascribed (i.e., a caste society) offers a high level of status-security. Presumably a part of the price we pay for our open-class society is the prospect that as individuals we may awake on some cold, gray dawn to the realization that for us "success" has indeed proved a dream. Despite the efforts of some educators to make it appear otherwise in the primary grades, there must be "also-ran's" in the steeplechase of upward mobility. Or stated positively, to have a feeling of status-security one should have the conviction that one is progressing satisfactorily to the statuses one aspires to achieve and that one's present and future ascribed statuses will prove acceptable at least, if not highly gratifying.

The child, the adult, and the aged all have their problems with status-security in American society. As the child emerges from the home and joins at play a group of his mates, he confronts a new set of expectations, a new set of criteria in terms of which to evaluate his adequacy. In his interaction outside the home, the child—and later the adult—meets an ever-shifting set of standards. At one age he may be judged by the fidelity of his representation of a cowboy hero; at another, by his prowess at baseball; at still another, by his ability with girls, by his ability to "con" the boss, and so on. It is by no means certain that a child who is proficient in meeting cultural expectations and derives recognition, approval, and security at one age level will do so at a later age or in adulthood when confronted with different standards. We may anticipate a later discussion by noting that, in part, this situation is a consequence of the existence of "cultural discontinuities," or the fact that the experiences at one age level do not necessarily train or prepare the child for the kinds of performance expected at the next level.

For the adult male there are two prominent aspects of American culture that facilitate the development of status-insecurity: its complexity and its competitiveness. When a man is dependent upon a self-sufficient farm, his economic difficulties can be attributed to a very limited number of somewhat easily comprehended sources: effort, climate, soil. When he is dependent upon an industrial economy and subject to the catastrophic consequences of depressions or other economic conditions, such as those related to technological and seasonal change, he may blame his difficulties on the "system." But the "system" is merely the name covering a network of extremely complicated relationships beyond the comprehension of the worker. It requires sophistication of a high order, for example, to grasp even a fraction of the intricate relationships between the movement of an armored column in Korea and a lay-off of workers in Keokuk. More generally stated, the psychic insecurity envisaged here is a consequence of the complexity of the socioeconomic organization and its responsiveness to a multitude of influences that the individual worker can neither understand nor foresee.

The individual, competitive ethos of American culture is a fertile field for the development of feelings of insecurity. The traditional "American dream" has embraced the concept of "self-realization," individually and competitively achieved. Achievement is registered in part through the improvement of status. By the nature of the case there is a limited number of higher socioeconomic statuses for a large number of competitors, and therefore some must be frustrated in their striving. That is, the nature of the system dictates that if all are striving, some must be frustrated. Many of those who fail are thrown into a state of status-insecurity, as are some of those who succeed but who still fear failure.

For the female—as child, adolescent, and young adult—one big question is whether or not she will marry. A correlative question of course is, assuming she will marry, how "well" will she (can she) marry?

It appears that a state of affairs conducive to status-insecurity occurs when a person has one or more high statuses but another one or more of low rank. The term "status-inconsistency" was introduced in Chapter 8 to refer to this state of affairs. Status-inconsistency exists, for example, when a person has a high level of education (such as training beyond the college level with a graduate or professional degree) but is in an unskilled occupation; the relatively uneducated man who is highly successful in business in another example. It has been theorized that a person with inconsistent statuses tends to develop conflicting expectations of his own and others' behaviors—that he will try to interact with another on the basis of his superior status(es) but that the other will try to interact with the first person on the basis of the first person's inferior status(es). Such conflicting expectations, according to this reasoning, should give rise to feelings of uncertainty and frustration, and the response of some persons to such status-insecurity should take the form of such physical symptoms as upset stomach, clammy hands, loss of weight, and palpitations. In support of this reasoning Elton Jackson reports that the amount of status-inconsistency is positively correlated with the number of psychophysiological symptoms where

1. Racial-ethnic rank is superior to occupational or educational rank.
2. For males, occupational rank is superior to educational rank.
3. For females, educational rank is superior to their husbands' occupational rank.[9]

[9] Elton F. Jackson, "Status Consistency and Symptoms of Stress," *American Sociological Review,* 27: 469–480 (1962).

Special problems concerning the family's capacity to afford emotional gratification arise with relation to the aged and to those whose marriages are broken. These are considered in Chapters 17 and 23, respectively.

INTERPERSONAL SECURITY

By feelings of interpersonal security or insecurity is meant the feelings of satisfaction or dismay a person has about the apparent esteem in which he is held by his associates. What is denoted is one's response to the evidence that one's associates regard one as acceptable, lovable, a good fellow, or as unacceptable, unlovable, a despicable fellow.[10] It should be emphasized that what is being evaluated is the more or less idiosyncratic behavior we speak of in terms of personality characteristics, not role performance or status-linked behavior.

The combination of individualism and competitiveness in American society creates a sense of isolation, a point that will be developed at greater length in connection with the concept of "separation anxiety." The impersonal nature of relationships in some types of urban settings tends further to foster feelings of alienation and to stimulate psychic insecurity and a need to "belong." Such a need is no doubt intensified by whatever doubts one may entertain as to one's moral worth.

The link between mental disorder and psychic insecurity has led psychiatrists and psychologists subscribing to the second view of man to be sensitive to signs of psychic insecurity. "Feelings of inferiority and inadequacy . . . a conviction of incompetence, of stupidity, or unattractiveness"[11] are subjective symptoms of psychic insecurity. The third view of man, on the other hand, focuses on psychic security and mental health, symptoms of which are that "basic needs for safety, belongingness, love, respect and self-esteem have been sufficiently gratified that the individual is motivated primarily by trends to self-actualization."[12]

There is a certain plausibility in construing the incidence of suicide as a rough index of the level of psychic insecurity. Late in the nineteenth century Durkheim showed that in Western Europe suicide occurred more often among the unmarried than among the married, and among childless men than among fathers. Durkheim interpreted these findings as showing that the number and integration of one's social relationships had an influence on the probability

---

[10] This concept of interpersonal security contains the ingredients of Cooley's concept of the looking-glass self: "the imagination of our appearance to the other person; the imagination of his judgment of that appearance, and some sort of self-feeling, such as pride or mortification."—Charles Horton Cooley, *Human Nature and the Social Order* (rev. ed.; New York: Scribner, 1922), p. 184.

[11] Karen Horney, *The Neurotic Personality of Our Time* (New York: Norton, 1937), pp. 36–37.

[12] Abraham Maslow, "Deficiency Motivation and Growth Motivation," in Marshall R. Jones (ed.), *Nebraska Symposium on Motivation* (Lincoln: University of Nebraska Press, 1955), pp. 1–30. Quotation is from p. 8.

that one would commit suicide.[13] This point has been corroborated in somewhat different ways by Henry and Short and by Gibbs and Martin.[14] Durkheim also noted that suicides tended to occur with a sudden change in one's situation, as in the death of a spouse (his anomic suicide).[15] Another study has shown that the suicide rate of elderly men is related closely to retirement and the consequent loss of occupational status. Using a twenty-year series of data from Tulsa County, Oklahoma, Powell found (1) that whereas the suicide rate of women went down slightly after the age of 65, the rate for men shot up dramatically, and (2) that the suicide rate for retired men over 65 was nearly twice that of all males of the same age bracket, and therefore presumably much higher with respect to the men over 65 who were still employed. Powell aptly speaks of retirement as "a virtual excommunication."[16] The obvious alternative interpretation is that in the older age brackets suicide might be related to the incidence of incurable diseases. There are national data that are relevant to this point. When the American population is double-dichotomized by race (white and nonwhite) and by sex and when the age-specific suicide rates are calculated for the resulting four categories, it turns out that three of the four curves rise to peaks and then taper off at the older ages, but the curve for white males increases with each successive age group. From age 35 on this curve is considerably higher than for nonwhite males, which in turn is higher than the curves for females of either race over almost all age categories.[17] Since it is unlikely that white males have a vastly higher incidence of incurable diseases than nonwhite males, but since it is plausible that white males gain more gratification from their work, these national data do seem consistent with Powell's interpretation.

WAYS OF ALLEVIATING PSYCHIC INSECURITY OUTSIDE THE FAMILY

As defined in this book (see Chapter 1), the religious function overlaps with that part of the function of emotional gratification having to do with the alleviation of feelings of anxiety. In Chapter 5 it is noted that religion is the most ancient and widely known way of providing psychic security on a society-wide basis. Chapter 5 also notes that religious beliefs vary from culture to culture, apparently in response to the nature of commonly experienced sources

---

[13] Émile Durkheim, *Suicide: A Study in Sociology* (trans. by John A. Spaulding and George Simpson; New York: Free Press, 1951), pp. 197, 208–209.
[14] Andrew F. Henry and James F. Short, Jr., *Suicide and Homicide: Some Economic, Sociological and Psychological Aspects of Aggression* (New York: Free Press, 1954); Jack P. Gibbs and Walter T. Martin, *Status Integration and Suicide: A Sociological Study* (Eugene: University of Oregon Press, 1964).
[15] *Op. cit.*, pp. 259–260.
[16] Elwin H. Powell, "Occupation, Status, and Suicide: Toward a Redefinition of Anomie," *American Sociological Review*, 23: 131–139 (1958), at p. 136.
[17] National Center for Health Statistics, *Suicide in the United States: 1950–1964*, Series 20, No. 5 (Washington, D.C.: U.S. Department of Health, Education, and Welfare, August 1967), Figure 3, p. 5.

of stress, and that secularization brings on a demand for functional equivalents of the religious structure. It was noted above that a heightened need to belong seemed to be a frequent response to feelings of psychic insecurity, and that this might motivate a person to assuage his insecurity through marriage. Other kinds of "joining," more or less irrespective of the kind of group, can be interpreted as a response to anxiety and in some sense a substitute for religious faith. The psychological similarity of political zealots and of religious evangelists is frequently remarked. But other kinds of memberships can also be anxiety reducing. Lodges, fraternities, labor unions, service clubs, ladies' aid societies, bridge clubs, and social groups in neighborhood taverns can confer a sense of "belonging" and thereby impart a sense of psychic security.

Gratification and the Third View of Man

To this point the chapter has considered insecurity, its origins and varieties, ways of alleviating it, and in particular the family's contribution in this respect. As we shift from the second view of man (seeking to resolve his anxieties, to relax his tensions, and to achieve Nirvana) to the third view (which locates gratification in conation or activity), it would be orderly to describe and to analyze the kinds of emotional gratification that the family has to offer occupants of the various familial roles: the roles of husband and wife, parent and child, and, indeed, the roles of the extended family. Whether or not it is for the reasons proposed above, however, there is very little scientific literature on positive affect associated with these roles, its causes and its consequences. Rather than try to collect the fragmentary evidence at this juncture, it seems preferable to present the material on marital happiness in connection with the analysis of marriage in Chapter 21 and the material on the gratifications of childhood in the sections on socialization, Part Five, especially Chapters 13 and 15. In the passage to follow, then, we shall offer a few observations about emotional gratification in parenthood.

Parenthood

To be or not to be a parent is a question that implies that children are neither inevitable nor necessarily desirable. The question also indicates that the culture contains some socially approved, or at least condoned, method of preventing their coming. The availability of contraceptives and of literature on their use shows that there is considerable support for the idea that pregnancies should be avoided without resort to sexual abstinence; on the other hand, the opposition to the spread of information on contraceptive techniques reveals conflict on this subject. Of course the topic of voluntary parenthood covers other questions than whether or not to be a parent. Assuming this question to be answered in the affirmative, there remain the further questions as to how many children one wants, and at what intervals, and also whether or not to adopt one or more children instead of, or in addition to, one's own.

The life goal of the Arapesh, according to Margaret Mead,[18] is to raise yams and children. Few contemporary Americans could give such a simple, concise statement of their life goals. "Happiness" seems to be the first approximation to an answer that members of our society are disposed to offer. Wilson reports that (in American society) the happy person tends to be well educated, well paid, to have high self-esteem, high job morale, and modest aspirations, and to be of either sex and of a wide range of intelligence.[19] From this characterization it is seen that one aspect of happiness concerns job, career, income, satisfying and remunerative employment, and (with respect to one's level of aspiration) "success." This is the set of considerations we noted in the concept of status-security. A second aspect concerns the companionship, esteem, and affection of intimate friends, and especially a marriage partner. These are elements in interpersonal security. Scrutiny of the first set of ends discloses that they are oriented to personal advancement, an individualistic end. Although the second set specifies association, the emphasis is upon the gratification the individual expects to derive from such association, again an individualistic end.

Zimmerman tells us that individualism leads to a declining birth rate and that neither of these phenomena is uniquely modern. He finds them present in the latter periods of the classical civilizations: post-Periclean Greece and imperial Rome. In these periods, he says, the use of birth control techniques was widespread, as was childlessness and consequent depopulation. In Rome, Augustus instituted a series of legal measures known as the *Leges Juliae*, which were designed to make it difficult for people of property to avoid either marriage or parenthood.[20] We have observed that for the century preceding the depression America had a declining birth rate and that for the quarter-century thereafter the birth rate shot up. Since that time it has fallen off again. Do these trends coincide with trends of waxing, waning, and waxing individualism? The writer knows of no data that can provide an answer. Let us, however, see what can be stated about the rewards and penalties of parenthood.

REWARDS OF PARENTHOOD

The literature on fertility has devoted considerably more space to the disadvantages than to the advantages of parenthood. This may lead the reader to the conclusion that such analysts are irresponsible cynics. A more appropriate interpretation is that the analysts have been confronted with the idea

---

[18] *Sex and Temperament in Three Primitive Societies*, in *From the South Seas* (New York: Morrow, 1939), p. 14.

[19] Warner Wilson, "Correlates of Avowed Happiness," *Psychological Bulletin*, 67: 294–306 (1967). Wilson also reports that the happy are young, healthy, extroverted, optimistic, worry-free, and religious. Cf. also Norman M. Bradburn and David Caplovitz, *Reports on Happiness* (Chicago: Aldine, 1965); and Derek L. Phillips, "Social Participation and Happiness," *American Journal of Sociology*, 72: 479–488 (1967).

[20] Carle Zimmerman, *Family and Civilization* (New York: Harper & Row, 1947), pp. 154–166.

that parenthood is "natural," and that what required explanation was the "unnatural" avoidance of parenthood. Some corroboration for this view comes from a survey in 1955 of some 2600 wives who were asked how many children they would want if they could live their married lives over again. Only 1.1 percent responded none.[21] In any case the result of the emphasis is a great lack of information on why people *do* want children. Dennison has reported the responses of a highly selected group (400 Princeton graduates). He found that 82 percent wanted children because of the companionship they would provide (more important for younger than for older parents); 66 percent wanted them in order to perpetuate the family line; 63 percent said that the creation and development of a new life was one of the main interests in living; and 48 percent thought children would provide companionship in old age. Other reasons for having children and the proportions giving these reasons were fulfillment of social obligation, 40 percent; the idea of having children is a social convention, 35 percent; birth occurred in spite of efforts at prevention, 15 percent; and opposition to artificial efforts at prevention, 7 percent.[22]

The American reader will probably not find the Princeton men's reasons for having children very surprising. A visitor from rural Ireland, however, might be astonished at the absence of expectation of economic benefits, and a visitor from traditional China might add that "the child helps the development of intimate relations between husband and wife, who are little acquainted with one another before marriage."[23] In America, except where child labor is permitted and/or where there is an expectation of support in old age, the evidence indicates that the rewards of parenthood are psychic rather than economic.

It was remarked above that most writers seemed to regard parenthood as so "natural" that it called for no explanation; only the avoidance of parenthood seemed to require explanation. For example, Schilder says: "The wish of an adult or of a child . . . to have a child . . . signifies . . . the wish to create something going out from themselves, something which has a life of its own yet remains a part of the parent."[24] Deutsch regards a woman's desire for a child as a part of normal femininity and points out that, although men are greatly advantaged in the occupational system, the ability to bear a child is the uniquely feminine mode of creativity. The exercise of this ability, she asserts, is a great source of gratification to women.[25]

---

[21] Ronald Freedman, Pascal K. Whelpton, and Arthur A. Campbell, *Family Planning, Sterility and Population Growth* (New York: McGraw-Hill, 1959), Table 7.2 and p. 223.

[22] C. P. Dennison, "Parenthood Attitudes of College Men," *Eugenical News*, 25: 65–69 (1940).

[23] Hsiao-Tung Fei, *Peasant Life in China: A Field Study of Country Life in the Yangtze Valley* (New York: Dutton, 1939), p. 31.

[24] Paul Schilder, *Goals and Desires of Man: A Psychological Survey of Life* (New York: Columbia University Press, 1942), p. 178.

[25] Helene Deutsch, *The Psychology of Women: A Psychoanalytic Interpretation* (New York: Grune & Stratton, 1945), Vol. II.

PENALTIES OF PARENTHOOD

An exception to the general run of writers presenting parenthood as so natural a phenomenon as to require no explanation is C. S. Ford, an anthropologist, who notes that pregnancy handicaps and frustrates a woman, that labor is painful and childbearing dangerous, that the child may be deformed or stillborn, and that if it arrives alive and healthy, the mother must then spend much of her time attending to its needs. "If people are to reproduce," he concludes, "social life must offer enough rewards for bearing children to more than outweigh the punishments involved in reproduction."[26]

In an analysis of social factors in birth control Heberle makes the following points: (1) As a result of industrialization, masses of people became dependent upon income in the form of wages and salaries. (2) Wage and salary workers do not have property in land or capital that they wish to pass on undivided to their heirs. (3) Unlike artisans or shopkeepers, who have an opportunity to build up capital throughout their productive years, the wage or salary worker rapidly reaches his maximum income and "must face the fact that at forty years of age . . . his income will remain at a stationary level or will begin to decrease precisely in those years in which the younger and adolescent children in a large family occasion expenses of great magnitude." (4) Where child labor is prohibited, birth rates decline. (5) Although women have always worked, industrialization has taken them out of the home. The transfer of women's work to the factory or office has produced an incentive to restrict the raising of large families.[27]

Lorimer reports that on any given income level the proportion of income spent on food rises with the number of children. It follows that families with children have less to spend on other commodities, and he states that in such families the father and mother spend less on their own clothing than do husbands and wives with fewer or no children. "If all families invested the same proportion of their total income in food it would appear that, in order to maintain the same consumption level, families with three or four children in Chicago would need just about twice the income of childless families, and even farm families of this size would need more than 50 percent larger incomes than childless families in the same area."[28] Lorimer's report indicates the cost of children when income is held constant. Because of the fact that children tend to prevent or render difficult the full-time employment of wives, however, this is an unrealistic assumption. When the earning potential of the wife is considered, the economic disadvantage of children becomes even more marked.

---

[26] Clelland Stearns Ford, *A Comparative Study of Human Reproduction* (New Haven, Conn.: Yale University Publications in Anthropology, No. 3, 1945), pp. 86–87.

[27] Rudolph Heberle, "Social Factors in Birth Control," *American Sociological Review*, 6: 794–805 (1941), at p. 799.

[28] Frank Lorimer, "The Effect of Children on the Economic Status of American Families," *Journal of Heredity*, 31: 300–303 (1940), at p. 301.

As of 1967, 39 percent of the married women who were living with their husbands and had no children under eighteen were in the labor force. This was nearly one-half greater than the proportion of those wives who had preschool children.[29]

The shifting nature of responsibilities between parents and children is another factor entering into the attitude toward parenthood. In Chapter 4 we noted what we believed to be a trend—that the sense of responsibility for the welfare of parents seemed to be diminishing, while that for the welfare of children seemed, if anything, to be on the increase. In bygone days, then, children were productive at an early age and were a source of security to the parents in the latters' declining years. Under the changed conditions children are a liability when young and an undependable source of security to their aged parents.

As in the ancient syllogism about Socrates, most of us have come to accept intellectually the idea of our own mortality. Religious doctrines of recent generations have come to stress less and less the kingdom of heaven, salvation, post-mortem rewards, and the immortality of the soul. For the more secular minded, immortality and the future life appear to have become more a figure of speech than a serious expectation held with strong conviction. But regardless of their convictions about the hereafter, it appears that most Americans wish to achieve a sort of immortality by leaving some mark on the world, some evidence to future generations that they have lived. Children and works are two ways of doing this; and for most, parenthood is more easily achieved than are buildings, reforms, books, works of art, and so on. Thus parenthood offers the prospect of a sense of continuity with generations past and future. Presumably this psychic payoff is greater in times when there is ease of empathy and identification between successive generations, i.e., in times of stable, rather than rapidly changing, values. Cicero's lament "O tempora! O mores!" reminds us that the "generation gap" is not uniquely modern. Yet it seems safe to conclude that as that gap widens to the point where parents feel little understanding of their children's goals, there is probably a substantial reduction in the rewards of parenthood and that this trend may carry on to the point where parenthood seems laden with penalties.

PERSONALITY AND PARENTHOOD

To this point our analysis of the rewards and penalties of parenthood has been in terms of societal and cultural elements. Now we shift to a psychological level of interpretation. Since societal and cultural inconsistencies are frequently reflected in personality structure and since there are both rewards and punishments with respect to parenthood, we might expect to find emotional conflict and ambivalence with respect to parenthood. In American cul-

[29] Women's Bureau Bulletin No. 294, *1969 Handbook on Women Workers* (Washington, D.C.: GPO, 1969), Table 12, p. 33.

ture, as in Western culture generally, sex practices, contraceptive techniques, and the topic of procreation have been overlaid with strong taboos. Accordingly, except at the most superficial level, there has been little study of the psychological aspects of procreation. By the same reasoning, moreover, it is more than probable that even if one could find a group of totally frank persons, they would not be able to divulge their complete views and feelings on the subject of parenthood because some part of their feelings would be on the unconscious level and not accessible in the usual interview situation. As is well known, one of the points that Freudian psychology has driven home with great force is that a considerable part of motivation is unconscious; although people may be able to verbalize reasons for their behavior, there are frequently additional reasons of which they are quite unaware. Much clinical evidence supports this thesis.

Since we are confronted with a field in which there is no tested knowledge concerning the whole society or any of its strata, we have the choice either to pass along without comment, or to pause for a few speculations that seem to be consistent with the facts of our culture and with current psychological theory. Therefore, with the warning that the following remarks are more speculative than factual, the writer will offer some hypotheses concerning more or less unconscious emotional bases of procreative performance in our culture.

First, it should be observed that various unconscious emotional considerations may work either for or against a desire for children. In fact, it should not be a cause for astonishment to find both pro and con emotional factors at work in the same individual; the consequence is an attitude of ambivalence toward parenthood.

In growing from childhood to adulthood one faces the task of self-validation. This means that one has to demonstrate that one has the attributes, attitudes, and skills appropriate to one's age, sex, and social class. Self-validation in terms of age and sex means establishing oneself as a "man" or a "woman." Parenthood is one manifest way of accomplishing this end, and the presumption is strong that some persons who may entertain unconscious (or even conscious) doubts as to their "femininity" or, probably more frequently, their "masculinity," will desire children to achieve this end in their own eyes and in the view of others. As it affects the attitude toward parenthood, a strong drive for self-validation in terms of socioeconomic status may of course have the opposite result. If the success drive is strong, parenthood and even marriage may be deferred or perhaps forfeited entirely to achieve this goal.

Self-validation may involve vastly more subtle considerations than those already enumerated. It may take the form of an attempt to demonstrate one's knowledge or power, or one's ability to love, or to be immortal. If it takes the form of a desire to demonstrate knowledge or power, the person may seek to express such desires directly and strive for a high professional or executive position. Or he may abandon any hope for direct expression and resort to vicarious achievement, and then he will greatly desire a child upon whom to project his ambitions. Moreover, most parents can appear to their children, at least during the early years of the latters' lives, as having great knowledge and power.

One of our cultural expectations is that everyone should be capable of loving and of being loved, a matter to which we shall presently give considerable attention. For reasons that we shall discuss,[30] not everyone is confident of his ability to fulfill this cultural expectation. This seems to be particularly true of persons who enter marriage with affectional expectations that are unrealistic (or at least prove to be unfulfilled), and whose marital experience may result in increased rather than in diminished doubts as to their capacity for love. Some seek to resolve their doubts via the divorce courts and successive marriages. To others parenthood appears the more attractive means for the successive testing and validation of their ability to love.

Our culture contains the expectation that one who reaches the age of adulthood should be emotionally "mature," in the sense of being no longer emotionally dependent upon any other person. Clinical evidence[31] shows that this expectation is far from fulfilled. In some cases the dependency of child upon parent proves a deterrent to the marriage of the offspring; in others, the marriage may be greatly delayed, frequently until after the death of the beloved parent. Where the marriage does take place, it is frequently found that the spouse becomes the focus of this emotional dependency. To such a person, it may appear (often unconsciously) that the prospect of sharing the affection, love, and attention of the spouse with one's children is so repugnant as to preclude any desire for children. Since the dependent claims of the infant and young child are directed largely toward the mother, it follows that to whatever extent the husband-father may have been making his own dependent demands on the wife-mother, the more legitimate claims of the infant must now take precedence. Accordingly it would seem that the disinclination to have children because of unwillingness to give up a relationship of high dependence on the spouse should be manifested more markedly and more repeatedly among men than among women. On the other hand, women who are highly dependent may wish to avoid parenthood because of an anticipation that they would prove emotionally incapable of providing all the nurturant care an infant requires.

(Considerations taken up in the previous paragraph may also be stated in the more sociological language of roles and positions. As one approaches chronological maturity, one has normally been socialized to understand that one is expected to adopt adult social positions. Among these are the familial positions of husband-father and wife-mother with the parental roles those terms denote. Social approval is the reward for conforming to these expectations.)

[30] In Chapter 16 and Part Six.
[31] For a presentation of evidence on tendencies of dependence among our fighting men see Roy R. Grinker and John P. Spiegel, *Men under Stress* (New York: McGraw-Hill-Blakiston, 1945).

There is a set of attitudes centering upon the physiological consequences of pregnancy. Of these, fear of death in childbirth is perhaps the most widespread. The basis for this fear has decreased greatly since 1915.[32] One innovation in prenatal care is an attempt to overcome this fear on the part of expectant mothers.[33] Where there is much emphasis upon women's appearance, moreover, women have an emotional basis for the development of negative attitudes toward pregnancy. A woman may feel that such loss in her physical attractiveness as might be the consequence of bearing children would make her relationship with her husband less secure. On the other hand, both husband and wife may feel that a child represents both an externally imposed and an internally created pressure to maintain their marriage. The phrase "externally imposed" refers to an increment of social pressure to keep a marriage intact where there is a child. The "internally created pressure" arises from the new common interest, the set of more or less shared task-oriented activities in caring for, training, and rearing a child, and ultimately from the sense of shared accomplishment as the offspring matures.

As we shall see in Chapter 14, over the last generation or more the literature on child care has centered on the theme that the personality of the child is influenced to a great degree by the kind and nature of his parental care. This emphasis may well cause some adults to ponder whether or not they are capable of giving the proper kind of care so as to avoid creating a warped personality. Bossard points out another aspect of the same problem, which may give hesitation to the prospective parent: "Adequate parenthood has become a complex and difficult challenge in all families, requiring knowledge not only of the intricacies of the world in which the child lives, but also of its social resources and how to use them effectively."[34]

The human psyche being as complex as it is, we can regard as no more than illustrative those psychic pressures we have noted—motivations that impel people to seek or to avoid parenthood, to seek what they anticipate as its gratifications or to avoid what they foresee as the anguish. There are in the clinical literature accounts of more unusual responses to the prospect and actuality of parenthood. For example, Benedek reports a case in which very

[32] In 1915–1919 the maternal mortality rate was a little over 7 per 1000 live births (7 per 1000 for whites and nearly 13 per 1000 for nonwhites). National Center for Health Statistics, *Infant, Fetal, and Maternal Mortality, United States—1963* (Washington, D.C.: GPO, 1966), Series 20, No. 3, Table 23, p. 56. For 1967 the corresponding rates were: for all races 3 per 1000, for whites 2 per 1000, and for nonwhites around 7 per 1000.— *Statistical Abstract of the United States: 1970*, Table 69, p. 55.

[33] Herbert Thoms, *Training for Childbirth: A Program of Natural Childbirth with Rooming-In* (New York: McGraw-Hill, 1950). Other aspects of this program of "natural childbirth" are to prepare the mother's body for labor by a course of exercises, and emotional preparation of the prospective father. Cf. also H. C. Walser, "Fear, an Important Etiological Factor in Obstetric Problems," *American Journal of Obstetrics and Gynecology*, 55: 799–805 (1948).

[34] J. H. S. Bossard, *The Sociology of Child Development* (New York: Harper & Row, 1948), p. 439.

strong feelings of guilt motivated a husband to want a child. While a Marine, he had developed considerable guilt because of having killed enemy soldiers. To assuage his guilt over killing he wished to create a life. His wife's first pregnancy terminated in a stillbirth; whereupon he developed a psychosis.[35]

In summary, after recalling that much of this discussion is speculative, let us note that for most Americans the desirability of having children seems to outweigh any negative feelings. It seems reasonable to presume, moreover, that to some degree at least both positive and negative considerations are present in all, and hence we can hardly help feeling some ambivalence concerning the value of parenthood.

We should note that for some persons who have parental impulses but are unable or unwilling to assume the responsibilities of parenthood a pet can become the psychic equivalent of a child. A person can find expression for his nurturant impulses in caring for a pet; he can obtain response of a noncompetitive, nonthreatening, and nonverbal character; he can impute "human" qualities to the animal and thereby create an "almost human" being.[36]

RELATIVE GRATIFICATIONS OF CHILDLESS AND PARENTAL MARRIAGES

It is interesting to contemplate what differences may exist in general with respect to the gratifications available to spouses in childless marriages as compared with the gratifications available to parents. There are two somewhat paradoxical findings: that the incidence of divorce is higher among childless couples than among couples with children and that, on the average, childless couples are reported as being as well adjusted maritally as those with children. Let us consider these points.

The paucity of data in this country makes it impossible to formulate precise statements about differential divorce rates. It is estimated, however, that in 1955 there were 1.6 divorces among childless couples for every divorce occurring among couples having children; or stated differently, divorces were 60 percent more frequent among the childless than among parental couples. Moreover, the divorce rate varies inversely with the number of children the couple has. These statistics, however, must be interpreted carefully. It is because divorces concentrate in the early years of marriage that such a high proportion of childless couples is involved.[37] Furthermore, in order to determine the effect of childlessness on marital stability, it would be necessary to take account of desertions and informal separations, for which data are not available. "Until the data are available," concludes Davis, "it is useless to assume the point proven, no matter how righteous it may seem."[38]

[35] Therese Benedek, *Insight and Personality Adjustment* (New York: Ronald, 1946), p. 227.

[36] J. H. S. Bossard, "The Mental Hygiene of Owning a Dog," *Mental Hygiene*, 28: 408–413 (1944).

[37] Paul H. Jacobson, *American Marriage and Divorce* (New York: Holt, Rinehart and Winston, Inc., 1959), pp. 132–135.

[38] Kingsley Davis, Harry C. Bredemeier, and Marion J. Levy, Jr., *Modern American*

If we should accept for purposes of argument that the rate of marital instability of all forms is higher in childless than in parental couples, then there remains the question as to just why. One possibility is that such a difference would reflect the satisfaction of having children. A second possibility is that parents who are unhappy with each other decline to separate because of a sense of duty to their children. A third possibility is that parents who would separate decide not to because of an anticipation that relatives and friends would feel that the parents have a duty to remain together, and thus the spouses would be exposed to unpleasant social pressures if they were to part. To the writer it seems inevitable that each of these interpretations applies in some cases, but at present there is no evidence as to the relative importance of these interpretations.

After reviewing the relevant data, Burgess and Wallin conclude that there is no consistent relationship between having children and marital happiness (they speak of it as "marital success"). They did find the desire for children to be positively correlated with marital adjustment. They phrase their conclusion as follows: "it is the attitude of men and women to having children that is associated with marital success and not whether they have any."[39]

It should be noted that the data upon which Burgess and Wallin base their conclusion are taken from young and middle-aged couples. It may be that the maximum gratification of parenthood is the antidote it offers to the loneliness of old age. It stands to reason that the couple with children, even though the family relationships be not wholly amicable, will have, as W. S. Thompson says, a greater "sense of participation in the future" than the couple without children. What is being referred to is not the financial support of the couple as they become old but rather that the presence of children may augment the feeling that "someone cares" what happens to one.[40]

A somewhat oblique attack on the relative gratification of marriages with and without children comes from the previously cited study by Freedman, Whelpton, and Campbell. We have noted that only 1 percent of the 2600 wives responded that they would want no children if they could start their married lives over again and choose the number they wanted. The effect of having a first child appears to have a temporarily depressing effect on the number of children wanted. The number of children wanted a year after the birth of the first child was substantially lower than at the time of marriage or at the time of the interview somewhat later. Freedman *et al.* interpret the finding as

Society: Readings in the Problems of Order and Change (New York: Holt, Rinehart and Winston, Inc., 1948), p. 682.

[39] Ernest W. Burgess and Paul Wallin, *Engagement and Marriage* (Philadelphia: Lippincott, 1953), p. 719. See the distinction drawn in Chapter 21 below among marital happiness, marital adjustment, and marital success.

[40] The childless marriage "reflects the condition of an urban society where blood is no longer blue, life is impersonal, children are a luxury and women must earn their own livings."—Walton Hamilton, "Institution," in *Encyclopaedia of the Social Sciences* (New York: Macmillan, 1932), VIII, 85.

the consequence of the wives' first experiencing the cares of motherhood.[41] One other strand of evidence comes from the correlation between economic indexes and the birth rate, from which it appears that when economic conditions are favorable, people are disposed to have more children than under conditions of economic strain. Thus the burden of evidence tends to support the conclusion that children are apparently viewed as sources of gratification.

Summary of This Chapter

Three views of man are currently in vogue: the Lockean or responding machine man, the Freudian man striving to work through his feelings of insecurity and achieve Nirvana, and the vitalistic man striving to get gratification from striving. Because of the state of the literature the topic of gratification has been developed largely in terms of the second of these views.

On the basis of the nature of the threat, feelings of insecurity may be classified as physical or psychic. Generally speaking, physical threats tend to come from outside the family and, except for the young child, protection against such threats in a mass society is also provided outside the family. Two varieties of psychic insecurity have to do with statuses and interpersonal relationships. Uncertainty and failure are factors contributing to insecurity with respect to achieved, but not with respect to ascribed, statuses. Since positions conferred by the family tend to be ascribed, whereas many conferred by other societal structures are achieved, the sources of status-insecurity are largely outside the family.

As we saw in Chapters 1 and 5, the religious structure has the individual-oriented function of alleviating anxiety. People do not universally turn to organized religion to find the antidote of insecurity, however. In a secular society formal religion is able to minister only to those who remain faithful; others will seek alternate sources of comfort—political ideologies, patriotic and vigilante organizations, and psychotherapy. (It should also be recalled that religious organizations can increase, as well as mitigate, feelings of insecurity by exacerbating the sense of guilt.) To some extent the interpersonal security the family is capable of providing can be used to compensate for status-insecurity.

Turning from the negative side of gratification to the positive, i.e., from the alleviation of anxiety to the enjoyment of zestful and creative activity, we find that parenthood offers rewards and penalties, gratifications and frustrations. The evidence seems to indicate that marriages with and without children offer approximately equal probabilities of marital happiness, but the qualification should be kept in mind that the studies underlying this conclusion were based upon young couples, whereas the gratifications of parenthood may be at a maximum when the parents are old. The available evidence

---

[41] Freedman, Whelpton, and Campbell, *op. cit.*, p. 225.

indicates a somewhat higher divorce rate among childless than among parental couples, but it is unknown what difference there is between these two classes of marriages when all forms of separation are taken into account. The difficulty of moving away from a position of agnosticism regarding the net gratifications of parenthood is inherent also in the observation that if it is true that the separation rate is higher among childless than among parental couples, there are other possible interpretations than the one involving the gratifications of parenthood. However, the expressions of desire for children and the correlation of the birth rate with economic indexes provide some evidence for the view that children are, all things considered, thought to be more gratifying than frustrating.

Summary of Parts Two and Three

How shall we think about the family as a source of gratification and reward relative to other structures in the society? Parts Two and Three suggest a way of thinking about the problem. Through these two parts has run the following theme: The basic societal structures fulfill basic societal functions. Basic societal functions have individual-serving as well as society-serving functions. Individual-serving functions are experienced as rewards. Rewards influence behavior. The capacity of a society's concrete structures to influence behavior is determined by their capacity to dispense and to withhold rewards.

In some times and places both the extended and the nuclear families have operated as virtually self-contained economic units. When this is so, the importance of the family to the individual member for the resources to survive and to be comfortable is obvious. For the most directly affected millions, industrialization has meant that production has been organized on a mass basis, and the family has ceased to have economic significance with respect to production. Urbanization has meant the separation of home and work. The urban-industrial complex has replaced a familial network of economic interdependence with a category of gainfully employed family members and a category of economic dependents. In an economic sense, then, not only does the family have no control over the economically independent, but persons in that category are better off, in the sense of not having to divide their resources, if they withdraw from the family. Where no other controls or pressures are operating, this frequently happens, as is shown by the frequency of desertion among lower-lower class families. A more or less parallel transfer of function out of the family has been noted with respect to the socializing-educational function; there has been less transfer with respect to the political and religious functions because these functions were not important in the American family.

The rise of the urban-industrial order in Western countries has resulted in an open-class system of stratification with its array of achievable statuses. The rise in the importance of achieved statuses reduces the relative importance of ascribed statuses and thereby is another loss of function for the family.

In the light of this presentation the "weakening" and "disintegration" of the family referred to in the opening paragraphs of this book are seen as stemming from the loss of basic societal functions with their individual-serving capacities and hence from a loss of control over rewards. Of course we do not conceive of function as present in, or absent from, the family in a categorical or "yes-no" sense. Since the family can hardly refrain from some sort of production, for example, we are always thinking of the presence or absence of function as a matter of degree.

The last two paragraphs would appear to sound the knell of the modern American family. Countervailing tendencies are discernible, however: (1) Through suburbanism the family, especially the family of the middle class, has sought to establish itself in a setting where the loss of functions could be not only halted but, at least modestly, reversed. (2) Aside from such substitute measures as joining protest movements, the person suffering from psychic insecurity has three categories of possible succor: the traditional (the church), the professional (the psychotherapeutic-counselling specialties), and the congeniality group. It may be that the loss of basic societal functions other than the familial makes it easier for the family to be a congeniality group, to provide psychic security, and thus to afford an emotional sanctuary in a bustling and occasionally threatening world.

In very unsociological phrasing the foregoing may be summarized as pointing to the importance of people in families "being nice to each other." A professional phrasing would refer to the mutual gratification to be derived from social interaction and the accompanying emotional interchange within the family. The relative importance to the family of the function of providing emotional gratification (i.e., in the light of the loss of other functions) is seen in several ways. For what reasons are marriages usually broken up in middle-class America—because of sterility or because the wife is a poor or unwilling worker? No, it is because she and her husband do not get on well together. What are thought to be the principal causes of the philandering of spouses and the running away of children? Again the answer seems to pertain to a failure to get emotional gratification from relationships within the family. What sort of service is provided by social agencies that work in the field of the family? In bygone times they conceived their task to be exclusively that of helping the poor. More recently some of the resources of the profession have been directed to the middle classes wherein they treat emotional problems of the family.

To this point the analysis of the function of emotional gratification has been incomplete. More will come in Chapter 12 and in Parts Five and Six.

PART FOUR

Elements in the Structure of American Family Forms

The present volume considers the family in terms of function and structure. Concretely the focus has been on the family (or if the reader prefers, on various familial forms) in American society. Where perspective could be deepened by so doing, the family has been considered in other cultural contexts. Let us recall that we are aiming not only to understand the family in America but, as students of sociology, to arrive at a set of principles that will explain family life in any setting, be it folk-primitive or urban-industrial or lunar or even intergalactic. At present we are able to enunciate some principles but they tend to fall short of the level of generality referred to in the latter part of the preceding sentence. As we consider the information in Part Four, which principally concerns the family in America, let us keep in mind our objective of a general sociology of the family and the corollary that in this sense the American family merely comprises a special case.

To this point, function and change in function have been our concepts of major concern. Now it seems generally to be true that a major shift in function will in due course be followed by a major shift in structure.[1] One such shift has already been examined—the reduction in family size through the decline in the American birth rate from 1790 to the middle 1930's.

Chapter 10 considers the ways in which mates are selected and nuclear families are established. In keeping with our effort to seek principles of generality we do not consider at this time the operation of love in mate-selection since love seems to be a mate-selective criterion only under special circumstances. The nature of love is taken up in Parts Five and Six, especially in Chapters 18, 19, and 20.

Chapter 11 examines the forms of the family in the United States. It concludes that three types can be discerned, and some correlates of these types are presented. Chapter 12 analyzes the structure of the American nuclear family with respect to positions and roles. (Further consideration is given to this topic in Chapter 21, where marital roles are scrutinized.)

---

[1] A more precise formulation of such a proposition would specify an initial state of equilibrium and would require a definition of "major." The above statement should not be interpreted as excluding the possibility of the converse—that a major shift in structure would be followed by a major shift in function.

10

Mate-Selection and the Field of Eligibles

Purpose of This Chapter

This chapter takes up the problem as to how husbands get wives and vice versa. No doubt some readers will be astonished to discover that although this chapter concerns marriage, it will scarcely mention love. (The nature of love as a mate-selective factor will be taken up in a later chapter.) Unlike Americans, most other peoples do not seem to have regarded love as essential —or indeed as relevant—to mate-selection. If love does not determine who marries whom, what does? It is our view that in all societies there are two principles that determine whom one *may* marry. We may call these the *principle of incest avoidance* and the *principle of ethnocentric preference*. Just how these principles operate does vary from one society to another, but in all societies it is the joint operation of these two principles that determines for each marriageable person his field of eligible spouse-candidates, or as we shall phrase it, his *field of eligibles*. To the extent that the principle of ethnocentric preference governs mate-selection there should be evidence of *homogamy*.[1] We shall consider dimensions along which mate-selection in the United States is demonstrably homogamous.

How the selection of a spouse is made from the field of eligibiles is also subject to intersocietal variation. It is our thesis that the basis upon which a spouse is selected depends upon the functional significance of the spouse. If the family is highly functional, then it is probable that the ability to perform functional tasks will become a criterion in mate-selection. If the extended family is a functional unit, it is likely that the parents of the bride and groom

---

[1] Homogamy (*homos,* same + *gamia,* marrying): marriage between spouses of similar characteristics.

and other relatives as well will evince a lively interest in the process of mate-selection. We should anticipate, moreover, that in such a society there would be strong sanctions favoring parental participation in the choice. On the other hand, where the family is relatively functionless, we should anticipate little participation by persons other than the bride and groom, and we should expect the choice to be made on the basis of mutual congeniality and mutual love.

Principle of Incest Avoidance[2]

In every known society there is a rule to prevent certain closely related persons from marrying each other. It is generally true that marriage is prohibited between mother and son, between father and daughter, and between brother and sister. Just how far this incest prohibition may extend, i.e., to what degrees of kinship, varies from one culture to another. In colonial New England, for example, it would have been thought incestuous if a man were to marry his deceased wife's sister. Among the ancient Hebrews, on the other hand, the custom of the levirate required that under certain circumstances a man had to marry his deceased brother's widow. Among Australian aborigines marriage was prohibited among persons of similarly named clans although they might live hundreds of miles apart and be entirely unrelated as we reckon kinship.

Principle of Ethnocentric Preference

Just as every society has its rules concerning the avoidance of incestuous marriages, so it also has some conception of preferential mating on the basis of ethnocentrism. The student of sociology is familiar with the idea that all societies tend to have some suspicion of outsiders, to regard strangers as barbarians who are dirty, immoral, and/or dangerous. The application of eth-

---

[2] The first part of this chapter is based on Linton C. Freeman, "Marriage without Love: Mate-Selection in Non-Western Societies," Chapter 2 in Robert F. Winch, *Mate-Selection* (New York: Harper & Row, 1958). Reprinted in Robert F. Winch and Louis Wolf Goodman, *Selected Studies in Marriage and the Family* (New York: Holt, Rinehart and Winston, Inc., 1968), pp. 456–469.

The literature on incest is extensive. Following are some titles of interest. David F. Aberle *et al.*, "Incest Taboo and the Mating of Animals," *American Anthropologist*, 65: 253–265 (1963); J. R. Fox, "Sibling Incest," *British Journal of Sociology*, 13: 128–150; Russell Middleton, "Brother-Sister and Father-Daughter Marriage in Ancient Egypt," *American Sociological Review*, 27: 603–611 (1962); Yonina Talmon, "Mate Selection in Collective Settlements," *American Sociological Review*, 29: 491–508 (1964); and Frank W. Young, "Incest Taboos and Social Solidarity," *American Journal of Sociology*, 72: 589–600 (1967).

nocentrism to mate-selection implies that a society will prefer to have its young people marry persons from their own locality and/or segment of society, or who are at least similar to themselves in social characteristics, and will look with disfavor upon marriages with outsiders or with persons of quite alien social characteristics. The principle of ethnocentric preference may forbid a person to marry outside his native village or it may penalize him for marrying outside his social class. In almost all societies this principle is evident in the cultural disapproval of marriages between persons of markedly different racial or cultural backgrounds.

Field of Eligibles Resulting from the Two Principles

The principle of incest avoidance rules ineligible as spouse-candidates certain individuals who are culturally defined as closely related to the self. The principle of ethnocentric preference states that the individuals who are highly similar to the self in social characteristics are especially eligible as spouse-candidates. In any society the relative strength of these two principles determines the composition of an individual's field of eligibles. In some groups or societies ethnocentrism may be very strong, with the result that a large proportion of marriages occur among people closely related to each other. This was true in the ruling classes of ancient Hawaii, Egypt, and the Incas, where marriages between brother and sister were common. In our own country ethnocentric preference resulting in the intermarriage of cousins has been reported in two quite different settings—among the "proper Bostonians" and among the highlanders of the southeastern states.[3] We can also point to examples where the field of eligibles is determined largely by the principle of incest avoidance. In traditional China one was forbidden to marry a person bearing the same family name as one's own, although in that populous country with its small number of surnames this rule might proscribe hundreds of thousands of spouse-candidates.

The eligibility of some man or woman to be one's spouse may well be conceived on an all-or-none basis where the possibility of incest is concerned. With respect to the operation of ethnocentric preference in our own culture, however, there seems to be a gradient of approval-disapproval rather than a sharp all-or-none distinction. Because of this the field of eligibles may have a somewhat vague boundary.

Having conceptualized the field of eligibles as the resultant of the two principles, let us now turn to the question as to how mates are selected within the field of eligibles.

---

[3] Cleveland Amory, *The Proper Bostonians* (New York: Dutton, 1947), chap. 1; J. S. Brown, "The Conjugal Family and the Extended Family," *American Sociological Review*, 17: 297–306 (1952).

Two Types of Mate-Selection

We shall distinguish two principal ways in which mates are acquired: by mutual volition and by arrangement. (In passing we may note a third way —marriage by capture—but Sumner and Keller have remarked that a person who becomes a spouse by capture has no customary rights and is "wholly the possession of the captor"; hence they conclude that marriage by capture is "really no marriage at all."[4])

Mutual volition is the mate-selective procedure familiar in middle-class America whereby a man and a woman select each other and agree to marry each other. They may or may not consult with and obtain permission from their respective families, but in any case the selection is made by the bridal couple. Where mutual volition is the basis upon which mate-selection takes place, it is frequently—perhaps usually—assumed that the selection is premised upon a pre-existing mutual love.

Arranged marriage is the mate-selective procedure that is the chief alternative to mutual volition. When marriages are arranged, mate-selection results from negotiations between the family of the groom and the family of the bride. With this procedure, moreover, there is frequently an exchange of property in the form of dowry or bride price. Furthermore, in a society where marriages are usually arranged it is not unusual for a specialized occupation of "go-between" or marriage broker to develop.

Familial Functionality and the Type of Mate-Selection

It is the point of view of this book that the type of mate-selection that prevails in a society is not the result of chance but in all likelihood is closely related to the functions of the family. Chapter 3 concludes tentatively that in societies, or segments thereof, wherein the extended family is highly functional, we should expect mate-selection to occur on the basis of arrangement

---

[4] W. G. Sumner and A. G. Keller, *The Science of Society* (New Haven, Conn.: Yale University Press, 1929), III, 1624. From his study of middle-class marriages in Tokyo, Blood reported that in that Westernizing segment of Japan, mate-selection tended to fuse the traditional form of arranged marriage with the Western form of "love-marriage." According to Japanese folk-wisdom, "Love matches start out hot and grow cold; arranged marriages start out cold and grow hot." Blood's conclusion, however, was: ". . . arranged marriages do start out cold; but they grow hot only from a short-range male viewpoint . . . [whereas for wives] arranged marriages start out cold, grow temporarily warm, and then freeze up. . . ." Cf. Robert O. Blood, Jr., *Love Match and Arranged Marriage* (New York: Free Press, 1967), chap. 3, esp. p. 94. Cf. also Ezra F. Vogel, *Japan's New Middle Class: The Salary Man and His Family in a Tokyo Suburb* (Berkeley: University of California Press, 1963), pp. 175–177.

because the attributes of the mate to be selected are important to the family as a whole and not just to the person acquiring a spouse. Since the person who is acquiring a mate is usually young and inexperienced, this person is regarded as not sufficiently wise to make a decision of such importance to the entire family. Where the extended family is minimally functional, on the other hand, the acquiring of a new member does not carry important consequences for the family as a whole. Therefore the attributes of the person to be selected become more a matter of indifference to the family as a whole, and selection can be left to the individual who is acquiring a mate. If the young person selects a mate foolishly in the latter case, it is chiefly or solely the young person—and not the entire family—who suffers.

The point of the preceding paragraph is illustrated very clearly by the two family forms that we used to anchor our conception of familial functionality. In Chapter 2 we noted that the family of the traditional Chinese peasantry was almost a small society and hence that it was maximally functional. In this case, moreover, we saw that the selection of the bride was of especial interest to the groom's mother, since many of the bride's roles were to place her in a relationship of subordinate and assistant to her mother-in-law. Here mate-selection was by arrangement, and the vitally concerned mother of the groom was especially active in choosing the bride.[5] In Chapter 3 we anchored the minimal end of the dimension of familial functionality to the example of the family in the Israeli kibbutz. Here we saw that love and mutual volition constituted the basis of mate-selection.

We have noted that an implication of a family structure of little functionality is that other structures in the society are carrying out important functions. In contemporary America the large corporation is such a structure. Let us recall the paradigm that function implies reward and reward implies the power to exercise social control. These considerations raise the prospect that the large corporation may be exercising some control over mate-selection. William H. Whyte, Jr., has introduced us to the "organization man" and to the distaff counterpart, the "company wife."[6] We shall consider Whyte's ideas

---

[5] A combination of the principles of incest avoidance and ethnocentric preference is seen in Indian marriages—both among Hindus and among Muslims—as reported by David Mandelbaum. The prospective spouse should be of the same caste and subcaste as oneself. One must not marry into one of the related families of the subcaste, however. In upper castes of northern India "a man may not marry a woman related to him through either the paternal or the maternal lines to the sixth or fourth degrees respectively."—David G. Mandelbaum, "The Family in India," in Ruth N. Anshen (ed.), *The Family: Its Function and Destiny* (rev. ed.; New York: Harper & Row, 1959), pp. 167–187; quotation is from p. 172. Where castes and subcastes have sections that are ranked, a woman may marry upward but not downward among these sections. Traditionally marriages are arranged. When seeking a spouse for a son or a daughter, a father looks for freedom from disease and from deformation. The reputation and standing of the family of the prospective spouse are also of concern.— K. M. Kapadia, *Marriage and Family in India* (2d ed.; Bombay: Oxford University Press, 1958), chap. 6.

[6] William H. Whyte, Jr., *The Organization Man* (New York: Simon and Schuster,

in some detail when we take up the differentiation of roles (in Chapter 12). For the present it is sufficient to note Whyte's assertion that the organization man's promotion has frequently been influenced by the degree to which his mate's characteristics meet the specifications of the company wife. It would seem to follow that as young men have come to believe that characteristics of their wives enter into their occupational success, corporations have influenced mate-selection. But since 1956 when Whyte was commenting on the "organization man" as well as the "silent generation," this writer believes there have been cultural changes with the seeming result that corporations have become less insistent on controlling the off-the-job behavior of their employees. To the extent that this is so, the corporation's influence on mate-selection has presumably waned.

Field of Eligibles and Method of Choice

We have stated that one's field of eligibles is defined in terms of the joint operation of the principle of incest avoidance and the principle of ethnocentric preference. How these two principles operate in any given society determines how broad will be the field of one's eligibles. We have noted the two principal methods of selecting a spouse from the field of eligibles—mutual volition and arrangement. If we consider simultaneously the ways in which both of these processes may vary, we can conceptualize four types of mate-selection, i.e., two kinds of field of eligibles from each of which selection may be made in one of two ways. Table 10.1 is from Freeman's presentation and shows where middle-class America falls. For cultural descriptions of the Yaruros, the Hottentots, and feudal Japan, the interested reader is referred to Freeman's treatment of this topic.

Mate-Selection in America

The analysis to this point represents mate-selection in middle-class America as based on mutual volition from a wide field of eligibles. We shall now consider the research literature on mate-selection in America for the purpose of getting some understanding as to how wide the field of eligibles actually

1956); "The Wives of Management," *Fortune*, October 1951, pp. 86–88, 204, 206–8, 210, 213; "The Corporation and the Wife," *Fortune*, November 1951, pp. 109–111, 150, 152, 155–156, 158; "The Wife Problem," *Life*, January 7, 1952, pp. 32–48 and, adapted, in Robert F. Winch and Louis Wolf Goodman (eds.), *Selected Studies in Marriage and the Family* (3d ed.; New York: Holt, Rinehart and Winston, Inc., 1968), pp. 177–188. In the later 1950's and early 1960's this theme was rebroadcast by other writers: Helen Hill Miller, "Ambassadresses of Good Will—or Ill: Personnel Officers Picking a Man for Foreign Service Now Ask, 'What's His Wife Like?' Here Is a Code for Government Wives Abroad," *The New York Times Magazine*, February 19, 1956, pp. 26, 74, 76; "Navy to Grade Officers' Wives for Social Graces and Conduct," *The New York Times*, March 9, 1962, pp. 1, 15; Sarah Boyden, "Are You a Help to Your Husband? Wives Are Important Too," *Sunday Midwest* (*Chicago Sun-Times*), August 4, 1957, pp. 4–5.

TABLE 10.1

Permutations of Preferential Mating and Arrangement of Marriage

DEGREE OF ARRANGEMENT OF THE MARRIAGE	PREFERENTIAL MATING	
	Highly Specified Preferences Leading to Narrow Field of Eligibles	*Little Specification of Preferred Mate Leading to Wide Field of Eligibles*
High: Parents or others select one's spouse	Yaruros	Feudal Japan
Low: Principal selects own spouse (mutual volition)	Hottentots	Middle-class U.S.A.

SOURCE: Linton C. Freeman, "Marriage without Love: Mate-Selection in Non-Western Societies," in Robert F. Winch, *Mate-Selection* (New York: Harper & Row, 1958), p. 39. Reprinted by permission of the publishers.

is. For the present we shall accept the popular notion that within the field of eligibles mate-selection is determined by the mysterious processes of love. In a later chapter that idea will come under critical scrutiny (see Chapter 18).

The present chapter will present numerous data about marriages. The reasons for this emphasis are (1) that we are here primarily concerned with describing the conditions under which new nuclear families are formed in contemporary America and (2) that we shall devote part of a later chapter to the topic of remarriage. The relation of first marriages to all marriages is suggested by the fact that data from the marriage-registration area show that well over three quarters of those being married in 1960 were entering first marriages.[7]

As will be seen from Table 10.2, the proportion of the adult population that is married has increased appreciably since 1890. By 1950 only about a quarter of the males over fourteen and about a fifth of the females had never been married. For Denmark, Sweden, and Switzerland, as well as for the United States, it has been shown that the increase in proportion married has been greater in urban than in rural areas, among those with more rather than less education, and among employees rather than among employers—thus among urban white-collar workers.[8] Whether it is cause or effect, the increase in the proportion married is related to an increase in the proportion of young

---

[7] National Center for Health Statistics, *Marriage Statistics Analysis: United States, 1963* (Washington, D.C.: GPO, 1968), Table 7, pp. 29–30. In 1960 the marriage-registration area consisted of thirty-three states.—*Ibid.*, p. 37.

[8] John Hajnal, "Analysis of Changes in the Marriage Patterns by Economic Groups," *American Sociological Review*, 19: 295–302 (1954).

TABLE 10.2

Percent Distribution of Persons 14 Years Old and Over, by Marital Status and Sex, Standardized for Age and Unstandardized, for the United States, 1960 to 1969, and for Coterminous United States, 1890 to 1955

	MALE				
YEAR	*Total*	*Single*	*Married*	*Widowed*	*Divorced*
Standardized for age					
1969	100.0	23.7	70.6	3.2	2.4
1966	100.0	23.9	70.8	3.0	2.3
1960	100.0	25.3	69.1	3.7	1.9
1955	100.0	25.4	68.4	4.4	1.8
1950	100.0	26.2	67.4	4.7	1.7
1947	100.0	27.2	66.5	4.8	1.5
1940	100.0	30.7	62.6	5.4	1.3
1890	100.0	31.9	61.8	6.1	0.3
Unstandardized					
1969	100.0	27.4	67.0	3.3	2.3
1966	100.0	26.9	67.9	3.0	2.2
1960	100.0	25.3	69.1	3.7	1.9
1955	100.0	24.0	69.9	4.3	1.8
1950	100.0	26.2	68.0	4.2	1.7
1947	100.0	28.2	66.2	4.1	1.6
1940	100.0	34.8	59.7	4.2	1.2
1890	100.0	43.6	52.1	3.8	0.2
	FEMALE				
	Total	*Single*	*Married*	*Widowed*	*Divorced*
Standardized for age					
1969	100.0	19.2	65.3	12.0	3.5
1966	100.0	18.7	66.1	12.0	3.2
1960	100.0	19.0	65.6	12.8	2.6
1955	100.0	19.1	65.2	13.5	2.2
1950	100.0	20.0	63.9	14.0	2.1
1947	100.0	21.4	62.5	14.1	2.0
1940	100.0	24.2	59.3	14.8	1.6
1890	100.0	23.8	58.1	17.7	0.4
Unstandardized					
1969	100.0	21.8	62.3	12.5	3.3
1966	100.0	20.9	63.7	12.4	3.1
1960	100.0	19.0	65.6	12.8	2.6
1955	100.0	18.2	66.8	12.8	2.3
1950	100.0	19.6	66.1	12.2	2.2
1947	100.0	22.0	64.2	11.6	2.1
1940	100.0	27.6	59.5	11.3	1.6
1890	100.0	34.1	54.9	10.6	0.4

SOURCE: U.S. Bureau of the Census, *Current Population Reports—Population Characteristics*, Series P-20, No. 198, March 25, 1970, Table F, p. 4. Standardization is on the basis of the age distribution in 1960.

married women who are employed. Glick and Carter assert that the more highly educated of the young married women "probably continue to work longer after marriage and to postpone childbearing longer than women with less education."[9]

Residential Propinquity as a Factor in Mate-Selection

In 1932 Bossard advanced the idea of "residential propinquity" as a basis for mate-selection. By this he meant that the probability that A and B will marry each other decreases as the distance between their residences increases.[10] In its simplest statement the idea seems somewhat obvious, for it is unlikely that a boy in Philadelphia will marry a girl in Walla Walla if neither moves out of his home town. As applied within cities, however, the truth of the idea was somewhat less obvious. Over the years numerous sociologists have studied residential propinquity (mostly within cities), and it is generally accepted that there is a demonstrable tendency for mate-selection to show a negative spatial gradient as predicted by Bossard's hypothesis.[11] Both the segregation of cultural aggregates and the cost, in time and energy, of travel seem to contribute to the residential propinquity of marriage partners.[12]

---

[9] Paul C. Glick and Hugh Carter, "Marriage Patterns and Educational Level," *American Sociological Review*, 23: 294–300 (1958), at p. 298.
[10] J. H. S. Bossard, "Residential Propinquity as a Factor in Marriage Selection," *American Journal of Sociology*, 38: 219–224 (1932).
[11] Ray H. Abrams, "Residential Propinquity as a Factor in Marriage Selection: Fifty Year Trends in Philadelphia," *American Sociological Review*, 8: 288–294 (1943); Alfred C. Clarke, "An Examination of the Operation of Residential Propinquity as a Factor in Mate Selection," *American Sociological Review*, 17: 17–22 (1952); M. R. Davie and Ruby J. Reeves, "Propinquity in Residence before Marriage," *American Journal of Sociology*, 44: 510–517 (1939); John S. Ellsworth, Jr., "The Relationship of Population Density to Residential Propinquity as a Factor in Marriage Selection," *American Sociological Review*, 13: 444–448 (1948); Daniel Harris, "Age and Occupational Factors in the Residential Propinquity of Marriage Partners," *Journal of Social Psychology*, 6: 257–261 (1935); Ruby J. R. Kennedy, "Pre-Marital Residential Propinquity and Ethnic Endogamy," *American Journal of Sociology*, 48: 580–584 (1943); Alan C. Kerckhoff, "Notes and Comments on the Meaning of Residential Propinquity as a Factor in Mate Selection," *Social Forces*, 34: 207–213 (1956); Marvin R. Koller, "Residential Propinquity of White Mates at Marriage in Relation to Age and Occupation of Males, Columbus, Ohio," *American Sociological Review*, 13: 613–616 (1948); J. R. Marches and G. Turbeville, "The Effect of Residential Propinquity on Marriage Selection," *American Journal of Sociology*, 58: 592–595 (1953); H. Y. McClusky and Alvin Zander, "Residential Propinquity and Marriage in Branch County, Michigan," *Social Forces*, 19: 79–81 (1940); Donald Mitchell, "Residential Propinquity and Marriage in Carver and Scott Counties, Minnesota, as Compared with Branch County, Michigan," *Social Forces*, 20: 256–259 (1941); G. J. Schnepp and Louis A. Roberts, "Residential Propinquity and Mate Selection on a Parish Basis," *American Journal of Sociology*, 58: 45–50 (1952).
[12] Alvin M. Katz and Reuben Hill, "Residential Propinquity and Marital Selection: A Review of Theory, Method, and Fact," *Journal of Marriage and the Family*, 20: 27–35

Dimensions of Ethnocentric Preference

Whereas, in its simplest form residential propinquity points to the mere probability that A and B will learn of each other's existence because of the consideration of physical space, the principle of ethnocentric preference implies that within the aggregate of persons who are spatially present or available, those persons of opposite sex whose social and cultural characteristics most resemble one's own will be perceived as one's most acceptable potential mates. Race, ethnoreligious affiliation, socioeconomic status (including the components of occupation and level of formal education), age, and previous marital status are dimensions of preference that have been studied.

RACE

In the United States the most obvious dimension of ethnocentric preference is race. Many of the states have had laws prohibiting marriages between persons of different races.[13] The strength of the deterrents to interracial marriages is sufficiently great, however, that where legal barriers have been removed, there has been no rush to intermarry. Over a one-year period following nullification of such a law in California the rate of interracial marriages for whites in Los Angeles, as measured by data from license applications, was slightly under one half of one percent,[14] and in the thirty-month period following nullification it was slightly over one half of one percent.[15] Golden summarizes the social forces tending to prevent marriages between whites and blacks as follows:

> the segregated social structure of our culture; the system of attitudes, beliefs, and myths which grow out of the social system and which serve to strengthen it; the laws which express the sex and marriage customs of the culture; institutional functionaries, such as clergymen, army officers, and governmental employees who attempt to discourage interracial marriage even in those states which have not legislated on the subject; the family, especially the immediate family, which uses affectional ties to prevent intermarriage.[16]

(1958); William R. Catton, Jr., and R. J. Smircich, "A Comparison of Mathematical Models for the Effect of Residential Propinquity on Mate Selection," *American Sociological Review*, 29: 522–529 (1964).

[13] In an article published in March 1958, Joseph Golden reported that as of the moment of writing twenty-eight states had laws prohibiting intermarriage.—"Social Control of Negro-White Intermarriage," *Social Forces*, 36: 267–269 (1958).

[14] Randall Risdon, "A Study of Interracial Marriages Based on Data for Los Angeles County," *Sociology and Social Research*, 39: 92–95 (1954).

[15] John H. Burma, "Research Note on the Measurement of Interracial Marriage," *American Journal of Sociology*, 57: 587–589 (1952).

[16] "Social Control of Negro-White Intermarriage," *loc. cit.*, p. 269.

TABLE 10.3

Number of Total Marriages and Interracial Marriages in Selected States of the Marriage-Registration Area, and Percentage Distribution of Interracial Marriages by Race of Bride and Groom, 1963

Total number of marriages in 32 MRA states and District of Columbia		796,827
Number of interracial marriages in same area		3,444
Interracial marriages as percent of all marriages		0.4
All interracial marriages ($N = 3444$)		100.0
Bride white		50.7
Groom black	22.5	
Groom other	28.2	
Groom white		46.7
Bride black	7.5	
Bride other	39.2	
Black bride and other groom + other bride and black groom		2.6

SOURCE: National Center for Health Statistics, *Marriage Statistics Analysis: United States, 1963* (Washington, D.C.: GPO, 1968), Table N, p. 20. The MRA for 1963 consists of thirty-five states plus the District of Columbia. Three states were omitted (California, New Jersey, and Ohio) because they did not request information on color or race or both.

Table 10.3 shows that when a black and a white marry, it is three times more likely to involve a black man and a white woman than the other way about. Drake and Cayton believe that one important reason why few white men marry black women is that "such marriages endanger the economic position of the white wage-earner even more than that of the Negro."[17]

Drake and Cayton assert that among blacks there is much disapproval of intermarriage. They state that there is practically no intermarriage within the black middle class and that to intermarry might well jeopardize the position of a black professional man, businessman, or politician. Blacks who do intermarry, they say, tend to be intellectual bohemians, members of the lower class, or members of some group having a specific philosophical or ideological motivation toward intermarriage. They cite the Baha'i movement and the Communist Party as the chief cases, respectively, of these two types of groups.[18]

When blacks and whites do intermarry, it is very difficult for the couple

[17] St. Clair Drake and Horace R. Cayton, *Black Metropolis* (New York: Harcourt, 1945), p. 137.
[18] *Ibid.*, pp. 138–139.

to participate in the community as a couple because each member of the couple is an outsider with respect to the spouse's racial group. In a series of black-white marriages that Golden studied in Philadelphia, he found that there was a high median age at marriage (28.3 years), many of the spouses had previously been married (some interracially), and there were relatively few children.[19]

After analyzing the rates of interracial marriages in states permitting such marriages and maintaining official records of those marriages, Heer concluded that—depending upon the assumptions made—complete amalgamation of the races would take from 13 to 1,000 generations, or from 351 to 27,000 years.[20]

RELIGIOETHNIC IDENTITY

Next we shall consider the significance for mate-selection of a person's being identified with one or another religious group and with one or another ethnic group. Because religious affiliation is frequently correlated with national origin and because, as we shall conclude, the significance of religious identity seems to vary with the obviousness, or visibility, of the ethnic identity, we shall consider the two kinds of identity simultaneously.

"Next to race," says Hollingshead, "religion is the most decisive factor in the segregation of males and females into categories that are approved or disapproved with respect to nuptiality."[21] Although it is contended in the present discussion that ethnic identity, especially in its status implications, is more important in mate-selection than is religious identity, it seems that Hollingshead is probably right insofar as his remark pertains to the overt expression of consciously held attitudes. The writer would like to propose that the widely held conviction as to the importance of religious endogamy[22] (and by implication, the *relative* unimportance of ethnic endogamy) is not so much a reflection of people's sensitivity to variations in the conception of God or in the details of religious ritual as it is of the fact that in most marriages there are two types of occasion when each spouse is called upon to make an explicit affirmation of religious identity, whereas ethnic identity is not tested in any such solemn occasion. The first of these occasions is the wedding ceremony.

---

[19] Joseph Golden, "Characteristics in the Negro-White Intermarried in Philadelphia," *American Sociological Review*, 18: 177–183 (1953). Drake and Cayton describe some of the circumstances and roles that impel members of interracial marriages to keep their marriages clandestine.—*Op. cit.*, chap. 7.

[20] David M. Heer, "Negro-White Marriage in the United States," *New Society*, 6: 7–9 (August 26, 1965); reprinted in Robert F. Winch and Louis Wolf Goodman, *Selected Studies in Marriage and the Family* (New York: Holt, Rinehart and Winston, Inc., 1968), pp. 481–486.

[21] August B. Hollingshead, "Cultural Factors in the Selection of Marriage Mates," *American Sociological Review*, 15: 619–627 (1950), at p. 622.

[22] *Endogamy:* marriage within some social group or category, such as family, clan, tribe, or social class. *Exogamy:* marriage between partners of different social groups or categories.

It appears that the overwhelming majority of wedding ceremonies in this country are officiated over by the clergy[23] and that Americans tend to regard civil ceremonies as lacking in the "proper" sentiment. The religious affiliation of the clergyman chosen to officiate thus implies, whether rightly or wrongly, some commitment on the part of the couple. The other occasion is the time at which the religious instruction of the first child is begun. Both of these are points on which it is difficult to compromise. Thus although couples are not called upon to make explicit decisions to raise their children in one or another ethnic tradition (as Poles, say, or as Italians), they are characteristically called upon to make some provision for the religious instruction of their young and hence to "raise their children" as Catholics, as Protestants, or as Jews.

Table 10.4 gives the percentage distribution of voluntary responses in a sample survey conducted by the Bureau of the Census to the question "What

TABLE 10.4

Percentage Distribution of Religion Reported for Persons 14 Years Old and Over, by Sex, for the United States: Civilian Population, March 1957

RELIGION	MALE		FEMALE	
	All Responses	Excluding "Other," "None," and "Not Reported"	All Responses	Excluding "Other," "None," and "Not Reported"
Total, 14 years and over	100.0	100.0	100.0	100.0
Protestant	64.7	69.1	67.6	70.0
Baptist	19.4		20.0	
Lutheran	7.1		7.0	
Methodist	13.5		14.4	
Presbyterian	5.3		5.8	
Other Protestant	19.3		20.4	
Roman Catholic	25.7	27.4	25.7	26.7
Jewish	3.2	3.5	3.2	3.3
Other religion	1.3		1.2	
No religion	4.1		1.4	
Religion not reported	1.0		0.9	

SOURCE: U.S. Bureau of the Census, *Current Population Reports—Population Characteristics*, Series P-20, No. 79, February 2, 1958, "Religion Reported by the Civilian Population of the United States: March 1957," Table 1, p. 6.

[23] In 1961, 80.2 percent of all marriages recorded in the marriage-registration area were solemnized by religious ceremonies. For first marriages the percentage was 85.1; for remarriages, 63.2.—National Center for Health Statistics, *Vital Statistics of the United States: 1961* (Washington, D.C.: U.S. Department of Health, Education, and Welfare, n.d.), Table 2-21.

is your religion?" The Bureau of the Census asserts that, given this distribution of responses, if marriages had occurred randomly (rather than homogamously) with respect to religious affiliation, the percentage of couples reporting both spouses as being in the same major religious group would have been 56. It is likely that the procedure used to arrive at this conclusion is that set forth in Table 10.5. Here the marginal totals are based on Table 10.4 and the cell

TABLE 10.5

Theoretical Percentages of Religious Intermarriage, Assuming Random Mate-Selection, with Marginal Totals Based on Columns 2 and 4 of Table 10.4[a]

FEMALES	MALES			
	Protestant	*Catholic*	*Jewish*	*Total*
Protestant	*48.4*	19.2	2.5	70.0
Catholic	18.4	*7.3*	0.9	26.7
Jewish	2.3	0.9	*0.1*	3.3
Total	69.1	27.4	3.5	100.0

[a] The percentages in italic type represent the theoretical values for endogamous marriages within each of the three major religious groups.

entries are computed on the basis of joint probability. Thus the "both Protestant" value of 48.4 percent in the upper-left cell is merely the product of "male Protestant" (i.e., column 1's total of 69.1 percent) times "female Protestant" (i.e., row 1's total of 70.0 percent). Then the 56 percent for the same religious group is the sum of the diagonal entries in Table 10.5 rounded off to the nearest whole percent. Instead of 56 percent, as would be predicted on a chance or random basis, however, the actual percentage was 94. (See Table 10.6.) The fact that the observed value of 94 percent for religious homogamy is so much greater than the chance value of 56 percent is strong evidence in support of Hollingshead's generalization about the strength of religious affiliation as a mate-selective factor.

Before accepting the evidence in favor of religious homogamy one factor must be taken into account. Census data are necessarily static; they record a state of affairs as of some particular time. The marriages that make up the percentage homogamous (i.e., the 93.6 percent in Table 10.6) are reported to have been similar with respect to major religious category as of March 1957. Lenski has reported, however, that for every interfaith (heterogamous) marriage found among Christians in his sample in Detroit there was at least one additional marriage that had been interfaith before the wedding but wherein one party had converted to the faith of the other. On the basis of Lenski's data

TABLE 10.6

Comparison of Theoretical (Random) Mating (Diagonals from Table 10.5) with Actual Mating (from Table 10.7)

RELIGION	THEORETICAL (RANDOM MATING)	ACTUAL
All married couples with husband and wife in a major religious group	100.0	100.0
Husband and wife in same religious group	55.8	93.6
Both Protestant	48.4	67.3
Both Catholic	7.3	22.9
Both Jewish	0.1	3.4
Husband and wife in different major religious groups	44.2	6.4

Yinger has estimated that about one fourth of the Catholics, one tenth of the Protestants, and one fifteenth of the Jews are intermarried.[24] These fractions, when multiplied by the proportions of the respective religious categories in the married population, give a heterogamous percentage about double that shown in Table 10.6—about 13 percent instead of 6.4 percent married heterogamously with respect to religion. It is seen that even with the Lenski-Yinger correction applied, this percentage falls greatly short of the 44.2 percent we should expect to be intermarried on a chance basis. Thus the evidence convincingly supports the conclusion that religious homogamy prevails.

It is generally appreciated that the Roman Catholic Church takes a very strong position in opposition to the marriage of its members to persons of other faiths. It is of some interest, therefore, to see from Table 10.7 that the Catholic rate of homogamy (78.5 percent) is lower than that of Protestantism or of Jewry (91.4 and 92.8 percent, respectively). Attitudinal data support the statement that a greater proportion of Catholics than of Protestants are tolerant of marriages outside their religious grouping. The *Catholic Digest* found that 19 percent of Protestants and 40 percent of Catholics reported to a sample survey that they would have no objection to having a member of the family marry outside the major religious grouping.[25] Similar results have been reported by the American Institute of Public Opinion. To a question as to whether or not the respondent would object to having a daughter or a son marry a member of

---

[24] Gerhard Lenski, *The Religious Factor* (New York: Doubleday, 1963), p. 54; and J. Milton Yinger, "A Research Note on Interfaith Marriage Statistics," *Journal for the Scientific Study of Religion,* 7: 97–103 (1968).

[25] "Catholic Poll Split on Mixed Marriages," *The New York Times,* July 18, 1953, p. 14.

TABLE 10.7

Percentage Distribution of Married Couples by Religion Reported for the United States: Civilian Population, March 1957

RELIGION	PERCENT
All married couples with husband and wife in a major religious group	100.0
Husband and wife in same major religious group	93.6
Both Protestant	67.3
Both Roman Catholic	22.9
Both Jewish	3.4
Husband and wife in different major religious groups	6.4
Either or both spouses Protestant	100.0
Both Protestant	91.4
One Roman Catholic	8.4
One Jewish	0.2
Either or both spouses Roman Catholic	100.0
Both Roman Catholic	78.5
One Protestant	21.2
One Jewish	0.4
Either or both spouses Jewish	100.0
Both Jewish	92.8
One Protestant	4.2
One Roman Catholic	3.0

SOURCE: U.S. Bureau of the Census, *Current Population Reports—Population Characteristics*, Series P-20, No. 79, "Religion Reported by the Civilian Population of the United States: March, 1957," Table 6, p. 8.

"opposite faith," the objectors numbered 23 percent among the Catholics and 35 percent among the Protestants.[26] As in the case of interracial marriages, there seems to be a considerable body of folk wisdom to the effect that marriages between persons of different religions "don't work." According to the Gallup Poll, 36 percent of Catholics and 46 percent of Protestants believe that marriages mixed with respect to religion do not work out as well as other marriages. Moreover, the young person contemplating this kind of marriage is exposed to articles bearing such titles as:

> "We Wouldn't Marry Each Other Again: A Catholic and a Protestant Reveal the Problems of a Mixed Marriage."[27]

[26] American Institute of Public Opinion, "Do Mixed Marriages Work?" *Chicago Sun-Times,* March 22, 1959, sec. 2, p. 3.

[27] *Parade,* November 14, 1954, pp. 6–7, 9. But one author reports no significant dif-

Kennedy has studied the marriage patterns within and between ethnic and religious aggregates in New Haven over the period from 1870 to 1950. She reports that whereas there was considerable intermarriage between ethnic minorities (e.g., between Italians and Poles), still these marriages were overwhelming *within* the three major religious groupings (so that the Italian-Polish wedding, say, would be between two individuals of the Catholic faith). Although she did report that religious endogamy had decreased since 1870, the earliest year on which she obtained data, still for 1950 Kennedy found endogamous marriages accounting for 70, 73,[28] and 96 percent, respectively, of all the Protestant, Catholic, and Jewish individuals being married.[29] Similarly Hollingshead found that 91 percent of 523 couples whom he studied in New Haven in 1948 had married endogamously within one of the three large religious groupings. This observation led Professor Kennedy to state that there was a "triple melting-pot" rather than a single one and Hollingshead to speak of the "three pots boiling merrily side by side with little fusion between them."[30]

Thomas has found considerable variation in the rate at which Catholics marry non-Catholics. He believes that three factors bear the major responsibility: the proportion of Catholics in the community, the presence of close-knit ethnic subgroups in the community, and the socioeconomic status of the Catholics in the community.

With respect to the proportion of Catholics in the community Thomas found that where Catholics are relatively sparse, their intermarriage rate is high.

> For example, in the dioceses of Raleigh, Charleston, Savannah-Atlanta, Nashville, and Little Rock, where the Catholic population is two percent

ference between the religiously intermarried and the in-married in number of areas of disagreement or of intensity of disagreement.—Richard N. Hey, "Dissimilarity of Religious Background of Marital Partners as a Factor in Marital Conflict," paper read at 1965 meeting of the American Sociological Association.

[28] Loren E. Chancellor and Thomas P. Monahan report virtually the same figure for Iowa in 1953: "Of all individual Catholics getting married, 27 in 100 marry non-Catholics." —"Religious Preference and Interreligious Mixtures in Marriages and Divorces in Iowa," *American Journal of Sociology*, 61: 233–239 (1955), at p. 237.

[29] Ruby Jo Reeves Kennedy, "Single or Triple Melting-Pot? Intermarriage in New Haven, 1870–1950," *American Journal of Sociology*, 58: 56–59 (1952).

[30] "Cultural Factors in the Selection of Marriage Mates," *loc. cit.*, p. 624. Consistent with the conclusions of Kennedy and Hollingshead is the finding that there has been only a slight decline in interethnic residential segregation (e.g., Irish from Italian immigrants) in cities of the United States since 1930, and that interethnic segregation remains high into the second generation (native born of native parents). According to the author of this study, "the strong prejudice against Negroes on the part of whites only compounds an existing separatism, for if Protestant Norwegians hesitate to integrate with Protestant Swedes, and Catholic Italians with Catholic Irish, then these groups are even less likely to accept Negro neighbors."—Nathan Kantrowitz, "Ethnic and Racial Segregation in the New York Metropolis, 1960," *American Journal of Sociology*, 74: 685–695 (1969). Quotation is from p. 695.

or less of the total, the mixed marriage rates are 76.3, 71.5, 70.3, 58.3, and 55.6 respectively. On the other hand in the dioceses of El Paso, Corpus Christi, Lafayette (La.), Providence (R.I.), and Santa Fe, where the Catholic population is fifty to seventy percent of the total, the mixed marriage rates are 8.7, 7.5, 14.2, 17.2, and 8.4 respectively.[31]

Thomas interprets this point as follows: "The scarcity of prospective marriage mates within one's own religious group leads to a high rate of intermarriage wherever ethnic and/or social status differences do not prevent occupational and social contacts."[32] Further corroboration of this point comes from a study reporting a rank correlation of —.86 between the rates of "valid" interfaith marriages involving Catholics and the percentage of Catholics in the population in each of the forty-eight states of that time. The same investigators show the inverse relationship to hold for the regions of the United States.[33] (See Table 10.8, in which the rank correlation by regions is —.75.)

TABLE 10.8

Percent Catholic of the Total Population and Percent Mixed Marriages, by Regions of the United States, 1955

REGION	PERCENT CATHOLICS	"VALID" INTERFAITH MARRIAGES AS PERCENT OF ALL "VALID" CATHOLIC MARRIAGES
New England	47	22
Middle Atlantic	33	24
East North Central	25	26
Mountain	21	29
Pacific	20	34
West South Central	18	23
West North Central	18	30
South Atlantic	5	50
East South Central	4	47

SOURCE: Harvey J. Locke, Georges Sabagh, and Mary Margaret Thomes, "Interfaith Marriages," *Social Problems*, 4: 329–333 (1957). These authors cite *The Official Catholic Directory* (New York: Kenedy, 1955). See note 33 for meaning of "valid."

[31] John L. Thomas, "The Factor of Religion in the Selection of Marriage Mates," *American Sociological Review*, 16: 487–491 (1951), at p. 489. "A diocese is a district presided over by a bishop and generally named after the city in which his residence is located. Very few dioceses cross state lines but there may be several dioceses within the same state."—*Ibid.*, p. 488.

[32] *Ibid.*, p. 489.

[33] Harvey J. Locke, Georges Sabagh, and Mary Margaret Thomes, "Interfaith Marriages," *Social Problems*, 4: 329–333 (1957). In their study "valid" marriages are defined

On the point concerning close-knit ethnic subgroups Father Thomas mentions San Antonio and Syracuse. In each of these dioceses about 30 percent of the population is Catholic. Yet San Antonio, which has an important ethnic subgroup of Spanish and Mexican Catholics, has an intermarriage rate only half as large as that of Syracuse, which has no such minority (14 and 27 percent, respectively).

Thomas used rental value as an index of socioeconomic status. For 51,671 families in thirty parishes of a large urban center he related this index to the percentage of mixed marriages. The results appear in Table 10.9, which shows

TABLE 10.9

Rental Areas and Percentage of Catholic Marriages That Are Mixed

TYPE OF RENTAL AREA	PERCENTAGE OF MIXED MARRIAGES
Lower	8.5
Mixed lower and middle	9.1
Middle	12.0
Mixed middle and upper	16.3
Upper	17.9
Suburban	19.3

SOURCE: John L. Thomas, "The Factor of Religion in the Selection of Marriage Mates," *American Sociological Review,* 16: 490 (1951). By permission of The American Sociological Association.

a distinct tendency for the rate of Catholic intermarriage to increase with higher socioeconomic status.

Rosenthal has found that the rate of intermarriage among Jews increases as the size of the local Jewish community diminishes. Also he finds that the rate of intermarriage is higher among the previously divorced than among the previously widowed and among those entering first marriages. Moreover,

as those approved by the Roman Catholic Church. Locke et al. cite Father Thomas to the effect that about 40 percent of the interfaith marriages involving Catholics are assessed as not "valid."

In view of the evidence of a strong negative relationship between proportion of interfaith marriages and proportion that a religious category constitutes of a community and in view of the fact that Jews comprise such a small percentage of the U.S. population, the reader may be astonished that the proportion of Jewish intermarriages is so low (3 percent in Table 10.7). At least part of the answer lies in the fact that the Jews are far from uniformly spread through the country. Over 60 percent of the Jews live in the New York, Los Angeles, Philadelphia, and Chicago areas, and in 1962 over 40 percent lived in New York City plus three suburban New York State counties. Cf. Alvin Chenkin, "Jewish Population in the United States, 1967," in Morris Fine and Milton Himmelfarb (eds.), *American Jewish Year Book* (New York: The American Jewish Committee, 1968), Vol. 69.

he cites a study of intermarriage in Washington in 1956 that shows a marked increase with succeeding generations—from 1 percent among foreign-born Jews to 10 percent for first generation native-born and 18 percent for second-generation native-born Jews.[34]

As we reflect on what might be called the "natural history" of immigrant groups in this country, we can add meaning to the conclusions of Thomas and Rosenthal. Our immigrants came in waves—the Germans, the Swedes, the Irish, the Italians, the Poles, and so on. As each nation's immigrants entered American society, it came bearing the stamp of its national culture. The foreign-born were distinguished from the native-born by appearance, customs, and language. These distinctions functioned as social stigmata since the immigrants were poor and largely ignorant with respect to skills needed to get on in American cities, and hence they entered American society in the lowest social strata. Successively the immigrants of each nation tended to rise in the stratification system of American society. The rise was easier for the children of the immigrants because they learned English as the natives spoke it, and they tended to learn American customs. By the time a considerable number of a group had risen to, say, upper-middle class, they had lost virtually all of their visible and attitudinal identity with the ethnic group. Accordingly, the interpretation runs that while they are still recent immigrants their religion is viewed to be as stigmatic as their accent, and both are stigmatic because the immigrants are at or near the bottom of the system of stratification. As the minority begins to rise and to lose some of its (social) stigmata, its members become generally more acceptable to the majority, and their various social characteristics, including their religion, become less salient in stigmatizing them as inferior to the majority. The "more enlightened" members of the majority begin to see that "after all, they [the minority] worship the same God we do," which implies that members of the minority are becoming acceptable, or at least conceivable, marriage partners. The sociologist's phrasing would run:

> With socioeconomic status becoming equalized and ethnic characteristics virtually gone, religious identity has lost most of its prejudicial and discriminatory salience.

Thus the sociologist sees the principle of ethnocentric preference, rather than that of Christian tolerance, at work.

SOCIOECONOMIC STATUS

Thus far we have seen that American marriages tend to be homogamous with respect to race and religioethnic identity. If, then, Americans marry for love, there seems to be some principle operating to determine that Americans

---

[34] Erich Rosenthal, "Studies of Jewish Intermarriage in the United States," in *American Jewish Year Book, 1963*, and "Jewish Intermarriage in Indiana," in *American Jewish Year Book, 1967*, both published by The American Jewish Committee, New York.

are more likely to love someone of their own than of a different race and religio-ethnic identity. Love, as we shall see, tends also to be sensitive to socio-economic status.

Frequently used indexes of socioeconomic status include occupation, residential area, and level of education. Data on homogamy will be presented for each of these indexes. (The writer knows of no evidence relating homogamy to level of income.)

Rubin has reanalyzed data gathered by the U.S. Bureau of the Census in March, 1962, and used by Blau and Duncan in their study of occupations.[35] There were roughly 25,000 married men in the sample for each of whom there were data on his own father's occupation and also on the occupation of his wife's father. Rubin presents these data using a fivefold classification of occupations.[36] The present writer has reworked Rubin's data so that the twenty-five cells (resulting from cross-tabulating own father's occupation with wife's father's occupation) show both the actual percentage of cases in each cell and also the percentage that would have appeared if the process of mate-selection had taken place on a completely random basis. The actual percentages appear in the top position in each cell, and the expected (chance) percentages appear in parentheses in the bottom position in each cell.

If mate-selection were a random process, the diagonal cells (from upper left to lower right) would contain a little over 22 percent of the marriages. The sum of the actual percentages in these diagonal cells is over 37 percent. The degree of socioeconomic homogamy is represented by the increment of the actual 37 percent over the expected 22 percent. If we expand the criterion for homogamy to include the cells immediately above and below the diagonal, 71 percent of the marriages are actually homogamous as compared with a chance figure of 57 percent. (See Table 10.10.)

A parallel mode of analysis was used in a considerably earlier (1949) study on social class as indicated by the residential area of the families of orientation of newly married husbands and wives in New Haven, Connecticut. Using six classes of residence (rather than the five used in the study of occupations), Hollingshead found 58 percent homogamy on the diagonal and 83 percent when he included the immediately adjacent cells.[37]

Glick has demonstrated homogamy with respect to the years of schooling completed by husbands and wives. See Table 10.11, wherein it is clear that the highest percentage in each row and column is either on or close to the diagonal. Here the percentages on the diagonal total 45, while the immediately adjacent cells bring the total up to 82.

---

[35] Peter M. Blau and Otis Dudley Duncan, *The American Occupational Structure* (New York: Wiley, 1967, 1968).

[36] Zick Rubin, "Do American Women Marry Up?" *American Sociological Review*, 33: 750–760 (1968).

[37] August B. Hollingshead, "Cultural Factors in the Selection of Marriage Mates," *American Sociological Review*, 15: 619–627 (1950).

TABLE 10.10

Percentage Distribution of Marriages Classified by Occupational Category of Husband's Father and Wife's Father: United States, 1962

CATEGORY OF OCCUPATION OF HUSBAND'S FATHER	CATEGORY OF OCCUPATION OF WIFE'S FATHER					
	I	II	III	IV	V	Total
I. Professional and managerial	2.1 (0.9)	2.4 (1.4)	1.8 (1.9)	1.8 (2.6)	1.1 (2.4)	9.2 (9.2)
II. White-collar	2.5 (1.6)	4.0 (2.4)	3.4 (3.3)	3.8 (4.5)	2.5 (4.3)	16.1 (16.1)
III. Upper blue-collar	2.0 (2.0)	3.0 (3.0)	5.5 (4.1)	6.2 (5.5)	3.1 (5.2)	19.8 (19.8)
IV. Lower blue-collar	1.9 (2.6)	3.4 (3.9)	6.0 (5.3)	10.4 (7.2)	4.1 (6.8)	25.8 (25.8)
V. Farm	1.5 (2.9)	2.4 (4.4)	3.8 (5.9)	5.8 (8.1)	15.6 (7.7)	29.0 (29.0)
Total	10.0 (10.0)	15.1 (15.1)	20.5 (20.5)	28.0 (27.9)	26.4 (26.4)	100.0 (99.9)

SOURCE: The immediate source is Table 1 (the two halves of which have been summed) of Zick Rubin, "Do American Women Marry Up?" *American Sociological Review*, 5: 750–760 (1968). The data were gathered by the U.S. Bureau of the Census and are reported in Peter M. Blau and Otis Dudley Duncan, *The American Occupational Structure* (New York: Wiley, 1967).

AGE

As would be expected, the older a spouse is at marriage, the older the mate is likely to be. From Table 10.12 it can be seen that approximately 40 percent of the marriages reported in 1961 were of men and women in the same five-year age bracket. (The diagonal cells total 42.1 percent.) Nearly another 40 percent consists of marriages wherein the man is in the next older bracket than the woman (38.1 percent). On the other hand, relatively few (5.7 percent) are in the cells where the woman is reported as in the next five-year bracket older than her husband. Homogamy with respect to age is demonstrated by the fact that the diagonal and immediately adjacent cells account for more than five sixths of all marriages (42.1% + 38.1% + 5.7% = 85.9%).

Table 10.13 shows that although the husband tends generally to be older than the wife, the magnitude of this difference increases with their age at marriage. (As Bowerman observes, this is more true in the case of men marrying single women than of men marrying widowed women.[38]) Thus, while 18-year-

[38] Charles E. Bowerman, "Age Relationships at Marriage, by Marital Status and Age at Marriage," *Marriage and Family Living*, 18: 231–233 (1956).

TABLE 10.11

Percent Distribution of Couples with First Marriages between January 1947 and June 1954, by Years of School Completed by Husband and by Wife.

YEARS OF SCHOOL COMPLETED BY HUSBAND	ALL RECENTLY MARRIED COUPLES	YEARS OF SCHOOL COMPLETED BY WIFE						MEDIAN SCHOOL YEARS COMPLETED
		Elementary		High school		College		
		Under 8	8	1–3	4	1–3	4 or more	
Total	100.0	7.0	9.6	24.3	43.2	9.1	6.8	12.2
Elementary								
Under 8 years	9.8	*3.8*	1.7	3.1	1.0	0.1	0.1	8.6
8 years	12.4	1.4	*4.0*	3.8	2.8	0.3	...	9.6
High school								
1 to 3 years	23.6	1.3	2.2	*9.2*	9.9	0.8	0.1	11.7
4 years	33.0	0.4	1.4	6.4	*21.2*	2.7	1.0	12.4
College								
1 to 3 years	10.0	0.1	0.1	1.3	*4.9*	2.4	1.1	12.7
4 or more	11.3	...	0.1	0.4	3.3	2.9	*4.5*	14.8
Median years completed	12.1	6.5	8.8	10.7	12.4	13.9	16+	

SOURCE: Reprinted with permission from Paul C. Glick, *American Families*, p. 117. Copyright 1957 by John Wiley & Sons, Inc. From National Office of Vital Statistics, *Vital Statistics—Special Reports*, Vol. 45, No. 12, Table 10, p. 322. The highest value in each row and column is in italics.

old husbands tend to choose wives only very slightly their junior, bridegrooms of 28 years are on the average nearly four years older than their brides. When we use age of wife at first marriage as our reference point, however, we find that the spread between her age and that of her bridegroom narrows at later ages: whereas the 16-year-old marries a man nearly five years her senior, the 23-year-old has a bridegroom, on the average, three years older than herself.

Table 10.14 is presented to show the variation in relative ages of husbands and wives both in first marriages and in remarriages. Greater variation is apparent in remarriages, or, as Glick phrases it, "men who remarry are somewhat more likely than those who enter first marriage to be younger than their wives and are much more likely to be far older than their wives. . . . For all couples with the husband in his first marriage, the husband is three years older than the wife, on the average; for all couples with the husband in a remarriage, the husband is six years older than the wife, on the average."[39]

[39] Paul C. Glick, *American Families* (New York: Wiley, 1957), p. 126.

TABLE 10.12

Percentage Distribution of Marriages by Age of Bride, by Age of Groom: Marriage-Registration Area of the United States, 1961

AGE OF BRIDE	AGE OF GROOM				
	Under 20 Years	20–24 Years	25–29 Years	30–34 Years	35–39 Years
Under 20	11.7	22.5	3.1	.5	.1
20–24	1.4	19.7	8.9	2.3	.8
25–29	.1	1.4	3.6	2.2	1.0
30–34		.2	.8	1.7	1.2
35–39		.1	.3	.8	1.1
40–44			.1	.3	.5
45–49				.1	.1
50–54					
55 and over					
Total	13.2	43.9	16.8	7.9	4.8
	40–44 Years	45–49 Years	50–54 Years	55 and Over	Total
Under 20	.1				38.0
20–24	.2	.1			33.4
25–29	.4	.2			8.9
30–34	.6	.3	.2	.1	5.1
35–39	1.1	.6	.3	.2	4.5
40–44	.8	.7	.4	.4	3.2
45–49	.3	.5	.6	.7	2.3
50–54	.1	.3	.4	.9	1.7
55 and over		.1	.2	2.6	2.9
Total	3.6	2.8	2.1	4.9	100.0

SOURCE: National Center for Health Statistics, *Vital Statistics of the United States, 1961*, Vol. III, Sec. 2, Table 2–9.

PREVIOUS MARITAL STATUS

Since there is a high positive correlation between the ages at marriage of husbands and of their respective wives, it should be expected that there would also be homogamy with respect to marital status—that single individuals would tend to mate with single persons, divorced with divorced, and so on. In Table 10.15 it is seen that the large values are again in the diagonal cells, and thus the evidence supports our expectation of homogamy with respect to previous marital status.

TABLE 10.13

Specified Age of Husband or of Wife by Median Age of Spouse at First Marriage of Both, for Couples Who Married between January 1947 and June 1954

SPECIFIED AGE OF HUSBAND	MEDIAN AGE OF WIFE	SPECIFIED AGE OF WIFE	MEDIAN AGE OF HUSBAND
18 years	17.9	14 and 15 years	20.1
19 years	18.5	16 years	20.9
20 years	18.9	17 years	20.9
21 years	19.7	18 years	21.6
22 years	20.3	19 years	22.2
23 years	20.7	20 years	23.3
24 years	20.8	21 years	23.8
25 years	21.7	22 years	24.6
26 years	22.0	23 years	26.0
27 years	23.4	24 years	26.4
28 years	24.2	25 years	27.8

SOURCE: National Office of Vital Statistics, *Vital Statistics—Special Reports*, Vol. 45, No. 12, September 9, 1957, Table L, p. 289.

Residential Segregation, Ethnocentric Preference, and the Field of Eligibles

We have found homogamy operative with respect to race, religioethnic identity, SES, age, and previous marital status. Thus far our remarks have been somewhat descriptive. Now let us try to tie together our observations into a statement of some theoretical coherence.

1. It is important to note that people are not spread through space in a random fashion with respect to social characteristics. It is a matter of common observation that within cities there are areas of high-cost housing, of slums, of recent migrants from one country or another, of blacks, and so on. Given the nonrandom way in which people are distributed through space, the probability is reasonably high that any given person is going to be living in close proximity to others who are somewhat like him in the characteristics of which we are speaking.

2. It is again a matter of common observation that when one needs to travel to accomplish a mission, he will ordinarily travel a shorter rather than a longer distance to do so. He will walk to his corner drugstore rather than to one on the opposite side of the city for a tube of toothpaste, for example. This has been studied under the rubric of "intervening opportunities" and the "time-

TABLE 10.14

Percent Distribution of Difference between Ages of Husband and Wife, for Couples with Marriages between January 1947 and June 1954

DIFFERENCE BETWEEN AGES OF HUSBAND AND WIFE	HUSBAND IN FIRST MARRIAGE	DIFFERENCE BETWEEN AGES OF HUSBAND AND WIFE	HUSBAND REMARRIED
Total	100.0	Total	100.0
Husband older than wife by:		Husband older than wife by:	
10 years or more	6.1	15 years or more	13.3
5 to 9 years	23.0	10 to 14 years	16.6
3 and 4 years	21.4	7 to 9 years	15.1
2 years	13.1	5 and 6 years	11.8
1 year	11.1	3 and 4 years	10.4
Husband and wife same age	10.7	1 and 2 years	10.6
Husband younger than wife by:		Husband and wife same age	4.4
		Husband younger than wife	17.8
1 and 2 years	8.9	Median years husband was older than wife	6.1
3 years or more	5.8		
Median years husband was older than wife	3.0		

SOURCE: Reprinted with permission from Paul C. Glick, *American Families*, p. 125. Copyright 1957 by John Wiley & Sons, Inc. From National Office of Vital Statistics, *Vital Statistics—Special Reports*, Vol. 45, No. 12, September 9, 1957, Tables 15 and 16. Based on Current Population Survey data collected by the Bureau of the Census.

TABLE 10.15

Percent Distribution of Marriages by Previous Marital Status of Bride and Groom, for the Marriage-Registration Area: 1961

	GROOMS			
BRIDES	Single	Widowed	Divorced	Total
Single	72.3	1.0	5.7	79.0
Widowed	1.3	2.4	1.7	5.4
Divorced	5.8	1.4	8.4	15.6
Total	79.4	4.8	15.8	100.0

SOURCE: National Center for Health Statistics, *Vital Statistics of the United States, 1961*, Vol. III, Sec. 2, Table 2–17.

cost function."[40] The literature on residential propinquity indicates that this kind of consideration functions in mate-selection. It has been shown, moreover, that not only is residential propinquity operative at the time of application for the marriage license but also in the "meeting and dating patterns of the couples."[41] Furthermore, the appropriateness of thinking of propinquity in terms of the cost of travel is suggested by findings that men of higher SES (in terms of occupation) travel farther to locate wives than do men of lower SES.[42]

3. From the first two observations it follows that one should expect homogamy to occur even if there were no sanctions in its favor.

4. It does appear, however, that there are sanctions in favor of homogamy. The most obvious example concerns the attitudes with respect to racial endogamy in the Southern states.

5. As Katz and Hill point out,[43] although age and previous marital status do not tend to be bases of residential segregation, nevertheless they do seem to be attended by homogamous sanctions. Especially is it frequently expressed that old and young persons ought not to marry each other.

With respect to race, religioethnic identity, and SES, then, it appears that people tend to marry homogamously, in part because they tend to find mates like themselves closer at hand than do persons of different characteristics. And people tend to mate homogamously, in part because of the more or less widespread belief in the "rightness" that one should marry within one's race, religion, and the like. This is the meaning of ethnocentric preference. These variables apparently tend to select for each of us an aggregate of people who are more or less like us with whom we associate at work, at play, at worship, and elsewhere.[44] For most of us, moreover, it takes an extra effort to

[40] Samuel A. Stouffer, "Intervening Opportunities: A Theory Relating Mobility and Distance," *American Sociological Review,* 5: 845–867 (1940); Daniel Harris, "Age and Occupational Factors in the Residential Propinquity of Marriage Partners," *Journal of Social Psychology,* 6: 257–261 (1935). Corroboration for the general point arises in another context, where it is shown that the ecology of interaction patterns and the development of friendships in a housing project are affected by the sheer distance between houses and the directions in which the houses face.—Leon Festinger, "Group Attraction and Membership," in Dorwin Cartwright and Alvin Zander (eds.), *Group Dynamics: Research and Theory* (New York: Harper & Row, 1953), pp. 92–101, esp. p. 95.

[41] Alfred C. Clarke, "An Examination of the Operation of Residential Propinquity as a Factor in Mate Selection," *American Sociological Review,* 17: 17–22 (1952), at p. 19.

[42] Koller, "Residential Propinquity of White Males," *loc. cit.;* Clarke, "An Examination of the Operation of Residential Propinquity," *loc. cit.*

[43] Alvin M. Katz and Reuben Hill, "Residential Propinquity and Marital Selection: A Review of Theory, Method, and Fact," *Marriage and Family Living,* 20: 27–35 (1958).

[44] After interviewing 97 New Haven families Sussman concluded that families influence the mate-selection of their children both through residential propinquity, i.e., living in the "right sort" of neighborhood, and through sanctions (or, as he phrased it, "persuasive" techniques).—Marvin B. Sussman, "Parental Participation in Mate Selection and Its Effect

arrange to associate with people quite different from ourselves; we probably do not know how to do it, and we might feel uncertain about being accepted if we were to try. In the sense that these variables determine for us with whom we shall associate it seems appropriate to think of them as defining for each of us a "field of eligible spouse-candidates," or more briefly a "field of eligibles," within which it is likely that each of us will choose his or her spouse.[45]

It has been shown that spouses tend to resemble each other with respect to certain psychological variables: intelligence, interests (e.g., religious, esthetic, political), values, attitudes (e.g., toward birth control and toward communism), neurotic tendency, and temperamental disposition. "The correlations are higher in the intellectual and attitudinal traits than in traits of temperament. None of the correlations, even in temperament, [is] reliably negative, as the theory of the attraction of opposites would require."[46] Such

---

upon Family Continuity," *Social Forces*, 32: 76–81 (1953). Not related to residential propinquity but to parental participation in mate-selection is a report from Italy concerning an organization known as the Pink Bows Association. This is a confederation of local clubs made up of fathers of unmarried daughters who are interested in saving the girls from spinsterhood. According to the report, each local club has its own projects to aid the unmarried girls. One club, for example, was reported to be considering two projects: a publicity program to advertise the girls' plight in a dignified manner, and a fund to provide a small pension to each girl who has not married by some specified age.—"Unwed Girls Get Assist from Dads: Italian Fathers Form Pink Bows Clubs to Help Their Daughters Get Beaus," *The New York Times*, February 22, 1959, p. 69.

[45] An intriguing, if morbid, extension of the concept of the field of eligibles is the evidence that in India murderers and their victims tend to be of the same caste, religion, and sex.—Edwin D. Driver, "Interaction and Criminal Homicide in India," *Social Forces*, 40: 153–158 (1961). Somewhat parallel is evidence from Chicago that when a murder occurs, the probability is about 1/2 that the murderer is a friend or other unrelated acquaintance of the victim, about 1/4 that the murderer is a relative of the victim (including the probability of 1/5 that the murderer is the spouse of the victim), and no more than 1/4 that the murderer and victim are unacquainted. "Murder Analysis for 1965," prepared by the Homicide, Sex and Aggravated Assault Section, Chicago Police Department. ". . . up to 85 per cent of all murders occur within families or among acquaintances. Murder . . . occurs where emotions are strongest—husband and wife, father and son. . . . If you are afraid of being murdered, there is more safety in deserting your family and having no friends than in additional police. . . ." Ramsey Clark, *Crime in America: Observations on Its Nature, Causes, Prevention and Control* (New York: Simon and Schuster, 1970), pp. 50–51.

[46] Helen M. Richardson, "Studies of Mental Resemblance between Husbands and Wives and between Friends," *Psychological Bulletin*, 36: 104–120 (1939), at p. 108. Some of the more important studies of this type are E. W. Burgess and Paul Wallin, "Homogamy in Personality Characteristics," *Journal of Abnormal and Social Psychology*, 39: 475–481 (1944); E. L. Kelly, "A Preliminary Report on Psychological Factors in Assortative Mating," *Psychological Bulletin*, 34: 749 (1937, abstract); E. Lowell Kelly, "Consistency of the Adult Personality," *American Psychologist*, 10: 659–681 (1955); James A. Schellenberg, "Homogamy in Personal Values and the 'Field of Eligibles,'" *Social Forces*, 39: 157–162 (1960); Mary Schooley, "Personality Resemblances among Married Couples," *Journal of Abnormal and Social Psychology*, 31: 340–347 (1936); R. R. Willoughby, "Neuroticism in Marriage, IV, Homogamy; V, Summary and Conclusions," *Journal of Social Psychology*, 7: 19–48

interspousal correlations—especially when account is taken of the low degree of these correlations—would seem to result from the selecting of mates from the field of eligibles. With respect to deeper-lying emotional motivation, however, Winch holds that mates tend to be attracted to each other on the basis of complementariness rather than on the basis of similarity.[47] This subject will be considered in Chapter 18.

Age at Marriage Related to Other Variables

Now that we have examined the evidence on homogamy, it is in order to look at age at marriage to see what is known about its change through time, to observe how it varies from one country to another, and to note how it covaries with urban versus rural residence and with indexes of socioeconomic status—education, income, occupation, and social class—and with Protestant versus Catholic religious affiliation.

The earliest year for which an official estimate is available for the median age at first marriage for men and women in the United States is 1890. Official data have shown a generally downward trend in age at first marriage from 1890 to 1960 followed by a slight upswing. (See Table 10.16.) Although official

TABLE 10.16

Median Age at First Marriage, by Sex, for the United States, 1890 to 1969

YEAR	MALES	FEMALES
1969	23.2	20.8
1960	22.8	20.3
1950	22.8	20.3
1940	24.3	21.5
1930	24.3	21.3
1920	24.6	21.2
1910	25.1	21.6
1900	25.9	21.9
1890	26.1	22.0

SOURCE: 1940–1969: *Statistical Abstract of the United States, 1970,* Table 75, p. 60; 1920–1930: *Statistical Abstract of the United States, 1968,* Table 77, p. 61; 1890–1910: U.S. Bureau of the Census, *Current Population Reports—Population Characteristics,* Series P-20, No. 114, January 31, 1962, Table D, p. 3.

(1936). In an unpublished study E. L. Clark has correlated a number of characteristics of 913 husbands and their wives, all of whom had been undergraduate students at Northwestern University. All correlations were positive. The correlations may be summarized as follows: height, .39; weight, .20; college grades, .26; rank in high school, .18; education of father, .19.

[47] Robert F. Winch, *Mate-Selection: A Study of Complementary Needs* (New York: Harper & Row, 1958).

figures have been criticized as being so laden with error as to be virtually meaningless,[48] some corroboration of the downward trend comes from a statistical series showing a recent increase in the proportion of young whites who are married—but it also shows a decrease in the proportion of nonwhites. (See Table 10.17.)[49]

It is a widespread impression that very early marriage was the pattern in our colonial and early national period.[50] As Ogburn and Nimkoff remark, "This opinion is very widespread, but it is not very precise; it does not tell us how much earlier, nor does it specify the exact dates."[51] They go on to point out that the bases for the impression are several: the writings of travelers from Europe, genealogies, and the fact that common law specified that the minimum ages for males and females to marry were 14 and 12 years, respectively.

If it is true that median ages at first marriage were quite young in the seventeenth and eighteenth centuries and that they have been going down during the present century, it would appear that they must have increased during the nineteenth century perhaps because of the great number of immigrants. Ogburn and Nimkoff cite data on Massachusetts for the latter half of the nineteenth century to support the view that such an upward trend took place at that time. From the time of the Civil War until the end of the nineteenth century they report that the median age for men to marry rose from 24.9 to 26.1 years and for women from 22.5 to 23.5 years.[52]

---

[48] Monahan, who has made a detailed criticism of the procedures used in deriving official estimates of age at marriage, concludes: "We do not know, therefore, what the average age at marriage is for the United States and how much it has changed one way or another."—Thomas P. Monahan, *The Pattern of Age at Marriage in the United States* (Philadelphia: Stephenson, 1951), pp. 99–136. Quotation is from p. 136. Cf. also Letters to the Editor of the *American Journal of Sociology* by Thomas P. Monahan and A. Ross Eckler, 56: 181–184, 184–187, 268–270 (1950).

[49] Another form of indirect and impressionistic evidence that an increasing proportion of the population is marrying at the younger ages comes from the concern of educational administrators with the "problem" of the married high school student. In bygone years the policy was widespread to expel any high school student whose marriage became known. Apparently the nub of the "problem" lay in the confusion of roles between the general conception of the high school student as a dependent adolescent and physical evidence of the assumption of the adult role of mother by married and visibly pregnant young women. The more "liberal" policy is apparently one of trying not to allow the role conflict to disturb the system. Some popular discussions are Rita Fitzpatrick, "Should You Wed in High School? Why Teen Marriages Are Headache Here," *Chicago Sun-Times*, March 4, 1959, p. 41; Samuel Grafton, "Why Teen-Age Marriages Are Falling Apart," *McCall's*, November 1959, pp. 88–89, 118–124; Lloyd Shearer, "Married Teenagers: Should They Be Allowed in High School?" *Parade*, September 6, 1959, pp. 4–7. Cf. also Lee G. Burchinal, "Research on Young Marriage: Implications for Family Life Education," *Family Life Coordinator*, 9: 6–24 (1960).

[50] Cf., e.g., A. W. Calhoun, *A Social History of the American Family* (New York: Barnes & Noble, 1945), II, 11.

[51] W. F. Ogburn and M. F. Nimkoff, *Technology and the Changing Family* (Boston: Houghton Mifflin, 1955), p. 64.

[52] *Ibid.*, p. 63. But Monahan contends that the data warrant none but an agnostic

TABLE 10.17

Percent of American Population 15–19 and 20–24 Years of Age
Ever Married, by Color and Sex: 1890–1966

	MALE				FEMALE			
	White		Nonwhite		White		Nonwhite	
YEAR	15–19	20–24	20–24	20–24	20–24	15–19	15–19	15–19
1966	NA[a]	48.7	NA	39.1	NA	68.6	NA	60.3
1950	3.2	40.5	4.4	45.3	16.5	67.6	21.1	68.8
1940	1.6	26.5	3.2	39.6	10.9	51.6	19.0	62.8
1930	1.5	27.1	3.6	41.7	11.8	51.9	21.9	66.9
1920	1.9	27.2	4.0	44.0	11.8	52.4	21.2	68.5
1910	1.0	22.9	2.3	38.8	10.7	49.6	18.4	65.1
1900	0.9	20.2	1.8	34.8	10.4	46.4	16.8	60.3
1890	0.5	17.3	0.9	33.5	8.8	46.2	15.1	61.9

[a] NA = not available.
SOURCE: 1966: U.S. Bureau of the Census, *Current Population Reports—Population Characteristics*, Series P-20, No. 159, January 25, 1967, Table 3, pp. 9–10; 1890–1950: adapted with permission of the author from Paul H. Jacobson, *American Marriage and Divorce*. New York: Holt, Rinehart and Winston, Inc. copyright, ©, 1959, Table 23, p. 62.

One important consequence of age at marriage concerns the number of children born. As Nimkoff observes: "Fertility is more closely related to age [at marriage] than to any other demographic factor."[53] Reference was made in Chapter 8 to an estimate that over 95 percent of the births in this country are legitimate. It is obvious that of the women who survive until, say, age 45, one who marries early will have a longer period to bear legitimate children than one who marries late. Nimkoff remarks that the probability of a woman's remaining childless is three times greater (although still only one in ten) if she marries at 20 or 21 years of age rather than at 18. He implies that this is due not so much to any difference in fecundity (potential capacity for reproduction) on the part of late-marrying women as to a greater tendency on their part to prevent conception. Corroboration of the negative correlation between fertility and age at marriage comes from a sample of the 1950 census of population: ". . . in the age group 40 to 44 years the women who had been married 20 years or more had 2,954 children per 1,000 women as compared with 2,041 for the women married 15 to 19 years."[54]

position: "The somewhat contradictory but often repeated assertions that American colonists married very early, and that the age at marriage is remarkably lower today than in former generations, are conclusions not supported by the facts."—*Op. cit.*, p. 346.

[53] Meyer F. Nimkoff, *Marriage and the Family* (Boston: Houghton Mifflin, 1947), p. 537.

[54] U.S. Bureau of the Census, "Fertility by Duration of Marriage: 1950," Series PC-14, No. 22, September 7, 1956, p. 2. Just as in the nineteenth century in Europe the control of

With respect to the ages at which women marry there is considerable variation among countries; within the United States there is variation among categories of the population when classified by urban versus rural residence, by education, by income, and by husband's occupation. The United States has a high proportion of women married in the younger age categories. Table 10.17 shows that during the 1940's the proportion of white American females who were married was in the range 12–17 percent for those 15–19 years old, and 53–68 percent for those 20–24 years of age. By contrast, Eire (the Irish Free State) has been a country with a high median age at first marriage and a very small proportion of young women married. For one of the years in the 1940's it had 1 percent and 12 percent married, respectively, in the 15–19- and 20–24-year-old age categories.[55] In our discussion of County Clare we noted something of the marriage customs of a rural part of this country. Deferral of marriage enables this relatively poor country, which has been exporting population for over a century, to adhere to Roman Catholic tenets about avoiding contraceptive practices and still avoid a high birth rate.

Some other relationships have been reported as follows. Urban people marry at a later average than do farm people. The relation between education and average age at marriage is curvilinear; i.e., the high median ages go with low education (less than high school) and with high education (four years or more of college). For urban residents of both sexes the lowest median age at first marriage is found in those who left high school before graduating.[56] Men with larger incomes marry later, on the average, than those with lower incomes.[57] Occupations with higher median ages at first marriage are the ones involving either a period of training or of experience or an accumulation of resources.[58] Consistent with the data on income and occupation is a report that higher social classes have later median ages at marriage than do lower classes.[59]

---

fertility was mainly achieved through social barriers to early marriage (cf. Frank Lorimer, *Culture and Human Fertility* [Paris: UNESCO, 1954], p. 206], so more recently governments have been undertaking to manipulate the birth rate by providing inducements or penalties for early marriages. In the 1950's it appears that Sweden was doing the former and Austria the latter.—"Swedish Couples Get State Loans: Government Plan to Furnish Homes Aimed at Increasing Marriage and Birth Rate," *The New York Times*, August 22, 1954, p. 26; "Taxes Make 40,000 Live Unmarried [in Vienna]," *Chicago Sun-Times*, December 11, 1955, p. 5.

[55] Metropolitan Life Insurance Company, *Statistical Bulletin*, Vol. 28, No. 2, February 1947, p. 9.

[56] National Office of Vital Statistics, *Vital Statistics—Special Reports*, Vol. 45, No. 12, September 9, 1957, Tables 24 and 27, pp. 339 and 348–350.

[57] Paul C. Glick and Emanuel Landau, "Age as a Factor in Marriage," *American Sociological Review*, 15: 517–529 (1950). Table is on p. 527.

[58] *Ibid.*

[59] W. Lloyd Warner and Paul S. Lunt, *The Social Life of a Modern Community* (New Haven, Conn.: Yale University Press, 1941), pp. 203, 255. Monahan has criticized Warner's data on the grounds that (1) Warner combined first and later marriages in the

Finally, Chancellor and Burchinal have analyzed data on all marriages (presumably including remarriages) that took place in Iowa during the years 1953–1957 between non-Jewish white persons. They found that with the occupational status of grooms either controlled or allowed to vary, the median ages at marriage of Catholic grooms and brides were higher than those of Protestants and of the religiously unaffiliated. Their major interpretation centers on the general adult opposition to teen-age marriages plus the strong emphasis of the Catholic Church on familial stability.[60]

Mate-Finding

In simple societies there is an opportunity for the person seeking a mate—whether the individual to be married or the representative of him or of his family—to know the field of eligibles. In some traditional societies where families, rather than principals, make the decisions, the specialized occupation of marriage-broker has developed. Traditional Chinese, Japanese, and Jewish societies are examples. In mass societies where mate-selection is volitional, rather than arranged, there is evidence of a need to supplement the ecologically based process reflected in the dimensions of homogamy that have been documented above. Various devices have been used to assist people in finding mates in such societies. Advertising has been widely used in Europe, e.g., in Germany and the United Kingdom, and in ethnic enclaves of European origin in the United States. The educational system has provided a meeting place in this country—both at the secondary and higher levels. Hotels, resorts, and housing developments have not overlooked the opportunity to attract a nubile clientele by offering "introduction" services. Marriage bureaus advertise their services in European newspapers, and perhaps it is characteristically American that their counterparts in this country should be called dating services and should involve the use of electronic computers—presumably programmed to match pairs with respect to similarities in a number of the dimensions shown to underlie the pattern of homogamy.[61] For those who are divorced or widowed and are seeking remarriages, opportunities to meet persons of similar marital status exist in such groups as Parents Without Partners.

---

same series and (2) he combined data on men and women. Monahan further complained that he was unable to obtain the data necessary to refine the presentation. Cf. Monahan, *op. cit.*, p. 262.

[60] Loren E. Chancellor and Lee G. Burchinal, "Status Levels of Grooms, Religious Affiliations and Ages of Brides and Grooms, Iowa, 1953–1957," unpublished manuscript.

[61] An official investigation in 1971 revealed that there were 28 dating services in the New York metropolitan area that used or claimed to use computers to match applicants on such attributes as age, education, creativity, hobbies, etc. Witnesses reported paying several hundred dollars and getting little in return. The attorney general of the state was considering the advisability of licensing this type of service. "Computer as Cupid Assailed by Clients," *New York Times*, January 9, 1971, p. 31.

Summary

Every society has some rules for the selection of spouses. The letter of the rule may vary from one society to another and from one stratum to another within a society. One set of rules concerns the degree of kinship that is tolerable in marriage. This is the rule of incest avoidance. Another set of rules concerns the avoidance of possible spouse candidates who are unacceptably different from oneself. This is the rule of ethnocentric preference. The joint operation of these two rules defines the field of eligibles. Customarily mates are obtained from the field of eligibles. There are two ways in which the selection may be made. It may be done by arrangement, usually by the parents of the principals, or it may be done volitionally, by the prospective bridal couple themselves. The functionality of the family determines the degree of importance to be attached to mate-selection. If the family is highly functional, mate-selection tends to be important to the family. In this situation it is likely that there will be arranged marriages and spouses will be selected on the basis of criteria important to the family. If the family is not highly functional, as in middle-class America, mate-selection can be volitional, i.e., it can be left to the inexperienced principals, who will tend to select spouses from the field of eligibles on the basis of love.

In middle-class America mate-selection is traditionally volitional, and dimensions of ethnocentric preference have been shown with respect to race, religioethnic identity, and socioeconomic status. These dimensions apparently function both unwittingly—through residential propinquity and segregation and through differential association at work, at play, and at worship—and wittingly through sanctions. With respect to age and previous marital status, homogamy is also observable; here, however, its functioning is apparently not so much a consequence of residential propinquity and segregation as of differential association and sanctions.

Variation in age at first marriage has both consequences and causes. Other things being equal, the later the average age at first marriage, the lower will be the birth rate. For this reason some governments seek to exercise control over fertility by making marriage either more or less attractive, depending upon whether higher or lower fertility is desired.

Customarily age at first marriage reflects the age at which people are able to assume the responsibilities of parenthood at their level of living; that is to say, the age at which they assume fully adult status. In Chapter 7 it was seen that in rural Ireland the son staying on the land did not achieve such status until the death or retirement of his father, with the result that sons frequently did not marry until they were in their late thirties. In American society the age at which a male achieves adulthood is associated with the amount of education he obtains and the kind of occupation he enters. High levels of education and occupations requiring long periods of training and experience result in late attainment of a fully adult status and hence in late age at first marriage. For the woman late marriage in American society is associated, among other things, with an avoidance of premarital pregnancy, and thus we are brought to see that early pregnancy is a way in which a female may expedite her attainment of adult status.

Where marriages are early, it seems probable that one or more of three situations obtain: (1) There is early assumption of the status of adulthood. This occurs where the men involved need little training, as in the unskilled occupations of the lower socioeconomic strata in this country. (2) The couple is being supported, as by an extended, especially a stem, family. It sometimes happens that the entity providing support and standing *in loco parentis* to the young couple is a large corporation that is training the husband to become a productive employee, or it may be the state rewarding him for entering an occupation where workers are in short supply. In this situation, even though the couple may quickly have children, they have not become fully adult in the American middle-class sense because of their continued dependence. (3) The attainment of fully adult status is deferred by the postponement of parenthood. This involves the availability of efficient means of contraception. It seems likely that many of the married couples with one or both members in college can be classified into either (2) or (3) or both.

11

Familial Structure and the Composition of American Families

Purpose of This Chapter

At one or another time the word "family" has been used to refer to a gamut of familial forms ranging from two related individuals occupying a single dwelling to a clan consisting of thousands of people occupying thousands of square miles. In this chapter it is our purpose to suggest some indexes that will enable us to measure an aspect of familial structure that will be called "extended familism." A second purpose will be to propose some correlates and hypothetical determinants of various familial forms. In other words, we shall try to specify conditions under which one or another familial form will exist. Third, we shall differentiate some familial forms in American society. And finally, we shall offer some descriptive statistics about the family in America.

The Range of Familial Structure

For practical purposes we may think of the range of familial forms as being indicated in Chapters 2 and 3 on, respectively, the family of traditional China and the family of an Israeli kibbutz. We noted in Chapter 1 that traditional China had the ideal of the joint family—a single household containing a father and a mother, all their sons and unmarried daughters, the wives of their sons, all of the sons' children except married daughters, and so on through as many generations as possible. As observed in Chapter 2, however, such large domestic families were usually possible only for the numerically small gentry, whereas peasant households had much less generational depth.

On the other hand, in Kiryat Yedidim—the kibbutz described in Chapter 3—the family consists of a parental couple and their minor children. If they had, say, one child under one and other around six, each of the children would be living in his own age-graded residence, and thus this family of four would be ensconced in three households.

Determinants of Familial Structure

Once we become aware of great variation in the structure of familial forms, it is in order to seek the conditions that result in one or another of the possible forms. Probably the most obvious variable to propose in looking for variation in familial structure is the way the economy is organized. Labeling this variable "subsistence-complexity," Winch and Blumberg have proposed that the elaborateness of familial structure is a curvilinear function of the level of subsistence-complexity. This means that at the simplest levels of subsistence-complexity, e.g., where subsistence is based on gathering and on hunting, familial structure tends to be small, i.e., nuclear (triadic) or dyadic.[1] As the level of subsistence becomes more complex—toward herding and settled agriculture—the form of the economy is favorable to larger familial organization, and the extended family prevails. With further advances in the complexity of the economy, however, i.e., with the development of mass-industrial societies, conditions tend to favor small families, and the nuclear form again becomes dominant. This last phase does not necessarily involve the isolation of the nuclear family; rather, it implies that interactiton and function will be more intense in the nuclear than in the extended family, and it leaves problematic the degree of isolation of the nuclear family.[2]

The reader may have interpreted the foregoing paragraph as implying that within societies the structure of the family would prove to be homogeneous. This is probably more false than true, and certainly it is more false, the more differentiated is the society. As societies become more complex, they develop not only specialized structures to carry out various functions, but they also evince variation in those structures. More particularly, the more highly developed societies, such as the United States, show within their borders a variety of familial structures. Three such varieties will be distinguished for the United States.

---

[1] See "nuclear family" and "nuclear dyad" in Table 1.1, p. 11 above.

[2] Robert F. Winch and Rae Lesser Blumberg, "Societal Complexity and Familial Organization," in Robert F. Winch and Louis Wolf Goodman (eds.), *Selected Studies in Marriage and the Family* (3d ed.; New York: Holt, Rinehart and Winston, Inc., 1968), pp. 70–92. Since both subsistence-complexity and degree of familial complexity are measured by ordinal, rather than interval, scales, it is more accurate to speak of the relationship between these two variables as non-monotonic than as curvilinear. Scales are discussed on pp. 11–12 of Winch and Goodman, *op. cit.*

Structure of the American Domestic Family (or Familial Household)

Unfortunately there are no data that would enable us to discover the structural history of the American family. What fragmentary data exist pertain not to families in general but to domestic families (or familial households). As we have indicated in Chapter 1, a family is a social system having functions and consisting of positions bearing kin relationships to each other. Of course this statement implies no specification as to the number of households a family may occupy. Historical statistics about the American family come mainly from the U.S. Bureau of the Census, which collects information not about familial systems as such but only about the related persons who share dwelling units, i.e., about domestic families. For this reason most of the following discussion will pertain to domestic families.

The median size of household appears to have shrunk by about two persons over the century and three quarters from 1790 to 1967. In 1790 the median was 5.4 persons; in 1969 it was 3.2.[3] Although the size of household appears to have diminished by about 40 percent over this period, the size of the familial structure does not seem to have been affected. (It will be recalled that the size of structure refers to the number of positions in the system and not to the number of incumbents of each position; by this formulation a family consisting of two parents and one child has the same size of structure [three positions] as one with two parents and ten children.) Toward the close of the eighteenth century, as we saw in Chapter 7, the average fertile married woman was bearing eight children; the current figure seems to be a bit under three. Moreover, life expectation at birth has just about doubled over this period. The result is fewer children per married woman, and a vastly higher proportion surviving into adulthood. Virtually all of the reduction in size of household can be accounted for by the reduction by two in number of children per household.

Recent Confusion about the Structure of the American Family

In the 1930's and 1940's, as is stated in the introduction to Chapter 6, American sociologists were writing that the American family was typically urban, isolated, and nuclear. It was thought by these writers that other forms of the family might exist within our national borders, but that they were probably among either rural people—especially those in the Southern highlands—and/or among unassimilated immigrants. The writers of this period

---

[3] U.S. Bureau of the Census, *Historical Statistics of the United States, Colonial Times to 1957* (Washington, D.C.: GPO, 1960), Table A 255–263, p. 16; *Statistical Abstract of the United States, 1970*, Table 40, p. 35.

saw such people destined to become urban and middle-class and their familial forms destined to evolve into the urban-isolated-nuclear structure.

Then in the 1950's came a spate of revisionist papers showing that urban people did have relatives, interacted with them, seemed to enjoy such interaction, and used their relatives as sources of succor in time of need. Thus American families, even though nuclear in household, and urban and middle-class, were no longer thought to be necessarily isolated.[4]

Some Findings about the Structure of the American Family

The issue that was posed by the allegations of the 1930's and 1940's and the seemingly contrary data of the 1950's concerned the structure of the family. Both sets of writers were talking about the domestic family. Without the benefit of systematic data the earlier set asserted that the conditions of urban life brought about the isolation of the domestic family from kinsmen. The latter writers had data that revealed that although some domestic families were indeed isolated, the majority were typically in touch with kinsmen from other households.

If, then, the earlier writers had meant to say that all urban domestic families were isolated, they had been proved wrong. But perhaps they meant that a greater proportion of families in urban areas would be isolated than in other areas. To test this hypothesis Winch and Greer reported data from a state-wide probability sample of 513 domestic nuclear families in Wisconsin. Since isolation constitutes only one end of an index of isolation, the term "extended familism" was used to designate the other end. With residence classified as metropolitan, rural, and other, it was found that urban respondents did not report significantly fewer households of kin in the community although they did interact less with those kin and did have less functional interaction with them. These differences, however, are related to migratory status; when neither spouse was a migrant, the differences between urban (metropolitan) families and the others disappeared, but the differences held up when one or both spouses were migrants.[5] Straus reports that rural housewives are more likely to interact with kin than are urban housewives and that wives of blue-collar workers are more likely to do so than are wives of white-collar workers.[6]

---

[4] Details and bibliography concerning this dispute appear in Winch and Blumberg, *op. cit.*, pp. 70–73, and Robert F. Winch, "Some Observations on Extended Familism in the United States," in Winch and Goodman, *op. cit.*, pp. 127–138, esp. pp. 127–131.

[5] Robert F. Winch and Scott A. Greer, "Urbanism, Ethnicity, and Extended Familism," *Journal of Marriage and the Family*, 30: 40–45 (1968). Key found no significant differences between rural and urban respondents with respect to participation in their kin networks.—William H. Key, "Rural-Urban Differences and the Family," *Sociological Quarterly*, 2: 49–56 (1961).

[6] Murray A. Straus, "Social Class and Farm-City Differences in Interaction with Kin in Relation to Societal Modernization," *Rural Sociology*, 34: 476–495 (1969).

A related study, based upon the responses of some three hundred wives of heads of households in an upper-middle-class suburb of Chicago, found the dimension of isolation-extended-familism to be strongly correlated with ethnicity and migratory status. Twenty-eight percent of the Protestants, 13 percent of the Catholics, and only 4 percent of the Jews reported being isolated in the sense of having no household of kinsmen in the Chicago metropolitan area. On the other hand, 78 percent of the Jews reported the presence of twelve or more households in the area, compared with 35 percent for the Catholics and 14 percent for the Protestants.[7]

The U.S. Bureau of the Census has collected data that illuminate the composition of American domestic families. Eleven out of every twelve Americans live in families. (See Table 11.1.) In 1968 it was estimated that there

TABLE 11.1

Percentage Distribution of Familial Status, by Sex, for the United States, 1966

		PERCENT DISTRIBUTION		
SEX	Total	In Families	Unrelated Individuals	Inmates of Institutions
Total	100.0	92.5	6.4	1.1
Male	100.0	93.8	4.9	1.3
Female	100.0	91.2	7.9	0.9

SOURCE: U.S. Bureau of the Census, *Current Population Reports—Population Characteristics*, Series P-20, No. 159, January 25, 1967, Table 4, p. 11.

were nearly fifty million domestic families, of which 87 percent were husband-wife families and 11 percent were families with female heads. The *number* of families with female heads is three times as great among whites as among blacks, but the *proportion* of families having female heads is three times as great among blacks (28 percent) as among whites (9 percent). In the central cities of metropolitan areas having at least three million inhabitants the percentages with female heads were 34 for blacks and 14 for whites.[8]

In 1967 the average size of family was 3.7 persons with 1.4 persons under 18 years of age and 2.3 persons being 18 or over.[9] Almost all married couples

---

[7] Robert F. Winch, Scott Greer, and Rae Lesser Blumberg, "Ethnicity and Extended Familism in an Upper-Middle-Class Suburb," *American Sociological Review*, 32: 265–272 (1967). Because the research interest in religious affiliation was in culture rather than theology, the writers speak of it as ethnicity.

[8] U.S. Bureau of the Census, *Current Population Reports—Population Characteristics*, Series P-20, No. 191, October 20, 1969, Table 1, pp. 10–17.

[9] U.S. Bureau of the Census, *Current Population Reports—Population Characteristics*, Series P-20, No. 173, June 25, 1968, Table 2, p. 13.

(98.3 percent) had their own households.[10] Most husband-wife families (57.6 percent) have at least one own child under 18; just under 40 percent have two or more own children under 18.[11] The average number of children per married couple is 1.4; the average per couple with children is 2.4.[12] Of those who live in households a quarter are male heads of households, a little less than a quarter are wives of heads, a sixteenth are female heads of households, a little over a third are related children under 18, and a tenth are relatives 18 or over. (See Table 11.2.) These statistics are consistent with the general notion that our households generally consist of nuclear families.

TABLE 11.2

Percentage Distribution of the Composition of American Households, March 1967

CATEGORY OF MEMBER	PERCENT		
Head: Male, Wife present	22.0		
Wife absent	2.4	24.4	
Female		6.1	30.5
Wife of Head			22.0
Other Relative: Under 18		36.1	
18 or over		10.2	46.3
Nonrelative			1.2
Total			100.0

SOURCE: U.S. Bureau of the Census, *Current Population Reports—Population Characteristics*, Series P-20, No. 173, June 25, 1968, Table 11, pp. 27–28.

Among whites most female heads of households are either widowed (50 percent) or divorced (20 percent); among nonwhites the corresponding percentages are considerably less—34 and 13, respectively. Among nonwhites the "separated" category, which presumably includes desertions, is considerably higher than among whites—33 percent as compared with 11 percent.[13] Among whites and blacks there is a negative correlation between family income and proportion of families with female heads. The gap between the races in proportion of families with female heads widens at the lower income levels and is widest below $3000—23 percent for whites, 42 percent for blacks.[14]

Black writers tend to interpret the greater relative frequency of the

---

[10] *Ibid.*, Table 2, p. 13.
[11] *Ibid.*, Table 4, pp. 16–17.
[12] *Ibid.*, Table 8, p. 24.
[13] U.S. Bureau of Labor Statistics, Report No. 332, *Current Population Reports—Social and Economic Conditions of Negroes in the United States*, Series P-23, No. 24, October 1967, pp. 67–78.
[14] *Ibid.*, pp. 70–71.

mother-child family among blacks than among whites as related historically to the conditions of slavery and currently to the depressed income of blacks and the special economic handicap of the black male:

> The powerlessness of the Negro man to protect his family for two and a half centuries under slavery has had crippling consequences for the relations of Negro men and women to this very day. . . . The strong hand of the slave owner dominated the Negro family, which existed only at his mercy and often at his own personal instigation.[15]

> . . . the proportion of families with women heads among both blacks as well as mulattoes was significantly smaller in Birmingham, where half of the men were in industrial occupations, than among both mulattoes and blacks in Nashville and Charleston, where Negro men were employed chiefly in domestic and personal service. In the latter two cities from a third to two-fifths of the families had female heads, whereas in Birmingham approximately a fourth of both the black and the mulatto families were in this category.[16]

> The Negro male . . . is required to face the fact that he cannot protect his children or be the agent through which they will be adequately fed or clothed or educated. What appears to be irresponsibility or neglect by the absent fathers can be seen rather as the anguished escape of the Negro male from an impossible predicament. He cannot function effectively as a husband and father, so he often does not function at all. Even his presence would not be significantly different from his absence. If he were present and unable to protect his wife and child, there would be psychological torment and the inevitable explosion into aggression. The additional tragic predicament of the Negro male is that his powerless status tends to be self-perpetuating. What the Negro boy learns first is that to be Negro and male is to be menial—and to be menial is to be defeated in the competition for socially desirable status and its constructive rewards. When these avenues are blocked, the individual must seek other avenues for attaining that minimal status essential for human life.[17]

Some Types of American Family Structure

In the foregoing section three types of American familial structure have been distinguished:

1. A nuclear family embedded in a network of extended kin

---

[15] Andrew Billingsley, *Black Families in White America* (Englewood Cliffs, N.J.: Prentice-Hall, 1968), p. 61.

[16] E. Franklin Frazier, *The Negro Family in the United States* (Chicago: University of Chicago Press, 1939), pp. 327–328.

[17] Kenneth B. Clark, "Sex, Status, and Underemployment of the Negro Male," in Arthur M. Ross and Herbert Hill (eds.), *Employment, Race, and Poverty: A Critical Study of the Disadvantaged Status of Negro Workers from 1865 to 1965* (New York: Harcourt, 1967), pp. 138–148. Quotation is from p. 147.

2. An isolated nuclear family
3. A mother-child nuclear family, sometimes with matrilineal extension

A comment will be made on each of these types.

As noted above, a suburban study has shown the embedded-nuclear family to occur more frequently among all social categories considered than the isolated-nuclear family, and to be highly characteristic of Jews, intermediately so of Catholics, and least so of Protestants. Eighty-five percent of the Wisconsin respondents reported at least one household of kin in the local community. This type of family was found in Wisconsin to be more frequent among Catholics and Lutherans than among other Protestants and among rural than urban residents. However, this type is not more characteristic of rural than of urban families if neither spouse is a migrant. Other social characteristics that are correlated with this type of family are that both spouses are living in the area where they were born and that the head of the house is in an entrepreneurial, rather than a bureaucratic, occupation.

If we define the isolated nuclear family as a nuclear family with no household of kin in the local area, we do find that this type exists. In the studies so far reported it is more frequent in the upper-middle-class suburb than in the state-wide sample, among "other Protestants" than among Lutherans or Catholics, and among Protestants than among Catholics or Jews. In none of these categories is it a majority pattern, however; it occurred in about one out of every five "other Protestant" families in Wisconsin and about one out of every four Protestant families in the suburb. Other characteristics related to the isolated nuclear family are a bureaucratic occupation for the head of the house and both husband and wife being migrants. With respect to the latter point, 94 percent of the couples in the Wisconsin sample who had no local kin were both-migrant couples.

The rubric introducing the mother-child family contains a phrase not previously considered—"sometimes with matrilineal extension." Ethnographic accounts indicate that frequently the maternal grandmother socializes and nurtures her grandchildren and runs the house while the young mother provides the funds through her employment. In the United States there are no official data as to the frequency of matrilineal extension for the previously cited reason that the Bureau of the Census enumerates only domestic households and does not take into account a familial system that is housed in two or more dwellings. If a maternal grandmother lives in the apartment next to her daughter and the latter's children, the grandmother is not a part of the mother-child bookkeeping of the Census, no matter how active the grandmother may be in keeping the family running.

Studies show the mother-child family to be widely distributed among the poor of the Caribbean and Latin America.[18] Adams presents data showing

---

[18] Richard Adams, "An Inquiry into the Nature of the Family," in Gertrude Dole and Robert L. Carniero (eds.), *Essays in Science of Culture in Honor of Leslie A. White* (New York: Crowell, 1960), pp. 30–49; Judith Blake, *Family Structure in Jamaica* (New

that in 1950 this type accounted for from one sixth to one quarter of all families in four Central American countries. In the United States the mother-child family is typically a phenomenon of poor urban blacks, although even among this category it is not the major pattern. About one quarter of black families as compared with one tenth of white families are headed by women. In what the Bureau of the Census calls "metropolitan poverty areas" about one third of the poor white families and one half of the poor black families have female heads.[19] Thus poverty seems to be one condition that is conducive to this familial structure. Another condition is the relatively greater economic marginality of the male than of the female.

Is This Typology Exhaustive?

Are there other types of American families beyond the three proposed here? There may be; we cannot be sure. It should be noted that these are types constructed from data (i.e., empirical types).[20] Since the data come from only one state out of fifty and from one suburb out of hundreds and thereby leave numerous categories of the population unrepresented, there are certainly possibilities that other types exist. Moreover, just two dimensions of differentiation have been used here:

1. Completeness versus incompleteness of the nuclear family
2. Isolation of the nuclear family versus extended familism[21]

But it is conceivable that we could use other variables for the analysis and emerge with different types. This is clearly a matter for further research. And of course many families will not fit neatly into one of these three types but

York: Free Press, 1961); J. Mayone Stycos and Kurt W. Back, *The Control of Human Fertility in Jamaica* (Ithaca, N.Y.: Cornell University Press, 1964); F. M. Henriques, *Family and Colour in Jamaica* (London: Eyre and Spottiswoode, 1953); T. S. Simey, *Welfare and Planning in the West Indies* (Oxford: Clarendon Press, 1946); and Raymond T. Smith, "Culture and Social Structure in the Caribbean," *Comparative Studies in Society and History*, 6: 24–26 (1963); and Nancie L. Solien Gonzalez, *Black Carib Household Structure: A Study of Migration and Modernization* (Seattle: University of Washington Press, 1969).

[19] U.S. Bureau of the Census, *Current Population Reports—Consumer Income*, Series P-60, No. 61, June 30, 1969), Table 3, p. 16.

[20] Robert F. Winch, "Heuristic and Empirical Typologies: A Job for Factor Analysis," *American Sociological Review*, 12: 68–75 (1947).

[21] It would appear that the Italian-American family as described by Campisi would fit into our nuclear-embedded type along with the Jewish family. It would also seem that the French-Canadian family and the working-class family of East London would fit this type.—Paul J. Campisi, "The Italian Family in the United States," *American Journal of Sociology*, 53: 443–449 (1948); Michael Young and Peter Willmott, *Family and Kinship in East London* (New York: Free Press, 1957); Philip Garigue, "French-Canadian Kinship and Urban Life," *American Anthropologist*, 58: 1090–1101 (1956).

will show properties of more than one. Although the writer has presented three empirical types, he has done so in the full realization that there are many intermediate cases.[22]

Conclusions and Summary

This chapter concerns familial structure. A familial system, like any other social system, has structure as well as functions. In Table 1.1 we saw that a social structure was conceived of as a network of social roles and positions. We also saw that a nuclear family has a structure consisting of three positions (husband-father, wife-mother, and offspring-sibling), but that an extended family has no one combination of positions.

One major line of inquiry in this chapter has been to see to which extent the American domestic family is without households of kin in the local community, and hence does not interact with kin, or, on the contrary, has households of kin and does interact with them. To investigate this topic the variable isolation-extended-familism was proposed. Ethnicity and migratory status were found to be highly correlated with this variable. Ruralism was correlated with amount of interaction with kinsmen, as well as with functionality of that interaction, but this is a correlation that disappears when neither spouse is a migrant.

Of all American domestic families 10 percent are nonwhite; but of all American domestic families with female heads 22.5 percent are nonwhite. Although this form occurs more often among whites than among blacks, the proportion among blacks is much greater, and the form seems most characteristic of poor urban blacks.

What causes one familial structure or another to prevail? This is a topic receiving attention from scholars, but not enough research has been reported to give a definitive answer. One plausible hypothesis is that the organization of the economy has something to do with familial structure. In particular, the evidence both in the United States and also in Latin America and the Caribbean suggests that the mother-child family occurs generally in a situation of poverty where the husband-father is economically more marginal than the wife-mother. Migratory status appears to be the most immediately explanatory variable with respect to the degree of extended familism shown by nuclear families in the areas studied. To what degree migratory status is economically determined is not yet clear. More specifically, the high extended familism of the Jews cannot be completely explained by this variable.

More generally it has been proposed that societies can be arrayed along a continuum of subsistence-complexity and that the elaborateness of familial

---

[22] For example, the modal pattern observed among white families in Greensboro, North Carolina, seems intermediate between our embedded-nuclear and our isolated-nuclear types.—Bert N. Adams, *Kinship in an Urban Setting* (Chicago: Markham, 1968).

structure is a curvilinear function of subsistence-complexity. This means that the most elaborate familial structure is hypothesized to coexist with middling subsistence-complexity—settled agriculture—and that simpler familial structure is hypothesized to coexist with the more developed industrial societies as well as with the simpler hunting and gathering societies.

The analysis concludes with the presentation of three empirically derived types of American family: a nuclear family embedded in a network of extended kin, an isolated nuclear family, and a mother-child family sometimes with matrilineal extension.

12

Role-Differentiation and Role-Strain

Introduction

As one reflects on the family as a social group whose basic societal function is that of replacement, one notices immediately that the functional conception implies differentiation of members of the family with respect to sex and age. For the function to be fulfilled there must be a male and a female; in consequence there will be adults and children. Differentiation with respect to sex and age carries implications for the division of labor. Because of primary sex differences certain types of activity can be performed better by men than by women. The usually superior strength of men better qualifies them for the more rigorous and strenuous physical tasks. Not being handicapped by menstruation, pregnancy, or nursing, moreover, men can roam far from home to hunt, fish, and herd. Although they are less categorical than sex differences, age differences present all societies with another ready-made basis for a division of labor. To the very old and the very young are generally allocated tasks requiring minimum strength and skill, while vigorous adults assume the heavier work of the society.

The present chapter takes up the consequences of these observations—the differentiation of familial roles and the strain consequent upon role demands.

Points of Emphasis

Some familial systems, such as the traditional Chinese, have a relatively large number of positions; some, like the American, have few. Some systems have highly differentiated roles, and others do not. The usually superior strength of men and the usual presence among women of physiological and domestic restraints upon mobility are the dimensions that differentiate the modal activities of the sexes. What ethnographers have called the "stage of the arts" may alter the effect of these factors, which then alters the degree and nature of the differentiation of the sex roles. The number of positions and the degree of differentiation of familial roles is affected by the functionality and size (number of persons) of the family, i.e., the less functional and/or smaller the family, the less, in general, will be the degree of differentiation among familial roles.

Every person in a society is concurrently caught up in a number of roles. Other things being equal, the more active one is, the more roles one is expected to carry out. Because of a variety of considerations—the most obvious of which is the conflict of the demands of two or more of one's roles—a person is exposed to role-strain. We shall consider some of the strains associated with familial roles and some of the devices for dealing with these strains.

In the present chapter we are interested in familial positions and roles, in conditions affecting the number of positions and the degree of differentiation of familial roles, and in strains in the roles of family members. Our analysis begins with a consideration of the relation between position and role; after an analysis of roles and role-differentiation in general it applies these concepts to the family.

Position, Status, Role, and the Differentiation of Roles

Because of the possibility of ambiguity and confusion it is advisable to recall that role is a concept subaltern to the concept of position and that status is a concept that emphasizes the invidious aspect of position. A social structure, as we observed in Chapter 1, is an arrangement of social positions. A person's social position places him in the social structure, i.e., in relation to all the other positions in the structure; his role places him in relation to one other individual or class of individuals filling the complementary role. Let us invent a Mr. Jones who holds a position of district sales manager in the equally mythical XYZ Corporation. With his position Mr. Jones assumes a number of roles: subordinate to the vice-president in charge of sales, supervisor of the district salesmen, perhaps sales representative to the major accounts in the district. It is evident that these roles have much bearing on Mr. Jones's occupational status.[1]

---

[1] Rommetveit distinguishes three meanings of role: shared frames of reference, standards of behavior, and pressures to conformity. Our definition involves the first two of these and implies the third. Cf. Ragnar Rommetveit, *Social Norms and Roles* (Minneapolis: University of Minnesota Press, 1955). According to Gross *et al.* the concept of role has three essential ingredients: the behavior of the actor, his social position, and the expectations of the role-definers. Cf. Neal Gross, Ward S. Mason, and Alexander W. McEachern, *Explora-*

A social role has been defined as a more or less integrated and distinctive set of social norms (or role-expectations). The expectations of the behavior of a district sales manager held by Mr. Jones's salesmen constitute one of his roles; the expectations held by his vice-president and the other executives of the company determine another; the expectations held by his customers comprise still another; and so on. We may speak of the company's salesmen, its executives, and its customers as Mr. Jones's role-definers, or norm-senders. Mr. Jones is said to have internalized the roles of the district sales manager when his expectations conform to the consensus of the various categories of norm-senders as to the role-performances of a district sales manager. To the extent that each norm-sender conceives of his own roles as deviating from those of the district sales manager, the roles associated with the latter position are differentiated.

The Division of Labor and the Differentiation of Roles

Let us picture two men hunting game. They adopt an efficient procedure whereby one startles their quarry and drives it toward the second, who now has an easy shot and kills the animal. Here we have a simple example of the division of labor into two operations. Wherever men are involved in the cooperative execution of tasks, we may look for and usually find a division of labor that renders the performance of the task more efficient than it would be if carried out by uncooperating individuals.[2] An increase in efficiency means a reduction in the cost per unit of product. Cost is thought of in terms of the amount of work (or energy) and materials involved. It is assumed that the benefits of the division of labor are sufficiently distributed to the participants so that the advantages of cooperation over solitary production are evident.[3]

---

tions in Role Analysis: Studies of the School Superintendency Role (New York: Wiley, 1958), chap. 1. Cf. also Theodore R. Sarbin and Vernon L. Allen, "Role Theory," in Gardner Lindzey and Elliot Aronson (eds.), The Handbook of Social Psychology (2d ed.; Reading, Mass.: Addison-Wesley, 1968), Vol. 1, pp. 488–567.

[2] Of course not all ways of dividing labor lead to greater efficiency than is achievable by the single actor. Our conceptual scheme involves the assumption that there is a disposition to try out various possible arrangements and to select an efficient procedure. Although this assumption seems generally to be borne out by observation, there occurs an occasional instance of unwillingness to make trials and even to accept new procedures of demonstratedly greater efficiency.

[3] Related to the above are the ideas of Homans, who speaks of interaction as an exchange of goods, material and nonmaterial, and of Thibaut and Kelley, who theorize that interaction is continued only if the rewards (equivalent to Homan's goods) realized meet standards of acceptability. Cf. George C. Homans, "Social Behavior as Exchange," American Journal of Sociology, 1958: 597–606 (1958); John W. Thibaut and Harold H. Kelley, The Social Psychology of Groups (New York: Wiley, 1959); Alvin W. Gouldner, "The Norm of Reciprocity: A Preliminary Statement," American Sociological Review, 25: 161–178 (1960); Peter M. Blau, Exchange and Power in Social Life (New York: Wiley, 1964).

Even in the simplest societies there is some division of labor such as that suggested in the above paragraph. Sooner or later the division of labor becomes more or less routinized. As the routine develops, there arises a set of expectations that people in one category (e.g., the hunters) will typically engage in behavior that is distinctive and different from the typical behavior of persons in other categories (e.g., the cooks). With the rise of such social norms we have social positions and with each position the associated social roles and the implied role differentiation. Moreover, it appears that the differentiation of positions and roles frequently gives rise to a set of understandings concerning the distribution of influence and rewards as reflected in the answers to the questions, Who gives orders to whom? How are the goods distributed? Who defers to whom? Here we have the invidious quality of status associated with the position and the deference, dominance, and submission involved in role-relationships.[4]

Conditions Affecting the Differentiation of Roles

What are the conditions that affect the degree to which roles are differentiated? In other words, what are the conditions that determine whether the number of roles in a given social system will be large or small? A necessary, but presumably not sufficient, condition for a high degree of differentiation would appear to be a large aggregate of persons. For example, a nuclear family would generally be unable to fill all the roles called for in order to form a baseball team, and certainly it would be too small to man a symphony orchestra.

A second condition relevant to the degree of role differentiation is the number and complexity of the tasks to be performed. In general, it seems true that the more numerous and the more complex the tasks, the more roles that will be differentiated. For example, an urban-industrial society produces a vastly greater array of goods and services than does a simple society; the greater role-differentiation of the urban-industrial society is evidenced in the hundreds of its occupational roles. In Chapter 1 five basic societal functions were postulated; related to these were a total of thirteen social roles. It follows from that analysis that in all societies—even in the simplest—there will be at least these thirteen social roles.[5] In most societies the number of roles will be vastly greater.

[4] Efforts have been made to examine such questions experimentally. See, e.g., Eugene A. Weinstein, William L. DeVaughan, and Mary Glenn Wiley, "Obligation and the Flow of Deference in Exchange," *Sociometry*, 32: 1–12 (1969).

[5] There is an arbitrary aspect to the number thirteen in the above context. The number of roles follows from the number of functions postulated and the manner in which the core relationships are conceptualized. Since functions and roles may be conceptualized in a variety of ways, there is no justification for asserting that the minimum number of social roles in all societies is exactly thirteen.

A third factor bearing on the degree of role-differentiation involves differences in the abilities of the participants in the social system. In his satirical fantasy *Brave New World* Aldous Huxley created an arrangement whereby persons were engineered to fit certain social roles by means of assigning them the appropriate combinations of genes at the moment of conception. In the observable, non-Huxleyan world people are categorized on the basis of characteristics that are more or less adequate indexes of ability. Two such categories that are universally recognized are those based on sex and age.

The Differentiation of Sex and Age Roles in Primitive Societies

All societies recognize some division of labor between the sexes. After an extensive survey of the cultures of 224 societies in various parts of the world, Murdock observes that men tend to engage in such activities as the catching of sea mammals, lumbering, hunting, fishing, and trapping. The women of these societies tend to specialize in more sedentary but equally important pursuits, such as grinding grain, cooking, preserving meat and fish, and gathering fuel and fruits and vegetables.[6] In sum, masculine pursuits are typically those demanding one or more of the following:

1. Strenuous physical exertion and strength
2. Spatial mobility and absence from home
3. Continuous effort for considerable blocks of time

By contrast, feminine pursuits typically

1. May require a considerable output of energy but are usually less demanding of great strength
2. Are local
3. Involve only a few hours at a time when they are carried out away from home

The primary sex differences noted in the opening paragraph of this chapter are consistent with the sex differences in pursuits.

With respect to age categories, it appears that all societies distinguish at least four: infancy, childhood, active adulthood, and old age.[7] In general the

---

[6] G. P. Murdock, "Comparative Data on the Division of Labor by Sex," *Social Forces*, 15: 551–553 (1937).

[7] The seemingly contrary view of Ariès requires interpretation. He states: "In medieval society the idea of childhood did not exist . . . as soon as the child could live without the constant solicitude of his mother, his nanny or his cradle-rocker, he belonged to adult society."—Philippe Ariès, *Centuries of Childhood: A Social History of Family Life* (New York: Knopf, 1962), p. 128. He goes on to relate that in the Middle Ages children were

most demanding activities are assigned to active adulthood. Old age is regarded as too feeble for strenuous exertion; childhood, as too unskilled for complex activities.

Activities Affecting Role-Differentiation in the Family

Functional analysis leads to the question, In which societal structures are the important activities going on, especially those involved in the basic societal functions? Our interest in the family leads to the further question, To what extent are these activities being carried on in the family? For example, we are interested in knowing how economic activity is organized, whether or not the family tries to feed itself from its own garden. As we discover the answers to such questions in any given society we imply some answers to the question, In terms of which roles do members of the family interact?

The core relationship between adult male and subadult male in the nuclear family is, of course, father-son. If production is carried on within the family, there is a strong likelihood that father and son have not only a parent-child relationship but also one we might call foreman-worker. If religious activities are carried on in the family, the priest-parishioner relationship is added to the father-son relationship. These observations imply that in the highly functional family, man and boy enact multiple roles with each other and are bound to each other by the important activities we have been calling functions. This state of affairs, according to Durkheim, results in what he has called organic solidarity; conversely, where there is little division of labor, where individuals do not have a number of differentiated roles, and where, therefore, they are more similar to each other, the solidarity is less binding and, in his words, more mechanical.[8]

The Parental Function and the Content of the Paternal and Maternal Roles

Once a child is born, there is considerable variation from one cultural context to another in the way he is cared for, in the duration of such care, and in the relationship to him of the person or persons responsible for that care. Owing to the protracted period of maturation the human being is dependent

---

generally socialized into adult roles through the system of the apprenticeship. To Ariès the absence of the idea of childhood followed from the practice of apprenticing young children, which he interpreted as treating them as little adults. In the view of this writer the recognition that children need to be taught adult roles implies recognition of the status of childhood.

[8] Émile Durkheim, *On the Division of Labor in Society* (trans. by George Simpson; New York: Macmillan, 1933), p. 131.

on others to minister to his needs for food, warmth, shelter, and so on, and to keep him out of danger. Accordingly we speak of the parental function as consisting of nurturance and of control.

Although it is usual in some societies for fathers to assume part of the responsibility for the care of the child from the child's early months of life (examples are the Mountain Arapesh of New Guinea[9] and the Trobriand Islanders of the same area[10]), still no degree of cultural ingenuity has served to nullify or to circumvent primary sex differences, and even the most ardent cultural relativist must agree that everywhere it is the women who become pregnant and go through childbirth. It is because of this that we have derived the three typical differences between the masculine and the feminine pursuits as applicable at least during menstrual periods, pregnancies, and confinements. These differences also apply during the period, which varies from one setting to another, over which the culture decrees that the mother has the primary responsibility for the care of her children. Aside from the kibbutzim (see Chapter 3), one of the shortest periods of immediate maternal responsibility on record comes from the Alorese, where the mother returns to her work in the fields a fortnight after delivery and leaves the infant in the care of a young girl.[11]

There is variation in the way in which the two parental responsibilities of nurturance and control may be culturally allocated. At least some of the content of the child's familial relationships hinges on just how these responsibilities are assigned. For each child there may be an arrangement whereby one adult has the primary responsibility for nurturance and another has the responsibility for control, or both responsibilities may be combined into a single parental role. Malinowski reports that among the Trobriand Islanders both the child's mother and father are highly nurturant and noncontrolling, whereas it is primarily the mother's brother who exercises control.[12]

As the child moves through the different ages, there is frequently some rearrangement in the assignment of parental responsibilities. This shift is exemplified by the practice in upper-middle and upper-class English families of removing the boy from the care of the mother (or governess as mother-surrogate) and sending him off to boarding school. With maturation, moreover, there is a marked shift in the kind of parental behavior called for. A six-day-old infant requires much nurturance and no control. A six-year-old boy calls for a different kind of nurturing and a good deal of control; the difference between these two cases and that of a sixteen-year-old is also great.

[9] Margaret Mead, *Sex and Temperament in Three Primitive Societies*, chaps. 1–8, in *From the South Seas* (New York: Morrow, 1939).

[10] Bronislaw Malinowski, *Sex and Repression in Savage Society* (New York: Meridian, 1955).

[11] Abram Kardiner, *The Psychological Frontiers of Society* (New York: Columbia University Press, 1945).

[12] *Op. cit.*, chaps. 2–4.

Familial Role-Differentiation Associated with Sex Differences in Ability

On page 311 it was noted that because of primary sex differences there were three universal distinctions between typically masculine and typically feminine pursuits. It is now in order to relate that discussion to the family. Again we turn to Murdock, who remarks that the specialization arising out of the sexual division of labor produces a level of skill for each sex that would otherwise not be achieved. Then Murdock continues that with their division of labor, the members of the man-woman dyad provide a sort of insurance for each other.

> The man, perhaps, returns from a day of hunting, chilled, unsuccessful, and with his clothing soiled and torn, to find warmth before a fire which he could not have maintained, to eat food gathered and cooked by the woman instead of going hungry, and to receive fresh garments for the morrow, prepared, mended, or laundered by her hands. Or perhaps the woman has found no vegetable food, or lacks clay for pottery or skins for making clothes, obtainable only at a distance from the dwelling, which she cannot leave because her children require care; the man in his ramblings after game can readily supply her wants. Moreover, if either is injured or ill, the other can nurse him back to health. These and similar rewarding experiences, repeated daily, would suffice of themselves to cement the union. When the powerful reinforcement of sex is added, the partnership of man and woman becomes inevitable.[13]

It is such observations as these that led W. G. Sumner to assert that marriage is primarily an economic matter, an arrangement of cooperation in the service of self-maintenance.[14] Following this line of interpretation Murdock concludes that "marriage exists only when the economic and the sexual are united into one relationship."[15]

At this juncture it is important to emphasize a point that has been implicit in our discussion of the differences in ability associated with being a man or a woman. These differences have been presented as consequences of primary sex characteristics, which means as consequences of the indispositions, confinements, and maternal responsibilities placed on women. This argument does not rest on any assumption that "natively" women are less competent than men to become physicians or physicists or to mold the destinies of nations. In this context "ability" is used in the pragmatic sense, denoting that a person can do something; if unable to do that something for whatever reason, the person is not able in this sense. We are noting that primary sex differences cause certain inabilities for women.

---

[13] George Peter Murdock, *Social Structure* (New York: Macmillan, 1949), p. 8.
[14] W. G. Sumner and A. G. Keller, *The Science of Society* (New Haven, Conn.: Yale University Press, 1929), III, 1505, 1508.
[15] *Social Structure.*

Tasks, Abilities, and Sex-Role Differentiation

Our theorizing now leads to some plausible observations as to conditions that maximize or minimize sex-role differentiation—both in the society and in the family. Our functional theory leads to the conclusion that sex-role differentiation should be maximized in a society that places high importance on tasks involving one or more of the three characteristics of masculine pursuits. By this reasoning societies in which hunting or soldiering is a regular and highly valued occupation should show a high degree of sex-role differentiation. Conversely, societies in which few or no important tasks demand great strength, mobility, or continuous effort should show little differentiation of sex roles.

A favorite topic of popular writers over the years has been to view with alarm an alleged narrowing of sex differences in the United States—the theme that American men are becoming softer and wearing aprons and that American women are becoming harder, donning pants, and usurping masculine pursuits. It is difficult to bring convincing data to bear on this point. As we look at the important tasks to be performed, however, we can see that the introduction of steam, electricity, and other forms of nonhuman power has greatly reduced the importance of human strength—the basis of our first distinction between masculine and feminine pursuits. Symptomatic of the elimination of backbreaking physical labor is the development of road-building equipment and mining machinery. As technology develops, the proportion of all jobs that are white-collar jobs increases.[16] The proportion of white-collar jobs has risen from 21 percent in 1910[17] to 49 percent in 1970.[18] By definition white-collar employment is not physically strenuous. In 1970 the proportion of males in white-collar occupations was 53 percent; in all other occupations it was 71 percent.[19] Thus the development of technology, which is an integral part of the rise of an urban-industrial social order, has brought about a decrease in the proportion of jobs involving manual labor, an increase in the proportion of white-collar jobs, and, in this sense, a "feminization" of the occupational structure. (Since white-collar workers are generally regarded as belonging to the middle classes, and manual—or blue-collar—workers as belonging to the working classes, another consequence, moreover, of this trend has been to increase the proportion of the population that belongs to the middle classes and to diminish the proportion belonging to the working classes.)

With the reduction in the importance of hard physical labor it follows that the task-determined differentiation of masculine occupational roles de-

---

[16] A. J. Jaffe and Charles D. Stewart, *Manpower Resources and Utilization* (New York: Wiley, 1951), p. 144.
[17] *Ibid.*, Table 22, p. 190.
[18] *Statistical Abstract of the United States, 1970*, Table 334, p. 225.
[19] *Ibid.*

pends more on the second and third criteria—mobility and the availability of blocks of time. This line of theorizing sheds some light on one observation made in Chapter 6. There the impression was reported that if the male head of the house remained in the suburbs during the day, a good explanation was required to avoid bringing shame on the family. Commuting is a form of mobility, and from our analysis it follows that it is more masculine to commute than not to commute. No doubt it is hyperbolic to equate the noncommuting male to a skeleton in the closet, but there does seem to be a feeling in the suburbs that those men who are in the suburbs during the day—tradespeople, city officials, people in the services and the professions—are somehow less hardy, less he-men, and less likely to be "in the bigtime" than those who "go into the city."

Both mobility and blocks of time are involved in jobs that call for traveling beyond the commuting range. The masculinity of such travel can be assessed by noting the sex composition of weekday first-class flights. Another matter that merits our speculative notice is that with spatial mobility goes the expense account, and it would appear that the expense account has become for many a means of asserting masculinity.[20]

The diminished importance of physical strength is not the only influence at work to reduce the functional distinction between the masculine and the feminine sex roles. Another factor has been the reduction, both absolutely and relatively, of the amount of a woman's life during which she is unable to participate in the labor force because of pregnancy and the need to care for small children. We have seen that the reduction in the average number of children ever born per married woman and the lengthening of her life expectancy have resulted in the reduction in the proportion of a woman's life devoted to parental responsibilities, and this reduction in turn has resulted in an increase in the percentage of women past forty in the labor force.

The foregoing remarks should not be construed as asserting that the increase in the proportion of white-collar jobs has wiped out the advantage of the male in the labor market. From the standpoint of the prospective employer of persons for professional and other skilled occupations there is a further set of considerations that leads the employer to differentiate between the two sexes. In view of the norm that a man works throughout his productive years —say from his early twenties to his middle sixties—a man is in a position to make a long-range emotional commitment to his job. A young woman, on the other hand, is frequently considering marriage or hoping to have an opportunity to do so. If she marries, there is a high probability she will bear children. If she has children, she will be lost to the employer for a considerable period, and it is doubtful that she will ever return. On the other hand, a middle-aged woman who has just raised a family may be a good prospect for a decade or so of service but cannot be expected to be conversant with recent developments

---

[20] Somewhat relevant is Ernest Havemann, "The Expense Account Aristocracy," *Life*, March 9, 1953, pp. 140–142, 145–146, 151–152.

in her profession. This gives the prospective employer the view that the man's first emotional commitment is to his job; a woman's, to her family; that for a man, his work is a career; for a woman, more an activity to take up the slack before bearing children or after completing her tour of duty in her maternal role.

Women in the Labor Force

In Chapter 4 it was reported that the proportion of married women who are in the labor force had jumped from 1 out of every 20 in 1890 to nearly 1 out of 3 in 1965. It will contribute to our understanding of the conditions under which women carry out their domestic roles if we notice certain additional facts about the participation of women in the labor force.

First, it seems that having one or more children under the age of six depresses the rate of participation in the labor force. Table 12.1 shows that

TABLE 12.1

Labor-Force Participation Rates of Wives (16 Years of Age and Over with Husband Present), by Income of Husband in 1966 and Presence and Age of Children, March 1967

		PRESENCE AND AGE OF CHILDREN		
INCOME OF HUSBAND	Total	No Child under 18	Children 6–17 Only	Children under 6[a]
Total	36.8%	38.9%	45.0%	26.5%
Under $1000	37.4	34.3	52.3	35.3
$1000 to $1999	27.0	23.6	45.9	31.4
$2000 to $2999	33.0	29.2	50.8	31.3
$3000 to $4999	41.4	41.0	52.0	34.4
$5000 to $6999	42.6	48.0	49.9	31.6
$7000 to $9999	37.9	46.6	46.9	21.9
$10,000 and over	28.8	36.6	32.9	15.7

[a] May also have older children in addition to one or more under six.
SOURCE: Women's Bureau Bulletin No. 294, *1969 Handbook on Women Workers*, (Washington, D.C.: GPO, 1969), Table 12, p. 33.

about one fourth of the mothers with husbands present and children under six are in the labor force; Table 4.2 revealed that for all women living with their husbands the ratio is two fifths.

Second, a negative correlation between husbands' incomes and rate of participation is quite evident among the mothers of small children: the rate of participation falls off for wives whose husbands received over $5,000 in

1966. A generally similar correlation prevails where there are children but none younger than six. Where there is no child under eighteen, the relationship is curvilinear with maxima at husband's income under $1,000 and in the $5,000–$7,000 bracket and minima in the $1,000–$2,000 and $10,000+ brackets.

Third, for the women with children the presence or absence of a husband in the home is an important determinant of her labor force status. See Table 12.2, in which it is seen that if the husband is absent, the participation of a

TABLE 12.2

Labor-Force Participation Rates of Mothers, by Marital Status and Age of Children, March 1967

	AGE OF YOUNGEST CHILD			
MARITAL STATUS	Under 18	6 to 17	3 to 5	Under 3
All women ever married	38.2%	48.6%	34.5%	25.0%
Married, husband present	35.3	45.0	31.7	23.3
Other women ever married[a]	64.0	75.0	58.8	44.2

[a] Refers to women who are widowed, divorced, or separated or whose husbands are absent for other reasons.
SOURCE: Women's Bureau Bulletin No. 294, *1969 Handbook on Women Workers* (Washington, D.C.: GPO, 1969), Table 16, p. 39.

mother with a child under six is nearly twice as frequent as where the husband is present.

Fourth, one of the most marked correlations is that between the woman's own educational level and participation in the labor force. Table 12.3 reveals that although the probability of a woman's participating in the labor force is greater if she is single than if she is married, within any marital status her probability of participation rises rapidly with the level of her education.

Finally, two graphs have been prepared to show labor force participation by sex and by three marital statuses: married, spouse present in Figure 12.1; and single and other marital status, both shown in Figure 12.2. The curve for married men living with their wives shows consistently higher participation than is shown in any of the other five curves. It carries no surprise except perhaps for the very high level of participation in the earliest age group. This does not mean, of course, that men who will ultimately marry enter the labor force early, but rather that those who marry early get into the labor force early. For example, of the married males in the 14–19 age group, 95.5 percent are in the labor force, whereas the proportion among single males of the same age group is only 36.0 percent. The participation curve for married women living with their husbands has two maxima. The first is in the 20–24 age group (presumably before the birth of the first child), and the second is in the 45–54 age group (when the children are no longer small). This maximum in the latter

TABLE 12.3

Labor-Force Participation Rates of Women (18 Years of Age and Over), by Educational Attainment and Marital Status, March 1968

YEARS OF SCHOOL COMPLETED	MARITAL STATUS			
	Total	Single	Married (husband present)	Other
Total	42.0	62.3	38.4	40.6
Elementary school:				
Less than 8 years	24.4	36.2	25.1	21.6
8 years	30.8	48.5	30.9	27.8
High school:				
1 to 3 years	39.6	46.6	37.0	44.3
4 years	48.1	72.6	41.5	58.0
College:				
1 to 3 years	45.5	54.4	39.7	54.9
4 years or more	58.4	81.8	51.3	61.4

SOURCE: Women's Bureau Bulletin No. 294, *1969 Handbook on Women Workers* (Washington, D.C.: GPO, 1969), Table 94, p. 206.

forties appears in none of the other five curves. This distinctive feature, moreover, is a recent development and signifies that married women have begun to return to the labor force in unprecedented numbers after their children are no longer small. In summary, then, Figure 12.1 reflects the care of children—a consistently high level of participation by men in the roles of husbands and fathers, withdrawal from the labor force by women while functioning actively in the role of mother, and the recent development—the re-entry of a considerable number of women after carrying out the maternal role.

Figure 12.2 presents a quite different picture. Here the curves for women are quite parallel to those for the men. Probably most of the difference in the height of curve between single women and those of "other" marital status is accounted for by women in the latter category who stay out of the labor force in order to care for their children.

Positions and Role-Differentiation in the American Family

Since the typical American family is nuclear, it has only three positions: husband-father, wife-mother, and minor, unmarried offspring (or four positions if we distinguish between sons and daughters). Since American marriages are

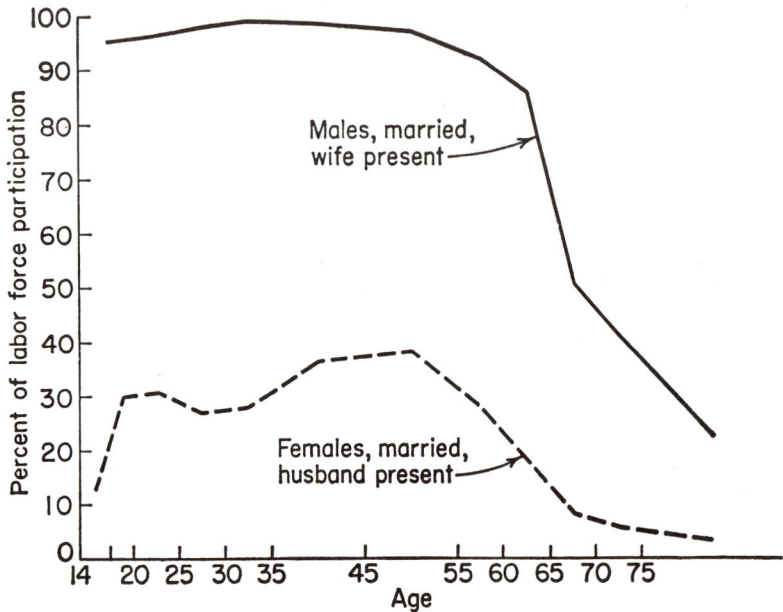

FIGURE 12.1

Percent of Labor Force Participation by Married Persons Whose Spouses Are Present, by Sex and by Age: March 1958

SOURCE: U.S. Bureau of the Census, *Current Population Reports— Labor Force,* Series P–50, No. 87, Table 2, p. 14.

monogamous, only one person may fill each of the first two positions. Since the number of children in completed families averages around two to three (see Tables 7.2 and 7.3), the usual American nuclear family with all positions filled consists of four or five persons.

Actually, of course, the family as a household (i.e., domestic families) may include additional positions. There may be one or more persons in the household from the grandparental generation, or there may be a collateral kinsman. There may be a married offspring with or without spouse and with or without children. From Table 11.2 it is seen that a little more than half (52.5 percent) of all persons in households are heads and wives of heads of households. Another 36.1 percent are "other relatives" of the head of household under the age of eighteen, and thus about seven of every eight residents of households are likely to be members of nuclear families (occupants of one of the three nuclear familial positions). As we have suggested above, American families with more than three positions seem generally to occur where there is some sort of pressure, such as that arising from the financial inability of a young couple to set up an independent household or of an elderly parent

FIGURE 12.2

Percent of Labor Force Participation by Persons Who Are Single and of "Other" Marital Status, by Sex and by Age: March 1958

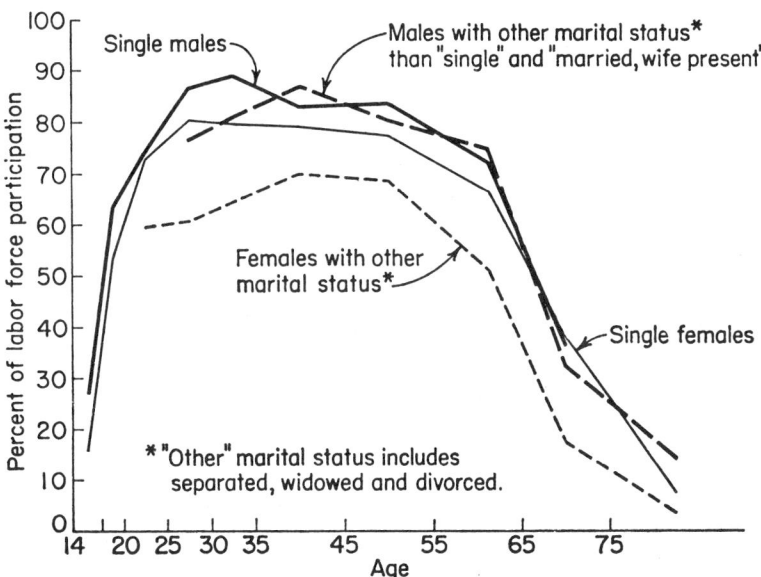

SOURCE: U.S. Bureau of the Census, *Current Population Reports—Labor Force*, Series P–50, No. 87, Table 2, p. 14.

to maintain one, or the pressure arising from the disability of some regular member of the family, especially of the wife-mother.

Some idea as to the structural simplicity of the ideal American family can be derived by comparing it with the traditional Chinese family, which provided ten positions if we include the deceased ancestors, and nine otherwise. (See Table 12.4.) The relation of age and sex roles to the structure of the family is evident. It will be recalled that Chapter 2 presented the traditional Chinese family, and Chapter 3, the family of the kibbutz, to exemplify extremes in familial functionality. Table 12.4 portrays those two and adds the American family. It can be seen that the Chinese family is extended and hence has continuity, which is provided through the male line. Consanguineal females are born into the family and marry out of it; affinal females are born out of it and marry in.[21] In contrast to the continuity of the Chinese family stands the life cycle of the American family, which reflects its neolocal formation by marriage, its nuclear structure, its growth with the coming of children,

---

[21] *Consanguineal*: related through "blood." *Affinal*: related through marriage.

TABLE 12.4

Familial Positions Resulting from Generation and Sex Categories in (a) Stem Family of the Traditional Chinese Peasantry, (b) American Middle-Class Family, and (c) Kibbutz Family

CHINESE STEM FAMILY			AMERICAN AND KIBBUTZ FAMILIES	
Stay in the home	*Join the home*	*Leave the home*	*Establish a new home*	*Leave the home*
Dead ancestors[a]				
Grandfather	Grandmother			
Father	Mother		Husband-father and wife-mother	
Eldest son	Wife of eldest son	Brothers and sisters of eldest son[b]		Their children[c]
Eldest son of eldest son		Other children of eldest son		

[a] The dead ancestors are included because "they are potentially present and spiritually active in the affairs of the household." This point was as true of the traditional Chinese family as of the traditional Japanese family described by Beardsley *et al.*, from whom the above representation was adapted. Cf. Richard K. Beardsley, John W. Hall, and Robert E. Ward, *Village Japan* (Chicago: University of Chicago Press, 1959), pp. 218 and 222.

[b] In the joint family of the traditional Chinese gentry, younger, as well as eldest sons would remain in the home.

[c] American children leave home in their late teens or early twenties—to get married or to take a job away from home; in the kibbutz reported in Chapter 3 children never live in the homes of their parents.

its shrinkage with their departure, and its ultimate disappearance with the deaths of the spouses. It should be noted that in either system not all positions are always filled. Still it is clear that the Chinese conceived of the family as having more positions than do Americans, and it seems likely that they usually had more than three positions filled at any one time.[22]

[22] Reverting from the structure of the family in terms of position and role to the size of the domestic family in number of persons, we may review some relevant statistics.

Another point regarding the simple structure and small size of the American family is that under some conditions it makes the woman's position a very lonely one. If the family has the American dream house on a wooded acre, and if there are small children, the situation tends to isolate the wife-mother from other adults during most of her waking hours. Here the popularity of the *Kaffeeklatsch* is comprehensible, as is the receptive attitude of some mothers to the chore of transporting children, which they say enables them to break their routine and to get out of the house. After having interacted with little people three feet high all day it is not astonishing that the woman may demand a sitter and an evening at the theater.[23]

It appears that the isolation of the wife-mother and of the entire nuclear family varies in kind and degree with socioeconomic status. Women in the higher strata tend to have more close friends and to belong to more clubs and organizations than do lower-status women.[24] People in the lower strata exceed those in the higher in the proportion of all their social contacts that are with relatives.[25]

Finally, the small size and simple structure of the American family have given rise to a novel way of arranging for substitute mothers. In many societies mothers have occasion to be away from even small children for a time—perhaps to go to market or to work in the fields. Where households are large or kinsmen are neighbors, it seems usual for a female relative to assume temporary responsibility for the nurturance and control of the children of the absent

---

In 1967, 87 percent of all domestic families in the United States were husband-wife families. Fifty-eight percent of all husband-wife domestic families had one or more own children under 18 in the home, with 18 percent having exactly one and 17 percent having exactly two. The average size of all domestic families was 3.7 persons and of households was 3.3 persons. U.S. Bureau of the Census, *Current Population Reports—Population Characteristics*, Series P-20, No. 173, June 25, 1968, Tables A and 2. In Chapter 2 four pre-World War II averages were given for size of the household in China: very small, 4.2 persons; medium, 5.5; large, 8.3; and very, very large, 10.7. Cf. note 7, page 00. For 27 nations Burch reports that average household size around 1960 ranged from 2.8 to 5.7 persons with a median of 3.9. He concluded that average size of household seemed more to reflect fertility than structure of the extended family.—Thomas K. Burch, "The Size and Structure of Families: A Comparative Analysis of Census Data," *American Sociological Review*, 32: 347–363 (1967).

[23] "As a group, housewives to-day suffer more from social isolation and loss of purpose than any other social group, except, perhaps the old . . . . many causes of marital friction and unhappiness would be removed if outside contacts and mental stimuli, as well as the whole income-earning power, were not practically the monopolies of one spouse."—Alva Myrdal and Viola Klein, *Women's Two Roles: Home and Work* (London: Routledge, 1956), p. 191.

[24] James H. Williams, "Close Friendship Relations of Housewives Residing in an Urban Community," *Social Forces*, 36: 358–362 (1958). Cf. also Joel Smith, William H. Form, and Gregory P. Stone, "Local Intimacy in a Middle-Sized City," *American Journal of Sociology*, 60: 276–284 (1954).

[25] Morris Axelrod, "Urban Structure and Social Participation," *American Sociological Review*, 21: 13–18 (1956). Cf. also Leonard Blumberg and Robert R. Bell, "Urban Migration and Kinship Ties," *Social Problems*, 6: 328–333 (1959).

mother. In this country many families participate in a cooperative arrangement, sometimes called a "sitting pool," whereby a mother "sits" for one or more others and builds up credit to have the service returned when she wishes free time. Such cooperative arrangements among neighbors and comparable mutual aid among relatives do not meet the demand, however, and a new occupation of "sitters" has grown up. The sitter seems usually to be an unrelated and sometimes unknown adolescent, especially female, who is hired to assume the control function and perhaps the nurturant function during the parents' absence. In some communities the demand for sitters has been great enough to encourage the establishment of agencies that organize and provide this service. Moreover, schools and other agencies have undertaken to train sitters in the rudiments of mothering, and some hotels advertise the availability of a "sitting" service.

Above we related the degree of differentiation within a structure to (1) the number of persons participating, (2) the number and complexity of the tasks, and (3) the abilities of the participants. Granting that there is considerable variation in the number of participants in the American family, let us concentrate on the ideal family with four persons occupying the three nuclear positions. By itself, then, the small size of the American family creates a situation of few positions tending toward relatively little differentiation of roles.

To inquire about the number and complexity of tasks is to ask about the functions performed. The slight degree to which the American family carries out the basic societal functions results in a relatively low number of differentiated tasks, and hence the number of core relationships with their associated roles is relatively small in the American family. Unlike his Chinese counterpart, the American son does not play worker to the father's role of foreman nor parishioner to his father's priest, and so on.

To the extent that the family *is* functional it appears that the importance of the activities leads members of the family to assess each other in terms of the quality of their performances of these tasks. To the extent that the family is *not* functional, on the other hand, it appears that members of the family can assess each other only on the basis of congeniality, affability, and other characteristics of personality.[26] (Some hold that recreation should be regarded as an important function and hence that we should use play as an index of familial functionality.[27] To this writer the argument seems spurious because a function should have a consequence thought to be important, e.g., the production of food, and because it should eventuate in role-differentiation, e.g., foreman-worker. The harsh realities of the extrafamilial world would sooner or

[26] Somewhat relevant evidence appears in Henry W. Riecken and George C. Homans, "Psychological Aspects of Social Structure," chap. 22 in Gardner Lindzey (ed.), *Handbook of Social Psychology* (Reading, Mass.: Addison-Wesley, 1954), II, esp. 789–790, and studies by Gilchrist, Homans, Jennings, and Schachter cited there.

[27] Nelson N. Foote, "Family Living as Play," *Marriage and Family Living*, 17: 296–301 (1955).

later disabuse a child of any belief that his father's competence at barbecuing or his golf handicap had far-reaching significance.)

Granting that there is little functionality of the basic variety to tie members of the American family to each other, let us look at the derived functions: position conferring and integration with the society, and emotional gratification. As we saw in Chapter 8, neither position-conferring nor integration with the society regularly involves intrafamilial interaction. Accordingly there is no reason for this function to produce role-differentiation within the family.

Emotional gratification is a function involving interaction between family members. Let us consider the potential of this function for role-differentiation. As we saw in Chapter 9, one kind of gratification comes from the alleviation of insecurity and other forms of psychic anguish. Insecurity is especially likely to be a response to a situation fraught with the prospect of failure, as is true in the arenas where statuses are achieved. The husband-father and also the children are more likely to be exposed to this sort of psychic hazard than is the wife-mother. The authors of *Crestwood Heights* observe that in the upper-middle-class suburb they studied, some husbands, especially those who were professional men, have a strong wish to use their homes as emotional havens, and these authors speak of the wife-mother as the "emotional hub of the family."[28] Somewhat akin is the formulation of Parsons and Bales, who speak of the wife-mother as assuming what they call the "expressive" role in the family. The expressive role is defined as involving "the maintenance of integrative relations between the members, and regulation of the patterns and tension levels of its component units."[29]

Zelditch adds some helpful elucidation by referring to the expressive role in the family as that of "the mediator, conciliator . . . soothes over disputes, resolves hostilities in the family . . . is affectionate, solicitous, warm, emotional to the children . . . is the 'comforter,' the 'consoler,' is relatively indulgent, relatively unpunishing."[30]

From the remarks to this point it would appear that in the American family the wife-mother fulfills the role of bandaging up the skinned knees of her children and applying balm to the scarred psyches of her husband and children. To the writer it seems clear that there is frequent need of such a function within the family, but it is not clear that the wife always, or even usually, has it. What has been omitted from the foregoing discussion is the situation of the woman, her frustrations and anxieties, and her consequent need for emotional gratification. To understand this let us consider the woman's dilemma.

[28] John R. Seeley *et al.*, *Crestwood Heights* (New York: Basic Books, 1958), pp. 177–178.

[29] Talcott Parsons and Robert F. Bales, *Family, Socialization and Interaction Process* (New York: Free Press, 1955), p. 47.

[30] Morris Zelditch, Jr., "Role Differentiation in the Nuclear Family: A Comparative Study," chap. 6, *ibid.*, cf. p. 318.

The Woman's Dilemma

Reference was made in Chapter 8 to certain changes in the status of women. To cast but one backward glance on this trend as evidenced in education, we may recall that in the seventeenth century women received very little formal education, and that, so far as they entered into this process at all, they were afforded treatment appropriate to a distinctly inferior caste. In the nineteenth century, women's colleges and coeducational universities came into being, and today there remain only a few vestiges of discrimination against women in the educational system.

It is usual that the improvement of the condition of an underprivileged minority brings to its members a host of new and generally unanticipated problems. The alteration in the status of women has brought them advantages and difficulties, opportunities for career and for insecurity. The young woman of a century or two ago could count on housekeeping as her lifework. If she should be so unfortunate as not to be married, housekeeping was the principal way of life for women anyway, and she would find employment in the home of a kinsman. No such simple formula confronts the young woman of today.

The relative emancipation of woman means that she no longer has a predestined role. The reduction in size of family and of household, and the increase in labor-saving devices in the home have combined to render the homemaking role a progressively less honorific one. Parsons, for example, speaks of home management as having been reduced to "a kind of 'pseudo-' occupation."[31] On the other hand, the fact that our educational system is largely coeducational means that boys and girls are exposed to very similar indoctrination with respect to values. It is true, of course, that girls learn that marriage is a desirable state and motherhood an honorable one. Still, when compared with the rewards of a man's world, child rearing appears to some to be dull and strenuous while housework may be viewed as downright degrading.[32]

---

[31] Talcott Parsons, "Age and Sex in the Social Structure of the United States," *American Sociological Review*, 7: 609 (1942).

[32] Robert S. Weiss and N. M. Samuelson, "Social Roles of American Women: Their Contribution to a Sense of Usefulness and Importance," *Marriage and Family Living*, 20: 358–366 (1958); and Seeley *et al.*, *op. cit.*, p. 180. The present curriculum of high schools and colleges has been criticized as being nonfunctional for women. Just what should be done, however, is not clear. It is true that most girls will get married and hence will find training in domestic skills useful. The individual girl, however, has no assurance that she will be married. There is a general conviction, moreover, that even for the girl who marries, education should be sufficiently general to equip her to establish common interests with her husband and to become an adequate citizen. Cf. R. G. Foster and Pauline Wilson, *Women After College: A Study of the Effectiveness of Their Education* (New York: Columbia University Press, 1942); Mirra Komarovsky, *Women in the Modern World: Their Education and Their Dilemmas* (Boston: Little, Brown, 1953); Katharine McBride,

In our society the male can choose a career and train for it with the expectation that his entering the field of his choice depends upon his ability, the state of the labor market, and the absence of a major disaster, such as war or depression. The first three quarters of this century have shown these contingencies to be by no means trivial. But the woman has additional difficulties to reckon with. The major known handicap is the discrimination against women in many occupations. Another problem is that during her school years she has no way of knowing whether she will marry or how long she will remain married.

The contemporary middle-class girl is confronted with three values: marriage, motherhood, and career. She may choose one or more, but she has no assurance that she will be able to realize her choice. If she chooses marriage, she must be able to find a man who will choose her. If she chooses motherhood, she is also normally choosing marriage, and the same contingency applies, plus the additional contingency of agreement with the husband on the desirability of children. If she chooses career only, she is denying herself a legally sanctioned normal sex life. If she chooses marriage and career, she must find not only a husband, but one to whom that combination (including the arrangement not to have children) is satisfactory. If she chooses all three, she must, again, find a man to whom this combination is satisfactory. Then she must decide between one of two further courses. Either she must retire from her vocation for the period while her children require her attention (a period whose terminus is very hard to define), or else she must arrange for someone else to care for her children. If she elects the latter course, irrespective of the adequacy of the arrangements, she may expect to encounter criticism for being a neglectful and indifferent mother. Moreover, she may have to reckon with her own feelings of guilt on this point. And finally her choice assumes either that she does not lose her husband (divorce is a more likely cause of loss than death in the early years of marriage) or that if she does so, she can replace him without undue delay. Since the assumption that the woman can continue to be married—whether to her original husband or to a satisfactory replacement—is problematic, moreover, the woman should take account of the prospect that she may be forced to rear her children without the moral, physical, or financial support of a husband.

Various writers have observed that the roles involved in a career are divergent from and contradictory to those of wife and mother. One writer asserts that a career "requires of the woman a great deal of drive, self-assertion, competitiveness, and aggression," whereas the roles of wife and mother call "for a relaxation of these assertive requirements in favor of those that can be

"What Is Women's Education?" *Annals of the American Academy of Political and Social Science,* 251: 143–152 (1947); Kate H. Mueller, *Educating Women for a Changing World* (Minneapolis: University of Minnesota Press, 1954); C. G. Spiegler, "Are Our Girls Getting Boys' Education?" *The New York Times Magazine,* May 14, 1950, pp. 29, 38, 42; John Willig, "Class of '34 (Female): Fifteen Years Later," *The New York Times Magazine,* June 12, 1949, pp. 10, 51, 53.

classified as protective or nurturing, passive and receptive."[33] Another writer who has studied girls attending an eastern college reports that they suffer emotionally from the uncertainty as to which is their appropriate and expected set of roles. This writer concludes: "Generally speaking, it would seem that it is the girl with a 'middle-of-the-road personality' who is most happily adjusted to the present historical moment. She is not a perfect incarnation of either [set of roles] but is flexible enough to play both."[34]

It seems reasonable to assume that if the marriage-motherhood-career question could be settled relatively early in the adolescent period, much uncertainty and subsequent psychic suffering would be eliminated. The actual situation, however, is that the age at marriage is relatively high among the middle classes.[35] In this situation of uncertainty the girl becomes aware of the advantages of each of the possibilities. As the culture is mediated to her, she comes to the view that "every girl wants a man." She comes to visualize herself cuddled in his strong, protecting arms. She contemplates the creative joy of motherhood, of seeing her likeness develop into a new personality. She can see the prestige and recognition accorded to women successful in the professions, in the arts, in entertainment, and in business. She may learn, too, that each of these three values has its negative as well as its positive aspect: that many marriages end in emotionally painful divorces; that babies represent round-the-clock responsibilities and are not very stimulating company; that many jobs, especially for women, turn into monotonous routines leading nowhere.

What seems to happen is that most women play perfunctorily at a job while awaiting their opportunities to be married. Then, whether they marry or not, they spend some time lamenting the fact that they did not elect some option or combination of options other than the one they chose. By contrast, while the lot of the middle-class adult male in the United States is not devoid

[33] Marynia Farnham, "Battles Won and Lost," *Annals of the American Academy of Political and Social Science*, 251: 119 (1947). In many middle-class occupations the recognition accorded to a woman's achievement is granted by males in terms of the degree to which she manifests behavior appropriate to the masculine sex role, i.e., she is being praised to the extent that she can be said to perform "just like a man." In the roles of wife and mother, on the other hand, she must succeed in appealing "to the personal sentiments of men."—Talcott Parsons in Lyman Bryson, Louis Finkelstein, and R. M. MacIver (eds.), *Conflicts of Power in Modern Culture* (New York: Harper & Row, 1947), p. 37. Both sets of conditions serve to impress upon her the degree to which she is in competition with other women and the degree of "inferiority" of her sex even in this equalitarian culture. It seems evident that this setting is favorable for the development of the "masculine protest" in contemporary middle-class women.

[34] Mirra Komarovsky, "Cultural Contradictions and Sex Roles," *American Journal of Sociology*, 52: 189 (1946). A similar study made at a university on the Pacific Coast reports less conflict and suffering deriving from this confusion. Cf. Paul Wallin, "Cultural Contradictions and Sex Roles: A Repeat Study," *American Sociological Review*, 15: 288–293 (1950).

[35] National Office of Vital Statistics, *Vital Statistics—Special Reports*, Vol. 45, No. 12, September 9, 1957, Tables 24 and 27, pp. 339 and 348–350.

of frustration, he is confronted with a clear expectation that he will qualify himself for and pursue some gainful occupation. He is not expected, moreover, to choose between family life and career. Such a situation as confronts the contemporary middle-class woman is relatively unknown in other societies and is fraught with unpleasant psychiatric possibilities. In the setting of this interpretation we are perhaps justified in mitigating the harshness of some writers' evaluation of the middle-class woman in terms of her "parasitism," "momism," and so on. The interpretation also renders intelligible the bitterness of some spokeswomen for the movement to liberate women as well as their fervor for the abolition of sex-role differentiation. Commenting on this outcome of the emancipation of women, one writer has observed that "women have conducted a magnificent campaign and won a Pyrrhic victory."[36]

One further thought concerns a question the perceptive young woman may ask herself: Is it more interesting to interact with a competent and attractive man in the home or in the office, to be largely responsible for the running of the home and family or to be his helper in the business setting, to discuss with him whether Junior needs orthodontia or an inept clerk needs firing; in other words whether it is more gratifying to be a man's wife or his secretary? And if the young woman makes the traditional choice, will she feel envy of the woman who is his secretary for working with the man during the part of his day that he finds most interesting, challenging, and creative? But if she is the secretary, will she not feel envy of the legal wife who enjoys the income and social position that the secretary—the "office wife"—believes she helped the man to achieve through her effort, commitment, and skill?[37]

We have considered the woman's dilemma in connection with the familial function of emotional gratification. What have we learned? We have noted Farnham's contention that the career-orientation implies aggressive traits, whereas family-orientation for the woman implies nurturant traits, and the latter is consistent with Zelditch's elucidation of the expressive role. The argument has been presented here that our society is not organized to give the nubile female assurance as to which kind of behavior she will find the more useful: whether or not she will have the opportunity to choose the familial roles and to remain in them.

Here, then, are some of the conditions under which American women,

---

[36] Farnham, "Battles Won and Lost," *loc. cit.*, p. 116. A Gallup Poll has asked whether respondents ever wished they had been of the opposite sex. Affirmative responses were four times as frequent among women (16 percent) as among men (4 percent). "Some Women Have Wanted To Be Men," *Chicago Sun-Times*, August 23, 1970, pp. 5, 30.

[37] Humorist Art Buchwald writes of secretaries taking over American business in a vein reminiscent of, but more lighthearted and amusing than, Philip Wylie's treatment of "momism." Quoting an unidentified friend, Buchwald writes: "My wife has to be nice to [my secretary], because if she isn't, my secretary won't let my wife speak to me. As it is, my secretary only lets her through 50 percent of the time. The other 50 percent she just says I'm in an important meeting, as if to imply that my wife should know better than to call the office when world-shaking events are going on behind the company's locked doors." —"America's New Amazons," *Chicago Sun-Times,* March 24, 1962, p. 23.

especially middle-class women, live and learn, are socialized into adult roles, or, perhaps we should say, are socialized into confusion about their adult roles. This is the context from which it seems reasonable to doubt that it is usual for American middle-class wives to achieve such a level of security and equanimity that they can typically and consistently assuage the anxieties, relieve the emotional tensions, and in other ways provide emotional gratifications for other members of the family. Rather, the situation seems better captured in the following passage:

> ... we found that most Americans look to the home for their greatest happiness and satisfaction ... it appears that for women the home also is a great source of distress, more so than for men; they are unhappier with marriage, more aware of problems with it. This holds true in their roles as parents as well as spouses; they feel more inadequate as parents and have more problems with their children. ... Their outlook on life is more negative and passive, more introspective and inwardly turned; they are more sensitive about their personal relationships with other people. Being more introspective and aware of themselves they suffer some of the distress that usually accompanies self-analysis.[38]

Consistent with this analysis of the roles of women and with the increment of role-strain seemingly involved in women's roles over men's is a report that, although the number of psychiatric referrals is greater for males before the years of adolescence, still females come out far ahead in psychiatric referrals after adolescence.[39]

Not all women are willing to accept the system that presents their sex with this dilemma. In vigorous language Alice Rossi has proposed that American society should "attempt to reach a state of full sex equality." She interprets "as a new and subtle form of anti-feminism" the views of such advice-givers as Dr. Spock that mothers should devote full time to child rearing. She believes this practice to be deleterious for children and mothers and, indeed, for fathers as well. Noting that there is "no evidence of any negative effects traceable to maternal employment," she asserts that it is urgently necessary to create social conditions to facilitate occupational careers for mothers. To accomplish this, she proposes the creation of an occupation of "practical mothers," the development of child-care centers, and the saving of travel time by encouraging middle-class families to live in central cities rather than in suburbs.[40]

---

[38] Gerald Gurin, Joseph Veroff, and Sheila Feld, *Americans View Their Mental Health: A Nationwide Interview Survey* (New York: Basic Books, 1960), p. xvi.

[39] Ruth E. Hartley, "Some Implications of Current Changes in Sex Role Patterns," *Merrill-Palmer Quarterly*, 6: 153–164 (1959–1960), esp. p. 162.

[40] Alice S. Rossi, "Equality between the Sexes: An Immodest Proposal," *Daedalus*, 93: 607–652 (1964). Quotations are on pp. 614, 616, and 617 respectively. Other authors who write with affect about the woman's dilemma include: Simone de Beauvoir, *The Second Sex* (New York: Knopf, 1953); and Mary Ellman, *Thinking about Women* (New York: Harcourt, 1968). Mrs. Ellman regrets much of the lot of women including their anatomy and physiology. She writes of breasts as being either engorged and "swelling into great red throbbing

Rossi has proposed the creation of institutional arrangements that would maximize the opportunities of women's careers through minimizing the consequence of their sex characteristics. That is, she would reduce the wife-mother's responsibility for the care of infants and small children by removing child care from the home. Another point that she did not emphasize would be to reduce the wife-mother's responsibility for the maintenance of the household by shifting some of the work to the husband-father. These ideas have been planks in the platform of sexual equality in socialist societies for a long while. Both the non-Marxist socialist countries of Scandinavia and the Marxist countries of Eastern Europe and Asia have given lip service to these ideas if they did not actually try to implement them. One effort along this line was described in Chapter 3 above. In Kiryat Yedidim, a Marxist community, there was a studied effort to break with the traditions of the shtetl and to establish the conditions of the equality of the sexes. From Spiro's account one gets the impression that this feature was working somewhat satisfactorily although the notion of men's work and women's work was beginning to reappear. Haavio-Mannila reports that in Finland the modern view of sexual equality prevails in the occupational system, but in the home the traditional division of labor persists. The fact that a full schedule of household chores awaits the wives after they finish their day's employment results in their being "dissatisfied with their husband's participation in household tasks."[41] A similar situation is reported for Russia. "Without replacing childrearing, food purchase and preparation . . . the Revolution simply brought an additional burden to women . . . it was the men who profited . . . by the new freedoms intended to bring equality to women."[42] On the other hand there is evidence that American husbands are more responsive to the pressure to increase their participation in domestic chores as a result of their wives' full-time employment.[43] How American mothers arrange for the care of their children is shown in Table 12.5.

It is this writer's opinion that in line with the Parsons-Bales-Zelditch

tumors of pain" or as "excess baggage . . . like two empty picnic hampers."—*Ibid.*, p. 182. See also the literature on the women's liberation movement in the United States, e.g.: Susan Brownmiller, " 'Sisterhood Is Powerful': A Member of the Women's Liberation Movement Explains What It's All About," *New York Times Magazine*, March 15, 1970, pp. 27, 128–130, 132, 134, 136, 140.

[41] Elina Haavio-Mannila, "Some Considerations on Sex Differentiation in Role Expectations and Performance," Institute of Sociology, University of Helsinki, Research Report No. 75, 1966. Quotation is from p. 25. Cf. also Elina Haavio-Mannila, "The Position of Finnish Women: Regional and Cross-National Comparisons," *Journal of Marriage and the Family*, 31: 339–347 (1969).

[42] H. Kent Geiger, *The Family in Soviet Russia* (Cambridge, Mass.: Harvard University Press, 1968), p. 60. On Yugoslavia see Olivera Buric-Cukovic, *Promene U Porodicnom Zivotu Nastale Pod Uticajem Zenine Zaposlenosti* (*Changes in Family Life Emerging under the Impact of the Wife's Employment*) (Beograd: Institut Drustvenih Nauka, 1968) (English summary).

[43] Lois Wladis Hoffman, "Parental Power Relations and the Division of Household Tasks," and Kathryn S. Powell, "Family Variables," both in F. Ivan Nye and Lois Wladis Hoffman, *The Employed Mother in America* (Skokie, Ill.: Rand McNally, 1963), pp. 215–230 and 231–240 respectively.

TABLE 12.5

Percentage Distribution of Arrangements of Working Mothers for the Care of Their Children under 14 Years of Age, by Ages of Children, 1965

TYPE OF ARRANGEMENT	AGES OF CHILDREN			
	Total	Under 6 Years	6 to 11 Years	12 and 13 Years
Total	*100*	*100*	*100*	*100*
Care in child's own home by	*46*	*47*	*47*	*38*
Father	15	15	15	14
Other relative	21	18	23	21
Under 16 years	5	2	6	5
16 to 64 years	13	13	13	13
65 years and over	4	3	4	3
Nonrelative who only looked after children	5	8	4	2
Nonrelative who did additional chores (maid, housekeeper, etc.)	5	7	4	2
Care in someone else's home by	*15*	*30*	*11*	*5*
Relative	8	15	5	3
Nonrelative	8	15	6	2
Other arrangements	*39*	*23*	*43*	*57*
Group care (day care center, etc.)	2	6	1	0
Child looked after self	8	1	8	20
Mother looked after child while working	13	15	12	11
Mother worked only during child's school hours	15	1	21	24
Other arrangements	1	1	1	1

SOURCE: Women's Bureau Bulletin No. 290, *1965 Handbook on Women Workers* (Washington, D.C.: GPO, 1966), Table 23, p. 49. Analysis refers to mothers who worked twenty-seven weeks or more in 1964 either full or part time.

formulation noted on page 325 above there is a conventional expectation that American wives and mothers will show somewhat more nurturing and comforting behavior than will husbands and fathers.[44] However, this opinion con-

[44] The kind of evidence on which this opinion is based is illustrated by a study asking college students to indicate the types of behavior they associate with males and females—

tinues, such expectations are not normative in the sense of carrying sanctions, but are loose and optional with the consequence that there is no institutionalized outrage if it is the husband-father who consoles the wife and encourages the children. Experimental support of this view comes from a study showing the instrumental-expressive difference in behavior to be more sex-linked among strangers than within families.[45] Such a formulation makes expressive behavior more a consequence of the personalities of the spouses than of their roles.

If we ignore the Parsonian question as to whether the sexes differ in the quality of their roles and if we attend only to accessibility, we should expect the mother to be more active in all aspects of child rearing simply because she is less likely to be away from home as much as the working father. Corroboration of this expectation comes from a study of English and American children (average age about eleven years in both samples), which shows that in both countries mothers are reported by the children as

> being the principal source both of emotional support and of day-to-day discipline and control, and with the father functioning as an occasional companion and helper to the children, especially to boys, as a kind of balance wheel in disciplinary matters to which he brings an element of principle and authority, and as the occasional agent of punishment.[46]

Housework and Child Rearing

Maintaining a household involves such activities as bringing in needed supplies, removing waste products, preparing meals, and keeping the residence and its grounds clean and attractive. Generally speaking, American culture assigns to the wife-mother responsibility for routine purchases, preparation of meals, and for all but the heaviest work done indoors. If some of these activities are carried out by domestic servants or by commercial services, then the wife-mother has supervisory responsibility. There seems to be consensus that heavy tasks and those done outside the house comprise part of the masculine familial role, but if such tasks are performed by servants or commercial services, their supervision is likely to fall to the wife-mother.

Some degree of ambiguity is introduced into the division of labor by such considerations as variation in the economic level of the family (with the corollary question as to whether or not others are hired to perform some or

in this case, of preschool age. The author of the study asserts that the data "fit the notion that the girl both is and is expected to be timid and more passive; the boy is and is expected to be aggressively forceful in our culture."—Robert I. Watson, *Psychology of the Child* (New York: Wiley, 1959), pp. 442–443.

[45] Robert K. Leik, "Instrumentality and Emotionality in Family Interaction," *Sociometry*, 26: 131–145 (1963). The data of Heiss are also congenial to this interpretation: Jerold S. Heiss, "Degree of Intimacy and Male-Female Interaction," *Sociometry*, 25: 197–208 (1962).

[46] Edward C. Devereux, Urie Bronfenbrenner, and Robert R. Rodgers, "Child-Rearing in England and the United States: A Cross-National Comparison," *Journal of Marriage and the Family*, 31: 257–270 (1969). Quotation is from p. 265.

most of the tasks some or all of the time), the amount of time the man spends on his job and the amount of traveling he does, the presence, age, and sex of offspring, and so on. To take a homely example of the latitude for dispute, let us assume a family wherein it is understood that the man has responsibility for taking out the garbage. If he is away overnight, should the garbage be saved for him to remove when he returns? If he is away for two or three days? If not, the wife has the opportunity to grumble about her having to carry out "his" garbage while he is eating prime-grade steaks and staying at luxury hotels at his company's expense.

In the upper-middle-class suburb of Crestwood Heights it is reported that many women view housework as degrading unless "balanced by intellectual and aesthetic pursuits." This assessment of their duties, according to the authors of that study, leads wives to intensive participation in P.T.A. and philanthropic activities.[47] Given this conviction, moreover, it is not surprising to read that in Crestwood Heights "many wives try by all possible means to involve their husbands in responsibilities around the house."[48] Husbands in this suburb are "ritually responsible" for such tasks as require considerable strength, e.g., putting on storm windows, but in practice the tasks are frequently delegated to commercial services. One wife experienced a glow of satisfaction when her effort to "involve" her husband succeeded to the extent that she got him to *pay* their gardener.[49]

It appears that norms leave the role of father nearly as ill defined as the role of husband. The immediate demands of the situation pretty well require the mother to be the source of both nurturance and control of young children —say of preschool age. Should the father backstop the mother in giving nurturant care? Should he give the extra treats? Should he be the ultimate source of control called upon to judge and punish incidents of grave misbehavior? There are no obvious situational determinants as to what should be the nature of the father's participation, nor are there clear-cut norms. Rather, we see a most intriguing ebb and flow of views, advice, and exhortations: from wanting the father to participate fully in the rearing of his children and almost in the bearing of them to fearing that he will lose his potency if he does; from wanting the father to become a pal to his children to indignant cries that the role of pal is sharply inconsistent with the role of father. It does not appear that the norms become much clearer as the children become older.

Marital Roles and Domestic Power

We have remarked that in the American nuclear family the main activity of the man is to earn a living and to make a success of his occupation, while the main activity of the woman is typically family-oriented: the supervision and rearing of children and the management of the household. By virtue of

[47] Seeley *et al., op. cit.*, pp. 180–181.
[48] *Ibid.*, p. 191.
[49] *Ibid.*

this situation alone it would seem that the woman should be in a position to exercise dominance and leadership over family affairs. To some extent the logic of the situation is offset by two other considerations: the tradition of masculine dominance, and the fact that it is easier for the man to leave the family and live either by himself or with a new woman than it is for the wife-mother because of her greater immediate responsibility for the children[50] and, probably also, because of her closer emotional tie to them. What E. A. Ross called the "law of personal exploitation" is involved here: that the person who is less involved and who has less at stake can demand more from the other for continuing to participate.

The force of the foregoing argument is to leave problematic whether the man or the woman will be the dominant spouse. Wolfe has sought to explain patterns of marital dominance by referring to the occupational experience and success of the spouses. With data from the Detroit Area Survey he has come to the following conclusions:

1. Husbands who achieve success and prestige on their jobs exercise more authority in their homes than do those who are not so successful. Another phrasing is that in the higher socioeconomic strata the husbands tend to be more dominant; in the lower strata it is the wives.[51]

2. Wives who are at work, or who have worked, outside the home have more authority in the family than wives who have never worked outside the home.[52]

3. Control of the family's finances is in the hands of the dominant figure in the family.

4. The relative power of the wife increases with age.[53]

These conclusions have been supported by studies in France[54] and West Ger-

---

[50] Again we can see the working of the second and, to some extent, the third of the criteria which distinguish masculine from feminine sex roles. Cf. page 311 above.

[51] Support for this correlation comes also from Marvin E. Olsen, "Distribution of Family Responsibilities and Social Stratification," *Marriage and Family Living*, 22: 60–65 (1960).

[52] Similar results on points 1 and 2 appear in David M. Heer, "Dominance and the Working Wife," *Social Forces*, 36: 341–347 (1958). On a point comparable to 2 above, however, some negative results appear in Robert O. Blood, Jr., and Robert L. Hamblin, "The Effect of the Wife's Employment on the Family Power Structure," *Social Forces*, 36: 347–352 (1958). One other study finds that working wives exercise more domestic power than do nonworking wives, but that this correlation disappears when the ages and number of children and the husband's occupation are controlled. Cf. Lois Wladis Hoffman, "Effects of the Employment of Mothers on Parental Power Relations and the Division of Household Tasks," *Marriage and Family Living*, 22: 27–35 (1960).

[53] Donald M. Wolfe, "Power and Authority in the Family," chap. 7 in Dorwin Cartwright (ed.), *Studies in Social Power* (Ann Arbor: University of Michigan Press, 1959), pp. 99–117. See also Robert O. Blood, Jr., and Donald M. Wolfe, *Husbands and Wives: The Dynamics of Married Living* (New York: Free Press, 1960).

[54] Andrée Michel, "Comparative Data Concerning the Interaction of French and American Families," *Journal of Marriage and the Family*, 29: 337–344 (1967).

many,⁵⁵ and by an account of life in traditional Japan.⁵⁶ Contrary findings have been reported for Yugoslavia and Greece, i.e., the higher the social status of the husband, the lower his domestic influence.⁵⁷ It seems likely, however, that this inverse correlation is a result of recent migration from rural areas and thus is a transitory vestige of traditional peasant culture. This interpretation is supported by a study in Japan.⁵⁸

Familial Roles and Role-Strain

As Goode has observed, it is usual for sociologists to think of roles as being enacted and of norms as integrated,⁵⁹ but in fact dissensus⁶⁰ and role-strain are as much a part of the experiential world as are consensus and role-integration.⁶¹ Let us consider some of the factors that create difficulty in the enactment of roles and prevent actors from carrying out the behaviors called for by their role-obligations.

Probably the most obvious source of role-strain—a source that has interested literary as well as sociological writers—is the difference in behaviors called for by two or more of an actor's roles. For example, a Christian young man may interpret his religious role as prescribing for him a life of nonviolent behavior and certainly of avoiding murder, but his role as a soldier may require him to kill. Such a conflict may occur in the family when a girl learns that her brother has committed a forbidden act. In her role as sister she is expected to show loyalty to her brother and to remain silent; in her role as daughter she is expected to show loyalty to her parents and report the misdeed.

Another more or less obvious source of role-strain is that between role-obligation and the disposition of the personality.⁶² We might assume that in

---

⁵⁵ Eugen Lupri, "Contemporary Authority Patterns in the West German Family: A Study in Cross-National Validation," *Journal of Marriage and the Family*, 31: 134–144 (1969).

⁵⁶ Takashi Koyama, *The Changing Social Position of Women in Japan* (Paris: UNESCO, 1961) p. 34.

⁵⁷ Olivera Buric and Andjelka Zecevic, "Family Authority, Marital Satisfaction, and the Social Network in Yugoslavia," *Journal of Marriage and the Family*, 29: 325–336 (1967); and Constantina Safilios-Rothschild, "A Comparison of Power Structure and Marital Satisfaction in Urban Greek and French Families," *Journal of Marriage and the Family*, 29: 345–352 (1967).

⁵⁸ Robert O. Blood, Jr., *Love Match and Arranged Marriage: A Tokyo-Detroit Comparison* (New York: Free Press, 1967), pp. 167–169.

⁵⁹ The present writer would add that such an assumption seems especially likely to be made by sociologists who proceed from functional premises.

⁶⁰ *Dissensus:* the antonym of *consensus.*

⁶¹ William J. Goode, "A Theory of Role Strain," *American Sociological Review*, 25: 483–496 (1960).

⁶² Goode refers to the same source of role-strain in noting that there are role-demands which are "onerous, difficult, or displeasing" and that the "individual's total role obligations are over-demanding."—Goode, "A Theory of Role Strain," *loc. cit.,* p. 485.

personality our hypothetical young Christian is gentle and somewhat timid. The role-demands of the combat soldier would prove discrepant with such personality traits. In the setting of the family such a role-strain would occur if an intelligent and well-coordinated but impatient mother would be confronted with the task of teaching a dull and awkward offspring.

What are the sources of role-strain in the American middle-class family? It should be clear that there are many possible sources. In the present passage we shall deal only with the most obvious source for each of the three positions in the nuclear family. A previous section in the present chapter, which is entitled "The Woman's Dilemma," points to a source of strain for the woman in her familial roles. It has been argued that the crux of the strain comes from the uncertainty as to whether or not the woman will be called upon to fill the roles of wife and mother and the quite different kinds of behavior patterns appropriate to the single career woman as compared with the woman who devotes her full time to being wife and mother.

Less attention has been given to a comparable source of strain for the man. From early in his boyhood the male is socialized into attitudes appropriate to vocation and upward mobility. He is constantly being queried as to "what he will be when he grows up." The successes and failures of his father's peers become a topic for domestic conversation, and hence the overriding importance of occupational roles is impressed upon him. To the extent that the man is a professional or an "organization man" he is called upon to commit almost all of his waking life and energies to his occupation. Hence such a commitment runs counter to an appreciable emotional investment in the roles of husband and father, and certainly to the efforts of the wife-mother to "involve" him in domestic routines.

For the offspring role-strain consists largely of the discrepancy between the role-demands of the peer group, or gang, and the demands of the roles of son and sibling. The strain seems roughly correlated with the age of the offspring, the maximum normally coming in adolescence. This point will be developed later.

How do actors respond to role-strains? Again Goode offers some suggestions. Among the ways he mentions for the reduction of role-strain are compartmentalization, delegation, elimination of role-relationships, extension, and barriers against intrusion. To this list we shall add aloofness, or the avoidance of intimacy. We shall consider each of these.

Rendering unto God those things that are God's and unto Caesar those that are Caesar's is a classic formulation of compartmentalization. What this involves, for example, is behaving like a Christian while attending church and like a soldier when in combat, and acting on the principle that each behavior is appropriate in its own setting and not in the other. Applied to the family setting, an example would be a gangster who employs violent and bloody sanctions in his occupation and who is kind, gentle, and considerate in his home.

Delegation is a technique whereby the actor arranges for someone else to carry out one of two discrepant role-performances while the actor is left in a conflict-free position to carry out the other role-performance. In the family setting a man might perceive as discrepant the exhibiting of expressive, even effusive, behavior if he had been socialized into the attitude that masculine roles call for a "strong, silent" demeanor. Yet such emotional and behavioral austerity might lead kinsmen and friends to regard the man as unfriendly and indifferent. By calling on his wife to show expressive behavior, the man is able to delegate the emotional show of solidarity with friends and relatives without compromising his masculinity as he understands that term.

By elimination of role-relationships Goode refers to a situation whereby, for example, a father who subscribes to the tenets of his culture's morality avoids endorsing the immoral and improvident behavior of a prodigal son by disowning him.

In extension the actor expands "his role relations in order to plead these commitments as an excuse for not fulfilling certain obligations,"[63] as when the husband-father volunteers to entertain a visiting customer and is thus able to avoid taking his son to a movie, or when a wife-mother accepts an office in the P.T.A. that requires her to be away from home at an hour when younger children must be bathed and put to bed.

Perhaps the commonest example of "barriers against intrusion" is the secretary who guards the entrance to her boss's office and shields him from being importuned into undesired role-performances.[64] In some homes a general understanding that each person is entitled to privacy (implemented perhaps by such devices as the individual room and a private telephone line for children) constitutes some protection against unwelcome role-demands among family members.

In military organizations there is an institutionalized avoidance of intimacy between enlisted men and their officers. This is an age-old device for preventing the commanding officer from developing bonds of affection with men he may have to order to their deaths. Consistent with this is the disposition to make the position of commanding officer a very lonely one. Presently we shall consider an example of emotional aloofness in the Chinese family.

Conformity or Hypocrisy? Role versus Personality

One form of role-strain, we observed above, can arise from a discrepancy between the demands of the role and the dispositions of the personality. Let us relate these terms to each other and note a few implications. We have defined a role as a set of more or less integrated expectations concerning the behavior of an individual with respect to one segment of the position he occupies: the district sales manager's behavior vis-à-vis his vice-president or the

[63] *Ibid.*, p. 486.
[64] Cf. note 37 above.

father's behavior vis-à-vis his son. The behavior referred to, then, is relationship-determined or situation-determined. That is, the occupant of the role is expected to behave in a specified manner when he is enacting that role. The concept of role contains no specification of what the actor will be doing when he is not enacting the role under consideration. Personality, on the other hand, is an abstraction that refers to the actor's behavior irrespective of the situation or relationship in which he finds himself. A person is spoken of as being active, energetic, dependent, or the like, and these adjectives refer to traits of his personality without the qualification of any setting in which they are appropriate or inappropriate.[65]

It has been observed that as society becomes more complex, the actor is called upon to assume an increasing number of roles. It appears that this is the reason why there is such an emphasis in contemporary society on "adjustability" as a trait to be cultivated, why schools report to parents the degree to which children are observed to "integrate" with their peers, and why undergraduate life seems to offer such an amazingly diverse range of activities, many of which lack academic content or intellectual orientation.

The phenomenon of conformity, which has been much publicized and criticized, can be seen as a consequence of the emphasis upon developing skill in assuming a role, abandoning it, and shifting quickly to another. This criticism appears in Riesman's writing under the rubric of the "other-directed" personality, in Whyte's as the "organization man,"[66] and by others has been called the "gray-flannel man with the button-down mind." What is being referred to here, of course, is the idea that the actor's behavior is largely a set of responses to the cues given by others rather than the responses to his own drives toward goals he defines for himself and pursues in his own unique style. In other words, the criticism may be phrased thus: there is too much role-performance, too little personality-originated behavior.

Whyte has emphasized the impact of the corporation's demand for conformity on the behavior of wives of men in the administrative hierarchy. His concept of the "company wife" stresses the idea that through her appearance, deportment, command of small talk, knowledge of etiquette, and sensitivity to the increments of deference associated with the company's hierarchical echelons, the wife can be an appreciable positive or negative influence on the career of her husband as an "organization man." The ideal company wife Whyte sees as not being a woman of great talent and/or energy in any very

---

[65] ". . . role directs our attention to behaviors and attitudes that are appropriate to a situation, irrespective of the actor, whereas personality directs our attention to behaviors and attitudes that are characteristic of the actor, irrespective of the situation." Robert F. Winch, "Determinants of Interpersonal Influence in the Late Adolescent Male: Theory and Design of Research," in Reuben Hill and Rene König, *Families in East and West* (Paris: Mouton, 1970), pp. 578–601. Quotation is from p. 582.

[66] David Riesman, *The Lonely Crowd* (New Haven, Conn.: Yale University Press, 1950); William H. Whyte, Jr., *The Organization Man* (New York: Simon and Shuster, 1956).

conventional sense. Rather, her accomplishment is presented as a consequence of temperamental blandness and the judicious use of blandishments—behavior adjudged to be expressively attractive without having much content, behavior that demonstrates "taste" but not intellect.[67]

This writer wishes neither to take up the chorus of the critics of conformity nor to shout them down, but merely to direct the reader's attention to ways in which what the layman calls conformity is related to what the sociologist calls role, role-obligations, and role-performance. When the salesman "butters up" a prospective customer whom he secretly loathes, he is enacting a role and may despise himself for doing so and berate destiny for having put him in a spot where he must do this in order to feed his family and get ahead. In the language of the layman, such behavior shows conformity, hypocrisy, and lack of integrity. Presumably the same observation can be made with respect to the intelligent but impatient mother of the slow-witted and awkward child. She understands that she must appear gentle, patient, and encouraging, whereas subjectively she may be seething with frustration and rage at the child's ineptitude. Presumably she too is showing conformity, hypocrisy, and lack of integrity. But the reader no doubt would agree that in the latter situation the mother has little choice but to carry out her role-demands.

One final observation pertains to the possible cost to the actor of diminished emphasis on personality and increased emphasis on role-performance. To the extent that such a trend exists we may offer the hypothesis that there should be a cost to the actor in a loss of sense of identity. Let us bear in mind that the term "personality" refers to continuities in a person's behavior. To the degree that his personality offers little resistance in the shift from one role to another, his personality also offers him little sense of continuity. Hence he has no way to answer his own question "Who am I?" except to list the totality of his roles. Beyond that he lacks the individuality that renders the question silly and meaningless.

Summary and Conclusions

In most operations of any degree of complexity there is a demonstrable advantage in dividing the task into two or more operations. Where this is done and the tasks are formalized into specialized activities, there is a consequent differentiation of positions and roles. A role is a more or less integrated set of expectations concerning the performance of an actor.

Primary sex characteristics provide a universal basis for differentiation of roles. Age differences provide another basis for the differentiation of roles. Al-

---

[67] William H. Whyte, Jr., "The Wife Problem," *Life*, January 7, 1952, pp. 32–48, reprinted in Robert F. Winch and Louis Wolf Goodman (eds.), *Selected Studies in Marriage and the Family* (3d ed.; New York: Holt, Rinehart and Winston, Inc., 1968), pp. 177–188.

though there is great variation in the way societies define their sex and age roles, the usual result is that active adult males are assigned those tasks having one or more of the following requirements: great physical strength, absence from home for considerable periods and/or distances, and continuous attention and effort for considerable blocks of time. With respect to the second (absence from home), it is in order to note that far from being an unprecedented consequence of the industrial order and suburban living and in that sense a recent development, the absence of the man from the home has been a common experience over the centuries, having been recorded at least as long ago as Homer wrote of the siege of Troy.

In many ways, however, the rise of an urban-industrial order has affected sex roles and their differentiation. An increasing number of the roles of the adult male—especially the most meaningful and significant roles—involve him in relationships outside the family. This implies that an increasing proportion of the man's time is being devoted to extrafamilial activities. As the technology that accompanies the urban-industrial social order introduces new forms of power, there is a consequent reduction in the importance of jobs depending upon the physical strength of the worker, and the proportion of white-collar jobs in the total occupational system increases. The increase in the number and proportion of white-collar jobs creates a demand for women in the labor force. The demand can be met because of the increasing life expectancy of women (as well as of men), the relatively small number of children ever born per woman ever married, and the effect of these factors in reducing the proportion of her life that the average woman devotes to the rearing of children. With a reduction in the importance of physical strength goes a reduction in the role-differentiation of the two sexes. In many countries, moreover, the reduction in the functional significance of sex-role differentiation has been accompanied by a claim that the concepts of equality and democracy call for the further reduction, and even ultimate abolition, of sex-role differentiation. The American conception of the equality of the sexes is expressed in classrooms where boys and girls sit together and learn the same skills and values. The effect of their receiving substantially similar education is that both sexes come to value positively the kinds of activities available to men and to depreciate many activities that are characteristically feminine. The major reason for the positive evaluation of men's activities is that the important roles of the society are normally carried out by men. A major reason for the negative evaluation of women's activities in the family is the recognition that families with adequate resources frequently hire domestics and governesses to perform many of the duties assigned to the wife-mother. The major exceptions are the woman's obligation to be the husband's sex partner, to bear her husband's children, and to be hostess to the family's visitors. Another reason for the negative evaluation of women's domestic activities is the rise of the domestic technology. Viewed positively, processed foods and household appliances reduce the time and energy required to maintain a household. But the negative side is that domestic technology has done much to remove the pride of workmanship, with the result that some wives feel their domestic roles call for the body of a woman and the mind of a child. (It should be recalled that the rise of domestic technology has also had the consequence of returning to the home some of the productive functions that had been lost—baking, laundering, and so on.)

The relative lack of functions within the American family affects the happiness of the individual member both negatively and positively. The negative consequence is that there is a relatively small number of role-relationships to bind members to each other, and thus a minimally functional family cannot be expected to have the solidarity of a highly functional one. The positive consequence is that the role-relationships are less complicated than they would be under conditions of greater functionality and the individual has greater freedom to come and go and to pursue his own individual goals. Let us trace some implications of these points.

As Table 12.4 shows, the Chinese family, whether of the stem or joint type, had indefinite continuity. Since the continuity of generations was traced through the male line and since the family was patrilocal, the mother was an arrival from another family and the daughters would soon depart. Thus the Chinese family gave prominence to the father-son relationship. In America, since the children leave to found their own nuclear families, the most enduring familial relationship is that between husband and wife (unless broken by divorce or premature death).

There is some reason to believe that the second most important familial relationship in American society is that of mother to her married daughter. The reasons advanced are several: since women are generally assigned the responsibility of being social secretary—of "keeping in touch"—they are the representatives of their respective nuclear families who interact with each other; since domestic activities constitute the main occupation of women and their "shop talk" concerns the treatment of colic and the price of beans, they have more in common than do males; and it is probable that the bond between the wife and her mother is usually stronger than that between her and her husband's mother because of a lifetime of intimacy and shared experience with her own mother and because of some tradition of hostility with her husband's mother, who may view the wife as successful rival and unwelcome successor in the affections of the husband.

The multiplicity of role-relationships between two individuals has its negative aspect in role-strain as well as its positive one in solidarity. It has been noted above that in China the father and the eldest son were extremely important to each other, that they had numerous role-relationships binding them together, that the continuity of the family hung on their relationship, and that the continuity of the family was the goal of their lives. As might be expected, however, the numerous functions threatened at times to overload the father-son relationship. The concept of filial piety operated to prevent overt conflict in this all-important relationship. Thus role-strain was relieved by creating emotional distance between father and son. "Respect, awe, and fear are terms . . . descriptive of the relationship as seen from the son's point of view," observes Levy, who continues that "from the father's point of view the relationship was also one of avoidance rather than one of intimacy."[68]

The American ethic of equalitarianism leads to a rejection of a reverential attitude toward the father. This smacks of Victorianism and of Middle European authoritarianism. As was noted above, there has been pressure to make of the American father the pal and confidant of his children. The relative lack of functional relationships between the American father and son makes their relationship freer of role-strain than that in the Chinese family. Therefore there is not as much need for a device, such as aloofness, to relieve role-strain. In the American family, then, there is a relative lack of a brake on the expression of affect. Without avoidance, awe, or reverence the relation becomes one of love and intimacy if the feelings are positive, or of hatred and rejection if they are negative.

One further implication of the relative lack of function in the American family is that familial roles are not clearly defined. It is not generally agreed as to just which tasks a husband should perform or which responsibilities a father should discharge. The concept of equalitarianism is interpreted by some to mean that there should be no role-differentiation between the sexes or, indeed, between the generations. The culture contains the proposition that it is satisfactory to break with tradition and that professional advice-givers are more knowledgeable authorities on familial role-obligations than are parents. In the light of these considerations it is not surprising that young people about to be married feel confused as to how to organize their families. Some seek answers in college courses on family life education, and many who do not get to college presumably are edified by columns of advice to the troubled and lovelorn, while paperback books of various persuasions are available to all who can read. Advice giving and its effects will be considered in Chapter 14.

[68] Marion J. Levy, Jr., *The Family Revolution in Modern China* (Cambridge, Mass.: Harvard University Press, 1949), pp. 172–173.

PART FIVE

Parental Functions and Intergenerational Relations:

the first phase of the affectional cycle

To this point we have considered the structure and functions of the family as resultants of the structures and functions of societies. In this section we turn to the nuclear family as a social system and examine its internal workings. We shall be much concerned with the parental functions: nurturance and control. We shall also be setting forth our structural analysis at points along the family's life cycle and noting variation in the positions and roles of family members vis-à-vis each other.

Descriptive statistics concerning the median life-cycle of the American nuclear family will give background to the more qualitative presentation of the next few chapters. Table V.1 shows the median ages of American women at certain points in the familial cycle and how these ages have varied over half a century. Age at first marriage and at the birth of the last child have gone down whereas age at death of one spouse has risen. By comparing the fourth and fifth rows of this table the reader can see that the median period the parental couple survives after the marriage of the last child has risen from about ten months ($57.0 - 56.2 = 0.8$) to about twelve years.

As noted in Chapter 4, it makes sense to speak of two segments of the population—the economically productive and the economically dependent. Just where to draw the two age boundaries—between the very young and the productive, and between the productive and the old—is a difficult question. Perhaps the best clue for the former boundary is afforded by the median years of school completed. In 1890 it was about $8\frac{1}{3}$ years; in 1967, about $12\frac{3}{4}$.[1] Thus it would not be far off the mark to regard the 15–19 age-category as productive in 1890 (i.e., at the left side of Figure V.1) but as becoming dependent by 1968 (at the right side of that graph). At the upper boundary it appears that the limit was a bit above the age of 65 in 1890[2] but had receded to 65 by 1940.[3] The young dependents (0–14) constituted about 36 percent in 1890, and (using the 0–19 age-category) about 39 percent in 1968. The old dependents were no more than 4 percent in 1890 and were 9.6 percent in 1968. Considered together, the two dependent categories constitute about 40 percent of the population at the beginning and nearly 50 percent at the end of the 78-year period covered by Figure V.1.

[1] Statistics on median years of school completed have been available only since 1940. Those who were 55 to 64 in 1940 had a median education of 8.3 years.—*Historical Statistics of the United States, Colonial Times to 1957*, Table H 395–406, p. 214. Those who were 20 to 24 years old in 1969 had a median schooling of 12.7 years.—*Statistical Abstract of the United States, 1970*, Table 160, p. 111.

[2] Figures show that 68.3 percent of the males sixty-five and over were in the labor force in 1890.—*Historical Statistics of the United States, Colonial Times to 1957*, Table D 13–25, p. 71.

[3] In 1940, 42.2 percent of the males sixty-five and over were in the labor force. *Ibid.* By 1969 the percentage was down to 26.2.—*Statistical Abstract of the United States, 1970*, Table 317, p. 214.

TABLE V.1

Median Age of Women at Selected Stages of the Family Life Cycle, for Women Born from 1880 to 1939, by Year of Birth

SUBJECT	YEAR OF BIRTH (BIRTH COHORT) OF WOMEN					
	1880 to 1889	1890 to 1899	1900 to 1909	1910 to 1919	1920 to 1929	1930 to 1939
First marriage	21.6	21.4	21.1	21.7	20.8[a]	19.9[a]
Birth of first child	22.9	22.9	22.6	23.7	23.0[b]	21.5[b]
Birth of last child	32.9	31.1	30.4	31.5	30.0–31.0[c]	(NA)[d]
First marriage of last child[e]	56.2	53.5	51.9	53.0	51.5–52.5	(NA)
Death of one spouse: For all couples[f]	57.0	59.4	62.3	63.7	64.4	64.4
For couples surviving to first marriage of last child[g]	69.2	63.1	67.8	68.2	67.2–68.2	(NA)

[a] Projected from partial experience on the assumption that 96 percent of the cohort will ultimately marry.

[b] Projected from partial experience on the assumption that 90 percent of all women in the cohort (including single) will ultimately become mothers.

[c] Projected as follows: Assuming that 48 percent of all women in this cohort (including single) will ultimately have a third child, partial experience to date indicates an ultimate median age of women at birth of the third child of 28.1 years. The median age of mothers in the cohort of 1900–1909 and 1910–1919 at birth of their last child of any order exceeded the median age at birth of their third child by an average of 2.4 years. This figure added to 28.1 gives 30.5 years, the center of the projection range shown.

[d] NA = not available.

[e] Assumes woman has last child at median age for cohort and last child marries at estimated median age of first marriage for children (see text).

[f] Assumes wife first married at median age for cohort to husband three years older.

[g] Measure applies to couples surviving jointly to median age of women at marriage of last child.

SOURCE: Paul C. Glick and Robert Parke, Jr., "New Approaches in Studying the Life Cycle of the Family," *Demography*, 2: 187–202 (1965); reprinted in Robert F. Winch and Louis Wolf Goodman (eds.), *Selected Studies in Marriage and the Family* (3d ed.; New York: Holt, Rinehart and Winston, Inc., 1968, p. 169).

With respect to intergenerational relations in the American family we can foreshadow two conclusions. In the first place, evidence is convincing that norms have been "coming unstuck," expectations have broken down, roles and positions have become fluid. Examples concern the role of mother (Chapters 13 and 14) and adolescent (Chapter 16) as well as filial responsibility for

FIGURE V.1
Percent Distribution of the Age Composition of the Population of the United States for Selected Age Categories: 1890–1968

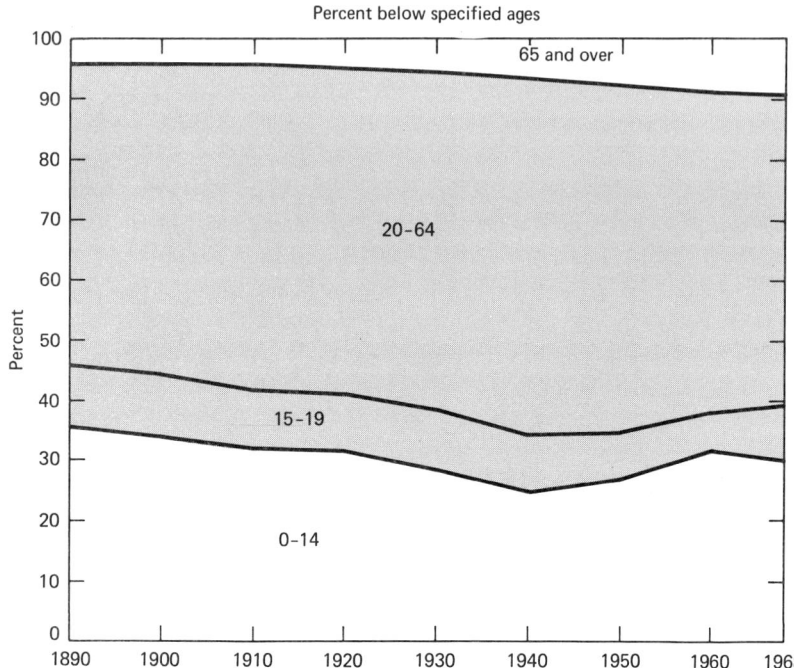

SOURCE: U.S. Bureau of the Census, *U.S. Census of Population: 1960. General Population Characteristics. United States Summary.* Final Report. PC(1)-1B (Washington, D.C.: Government Printing Office, 1961). For 1968—U.S. Bureau of the Census, *Current Population Reports—Population Characteristics,* Series P-20, No. 181, April 21, 1969, Table 1, p. 10.

dependent parents (Chapter 17). The second conclusion is a corollary of the first: where norms have disintegrated, family members grope for the "right" way to behave toward each other, for the "right" thing to expect of others. In this age when tradition is no longer the guide to wisdom, there is a quest for a new source of guidance. To some the answers appear derivable from science —or from what appears to the layman to be scientific, or at least "expert," opinion. To others science seems a false and unethical god, and wisdom comes from nonrational sources—from revelation and from the realm of the occult. The great volume of discussion and writing on such topics as interpersonal ethics, the "generation gap," and communal living is evidence of man's abhorrence of the normative vacuum.

What implications have these remarks for the level of our analysis? Sociological analysis is relevant where behavior is patterned, i.e., where the domain under scrutiny is one or more social systems with their attendant configurations of positions and roles. The first four parts of this book consist of such sociological analysis. Parts Five and Six, however, pertain respectively to interaction between parent and child and between husband and wife in a somewhat anomic (normless) context. To the extent that norms are absent, this writer holds that the proper level of analysis is social-psychological. The reader is invited to recall a formulation in Chapter 1 to the effect that social functions are Janus-faced in the sense that they eventuate in both group-serving and individual-serving consequences. To the extent that the latter become desired (e.g., a mother's love, a family's prestige, etc.) the functionality of the family results in rewards. Through control of these rewards, according to this theory, the family can control its members. Conversely, to the degree that the family is nonfunctional or to the degree that it does not use its resources selectively to reward behavior, it lacks influence over its members.

13

The Nurturant Function and the Infant

Introduction

The birth of the first child is in many societies the occasion on which a couple is recognized as having achieved the standing of adult and fully participating citizens. In view of our postulate that replacement is the basic societal function of the family this is not surprising. The arrival of a child immediately calls into play two of the family's derived functions: position-conferring and nurturance.

As Chapter 8 explained at some length, birth into a family is the normal means by which an individual acquires ascribed positions in certain structures of his society. Through being born into a family he is the son of someone (not a *nullius filius*) and is thereby legitimate. In American society the birth certificate symbolizes this fact. For Christians the baptismal ceremony marks the ascription to the newborn of his position in the religious structure (and other faiths mark the ascription with kindred rites).

Since our major concern in the present chapter is the infant, the function of nurturance is in the forefront of our thinking. One of the most fascinating and least-understood problems in social science concerns the importance of the experiences of the early months and years in general, and of maternal nurturance in particular, on the later behavior and personality of the individual. After some observations on the valuation of parenthood, we shall present evidence concerning mother-infant interaction and attempt to portray the state of our knowledge and of our ignorance on this topic. Further assessment of this evidence appears in Chapter 14.

Parenthood and Culture

In Chapter 9 we considered parenthood as a source of emotional gratification. Features of culture and of personality that serve to make parenthood more or less attractive were presented as pointing to rewards and penalties of parental roles. Because such considerations bear upon the way in which adults fulfill the parental functions of nurturance and control, that theme is reviewed and further developed in the following paragraphs.

In any setting parenthood involves disadvantages as well as satisfactions. On the negative side, we may remind ourselves that children need to be cared for, and the newborn requires around-the-clock attention. The parents are obliged to invest a certain portion of their energies and other resources in the child. The portion, of course, is influenced by such considerations as the wealth of the parents, their pre-existing commitments (including the number of children they may already have), and their interest in children. Positive considerations appear where the culture values parenthood as the badge of adulthood and where the status of the woman is improved by becoming a mother. Under such conditions there is relatively little basis for parents to develop negative feelings about parenthood. The positive side of the picture is intensified, of course, where the social organization is well geared to child rearing, where children are economic as well as social assets, and especially where children represent security for the parents in their declining years.

In the societies described in Chapters 2 and 3 conditions were generally conducive to the development of attitudes favorable to parenthood. Conditions are quite different in contemporary American cities, however. The social life of the city is organized for the participation of active adults; it is unfriendly to the very young and the very old. The migration of urban-oriented people to the suburbs is largely motivated, as we saw in Chapter 6, by the desire to find a setting more hospitable to the rearing of children.

Most cultures, and certainly the American culture is no exception, contain the expectation that a woman will marry and bear children. As we saw in Chapter 12, some women, especially in the more highly educated segment of the American middle class, are also given the expectation that they should, or may, become professionally productive. The interaction of the former and latter expectations may produce a considerable sense of role-conflict. For a period, at least, parenthood means that the woman's life will be circumscribed, that her participation in cultural activities will be restricted, that whatever vocational or professional skills she may possess may become atrophied.

Other attitudes that may color a woman's valuation of motherhood include a fear of pregnancy because of the attendant sickness, because of her fear of loss of attractiveness and its implications in terms of her husband's affections, or because of the possibility of death in childbirth. To her the coming of a child may signify the cementing of a strong relationship with her husband or the bolstering of a weak one, or she may view the coming child as an unwelcome vestige of an already doomed marriage. The child may come to symbolize a common interest of transcendent importance to husband and wife; it may be foreseen and utilized as a substitute love-object when the relationship between spouses has weakened or never was vital; it may achieve the status of competitor for the love and affection of the spouse. The wife may see procreation as the acme of self-expression or as the anonymity of motherhood.[1]

Some of these same considerations may also color the husband's attitudes toward parenthood. In general, it seems fair to say that for him the significance of parenthood is painted in less vivid hues than they are for the wife. To him children represent current expense and the necessity for fiscal planning; they may also represent restriction of mobility and of leisure-time activities. At the same time most of the husband's waking hours are spent out of their presence and are therefore unaffected in an immediate way by either the joys or vicissitudes of parenthood. For the husband, then, parenthood represents a network of relationships and obligations; for the wife it is also a vocation and a way of life.

Because of differences in socioeconomic and ethnoreligious background and in sex as well as in numerous other social characteristics the effect of the cultural impress is very uneven. For these reasons the following conclusions seem appropriate: Most Americans desire children for numerous reasons, the relative strength of which varies from one social class, ethnoreligious identity, and, indeed, person to another. In some the negative attitudes toward parenthood are stronger than the positive. To some degree at least, both positive and negative considerations are present in all; hence we can hardly help feeling some ambivalence concerning the cultural value of parenthood.

Relevant to this line of theorizing is a study by LeMasters, who hypothesized that the arrival of the first child would prove to be a crisis. He found that the great majority of the young couples he interviewed (38 of 46 couples) had experienced the arrival of their first-born as either an "extensive" or a "severe" crisis. According to the author of the study this high incidence of crises was apparently not the consequence of the child's being unwanted, of the parents' being neurotic, or of the marriage's being shaky. Rather, the source of the crises seemed to be that the couples felt that they had had very little preparation for their parental roles, that this lack of preparation was naturally experienced more profoundly by the mothers than the fathers, that the mothers worked hard and were chronically tired and felt they were fulfilling their maternal roles poorly, that these mothers developed feelings of

---

[1] There is another aspect of this general topic that merits consideration: the parent's attitude toward the specific child as contrasted with the attitude toward parenthood in general. This point is considered in Chapter 15 under the heading "The Individual Child."

guilt because they believed they were inadequate mothers as well as poor housewives, and, finally, that these women experienced misgivings over what they felt was a deterioration in their appearance.[2]

When all the studies on this topic are considered, however, it is not clear just how much of a crisis parenthood usually is. There are two studies that report results that are roughly similar to those of LeMasters,[3] but there are two other writers who find few major crises among their subjects.[4]

No doubt most mothers are convinced that the gestation period of humans is quite long enough. Yet the fact remains that the human infant is, by mammalian standards, relatively undeveloped at birth. The basic fact of human parenthood is that not only is the human infant helpless at birth but remains dependent for such a long time. Keeping that fact and the data of LeMasters and the related follow-up studies in mind, let us investigate the nature of the human animal by considering the topic of motivation, then look into the subject of the nurturant function, and conclude with some speculation as to the way in which human beings learn to love.

The Biophysical Basis of Activity

To account for activity on the part of any animal, including man, it is presumably necessary to postulate some internal source of motive power or "drive." A drive-reduction theory (or model) is useful to account for some —but definitely not all—of man's behavior. According to this model, tension arises in the organism as the consequence of recurring states of physiochemical imbalance. Such tension is experienced as "unpleasure." The organism responds to this uncomfortable state with activity. According to this model the purpose of activity is to restore the state of physiochemical balance (homeostasis). Thus activity is conceived as an adjustment on the part of some animate form to achieve homeostasis, at which point, presumably, activity ceases until there

---

[2] E. E. LeMasters, "Parenthood as Crisis," *Marriage and Family Living*, 19: 352–355 (1957).

[3] Everett D. Dyer, "Parenthood as Crisis: A Re-Study," *Marriage and Family Living*, 25: 196–201 (1963); and Joseph H. Meyerowitz and Harold Feldman, "Transition to Parenthood," *Psychiatric Research Report 20*, American Psychiatric Association, February 1966, pp. 78–84.

[4] Daniel F. Hobbs, Jr., "Parenthood as Crisis: A Third Study," *Journal of Marriage and the Family*, 27: 367–372 (1965); Daniel F. Hobbs, Jr., "Transition to Parenthood: A Replication and an Extension," *Journal of Marriage and the Family*, 30: 413–417 (1968); cf. also study by David Beauchamp reported in Arthur P. Jacoby, "Transition to Parenthood: A Reassessment," *Journal of Marriage and the Family*, 31: 720–727 (1969). A survey of the attitudes of low-income mothers of newborn babies was made in Jersey City, N.J., and it was found that happiness about being pregnant correlated positively with its being a first pregnancy and with the woman's being of the Catholic religion. Cf. W. Godfrey Cobliner, "Some Maternal Attitudes towards Conception," *Mental Hygiene*, 49: 550–557 (1965).

recurs an imbalance, resulting in tension, which in turn results in more activity. Thus activity accounted for by the drive-reduction model runs through what we may call a tension-equilibrium cycle.

The common psychic attribute of all states of drive (or tension or need[5]) is dissatisfaction or "unpleasure." Satisfaction or pleasure is derived from the reduction of tension. When the reduction in need or tension is relatively rapid, the pleasure is relatively intense.[6]

In the form just stated, the drive-reduction model based upon the hedonic premise[7] is not adequate to account for all behavior. Consider, for example, a man who goes for a walk before dinner in order to "work up" an appetite. At first it appears that such behavior stands the preceding model on its head: the activity is designed to increase tension rather than to lower it. On reflection, however, it can be seen that this behavior calls for extension rather than rejection of the drive-reduction model. What can be seen here is that the animal (the strolling gentleman in our example) has learned the pleasure to be derived from a specific tension-activity-equilibrium cycle (in this case being hungry and then eating) and undertakes to increase the relevant tension in order to enjoy its reduction. Thus the preprandial walk is the response to a secondary (or acquired or learned) drive to be hungry in order to enjoy eating. Since such drives are learned, it is evident that they are less relevant to early infancy than to later periods.[8]

What Is Nurturance?

Infants are helpless, and their visceral processes dominate their lives. Moreover, they have not yet acquired much in the way of secondary drives. For these reasons the presence of an infant in the household creates the demand for nurturant care.

---

[5] At the biophysical level we may conceive of drive, tension, need, and motive as equivalent terms.—Gardner Murphy, *Personality: A Biosocial Approach to Origins and Structure* (New York: Harper & Row, 1947), p. 89. H. S. Sullivan writes: ". . . euphoria refers to a polar construct, an abstract ideal, in which there is no tension, therefore no action—tantamount in fact perhaps to something like an empty state of bliss. . . . Terror is perhaps the most extreme degree of tension ordinarily observable; the deepest levels of sleep, perhaps the nearest approach to euphoria."—H. S. Sullivan, "Multidisciplined Coordination of Interpersonal Data," in S. S. Sargent and M. W. Smith (eds.), *Culture and Personality* (New York: Viking Fund, 1949), p. 180. The standard work on homeostasis is W. B. Cannon, *The Wisdom of the Body* (New York: Norton, 1939).

[6] H. A. Murray *et al., Explorations in Personality* (New York: Oxford, 1938), p. 92.

[7] The premise that man, and other animals as well, seek pleasure and avoid pain.

[8] For a formulation that represents a rather sharp break with drive-reduction theory see Robert W. White, "Motivation Reconsidered: The Concept of Competence," *Psychological Review*, 66: 297–333 (1959). Cf. the introduction to Chapter 9 above and the works cited in note 4 of that chapter; cf. also Neal E. Miller, "Some Reflections on the Law of Effect Produce a New Alternative to Drive Reduction," and Karl H. Pribram, "Reinforcement Revisited: A Structural View," in Marshall R. Jones (ed.), *Nebraska Sym-*

The Freudian emphasis on the erogenous zones and, in particular, on the "oral" stage of human development has stimulated numerous studies of the outcomes of different feeding practices. It was believed, for example, that frustration in the sucking experience would tend to prolong sucking.[9] Unfortunately, however, these studies have not led to any firm conclusions concerning the relationship between the type and/or schedule of infant feeding and outcomes with respect to the personality of the child.[10]

As long as we have the vital processes in mind, the behaviors denoted by "nurturance" are reasonably clear—feeding the infant, keeping him warm, clean, and dry, and so on. Let us speak of these denotations as constituting a "narrow" conception of nurturance. To many persons, however, nurturance has a far broader set of denotations whereby it includes not only the ministration to the vital processes, but also such behaviors as making "soothing" sounds, stroking the infant's skin, and so on. As one moves from the narrow to the broad conception of nurturance, it becomes increasingly difficult to distinguish the nurturing function from the function of providing emotional gratification.

SOME STUDIES BEARING ON THE NARROW CONCEPTION OF NURTURANCE

As we shall see in this and the following chapter, some of the more interesting studies on the nature and consequences of nurturance have employed animals as subjects. In one such study it was reported that dogs whose sucking was interfered with engaged in nonnutritional sucking.[11] In another study, it was found that, in contrast to rats that were not deprived in infancy, those that were frustrated in their feeding during their infancy showed hoarding behavior as adults.[12] In human beings, however, the results were less clear-cut. A well-controlled study to determine the consequence of not rewarding sucking activity (through feeding the human infants by cup) showed generally nonsignificant results except that infants who sucked at the breast developed a stronger sucking reflex than did those who either sucked bottles or were fed by cup.[13] The findings of a subsequent study were interpreted as supporting

posium on Motivation (Lincoln: University of Nebraska Press, 1963), pp. 65–112 and 113–159 respectively.

[9] Margaret A. Ribble, "Infantile Experience in Relation to Personality Development," in J. McV. Hunt (ed.), *Personality and the Behavior Disorders* (New York: Ronald, 1944), pp. 621–651; D. M. Levy, "Finger Sucking and Accessory Movements in Early Infancy," *American Journal of Psychiatry,* 7: 881–918 (1928).

[10] Bettye M. Caldwell, "The Effects of Infant Care," in Martin L. Hoffman and Lois Wladis Hoffman (eds.), *Review of Child Development Research* (New York: Russell Sage Foundation, 1964), pp. 9–87, esp. pp. 40–41.

[11] D. M. Levy, "Experiments on the Sucking Reflex and Social Behavior of Dogs," *American Journal of Orthopsychiatry,* 4: 203–224 (1934).

[12] J. McV. Hunt *et al.,* "Studies of the Effects of Infantile Experience on Adult Behavior in Rats," *Journal of Comparative and Physiological Psychology,* 40: 291–304 (1947).

[13] H. V. Davis, R. R. Sears, H. C. Miller, and A. J. Brodbeck, "Effects of Cup, Bottle and Breast Feeding on Oral Activities of New-Born Infants," *Pediatrics,* 3: 549–558 (1948).

a hypothesis of Freud that "securing food by sucking increases the erotogeneity of the mouth (increases oral drive)." Furthermore, although the authors of this study saw no reason to regard such an outcome as "seriously harmful," they found that late weaning caused more frustration than did early weaning.[14] This result appears to be contrary to the beliefs of those who, like Ribble (to be considered shortly), subscribe to the "deficit" school of thought.

SOME STUDIES BEARING ON THE BROAD CONCEPTION OF NURTURANCE

Theories about the influence of maternal nurturance broadly conceived have come largely from the writings of psychoanalysts and psychiatrists, who by the nature of their work tend to see cases only when "something goes wrong" and are dependent upon the clinical method. With the clinical method the scientist is confronted with one or more individuals in whom he observes that some condition exists, and he attempts to discover the process that led to the observed condition. The clinical method stands in contrast to the experimental method, in which the scientist makes observations before and after an experimental treatment while he tries through controlling the conditions of the experiment to prevent the intrusion of extraneous influences. When the clinical method is followed, the only evidence concerning the correctness of the clinician's interpretation is the disappearance of the morbid condition (or "cure"), but the patient may get well for quite different reasons. The experimental method provides much greater opportunity to neutralize those different reasons (or extraneous influences). Accordingly, conclusions based on the clinical method have a lower truth value than those based on the experimental method.[15]

With respect to mother-infant interaction the basic generalization to which clinicians seem generally to subscribe is that not only do the infants react differently, depending upon the quantity and quality of maternal care but also that these differential reactions have lasting effects, so that the way in which mothers carry out the function of maternal nurturance may well be reflected in the behavior of their offspring after the latter have become

[14] R. R. Sears and G. W. Wise, "Relation of Cup Feeding in Infancy to Thumb-sucking and the Oral Drive," *American Journal of Orthopsychiatry*, 20: 123–138 (1950). Blau and Blau painstakingly studied the responses of one infant and found more prolonged nonnutritive sucking when the infant was fed slowly than when feeding was rapid.—Theodore H. Blau and Lili R. Blau, "The Sucking Reflex: The Effects of Long Feeding vs. Short Feeding on the Behavior of a Human Infant," *Journal of Abnormal and Social Psychology*, 51: 123–125 (1955).

[15] For a discussion of the clinical and experimental methods see Robert F. Winch and Louis Wolf Goodman, *Selected Studies in Marriage and the Family* (3d ed.; New York: Holt, Rinehart and Winston, Inc., 1968), chap. 1. For a general discussion of the logical pitfalls involved in the design of research see Donald T. Campbell and Julian C. Stanley, *Experimental and Quasi-Experimental Designs for Research* (Skokie, Ill.: Rand McNally, 1968).

adults.[16] Studies by Ribble, Spitz, and Goldfarb are frequently cited in this connection. As we shall see, however, these studies are not sufficiently longitudinal to produce data on the adult consequences of experiences in infancy and childhood.

In a widely discussed study Margaret Ribble[17] holds that because of the transition of the infant at birth from a liquid to a nonliquid environment, the loss of physical support provided by the liquid medium should be compensated for by the physical support involved in "mothering," or physical handling. She deplores the emphasis in some hospitals upon sterile practices and the avoidance of infection, of separating mother and infant as much as possible, and of leaving the infant supported most of the time only by a flat surface. Dr. Ribble believes that not only the support but also the tactual stimulation of "mothering" is desirable for both the emotional and physical development of the infant. She holds that a condition known as "marasmus" (from the Greek word meaning "wasting away") is a consequence of the lack of "mothering." Not more than forty years ago, she says, marasmus under the name of "debility" or "infantile atrophy" was responsible for nearly half the infant mortality rate. The symptoms of marasmus are skin pallor, poor muscle tone, protruding abdomen, gaseous distention of the intestines, and, sometimes, congestion of the liver.[18]

In her study of six hundred newborn infants Dr. Ribble reports that about 30 percent manifested patterns of exaggerated muscular tension. This tension appeared to be relieved under the following conditions: when the infant was sucking, when it was placed in close contact with the body of the mother, by having its head and face stroked, by being placed in a secure position either by being held in its mother's arms or by being supported with pillows and wrappings, by being rocked, by having a warm bath, or by having its head lowered. These activities Dr. Ribble subsumes under the term "mothering" and she observes: "Such mothering definitely fosters functional integration. From my own observations I have found that infants who do not get this sort of mothering show increasing and persistent muscular tension. . . ."[19]

Equally dramatic is evidence reported by René Spitz, who compared infants in a nursery home with others in a foundling home. He found that the infants in the former setting were much better off physically and mentally

---

[16] Some authorities believe that the psychological state of the mother affects the fetus. It is quite possible that this may leave a lasting impression on the personality of the child subsequently to be born. Cf., for example, L. W. Sontag, "Differences in Modifiability of Fetal Behavior and Physiology," *Psychosomatic Medicine*, 6: 151–154 (1944); Antonio Ferreira, "The Pregnant Woman's Emotional Attitude and Its Reflection on the Newborn," *American Journal of Orthopsychiatry*, 30: 553–561 (1960); "Placenta Is No Barrier to Host of Agents: Tufts Pediatrician Reports Many Drugs Taken by Mother May Threaten Fetus," *Medical World News*, March 10, 1967, pp. 116–117.

[17] Margaret A. Ribble, "Infantile Experience in Relation to Personality Development," in Hunt, *op. cit.*, pp. 621–651.

[18] *Ibid.*, p. 634.

[19] *Ibid.*, p. 629.

than those in the foundling home, which did not provide a mother, "not even a substitute-mother, but only an eighth of a nurse." Spitz concluded that infants in the foundling home had virtually no opportunity for what he called "emotional interchange," with the result that they tended to suffer from what he called "anaclitic depression."[20]

Goldfarb studied emotional deprivation through comparing children whose major life experience had been in institutions with children who had been in foster homes most of their lives. At the time of the study the children ranged in age from three to twelve years. He found the institutional experience to be depriving, to constitute "an extreme meagerness of stimulation." He concluded that infant deprivation resulted in the child's being passive and emotionally apathetic.[21] The studies by Ribble, Spitz, and Goldfarb strongly suggest that early deprivation and the absence of stimulation lead to the apathetic, limp, supine, immobile, expressionless kind of individual described by Kingsley Davis as a case of "extreme social isolation."[22] Such studies have led Bowlby to conclude that "when deprived of maternal care, the child's development is almost always retarded—physically, intellectually, and socially—and that symptoms of physical and mental illness may appear."[23]

SOME NEGATIVE VIEWS

Writers who subscribe to the view that parent-child interaction in general —and maternal nurturance, especially—is a (if not *the*) major determinant of the child's personality tend also to adhere to the correlative Freudian principle that the structure of the personality is determined in the first few years of life. There is little evidence on this point. One study reports that judges did better than they should have by chance alone in an effort to pair per-

---

[20] See the following papers by René A. Spitz: "Hospitalism," in *The Psychoanalytic Study of the Child* (New York: International Universities Press, 1945, 1946), I, 53–74 and II, 113–117; "Anaclitic Depression," *ibid.*, 313–342; and "The Role of Ecological Factors in Emotional Development in Infancy," *Child Development*, 20: 145–155 (1949).

[21] W. Goldfarb, "Psychological Privation in Infancy and Subsequent Adjustment," *American Journal of Orthopsychiatry*, 15: 247–255 (1945). Heinicke compared seven two-year-old children in a day nursery with six in a residential nursery and found more sickness and emotional disturbance in the latter group.—Christoph M. Heinicke, "Some Effects of Separating Two-Year-Old Children from Their Parents: A Comparative Study," *Human Relations*, 9: 105–175 (1956). Burlingham and Freud view the institutional setting as presenting the infant and small child with a favorable experience in the narrow conception of nurturance but with an unfavorable one in the broad conception.—Dorothy Burlingham and Anna Freud, *Infants without Families: The Case for and against Residential Nurseries* (London: G. Allen, 1943), pp. 18–21.

[22] "Extreme Social Isolation of a Child," *American Journal of Sociology*, 45: 554–565 (1940); "Final Note on a Case of Extreme Isolation," *American Journal of Sociology*, 52: 432–437 (1947).

[23] John Bowlby, *Maternal Care and Mental Health* (Geneva: World Health Organization, 1952), p. 15. Cf. also Leon J. Yarrow, "Separation from Parents during Early Childhood," in Martin L. Hoffman and Lois Wladis Hoffman, *op. cit.*, pp. 89–136, esp. p. 127.

sonality sketches of seventeen-year-olds with sketches on the same boys and girls based on observations over the first two years of life. Needless to say, the pairing was far from perfect.[24]

Not all psychologists believe that the infant is so sensitive to his early experiences or that his personality is permanently molded by them. For example, John Anderson holds that Ribble's point of view misrepresents the facts. He contends that the child is not as passive nor as responsive to stimulation, nor as delicate and tender as Ribble suggests.[25] Pinneau has written a more detailed, exhaustive, and devastating critique of Ribble's work. He contends that a review of the related empirical studies in physiology and psychology shows Ribble to be wrong in practically all her conclusions.[26] Sewell found that five- and six-year-old children who had been breast-fed did not differ significantly on several measures of personality from children who had been bottle-fed, that those who had been fed on a self-demand nursing schedule did not differ from those fed on a regular nursing schedule, and that those who had been weaned gradually did not differ from those who had been weaned abruptly.[27]

Reactive Outrage

Those who are amused by intellectual donnybrooks may be interested in following the reaction to the foregoing type of criticism. One line of defense has been to make a virtue of the methodologically weak clinical method and to assert that nonclinicians lack the skill and sensitivity to make the necessarily subtle observations. The theory, too, is represented as so subtle that the critics are seen as lacking the sophistication even to understand the propositions they have the temerity to test. A good example is a book by Brody in which she criticizes Pinneau's critique of Ribble on the ground that Pinneau "cannot deal with [cannot understand? is unwilling to accept for some reason?] the concept of a psychic experience in infancy, except in mechanistic terms" (a criticism that no doubt has clear meaning to the clinical in-group).[28] But

[24] Patricia Neilon, "Shirley's Babies after Fifteen Years: A Personality Study," *Journal of Genetic Psychology*, 73: 175–186 (1948). In another study there were very few significant correlations between maternal nurturance (narrowly and broadly conceived) in infancy and projective test results of the offspring at ages 9, 12, and 18 years.—M. I. Heinstein, "Behavioral Correlates of Breast-Bottle Regimes under Varying Parent-Infant Relationships," *Monographs of the Society for Research in Child Development*, Vol. 28, No. 4, 1963.

[25] J. E. Anderson, "Personality Organization in Children," *American Psychologist*, 3: 409–416 (1948).

[26] S. R. Pinneau, "A Critique on the Articles by Margaret Ribble," *Child Development*, 21: 203–228 (1950).

[27] William H. Sewell, "Infant Training and the Personality of the Child," *American Journal of Sociology*, 58: 150–159 (1952).

[28] Sylvia Brody, *Patterns of Mothering; Maternal Influence during Infancy* (New York: International Universities Press, 1956), pp. 81–82; introduction by René A. Spitz.

thereupon Brody admits that knowledge of the process through which maternal influences take effect is meager; indeed, her own study can be interpreted as showing little support for theorists of the Ribble-Spitz school.[29]

Where Do We Stand? Agnosticism or Synthesis?

Naturally one wonders what is the most judicious position to take in this matter. To this writer it seems perfectly possible, even importuningly obvious, to come to an agnostic position, i.e., that because the theories, evidence, and beliefs of the experts are contradictory, there is nothing on which to base belief at this time. It should be emphasized, however, that to accept the agnostic position is to accept the proposition that our knowledge adds up to zero. After some further presentation of the views of experts in Chapter 14, it will be argued that it is intellectually respectable—although not evidentially necessary—to avoid the agnostic position.

For the moment, then, let us turn away from the topic of a deficit in nurturance and its long-range consequences and take up instead a short-range consequence of maternal nurturance narrowly conceived.

The Maternal Role as the Biosocial Basis of Infantile Love

Because of his helplessness the human infant can achieve tension reduction only with the assistance and cooperation of another person or persons. The ministering to the needs of the infant—the providing of food, warmth, dryness, and so on—constitutes the nurturing function—one of the two parental functions. This function is usually carried out largely by the mother. Since it is usually the mother who provides the infant with tension reduction, there exists the opportunity for the infant to associate the pleasurable achievement of equilibrium with the presence and activities of the mother. Within the first three weeks the infant is capable of recognizing the mother's voice. Because of the slowness of development of the visual apparatus, visual recognition of the mother comes somewhat later.[30] (Orientation to objects appears to be developed by the end of the fourteenth month.[31]) As awareness develops in the infant, he becomes cognizant that the mother is the principal means of inducing pleasurable states in his own organism. Lois Murphy writes: ". . . the immediate oral stimulus of milk is associated with satisfaction, the tactual-

---

[29] *Ibid.*, pp. 344–346.

[30] Gardner Murphy, Lois Murphy, and T. M. Newcomb, *Experimental Social Psychology* (New York: Harper & Row, 1937), p. 217.

[31] J. S. Watson, "Perception of Object Orientation in Infants," *Merrill-Palmer Quarterly*, 12: 73–94 (1965).

olfactory stimulus of breast is a sign of the imminent availability of milk, and subsequently there emerges the multi-sensory perception of mother, whose image, rich and complex, ultimately becomes a symbol of all nurturance."[32]

This recognition of the mother or mother-substitute as the agent of the pleasurable sensation of tension reduction provides the basis for the infant's positive feeling (or positive affect) toward the mother figure. It is the writer's view that the earliest form of human love[33] is the positive affect that coincides with tension reduction, and that is associated with the mother figure. In terms of the considerations introduced thus far, therefore, it appears that we have the conditions from which the infant's love of his mother develops, namely, recurring tension in the organism of the infant, his awareness of the tension, his awareness that the mother is the means of relieving it.

As the foregoing observations imply, the very young infant is largely a reacting machine. Early in infancy he responds to almost nothing but his own visceral processes. The development of the senses provides the neural conditions necessary for the beginnings of external orientation, the growing awareness of external objects, and, more important for our purposes, the growing awareness of social objects (i.e., objects that respond). It appears that as the infant begins to learn that persons have the capacity to gratify his needs, they begin to assume for him the power to evoke needs.

The needs that persons can evoke are in part old, and in part new. For example, the conditioning process to which we have referred may well develop to the point where the approach of the mother stimulates the erstwhile quiescent infant to cry. His cessation of crying upon receiving the breast or bottle suggests that the external stimulus of the mother has evoked the hunger need.

Freud asserts that as the infant learns to distinguish between himself and his environment, he loses an infantile sense of omnipotence and becomes gradually aware of his great dependence on others.[34] Whether or not such awareness develops in just the manner Freud believed, it does seem clear that unless nurturance is so complete as to reduce each of the infant's tensions before it develops to an uncomfortable level, the infant must learn that he is dependent on others who are not always able or willing to respond immediately to his summons. It seems probable that this awareness of dependence is a necessary but not a sufficient condition to cause the infant (1) to become increasingly responsive to a greater variety of cues in the behavior of persons around him and (2) to develop new needs that are social in nature.

Physical needs are distinguished from social needs in that (1) the former are necessary to the operation of vital processes whereas the latter are not; and (2) the former are present in the organism at birth or develop in the

---

[32] Lois Barclay Murphy, *Personality in Young Children*, Vol. I, *Methods for the Study of Personality in Young Children* (New York: Basic Books, 1956), pp. 18–19.

[33] Love is defined on page 483 below.

[34] Sigmund Freud, *Civilization and Its Discontents* (3d ed.; London: Hogarth, 1946), pp. 11–14.

course of maturation, whereas the latter develop in social interaction. The very young infant manifests only physical needs; such social needs as those for affection, response, recognition, and reassurance are quite evident in older children, adolescents, and adults.

Such studies as those of Spitz, considered above, suggest that another condition, in addition to awareness of dependence, enters into the infant's responsiveness. This is the belief on the part of the infant that others in the environment will respond—part of the time, at least—in such fashion as to reduce the infant's tensions. Thus it is proposed that the two conditions—awareness of dependence *and* belief in the nurturance of others—are sufficient for the infant to develop social awareness and social needs.

Summary

Chapter 13 may be summarized in the following points:

1. In any society parenthood involves both positive and negative values. We have presented evidence to suggest that conditions in American cities have emphasized the negative values, whereas the migration to the suburbs has been motivated by a wish to shift the balance toward the positive values while retaining many of the advantages of the city (see Chapter 6).

2. The conflict in the cultural definition between positive and negative values of parenthood is reflected in the parents' personalities through their ambivalence toward the child.

3. The nature of the parent-child relationship is such as to produce in the infant (and also in the parent) frustration and anxiety as well as gratification.

4. To a considerable degree, especially in the infant, the biophysical basis of activity is tension and the drive to achieve homeostasis.

5. Tension is unpleasurable and its release, especially at a relatively rapid rate, is pleasurable.

6. During infancy the child comes to associate external objects and persons, especially the mother, with the release of tension.

7. The association of social objects, especially the mother, with the pleasure derived from the release of tension, is the sociopsychological basis of infantile love.

14

Rearing by the Book

Introduction

In this chapter, as in Chapter 6, we depart more than usual from the purpose of building a general theory of the family and consider a state of affairs that seems characteristically American. This is the uncertainty of parents about how to raise children and institutional responses to this uncertainty with respect to family-life education and advice giving to parents.

After noting something of the magnitude of advice-giving activities and of the intensity of the demand implied in the scale of these enterprises, we shall look at the history of such advice in this country. Perhaps the most conspicuous historical fact concerns the vacillations over the years in the content of the advice given. These shifts seem to be related to different assumptions as to the original nature of man and also to the dearth of scientific evidence upon which to base practical advice. We shall examine a major point of disagreement in the advice that has been given and see what the available evidence leads us to conclude.

It should be noted that this chapter concerns the advice that has been given to parents of infants and young children; it does *not* consider the child-rearing practices themselves.

Examples of Advice Giving

Many modern American parents express doubt as to just how they should rear their children, how to handle problems of discipline, of incentive, and the like. The number of people in parental quandaries has seemingly resulted in a widespread demand for advice. In response to this demand professionals from a variety of occupations have moved in to take over the function of advising parents in problems of child rearing. It will be evident that the verb "advise" is being used in a broad sense since it refers to the gamut of functionaries from psychiatrist and pediatrician through social worker, minister, and teacher, to journalist; to the range in competence from research scientist to charlatan; and to organizations from the child guidance clinics through the schools to the PTA's. That Dr. Spock has become a household name suggests the degree of his success in displacing grandmother as the authority on child rearing. The degree to which Dr. Spock has become a household name is indicated by the fact that 21 million copies of his *The Common Sense Book of Baby and Child Care* have been sold.[1]

More modestly packaged advice comes in syndicated and local newspaper columns. Some years ago a representative list of questions parents wanted answered—or at least that the editors of parents' magazines thought parents wanted answered—included the following problems:

We made our child behave
I stopped spanking when I found out why I did
What happened when my child wanted a puppy but I didn't
I've stopped yelling
Hostility—how it develops in children and how it should be handled
When and how to wean your baby
What you should know about selecting a bike or trike
If your child says "Teacher and I don't get along"
If your child threatens to run away
What to do if you are all tired out
How to start a school camp[2]

(Of course other relationships than those between parent and child come in for public scrutiny and journalistic counseling. An analysis in the 1950's of some six thousand letters to one advice-to-the-worried columnist revealed a major emphasis on man-woman problems, both within and outside marriage. The problems presented, in order of frequency, were premarital intercourse, unfaithfulness of the second party, alcoholism of the second party, sexual incompatibility with the mate, religious difference, and age difference.[3])

For more than half a century the U.S. Children's Bureau has published a

---

[1] The first edition was published in hard covers in 1945 by Duell, Sloan & Pearce–Meredith Press (New York) and in paperback in 1946 by Pocket Books (New York). A second major revision was published in 1968 in hard covers by Meredith Press (Des Moines, Iowa) and in paperback by Pocket Books. A review of the new features of this revision appears in Katharine Davis Fishman, "The Less Permissive Dr. Spock," *The New York Times Book Review*, February 16, 1969, pp. 4–5, 32. That his book has been translated into twenty-nine languages implies that the questions he addresses may not be uniquely American.

[2] Donald Brieland, "Uses of Research in Recent Popular Parent Education Literature," *Marriage and Family Living*, 19: 60–65 (1957), at p. 62.

[3] Christine H. Hillman, "An Advice Column's Challenge for Family-Life Education," *Marriage and Family Living*, 16: 51–54 (1954).

series of pamphlets of advice on child rearing. (Below we shall take up Martha Wolfenstein's and Michael Gordon's analyses of trends in one of these pamphlets—*Infant Care*.) Numerous other series of pamphlets are available, for example: those of Science Research Associates in Chicago, Child Study Association in New York, and the Louisiana Association of Mental Health (publisher of the "Pierre the Pelican" series).

To this point the discussion of the present chapter has been couched in popular language. It will deepen our understanding of the situation to rephrase the phenomenon in the jargon of sociology. The roles of parents, as our analysis has been emphasizing, center on the nurturing and controlling of children. As we shall see, the uncertainty centers about the manner of performing these parental functions. To know how to nurture and to control a child in the manner approved by one's society—if there is consensus on the topic—is to know the crux of the parental roles as defined in that society. How does it happen that our society appears to bumble and muddle its way through in the task of socializing its members into parental (and other familial) roles?

Breakdown of Tradition and Demand for Advice

Generations ago mothers learned from *their* mothers the "right" ways of nursing, weaning, toilet training, and rearing children in general. (Although we can trace advice-to-parents back into the eighteenth century, still advice giving apparently did not become a large-scale operation until the twentieth century.) In the present context we are not concerned with the question as to whether the child-rearing practices of two or three centuries ago seem to be right or wrong by contemporary standards. Rather, our point is that at that time techniques of child rearing were quite firmly established in the folkways. Whatever the techniques, maternal grandmother could feel secure in teaching them to her daughter, and there would be no ground for the young mother to feel anxiety in putting those procedures into practice. As the authority of tradition has been breaking down, however, and as the elders have come to be regarded as fogies rather than as storehouses of wisdom, mothers have become progressively uncertain and insecure about the techniques of parenthood. As Martha Wolfenstein observes, "in a changing culture the elders lose their infallibility,"[4] to which we may add that it is under this condition that Dr. Spock supersedes grandmother.

[4] Margaret Mead and Martha Wolfenstein (eds.), *Childhood in Contemporary Cultures* (Chicago: University of Chicago Press, 1955), p. 145. That such a breakdown of tradition with resulting parental uncertainty is not unique to the United States is indicated by a study of the Japanese family that concludes: ". . . Japanese parents of today, irrespective of where they live, are at a loss to know how they should bring up their children, and this applies equally to the parents of infants, of young schoolchildren and of adolescents."— Kazuo Aoi *et al.*, "A Comparative Study of Home Discipline: Rural-Urban, Sex and Age Differences," paper presented before the Ninth International Seminar on Family Research. Tokyo, Japan, September 1965, p. 20.

Advice Giving

SUNLEY ON THE NINETEENTH CENTURY

It appears that historical perspective is usually useful in illuminating a contemporary phenomenon. Except for a thirty-year gap (1860–1890) the child-rearing literature in the United States has been subjected to analysis for the period from 1820 until about 1950. The most obvious and fascinating finding of these studies is that the content of advice to parents has shifted widely—probably "vacillated" is a more precise word.

Robert Sunley has analyzed American child-rearing literature over the forty-year period immediately preceding the Civil War.[5] Bottle feeding had just become popular in the United States by the beginning of this period. The rubber nipple was patented in 1845, and the first good formula was developed about 1860.[6] Mothers were advised to breast-feed their children and were cautioned against using wet nurses on the ground that they might alienate the baby's love. Moreover, since it was thought that fretfulness of children of the poor was often a consequence of "the mother's ill-governed passions transmitted through the milk," it followed that the wet nurse, who was frequently from a poorer class, might have an adverse effect on the infant.[7]

Sunley reports that contradictory themes in advice were evident in the nineteenth century. As in the twentieth century, there were exponents of indulgent treatment (with advocacy of demand feeding and providing a happy childhood) and of stern discipline (let the baby cry, toilet-train it early, break its will). Solitary prayer and Bible reading were proposed "to counteract the child's desire to masturbate."[8]

STENDLER ON "SIXTY YEARS OF CHILD TRAINING PRACTICES"

After a lapse of thirty years from 1860 the message of American child-rearing literature is again under scrutiny—this time by Celia B. Stendler,[9] who analyzed, by ten-year periods, the articles on child rearing that appeared from 1890 to about 1950 in three magazines: *Ladies Home Journal, Woman's Home Companion,* and *Good Housekeeping.* Judging by the number of articles appearing in 1890 and at the end of the period under study Stendler concluded that there was just about the same amount of interest in the topic of child rearing. In 1890 there was a strong emphasis on what was spoken of as "character development." The concept of "personality development" had not yet

---

[5] Robert Sunley, "Early Nineteenth-Century American Literature on Child-Rearing." chap. 9, in Mead and Wolfenstein, *op. cit.,* pp. 150–167.

[6] *Ibid.,* p. 154.

[7] *Ibid.,* pp. 153–154.

[8] *Ibid.,* p. 158.

[9] "Sixty Years of Child Training Practices," *Journal of Pediatrics,* 36:122–134 (1950).

appeared. "Good moral character" was manifested in the Victorian ideals of courtesy, honesty, orderliness, industry, and generosity. "Sixty-one per cent of the articles published during [1890] emphasized the importance of a good Christian atmosphere in the home with Mother seen as the crucial person in the formation of good character."[10] The emphasis on the mother as the important parent in character formation had already been evident in the early part of the nineteenth century.[11] In contrast to earlier generations, which had perceived woman as the less moral sex and had accepted Eve as her symbol, the 1890's, says Stendler, "exalted [motherhood] as never before," as, for example, by Whitman in poetry and by Whistler on canvas. Stendler interprets this phenomenon as follows: In 1890 business enterprise was enjoying success, but business—the arena of Father's activity—was seen as sordid, an arena in which the traditional morals were not operative. "To offset this sordidness, women were put on a pedestal. Maternal love and affection were emphasized as a possible check on the evils of materialism. A romantic and sentimental picture of women in general was built up and mothers in particular basked in this new glory."[12]

Relatively speaking, the advice of 1890 was rather indulgent. References to feeding advocated a loosely scheduled procedure, and "discipline" involved the use of rewards. By 1900 the pendulum had begun to swing away from indulgence. The danger with love and affection was that the children "were getting away with too much," and by 1900 "discipline" had come to mean punishment. Through the early years studied by Stendler (1890, 1900, and 1910) there was frequent reference to God—as the source of the wee ones and of guidance in developing sound moral character. There was little reference to the Divine after 1910.

In 1910 good moral character was still the prime objective, but the prescribed mixture of discipline (= punishment) and of affection had altered—much more of the former and much less of the latter. The physical manifestation of love through handling the infant was thought to "lead to precocity in the older child and dullness in the man." Picking up the baby spent his strength, which it was thought he needed for growing. "Mothers were admonished to insist upon obedience at all times, and if temper tantrums resulted, they should be ignored."[13] It seems consistent with the tenor of the foregoing, moreover, that during the decade 1900–1910 there had been a marked increase in the prescribing of strict scheduling—less than one quarter of the articles advocated the strict schedule in 1900, more than three quarters did in 1910.

By 1920 the articles dealing with infant disciplines were unanimously advising rigid feeding schedules, early toilet training, and letting baby cry it

[10] *Ibid.*, p. 125.
[11] Sunley, in Mead and Wolfenstein, *op. cit.*, p. 152.
[12] Stendler, "Sixty Years of Child Training Practices," *loc.i cit.*, p. 126.
[13] *Ibid.*, p. 128.

out. Although this general theme was familiar in 1910, its intensity had become stronger by 1920. But most noteworthy was the fact that the "reason" for following this prescription had changed. In 1910 children were not to be handled "because stimulation might lead to precocity or because that was the way Nature intended them to be raised," but the influence of J. B. Watson and his behavioristic psychology led to the interpretation in 1920 that to pick up the crying infant would result in conditioning the baby to future crying.

The major interest of the articles in 1920 (as well as in 1930), however, was in physical development and nutrition. Mothers were advised to initiate height-weight charts for their children. In 1930, reports Stendler, "the up-to-date mother was one who knew her calories and her vitamins."[14]

The high point in antiseptic sternness was reached (for this cycle) in 1930. Stendler believes that some reaction against extreme applications of Freudian views may have paved the way for the prevalence in 1930 of the "feed-'em-on-schedule, let-'em-cry-it-out" school of thought.

During the latter half of the 1930–1940 decade the pendulum began its return trip toward the indulgent terminus. Margaret Ribble[15] was a widely quoted apostle of the return to a "cuddling" conception of "mothering." It will be recalled that in Chapter 13 we considered the views of Ribble, who held that thousands of infants had died because they had not been treated with maternal indulgence. By 1940 two thirds of the articles that dealt with infant disciplines were advising self-regulatory, permissive procedures, and the "mothering, delayed-toilet-training, wean-'em-late" school of thought was still ascendant in the late 1940's, when Stendler concluded her study. As Vincent has phrased it, the period 1935–1945 might be called "baby's decade"—a period when the interests and authority of the mother "become secondary to . . . baby's demands . . . 'Momism' and *cherchez la mère* become thematic."[16]

WOLFENSTEIN ON "INFANT CARE"

Somewhat similar in method and conclusions is a study by Martha Wolfenstein.[17] In 1914 the U.S. Children's Bureau began publication of the pamphlet "Infant Care," which in its various editions has been circulated by the millions of copies. Wolfenstein examined every edition of which she could locate a copy (1914, 1921, 1929, 1938, 1942, 1945, and 1951) in order to determine the trends in advice given. She was unable to locate copies of the editions of 1926 and 1940. As did Stendler, Wolfenstein turned up numerous reversals in doctrine. For example, in the 1920's bowel training was to be *completed*

---

[14] *Ibid.*, p. 130.
[15] Citations to the relevant work of Ribble appear in the last chapter.
[16] Clark E. Vincent, "Trends in Infant Care Ideas," *Child Development*, 22: 199–209 1951), at p. 205.
[17] Martha Wolfenstein, "Trends in Infant Care," *American Journal of Orthopsychiatry*, 23: 120–130 (1953); "Fun Morality: An Analysis of Recent American Child-Training Literature," chap. 10 in Mead and Wolfenstein, *op. cit.*, pp. 168–178.

by the time the baby was eight months old; in the 1940's bowel training was to be *begun* when the baby was eight months old. In 1938 thumb-sucking was bad, and the pamphlet proposed a stiff cuff that would prevent the baby from sucking his thumb; in four years—the edition of 1942—thumb-sucking had become a harmless pleasure, and mothers were advised not to interfere with it.

Wolfenstein notes a period of strict scheduling with respect to weaning and bowel training in the 1929 and 1938 editions. The reasoning that supports this policy has to do with the assumptions that mother and infant are engaged in a struggle for domination and that it is bad for the baby to dominate the mother; strictness of scheduling, it is reasoned, gives the tactical advantage to the mother. In the next two editions (1942 and 1945), however, the child had become harmless, "in effect devoid of sexual or dominating impulses,"[18] and thus the danger that the baby would dominate the parents had become meaningless. In the later editions it seems that attention and care, "far from making him a tyrant, will make him less demanding later on." Here it seems that we can almost see a problem sufficiently clearly stated to be researchable. This particular bit of confusion could be stated in terms of the consequence of gratification (assuming that it is possible to identify those acts that are gratifying). Then we might ask, Over the long haul will taking care of the child when it cries build up its security and level of gratification so that it will become generally less fretful and better tempered and thus cry less, or will this care reinforce the crying, make crying an autonomous motive, and thereby increase the frequency of the child's future crying? Perhaps the problem is still too fuzzily conceived to be immediately researchable, but the direction to an answer does appear to be discernible.

In one paragraph Wolfenstein summarizes the range of the recommendations that mothers have received on the subject of the child's masturbating:

> In the 1914 edition of *Infant Care* (p. 62), masturbation is called an "injurious practice"; it "easily grows beyond control . . . children are sometimes wrecked for life." "It must be eradicated . . . treatment consists in mechanical restraints." In the 1921 revision (pp. 45–46), this is already toned down a bit: "a common habit . . . it grows worse if left uncontrolled." The mechanical restraints are slightly moderated; the nightgown sleeves must still be pinned down, but it is no longer specified (as it was in 1914) that the child's legs should be tied to opposite sides of the crib. In 1929, the atmosphere is much more relaxed: this "early period of what may be called sex awareness will pass away unless it is emphasized by unwise treatment on the part of adults." Physical restraints are now considered of little value. "Occupation and diversion" are the best treatment. The baby may be given a toy to hold until he goes to sleep (1929 ed., pp. 60–61). The 1938 revision (p. 49) anticipates the exploratory theme which subsequently becomes central: children "discover accidentally" that they can get pleasure from touching their genitals. The point about spontaneous discovery is repeated. In 1942, we are told: "Babies want to

---

[18] "Trends in Infant Care," *loc. cit.*, p. 121.

handle and investigate everything that they can see and reach. When a baby discovers his genital organs he will play with them. . . . A wise mother will not be concerned about this." Also, "see that he has a toy to play with and he will not need to use his body as a plaything" (1942 ed., p. 60). There is no change in 1945. In the 1951 edition (p. 87), we read: "Sometimes a baby handles his genitals when he is sitting on the toilet, or at other times when he is undressed. This is a common thing, and usually will not amount to anything if let alone. But sometimes it is disturbing to mothers, so if you feel uncomfortable about it you can try giving him a toy to hold while he's on the toilet seat. Don't confuse him by saying, 'No, No.'" The increased moderation in handling masturbation in the course of these years is accompanied by an increasingly diluted version of the activity. From expressing an urgent and dangerous impulse of the child, masturbation becomes an act about which the child has no feelings and which is only inexplicably embarrassing to the mother.[19]

And so Martha Wolfenstein has shown us that over four decades the *Infant Care* bulletins of the U.S. Children's Bureau have expressed just about the complete range of views on the subject of masturbation. But vacillation has occurred as well with respect to other "problems" of child rearing, and she has summarized the trends in the following table:[20]

SEVERITY IN THE HANDLING OF	1914 TO 1921	1921 TO 1929	1929 TO 1938	1938 TO 1942–45	1942–45 TO 1951
Masturbation	Decreases	Decreases	Constant	Decreases	Constant
Thumb-sucking	Constant	Decreases	Constant	Decreases	Decreases
Weaning	Increases	Increases	Constant	Decreases	Constant
Bowel training	Increases	Increases	Decreases	Decreases	Decreases
Bladder training	Increases	Decreases	Decreases	Decreases	Decreases

In addition to documenting the vacillation in expert advice, Wolfenstein has brought to our attention what seems to be the most recent tack. This is suggested in the last sentence of the paragraph quoted above—the disposition to interpret a problem not as "real" but as attitudinal on the part of the parent. In discussing what she calls "fun morality" she asserts that to have fun "has tended to become obligatory" in American culture. The implication for infant care is that a mother is supposed to "enjoy" her baby. If mother objects to thumb-sucking, the question is not why does the baby suck his thumb and what should be done about it, but why does mother object. If baby handles

---

[19] Martha Wolfenstein, "Trends in Infant Care," *American Journal of Orthopsychiatry*, 23: 120–130 (1953), at p. 122. Reprinted by permission of the Journal. In a book of advice on child rearing published in 1913 masturbation is not listed in the index, but the behavior is listed under self-abuse. Subtitles under self-abuse include brings disease, girls cannot afford, high thoughts possible, hope for all, invites cholera, perseverance will cure, and weakens memory.

[20] *Ibid.*, p. 129.

his genitals while sitting on the toilet and mother feels uncomfortable, she should hand him a toy—to dispel her discomfiture.

In the 1955 edition of "Infant Care" (published after the period covered by Wolfenstein's analysis) we can see the theme concerning the importance of the mother's attitude applied to the topic of feeding: "It matters much less ... whether you feed your baby by breast or by bottle than that you feel easy and relaxed and confident in your ability to provide for him. If you can nurse him, and want to, fine. If not, his progress on a bottle can be just as successful. It is the spirit in which you feed your baby that counts, rather than the particular kind of milk he gets."—P. 11. ("Counts" with respect to what, we wonder?)

Michael Gordon has extended the survey of *Infant Care* through the edition of 1963, which, he says, represents a major revision. According to his analysis, however, there was no major change since Wolfenstein's study, which terminated with the 1951 edition: ". . . gradualism and gentleness are stressed. . . ." He adds that he sees no evidence of a movement away from permissiveness.[21]

Child Rearing and Original Nature: The Puritan and more recent views

It is useful to think of any society's regimen of child rearing as involving —implicitly or explicitly—three basic conceptions: (1) of original nature, (2) of the ideal adult member of that society, and (3) of the procedures to mold the raw material (1) into the finished product (2). Because the colonial Puritans offer a rather obvious and easily understood example, it will be instructive to consider their views.

Puritan culture bore a heavy cast of the theology of the Old Testament. Children were thought to be depraved at birth. If left to their own designs, it was thought that they would grow up to be pleasure-seeking adults. The approved adult was industrious, pious, and, above all, self-denying. Therefore, it seemed to follow that the child-rearing regimen should be one of sternness, work, and denial of the flesh. The theory of the depravity of child nature, which was reflected in Puritan methods of training and disciplining children, is seen in Cotton Mather's account of an interview with his daughter which occurred some thirty years before his death:

> I took my little daughter Katy [age four] into my study and there told my child that I am to dy shortly and she must, when I am dead, remember everything I now said unto her. I sett before her the sinfull condition of her nature and charged her to pray in secret places every day. That God for the sake of Jesus Christ would give her a new heart. . . .

[21] Michael Gordon, "*Infant Care* Revisited," *Journal of Marriage and the Family*, 30: 578–583 (1968). Quotation is from p. 583.

I gave her to understand that when I am taken from her she must look to meet with more humbling afflictions than she does now she has a tender father to provide for her.[22]

Another example of the child-rearing regimen is the following quotation from a book of etiquette circulated in colonial days for the edification of children:

> Never sit down at the table till asked, and after the blessing. Ask for nothing; tarry till it be offered thee. Speak not. Bite not thy bread but break it. Take salt only with a clean knife. Dip not the meat in the same. Hold not thy knife upright but sloping, and lay it down at right hand of plate with blade on plate. Look not earnestly at any other that is eating. When moderately satisfied leave the table. Sing not, hum not, wriggle not. Spit nowhere in the room but in the corner. . . . When any speak to thee, stand up. Say not I have heard it before. Never endeavor to help him out if he tell it not right. Snigger not; never question the truth of it.[23]

A corollary of the conception of the original depravity of children was the idea that children were to be treated sternly until they were "broken." Parents, teachers, and ministers joined in the doctrine that "foolishness is bound up in the heart of the child" and that the only cure for that foolishness lay in plenty of useful work, stern repression, sharp correction, and, most important, the rod. Thus it is reported that "stern old grandfathers whipped their children at home for being whipped at school."[24] The Pilgrim preacher, John Robinson, wrote: "Surely there is in all children . . . a stubbernes and stoutnes of minde arising from naturall pride which must in the first place be broken and beaten down [so that] the foundation of their education being layd in humilitie and tractablenes other virtues may in their time be built thereon."[25]

Puritan parents were not to love their children "too intensely." A couple, having lost two children by drowning, interpreted the tragedy as God's retribution for their having been too indulgent with them.[26]

We may summarize the views of the colonial Puritans as follows:

> To them the human infant was conceived in sin and born an immoral little beast.
> If allowed to develop in conformity with his natural bent, he would become the victim of his passions.
> The desired adult was one who saw clearly the distinction between good and evil and never gave expression to his passions.
> Consistent with these conceptions was their regimen of strictly enforced obedience to the point of breaking the will of the child as the approved

---

[22] Quoted in A. W. Calhoun, *A Social History of the American Family* (New York: Barnes & Noble, 1945), I, 75–76.

[23] *Ibid.*, pp. 112–113.

[24] A. M. Earle, *Child Life in Colonial Days* (New York: Macmillan, 1899), p. 197.

[25] *Ibid.*, pp. 191–192.

[26] John Winthrop, *The History of New England from 1630 to 1649* (Boston: Little, Brown, 1853), II, 411.

method of producing a conforming moral adult from a sin-laden, passion-ridden babe.

Another example of the way in which the conception of original nature has provided a rationalization for child-rearing procedures comes from four Eastern European cultures. Infants were swaddled in each of the four societies, but for different "reasons." The Russian reason was to prevent self-mutilation, and this reason betrayed a conception of dangerous strength in the infant. The Poles sought to prevent the infant from playing with "bad" parts of his body: toes and genitalia. Here is revealed the idea that the body is partly "good" and partly "bad." Jewish Poles swaddled to protect the infant against the cold and menacing outer world. This idea suggests the vulnerability of the infant to the cruelties of anti-Semitism. The Rumanian reason was to prevent the child from deriving pleasure from his body and involved the conception that such pleasure would be sinful.[27]

Over the last fifty years it appears that we can differentiate at least three different conceptions of original nature in American society, and it seems reasonable to presume that there are plenty of exponents of each of these three conceptions today. We have already noted the first—the Calvinist-Puritan view implied in the "hell-fire and brimstone" sermons of our more fundamentalist preachers. Wolfenstein has called our attention to one manifestation of this conception—the 1914 conviction that havoc would be wrought by the infant's savage sexual impulses if he were permitted any masturbatory gratification.

A second view is that the infant, rather than being originally evil, is originally innocent. This Rousseauan concept of original goodness carries the idea that the "world," as contrasted with the child, is full of vice and wickedness, sorrow and tragedy. Since purity is desirable, it follows that the child should be "sheltered" from the world of evil and sorrow. Accordingly, the child should be "protected" from both direct experience with and even knowledge about sex, drinking, smoking, profanity, and other "vices." It is this conception of original nature that Margaret Mead has in mind when she asserts that American parents believe they should present themselves to their children as considerably more moral than they actually are.[28] This view seems to have been a major premise of the youth culture of the latter 1960's—a *Weltanschauung* of the pure, altruistic, loving individual pitting his puny strength against the wicked, cruel, aggressive, greedy social structures of his society—against the "establishment" and the "military-industrial complex."

The third conception of original nature may be seen as a variant of the second: that the infant is not only originally innocent but also rich in potentiality while at the same time being very fragile and responsive to both good and bad treatment. According to this third conception a favorable environ-

---

[27] Ruth Benedict, "Child Rearing in Certain European Countries," *American Journal of Orthopsychiatry*, 19: 342–348 (1949). Discussion by Margaret Mead, pp. 349–350.

[28] Margaret Mead, *And Keep Your Powder Dry* (New York: Morrow, 1943), p. 127.

ment during the first few months and years of life, especially a favorable experience with a warm, nurturing mother, enables the many potentialities born in the infant to develop so that the resulting adult will be spontaneous, creative, warm, kind, friendly, and secure. Correlatively it is believed that an unfavorable experience in infancy and childhood, again especially in the maternal relationship, will produce the opposite kind of adult—rigid, cruel, insecure. Probably the most dramatic spokesmen for their views on good maternal care have been Ribble and Spitz, who have held up the prospect of marasmus and anaclitic depression, respectively, as the outcome of inadequate mothering.[29]

The Traditional and the New Developmental Points of View

From the standpoint of immediate parent-child interaction a very important dimension is that of directiveness versus permissiveness, or, as the child psychologists phrase it, the traditional versus the developmental point of view. The traditional point of view involves ordering and forbidding procedures; it involves being directive with the child, the presumption that the child is less wise than the parent, and that the parent should make many decisions for the child. The developmental point of view implies a relatively permissive atmosphere, the idea that the child should be allowed to evolve from his own potentialities, to make his own mistakes, to develop into a unique and creative person. From the researches of Stendler and Wolfenstein it seems clear that over a period of perhaps twenty-five years or so and beginning in the middle thirties, the direction of advice to parents has been toward the developmental, permissive, indulgent point of view. Sibylle Escalona has thus summarized this philosophy of child rearing:

> To select a few representative items: It is now thought that it is up to us as adults to meet the needs of the younger child, rather than to expect early adaptation from him. To wit, self-demand schedules and all that goes with them. Among the needs of the young child we recognize the need for affection and for an intimate relationship with the mother as of very great importance, tending to evaluate it as more crucial than the need for good physical care. We prize self-expression, sincerity of feeling, and spontaneous interest above good manners, self-restraint, or intellectual accomplishment.[30]

Judged from the "old" or traditional point of view, an obedient and reserved child reflects credit on his parents. From the "new" or developmental

---

[29] That all three of these conceptions of original nature were present in nineteenth-century America is reported by Sunley in Mead and Wolfenstein, *op. cit.*, p. 163.

[30] Sibylle Escalona, "A Commentary upon Some Recent Changes in Child-Rearing Practices," *Child Development*, 20: 157–162 (1949), at p. 160.

point of view such a child is the inhibited (and hence unfortunate) product of a repressive (and hence undesirable) home. It is clear that the "new" approach places much more emphasis on the welfare of the child than did the "old," and much less on the pleasure and convenience of the parent. Escalona has offered the interesting hypothesis that parents have been taking up the indulgent-developmental technique of child rearing not only because of the considerable promotion it has received from psychoanalysts, psychologists, and others, but also because many parents feel a load of unconscious guilt about the failure of the parental generation to provide an acceptable world for the children to live in. As she also points out, the indulgent method of child rearing with demand-feeding and related features can be very wearing on the parent: "Self-demand, especially when the baby is breast-fed or when it is believed that close contact between mother and child at feeding time is important, means that all other activities must be adapted to the child's rhythm and makes it almost impossible to get away from home. Giving the child free scope to explore the world means endless patience and labor in cleaning up messes and in countless other ways."[31] As a consequence of the fatigue and frustration, a considerable negative feedback can be expected to build up in the parent. To the extent that such a feedback does build up, it should constitute motivation for a reversal of child-rearing procedures. Parents who have this experience, according to this reasoning, should become receptive to a plea for a return to the ordering-and-forbidding techniques.

Not only should the frustration and fatigue, the "endless patience and labor in cleaning up messes," motivate parents to become receptive to abandoning the developmental point of view; our overview of a century and a third leads us to expect that "experts" will come forward with "reasons" to support whatever doctrine is advocated to supersede the developmental view on the basis of the "discovery" that the new direction in child-rearing will be beneficial to the child. (We might note that psychiatrists and other leaders of opinion in this field are frequently parents and thus have their own frustrations to respond to as well as those of their patients.)

The New-New View

To the extent that the writer can read the signs of the times, the change foreshadowed in the above paragraphs is taking place. The pendulum does seem to be moving away from the indulgent-permissive end of its swing toward the ordering-and-forbidding end. What is more, it has been discovered that firmness and strictness on the part of parents is good for children: it adds to their sense of security. Here are some examples of arguments in support of the new-new view:

[31] *Ibid.*

> ... love alone ... cannot and should not be expected to counteract the effects of all the temptations and frustrations that surround so many children today.[32]

> The magnificent promise of progressive education has been dimmed by those who incorporated a rebellion against and hatred of their own society into their plans for freeing children to learn more spontaneously. Pediatricians who share the cultural belief in the need to teach self-control have twisted the invention of a self-regulatory schedule ... to a method of spoiling the baby by giving it its own way.[33]

> ... many teachers ... have ... exemplified a specious egalitarianism, which belies the true relation between child and adult ... the child ... wants the adult's help in controlling his impulses ... he needs to feel that the adult has achieved a more sure mastery of impulses ... egalitarian tendencies of adults express a one-sided perception of children's feelings toward authority.[34]

Surveying some women's magazines for selected years over the period 1892–1959, Maccoby found:

> ... a kind of cyclic fashion in the permissiveness-restrictiveness dimension of advice ... in 1959 restrictiveness shows a definite increase but has nothing like the amount of attention it enjoyed in earlier years.[35]

And so in our era it seems that the pendulum of fashion never rests. It is characteristic of the faddism in child rearing that before acquaintance with the "new" doctrine of permissive mothering was universal, a "new-new" doctrine has appeared. To the extent that the writer can discern its outlines, the following aspects of the emerging doctrine seem fairly clear:

1. Parents have rights to gratify their own impulses as well as duties to provide such care as will ensure the proper development of their children's personalities.
2. As offspring have become more assertive and their behavior more flagrantly contrary to parental norms, there is some misgiving that past leniency has contributed to present disorders.
3. The child-rearing regimen should not be completely permissive, as the child must incorporate inhibitions as well as develop creativity and spontaneity.

---

[32] Dorothy Barclay, "The Care and Handling of Young Rebels," *The New York Times Magazine*, December 9, 1956, p. 48.

[33] Mead, "Implications of Insight—II," in Mead and Wolfenstein, *op. cit.*, pp. 453–454.

[34] Wolfenstein, "Implications of Insight—I," *ibid.*, p. 446.

[35] Nathan Maccoby, "The Communication of Child-Rearing Advice to Parents," *Merrill-Palmer Quarterly*, 7: 199–204 (1961); reprinted in Robert F. Winch and Louis Wolf Goodman (eds.), *Selected Studies in Marriage and the Family* (3d ed.; New York: Holt, Rinehart and Winston, Inc., 1963), pp. 254–259. Quotation is from p. 255 in latter version.

The Present Status of Family-Life Education

Instruction on marriage, parenthood, and family life in general is widespread in America today. Books, the pamphlet series of the U.S. Children's Bureau, magazine articles, and newspaper columns of advice have already been mentioned. Many classes and study groups are organized by a variety of organizations, chiefly religious in their affiliation. Formal courses are widespread in the high schools and colleges of America. Educators speak of such courses as "functional." Lest the unwary reader be assuming that all courses are functional (or are at least intended by their instructors to be so), it should be added that a functional course is distinguished from the more traditional, or "academic," course. A conventional "academic" course on such a topic as marriage would be expected to examine what is known of the history of the topic, present evidence on variation in marriage customs, consider the concepts with which scholars organize their subject matter and the research they have done on it. On the other hand, the functional course "starts where the student is": asks him to state his problems, urges him to conjure some up if he believes he has none, and then undertakes to "deal with" such problems. In sociological phrasing, the objective of such courses would seem to be to socialize the students into acquiring the behaviors appropriate to their familial roles—present and prospective—and to understand reciprocal roles and some of the conditions under which one's own behavior and the behavior of others deviate from role-expectations. This can be seen in the following phrasing of appropriate objectives for a functional college course in preparation for marriage:

> Knowledge of the behavior of others
> Knowledge of the consequences of behavior
> Knowledge of social norms
> Knowledge about potential problems and achievements in marriage
> Knowledge of means of achieving marital goals
> Self-insight
> Personal growth[36]

Topics frequently treated in high school courses on education for family life include dating and courtship, implications of early marriage, love and romance, preparation for marriage, sex education, marital adjustment, and parenthood.[37]

It has been estimated that in 1956 well over 100,000 students were enrolled in marriage and family courses in American colleges and universities.[38]

---

[36] Robert O. Blood, Jr., *A Teacher's Manual for Use with "Anticipating Your Marriage"* (New York: Free Press, 1956), pp. 5–7.

[37] Reuben Hill, "Education for Marriage and Parenthood in the United States," paper presented at the Social Scientists' Advisory Meeting sponsored by the Social Security Administration of the U.S. Department of Health, Education, and Welfare, June 20, 1960, p. 12.

[38] Judson T. Landis, "The Teaching of Marriage and Family Courses in Colleges," *Marriage and Family Living*, 21: 36–40 (1959).

Although this is a sizable number, it is a small fraction of the 2.7 million undergraduate students in American institutions of higher education at that time.[39] Less is known about the availability and use of instruction in secondary schools. Hill reports that homemaking education is annually elected by more than 1.5 million girls and that more than 50,000 boys take some work in homemaking each year.[40] A report from Iowa in the 1950's indicates that just 11 percent of the high schools about which data could be obtained offered a course in family living,[41] but over 90 percent of the high schools reporting in Indiana were said to be offering some kind of family-life education.[42]

Attempts to Assess Effectiveness of Education for Family Life

After reviewing nearly two dozen studies on the results of parent-education efforts, Brim finds that the results have been inconclusive. Of the three studies using control groups and thereby best designed to produce conclusive findings, the first sees an increment in the knowledge of parents but no change in their attitudes, the second reports definite improvement in attitudes, and the third reveals "no improvement on one attitude measure, a significant improvement on subscales of another, and a change paralleled by change in the control group on still a third."[43] This confusing state of affairs leads Brim to assert: "The issue of how effective is parent education in changing parents or children therefore remains unresolved at present."[44] A similar note is struck by Kerckhoff in his review of family-life education. "Attempts at evaluation," he writes, ". . . have simply been inadequate."[45]

[39] *Health, Education, and Welfare Trends* (Washington, D.C.: U.S. Department of Health, Education, and Welfare, 1960), p. 58.

[40] *Loc. cit.*

[41] W. F. Kenkel, "A Survey of Family Life Education in Iowa High Schools," *Marriage and Family Living*, 19: 379–381 (1957).

[42] E. Z. Dager and G. A. Harper, "Family Life Education in Indiana Public High Schools: A Preliminary Report," *Marriage and Family Living*, 21: 385–388 (1959).

[43] Orville G. Brim, Jr., *Education for Child Rearing* (New York: Russell Sage, 1959), p. 311.

[44] *Ibid.*, p. 312. Hill points out that functional courses in marriage education point to changes in the student himself, whereas in parent education it is expected that the instruction of the parent will be reflected in the behavior or attitudes of the children of the student. Since the former course has the more modest task, Hill continues, it should be expected that it should be easier to demonstrate that it is followed by change. Indeed, Hill seems to believe change *is* demonstrated although he seems also to admit that studies done so far are generally not adequate in design to show convincing results.—Hill, "Education for Marriage and Parenthood in the United States," pp. 31–37. This calls to mind the young matron, married six years, who applied to a marriage counseling service because of the extreme unhappiness she was experiencing in her marriage and who expressed total mystification as to how she could have made such a mess of her marriage since she had received an "A" in her college course on marriage.

[45] Richard K. Kerckhoff, "Family Life Education in America," in Harold T. Christensen

How Scientific Have Been the Advice Givers?

As a society becomes urban and industrial, it substitutes rational knowledge for traditional wisdom. In American society it is the expert rather than the elder who is regarded as having authoritative knowledge. We have been examining the advice parents have been receiving since 1820, and presumably this advice has been based upon the opinions of experts. Then, one may ask, if the advice has been based on expert knowledge, why have there been such violent swings in the advice given?

To summarize what we are referring to as swings of the pendulum let us note (1) the swing from tender indulgence around 1890 to regulated sternness around 1900–1920, (2) the swing back to indulgence around 1935–1945, and it looks as though we are justified in adding (3) a more recent return toward sternness.

As we have indicated, three elements enter into the content of the advice: the presuppositions about original nature, the kind of adult desired, and the understanding as to the principles by which the desired type of adult is molded from the available raw material. Presumably a significant change in any of the three would result in a marked change in the advice. To this writer it appears there has been least change in the type of adult desired, in other words, he should be responsible, hard working, moral, and so on. It is true that there have been some changes, such as the evaluation of spontaneity—disapproved, officially at least, in Puritan culture and approved, officially at least, in contemporary middle-class culture—but there appears to be a large core of middle-class values on which all generations have agreed.[46] On the other hand, we have seen that there has been a marked shift in the conception of original nature, and it is plausible that much of the variation in advice resulted from varying conceptions as to whether the human infant was a little devil or a little angel or in some intermediate category.

The most obvious place for science to play a role in advice giving is with respect to the last of the three elements—the principles by which the desired type of adult is created from the raw material. Here we are posing a broad

(ed.), *Handbook of Marriage and the Family* (Skokie, Ill.: Rand McNally, 1964), pp. 881–911. Quotation is from p. 908.

[46] It appears that there was more emphasis in the United States on hard work in the nineteenth century than since 1900. One study analyzed fourth-grade textbooks over the period 1800–1950 for their achievement imagery and moral teaching. There was a sharp rise in achievement imagery from 1800 to 1890 followed by almost as steep a decline to 1950, the last year studied. Cf. Richard deCharms and Gerald H. Moeller, "Values Expressed in American Children's Readers: 1800–1950," *Journal of Abnormal and Social Psychology*, 64: 136–142 (1962). Another study analyzed the content of stories in the *Saturday Evening Post* over the period 1901–1961 and found that the emphasis on achievement declined over this period. Cf. Nancy M. Henley, "Achievement and Affiliation Imagery in American Fiction, 1901–1961," *Journal of Personality and Social Psychology*, 7: 208–210 (1967).

problem in behavioral science: to account for the child's subsequent behavior in terms of variation in his previous experiences. If we take the publication of William James's *Principles of Psychology* in 1890 as one of the events heralding the birth of behavioral science in America,[47] then the first seventy years of the period covered by our survey, the period from 1820 to 1890, lacked any psychology or sociology to offer principles on which to base advice. Although there were scholars who were developing the relevant sectors of psychology, social psychology, and sociology from 1890 on, the first scientist to make a major impact was the psychologist Watson in the 1920's. Thus the only really scientific impact, or the only period during which there was impact by persons thought to be scientists, was over the years following 1920.

It is in the period since 1920 that disputes over child-rearing procedures have become most violent. In the last chapter it was noted that such psychologists as Watson and Anderson expressed views that were in fundamental disagreement with those of such psychoanalysts as Ribble and Spitz as to the principles involved in converting the human infant into the socialized adult. At that point this question was posed: Should we come away with a completely agnostic point of view, or is there a tenable alternative to saying that we know nothing? At this juncture it seems correct to say that if one insists upon a high order of scientifically respectable evidence before he will accept a belief, agnosticism is the only correct belief. Our available evidence is simply not good enough to accept any other view.

The present writer would propose reserving judgment (which implies momentary acceptance of the agnostic attitude) but entertaining a hypothesis that undertakes to reconcile some of the seemingly contradictory evidence and claims. First, let us try to recapitulate simply the Watsonian view, then that of Ribble and Spitz, and finally see whether or not these views can be reconciled.

Earlier in the present chapter we noted that Watson advised against picking up a crying infant because to do so would reinforce the crying and would result in increasing the frequency with which the child would cry thereafter. Let us speak of the maternal act of handling the infant in this way, giving tactile contact, and so on, with the loose and undefined term "mothering."[48] Let us think of the infant's crying as a manifestation of dependence. We may well be going beyond what Watson would have subscribed to, but it seems in the spirit of his theorizing to represent the relation between "mothering" and the child's *in*dependence by the regression line in Figure 14.1, where it is seen that as "mothering" increases, the independence of the child diminishes. Levy's study of maternally overprotected boys can be interpreted as consistent with this relationship.[49]

---

[47] At that time in Europe, Freud was at work on the manuscript that was to be published as *Studies on Hysteria;* the development of psychoanalysis was in its fetal period.

[48] It is seen that "mothering" refers more to physical contact than to feeding; we might speak of it as nonnutritive nurturance.

[49] D. M. Levy, *Maternal Overprotection* (New York: Columbia University Press, 1943).

Now let us turn to the Ribble-Spitz point of view. Here it is argued that unless the child is given a good deal of "mothering," he will remain apathetic, undeveloped, sick, and dependent. Perhaps we are oversimplifying the views of these writers in Figure 14.2, but it would appear to follow from their analyses that there should be a positive correlation between "mothering" and the independence of the child. Harlow's fascinating experiments with monkeys can be interpreted as providing some convincing evidence for the Ribble-Spitz thesis. After subjecting some infant monkeys to "wire mothers" (unpadded frames giving milk and warmth) and others to "cloth mothers" (frames giving milk and warmth and covered with sponge rubber and terry cloth), Harlow found that the latter monkeys responded with greater "security" to strange objects than did the former.[50]

Comparison of Figures 14.1 and 14.2 leads to the conclusion that they flatly contradict each other. Yet it is possible that both can be correct if it is understood that they apply to different values or ranges of "mothering." Recalling that Ribble and Spitz, because of their being psychiatrists, were more likely to see extreme and morbid cases, we may hypothesize that they were observing an extremely low level of "mothering"—a lower level than Watson had in mind—and perhaps when "mothering" is at such a low level, the relationship they speak of does obtain.[51] In other words, we are proposing that the range of "mothering" over which Watson was generalizing was much higher. Accordingly, let us combine these two ideas by putting the Watsonian and the Ribble-Spitz views end-to-end in Figure 14.3. The solid straight line on the left of this figure represents the Ribble-Spitz view, and the solid straight line on the right represents the Watsonian view. The dotted line superimposed on the two straight lines represents a hypothetical curvilinear relationship whereby with middling "mothering" the child achieves maximum independence, but with very little or very much he remains highly dependent.[52] Al-

[50] Harry F. Harlow, "The Nature of Love," *American Psychologist*, 13: 673–685 (1958).

[51] From the clinical point of view Wolfenstein writes: "We have slowly come to realize . . . that insights which are based on trauma, failure, casualties of all sorts are at best only half the story; that we can make no complete plans without a second set of insights based on blessing, gift, success, upon a study of those happy combinations which produce something more than mere 'adjustment'; and that from experience the growing child gains not only wounds and vulnerabilities but also extra strengths and blessings."— Wolfenstein, "Implications of Insight—II," in Mead and Wolfenstein, *op. cit.*, p. 451. With a line drawing of two signs reading "Pansyvale Primary School (Infants)" and "Chimneys Cleaned," *Punch* records the trend as follows: "A psychologist has discovered that simple admonition is not always enough to train children up in the paths of virtue, and may need 'primary negative reinforcement'—that is to say spanking. This is another ripple in the returning tide of Victorian illiberalism. I suppose it won't be long before we find psychologists recommending fagging, compulsory games, and eventually child labour, all softened of course by new names. I suggest, respectively, 'organisational stratification practice,' 'physico-social integration' and 'adult economic responsibility acceptance imitation.'"— "Charivaria," *Punch,* May 9, 1962, p. 703.

[52] Sears has advanced a similar curvilinear hypothesis concerning the relation between

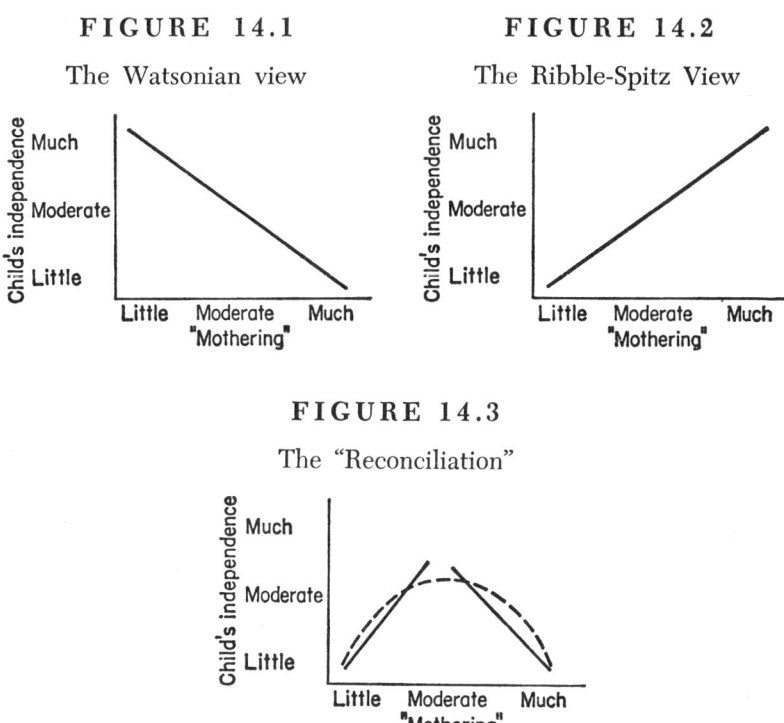

FIGURE 14.1 The Watsonian view

FIGURE 14.2 The Ribble-Spitz View

FIGURE 14.3 The "Reconciliation"

though there is plausibility in the proposition that the extremes in mothering behavior—both too little and too much—are associated with, and may be the cause of, continuing dependence in the child, let us bear in mind that this remains a hypothesis. The inadequacy of the knowledge in this area has been dramatized by an effort to replicate one of the most cited and respected studies in the literature of child development. The replication has led to the conclusion that methodological difficulties render virtually untenable the major findings of that study.[53]

maternal affection and the child's identification with the mother. He hypothesizes that the identification of the child with the mother will be stronger (1) the greater the degree of affectionate nurture given by the mother, (2) the more the child is required to substitute for her, and (3) the more the mother uses the withdrawal of love as a disciplinary technique. To reconcile an apparent paradox between (1) on the one hand and (2) and (3) on the other, it may be reasoned as follows: if mother is always gratifying, there will be no opportunity for the child to enact maternal behaviors; if she is never gratifying, the child has no instigation to act like her.—R. R. Sears, "Identification as a Form of Behavioral Development," in D. B. Harris (ed.), *The Concept of Development* (Minneapolis: University of Minnesota Press, 1957), pp. 149–161.

[53] Marian Radke Yarrow, John D. Campbell, and Roger V. Burton, *Child Rearing: An Inquiry into Research and Methods* (San Francisco: Jossey-Bass, 1968).

Summary

In this country Spock and Pierre the Pelican have replaced grandmother as the repository of wisdom as to how a young mother should rear her children. This signifies some degree of transfer from the family of the function of transmitting wisdom concerning the content of familial and, especially, parental roles. Advice in popular media has been traced back to 1820. Over the century and a half there have been quite pronounced changes in the advice given as to the best procedures to be followed in rearing children, including the care of infants. Although at any one time there were conflicting views, there was also a dominant point of view that emphasized indulgence in 1890, antiseptic aloofness in 1925, indulgent "mothering" in 1945, and subsequently rediscovered the rights of parents as the pendulum once again swung away from the indulgent extreme.

Our concern has not been with trying to determine which ideas were "right" or "wrong" but to understand how "expert" advice can be subject to such fluctuations. It is likely that assumptions concerning the nature of original nature influenced the content of the advice. Thus to the Puritans the infant was an immoral little creature and socialization centered on the problem of "breaking the spirit" of the child. In recent times it has been customary to distinguish between the "traditional" (or "old") and the "developmental" (or "new") points of view in child development. With the former point of view the parent is assumed to be wiser than the child and to exercise considerable direction with the child; with the latter it is assumed that the child will flourish if allowed more or less freely to develop his potentialities, especially for creativity and spontaneity. More recently authorities have been advising that to foster the child's feelings of security it is advisable to modify the "new" developmental view by subtracting a bit of the indulgence and adding a little more discipline. This "new-new" view can be seen as a return to an earlier position justified in modern phrasing.

Even though we interpret some of the variation in advice giving as the consequence of differences in assumption about original nature, it is clear that differences as to principles of child development have existed among writers recognized as authoritative. Since it seems unlikely that skilled and intelligent researchers are totally wrong in their perceptions, the present chapter has closed with a hypothesis that attempts to reconcile a set of seemingly inconsistent views on the consequences of "mothering."

15

Nurturance, Control, and Parent-Child Relations

Purpose of This Chapter

Let us consider childhood as roughly the period of life from the time the child begins to walk until the society stops regarding him as a child—usually a span of some ten to twelve years or perhaps more. During the early part of this period, when his life is still circumscribed by the family, the child learns the culture as it is mediated by the family. As he emerges from the family, the child enters the community and encounters new and perhaps divergent models after which to pattern his behavior. In Chapter 5 we noted aspects of the process of socialization that take place outside the family. In the present chapter the emphasis is on the parental functions of nurturance and control and on the aspects of socialization that take place within the family.

Points of Emphasis

With age comes the ability of the child to get into danger but before he has the experience to recognize danger. In all societies there are some techniques of controlling the child's behavior. With maturation, moreover, comes the capacity for learning increasingly complex social behavior. The process of socialization includes learning goals to be pursued and those to be avoided; it includes a conception of approved and condemned techniques for pursuing goals and for permitting and inhibiting the expression of impulses. The nature of the controls the child experiences and the content of what he learns are influenced by a number of factors. Among these we can distinguish the society into which the child is born and the nature of its culture, the family's position that society and the subculture associated with that position, the structure of the child's family, the personalities of his parents, and the original endowment of the child.

The Key Skills of Childhood

One of the most obvious facts about childhood is that its beginning is characterized by the acquisition of skills that result in a profound change in the child's way of life: the skills of manipulation, locomotion, and speech. Through enabling the child to bring an object close for inspection, the skill of manipulation allows the child to learn about the environment and his own body; through enabling him to throw the object out of sight, manipulation enables him to distinguish between the environment and his body. The skill of locomotion enables the child to change his environment and thereby to acquire new conceptions of the relations between his body and his setting; locomotion enables the child to develop acquaintance with his body through kinesthesia. The skill of speech enables the child to acquire a conception of the way in which others regard him and thus to develop an objective attitude toward himself; this process, which may be observed in the disposition of young children to speak of themselves in the third person, is called "acquiring a self" by G. H. Mead.[1]

Changing Needs and Parental Functions

With the development of the key skills, the child is increasingly able to provide direct gratification of his physical needs (to get food from cup to mouth and then from plate to mouth, to tie shoes, button clothes). With the development of the self, the social needs become more evident. The rapid learning now going on causes him to perceive some persons and objects with pleasurable anticipation and others with fear. The skill of speech enables the child to communicate with increasing clarity his desires and his feelings of anger, fear, vexation, pleasure, and so on. Correlatively, the parent becomes progressively aware that such expressions indicate needs that can be gratified at the symbolic level. For example, if a child has learned to fear a neighbor's dog, his fear may be dissipated in some cases by his being told that the dog cannot enter the house. More generally, the focus of the parental function of nurturance begins to shift from ministering to the child's physical needs by keeping him fed, warm, and dry, to ministering to his psychic needs by allaying fear, bestowing praise, or communicating affection.

The key skills of childhood also make the child able to get into hazards

---

[1] George H. Mead, *Mind, Self and Society* (Chicago: University of Chicago Press, 1934).

he is unable to recognize. It is at this point that control, the second parental function, comes prominently into play.

To summarize the argument to this point, maturation fosters independence, and with autonomy the child's dependent needs—those requiring parental responses—change from being primarily physical to being largely psychic. For the young child at this stage perhaps the most nurturant parental behavior is that which we speak of as "emotional warmth." It seems that warmth in interpersonal relations is a property that virtually everyone knows and recognizes but few can define. In a study based on interviews with 379 mothers of five-year-old children, Sears, Maccoby, and Levin conceive of maternal warmth as including acceptance of the child's dependency, using reasoning as a method of training, finding time to play with the child, and showing affectionate demonstrativeness in interaction with the child. They believe that the effects of maternal warmth—or, more precisely, of its opposite, maternal coldness—are marked: "Maternal coldness was associated with the development of feeding problems and persistent bed-wetting. It contributed to high aggression. It was an important background condition for emotional upset during severe toilet training, and for the slowing of conscience development."[2] Although the practical difficulties of arranging to include fathers in research on child development have resulted in concentrating on the mother-child relationship, there is a study of paternal nurturance in which it was found that warmth on the part of fathers was associated with masculinity in five-year-old boys.[3]

The point has been made that the behavior of the child must be controlled, restrained, and directed in the interest of the child's own safety. Of course, safety is not all that is involved. Parents are also interested in seeing signs that their children are developing in the direction of becoming acceptable adults, of learning acceptably the behaviors involved in adult roles. From the viewpoint of the child the psychological basis of the controlling function is quite different from that of the nurturant function. In nurturance the typical sequence is that the child feels a need, expresses it, and thereby initiates the nurturant behavior of the parent, which tends to be experienced by the child as pleasurable. In control the initiative typically comes from the parent, who sees the child in a hazardous or otherwise undesirable situation and sets about changing it. Offering the feeding and toilet-training situations as examples evocative of the nurturant and controlling functions, respectively,

---

[2] Robert R. Sears, Eleanor E. Maccoby, and Harry Levin, *Patterns of Child Rearing* (New York: Harper & Row, 1957), p. 483. This finding must be qualified, however, by a seemingly contrary report of nonsignificant correlations between maternal warmth and measures of aggression. Cf. Marian Radke Yarrow, John D. Campbell, and Roger V. Burton, *Child Rearing* (San Francisco: Jossey-Bass, 1968), pp. 66–67.

[3] See the discussion of the study by Mussen and Distler in the section appearing later in this chapter under the title "Correlates in Children's Responses of Some Variations in Familial Structure and Functions." See also the discussion of the influence of the father in the section immediately preceding "Correlates . . ." and bearing the title "Social Class and Child Rearing."

Sears and associates point out that whereas in the former the child has a need, in the latter he has "no initial desire to use the potty."[4]

As the child pushes on from infancy to the older age levels of childhood he learns increasingly complex skills and concepts. From about the age of five on through adolescence the growing psyche is confronted with a number of tasks: (1) the incorporation into his behavior of a sufficient proportion of the parental discipline to enable the child to achieve a workable level of adjustment with the parents; (2) as a corollary of this, acceptance of the idea that a considerable number of "immediate" pleasures are to be foregone in the interest of some "future" gain; (3) the creation of an image of himself as he would like to be (ideal self) and the beginning of the struggle to realize it; and (4) integration into the appropriate age and sex groups.

Internalization of Discipline: Development of conscience

According to our model of man, the behavior of the infant is pleasure-oriented, i.e., his behavior is directed to the immediate gratification of his own needs or tensions. With the progressive awareness of the nonself and the cognition of social objects, however, he comes gradually to take account of the behavior of others. As the child develops speech patterns, he becomes increasingly aware of the meaning of parental discipline. The concepts of "right" and "wrong," with their implications of reward and punishment, begin to emerge. In time he learns that others have the power to grant or deny his wishes, and ultimately, that accession to or denial of his wishes is correlated with his own behavior and the evaluation made of his behavior by others, chiefly by parents.

Kohlberg believes that there is an invariant developmental sequence whereby children acquire moral judgment. This sequence consists of three levels of morality subsuming six types of moral judgment, each type having its distinctive motivation. (See Table 15.1.) In a study of 72 boys aged 10–16, Kohlberg found that these stages correlated moderately with IQ ($r = .31$) and, as is suggested by its being a stage theory, somewhat highly with age ($r = .59$ with intelligence controlled).[5] Concerning age trends Kohlberg asserts:

> ... the first two types decrease with age, the next two increase until age thirteen and then stabilize, and the last two continue to increase from age thirteen to age sixteen. These age trends indicate that large groups of moral concepts and attitudes acquire meaning only in late childhood and

---

[4] R. R. Sears *et al.*, "Some Child-Rearing Antecedents of Aggression and Dependency in Young Children," *Genetic Psychology Monographs*, 47: 135–234 (1953).

[5] Lawrence Kohlberg, "Development of Moral Character and Moral Ideology," in Martin L. Hoffman and Lois Wladis Hoffman (eds.), *Review of Child Development Research*, vol. 1 (New York: Russell Sage, 1964), pp. 383–431.

TABLE 15.1

Kohlberg's Formulation of Levels and Types of Moral Judgment and of Corresponding Motivations

LEVEL AND TYPE OF MORAL JUDGMENT	MOTIVATION
Level I. Premoral	
Type 1. Punishment and obedience orientation	Obey rules to avoid punishment
Type 2. Naive instrumental hedonism	Conform to obtain rewards, have favors returned, and so on
Level II. Morality of conventional role conformity	
Type 3. Good-boy morality of maintaining good relations, approval of others	Conform to avoid disapproval, dislike by others
Type 4. Authority maintaining morality	Conform to avoid censure by legitimate authorities and resultant guilt
Level III. Morality of self-accepted principles	
Type 5. Morality of contract, of individual rights, and of democratically accepted law	Conform to maintain the respect of the impartial spectator judging in terms of community welfare
Type 6. Morality of individual principles of conscience	Conform to avoid self-condemnation

SOURCE: Lawrence Kohlberg, "Development of Moral Character and Moral Ideology," in Martin L. Hoffman and Lois Wladis Hoffman (eds.), *Review of Child Development Research*, vol. 1 (New York: Russell Sage Foundation, 1964), p. 400.

adolescence, and require the extensive background of cognitive growth and social experience associated with the age factor.[6]

To develop self-control and morality in their children some parents proceed directly—they order, they forbid, and they punish undesired behavior. Other parents proceed in a less direct manner, tending to reward desired behavior but being less reactive to behavior of which they disapprove. Probably most parents do some of both. There has been a considerable study of the relative merits and consequences of methods of parental discipline. After reviewing considerable literature, one writer concludes that

> . . . approaches to discipline which focus on using the love relationship with the child to shape his behavior are more likely to be correlated with

[6] *Ibid.*, p. 402.

internalized reactions to transgression (feelings of guilt, self-responsibility, confession) and with nonaggressive or cooperative social relations. On the other hand, power-asserting techniques in controlling the child are more likely to correlate with externalized reactions to transgression (fear of punishment, projected hostility), and with non-cooperative, aggressive behaviors.[7]

Tightness of control is another variable in parental behavior. Restrictive parents tend to foster behavior in their offspring that is well controlled but also dependent, submissive, and covertly hostile. Permissive parents, on the other hand, tend to have assertive, aggressive children, who are also outgoing and sociable.[8]

Traditionally the subculture of the middle class has been distinguished from that of the lower class by an ethical imperative to work for long-range goals. Because of this subcultural difference it has been usual for middle-class persons to view members of the lower class as incomprehensibly "shortsighted," "wasteful," "lustful," and the like. Deprivation in the present means "saving"; savings become capital; with capital one can make a fortune; and on some future day one can luxuriously enjoy vastly more of the fruits of life than by indulging oneself today. This general line of thought, perhaps best epitomized in *Poor Richard's Almanac*, is implicit in many of the conceptions of middle-class subculture. When animals and young children are hungry, they want food *now!* They cannot be placated by reference to a bountiful dinner in an hour or two. It is a task of parental discipline to train the child to accept the idea of deferred gratification, to forgo immediate pleasure in order to realize greater pleasure or less pain at some future time. A person going for a dental checkup realizes that the dentist may find a cavity, and, if he does, that the drill will hurt, but that a filling at the present time may prevent an extraction at a later date. The subculture of the middle class contains vastly more future rewards for present self-denial than does the subculture of the lower class. It is consistent with these differences in rewards that middle-class morality has emphasized thrift, prolonged vocational training, striving for occupational achievement, and other versions of deferred gratification.[9] This is part of what is implied in the conception of man as a "time-binding animal." A part of the morality, then, that parents in general and middle-class parents in particular seek to impart to their children concerns the idea of deferred gratification.

[7] Wesley C. Becker, "Consequences of Different Kinds of Parental Discipline," in Hoffman and Hoffman (eds.), *op. cit.*, pp. 169–208. Quotation is from p. 177.
[8] *Ibid.*, p. 197.
[9] Allison Davis, "American Status System and the Socialization of the Child," *American Sociological Review*, 6: 346–354 (1941), esp. pp. 353–354. With increasing affluence, however, the emphasis in the middle class on thrift seems to have diminished, and we have noted in Chapter 14 that the theme of achievement has been receiving less emphasis in the twentieth century. It may also be noted that when the attainment of long-range goals is thrown into substantial doubt, as in depression or in war, there is noted a "regression" in these themes of morality. The wartime attitude of "live today, for tomorrow we may die" is clearly in contradiction to these themes.

Development of Goals:
The ideal self

The foregoing section has considered the internalization of controls from a negative standpoint, i.e., building into the child, dispositions to delay or to avoid behaviors that offer the prospect of immediate gratification. It should be emphasized that the internalization of controls has a positive, or motivating, side as well as the negative, or inhibiting.

Numerous writers[10] have observed that a person, especially when young and small, is not satisfied by what he perceives himself to be. As the young child becomes aware—presumably in a somewhat vague and inarticulate way —of his own deficiencies and defects, his weaknesses and foibles, he constructs a second self, which is imaginary and a paragon of values and virtues, of strengths and skills and beauty. This paragon epitomizes the aspirations he has for himself. The precise content of this paragon—sometimes called the ego-ideal or the ideal self—typically varies through time. Since they loom so large in the life of the small child, parents seem usually to be the earliest models, and the child typically idealizes them into omnipotent, omniscient, and otherwise perfect creatures. This childish conception of the parents' perfection does not, however, withstand the day-to-day process of reality-testing. As the child comes gradually to sense his parents' lack of perfection, he seeks other models. These are ordinarily of superior status and have such roles as doctor, teacher, or minister.[11]

Lasting Effects of Parental Control:
Identification

From the standpoint of the social psychology of the family some of the most fascinating questions are: Under what conditions does the offspring become much like one or the other parent, and under what circumstances does he not? What determines which of a parent's behaviors a child tries to reproduce and which he does not? Actually, these may be seen as specific forms of the more general question: Under what conditions and with respect to which behaviors does any person A exert more or less lasting influence on the be-

---

[10] Cf., e.g., Sigmund Freud, "On Narcissim: An Introduction," *Collected Papers* (London: Hogarth, 1925), IV, 30–59.

[11] For an account of changes in the content of the ideal self, see R. J. Havighurst, Myra Robinson, and Mildred Dorr, "The Development of the Ideal Self in Childhood and Adolescence," *Journal of Educational Research*, 40: 241–257 (1946). For a review of literature on the self through the 1950's see Ruth C. Wylie, *The Self Concept* (Lincoln: University of Nebraska Press, 1961). Delightful accounts of fantasies emanating from the ideal self appear in James Thurber's fictional Walter Mitty and in Steig's cartoons captioned "Dreams of Glory."

havior of another person B? Here "influence" includes not only the behaviors of B that are similar to those of A but also the behaviors of B that are related in other ways to those of A, as in being reciprocal to or opposite from those of A. These are questions about which relatively little is known. In the following paragraphs an effort will be made to develop a theory that is, so far, untested but that seems to fit the few available data.

The term "identification" is frequently used to denote the process by which a child selects an attractive adult as a model and attempts to simulate some segment, large or small, of the model's behavior. Scrutiny of the literature reveals, however, that there are many other denotations of identification —so many in fact and with such consequent confusion that some writers have counseled their colleagues to abandon the term. Among the additional denotations is that the identifier may exhibit behavior that is related to the model's behavior in some way other than in being similar, i.e., in being reciprocal to or opposite from the behavior of the model. Thus Freud has spoken of a "primary identification" of the sucking infant with the nursing mother. Here the behavior of the identifier, the infant, is reciprocal to that of the model. Also, the literature contains the concept of "negative identification," which denotes a situation wherein, because of dislike of the model, the identifier exhibits behavior opposite to that of the model. An example would be the dissolute son of a rigidly pious father. Furthermore, the term is sometimes used to refer not to the *process* by which the identifier acquires some behavior functionally related to that of the model but rather to the acquired behavior itself, i.e., to identification-as-*product*.

In the paragraphs to follow we shall be using the term "identification" to refer both to the behavior acquired and to the process of acquiring it; to behavior not only similar to the model's but related in either of the other ways —reciprocally or oppositely. Should the reader feel that identification is not what is here discussed, no harm will be done if he will substitute for that word the phrase "more or less lasting influence of one person on another."[12]

From theories of learning and from experimental corroboration of those theories it is clear that there is a close connection between being rewarded for a particular behavior and learning to reproduce that behavior.[13] To reward

[12] Socialization is another concept that refers to a process whereby behaviors, especially those involved in roles, are acquired. In general usage, socialization differs from identification in that the former emphasizes the behaviors acquired and does not stress the model(s) from whom acquired, whereas identification directs our attention both to the behaviors acquired and to the interpersonal feature of acquiring them. Cf. the distinctions drawn between socialization and identification and between positional and personal identification in Robert F. Winch, *Identification and Its Familial Determinants* (Indianapolis: Bobbs-Merrill, 1962), pp. 15–25.

[13] That the connection is not perfect is emphasized by Mowrer, who observes that some people sometimes persist in unrewarded behavior and others sometimes do not persist in rewarded behavior.—O. H. Mowrer, *Learning Theory and Personality Dynamics* (New York: Ronald, 1950), p. 486. Kelly resolves this "neurotic paradox" on a phenomenological basis, i.e., by suggesting that the theory continues to be sastifactory but that the error lies

a person is to give him a resource, that is, something he desires. A resource may be intangible (for example, maternal love) as well as tangible (candy). A resource becomes a reward when it increases the probability that the person receiving it will emit a given behavior. From the connection between reward and learning it follows that any person who selects behaviors from a child's repertory to reward is exerting control over the behavior of the child.

From the argument presented in Chapter 1 it follows that, other things being equal, maximally functional families are more likely to possess resources than minimally functional families. The first hypothesis of our theory of identification follows from this reasoning:

H_1: The more functional the family, the greater is the probability that the child will form identifications within the family; conversely, the less functional the family, the greater is the probability that the child will form identifications with persons outside the family.

This argument has already been anticipated in Chapter 1, where it was suggested that a football coach might outrank a boy's father as a model because of the resources the coach can convert into rewards. Since it is clear also that a person usually has to be present in order to serve as a model,[14] we have the following hypothesis:

H_2: The identifications the child makes within the family depend upon the structure of the family, i.e., upon what positions and roles are filled and thus provide the child with models with whom to identify.

We can now add a statement relating identification to culture and then summarize its relation to familial function and structure:

Culture determines which behaviors adults will approve and hence be disposed to reward.
Function of the family provides resources that will be available for the adults to employ as rewards.
Structure of the family determines for which roles there will be occupants who will be available for the child to identify with.

Culture, Subculture, and the Content of Learning

The capacity to learn is built into the organism. What is learned, however, is subject to great variation. As we saw in Chapters 2 and 3, the content of learning and hence the process of socialization vary from culture to culture. In

in assuming that one man's reward is necessarily another's.—George A. Kelly, "Man's Construction of His Alternatives," in Gardner Lindzey (ed.), *Assessment of Human Motives* (New York: Evergreen, 1960), pp. 54–55.

[14] The adverb "usually" implies the possibility of identification where the model is not physically present. Identifications do occur with folk heroes and with figures of history and of fiction.

Chapter 8 we noted some dimensions of subcultural variation within American society. All societies present a somewhat different content of learning to the two sexes.

What is learned is not only the intellectual and motor skills, but also the appropriateness of striving toward certain goals and of experiencing particular emotions in specified situations. In the present section we shall note some of the more relevant aspects of cultures and subcultures, how these aspects are mediated by families, and the ways in which they are learned and incorporated into personality.

One approach to socialization is to view it as a process in which the child learns the cultural expectations related to his age, sex, and other roles and seeks to conform to those expectations. In American culture some of the most marked expectations concern the expression of aggressive impulses and their correlates in competition and achievement, the expression of sexual impulses, and the integration of the child into his peer group.

Whether or not American middle-class parents have become increasingly permissive since World War II, as some writers believe,[15] still it seems probable that techniques of expressive aggression are rather rigidly circumscribed in the middle and upper classes. The small boy is typically instructed that it is not fitting to "pick" a fight, particularly with someone smaller or with a girl. (Of course, the little girl is taught that fighting is "unladylike.") On the other hand, to fail to defend oneself is to fail to protect one's self-concept and frequently the self-concepts of one's parents. Therefore the child must learn to inhibit his aggressive propensities in many situations, and to appear aggressive in others, whether or not he actually feels aggressive in those situations.

By contrast, in the lower class, "the level below the common man,"[16] there is little cultural pressure to inhibit physical aggression; indeed, the pressure is in the opposite direction. Both boys and girls are expected to protect themselves with verbal or physical violence on any provocation; it is reported that the child who does not develop such patterns of behavior is regarded as either weak or sly and underhanded. "In . . . slum society, physical aggression is a normal part of life. Readiness to fight is therefore a normal part of personality there, and *is developed in children from two or three years of age.*"[17]

Psychologically speaking, competitive achievement is a close relative of aggression. Physical violence and verbal altercation are direct expressions of

---

[15] Cf. especially Urie Bronfenbrenner, "Socialization and Social Class through Time and Space," in Eleanor E. Maccoby, Theodore M. Newcomb, and Eugene L. Hartley (eds.), *Readings in Social Psychology* (New York: Holt, Rinehart and Winston, Inc., 1958), pp. 400–425. In the opinion of the present writer the data that have been interpreted as denoting trends in child-rearing *practices* (as contrasted with trends in *beliefs* about child-rearing practices) are too insubstantial for very credible inferences to be drawn.

[16] Reference is not to the stable blue-collar working class but to slum dwellers. Cf. pages 209–210.

[17] Allison Davis and R. J. Havighurst, *Father of the Man: How Your Child Gets His Personality* (Boston: Houghton Mifflin, 1947), p. 18. Italics in original.

aggression; competitive achievement is a converted, controlled form of aggression that is approved in selected cultural settings. It is not astonishing that the subculture of the middle class, which largely interdicts physical aggression, encourages competitive achievement. Praise or criticism may come to the child contingent upon whether or not he exceeds his peers in the age of acquiring speech and of being toilet-trained, in his grades, in the distance he can hit a ball, and in the degree of his popularity.

It has been suggested that the socializing modes of the middle class build into the modal personality an anxiety that is adaptive in the sense that it provides the drive for striving behavior.[18] A study purporting to show a process by which the offspring acquires a disposition to achieve reports that mothers of a group of high-achievement-oriented schoolboys tended to make greater demands for achievement upon their sons than did the mothers of a group of low-achievement boys.[19] That the inducing of anxiety is the dynamic by which these mothers attained their objective of fostering their sons' striving is suggested by the fact that a follow-up study with the same subjects showed a much higher correlation between mothers' attitudes at first testing and sons' test-anxiety six years later ($r = .75$) than between sons' achievement-test scores at the two times ($r = .38$).[20]

Evidence that middle-class adolescents differ from lower-class adolescents in valuing achievement for its own sake comes from a study in which the subjects established a level of performance on being rewarded; middle-class subjects tended to carry on at a high level of performance when the reward was withdrawn whereas lower-class subjects did not.[21]

The drive to achieve seems correlated with ethnoreligious affiliation as well as with social class. The most conspicuous arena of competitive achievement in this country is in the occupational system, and it is reported, as might be expected, that Italian parents are seen by their sons as more accepting of lower-status occupations than are Jewish parents by their sons.[22] It has been

[18] Allison Davis, "Socialization and Adolescent Personality," in Theodore Newcomb and Eugene L. Hartley (eds.), *Readings in Social Psychology* (New York: Holt, Rinehart and Winston, Inc., 1947), pp. 139–150. From a study in a quite different context Sweetbaum has concluded that drive is, in part, a function of anxiety.—Harvey A. Sweetbaum, "Comparison on the Effects of Introversion-Extraversion and Anxiety on Conditioning," *Journal of Abnormal and Social Psychology*, 66: 249–254 (1963).

[19] Marian R. Winterbottom, "The Relation of Need for Achievement to Learning Experiences in Independence and Mastery," in John W. Atkinson (ed.), *Motives in Fantasy, Action, and Society: A Method of Assessment and Study* (Princeton, N.J.: Van Nostrand, 1958), pp. 453–478. Cf. also Bernard C. Rosen and Roy D'Andrade, "The Psychosocial Origins of Achievement Motivation," *Sociometry*, 22: 185–218 (1959).

[20] Sheila C. Feld "Longitudinal Study of the Origins of Achievement Strivings," *Journal of Personality and Social Psychology*, 7: 408–414 (1967).

[21] Elizabeth Douvan, "Social Status and Success Strivings," *Journal of Abnormal and Social Psychology*, 52: 219–223 (1956).

[22] F. L. Strodtbeck, Margaret R. McDonald, and B. C. Rosen, "Evaluation of Occupations: A Reflection of Jewish and Italian Mobility Differences," *American Sociological Review*, 22: 546–553 (1957). In a subsequent publication, however, Strodtbeck asserted

found, moreover, that the proportion of Jews in higher-level occupations (e.g., clerks, managers, professionals) is about twice as high as the proportion in the population as a whole.[23]

How children are to be trained with respect to the expression of sexual impulses is another problem for which each culture must provide an answer. (How this problem concerns adolescents and adults will be considered in Chapters 16 and 19.) We may begin our consideration of sexual expression by harking back to concepts of original nature. If the concept of original innocence is combined with the idea that sex is evil, the implication is reached that the child will not manifest an interest in sexual matters, especially in overt sexual expression, unless he has been corrupted by others. Accordingly, any sort of masturbatory activity is to be regarded as evidence of moral taint—to be severely disapproved. Typical techniques of enforcing parental sanction against masturbation include threats of castration and of impending insanity. It now seems clear that masturbation in itself is harmless, but that considerable insecurity can be provoked by the threats. Around the time of World War II, according to Kinsey, most of the less educated people in this country still regarded masturbation as abnormal and immoral.[24]

In the middle classes the cultural ideal has apparently been to rear children to adulthood with no notice ever having been taken of the physical side of sex. In accordance with the concept of original innocence it was apparently believed that if no one "contaminated" the child, he would grow up sexually innocent and, since sex was regarded as evil, such an outcome was highly desirable. It seems to be a feature of the "new view" reported in the last chapter, however, to favor giving sex information to the child as he becomes interested in the topic. But from the standpoint of positive social approval the increase in sexual freedom is largely at the verbal level. While the new view does include a relaxation of the disapproval of masturbation, it does not give positive approval to homosexual relations at all or to heterosexual intercourse outside marriage.[25] In this situation it is not astonishing that Kinsey found a high incidence of masturbation among middle-class males. By contrast, in the lower class, where masturbation was still regarded as immoral and abnormal, the sanctions against premarital heterosexual intercourse were less strong.[26]

---

that when socioeconomic status was controlled, there remained no visible differences between Italian and Jewish parents with respect to the evaluation of such achievement as measured by a specially constructed scale.—F. L. Strodtbeck, "Family Interaction, Values, and Achievement," in D. C. McClelland *et al.*, *Talent and Society: New Perspectives in the Identification of Talent* (Princeton, N.J.: Van Nostrand, 1958), pp. 135–194.

[23] F. L. Strodtbeck, "Jewish and Italian Immigration and Subsequent Status Mobility," in McClelland *et al.*, *op. cit.*, pp. 259–266, esp. Table 1, p. 262.

[24] A. C. Kinsey, W. B. Pomeroy and C. E. Martin, *Sexual Behavior in the Human Male* (Philadelphia: Saunders, 1948), p. 223.

[25] As recently as 1960 a member of a faculty of a state university in the Midwest was discharged for advocating premarital sexual intercourse for college students.

[26] Kinsey, Pomeroy, and Martin, *op. cit.*, pp. 223, 375–377, and chap. 14. See also Chapter 19 of this book.

Again the slum culture stands in contrast with that of the middle class. As Havighurst says, "privacy is class-typed."[27] When large families live in the cramped quarters of one, two, or three rooms, it is difficult to arrange privacy for the sexual or any other aspect of life. There is much less inhibition concerning the discussion of sex; there is opportunity to observe, or at least to know about, the sexual activities of the members of the family. "Everybody does it and everybody sees it."[28] Conditions in the home, therefore, typically provide the slum child with an opportunity to acquire more than a verbal acquaintance with the subject of sex.[29]

Every culture contains expectations regarding differences in behavior between the two sexes. Expectations of such sex-typed behavior are encountered quite early and are experienced with varying degrees of intensity throughout life. For example, the father will typically act toward a male infant with hearty jocularity but toward a female infant with a show of tenderness. Evidence of early learning about sex roles is seen in a Midwestern sample of 20 boys and 20 girls aged 30–40 months who recognized as masculine or feminine with 75 percent accuracy a set of cultural artifacts (e.g., screwdriver, tool box, dustpan, and spatula).[30] The cultural expectation of sex-typed behavior is reinforced by the schools. According to one study, children's textbooks regularly show boys as active, and oriented to achievement and adventure. Girls, on the other hand, are presented as kind, timid, and less creative.[31] These characteristics of sex-typed behavior represent middle- rather than lower-class conceptions. In contrast with the culturally defined sex types of the middle class, that of the slum boy is "more male: coarser, more aggressive physically, more openly sexual"; that of the slum girl is "more outspoken, bolder sexually, more 'female,' more expressive of her impulses and her emotions."[32] We shall give further consideration to cultural expectations with respect to sex-typing in the next chapter.

As we pass from the consideration of cultural expectations to studies of actual behavior, we begin with a study that seems to indicate that sex differ-

---

[27] Robert J. Havighurst, "Cultural Factors in Sex Expression," in Jerome Himelhoch and Sylvia Fleis Fava (eds.), *Sexual Behavior in American Society: An Appraisal of the First Two Kinsey Reports* (New York: Norton, 1955), pp. 191–205. Quotation is from p. 202.

[28] *Ibid.* On the other hand, Blake cites her own study in Jamaica as well as others in Puerto Rico and among tenant farmers in the South to support the belief that "the degree of privacy attempted [in lower-class family life] and the amount achieved seem to have been underestimated."—Judith Blake, *Family Structure in Jamaica* (New York: Free Press, 1961), p. 53.

[29] It seems probable that at all class levels much of the sex education of children has been provided in the child's peer group, especially where parents have avoided the topic.

[30] Arthur M. Vener and Clinton A. Snyder, "The Preschool Child's Awareness and Anticipation of Adult Sex-Roles," *Sociometry*, 29: 159–168 (1966).

[31] I. L. Child et al., "Children's Textbooks and Personality Development: An Exploration in the Social Psychology of Education," *Psychological Monographs*, Vol. 6, No. 3 (1946).

[32] Davis and Havighurst, *op. cit.*, p. 26.

ences in primates are present before the onset of hormonal changes of puberty: when preadolescent rhesus monkeys were placed in the company of an infant of their species, males tended toward hostile behavior and females toward positive social behavior.[33] With respect to humans we encounter the report that among three-year-olds, sex differences in behavior are not yet grossly apparent.[34] L. B. Murphy cites her own work[35] and that of Hattwick[36] to document the point that play groups are often mixed with respect to sex and that the roles of policeman, fireman, or mother are shared by boys and girls alike. Boys begin to develop conceptions of masculine roles around four or five, and the behavior of the more aggressive assumes the exaggerated "masculinity" of "bravado, swashbuckling, bullying behavior."[37] At about the same time (before the end of the sixth year) girls are typically becoming interested in the overt characteristics of "femininity," such as dress, accessories, and cosmetics.[38]

Subculture, the Position-Conferring Function, and the Child's Test of "Reality"

From time to time we have noted

That each family has a location in the structure of the total society.

That associated with each location, or set of positions, in the society there tends to be a more or less distinctive subculture, with its own values, manners, skills, and so on.

That through its location in the society the family confers on its young a position in the society.

That invidiously considered, this position and its attendant roles may be thought of as statuses.

That because of the foregoing, as the child goes forth from the family into the community, he bears the marks of his family's statuses—ethnic, religious, socioeconomic, and so on.

As the child emerges from the family into the community, he is confronted

---

[33] A. Chamove, H. F. Harlow, and G. Mitchell, "Sex Differences in the Infant-Directed Behavior of Preadolescent Rhesus Monkeys," *Child Development*, 38: 329–335 (1967).

[34] L. B. Murphy, "Childhood Experience in Relation to Personality Development," in J. McV. Hunt (ed.), *Personality and the Behavior Disorders* (New York: Ronald, 1944), pp. 652–690.

[35] L. B. Murphy, *Social Behavior and Child Personality* (New York: Columbia University Press, 1937).

[36] L. A. Hattwick, "Sex Differences in Behavior of Nursery School Children," *Child Development*, 8: 343–345 (1937).

[37] L. B. Murphy, "Childhood Experience in Relation to Personality Development," in J. McV. Hunt (ed.), *Personality and the Behavior Disorders* (New York: Ronald, 1944), p. 674.

[38] *Ibid.*, p. 675.

with the necessity of finding or earning a place in a system of peers. Since in the usual nuclear family a child has no age peer, he is moving from the familial setting, where he is more or less one of a kind and thereby peerless, into situations filled with peers, where his task is to establish his status in the pecking order of one or more peer groups.

At this time the child begins to learn that his standing is determined in part by his ascribed statuses and in part by what he can achieve. He learns that the other children make some ascriptions to him on the basis of his reputation, some on the basis of his appearance, and some on the basis of his behavior. At his age level, as at others, the degree to which his standing is affected by his achievements reflects the openness of the system of stratification. An example of reputational ascription would be that the other children know he is a Catholic because they have heard their elders speak of the religion of his family. Reflecting their parents' stereotypes, moreover, the other children would no doubt "know" that because of his religion the boy would be honest or dishonest, aggressive or agreeable, or whatever. They would probably attach a positive or negative value to such ascribed characteristics, i.e., an initial attitude of approval and acceptance or of disapproval and therefore of rejection. With respect to appearance the children might use as their cues skin color and hair texture, or perhaps cleanliness, or style of dress and quality of clothing. And on the basis of these cues they could then ascribe honesty or dishonesty as before. Thus before the child has begun to behave in his newfound social groups, he is being placed by his ascribed characteristics. And as soon as he begins to behave, his actions are assessed for beliefs and attitudes.

In this way the child has a variety of opportunities to test what he has learned within the family against his experiences on the outside, or, in other words, to try out the wisdom and correctness of his parents' views. If the child could express this aspect of his experience, he might phrase it thus: "Is what my parents have taught me myth or reality?" Where the subculture of the community differs from that of the family (as frequently happens with the children of immigrant parents), the child may well conclude that the parents are in many ways wrong. To conclude that one's parents are wrong implies that one will reject them as models.

The child's standing in his peer-group is only partially determined by ascribed characteristics, and accordingly his skills and adaptability come into play. In American society and in others the individual goes through a series of experiences where he begins as a "small" member of a group with low status and over a period of time increases in stature and status, only to be "promoted" out of the group and to find himself at the bottom of the status hierarchy in the next chronological group. This experience occurs at the transitions between nursery school and primary school, between primary and junior high school, between the latter and high school, on entering college, and on entering an occupation. The successive play groups, school groups, adolescent gangs and crowds have their criteria for self-validation in terms of strengths and skills, but, as we shall see, these criteria change from one age level to another. Accordingly the grade school child, the early adolescent, and the late adolescent are each confronted with new problems of self-validation. Dependent upon his adequacy, or rather on his inadequacy, the child is confronted at each level with an anxiety-provoking situation. At the same time, the child is progressing from the policeman-fireman-cowboy stage of ambition to a conception of a goal characterized by less action and drama and by more income and higher social status.[39]

To the extent that a child is able to establish himself in a succession of peer groups having varying criteria of acceptability (whether on the basis of age grades or of subcultural variation or both), he is showing adaptability in social skills. In a culturally plural and considerably secularized society such as ours, where cultural relativism has displaced categorical morality, adaptability is rewarded and the social chameleon is fostered.

With respect to the atmosphere in which the child undertakes to achieve integration into his peer group one final point concerns the attitudes of his parents. For many young people the corporation continues to be a probable occupational destination, and for a considerable proportion of this number the corporation represents upward mobility. It is not surprising, then, that the subculture of the middle class, which is quite oriented to the corporation and which values upward mobility, should also value a role-expectation believed conducive to a high level of acceptance within the corporation, i.e., the "organization man." The high rate of technical obsolescence has rendered questionable the wisdom of training for some categories of occupations because of the prospect that such job classifications may not exist long enough for the trainees even to become established in them. These and other considerations have led to an emphasis on social skills, so that the young person will "fit" into an organization and become a good "team" person. Such an outlook leads to parental concern for the popularity and adaptability of the young person and creates for the young person the conditions from which an "identity crisis" may develop. This topic will be examined in the next chapter. For the present suffice it to say that there has been some evidence of reaction against the pressure to force all middle-class children into the mold of the extrovert.[40]

Social Class and Child Rearing

There seems to be consensus that, in America, child-rearing practices vary with social class. Just how the practices vary, however, remains somewhat problematic. In 1946 a paper was published that attracted much attention. This article presented evidence from which the authors concluded that lower-class

---

[39] Eugene A. Weinstein, "Weights Assigned by Children to Criteria of Prestige," *Sociometry*, 19: 126–132 (1956).

[40] Evidence appears in the content of the "Parent and Child" in *The New York Times Magazine*. Cf., e.g., Dorothy Barclay, "Too Much Popularity," *The New York Times Magazine*, October 19, 1952, p. 54.

parents tended to be warm and permissive, whereas middle-class parents were generally less nurturant and more strictly controlling.[41] These conclusions were contradicted by a paper that appeared eight years later. The second paper reported that parents in the middle class were warmer and allowed their children greater freedom than did parents in the lower class.[42] In general, subsequent studies have tended to confirm the latter view. In other words, the weight of the presently available evidence indicates that the image of child rearing in the lower class as casual and carefree is a (quite possibly romanticized) myth, and that the experiences of the lower-class child generally add up to a relatively stern regimen studded with physical punishment and little show of affection from the father, whereas the middle-class child is treated with relative indulgence.[43] There has been an attempt to reconcile the conflicting conclusions on the ground that each was correct at its point in time, i.e., that the lower-class pattern was indulgent around the time of the beginning of World War II and has become less so, whereas the pattern of middle-class parents was less indulgent in the earlier period and has become more so.[44] In the judgment of the present writer the credibility of such trends must remain in doubt because of the inadequacy of the data, although the evidence for such a trend among middle-class parents is somewhat more credible than for the countertrend among lower-class parents.

The available evidence does suggest that middle-class children are more likely to have a relationship of warmth and affection with their parents than is true in lower strata.[45] Furthermore, the evidence points to certain differences between the classes in the manner of exercising the parental function of control as follows:

1. Middle-class parents tend to be more tolerant of the child's expressed impulses and desires than is true of parents of lower status.[46]

2. Middle-class parents tend to discipline a child in terms of the apparent

[41] Allison Davis and Robert J. Havighurst, "Social Class and Color Differences in Child-Rearing," *American Sociological Review*, 11: 698–710 (1946).

[42] Eleanor E. Maccoby and Patricia K. Gibbs, "Methods of Child-Rearing in Two Social Classes," in William E. Martin and Celia Burns Stendler (eds.), *Readings in Child Development* (New York: Harcourt, 1954), pp. 380–396.

[43] Bronfenbrenner, "Socialization and Social Class Through Time and Space," in Maccoby, Newcomb, and Hartley, *op. cit.*

[44] *Ibid.*

[45] Maccoby and Gibbs, "Methods of Child Rearing in Two Social Classes," in Martin and Stendler, *op. cit.*, p. 391. In this and some of the following comparisons the lower status group is presented as "working class" rather than "lower class." Cf. Sears, Maccoby, and Levin, *op. cit.;* Melvin L. Kohn, "Social Class and the Exercise of Parental Authority," *American Sociological Review*, 24: 352–366 (1959). This raises a question as to the comparability of the socioeconomic strata from one study to another. If the gradients across strata are monotonic, no great problem exists; the hazard arises only in the event that the gradients have points of inflection, which seems unlikely in the light of Kohn's research. Cf. Melvin L. Kohn, *Class and Conformity: A Study in Values* (Homewood, Ill.: Dorsey, 1969), chap. 8.

[46] Bronfenbrenner, in Maccoby, Newcomb, and Hartley, *op. cit.*, p. 424.

intent of a behavior and to value self-direction in a child; parents of lower status tend to discipline children in terms of the consequences of the behavior and to value the child's conformity to external authority.[47]

3. Lower-status parents are more likely to use physical punishment than are middle-class parents, who tend to rely more on reasoning, isolation, appeals to guilt, and to other methods involving the threat of the loss of parental love.[48]

4. Parents of the middle class tend to have higher expectations for the child than do parents of lower status, e.g., to learn to take care of himself at an early age, to accept more responsibilities around the home, and especially to progress further in school.[49]

The four points just above are conclusions from some empirical evidence concerning differences in child-rearing practice between parents of the middle class and parents in lower statuses. But, the reader may inquire, why do such differences exist? The "why" is indeed a legitimate question. In the present state of our lack of knowledge, however, the answer can only be speculated about, but sociological and psychological theories do permit some sophisticated guessing. In Chapter 1 we tied reinforcement theory of psychology to functional theory of sociology. The same line of theorizing can be invoked at this point. Reinforcement necessitates the control by the reinforcer of some resource that the subject (or child) will view as a reward. It seems reasonable to argue that, relative to middle-class families, those of lower status have fewer resources they can convert to rewards for the control of the child's behavior. Two kinds of differentially scarce resources come to mind. The most obvious is physical goods—especially toys of all sorts—that cost money. Scarcely less obvious is parental time to devote to the child. Poverty causes many a mother to go into the labor force and thus to be away from home when otherwise she might be rewarding and thus controlling her child's behavior.[50] Similarly it appears that lower-status fathers are much more frequently engaged in "moonlighting" than are upper-status fathers, and the second and third jobs keep them away from their children.

Having noted the logical chain that leads from resource to reward to parental control over the child's behavior, we may now ask two questions: What is the consequence for the child's identification of such a shortage of resources as has just been attributed to the lower class? What does a parent do to control the behavior of the child when the parent lacks the ability to grant or to withhold resources?

With respect to the first question, it would follow from our theoretical development that the child would be relatively unlikely to identify (except

---

[47] Kohn, *Class and Conformity*, pp. 21, 34, 71.
[48] Bronfenbrenner, in Maccoby, Newcomb, and Hartley, *op. cit.*, p. 424.
[49] *Ibid.*
[50] As we shall see below, however, Hoffman's review of studies on the consequences of the employment of mothers shows them to have been somewhat inconclusive.

perhaps oppositely) with the parent but, rather, would seek as models persons having resources under their control. This leads to the hypothesis:

H_3: The probability that a child will form similar and/or reciprocal identifications with a parent is positively correlated with socioeconomic status.

Very tentative results from the writer's study of members of college fraternities on five American campuses support the conclusion that identification of son with father is positively correlated with socioeconomic status.[51]

With respect to the question as to what the parent does, two major courses come to mind: the parent may use physical punishment to divert the child from behaviors of which the parent disapproves, or the parent may give up the goal of trying to control the child's behavior. It appears that in the lower statuses some parents use physical coercion, some give up, and perhaps most alternate between these two courses. In economically depressed areas both the necessity of working long hours and the frequency of marital ruptures tend to produce parentless situations, so that the child with a housekey on a string around his neck becomes a commonplace in such areas.

It has been argued that a further element in the familial system of the lower class is a displacement of aggression from extrafamilial sources of frustration:

> The parent at the lower level receives less from society in the way of esteem, security, and material comforts . . . [and] probably receives more hostility from his peers and society in general. The absence of resources and receipt of aggression result in a "poverty" of positive affect. The economy of the psyche can be maintained only by dispelling this hostility to more vulnerable targets (e.g., the child).[52]

Finally, Kohn has found that middle-class parents differ from working-class parents in that the former tend to see themselves as competent members of a benign society whereas the latter tend to feel less competent and see the society as indifferent or threatening. (See p. 87 of the work cited in n. 47.)

---

[51] A statement of the theory underlying this study appears in Robert F. Winch, *op. cit.*; and by the same author, "Determinants of Interpersonal Influence in the Late Adolescent Male: Theory and Design of Research," in Reuben Hill and René König (eds.), *Families in East and West: Socialization Process and Kinship Ties* (The Hague: Mouton, 1970), pp. 578–601.

[52] Donald Gilbert McKinley, *Social Class and Family Life* (New York: Free Press, 1964), pp. 57–58. Another study concludes that fathers who present themselves as deviant and aggressive models for their sons tend to produce antisocial aggressiveness in their sons.—Joan McCord, William McCord, and Alan Howard, "Family Interaction as Antecedent to the Direction of Male Aggressiveness," *Journal of Abnormal and Social Psychology*, 66: 239–242 (1963).

Correlates in Children's Responses of Some Variations in Familial Structure and Functions

The term "familial structure" refers to the number and nature of the differentiated positions within the familial system and the number of persons occupying each position. As Table 12.4 signified, there are three positions in the American nuclear family system: husband-father, wife-mother, and sibling-offspring. The argument connecting familial structure and identification of offspring simply asserts that familial structure determines which models and how many the family presents to the child whose behavior the child may simulate, relate to reciprocally, or possibly come to reject, and hence with whom to develop similar, reciprocal, and/or opposite identifications. For illustrative purposes we shall consider studies reporting the correlates of (1) having the father present or absent and (2) having the sibling of the same or of opposite sex in two-child families.

The layman's conception of the paternal function in the family includes the idea that the father backstops the mother in providing discipline in the instances of serious breaches of conduct and that he provides an appropriate masculine model, which is relevant to the development of children of both sexes but is essential for the proper development of boys into men. Perhaps it is possible to make some check on these ideas by seeing what the research literature has reported as to the correlates of paternal absence.

Kohn finds that the image of differentiated parental roles is present in working-class families with mother cast as the nurturing parent and father as the controlling one. In some working-class families, Kohn says, it actually works out this way; in many others the mother rears (both nurtures and controls) the children while the father supports the home. In middle-class families there tends to be less differentiation of parental roles; both parents emphasize nurturance with each parent "taking special responsibility for being supportive of children of the parent's own sex."[53]

A study has been made of eight- and nine-year-old children of some Norwegian sailors who were away from home for periods up to two years and even longer. For controls a comparable set of children in father-present families was studied. The children responded to a doll-play test. The absence of the father seemed to affect the boys more than the girls. The differences between the responses of the father-absent and the father-present boys were interpreted as showing that the former had developed compensatory strivings toward masculinity and father-identification.[54] Other studies using a com-

---

[53] Kohn, *Class and Conformity*, p. 125.

[54] Erik Grønseth and Per Olav Tiller, "Father Absence in Sailor Families," in Nels Anderson (ed.), *Studies of the Family* (Göttingen: Vandenhoeck & Ruprecht, 1957), pp.

parable test on American children have shown father-absent boys to give less aggressive responses than father-present boys and to have fantasies about father that were more similar to those of girls than to those of father-present boys.[55] Kindergarten-age boys from father-absent homes are reported to be less masculine in a projective test of sex-role orientation but not in overt behavior than boys from father-present homes.[56] At the high school level we have reports that the absence of father correlates with reduced self-esteem[57] and with depressed scores on college entrance examinations.[58] In a study of male college students it was found that those whose fathers had been absent for three or more years early in the offspring's life tended to score relatively low in mathematics.[59]

According to one study, if the father left after the son was five years old, the boy's sex-typed behaviors were similar to those of boys in father-present homes.[60] This finding seems in some conflict with a result from another study wherein the boy tended to behave in a feminine and aggressive manner if the father left when the boy was in the six- to twelve-year age bracket.[61] The previously cited study of self-esteem found a complex relationship between this variable and the age of the boy at the father's departure:

> If the child was young when the family dissolved, then he will tend to have low self-esteem whether or not his mother remarried. If, on the other hand, the child was older at the time the marriage dissolved, then his self-esteem will be normal if his mother did not remarry but will be below normal if she did remarry.[62]

Of course, since the husband-father is normally the prime breadwinner,

---

97–137; David B. Lynn and William L. Sawrey, "The Effects of Father-Absence on Norwegian Boys and Girls," *Journal of Abnormal and Social Psychology,* 59: 258–262 (1959).

[55] Robert R. Sears, Margaret H. Pintler, and Pauline S. Sears, "Effect of Father Separation on Preschool Children's Doll Play Aggression," *Child Development,* 17: 219–243 (1946); Henry B. Biller, "A Note on Father Absence and Masculine Development in Lower-Class Negro and White Boys," *Child Development,* 39: 1003–1006 (1968); George R. Bach, "Father-Fantasies and Father Typing in Father-Separated Children," *Child Development,* 17: 63–80 (1946).

[56] Henry B. Biller, "Father Absence, Maternal Encouragement, and Sex Role Development in Kindergarten-Age Boys," *Child Development,* 40: 539–546 (1969).

[57] Morris Rosenberg, *Society and the Adolescent Self-Image* (Princeton, N.J.: Princeton University Press, 1965), chap. 5.

[58] B. Sutton-Smith, B. G. Rosenberg, and Frank Landy, "Father-Absence Effects in Families of Different Sibling Compositions," *Child Development,* 39: 1213–1221 (1968).

[59] Lyn Carlsmith, "Effect of Early Father Absence on Scholastic Aptitude," *Harvard Educational Review,* 34: 3–21 (1964).

[60] E. Mavis Hetherington, "Effects of Paternal Absence on Sex-Typed Behaviors in Negro and White Preadolescent Males," *Journal of Personality and Social Psychology,* 4: 87–91 (1966).

[61] Joan McCord, William McCord, and Emily Thurber, "Some Effects of Paternal Absence on Male Children," *Journal of Abnormal and Social Psychology,* 64: 361–369 (1962).

[62] Morris Rosenberg, *op. cit.,* pp. 104–105.

his absence frequently depresses the economic circumstances of the family. That this may be a critical part of the impact of the loss of father is suggested by a study that shows few differences between father-absent and father-present children when socioeconomic status is controlled.[63]

In one study absence of father has been found to be unrelated to the son's sex-typing.[64] The absence of father has also been reported to be unrelated to the incidence of emotional disturbance of male subjects[65] and to children's perceptions of their parents.[66] (Of course when a researcher finds a statistically nonsignificant relationship between a pair of variables, there is always the possibility that a significant result might have appeared with a bigger or different sample, with more valid and more reliable tests, and so on. Reference has been made above to the way one should view a statistically significant result.)

There is one study that relates boys' perceptions of their fathers' paternal functioning to the boys' identification. From a group of thirty-eight kindergarten boys two sets of ten each were distinguished on the basis of scores denoting "strong" and "weak" masculine identification. The boys had responded to a projective (picture) type of test. On the average it was found that boys in the strong-masculine-identification set perceived their fathers as higher in fulfilling the parental functions of nurturance and control than did the boys in the weak-masculine-identification set. This finding suggests that control, as well as nurturance, has reward value for the child and is consistent with the hypothesis that functionality of the parent produces identification in the child.[67]

Do the studies on the consequences of father-absence add up to anything? The answer seems to be that there are conflicting findings and no very strong conclusions. Then does the absence of the mother make any difference? Before undertaking to answer that question, it is advisable to consider the difference between father-absence and mother-absence. When children live

---

[63] Mary Margaret Thomes, "Children with Absent Fathers," *Journal of Marriage and the Family*, 30: 89–96 (1968).

[64] Jules M. Greenstein, "Father Characteristics and Sex Typing," *Journal of Personality and Social Psychology*, 3: 271–277 (1966).

[65] Frank A. Pedersen, "Relationships between Father Absence and Emotional Disturbance in Male Military Dependents," *Merrill-Palmer Quarterly*, 12: 321–331 (1966).

[66] Alan J. Crain and Caroline S. Stamm, "Intermittent Absence of Fathers and Children's Perceptions of Fathers," *Journal of Marriage and the Family*, 27: 344–347 (1965).

[67] Paul Mussen and Luther Distler, "Masculinity, Identification, and Father-Son Relationships," *Journal of Abnormal and Social Psychology*, 59: 350–356 (1959); and "Child-Rearing Antecedents of Masculine Identification in Kindergarten Boys," *Child Development*, 31: 89–100 (1960). The findings of these studies have been rephrased slightly to fit the conceptual scheme here advanced. The authors of the study characterize the fathers of the masculine-identified boys as being perceived as "more rewarding and nurturant" and "more punitive and threatening." Although identification as measured by Mussen and Distler is not the operational equivalent of identification as defined in this book, it is plausible to assume a positive correlation between the two.

with only one parent, that parent is nine times more likely to be the mother than the father. Of all children under eighteen who live with one or both parents 90 percent live with both parents, 9 percent with the mother only and 1 percent with the father only.[68] For this reason the only kind of maternal absence that is at all common is the daily absence occasioned by the mother's employment. Proportions of American mothers in the labor force are: 38 percent of those with children under 18, 29 percent of those with children under 6, and 25 percent of those with children under 3.[69] In the light of these facts researchers tried to discover the effects on children of having their mothers employed. Although a considerable number of studies have been done, no dramatic correlations have appeared, and the best conclusion to date seems to be that there are no very strong effects on the children because of their mother's employment.[70] Between categories of mothers, however, a few differences have been detected in their children. Hoffman enumerates the following as categories related to these differences: social class, full-time versus part-time maternal employment, age of child, sex of child, and mother's attitude toward employment. For example, when social class is not controlled, the children of working mothers are reported as not significantly more delinquent than the children of nonworking mothers; within the middle class, however, greater delinquency is reported among the children of working mothers.[71]

If a married couple is in the throes of marital conflict and if they have children, the question typically arises as to whether the children would be better off if the couple were to remain together than if they were to part. To remain together would presumably amount to an armed truce, whose chief positive sanction would be the welfare of the children, with a considerable probability that the truce would be punctuated with episodes of open conflict but with some possibility of a reconciliation. To part would be to relieve the spouses of the distress associated with each other's company but also to deprive the children of a parent and to increase the cost of maintaining the set of individuals. It has been a timeless cliché of sociology that the delinquencies of minors have been related to broken parental marriages, but the directive implied in this cliché is neutralized by another that assures us that children are emotionally damaged by living in the presence of marital conflict. After a careful scrutiny of evidence Toby has concluded that although there is a discernible correlation between broken homes and delinquency, the association becomes much stronger when the offspring is an adolescent girl or a pre-

---

[68] U.S. Bureau of the Census, *Current Population Reports—Population Characteristics*, Series P-20, No. 100, April 13, 1960, Table 2, p. 9.
[69] Women's Bureau, *1969 Handbook on Women Workers* (Washington, D.C.: GPO, 1969), Table 16, p. 39. Cf. also Table 12.2 above.
[70] Lois Wladis Hoffman, "Effects on Children: Summary and Discussion," in F. Ivan Nye and Lois Wladis Hoffman, *The Employed Mother in America* (Skokie, Ill.: Rand McNally, 1963), pp. 190–212.
[71] *Ibid.*, pp. 192–196.

adolescent of either sex than in the case of an adolescent boy.[72] But there is also evidence that marital conflict complicates the personality development of children, especially evidence that when the mother deprecates the father, the son has difficulty in achieving the appropriate masculine identification.[73] Thus it appears that neither solution assures the child of a peaceful and secure development.

The way in which familial interaction is patterned can have a marked influence on the way in which the child experiences the family. Bronfenbrenner reports that relatively irresponsible boys and girls tend to come from homes where there is relatively little differentiation of parental roles.[74] Henry finds that the eldest child tends to perceive the father as the principal disciplinarian and the youngest sees the mother in this role. Moreover, he states that females are more likely to see the mother as the principal disciplinarian.[75] In a previous study confined to male subjects he found a tendency for males perceiving mothers as principal disciplinarians to report reacting to a situation of interpersonal misunderstanding with self-blame, whereas males perceiving fathers as principal disciplinarians would tend to blame the other person.[76] With respect to the consequences of variation in ordinal position Pauline Sears has summarized some results from Helen Koch's elegantly designed study of two-child families:

> (a) Ordinal position differences are most strongly influenced by the child's relation to his sibling when the spacing between children is least. The greater the spacing, the greater the relative influence of parent-child relations. (b) The two- to four-year spacing, especially for males, seemed to be clearly the most stressful and stimulating. (c) Having an opposite-sexed sibling is more stimulating and more security-taxing than having a same-sexed sibling, especially for first-borns. (d) A boy with a much older sister is distinctly more withdrawn and dependent than a boy with a much older brother. (e) The social expansiveness of males varies positively with the distance between the child and his sibling.[77]

[72] Jackson Toby, "The Differential Impact of Family Disorganization," *American Sociological Review*, 22: 505–512 (1957). See also Thomas P. Monahan, "Family Status and the Delinquent Child: A Reappraisal and Some New Findings," *Social Forces*, 35: 250–258 (1957).

[73] M. M. Helper, "Learning Theory and the Self Concept," *Journal of Abnormal and Social Psychology*, 51: 184–194 (1955); Pauline S. Sears, "Child-Rearing Factors Related to Playing of Sex-Typed Roles," *American Psychologist*, 8: 431 (abstract; 1953); A. Bandura and R. H. Walters, *Adolescent Aggression: A Study of the Influence of Child-Training Practices and Family Interrelationships* (New York: Ronald, 1959), p. 257.

[74] Urie Bronfenbrenner, "Parental Behavior and Adolescent Responsibility: A Reorientation," paper presented at the Symposium in the Development of Standards, Values, and Moral Behavior in American Children at the 1959 meetings of the American Psychological Association.

[75] Andrew F. Henry, "Sibling Structures and the Perception of the Disciplinary Roles of Parents," *Sociometry*, 20: 67–74 (1957).

[76] Andrew F. Henry, "Family Role Structure and Self Blame," *Social Forces*, 35: 34–38 (1956).

[77] Pauline Snedden Sears, "Developmental Psychology," in *Annual Review of Psy-*

A further analysis of these data led to the conclusion that "cross-sex siblings will have more traits of the opposite sex than will same-sex siblings, and . . . this effect will be greater for the younger . . . sibling."[78]

The consideration given above to the age- and sex-distribution of siblings within nuclear families calls to mind the point that there are familial systems in which more than one woman can fill the role of wife-mother in a given nuclear family. The question then arises: What effect may plural parent-figures have on children?

A study of child-rearing practices in societies practicing monogamy, sororal polygyny,[79] or nonsororal polygyny concluded that societies with sororal polygyny tend to be more indulgent in the initial care of the young child and less severe in subsequent socialization than monogamous and nonsororally polygynous societies. This is interpreted on the ground that the sisters, who are wives of the same husband, have learned patterns of cooperation in their families of orientation and carry them forward into their families of procreation.[80] In this setting we can observe familial structure affecting the carrying out of parental functions, and we have already hypothesized a relationship between function and identification and presented some fragmentary evidence to support the hypothesis.

Reference to the definitions of our basic concepts in Table 1.1 reveals that a man and his two wives—whether in sororal or nonsororal polygyny—constitute just two positions in the nuclear family. The reason is that no criteria of differentiation have been stipulated between the two female positions.[81] Among the Trobriand Islanders, however, a child has a mother and two

chology (Palo Alto, Calif.: Annual Reviews, Inc., 1958), IX, 119–156. Quotation is from p. 127.

[78] Orville G. Brim, Jr., "Family Structure and Sex Role Learning by Children: A Further Analysis of Helen Koch's Data, "*Sociometry,* 21: 1–16 (1958), at pp. 14–15. In Koch's original study teachers had rated the five- and six-year-old children on 58 traits. Brim classified each of these traits as masculine or feminine contingent upon whether it seemed to be more instrumental or expressive, respectively. For example, he judged dominance and aggression to pertain to the instrumental role, whereas affection and the absence of negativism were classified as expressive. Strodtbeck and Creeland have interpreted a set of their data as not supporting the finding of Brim reported in the text above. Cf. Fred L. Strodtbeck and Paul G. Creelan, "The Interaction Linkage between Family Size, Intelligence, and Sex-Role Identity," *Journal of Marriage and the Family,* 30: 301–307 (1968). Because of gross differences between the two studies, however (especially with respect to ages of subjects and measures of masculinity), it is not clear what relation the two studies have to each other.

[79] A marriage of one man to two or more women is said to be polygynous. In a marriage of sororal polygyny the wives are sisters.

[80] John W. M. Whiting and Irvin L. Child, *Child Training and Personality: A Cross-Cultural Study* (New Haven, Conn.: Yale University Press, 1953), p. 311.

[81] Of course it would be possible to specify one or more criteria of institutionalized differentiation between the two wives, e.g., senior wife and junior wife. This single criterion of seniority-juniority suffices to create the two differentiated positions of wife-mother.

fathers, and the latter are differentiated from each other. The mother's husband (i.e., the child's "real" father by Western reckoning) is in a kindly, avuncular relationship to the child; the mother's brother is responsible for disciplining the child. Thus the two men divide the nurturant and controlling functions, and certainly we should anticipate this arrangement to have consequences for the child's emotional development generally as well as for his identifications.[82]

Margaret Mead's treatise on the Samoans asserts that it is commonplace for several nuclear families to live in the same household. Since the child relates to each adult male in the household as to a father and to each adult female as to a mother, the child has a plurality of parent-figures over whom to spread his dependency.[83] Mead believes that "most children need the safety of several parental substitutes,"[84] and that the Samoan arrangement generates a sense of security in the child. If Mead is correct, it follows that to have only two parents is more anxiety producing and provides "a very narrow ledge" from which to view the world.[85] And by extension, this reasoning leads to the conclusion that the one-parent family (resulting from divorce, desertion, separation, or death) should be still more anxiety producing for the young child.

A cross-cultural study of primitive societies concludes that the presence of grandparents in the household tends to make for more stern imposition of the basic moral rules of the society.[86] On the other hand, the presence of a sympathetic grandparent in the home may provide the child with a sense of security and refuge when under a ban of parental displeasure.

There is one other feature of familial structure that seems to have some effect on the child—birth order. A comparison of four first-born adolescent monkeys with a like number of monkeys of the same age but of later birth order led to the conclusion that the later born were more relaxed—perhaps

[82] Bronislaw Malinowski, *Sex and Repression in Savage Society* (New York: Meridian, 1955), chap. 2.

[83] Margaret Mead, *Coming of Age in Samoa* in *From the South Seas* (New York: Morrow, 1939).

[84] Margaret Mead, "Implications of Insight—II," in Margaret Mead and Martha Wolfenstein (eds.), *Childhood in Contemporary Cultures* (Chicago: University of Chicago Press, 1955), pp. 449–461. Quotation is from p. 452. A study comparing subjects having three or more parent-figures with those having two concludes that the former have self-conceptions that are more "social" and extended and more homogeneous than do the subjects not having multiple parent-figures.—Theodore R. Sarbin, "Role Theory," in Gardner Lindzey (ed.), *Handbook of Social Psychology* (Reading, Mass.: Addison-Wesley, 1954), I, 223–258, esp. 243–244.

[85] James H. S. Bossard and Eleanor Stoker Boll, *The Sociology of Child Development* (3d ed.; New York: Harper & Row, 1960), p. 56.

[86] G. P. Murdock and J. W. M. Whiting, "Cultural Determination of Parental Attitudes: The Relationship between the Social Structure, Particularly Family Structure, and Parental Behavior," in M. J. E. Senn (ed.), *Problems of Infancy and Childhood* (New York: Josiah Macy, Jr., Foundation, 1951), pp. 13–34.

because their mothers had been more experienced.[87] In a mother-child study with four-year-old children the mothers who had only one child were found to be more interfering and more demonstrative of affection than the mothers who had two or more children. The mothers who had only one child were also more disposed to give and to withdraw approval as the child succeeded and failed.[88] The evidence about birth order seems consistent with an interpretation that the mother of an only-child tends to prize that child greatly, to feel unsure of her maternal competence, and to be anxious lest the child be unsuccessful. As the mother acquires experience and self-confidence and as she learns that a child is not as fragile as she may have thought, she can be more relaxed with her subsequent children.

Parents' Experiences

We have cited evidence and opinions of clinicians to the effect that the personalities of parents affect those of their children. If this is true, or to the extent that it is true, the personalities of grandparents affect directly those of parents and indirectly those of the parent's children. Occasionally we need to be reminded that parents have in turn had parents.

A pattern of "alternation of generations" has been presented by Flugel[89] and subsequently by Symonds.[90] According to this formulation a highly self-confident or masterful parent may cause the child to be yielding and submissive. When the latter becomes a parent, however, his lack of energy and of authority causes the child of the third generation to rely upon his own powers, a situation that may conduce to the development of a self-confident and masterful person. More generally stated, the mediate or indirect influence of the grandparent on the child through the parent acts either through the similar or the opposite identification of the parent with the grandparent. In the former case the parent seeks to reproduce his own (presumably pleasant) childhood experiences for his child. One manifestation of this occurs when persons brought up religiously later become irreligious (this change representing some decay of the similar identification), and then, as parents, introduce their children to religion for the avowed purpose of enriching the children's lives. Parents who have made opposite identifications with their own parents have rejected their parents as models with such vigor that they pass

---

[87] G. D. Mitchell *et al.*, "Long-Term Effects of Multiparous and Primiparous Monkey Mother Rearing," *Child Development*, 37: 781–791 (1966).

[88] Irma Hilton, "Differences in the Behavior of Mothers toward First- and Later-Born Children," *Journal of Personality and Social Psychology*, 7: 282–290 (1967).

[89] J. C. Flugel, *The Psycho-Analytic Study of the Family* (London: Hogarth, 1921), pp. 62–63.

[90] P. M. Symonds, *The Psychology of Parent-Child Relationships* (New York: Appleton, 1939), pp. 168–169.

the latters' influence on to their children in negative, or opposite, form. If, for example, they regarded their parents as having been overly repressive, they tend to be lenient with their children; if they felt their parents not to have been interested in them, they try to be greatly interested in their children; and so on. Ingersoll states that where the childhood patterns of domination were similar (i.e., both had either father-dominated or mother-dominated homes), the parents tend to reproduce the pattern for their children. If the patterns in the childhood of the two parents were different, however, they tend to create a more equalitarian authority pattern for their children.[91]

The gratifications that the parent receives both within and outside the home may be expected to affect the nature of the parent-child relationship. Bernard Glueck has pointed out the influence of the gratification received by the husband-father in his vocational activities for marital and family interaction:

> Unless his business relations reach a certain degree of warmth, unless he is constantly given evidence by his superiors or associates that they think well of him as a person, that they value him as a friend as well as a business associate, he has a keen sense of privation. Such a person is not apt to promote his opportunities for getting out of life sufficient ego satisfactions. In consequence, he is apt to seek compensatory satisfactions of this type in the circle of the home. He is then apt to exaggerate the virtue and importance of obedience and submissiveness on the part of the children; he is apt to be unduly tyrannical and egotistical in the exercise of parental authority; and he will in consequence either transmit his own sense of inferiority and timidity to his children or provoke in them a negativistic and rebellious attitude toward sources of authority. Moreover, the marital relations between two people one or both of whom are disposed in this manner are apt to be unhealthy and ineffectual and conducive to an unhealthy home atmosphere.[92]

It will be recalled that the harsh treatment of lower-class children by their fathers has been attributed to a lack of gratification in the occupational system. (See the end of "Social Class and Child Rearing" earlier in this chapter.)

In the literature that purports to set forth the effect upon the child of various types of parental personalities the general burden of the argument is to the effect that a relationship of emotional security between mother and father and between parents and children is a setting in terms of which the child grows up with emotional security.[93] When these conditions are not realized, it is believed there is a strong possibility that the child will suffer

---

[91] Hazel Ingersoll, "A Study of the Transmission of Authority Patterns in the Family" *Genetic Psychology Monographs*, 38: 225–302 (1948).

[92] Bernard Glueck, "The Significance of Parental Attitudes for the Destiny of the Individual," *Mental Hygiene*, 12: 722–741 (1938), at pp. 733–734.

[93] Therese Benedek, *Insight and Personality Adjustment* (New York: Ronald, 1946), p. 32.

emotionally. To the extent that this is so, it is frequently argued that the gratification each spouse gets from the marriage represents money in the child's emotional bank. We have already noted one aspect of this argument in our remarks about divorce in the preceding section. The dynamics of the marital relationship will be considered in Part Six.

Parenthood as a Value

Whether or not a parent has religious faith and believes in life after death, the child can be viewed as a representation of immortality through constituting the link between the parent and posterity. This fact and the further consideration that the child is "one's own flesh and blood" make an offspring, generally speaking, the most important thing a parent has. In trying to understand parental behavior it is useful to recall William James's conception of the "social self" as being extended to one's wife and children, one's home, and to the end of one's walking stick. In this formulation James gave expression to the involvement of parents in the careers of their children. Since parents of the middle class are very much involved in a competitive social order, the comparative standing of their children becomes a matter of major concern. This appears to be especially true of mothers. For fathers of this class, the occupational system is the arena of competition. For most mothers, housewifery and motherhood constitute their career. Where the mother of an earlier generation might have expressed her competitive spirit in the immaculateness of her housekeeping and in taking prizes at a baking contest, labor-saving devices have reduced the competitive value of housekeeping, while "mixes" and commercially produced goods have done the same for baking. Since technology has reduced the area of competition in housewifery, children assume greater competitive significance. It is not astonishing, therefore, to hear mothers compare the precise ages at which their children uttered their first intelligible sounds, or first became "housebroken."

Because of the high degree of involvement of parents with their children it is not surprising that some seek to direct their children into occupations or marriages of the parents' choice, or, more generally, that parents should seek to be so directive over many areas of their children's activities as to be experienced by their children as dominating fathers and overprotective mothers. The clinical literature is replete with examples of the unfortunate consequences of such parental behavior. The disposition of the parent to force a child into an occupation of the parent's choice and thus to give expression to the parent's projected ambitions may result in the withdrawal of the child and his failure in school.[94] The father who dominates the child tends to produce children

---

[94] Kimball Young, "Parent-Child Relationships: Projection of Ambition," *The Family*, 8: 67–73 (1927).

who deviate from normality in being either passive and submissive or rebellious and resentful.[95] Somewhat comparable results are obtained by the overprotective mother.[96] But the clinical literature finds baleful consequences outside, as well as within, the family as we saw in Chapter 13. Thus there is literature that suggests that children who grow up outside the family situation suffer from intellectual deficiency and emotional coldness.[97]

The Individual Child

At various points in this chapter and preceding ones attention has been given to parents' attitudes to the general idea of parenthood. It is also in order to note the relevance to the parent-child relationship of the parents' attitude toward the specific child. Insofar as the child is an extension of the parent's own self, the parent is disposed to look in the child for physical features, emotional traits, mannerisms, and aptitudes that will reflect his own strengths or weaknesses, for the positive aspects from his own parents whom he admires or for negative ones from those whom he dislikes, for attractive features from his own antecedents or for unattractive ones from "the other side of the house."

The literature on individual differences enumerates a great many variables that enter into the way in which the child responds to stimuli, including, of course, the behaviors of his parents. These individual differences enter also into the way people respond to the child. There are reports that the subjective significance of the same objective experience varies with individual differences in original activity level,[98] sensitivity,[99] and reaction to cuddling.[100] Because of this variation in original equipment a type of mothering that might constitute rejection for one child may appear to another as stifling overprotection, and reciprocally a child who enjoys cuddling will elicit maternal responses different from those elicited by the child who is annoyed by such behaviors.[101]

The sex of the child is one of the most obvious characteristics to evoke differential responses. As Plant observes, we "hope it will be" a boy (or a

[95] D. D. Mueller, "Paternal Domination: Its Influences on Child Guidance Results," *Smith College Studies in Social Work*, 15: 184–215 (1945).

[96] D. M. Levy, "Maternal Over-Protection," *Psychiatry*, 1: 561–591 (1938).

[97] William Goldfarb, "Psychological Privation in Infancy and Subsequent Adjustment," *American Journal of Orthopsychiatry*, 15: 247–255 (1945).

[98] M. E. Fries and B. Lewi, "Interrelated Factors in Development: A Study of Pregnancy, Labor, Delivery, Lying-In Period and Childhood," *American Journal of Orthopsychiatry*, 8: 726–752 (1938).

[99] Mary Shirley, "A Behavior Syndrome Characterizing Prematurely Born Children," *Child Development*, 10: 115–128 (1939).

[100] R. W. Washburn, "A Study of the Smiling and Laughing of Infants in the First Year of Life," *Genetic Psychology Monographs*, 6: 397–537 (1929).

[101] Rose W. Coleman, Ernst Kris, and Sally Provence, "The Study of Variations of Early Parental Attitudes," in Ruth S. Eissler *et al.* (eds.), *The Psychoanalytic Study of the Child* (New York: International Universities Press, 1953), VIII, 20–47.

girl), "lacking the courtesy to await the child's arrival before we begin to pick the part it is to play."[102] Other obviously relevant characteristics include the size, body type, and general appearance of the child. It hardly seems disputable that some portion of the individual differences in intelligence is inborn. It has been shown that intelligence is positively correlated with a person's total activity rate, his leadership, and popularity.[103] Activity is correlated with body type, and boys with a muscular body type tend to be overrepresented among those classed as delinquent, just as the thin, fragile-boned boys are underrepresented.[104] These and other features enter into the way others respond to the child, to the impression he has of what others think of him, to the "self-feeling" that derives from these impressions,[105] and to the way in which he responds by presenting himself.[106]

Such considerations as these can be seen very clearly in a two-child family in which one child strongly resembles the mother and is spoken of as "her child," while the other child is regarded as the father's. This pattern creates the temptation for the parents to express hostility toward each other by punishing or depriving the favorite of the spouse. In such a situation it is evident that the two children will have different concepts of their parents and of family life in general. An example of this pattern may be drawn from the writer's research. Mrs. A has one sibling, a brother two years her junior. At an early age she understood that she was her father's favorite and that her mother preferred her brother. The father was a passive, dependent man, and he and both children were under the domination of the mother. Mrs. A felt sorely handicapped at having been her father's favorite since it was the mother who was the locus of power. Accordingly, she found herself rejecting her role as father's favorite and competing with both her brother and her father for her mother's favor.

Summary

In infancy nurturance is the important parental function. With the emergence of the key skills of childhood—manipulation, speech, and locomotion—comes the need to exercise the parental function of control. These skills enable the child to become somewhat more self-reliant,to extend his experience, and

---

[102] J. S. Plant, *Personality and the Cultural Pattern* (New York: Commonwealth Fund, 1937), p. 35.

[103] Richard D. Mann, "A Review of the Relationships between Personality and Performance in Small Groups," *Psychological Bulletin*, 56: 241–270 (1959).

[104] Sheldon Glueck and Eleanor Glueck, *Physique and Delinquency* (New York: Harper & Row, 1956).

[105] Cf. Cooley's concept of the "looking-glass self."—C. H. Cooley, *Human Nature and the Social Order* (New York: Scribner, 1922).

[106] Erving Goffman, *The Presentation of Self in Everyday Life* (New York: Doubleday Anchor Books, 1959).

to develop a social self. As the need for control arises, then, the child has less need of nurturance in the form of purely physical care, but his development into a social being generates a need for nurturance in the more symbolic form of ministration to his social needs for acceptance and reassurance.

Since the parents contribute to a large portion of the child's social interaction during the early years, the child acquires his first cultural elements while in the context of the family. For this reason what the child learns depends upon the social class and ethnoreligious affiliation of the family, i.e., upon the location of the family in the structure of the society and upon the associated subculture. Important elements in the culture concern expectations about the expression and inhibition of aggressive and sexual impulses. In this country expectations concerning achievement and integration into peer groups are also emphasized. Such norms and the child-rearing practices that implement them vary by social class and ethnoreligious affiliation. Relatively speaking, the middle class tends toward indulgence and love-oriented discipline directed at the intent of the child's behavior, whereas the lower class tends toward sternness, physical punishment, and discipline directed at the consequence of the child's behavior. With respect to ethnoreligious affiliation Jewish and Protestant families emphasize achievement more than do Italian and black families, but these differences may disappear when social class is held constant.

Socialization and personality development depend heavily upon the learning process. Learning involves cognition of the nature of the group's expectations concerning the child's expression and inhibition of impulses, the acquisition of behaviors appropriate to his present and future roles, and so on. The parental function of control is conceived not only in the negative sense of the internalization of discipline but also in the positive sense of acquiring goals and a sense of an ideal self.

We may think of identification as the more or less lasting influence of one person on another. In the present context we are especially interested in parents as models and children as identifiers. Typically a parent serves as the child's original model, but the child comes to displace the original model with others encountered outside the family circle. Psychological theories suggest that the child will find persons in control of rewards attractive as potential models. Our sociological theory (set forth in Chapter 1) asserts that the more functional the family, the more resources it will have at its disposal to convert into rewards, and hence the greater the probability that a parent in a highly functional family will serve as the offspring's model. The correlation between control of resources and socioeconomic status leads to the prediction that there will be a greater disposition for upper-class children to identify with their parents than will be the case in lower socioeconomic strata. It is proposed that the structure of the family determines the positions the family presents to the child as potential models, and the functions of the family determine the nature of the interaction between the child and the occupants of the various positions. Hence it is theorized that familial structure and function influence the nature of the child's identifications. Tentative findings from one study support the hypothesis that functionality leads to identification in boys; with girls the proposition awaits substantiation. Having an older sibling of the opposite, rather than the same, sex seems to complicate the task of achieving the appropriate sex-type identification.

If it is true that the behavior (and personality development) of a child is determined to a considerable degree by the behavior (and personality) of his parents, it is similarly important to notice the implication that the behavior of parents also has its determinants. This point directs our attention to (1) the experiences parents have had in *their* families of orientation (i.e., parents, too, have had parents) and (2) the experiences they have outside the familial setting. Additional influences on parent-child interaction are (3) the nature of the marital interaction and (4) the attractiveness of the individual child.

16

The Adolescent and the Fusion of the Parental Functions

Purpose of This Chapter

"Half man, half child" is the adolescent. The transition from childhood to adulthood occurs everywhere, but does adolescence always have the same meaning? Indeed, must it always occur? Where it does occur, is it a period of "storm and stress"? Is it *necessarily* so? What are the tasks of the adolescent? What is his position in his society? in his family? In which manifestations are the parental functions relevant to adolescence? What is the role of the parent of an adolescent? These are questions that we shall consider in the present chapter.

Points of Emphasis

It is possible to define adolescence as a period of sexual maturation.[1] For our purposes, however, it is preferable to rely on cultural definitions as referring to that phase in the human life cycle when a person is thought too old to be a child and too young to be an adult. It follows that if a society provides for its young to be admitted into adulthood at the conclusion of childhood, that society has no adolescence.

Since departure from adolescence means entry into adulthood, the serious business of adolescence is the acquiring of the skills, attitudes, and credentials that make such passage possible. In all societies adults are classified by sex; accordingly one adolescent task is to acquire the appropriately sex-typed be-

---

[1] Cf. Clellan S. Ford and Frank A. Beach, *Patterns of Sexual Behavior* (New York: Harper & Row, 1952), pp. 161–172.

haviors and attitudes. In advanced societies adults are classified by occupation, and it is expected that the adolescents who intend to enter the labor force will become occupationally oriented and prepare themselves to enter their occupations or at least begin the course of preparation. It is expected, moreover, that adolescents will become oriented to marriage and to making themselves desirable for the marriage market. The intensity of the expectations is greater for boys with respect to occupations and for girls with respect to marriage.

Since virtually all positions of superordination, influence, and responsibility in basic societal structures (see Table 1.2) are filled by adults, and since children and adolescents are thereby spectators and/or minor participants, adolescents have less involvement with, as well as less experience with, these structures. Despite their naïveté and because of their uninvolvement some adolescents can make more objective observations than some of their seniors. Being uninvolved and inexperienced, moreover, they are not in a position to empathize with an official experiencing role-conflict nor to condone his resulting behavior, which their objective perceptions assess as hypocritical and perhaps corrupt. Indeed the perceptions of adolescents can influence whether or not they will become involved and participating adults. The bohemians of the twenties, the beatniks of the fifties, and the hippies and the yippies of the sixties all were implying that they rejected the society in which they had been expected to assume positions of adult responsibility. Rebellion and rejection by those on the brink of entering the system (or "establishment") as adults are not new; somewhat novel, however, is that in more recent years some of the older generation appear to have been listening.

Ambiguity of Adolescence in American Society

Let us conceive of a society in which every member is trained to assume his or her adult roles by the time he or she has passed through puberty and in which everyone does exactly this. That is, he marries, founds a nuclear family, assumes adult economic responsibilities, and so on. In this setting there would be no adolescence.[2] What, then, is adolescence?

---

[2] Ariès has concluded from his studies of painting and diaries of four centuries in western Europe that during the Middle Ages and, especially in the lower classes, for some time thereafter, children became adults by cultural definition not long after the age of seven. The development of a system of formal education, he believes, was very important in creating both the concept of (postinfancy) childhood and of adolescence. Cf. Philippe Ariès, *Centuries of Childhood: A Social History of Family Life* (New York: Knopf, 1962).

It appears that the Jewish custom of *bar mitzvah* arose in a society without a concept of adolescence and has been adapted to one having this age category. Traditionally this ceremony has marked the achievement by a male at the age of thirteen of the right to participate in religious services. This implies that the male was seen as becoming an adult at the age of thirteen. As currently practiced among middle-class Jews in this country, however, *bar mitzvah* serves rather to mark the passage of the male from childhood into adolescence.

Since in the popular view the cultural phenomenon of adolescence is linked with the physiological events of puberty, there is some disposition to think of adolescence as in part a consequence of the rising sexuality of postpubertal youth and to interpret the beginning of dating as a benchmark for timing the onset of adolescence. Among studies that have recorded the phenomenon is one in a Southern city showing that boys and girls were generally dating by the time they were in the seventh grade.[3] Variation from one social setting to another in the age at which dating is begun, however, indicates that the relationship between puberty and the onset of adolescence is not a perfect one.[4]

Ambiguous as it is, the beginning of adolescence is probably easier to recognize in American society than is the end. Unlike some primitive tribes that utilize initiation ceremonies to mark the entry into adulthood, we observe no uniform rites. There are, however, practices affecting various social classes and ethnoreligious groups that mark this alteration in status with varying degrees of explicitness. Examples are the debut, marriage, graduation from high school or college, finishing an apprenticeship in a trade or a profession, going to work, assuming responsibility for supporting oneself, moving from the parents' home, entering military service. Some of these practices are attended by ritual; others are not. It must be immediately added that *none* of them *always* symbolizes the attainment of full and permanent adult status. Legal adulthood (majority) comes to all classes on the attainment of a birthday (usually the twenty-first). Social maturity, on the other hand, is much more variable.

Probably the most explicit ritual marking the attainment of adulthood is the debut.[5] This ceremony (or "rite of passage") is used to mark the achievement of adult status by the upper-class girl and to announce that she has entered the marriage market.

Marriage is frequently construed as implying the assumption of adult re-

---

[3] Carlfred B. Broderick and Stanley E. Fowler, "New Patterns of Relationships between the Sexes among Preadolescents," *Marriage and Family Living*, 23: 27–30 (1961).

[4] Physiological criteria seem not to offer much more precision than cultural definitions in specifying the beginning of adolescence. One difficulty results from a lack of consensus as to just which event signals the onset of puberty; another difficulty results from variation in the ages at which individuals experience any given physiological development. Among the male subjects studied by Kinsey first ejaculation occurred at a median age of 13.9 years. Cf. A. C. Kinsey, W. B. Pomeroy, and C. E. Martin, *Sexual Behavior in the Human Male* (Philadelphia: Saunders, 1948), p. 187. For females he preferred to use the appearance of pubic hair, which occurred at a median age of 12.3 years, rather than the more usual index of first menstruation, which occurred among his subjects at a median age of 13.0 years. The range in age at first menses was from 9 to 25 years. Cf. A. C. Kinsey *et al.*, *Sexual Behavior in the Human Female* (Philadelphia: Saunders, 1953), pp. 123–124. Regular ovulation probably does not begin until around 16 to 18 years of age; it is the period between the onset of menses and regular ovulation that constitutes the period of so-called adolescent sterility.—*Ibid.*, p. 125.

[5] Cf. J. H. S. Bossard and Eleanor Boll, "Rites of Passage—A Contemporary Study," *Social Forces*, 26: 247–255 (1948); and Stephen Birmingham, "Our Debutante Daughters," *Holiday*, November 1958, pp. 63–67, 202, 204–205, 207–208, 210.

sponsibilities and marking the passage into adult status, but this is not always the case. As we have seen in Chapter 10, there is much variation with respect to age at marriage. Some individuals are already well established in responsible positions when they marry; some never marry. Others, especially in the upper class, marry while still dependent upon their parents. To a lesser degree the same qualifications may be stated concerning parenthood as a mark of adulthood.

Leaving school is frequently a necessary but seldom a sufficient condition to mark the end of adolescence. If, as seems usually to be the case, the act of ending formal education is attended by becoming gainfully employed and assuming responsibility for one's own maintenance, the probability is much greater that adulthood is being achieved.

In recent years millions of young men and thousands of young women have been in military service. For males, registration by the Selective Service board continues to be one indication of the attainment of adulthood. For those who have entered the service while still regarded as adolescents there has been a disposition to conceive of the induction into the service as an initiation into adult status. (This has been explicitly recognized by the widespread reduction of the minimum voting age to eighteen.) This calls to mind the story of a bomber pilot who went home on leave during World War II and was denied the privilege of driving his father's automobile because he was too young to obtain a driver's license.[6]

In general, then, no one of the practices mentioned above suffices to mark the individual's passage into adulthood. Rather, the attainment of adulthood comes at the end of such a sequence as leaving school, going to work, becoming self-supporting, getting married, and moving out of the parents' residence. Customarily, therefore, the passage is more a gradual transition than an abrupt change.

The sequence of stages, the usual age of attaining adulthood, and, as we shall see, the conception of adulthood tend to vary with the social class. Where occupations require little or no training or education and where it is customary to leave school at an early age, as in the lower class, adult status can be achieved early. College and professional education and training in the

---

[6] And indeed in some areas the obtaining of the driver's license seems to be regarded as *the* rite of passage into adulthood.

Following are two related anecdotes. A soft-drink reception in California following the wedding of a 16-year-old male and a 14-year-old female had to be cut short because of a juvenile curfew law.—"Bride Is Only 14," *Chicago Sun-Times,* February 29, 1956, p. 16. A 15-year-old father was denied the privilege of seeing his newborn child in Illinois because the rules of the hospital required visitors to be at least 16.—"Rule Checks Father at 15," *Chicago Sun-Times,* February 17, 1956, p. 6. In Needles and Oakton Hollows in the Blue Ridge Mountains of Virginia the possession of a gun is the badge of emancipation "from the domination of women."—Mandel Sherman and Thomas R. Henry, *Hollow Folk* (New York: Crowell, 1933), p. 105. The reader is reminded that the rural residents of County Clare are "boys" and "girls" until they attain full adult status through marriage and succession to the parental farm—usually around the age of 35.

upper reaches of the middle class necessitate prolonged dependence on parents and delayed adulthood. When the offspring leaves home to obtain his education or training, the departure serves to mitigate his emotional dependence upon the parents even though his financial dependence upon them may be increasing sharply. In other words, going to college provides a sort of emotional weaning.

In the upper class, by contrast, property rather than occupation is the economic basis of socioeconomic status. This status derives from identification with family (ascribed status) rather than from individual accomplishment (achieved status). For this reason, the upper-class family tends to foster dependence of its offspring, and autonomy in the upper class tends to be retarded.

This discussion has endeavored to present the indefinite and amorphous nature of the passage from adolescence to adulthood in our society. Adolescence, therefore, is necessarily a somewhat vague concept. We shall see that the ambiguity of the nature and duration of adolescence contributes to make it a difficult period.

Some Problems of the Adolescent as an Individual

Childhood and adolescence present the growing individual with shifting criteria for self-validation. Those who have achieved high status at an earlier age may prove inept in the status struggle of adolescence.[7] We may illustrate the shifts in criteria from a report on the California Adolescent Study.[8] For both sexes Tryon has investigated the kinds of behavior correlated with high evaluations in status by classmates for the ages of 12 and 15. Groups of 12-year-old boys rated their peers highly for showing hyperactivity, aggressiveness, boisterousness, and competence in group games. Three years later the boys still prized skill in games, but were also according high ratings to those showing social ease and poise in heterosexual situations; while cheerfulness and a good sense of humor were values, boisterousness and hyperactivity were disapproved. High rating among the twelve-year-old girls fell to the "little lady"—friendly, but demure and docile. Tomboyishness was acceptable but raucous noisiness was not. After three years the girls were giving each other high ratings on one of two counts: aggressive good-fellowship with both sexes, or the ability to attract boys through sophistication and glamour. There is no certainty, to take one example, that the girl who achieves acceptance by her peers through her demureness at the age of twelve will be equally applauded at fifteen for aggressive good-fellowship. In a study of ten midwestern high

[7] Gardner Murphy, *Personality: A Biosocial Approach to Origins and Structure* (New York: Harper & Row, 1947), pp. 507–508.
[8] Caroline Tryon, "Evaluations of Adolescent Personality by Adolescents," in R. G. Barker, J. S. Kounin, and H. F. Wright (eds.), *Child Behavior and Development* (New York: McGraw-Hill, 1943), chap. 31.

schools Coleman found that membership in male elites went first to athletes, second to "ladies' men," and third to scholars. Popularity with boys went primarily to girls "with brains" in working-class high schools and to girls "with beauty" in middle-class schools.[9]

Developmental Tasks of Adolescence in the Middle Class

The subculture of the middle class confronts the adolescent with a variety of difficult goals and with strong pressure to achieve them. This is one of the reasons why adolescence is thought of as a period of "stress and strain." The two most important goals are success, or upward mobility; and the achievement of the appropriate "masculine" or "feminine" repertory of behaviors, or the correct sex-type. The importance of these goals may be seen in the fact that a middle-class person can evaluate his career in terms of the degree of his success in achieving them.

We have already noted that in the middle class the parent's exhortations to the child to be obedient are based on an expressed or implied threat to withhold their love and approval if the child should prove disobedient. Such punishment implies the possible further loss of the material benefits of their love, such as food, shelter, money, opportunity to prepare for a profession, and so on.

THE "SUCCESS" IMPERATIVE

A traditional characteristic of the middle classes has been an emphasis on upward mobility, on improving the socioeconomic status conferred by one's parents, on "making good." For many parents children represent the vicarious road to their own self-validation. As Plant remarks:

> What in the years of youth we plan and dream for our children, grows stronger as the years pass until—when we become parents—it becomes an imperious urge that the next generation live as we wish that we had lived, accomplish what we had hoped ourselves to do. . . . The girl who is a drudge must be assured a butterfly daughter; the man who didn't go to college, this experience for his son.[10]

A study of the American occupational structure finds that the socioeconomic level of the family "into which a man is born exerts a profound influence on his career, because his occupational life is conditioned by his educa-

---

[9] James S. Coleman, *The Adolescent Society: The Social Life of the Teenager and Its Impact on Education* (New York: Free Press, 1961), pp. 153, 157, 170–171.

[10] J. S. Plant, *Personality and the Cultural Pattern* (New York: Commonwealth Fund, 1937), p. 262.

tion, and his education depends to a considerable extent on his family."[11] Being reared in a broken family, moreover, leads to a lowered probability of concluding a high level of education and thereby constitutes a handicap for upward mobility.[12]

The whole social environment of the middle-class juvenile is stimulating him to develop images of what "he will be when he grows up." A sharp contrast is presented in the testimony of little girls in a remote region in the Blue Ridge Mountains of Virginia. When asked what they expected to be when they grew up, the response was "Wimmin."[13]

THE SEX-TYPE IMPERATIVE

In Chapter 12 we considered the general topic of the differentiation of roles with special reference to familial and sex roles. The present section is concerned with the process whereby a child acquires the behaviors and attitudes appropriate to his or her sex and the stress attendant to the process. We saw in Chapter 15 that distinctively masculine and feminine behavior began to appear in children by the age of four or five. From early childhood to adulthood individuals are learning which behaviors are appropriate to their sex categories and to produce such appropriate behaviors. There seems to be an intensification of this process in later childhood and adolescence, and although recent years have seen some mitigation of this point, the norms of sex-typed behavior tend to carry cruel sanctions in adolescence.

Some of the conclusions from the numerous studies on this general topic are as follows:

1. the degree to which one achieves behavior patterns appropriate to one's sex is correlated with the pleasantness and desirability of childhood experiences;[14]
2. for men (the study covered men only) sex-typed behavior is correlated with having masculine body structure;[15] although another study failed to support this conclusion;[16]
3. in adolescence skeletally accelerated boys are rated as more attractive

---

[11] Peter M. Blau and Otis Dudley Duncan, *The American Occupational Structure* (New York: Wiley, 1967), p. 330.

[12] *Ibid.*, p. 359. Cf. also William H. Sewell, Archibald O. Haller, and Alejandro Portes, "The Educational and Early Occupational Attainment Process," *American Sociological Review*, 34: 82–92 (1969).

[13] Sherman and Henry, *op. cit.*, p. 104.

[14] L. W. Ferguson, "The Cultural Genesis of Masculinity-Femininity," *Psychological Bulletin*, 38: 584–585 (1941).

[15] C. C. Seltzer, "The Relationship between the Masculine Component and Personality," in Clyde Kluckhohn and H. A. Murray (eds.), *Personality in Nature, Society, and Culture* (New York: Knopf, 1948), pp. 84–96.

[16] Nancy Bayley, "Kuder Masculinity-Femininity Scores in Adolescent Boys and Girls Related to Their Scores in Somatic Androgyny," *American Psychologist*, 4: 251 (1949).

in appearance and are more likely to be student leaders than those who are less advanced in skeletal development;[17]
4. late maturing boys are more likely than the early developers to have feelings of inadequacy and negative self-conceptions;[18]
5. hence it is not surprising to learn that adolescents are very much concerned about their physical development;[19]
6. early maturing boys tend to become achieving, conforming, non-neurotic men, whereas late maturing boys tend to be independent, perceptive and humorous, but also fearful and vulnerable to threat;[20] but by age 33 the physical differences have tended to disappear;[21]
7. those who feel that they have achieved their sex-type are more optimistic than others,[22] but
8. it has also been found that among sixth- and seventh-graders those who were high in anxiety showed significantly more sex-appropriate behavior (as reflected by the perceptions of peers) than those low in anxiety;[23]
9. traits judged to be masculine by college students are thought by students of both sexes to be generally superior to traits they judged to be feminine;[24]
10. girls express more negative attitudes toward their own sex as they grow older;[25]
11. irrespective of the sex of the person, the more masculine he or she rates on conventional tests of masculinity-femininity, the better he or she tends to be at problem-solving skills;[26]
12. a substantial proportion of college women feel called upon to pretend

---

[17] Mary Cover Jones and Nancy Bayley, "Physical Maturing among Boys as Related to Behavior," *Journal of Educational Psychology*, 41: 129–148 (1950).

[18] Paul H. Mussen and Mary Cover Jones, "Self-Conceptions, Motivations, and Interpersonal Attitudes of Late- and Early-Maturing Boys," *Child Development*, 28: 243–256 (1957).

[19] Alexander Frazier and Lorenzo K. Lisonbee, "Adolescent Concerns with Physique," *School Review*, 58: 397–405 (1950).

[20] Mary Cover Jones, "Psychological Correlates of Somatic Development," *Child Development*, 36: 899–911 (1965).

[21] Mary Cover Jones, "The Later Careers of Boys Who Were Early- or Late-Maturing," *Child Development*, 28: 113–128 (1957).

[22] R. N. Sanford, H. S. Conrad, and K. Franck, "Psychological Determinants of Optimism Regarding Consequences of the War," *Journal of Psychology*, 22: 207–235 (1946).

[23] Susan W. Gray, "Masculinity-Femininity in Relation to Anxiety and Social Acceptance," *Child Development*, 28: 203–214 (1957).

[24] John P. McKee and Alex C. Sherriffs, "Men's and Women's Beliefs, Ideals, and Self-Concepts," *American Journal of Sociology*, 64: 356–363 (1959).

[25] Dale B. Harris and Sing Chu Tseng, "Children's Attitudes toward Peers and Parents as Revealed by Sentence Completions," *Child Development*, 28: 401–411 (1957).

[26] G. A. Milton, "The Effects of Sex-Role Identification upon Problem-Solving Skills," *Journal of Abnormal and Social Psychology*, 55: 208–212 (1957).

to be inferior to men while actually believing themselves to be equal or superior to men;[27]

13. when confronted with a common task implying no division of labor, men and women who are strangers tend to show sex-typed behavior, but men and women of the same nuclear family do not;[28]

14. and having distinguished among sex-role *preference* ("the desire to adopt the behavior associated with one sex or the other"), sex-role *identification* ("actual incorporation of the role of a given sex, and . . . the unconscious reactions characteristic of that role"), and sex-role *adoption* (showing "overt behavior of a given sex"), Lynn believes that the extant studies provide support for the following hypotheses:

   a. With increasing age males become relatively *more* firmly identified with the masculine role, and females relatively *less* identified with the feminine role.
   b. A larger proportion of females than of males shows preference for the role of the opposite sex.
   c. A higher proportion of females than of males adopts aspects of the role of the opposite sex.
   d. Males tend to identify with a cultural stereotype of masculine role, whereas females tend to identify with aspects of their own mother's role specifically.[29]

One other theme in the literature concerns the degree to which behaviors connoted by the adjectives "masculine" and "feminine" vary from culture to culture. Margaret Mead's study of three primitive societies in New Guinea begins with the observation that "no culture has failed to seize upon the conspicuous facts of age and sex in some way, whether it be the convention of one Philippine tribe that no man can keep a secret, the Manus assumption that only men enjoy playing with babies, the Toda prescription of almost all domestic work as too sacred for women, or the Arapesh insistence that women's heads are stronger than men's."[30]

In qualification of the view that sex-role prescriptions are infinitely variable it is relevant to recall Murdock's study cited in Chapter 12 to the effect that feminine roles typically involve sedentary activities while the most

---

[27] Paul Wallin, "Cultural Contradictions and Sex Roles: A Repeat Study," *American Sociological Review*, 15: 288–293 (1950). See also Mirra Komarovsky, "Cultural Contradictions and Sex Roles," *American Journal of Sociology*, 52: 184–189 (1946).

[28] Robert K. Leik, "Instrumentality and Emotionality in Family Interaction," *Sociometry*, 26: 131–145 (1963). Cf. also Jerold S. Heiss, "Degree of Intimacy and Male-Female Interaction," *Sociometry*, 26: 197–208 (1962).

[29] David B. Lynn, "A Note on Sex Differences in the Development of Masculine and Feminine Identification," *Psychological Review*, 66: 126–135 (1959).

[30] Margaret Mead, *Sex and Temperament in Three Primitive Societies* in *From the South Seas* (New York: Morrow, 1939), p. xi.

vigorous and nomadic activities fall within masculine role prescriptions. Variable though culture is, it can hardly overcome the physiological fact that only women bear children.[31]

From the foregoing studies as well as from the analysis presented in Chapter 12[32] it appears that in the middle strata of American society the prescriptions for the roles of both sexes have become less differentiated, more amorphous and fluid. When we take account also of the superior evaluation accorded to masculine behaviors, it becomes understandable that women should have taken on a considerable number of masculine behaviors (smoking, drinking, participating in sports, wearing masculine garments, and so on). In the youth culture there seems also to have been some revulsion against the strongly athletic, crew-cut concept of masculinity (perhaps in large measure because of rejection of America's participation in the war in Viet Nam and of the police as representatives of the social order responsible for that war). In any case the end of the sixties saw a comparative submergence of sex-typical characteristics in dress, speech, attitudes, and behavior. The "unisex" style of dress—bell-bottom trousers and long hair for both sexes—made classification by gender not at all obvious and forced the observer to look for such cues as presence of a beard or handbag.

From the evidence it appears that (1) sex-typed behavior varies with the culture; (2) most infants have sufficient psychic plasticity to develop in a number of different ways; (3) because of this plasticity most infants have the capacity to achieve an acceptable approximation of the appropriate sex-type; and (4) the achievement of the behavior patterns and personality type consonant with one's sex depends upon one's musculature, glandular function, culture, and unique experiences within the cultural context.[33] It appears that for some individuals these factors combine in such fashion as to make achievement of the sex-typed personality painless and free from anxiety. For others, the sex-typed personality is never achieved. Sexual inverts and transvestites[34] are the most conspicuous examples of the latter group. It appears that in the American middle class there is an appreciable number of persons who almost completely achieve the overt manifestations of the traits defined as appropriate to their sex, but do so with varying degrees of strain and anxiety.

---

[31] In a later book Mead seems to have taken a position of less extreme cultural determinism on this point. Cf. *Male and Female: A Study of the Sexes in a Changing World* (New York: Morrow, 1949). Cf. also Amram Scheinfeld, *Women and Men* (New York: Harcourt, 1943).

[32] Cf. especially "Tasks, Abilities and Sex-Role Differentiation" and "The Woman's Dilemma."

[33] Relevant here is the study by Grønseth and Tiller of the sailors' sons who showed signs of compensatory strivings toward masculinity and father-identification. Cf. pages 404–405.

[34] *Transvestite:* one who is addicted to wearing clothing of the opposite sex.

Some Sources of and Reactions to Adolescent Conflict in the Middle Class

By the middle teens the adolescent has acquired many of the marks of physical maturity. Normally persons of both sexes have attained an approximation of their eventual height. By this age adolescents are physically able to engage in sexual intercourse and to procreate.

It has been the tradition in American middle-class culture that children should learn major goals of individual development—especially those of upward mobility and attainment of the appropriate sex-type—and that the adolescent should show progress toward these goals but should stop short of consummation. That is, it has not been expected that while still an adolescent the offspring should achieve a status higher than that of his parents, but only that he should prepare to do so through learning attitudes of industry and thrift and through making progress at school.[35] Moreover, the adolescent was expected to show progress toward sex-typed adulthood but was not expected to engage in actual sexual intercourse.

The preceding paragraph specifies conditions of conflict—arousal of the young to a set of goals, setting them on the road toward attaining those goals, but then insisting that the gratification of goal-attainment could not be experienced until adulthood. For those attending college the period of conflict, i.e., the duration of adolescence, was about ten or a dozen years. The resulting plight of the adolescent was something like that of a dog held on short leash while a piece of meat was held out of reach but not out of range of sight or smell. One would hardly expect the dog to be collected and quiescent under such circumstances.

The combination of physical capability, knowledge of the possibilities of gratification, and denial of access to them is familiar as the plight of minority groups. Presumably, then, it should not be surprising to find adolescents behaving like a minority—developing its own argot, values, customs, and status system, and either depreciating or completely rejecting the value system of the adult majority. "Youth, standing outside the [established social order] and not responsible for its defects, is likely to oscillate between what seems to adults an overdemanding idealism and a merciless cynicism."[36] It appears that adolescents arrive at a point where they "outgrow" the family of orientation and are not yet allowed to found the family of procreation. More precisely, this means that they look outside the family of orientation for rewards. Cole-

---

[35] Furthermore, the middle-class norm that it is wrong for parents to propose an occupation to an offspring typically leaves the offspring free to choose his career line, but freedom of choice among so many options as are provided in a contemporary developed country may induce conflict in the chooser.

[36] David Matza, "Subterranean Traditions of Youth," *Annals of the American Academy of Political and Social Service,* 338: 102–118 (1961), at p. 103.

man quotes with apparent approval an informant who asserts that adolescents lack the experience to understand adult roles; he sees teen-agers as living in a world apart and asserts that they look to each other rather than to the adult community for their social rewards.[37] In a sense, then, the peer group serves the adolescent as an interim kin group between the family of orientation and the family of procreation.

A classical response to such frustration as is outlined in the foregoing paragraphs is depreciation of the promised but withheld rewards. This has been precisely the attitude of a varying proportion of adolescents and young adults for at least half a century of American history, beginning with the bohemians of the early post–World War I period. Although bohemianism can be traced back into the nineteenth century,[38] it seems likely that the proportion of young people caught up in the movement and also the degree of rejection of middle-class values became greater in the later sixties than ever before.[39]

According to the ideology of the rebels of that period, the pill had outmoded the middle-class mandate to confine sex to the marital relationship, which was only hypocritically observed anyway since many who preached premarital chastity and marital fidelity engaged in clandestine adventures. Rebellious boys rejected upper-middle-class occupations (professional, executive) as dull and meaningless.[40] For girls the ideology involved rejection of the position of middle-class wife-mother as life in a gilded suburban prison. For both sexes there developed a cultivation of a Franciscan ethic of poverty—anathema were Madison Avenue and the consumers' goods it sells. Security came from seeing how much one could get along without. And the ethic of learning and preparing was rejected: "Why prepare, if there will be so few satisfying jobs to prepare for?"[41]

Since the word "rebels" appears in the preceding paragraph, it is in order to consider the nature of the rebellion. Has the rebellious generation—or segment of a generation—been rejecting its parents and their values, or the larger social order, or both? Braungart has noted the existence of two interpretations: (1) that campus radicals were rebelling against their conservative or middle-of-the-road parents, or (2) that the campus radicals had been socialized into their attitudes by parents of similar persuasion (the "red-

---

[37] *Op. cit.*, pp. 7–11.

[38] Bennett M. Berger, "Focus on the Flower Children: Hippie Morality—More Old than New," *Trans-action* 5: 19–23 (December 1967).

[39] No doubt the war in Viet Nam, the increasing impersonalization of bureaucracies (including the universities), pollution, discriminatory treatment of minorities, and other social problems have contributed to this attitude.

[40] When work was necessary, jobs that resisted the imputation of uselessness or exploitation were: farm labor, hauling boxes, janitoring, serving, dishwashing, and messenger. Cf. Lewis S. Feuer, *The Conflict of Generations: The Character and Significance of Student Movements* (New York: Basic Books, 1969), p. 406.

[41] Fred Davis, "Focus on the Flower Children: Why All of Us May Be Hippies Someday," *Trans-action*, 5: 10–18 (December 1967).

diaper" or "political-diaper" theory). After analyzing responses from more than a thousand students at ten major eastern universities, Braungart concluded that in the main the students were not revolting against their parents' views but, rather, were following political orientation given them by their parents.[42]

This section has been considering some sources of, and responses to, adolescent conflict in the United States. Frequently the question is asked: what is the proportion of American adolescents who react to their adolescence with behavior that appears to reject their parents and their values? In early 1971 *Life* published results from a nation-wide survey on this topic. Unfortunately the survey took a wide age-bracket for this purpose—15–21 years—and the results were not routinely broken down into narrower age categories.

The level of rebellion and disaffection appeared to be quite low. A large majority indicated approval of their parents: 73 percent reported they accepted and agreed with their parents' values and ideals; 66 percent said they did not have trouble communicating with their parents; and 90 percent said their lives to date had been happy. Hardly the testimony of a rebellious, alienated generation.

For some questions *Life* published the percentages for high school and college students separately. College students were less success-oriented, less religious, more liberal on sex and the use of marijuana.

Of course the Life survey does not deny that there are some youth who have rejected parental values and morals, who have dropped out of school and their families' lives, who have rejected the orientation to competitive achievement and the aspiration of occupational success, who have sought refuge in hallucinogenic drugs and/or some form of group experience emphasizing love and service. What the *Life* survey offers is the estimate that by early 1971 the overwhelming majority of the generation of youth (15–21 years of age) were giving responses that sounded conventional and conforming rather than rebellious and alienated.[43]

The Parent of the Adolescent

The stereotyped conception of the parents of the adolescent is one of confused helplessness. To nurture the infant and the young child, they thought, was an arduous but clear-cut task. The adolescent does not make heavy demands for nurturance in the form of physical care, but the nature of the parental responsibilities—for nurturance and especially for control—becomes ambiguous and anxiety producing. Size of allowance; size, quality, and nature of wardrobe; driving privileges, and perhaps a car of his own—these are some

---

[42] Richard G. Braungart, "Family Status, Socialization and Student Politics: A Multivariate Analysis," paper presented at the annual meeting of the American Sociological Association, September 1969.

[43] "A New Youth Poll," *Life,* January 8, 1971, pp. 22–27, 30.

of the problems in (largely material) nurturance for which the parent may have no guideline. With respect to control we recall first that the adolescent goes out of the home for educational, religious, and recreational purposes. Moreover, the artifacts of our culture further complicate the situation. The anxious parent will find some basis in reality for regarding the automobile as a means of destruction and a site for seduction.[44] Commenting over a generation ago upon late hours and the use of the family car as points of contention between the generations, the Lynds remarked that "a prevalent mood among Middleton parents is bewilderment, a feeling that their difficulties outrun their best efforts to cope with them."[45] If the boy's performance at the wheel suggests that he thinks of driving as a competitive sport, he may excite the admiration of his peers but not of his parents. Josselyn believes that the set hour for the return of a girl from a date serves for the parents as the psychic equivalent of a chastity belt.[46] On both of these questions the adolescent's drive to gain the approval of peers results in behavior contrary to parental norms.

When the parent sees his child struggling for self-expression and questioning parental authority, he recalls that it was "not long ago" that the adolescent was in diapers, and it "seems only yesterday" that he was trying to make the "little league" baseball team. Consciously, the parent may see his problem as getting his daughter married before she becomes pregnant, or of not having his son become addicted to drugs.

The foregoing parental concerns have not been relieved by an increasing libertarianism in American culture whereby the influence of church and school in enforcing middle-class norms has been called into question. In particular, it has been understood in bygone years that the high school and the college would stand *in loco parentis* to prohibit proscribed behavior (sexual, drinking, and so forth). Challenges by students have caused college officials to abandon their roles as surrogate parents with the consequence that in the sense of becoming responsible for their own behavior, more and more young people are becoming adults before finishing their formal education.

Unconsciously, it appears that there are other considerations at work. First, it not infrequently happens that the adolescent exceeds the parents in stature, strength, and attractiveness. To the parent of the same sex, this may bring envy, or identification and an opportunity to relive the now idealized "golden age" of his or her own adolescence. The opposite sex parent may come suddenly to appreciate the attractions of the offspring and to compare them to the aging appearance of the spouse. The ripening adolescent may be regarded

---

[44] A study of high school students in an upper-middle-income community reports that the use of a car is followed by a drop in the student's grades.—Cf. J. Keith Kavanaugh, Warren A. Kemper, and Edward R. Klamm, "The High School Student and the Automobile," *Traffic Safety*, 4: 4–11 (1960).

[45] R. S. Lynd and H. M. Lynd, *Middletown* (New York: Harcourt, 1929), p. 151.

[46] Irene Josselyn, *Psychosocial Development of Children* (New York: Family Service Association of America, 1948), pp. 105–109.

as a threat to parental authority and a progressively stronger competitor for the spouse's affections, or as a vehicle for vicarious gratification. Particularly does the latter appear in the mothers of girls who take a conscious interest in their daughter's dates in order to be sure that they are of the "right sort," and unconsciously enjoy the participation it allows them in the direction of reliving their own dating experiences.

Conflict between Adolescent and Parents

The adolescent period probably strikes the high point in the conflict of the generations. It is at this point that parental discipline is felt most keenly, that the interests of the generations are experienced as diverging most widely. It is at this point, Murphy says, that parents have "neither the closeness, the authority, nor the know-how to maintain the earlier parent-child relations."[47] It is at this point that children practically institutionalize their struggle for emancipation through the "crowd," with its specialized interests, activities, language, and secrets. The nature of the gang activities, including the specialized slang, gives implicit recognition to the feeling that the parents constitute an "out-group," almost an enemy group. The fact that the member of the adolescent gang is widely known outside America—as a Teddy-boy in London, as a hooligan in Moscow, as a *gyangu* in Tokyo[48]—implies that something more general than American culture is involved.

There are good reasons why middle-class adolescence involves conflict with authority in general and with parental authority in particular. The parental function of control places responsibility on the parents for the morality of their children. For this reason parents frequently find themselves opposing and forbidding just those behaviors from which the adolescent gains such acceptance. To the extent, therefore, that the parents try to enforce moral standards that conflict with the expectations of the adolescent peer group, they are seen by the adolescents as threatening their social acceptance.

It is well to bear in mind Murphy's remarks about parental ineptitude in dealing with adolescents. When a parent denies permission to his adolescent to participate in some activity, the parent no doubt feels that he is saving the adolescent from the latter's foolish impulses and that, at worst, the loss is only one evening's fun. But as we shall argue, although the adolescent may not be able to express it, the loss is not regarded as only momentary; it is felt to be far more significant.

In various ways, subtle and otherwise, some middle-class children come

[47] Gardner Murphy, *Personality: A Biosocial Approach to Origins and Structure* (New York: Harper & Row, 1947), p. 512.

[48] Robert Trumbull, "Japan Turns against the 'Gyangu,'" *The New York Times Magazine*, November 30, 1958, pp. 66, 69–70, 72, 74. See also *Juvenile Delinquency, Report of the Committee of the Judiciary, United States Senate, 86th Congress, 2nd Session, Report No. 1593* (Washington, D.C.: GPO, 1960), pp. 54–56.

to be indoctrinated with the notion that the road to success for male and female lies to a great degree in the ability to "manipulate personalities."[49] Various roads to occupational success are thought to involve the manipulation of personalities—either directly through managerial activities or less directly through communications, as in public relations and advertising. Perhaps the salesman has been the most characteristically American occupational type, and probably the most pungent statement of the "American tragedy" of the middle-class male is Arthur Miller's play *Death of a Salesman,* in which the suicide of the salesman seems to follow inevitably from the loss of his technique—manipulating personalities. The technique of manipulation is especially important to middle-class girls and women. The competence with which they can execute it may determine whether they will marry and at which class level.

In the middle class, then, there exists the theme that the ability to manipulate personalities is the road to power, and that being liked, being able to "mix," and being accepted are necessary aspects of the ability to manipulate. Because he has been taught to believe that so much of his future hangs on this ability, the adolescent is anxious to determine whether or not he has it, and to develop it if he has not. To gain the approval of his peers is to be reassured on this point. Here the approval of parents is vastly less important; they are supposed to love him whether he has know-how or not. Indeed, a corollary of emotional emancipation from the family is increasing sensitivity to the opinions of persons outside the family and decreasing concern over the evaluations placed on one's behavior by parents. One technique of obtaining the approval of peers is conformity to group standards. As would be expected, therefore, there is great emphasis among middle-class adolescents upon conformity to group standards in dress, speech, manner, and other forms of behavior. Adolescent behavior that is strange, bizarre, and unintelligible in parental eyes may only be conformity to the expectations of the peer culture.

For these reasons, therefore, parental control and prohibition have broader significance than the deprivation of immediate gratification. They signify also a loss in the opportunity to test social skills and to build up the ability to manipulate personalities, which are seen as essential to the "success" of the middle-class adolescent.

The lack of uniformity in the specification of the rights and duties of adolescents complicates the parent-child relationship. The disciplinary pattern is irregular from community to community, from family to family, and, indeed, for successive siblings in the same household. It is not difficult to see the basis for an irregular pattern within a community: the parents probably do not constitute a primary group and probably are not in touch with each other, they may not know each other and may not subscribe to the same subcultures,

---

[49] As Arnold Green has observed, the job-technique of the middle class revolves "around manipulating the personalities of others, instead of tools."—Arnold Green, "The Middle-Class Male Child and Neurosis," *American Sociological Review,* 11: 31–41 (1946), at p. 35.

and thus they tend to be establishing rules to govern the behavior of their offspring with their (not entirely objective) offspring as the principal source of information concerning community standards. There has been a disposition in some communities—especially after a tragic accident or a noisy and destructive party—for the parents to cooperate in the preparation of a code of behavior for teen-agers.

Another factor that complicates the relations of American middle-class adolescents and their parents is the absence of a clearly defined terminal point. Adolescence is a period when the child is supposed to go through the process of emancipating himself from parental control, but there is no systematic procedure for a concomitant relaxation of this control. Very frequently the problem of when parental discipline should terminate is resolved by the device of the adolescent's moving out of the household—to go to college, to work elsewhere, or to get married.

Is Adolescence Necessarily a Period of "Storm and Stress"?

We have considered a number of aspects of the middle-class subculture that combine to make adolescence a period of conflict. Some writers interpret this conflict in terms of the bodily changes of puberty. There remains the question as to whether or not the "storm and stress" of adolescence is as necessary and inevitable as the physiological explanation implies.

From her studies of the Samoan and Arapesh cultures Margaret Mead asserts that the answer lies in the negative. In these societies, one of which approves premarital sexual relations and the other of which does not, the adolescent proceeds into adulthood smoothly and rapidly. He is not held on short leash to witness and be tantalized by adult pursuits; he achieves adulthood at an early age. Dr. Mead concludes that whether or not adolescence is a period of "storm and stress" is determined by the nature of the social organization.[50]

At the present stage of our knowledge, Mead's conclusion sounds plausible but must still be regarded as tentative. There is an unfortunate dearth of comparative evidence about the degree of conflict in adolescence in various cultures and in the subcultures of our own country. Superficial scrutiny of the upper- and lower-class subcultures does suggest, however, that adolescence should have different psychic significance at the different class levels.

The middle-class subculture holds love of parents to be a virtue, and then holds up rewards in the pursuit of which the adolescent runs into conflict with parents, their authority and responsibility. The upper-class adolescent,

---

[50] Margaret Mead, *Coming of Age in Samoa* and *Sex and Temperament in Three Primitive Societies,* in *From the South Seas* (New York: Morrow, 1939).

on the other hand, is rewarded not for being independent and emancipated, but for being conforming to adult values and indeed for continuing to be dependent. He receives his upper-class status as a member of his family. Because his socioeconomic status is both high and ascribed, he need not struggle. Through gift or inheritance the property will be his one day in title. In the meantime his situation calls for dignified patience rather than anxious striving. The selection of a spouse calls for more prudence and probably less romance than in the middle class. Because of the control exerted by the extended family, a marriage involves numerous "interested" persons who will wish to know about the status and property of any prospective spouse. Here we have some of the attributes of the arranged marriage. Alienation of family would probably mean loss of the privileges of his class. For these reasons, family control over behavior is more prolonged in the upper class.[51] Unlike the middle-class adolescent, moreover, the adolescent of the upper class is not typically confronted with relatively sudden responsibilities. In this regard, his situation is more nearly similar to that of the traditional Chinese male of the gentry, who assumes his greatest responsibilities relatively late in life as a patriarch, who spends several decades preparing for the assumption of such responsibilities, and who is assisted in handling them by other members of the family.

In the lower class, adolescence appears to be shorter than in the middle class and to involve fewer discontinuities. Extensive occupational training is not customary. A physically sound adolescent can soon equal the earnings of an unskilled father. The absence of long-range goals means that the "leash" concept of adolescence is not applicable. In childhood, adolescence, and adulthood physical aggression is rewarded and sexual relations may be permitted. As Davis says, "Mothers try to prevent daughters from having children before they are married, but the example of the girl's own family is often to the contrary."[52]

From a superficial examination of the subcultures, therefore, one would surmise that there should be more "storm and stress" among adolescents in the middle class than in the other two classes.

Other things being equal, it appears that adolescence will be free from stress to the degree that

1. The society designates clearly which adult position the adolescent will fill and permits no alternative.
2. That position and its constituent roles are seen as attainable and highly rewarding.
3. The course of preparation for that position is not viewed as either too

[51] Cf. Allison Davis, B. Gardner, and M. R. Gardner, *Deep South* (Chicago: University of Chicago Press, 1941), pp. 95–99.

[52] Allison Davis, "Socialization and Adolescent Personality," in T. M. Newcomb and E. L. Hartley (eds.), *Readings in Social Psychology* (New York: Holt, Rinehart and Winston, Inc., 1947), p. 148.

long or too costly relative to the prospective rewards (with respect to time, energy, and/or deferred gratification).
4. The culture provides a means for the individual to be aware of the time when he passes into adulthood.

Orienting the Adolescent to the Adult System

If the society is to continue on course, the adolescent must sooner or later make peace with the adult world and adopt its values and status system.[53] A part of the adolescent dilemma inheres in the variety of goals from which choices must be made, and a part of the task is that of self-evaluation in terms of the available choices. The male must select an occupation, and that selection should be suited to his socioeconomic aspirations, his personality, and his aptitudes. In selecting a wife, he must make choices: glamorous or maternal; intellectual, artistic, or domestic—or will he try for all these characteristics? The girl is confronted with comparable choices but, as we have seen, with less assurance that she will have the opportunity to choose. Accordingly, the adolescent is confronted not only with the task of hitting upon rewarding techniques but also of defining the precise rewards he seeks.

As Benedict has observed,[54] nature ordains a discontinuity in the life cycle. Every man must be a son before being a father. The son's position involves dependence; the father must provide security for others. A cultural discontinuity involves a behavior that is learned at one stage in life and must be unlearned at a later stage. Such discontinuities are universal, but American culture, Benedict holds, contains extreme contrasts in its expectations concerning the behavior of the child and of the adult. She points out that children are supposed to be nonresponsible, submissive, and sexless, but are supposed to mature into responsible,[55] dominant, sexually adequate adults. She interprets

---

[53] An interpretation of Hitler's attractiveness to Nazi Germany as a national case of unresolved adolescence appears in Erik H. Erikson, *Childhood and Society* (New York: Norton, 1950), chap. 9.

[54] Ruth Benedict, "Continuities and Discontinuities in Cultural Conditioning," *Psychiatry*, 1: 161–167 (1938).

[55] Note that "categorical employability" reinforces the "responsible-nonresponsible" discontinuity. (Cf. pages 88–90 above.) We have remarked that categorical employability is a typically urban phenomenon. It is consistent, then, that the discontinuity between "nonresponsible" childhood and "responsible" adulthood should be more marked in urban than in rural situations. Both these considerations appear to be related to the greater degree of "sophistication" in urban than in farm adolescents. In this context the term "sophistication" usually denotes possession of social graces and an ease in social relations, especially with persons of the opposite sex. Since the normal out-of-school activities of the urban middle-class adolescent are recreational rather than productive, there is opportunity for this kind of sophistication to develop. There is greater demand for the farm adolescent to be productive, and hence, while the urban boy and girl are learning *savoir-faire*, the farm boy and girl are acquiring the skills needed for adult life on the farm. To the degree that

the "storm and stress" of adolescence as part of the psychic cost of such cultural discontinuities. In the struggle to achieve adulthood, aspiration fights a running battle with doubt. Although the adolescent wishes to be independent, independence is frightening.[56]

Resources and the Relative Influence of Parents and Other Adults on Adolescents

There are some questions whose answers are critical in determining the nature of parent-adolescent relationships:

1. What adult roles do the adolescents see as available and what are their options? Do the parents see the same set of options?

2. What is the relative attractiveness of each option? Do parents and offspring agree on the hierarchy of relative attractiveness of the available range of adult roles?

3. With respect to what adult role does the adolescent see the optimum combination of accessibility and attractiveness? In this sense will some adult other than a parent appear to the adolescent to be the most attractive model?

4. Is it possible that no adult role is sufficiently attractive (or that all are sufficiently unattractive), with the result that the adolescent avoids learning the behaviors of any adult role?

As an example of maximum paternal influence let us think of a setting in which occupations are hereditary and hence question 1 is answered that a son has only a single occupational role available to him. Since there is no option, question 2 is irrelevant. In this setting it seems likely that the son will see the paternal role as offering the maximum probability of successfully guiding him into his adult occupational role. By contrast let us imagine an American born son of an immigrant, unskilled laborer. In this setting the son may see an extensive set of occupational roles, all of which are more attractive than his father's and many of which are accessible. If the son aspires to a white-collar occupation, it is unlikely that the son will perceive the paternal role as maximizing the guidance factor; it is more likely that he will seek guidance from the occupant of some other role, say, the teacher. But perhaps he will become convinced that the entire set of attractive roles is inaccessible; then he may seek to perpetuate his adolescent male role by gang activities. One other way the fourth point may operate is to bring about an "alienated"

categorical employability and this specific cultural discontinuity exist, then, we may conclude that their results are that the farm boy and girl will tend to be quite well prepared for adult life on the farm; the urban boy and girl will tend to have little comparable preparation for career and housewifery but will tend to be reasonably adept in their social relations (which may in itself be related to their subsequent careers).

[56] Josselyn, *op. cit.*, p. 95.

adolescent, that is, one who is egocentric, distrustful, pessimistic, anxious, and resentful.[57]

Once again our theorizing points to a linkage between the model's possession of, and control over, resources (ability to guide the adolescent to an attractive goal) and influence over the young person. Once again we can see how it should be that the degree of influence of parent over offspring should correlate positively with socioeconomic status.

Summary

An adolescent is a person defined by his society as too old to be a child and too young to be an adult. If adulthood is achieved at or soon after puberty, there is little or no adolescence. In the middle strata of American society the termination of adolescence is not marked by any ceremony, but its duration can be estimated for those who graduate from college as roughly ten or a dozen years. In this cultural setting the adolescent is supposed to learn adult roles but is forbidden by the official morality from practicing them. Two important foci in adolescent socialization concern the acquisition of sex-typed behaviors and preparation for occupations.

It appears that not all cultures develop "storm and stress" for the adolescent but that a fair degree of anxiety and emotional turbulence is generated in the subculture of the American middle class. Among the factors that appear to contribute to the stress are cultural discontinuities, difficulty of achieving appropriate sex-typed behaviors, high level of parent-child conflict, and lack of a clear-cut terminus to adolescence. A cultural theme of the manipulation of personalities as a technique of achieving adult goals has the corollary that the peer group, and not the parents, can validate the adolescent's acquisition of the relevant social skills; this drives the adolescent into peer-conforming and parent-frustrating behaviors. To varying degrees the subcultures of American society provide conditions for the disaffection of adolescents. The results of a survey seem to indicate that a substantial majority of American adolescents are not rebellious but that the proportion of rebellious responses is somewhat higher among college-level than high school respondents.

When parent and offspring share a common goal-system, the parent may feel obliged at times to engage in a cop-and-robber relationship with the offspring in order to enforce the norm of deferred gratification, to ensure that his son is progressing toward an appropriate occupation, or to try to prevent his son's impregnating a neighbor's daughter. Such parental control is seen as in the service of keeping the offspring on course toward goals of which both parent and offspring approve. At times, however, and among sizable propor-

[57] Anthony Davids, "Generality and Consistency of Relations between the Alienation Syndrome and Cognitive Processes," *Journal of Abnormal and Social Psychology*, 51: 61–67 (1955).

tions of the offspring generation there is rejection of prevailing norms resulting in a challenge to the traditional middle-class goals specified above—the value of achievement and upward mobility, and of premarital chastity. Where parent and offspring differ about the goal-system, they find it difficult to communicate with each other for the lack of a common set of tacit premises.

17

The Adult and His Parents

Purpose of This Chapter

The preceding chapter has foreshadowed the burden of argument of the present one. A major theme has to do with the achievement of independence. Or to state it differently, it has to do with the nurturing and controlling relations between the young adult and his or her parents. The degree and kind of independence and the manner of fulfilling or not fulfilling the parental functions vary with societal and familial structures and with culture. We shall note the evaluation of age categories and the nature and frequency of intergenerational interaction as the older and younger generations move through their life cycles. We shall also consider filial responsibility with respect to the care of the aged.

Adulthood, Independence, and the Parental Functions

Like most cultures, ours dictates that the adult should become independent of his parents. What, then, is independence? Throughout this book it has been emphasized that there are two parental functions: nurturance and control. An offspring is dependent on a parent to the degree that he seeks either nurturance or control or both from that parent. Some offspring seem to continue to need support in the sense of being cared for, of being given to; others need support in terms of having someone make decisions for them, of providing guidance. To the extent that such needs are expressed by the offspring toward one or both parents, that offspring is registering dependence.

Conversely, the person who is capable of caring for himself and making his own decisions and who does so is manifesting independence.

We may speak of a person with a strong need to be nurtured as a *receptive* person, and of one who has a strong need to be controlled as a *submissive* person.[1] In the present context *dependence* includes both receptive and submissive dispositions and behaviors. Therefore a *dependent* person is viewed here as one who is either receptive or submissive or both.

Generally speaking, American culture demands a relatively high degree of economic and emotional independence. This can be seen as related to the individualistic nature of American culture, the emphasis on neolocal residence of newly married couples, and the autonomy of nuclear families from the extended kin group. Overt evidence that the individual has become adequately emancipated consists largely in his establishing himself vocationally, which means holding a job "with prospects," and in manifesting the dress and behavior appropriate to an adult of his or her sex. In the preceding chapter we have noted the relevance to the achievement of independence of such overt indicators as the debut, marriage, graduation from school or college, going to work, assuming responsibility for supporting oneself, moving from the parents' home, and entering military service. If we look at independence psychologically, we may say that a man's failure to achieve the expected degree of emancipation may prevent him from marrying, or, if he does marry, it may serve to complicate his relationship with his wife. Until we can develop more precise and agreed-upon measures of nurturance and control than now exist, it is not entirely clear whether most adult female roles demand as much independence as do those of the male. The expectations regarding the performance of women in occupations seem generally that they will be somewhat more dependent than men, and the role of wife does not seem to demand as much independence as that of husband; but the role of mother seems quite demanding.

Rewards and Penalties

SOCIAL CLASS

The process by means of which the individual strives to achieve adulthood (independence, emancipation, autonomy) can best be understood if we consider cultural definitions of adulthood and the rewards and penalties involved. In this discussion we shall again take the class structure into account.

We have seen that the rewards of the upper class are high status and

---

[1] The term "dependence" is sometimes used to denote a disposition toward receptive behavior without implying submissiveness and sometimes toward submissive behavior without implying receptiveness. Murray uses "succorance" to denote a disposition toward both types of dependent behavior.—H. A. Murray *et al.*, *Explorations in Personality* (New York: Oxford, 1938), p. 182.

property. The status, being ascribed, is conferred upon the person at birth. Since the wealth is in the form of property rather than earned income, it may be collectively owned, or if individually owned, it may be acquired through gift and inheritance. These rewards are acquired not through the exercise of independent initiative, but rather through conformity to such expectations of family and class as the maintenance of strong family ties, recognition of extended kinship relations, and attitudes of reverence toward the ancestors from whom flow the blessings of property and high status. The extreme penalty for nonconforming behavior is deprivation of status and property through being disowned and disinherited. In this sense the institutions of the upper class reward submissiveness and present no reason for an offspring to withdraw from a position of receptiveness within a continually nurturing family.

Since upward mobility is a major value in the ideology of the middle class, its subculture emphasizes independence, initiative, and judiciously controlled aggressiveness[2] as instrumental virtues leading to higher socioeconomic status. Coexisting with this ideology, however, is the fact of giant corporations with their vast bureaucracies and demand for armies of white-collar personnel. For young men of the middle class the corporation frequently stands in a relationship parallel to that of the upper-class family: it creates the expectation that if the young man is assessed as "loyal" and "industrious," he will be taken care of and may even prosper. In this fashion the corporation rewards submissiveness and fosters the receptive type of dependence.[3] Such is the setting that causes critics of our times to lament the rise of "conformity" and the "organization man."[4] To the extent that the "system" fosters the dependence of the middle-class male on the corporation it may alienate him from his family—perhaps his family of procreation as well as his family of orientation. A good organization man is free to spend as much time on the job as the

---

[2] Cf. Talcott Parsons, "Certain Primary Sources and Patterns of Aggression in the Social Structure of the Western World," in Lyman Bryson, Louis Finkelstein, and R. M. MacIver (eds.), *Conflicts of Power in Modern Culture* (New York: Harper & Row, 1947), pp. 29–48.

[3] The reader may demur on the ground that the corporation also rewards "idea" men. The reply is that although the demand for "idea" men varies with the times and the situation, most corporations as bureaucracies must have vastly more functionaries to handle routine work and can tolerate at any one moment only an insignificant proportion of its personnel as "idea" men.

The carryover of familial attitudes to the occupational system is especially marked in Japan. In large bureaucracies of business or government it is customary for a white-collar man (a "salary man") to remain for his entire work-life with the organization where he gets his first job. "Japanese firms value loyalty and prefer to recruit and train their own white-collar workers who become skilled in the way their particular firm operates rather than to take on employees who have acquired different habits in other firms."—Ezra F. Vogel, *Japan's New Middle Class: The Salary Man and His Family in a Tokyo Suburb* (Berkeley: University of California Press, 1963), p. 8. Cf. also T. Fukutake, *Man and Society in Japan* (Tokyo: University of Tokyo Press, 1962).

[4] E.g., William H. Whyte, Jr., *The Organization Man* (New York: Simon and Schuster, 1956). In some contexts adjustability and adaptability are synonyms for conformity.

corporation requests and to move about the country or around the world at its whim. In this subculture the reward system is conducive to the achievement of independence from the parental family and may place a strain on the degree to which the man can function as husband and father. Thus the middle class is in a somewhat conflictful situation with an official ideology extolling initiative and autonomy and a structure in which some of the most manifest rewards are for the submissively dependent.[5]

During childhood and adolescence some of the conditions of socialization in the lower class are such as to create at least an equal if not a greater degree of independence from the family than occurs in the middle class. At an early age the child is introduced to the grim rigors of the struggle for survival. On the other hand, he is also taught that in time of trouble the extended family will give aid, if able, and that public assistance and private charity are available. Although the subculture of the lower class undoubtedly fosters considerable independence in adults, therefore, it is not clear whether it does so to a greater or less degree than it does in the middle class.

THE PERIOD OF YOUNG ADULTHOOD

Having noted the relevance of class differentials to the culture of the adult, we turn now to the significance of age and sex categories. Since our knowledge is most complete with respect to the middle class, the following discussion will pertain to this class except where otherwise noted.

The period of young adulthood, say from 20 to 30 or 35, is one in which the man is "normally" getting his vocational start. It is a period during which he is presumed to apply himself with great vigor and concentrated assiduity to the business of carving out his career and "getting ahead." During this period it is expected that he will marry, establish an independent home, and begin to raise a family.

As indicated in the section on "The Woman's Dilemma" in Chapter 12 above, the contemporary middle-class girl is confronted with three values: marriage, motherhood, and career. It appears that an increasing proportion of women is seeking to pursue all three goals as simultaneously as possible. The women's liberation movement may be seen as an organizational response to the frustrations that arise in the simultaneous pursuit of these three goals.

---

[5] The reader will understand that the foregoing remarks pertain to what have been called "bureaucratic" occupations. "Entrepreneurial" occupations, on the other hand, demand initiative, enterprise, and willingness to take risks rather than adaptability and aptitude for teamwork. To the extent that the corporate bureaucracy demands total commitment of its executive and managerial personnel it may be likened to what Goffman has called a "total institution" in the sense that it asks for virtually all of the energy and loyalty of the husband-father and, in return, meets virtually all of his needs. Cf. Erving Goffman, *Asylums: Essays On the Social Situation of Mental Patients and Other Inmates* (New York: Doubleday, 1961). To the extent that the counterculture of the adolescent generation rejects the purposes and procedures of the corporation, this contributes to the "generation gap" between adolescents and fathers in corporate bureaucratic jobs.

It appears that for most women the choice continues to be marriage and parenthood. For these women the period of young adulthood tends to mean a brief fling at a profession or at business, but the serious business is that of mating. For her, as for the man, it is anticipated that this period will "normally" result in marriage, home, and children. For both sexes young adulthood is conceived of to be a period of maximum physical vigor and creativeness. With respect to physical well-being and the joy of living it is thought to be the "golden period" of life.[6]

Except for the career woman, the age of recognition of the female is that of late adolescence and early adulthood up to her wedding day. This is a period combining freedom from restraint with freedom from responsibility. It is not intended to suggest that other ages of females are lacking in rewards, but it is the young, unmarried, adult female who is toasted in song and celebrated in advertising. Overtly, it is a period when males seek her company for glamorous activities. Covertly, however, this may be a period of tension, strain, and insecurity if her social success falls considerably short of her standard. It is during this period that the culture defines the "normal" goal of the young woman to be marriage—as "good" a marriage as she can make. On her wedding day she announces to the world the degree of her success in this enterprise. On marrying, then, she gives up the more glamorous and exciting occupation of mate-seeking, yields much of her identity and her name, hitches her status to that of her husband, and passes into the relative anonymity of wifehood and prospective motherhood. For middle-class women who do not pursue careers it seems fair to say that by external criteria the "golden period" is that of the young maid rather than that of the matron.[7]

THE MIDDLE YEARS

The time at which the "middle years" arrive varies from class to class and from one occupation to another. For occupations requiring little preparation and considerable vigor, middle years may come early. Professional athletes are "old men" at thirty-five. In some plants industrial workers are "old" at forty-five. In business, and especially in the learned professions, however, "middle age" is chronologically later. In bygone days young physicians grew beards in their effort to appear older than their years and looked upon premature baldness as an economic advantage. The cultural conception is that the middle years should begin, at least, to reflect the degree of one's success in one's

---

[6] R. G. Kuhlen, "Age Trend in Adjustment during the Adult Years as Reflected in Happiness Ratings," *American Psychologist*, 3: 307 (1948); J. T. Landis, "What Is the Happiest Period in Life?" *School and Society*, 55: 643–645 (1942); John Sirjamaki, "Culture Configurations in the American Family," *American Journal of Sociology*, 53: 467 (1948).

[7] Sirjamaki, "Culture Configurations in the American Family," *loc. cit.*, p. 466; Weston LaBarre, "Social Cynosure and Social Structure," *Journal of Personality*, 14: 169–183 (1946).

efforts at self-validation. This is the "serious" period of life, and all the previous efforts at self-validation in childhood and adolescence can now be regarded as mere "trial runs." This is the period when the man who is destined to make his mark will achieve the status of "junior executive." A few outstanding individuals rise to top executive positions in this period. Although there is a general recognition of a reduction in physical vitality, this is not regarded as sufficient to impair performance in the white-collar occupations of the middle class. On the contrary, the attributes regarded as relevant to middle-class success are thought to reach their optimum at this time: the combination of intellectual vigor and seasoned judgment; the mature, but not yet senescent, appearance, which commands respect. Since it is the period when the eventual outcome of the competitive struggle for status can be foreseen, it is regarded as a time in which the power of socioeconomic status achieved through upward mobility is combined with a relatively undiminished physical vigor. For the man, at least, this is the "prime of life."

For the wife, socioeconomic status is generally determined by the husband's performance. The occasional woman who achieves a higher status than that of her husband through her own vocational efforts may be regarded as having "unfortunately" married a "weak" man. For the woman who marries and devotes her efforts to the career of housewifery and motherhood, however, this is somewhat past the "prime of life" in terms of the cultural definition. Officially, the culture greatly approves the role of mother, but unofficially concedes that the bearing of children is an attribute common to all classes of mankind and, indeed, to mammals, and hence, unlike success in business or the professions, is hardly to be regarded as evidence of unusual aptitude or of meriting the reward of high status. The culture grants some measure of approval to the mother whose children's deportment conforms to cultural expectations, but the rewards of the culture along this line are more negative than positive in the sense that "good" children are expected, and special notice, connoting disapproval, is largely reserved for the parents of nonconforming children. Special problems confronting the adult woman have been considered in Chapter 12.

THE AGED

Generally speaking, the culture does not define old age as a desirable category. It is a period of declining productivity and vitality, and frequently of dependency. To enhance our perspective, it is appropriate to recall that this is not a universal conception of old age. Some cultures have taken notice of the declining productivity of the elders by killing them or by allowing them to die of exposure. On the other hand, the traditional Chinese culture looks upon the aged as being but one step from the gods, as being a repository of wisdom and knowledge, and as meriting an attitude of reverence.[8]

[8] Linton holds, however, that even in the societies that accord respect and power to

In view of the fact that our culture places a heavy emphasis upon achieved status, and because the opportunities for achievement in old age are relatively slight, the socioeconomic status of the aged is generally determined by the achievements of earlier years. In their declining years the aged are generally dependent upon savings, pensions, relatives, public assistance, or private charity. In the upper classes, however, where economic condition is grounded in property rather than in employment, the title of the property frequently resides in the aged. In this event the aged person is in a position to become a venerated patriarch and a dispenser of favors, a condition serving to maintain and increase high status. Intermediate between these extremities of status are those who reach old age with sufficient resources to maintain themselves, perhaps with a substantial reduction in the level of living, and hence need make no or few financial demands upon their children.

The Adult Offspring and the Family Cycle

In Part Five we have been taking the family through a cycle—from the point at which the young married couple first become parents (in Chapter 13) to the time when they become grandparents and are retiring. The subject of the present chapter is the nature of the relationship between the parents and their now adult offspring. In a society with a high life expectancy, such as ours, the period embraced by the present chapter is much longer than those envisaged in the chapters on infancy and childhood. For this reason it is helpful to have some way of keeping track of the relative ages, on the average, of the members of the two generations as the offspring marries and founds his own family of procreation.

Table 17.1 presents average ages of the parents of the offspring, whom we denote as "ego,"[9] at various points in the cycle and under different assumptions: ego may be male or female and ego may be the first or the last child of ego's parents. For example, if ego is the first-born and a female, it turns out on the average that at the time of her marriage her father is 45 and her mother 42.5; if ego is the last-born and a male, when he is married his parents are likely to be 55 and 52.5, respectively. It will be appreciated that the figures represent averages for the country as a whole as of the latter 1960's. In upper strata the age at first marriage is above the national average, and the length of a generation is longer than that shown. This factor causes the ages to be slightly higher in those strata than the ages the table shows. We shall be referring to these age relationships as we consider the final stages of the family cycle.

---

the aged, this is "a consolation prize which does not compensate for a consciousness of waning strength and increasing physical disabilities."—Ralph Linton, "Age and Sex Categories," *American Sociological Review*, 7: 599 (1942).

[9] More generally, "ego" used in this sense denotes the person or position of reference.

THE OFFSPRING'S FEELINGS ABOUT THE PARENTS

As the young middle-class person approaches adulthood, he or she may be expected to evaluate the parental family (or family of orientation) in terms of the degree to which it facilitates or hinders the prospective goals of career and marriage. The evaluation of the parents may be tinged with negative feelings if they have provided the young adult with a socioeconomic status below that to which he aspires, or if they represent actual or potential dependents. Upper-class parents, on the other hand, may be positively evaluated for their ability to facilitate the achievement of the young person's goals through their status, "connections," and property. The young woman who uses her parental home as a base of operations from which to be married is quite dependent upon and frequently very sensitive to the resources and status of her family. For her, parental dependence may prove crucial in determining whether or not it will be possible for her to marry.

In the preceding chapter we described the adolescent period as the high point in the conflict between the generations. Transition from adolescence to adulthood is normally characterized by a shift in the parent-offspring relationship from conflict to accommodation, a reduction in the intensity of feeling-tone consequent upon the recognition by parents and offspring of the latter's new status. This seems usually to be followed by a more detached, objective relationship and perhaps, ultimately, by sentimentally colored feeling on both sides.

From personal documents the writer has derived the impression that the college period, if spent away from home, provides an excellent opportunity for emotional weaning. Although sufficient cases have not been analyzed to establish the following generalizations, there is impressionistic evidence to suggest that this phase of the developmental process is somewhat as follows: During childhood and early adolescence the offspring has been especially dependent upon and preferential toward one of his parents—usually the parent of opposite sex. During his college years he is no longer in continuous physical proximity with his parents. Moreover, he has time in which to reflect upon his experiences within the family, and to relate these reflections to his own future course. In this process he comes to be more objective about his family situation, to see that the relationship between the parents was not of the "black and white" character, that each had faults, and that perhaps the preferred parent gave the nonpreferred parent a somewhat rough time. As he looks ahead in his own life, he sees that he will one day confront many of the problems that beset his same-sex parent, and here we find a continuation of the identification process. It seems quite clear, however, that this identification is more detached and thoughtful than the "my-daddy-can-beat-your-daddy" identification of early childhood.[10]

[10] Similar opinions appear in Nevitt Sanford, "Developmental Status of the Entering Freshman," in Nevitt Sanford (ed.), *The American College: A Psychological and Social*

TABLE 17.1

Median Ages of Ego's Parents at Time of Their Marriage, at Time of Ego's Birth, and at Various Points in the Establishment and Development of Ego's Family of Procreation: by Sex and Birth Order of Ego, Based on Rates Prevailing around 1965–1970

	IF EGO IS			
	Male and His Parents'			
POINT IN FAMILY CIRCLE	First Child		Last Child	
	Father	Mother	Father	Mother
Marriage of Ego's parents	23.0	20.5	23.0	20.5
Ego is born	24.5	22.0	32.0	29.5
Ego leaves parental home and is married	47.5	45.0	55.0	52.5
Birth of Ego's				
First child	49.0	46.5	51.4	48.9
Last child	56.5	54.0	64.0	61.5
Last child starts school	62.5	60.0	70.0	67.5
First child marries and leaves home				
If male	72.0	69.5	79.5	77.0
If female	69.5	67.0	77.0	74.5
Last child marries and leaves home				
If male	79.5	77.0	87.0	84.5
If female	77.0	74.5	84.5	82.0
Ego is				
35 years old	59.5	57.0	67.0	64.5
50 years old	74.5	72.0	82.0	79.5
65 years old	89.5	87.0	97.0	94.5

SOURCE: These data are medians rounded to the nearest half-year for recent years. Median ages at first marriage: males, 23; females, 20.5. Cf. *Statistical Abstract of the United States, 1968*, Table 77, p. 61. Median interval from first marriage to birth of first child and of last child: 1.5 and 9 years, respectively. Cf. Paul C. Glick and Robert Parke, Jr., "New Approaches in Studying the Life Cycle of the Family," *Demography*, 2: 187–202 (1965); reprinted in Robert F. Winch and Louis Wolf Goodman (eds.), *Selected Studies in Marriage and the Family* (3d ed.; New York: Holt, Rinehart and Winston, Inc., 1968), pp. 166–177, esp. pp. 168–169.

Interpretation of the Higher Learning (New York: Wiley, 1962), pp. 253–282, esp. pp. 266–271; and Douglas H. Heath, *Growing Up in College* (San Francisco: Jossey-Bass, 1968), pp. 212–215.

TABLE 17.1 (Continued)

POINT IN FAMILY CIRCLE	IF EGO IS Female and Her Parents'			
	First Child		Last Child	
	Father	Mother	Father	Mother
Marriage of Ego's parents	23.0	20.5	23.0	20.5
Ego is born	24.5	22.0	32.0	29.5
Ego leaves parental home and is married	45.0	42.5	52.5	50.0
Birth of Ego's				
First child	46.5	44.0	48.9	46.4
Last child	54.0	51.5	61.5	59.0
Last child starts school	60.0	57.5	67.5	65.0
First child marries and leaves home				
If male	69.5	67.0	77.0	74.5
If female	67.0	64.5	74.5	72.0
Last child marries and leaves home				
If male	77.0	74.5	84.5	82.0
If female	74.5	72.0	82.0	79.5
Ego is				
35 years old	59.5	57.0	67.0	64.5
50 years old	74.5	72.0	82.0	79.5
65 years old	89.5	87.0	97.0	94.5

It is a common-sense observation that the scope of common interests should be least and the conflict of generations should be greatest where there are marked cultural differences between them. According to this view great differences between the generations should occur in the cases of lower-class, poorly educated parents, whose children enter the professions, especially if the parents are foreign-born and have not assimilated American culture to any appreciable extent. Yet a study based on responses of the older generation shows the greatest proportion reporting "closeness" with offspring where they also report the offspring to have been "more successful" than themselves. The authors of the study interpret the result tentatively as showing vicarious achievement.[11] It is possible that this finding reflects a generally asymmetrical disposition for the older generation to place greater emphasis on affectional ties to their adult offspring than do the latter on affectional ties to their

[11] Gordon F. Streib and Wayne E. Thompson, "The Older Person in a Family Context," in Clark Tibbitts (ed.), *Handbook of Social Gerontology: Societal Aspects of Aging* (Chicago: University of Chicago Press, 1960), pp. 447–488, esp. pp. 482–483.

parents.[12] Of course it is still possible that intergenerational conflict may be relatively severe in the comparatively few cases of greatest mobility, i.e., where intergenerational differences in subculture and style of life are most marked.

THE VIEW FROM THE PARENTS' SIDE

From the standpoint of the parents, the attainment of adulthood by their children is an event that may be expected to call forth mixed emotions. On the positive side, there is the feeling of a job accomplished, the realization of the reduction of one's responsibilities, of the demands to be made on one's time, energy, and resources. There is the possibility (perhaps one should say "hope") of the vicarious gratification of frustrated ambitions through the career of the offspring. With the fulfillment of the parental role and the consequent reduction of responsibilities comes the promise of a more relaxed mode of life and the ultimate leisure of retirement. There is the prospect that one's spouse will turn back to oneself and again be "husband" or "wife" rather than "father" or "mother" to one's children, with the division of affection and the diffusion of attention that the latter terms imply.

The same considerations can be stated with their negative connotations, however, and seem frequently to be so viewed by the parents. The "empty nest" psychology implies that since the parents' job is completed, they are no longer needed. They may look forward to declining strength, declining productivity, declining health, and, usually, in retirement to diminished income. The turning back of spouses to each other is not necessarily a tender embrace to the accompaniment of legato violins. Some husbands and wives find that the distinctiveness of their roles during their parental years has fostered a certain separateness of activities and interests, and with the removal of their major common activity and interest they discover to their consternation that they now have little in common. And there are some couples who discover early in their family life that they are quite incompatible and agree to carry on in a sort of armed truce "for the sake of the children." Two possible outcomes for couples in this situation is that they look forward with misgiving to having only each other in the home or else they view the future with pleasure because at last they feel free to get divorced.

On balance the maturing of the offspring means that the parents are released from responsibility, but it implies also that their child has become an adult and that the parents are in the process of moving from the status of parents to that of potential or actual grandparents. This in turn is frequently construed as signifying that the parents have begun to pass through their declining years even though we see from Table 17.1 that the median age for a mother to become a grandmother is 44 if her first child is a girl or 46.5 if

---

[12] Gordon F. Streib, "Intergenerational Relations: Perspectives of the Two Generations on the Older Parent," *Journal of Marriage and the Family,* 27: 469–476 (1965).

her first is a boy. The corresponding ages for becoming a grandfather are 46.5 and 49, respectively, and thus the median father may still have 15 or 20 productive years after becoming a grandfather.

GRANDPARENTHOOD

Good feeling between alternate generations is a phenomenon that has been remarked upon in the anthropological literature. Radcliffe-Brown says that this phenomenon is built into the kinship systems of Australian tribes and of some Melanesian peoples with the consequence that a male is classified as belonging to a social division with his father's father, with his sons' sons, and with his brothers; his father and his sons belong to another social division.[13] A "condition under which" the good feeling prevails between alternate generations is reported by Apple. She finds that a joking relationship of friendly equality exists between them only when the grandparents have no authority or responsibility for the grandchildren.[14] Generally speaking, American grandparents do not have parental responsibility with respect to their grandchildren,[15] and we have the stereotype of the doting grandparent.

In the child-grandparent relationship in America we can see some ground for ambivalent feelings on the part of the grandparent, but the objective conditions seem less conducive to evoking the hostile aspect of the ambivalence in the relationship to grandchild than in the relation to the grandparent's own son or daughter. On the negative side with respect to the grandchild is the very real consideration that the mere existence of the child is tangible evidence of the grandparent's passing from the treasured years of vigorous adulthood into the less desirable period of old age. On the positive side there are several important considerations. The grandchild represents assurance that the line is being carried on. In a sense, moreover, the grandchild allows the grandparent to relive vicariously the pleasant aspects of parenthood without being charged with the expense, worry, and responsibility that constitute the negative aspects. It seems plausible that the grandparent may derive some gratification, consciously or unconsciously, from observing his own offspring (the parent) fulfill the obligations of parenthood and thus come to realize the "obligations" the parent "owes" the grandparent. From the child's standpoint,

---

[13] A. R. Radcliffe-Brown, "Introduction" in A. R. Radcliffe-Brown and Darryl Forde (eds.), *African Systems of Kinship and Marriage* (New York: Oxford University Press, 1950), pp. 1–43.

[14] Dorrian Apple, "The Social Structure of Grandparenthood," *American Anthropologist*, 58: 656–663 (1956).

[15] In the black lower class, however, maternal grandmothers frequently exercise parental authority over their grandchildren. Cf. E. Franklin Frazier, *The Negro Family in the United States* (Chicago: University of Chicago Press, 1939), chap. 8; and Lee Rainwater, "Crucible of Identity: The Negro Lower-Class Family," *Daedalus*, 95: 172–216 (1965), reprinted in Robert F. Winch and Louis Wolf Goodman (eds.), *Selected Studies in Marriage and the Family* (New York: Holt, Rinehart and Winston, Inc., 1968), pp. 102–127.

too, this may be a pleasurable relationship. The stereotypic grandparent provides gratification for the child but does not punish him. In this way the grandparent serves as a kind of parent—but only as pleasure-giving parent (performing the nurturant function), and not as pain-causing (not performing the controlling function). Thus, as we have seen, both child and grandparent have basic reasons to feel hostile (as well as affectionate) toward the parent, while, generally, they do not have strong basic reasons to feel hostile toward each other. In this sense, then, the parent has the role "in the middle" and is a common focus of hostility.[16]

RETIREMENT

Under the Chinese family system described in Chapter 2 the hardest physical labor was performed by the young men and women at the peak of their physical condition. As they aged and their offspring grew to maturity, the parents could assume more administrative and supervisory duties for which their more vigorous duties of earlier years were a sort of apprenticeship. As the strength ebbed from the bodies of the older generation, the following generation was (at least, ideally) ready to take over. To some extent this sort of gradual tapering of duties within the individual career and smooth transition of tasks from one generation to the next is possible on the American family farm and wherever else the family is highly functional and has a three-generational structure.

By contrast the American urban setting, with its categorical employability,[17] presents a series of critical points requiring adjustments. By the middle or late thirties the median mother has her last child in school and by her early fifties her last child has married and left home. (See Table 17.1.) Accordingly, the median wife-mother finishes her parental duties well before her husband reaches retirement age at, say, sixty-five. If we think of motherhood as the principal activity in the lives of most women, then it is reasonable to view as a retirement problem the question as to what she should do with the time and energies released by her fulfillment of the maternal function. One part of the answer comes from Cumming and Henry: ". . . women act the roles of daughter, mother, and grandmother, shifting back and forth, from helping to being helped, in mutually dependent and closely knit relationships thoughout their life cycle. There is no discontinuity; only the emphasis changes."[18] The other part of the answer appeared in Chapter 11, where we saw evidence that an increasingly popular adjustment to this situation is to enter or re-enter the labor force. In 1967 the proportion of married women with husbands

---

[16] Cf. J. C. Flugel, *The Psycho-Analytic Study of the Family* (London: Hogarth, 1921), pp. 160–161, and Bernice L. Neugarten and Karol K. Weinstein, "The Changing American Grandparent," *Journal of Marriage and the Family*, 26: 199–204 (1964).

[17] See Chapter 4.

[18] Elaine Cumming and William E. Henry, *Growing Old: The Process of Disengagement* (New York: Basic Books, 1961), p. 149.

present who were in the labor force was 34 percent for the age category 25–29, and the proportion rose to 45 percent for the age category 45–54.[19] This modest difference undoubtedly underestimates the efforts of the older women to seek new roles to replace the now fulfilled role of mother. Another bit of evidence is that the proportion of women with husbands present who were in the labor force in 1967 was 23 percent for those with children under 3, 32 percent for those with children 3–5, and 45 percent for those with children in the 6–17 age bracket.[20] No doubt there are other ways in which women adjust to the completion of the maternal role, e.g., by taking up volunteer work, becoming active in clubs, and so on. It is reported that the level of dissatisfaction is especially high among middle-aged women who do not enter the labor force.[21]

For a considerable number of men, especially among those in urban occupations, the passage from active, productive adulthood into retirement occurs very abruptly as, for example, on some arbitrarily designated birthday. A manifestation of such categorical employability may be seen in Table 17.2. The rows of special interest are the second and fourth. Whereas there is almost no variation between them in the percentage "not able to work," there is considerable variation in the proportion "in labor force"—40 percent in

TABLE 17.2

Labor-Force Status, Males 65 and Over, by Type of Community, April 1952

(*Percentages*)

TYPE OF COMMUNITY	TOTAL	IN LABOR FORCE	NOT IN LABOR FORCE		
			Total	*Able to Work*	*Not Able to Work*
All types	100	42	58	43	15
Urban	100	40	60	45	15
Rural nonfarm	100	33	67	54	13
Farm	100	58	42	27	16

SOURCE: Adapted from Peter O. Steiner and Robert Dorfman, *The Economic Status of the Aged* (Berkeley: University of California Press, 1957), Table 4.5, p. 42, which is based on an unpublished tabulation of the *Current Population Survey*, April 1952. Reprinted by permission of the publisher.

---

[19] Women's Bureau Bulletin No. 290, *1965 Handbook on Women Workers* (Washington, D.C.: GPO, 1966), Table 10, p. 24.

[20] See Table 12.2.

[21] Arnold M. Rose, "Factors Associated with the Life Satisfaction of Middle-Class, Middle-Aged Persons," *Marriage and Family Living*, 17: 15–19 (1959).

urban communities and 58 percent in farm areas. (Since rural nonfarm communities are locations of retirement, the data in the third row are not relevant to our point.) Commenting on this table, Steiner and Dorfman speak of the farm economy as "being hospitable to the talents of older persons."[22] Categorical employment is also evident in Table 17.3, where the highest propor-

TABLE 17.3

Percentage Distribution of Males 65 and Over in Labor Force and Voluntarily and Involuntarily Retired, by Occupation Engaged in for Longest Time, April 1952

OCCUPATION GROUP ENGAGED IN LONGEST	IN LABOR FORCE	VOLUNTARILY RETIRED	INVOLUNTARILY RETIRED
Total	41	46	14
Professional and technical	67	21	13
Farmers and farm managers	43	50	7
Managers and proprietors	53	38	10
Clerical	31	43	26
Sales	49	35	16
Craftsmen, foremen, etc.	33	45	22
Operatives	36	50	14
Service, except household	35	46	18
Farm labor	35	60	5
Labor, except farm and mine	31	52	17

SOURCE: Adapted from Steiner and Dorfman, *The Economic Status of the Aged,* Table 4.9, p. 50.

tion of the voluntarily retired is among farm laborers and the lowest proportion is among professional and technical occupations. On the other hand, it should be noted that even in urban areas 40 percent of the males over sixty-five are still in the labor force, and even in the clerical and laboring occupations 31 percent are. (See Tables 17.2 and 17.3.) In their study of healthy, economically secure old people, Cumming and Henry report that in many cases "men . . . do not retire abruptly . . . but slip in and out of the labor market as if trying to get used to the change in role they are experiencing."[23]

For the reasons noted on the preceding page women who are active in the network of kinship tend to have no "problem" of retirement. However, since the question of what the husband "will do" tends to be resolved by his either competing with the wife for the socioemotional (expressive) role or else

[22] Peter O. Steiner and Robert Dorfman, *The Economic Status of the Aged* (Berkeley: University of California Press, 1957), p. 43.
[23] Cumming and Henry, *op. cit.,* p. 67.

finding some instrumental task, the retirement of a husband and his consequent presence in the home may generate a problem for his wife.[24]

Because the wife is the key worker with respect to domestic chores, she retains her usefulness as long as she is able to carry out such chores. Hence whether she is gainfully employed or not, her retirement from the totality of her roles tends to be gradual. This means that the wife's activities become more important than the husband's after his retirement. From this it might be expected that where the husband's employment is categorical, the wife's domestic power would increase with time. There is some evidence in favor of this proposition.[25]

Related to the topic of retirement is widowhood, which is considered in Chapters 22 and 23.

DISENGAGEMENT

Cumming and Henry conceptualize old age as a process of disengagement. They define disengagement as "an inevitable process in which many of the relationships between a person and other members of society are severed, and those remaining are altered in quality."[26] They point out that occupation and kinship are the prime social systems in which the husband and wife, respectively, are engaged in their vigorous years and that the respective rewards of these systems are approval and love. Cumming and Henry find that approval-seeking and love-seeking behaviors diminish with age. Because the ties of the family are based on ascription, old people are able to continue functioning as family members long after they have had to relinquish achievement-based ties in other areas of social participation.[27]

NURTURANCE AND THREE STAGES OF GRANDPARENTHOOD

How long, on the average, is the period of grandparenthood? Should it be thought of as consisting of stages?

For those who survive to the median age of becoming grandparents—about 55 for men and 53 for women—the expectation of life is to about age 75. It seems useful to distinguish three phases of grandparenthood—or relations between the older couple and their adult offspring—on the basis of the nature of nurturance, or the direction of dependency.

Early grandparenthood consists of the period (roughly a decade) between

---

[24] *Ibid.*, p. 147. Cf. quotation from Townsend on p. 233 above and also the discussion of instrumental and expressive roles, p. 325.

[25] D. M. Wolfe, "Power and Authority in the Family," in Dorwin Cartwright (ed.), *Studies in Social Power* (Ann Arbor: University of Michigan Press, 1959), pp. 99–117.

[26] *Op. cit.*, p. 211.

[27] Elaine Cumming, "Further Thoughts on the Theory of Disengagement," *International Social Science Journal*, 15: 377–393 (1963), reprinted in Winch and Goodman (eds.), *op. cit.*, pp. 416–430.

becoming a grandparent for the first time and the retirement of the husband. Typically the grandparental couple is still vigorous and productive. Presumably it is during this period that the grandparental generation is of the most help to their own offspring in providing services (such as help at the time of births, babysitting, and so on) and money.

The middle phase of grandparenthood consists of the first decade or so of retirement, or until the husband is about seventy-five. During this decade the elderly couple tend to continue living in their own household. With their children in middle age and, hopefully, economically established, demands for service and money should be greatly reduced, and thus the grandparents should now be freed from parental responsibilities. It seems likely that during middle grandparenthood there is a considerable reduction in the flow of nurturance.

Depending upon the state of their health and finances, those who survive middle grandparenthood enter late grandparenthood around the age of 75 or 80—perhaps earlier or even later. This phase is marked by a decline in the health and strength of the grandparents plus the rising probability of the loss of the spouse. These conditions cause the direction of dependency to be reversed, and now the offspring feel some responsibility for nurturing their parents.[28]

Of course the above stages contain some assumptions that are reasonable in middle-class America but probably quite outrageous in a village in India. These assumptions involve: (1) life expectation, (2) length of a generation, and (3) degree of health in the later decades of life. For any given individual in the United States, moreover, the above formulation might prove inapplicable as, for example, if he were not to have his first child until age 40, if his offspring were also late in having their progeny, and if his health should begin to deteriorate seriously by, say, age 50.

IS THE GRANDPARENTAL GENERATION ISOLATED?

Because the neolocal pattern of marriage sets up the adult offspring and his parents in separate households and because the American urban-industrial society fosters spatial mobility with the implication of a considerable probability that adults and their parents will not live near each other, Parsons holds that "the parental couple is left without attachment to any continuous kinship group."[29] We can get some idea as to the degree of justification of

---

[28] For further discussion of these stages see Wayne E. Thompson and Gordon F. Streib, "Meaningful Activity in a Family Context," in Robert W. Kleemeier (ed.), *Aging and Leisure: A Research Perspective into the Meaningful Use of Time* (New York: Oxford, 1961), pp. 177–211, reprinted in Winch and Goodman (eds.), *op. cit.*, pp. 433–448.

[29] Talcott Parsons, "Age and Sex in the Social Structure of the United States," *American Sociological Review*, 7: 615–616 (1942). Cf. also Ivan Belknap and H. J. Friedsam, "Age and Sex Categories as Sociological Variables in the Mental Disorders of Later Maturity," *American Sociological Review*, 4: 367–376 (1949).

Parsons' statement for America by checking the proportion of Americans who, in their old age, do not live in families and do not live with spouses.

As of 1968, 93 percent of the men and 96 percent of the women in the 35–44 age category lived in familial households. At older ages the proportion dropped—gradually for men, more sharply for women. Eighty-nine percent of the men in the 55–64 category, 84 percent of those 65–74, and 73 percent of those over 75 lived in familial households. The corresponding percentages for women were 80 percent of those 55–64, 65 percent in the 65–74 category, and 55 percent among those over 75.[30] The lower proportions of older women in families reflect two basic demographic facts: (1) women generally marry men older than themselves, and (2) women have higher life expectancies than men. Even more dramatic evidence of these demographic facts appears in Table 17.4. There we see that in 1968, 86 percent of the men 40–44 years old were reported as "married, wife present." This percentage remained quite steady through the 55–64 age bracket but then fell to 78 and 56 percent for the 65–74 and 75-and-over brackets, respectively. Among the women the maximum percentage with "husband present" was 84 in the 30–34 age category. The percentage declined gradually to 78 percent in the 45–54 bracket, but then the decline became sharper—65 percent in the 55–64 category, 45 percent in the 65–74 group, and a mere 19 percent in the bracket over 75. Over the age of 75, then, one out of every two men had a mate present, but only one out of every five women did. Finally, a study of old age in the United States, Britain, and Denmark provides the conclusion that the proportion of old people who were isolated in the sense of not having daily human contact was very small—under 5 percent in each country.[31]

CONTACT BETWEEN THE PARENTAL AND GRANDPARENTAL GENERATIONS

Two types of data that can illuminate this topic are census data on living arrangements, and sample survey and community data on interaction patterns.

Schorr has observed that there is a long-term declining trend in this country with respect to the proportion of aged people living with their children. In 1957 the proportion is reported to have been 28 percent.[32] The same writer concludes that "it is the currently nonmarried and especially the women who are most likely to share living arrangements" and further that "23 percent of all aged couples, 27 percent of the nonmarried men, and 37 percent of the nonmarried women" were living with their children in 1957.[33] These data in-

[30] U.S. Bureau of the Census, *Current Population Reports—Population Characteristics*, Series P-20, No. 187, August 11, 1969, Table 2, p. 16.

[31] Peter Townsend and Sylvia Tunstall, "Isolation, Desolation, and Loneliness," in Ethel Shanas *et al.*, *Old People in Three Industrial Societies* (New York: Atherton, 1968), chap. 9.

[32] Alvin L. Schorr, *Filial Responsibility in the Modern American Family* (Washington, D.C.: GPO, 1960), p. 8.

[33] *Ibid.* "Nonmarried" includes the divorced and widowed.

TABLE 17.4

Percent Distribution of the U.S. Population by Marital Status, by Age and Sex: March 1968

SEX AND MARITAL STATUS	14–17 YEARS	18–19 YEARS	20–24 YEARS	25–29 YEARS	30–34 YEARS	35–39 YEARS
Male: total	100.0	100.0	100.0	100.0	100.0	100.0
Single	99.8	91.9	55.1	20.8	10.5	8.9
Married						
Wife present	0.2	6.9	42.2	74.8	84.2	85.1
Wife absent	(z)	1.2	2.0	2.3	2.5	3.0
Separated	—[a]	0.3	0.9	1.5	1.7	1.9
Other	(z)[b]	0.9	1.1	0.7	0.8	1.0
Widowed	—	—	(z)	0.1	0.2	0.3
Divorced	(z)	0.1	0.7	2.1	2.6	2.7
Female: total	100.0	100.0	100.0	100.0	100.0	100.0
Single	97.6	76.8	35.9	10.3	5.9	5.1
Married						
Husband present	2.0	19.9	56.9	80.8	83.6	83.5
Husband absent	0.4	3.1	4.7	5.3	5.3	4.9
Husband in armed forces	0.2	1.8	1.8	0.8	0.7	0.4
Separated	0.1	0.8	2.1	3.7	3.5	3.3
Other	0.1	0.5	0.9	0.9	1.2	1.2
Widowed	—	0.1	0.3	0.5	1.4	1.8
Divorced	(z)	0.2	2.1	3.0	3.9	4.7

[a] The dash represents zero.
[b] (z) = less than 0.05 percent.
SOURCE: U.S. Bureau of the Census, *Current Population Reports—Population Characteristics*, Series P-20, No. 187, August 11, 1969, Table 1, p. 12.

dicate that in America one out of every three or four people over sixty-five lives with an offspring. Conversely, between two thirds and three fourths of the older adults do not live with their children. One of every six men over sixty-five and one of every three women in the same bracket were not living in families in 1968.[34] Is this isolation or is it not? We have yet to consider separate but proximate dwellings.

The study of old age in the United States, Britain, and Denmark presents

[34] U.S. Bureau of the Census, *Current Population Reports—Population Characteristics*, Series P-20, No. 187, August 11, 1969, Table 2, p. 16. ". . . one should not conclude that only poor, sick, old widows live with children, for though the numbers of men, of couples, and of well-to-do who live with children are smaller, they are noticeable. Women prove to be pivotal in live-together arrangements. Aged parents are more likely to live with their daughter and her husband and children, if any, than with a son and his family. Young

TABLE 17.4 (Continued)

SEX AND MARITAL STATUS	40–44 YEARS	55–64 YEARS	45–54 YEARS	65–74 YEARS	75 AND OVER
Male: total	100.0	100.0	100.0	100.0	100.0
Single	7.1	7.0	5.9	6.3	6.5
Married					
Wife present	85.9	84.7	83.5	77.6	56.2
Wife absent	2.7	3.1	2.8	2.5	3.4
Separated	2.0	2.0	1.8	1.3	1.6
Other	0.7	1.1	0.9	1.2	1.8
Widowed	0.8	1.7	4.3	11.0	31.4
Divorced	3.6	3.5	3.5	2.6	2.5
Female: total	100.0	100.0	100.0	100.0	100.0
Single	4.9	4.9	5.9	7.7	8.0
Married					
Husband present	81.4	78.4	64.6	44.6	18.8
Husband absent	4.5	4.0	3.1	1.9	1.7
Husband in armed forces	0.3	(z)	—	(z)	—
Separated	3.3	3.0	2.1	1.0	0.3
Other	0.9	1.0	1.1	0.8	1.4
Widowed	3.7	7.9	22.0	43.3	70.0
Divorced	5.6	4.8	4.4	2.5	1.4

data on the residential location of those respondents over sixty-five who had living children. In Britain about as many lived with their children as lived near them; in Denmark and the United States there were considerably more who lived within ten minutes' travel of their children than who lived with them. Together these categories accounted for about three fifths of the Danish respondents and nearly three fourths of the British and American subjects. It should be emphasized that the base for these proportions excludes those without living children.

Several community studies in England have provided interesting information on the familial status of the aged. In Wolverhampton, a manufacturing town of approximately 150,000, it is reported that "4 per cent of the old people . . . have children actually living next door. Ten per cent of the old people have children actually living in the same street. Twenty per cent of them have

couples starting out are more likely to live with the wife's family than with the husband's. Aged women with low incomes will tend, if they have children, to live with them. Men's choices are apparently dependent on other factors; they are as likely to live alone, whether or not they have children."—Schorr, *op. cit.*, p. 8.

relatives living within half-a-mile, or within such a distance that a hot meal can be carried from one house to the other without needing re-heating."[35]

A study of people of pensionable age (over 65 for men, over 60 for women) in Bethnal Green, a working-class borough of East London, looked into opinion concerning living arrangements of adults and their parents. The prevalent attitude was that it was good for the aged to have their separate and independent establishments but to have their children living nearby.[36] Just under a fifth of the sample had no surviving children; of those with children more than 80 percent had a child living within a mile, and over half had a child in the same dwelling.[37] Of those who had sons about one half saw the son daily; of those with daughters the proportion having daily contact rose to two thirds. And of those having both sons and daughters three fourths saw either a son or a daughter (or conceivably both) daily.[38] These facts seem to warrant the conclusion of the study: "Very few old people [in Bethnal Green] are isolated from all their children."[39]

Twenty-two of the 203 subjects in the foregoing study reported that they were "sometimes lonely" and an additional 5 reported being "very lonely." It was found, however, that there was less disposition of those who had been living alone to report being "very lonely" than among those who had recently lost a spouse. On this basis Townsend drew a distinction between isolation and desolation.

This working-class borough in East London shows two out of five persons of pensionable age with an offspring living in the same dwelling and another one out of the five having a child within a mile of his residence. How typical is such a set of findings? Or under what conditions may we expect them to vary?

A study was undertaken in Woodford, a suburb of London having both working-class and middle-class residents. Some differences were found between these two suburban samples and the working-class borough, Bethnal Green, with respect to interaction between the generations. The elderly people in East London were found to live nearer to and to see more of their relatives than did either class in Woodford. Furthermore, members of the working class in Woodford lived closer to and saw more of their relatives than did the middle-class persons in that suburb. It was also found that mobility appeared to decrease the amount of intergenerational contact for men but not for women. "The tie between mother and daughter seems to have the strength to resist the effect of occupational change."[40] And so some correlates of social

---

[35] J. H. Sheldon, "Old-Age Problems in the Family," *Millbank Memorial Fund Quarterly*, 27: 119–132 (1949), at p. 121.
[36] Peter Townsend, *The Family Life of Old People*, pp. vi, x.
[37] *Ibid.*, Tables 1 and 6, pp. 8 and 32, respectively.
[38] *Ibid.*, p. 37.
[39] *Ibid.*, p. xi.
[40] Peter Willmott and Michael Young, *Family and Class in a London Suburb* (London: Routledge, 1960), p. 86.

stratification turned up in the English data.⁴¹ In one paragraph the study of Bethnal Green presents a good summary of the intergenerational relations found in that working-class borough:

> We started by asking how far in fact old people were isolated from family life, and found that they often lived with relatives but preferred a "supported" independence. Those not sharing their homes rarely lived alone in a literal sense. Three generations of relatives were generally distributed over two or more households near one another and old people had very close ties with their families. Those interviewed had an average of 13 relatives within a mile and they saw three-quarters of all their children, both married and unmarried, once a week, as many as a third of them every day. We found old people getting a great deal of help, regularly and in emergencies, from their female relatives, particularly their daughters, living in neighbouring streets. The remarkable thing was how often this help was reciprocated—through provision of midday meals, care of grandchildren and other services. The major function of the grandparent is perhaps the most important fact to emerge from this book. If confirmed elsewhere we may have to re-examine many of our ideas about the family, child-rearing, parenthood and old age.⁴²

In view of the three stages of grandparenthood distinguished above, one may surmise from Townsend's astonishment that he had in mind what we have called "late grandparenthood," but that his subjects probably included a number of cases of "early grandparenthood." In any case, Townsend concluded that in East London the generations are "side by side throughout life, and at every stage kinship provides aid and support." In Woodford, on the other hand, aid is much less reciprocal in that the younger generation gives more than it receives. By way of explanation Willmott and Young point out that during what we have called "early grandparenthood" the older generation in Woodford is much less in contact with the younger than its counterpart in East London, but as they pass into "late grandparenthood" and become infirm and widowed, the residents of Woodford move near or with their children and see them oftener than before. Here we see the functional significance of the age distinction.⁴³ Consistent with this conclusion is a study of persons in the age brackets 50–69 and 70 and over, which led to the hypothesis that with age comes a progressive absorption with the self and withdrawal from others, or

---

⁴¹ From interviews with parents in ninety-seven New Haven families, Sussman has concluded that when children marry individuals of their own socioeconomic stratum, relations of the marital couple with their parents tend to be more harmonious than those where some socioeconomic heterogamy prevails.—Marvin B. Sussman, "Family Continuity: Selective Factors Which Affect Relationships between Families at Generational Levels," *Marriage and Family Living*, 16: 112–120 (1954).

⁴² Townsend, *The Family Life of Old People: An Inquiry in East London* (London: Routledge and Kegan Paul, Ltd., 1957), pp. 204–205. Reprinted by permission of the publishers.

⁴³ Willmott and Young, *op. cit.*, pp. 39–40.

what is called a "decrease in the social life space."[44] The postulating of the age categories immediately suggests a query as to which category is being referred to when we read that the "balance of financial aid proves to be 'greater in the direction of helping children'"[45] or that "dependence on children for subsidy weakens the family, for the family is partly built on *reciprocal services*."[46]

DEPENDENCY IN THE OLDER GENERATION AND FILIAL RESPONSIBILITY

It is time to address explicitly a theme that has been running through the preceding pages: that with the passage of time the older generation may become dependent on the younger and thereby bring about a reversal of roles. As the offspring comes to his physical prime and social adulthood, the physical strength of his parents is declining. His assumption of adult status implies that he no longer needs to be nurtured; having become responsible for his own acts, he need no longer be controlled. Many parents find themselves needing some sort of nurturant care—some in terms of company and affection, some in terms of nursing care, and others in terms of money. Senility sometimes brings parents to the point where someone must supervise and control their behavior. Whether or not the parent becomes dependent on the child and if so, in what sense, depends on diverse circumstances—the wealth and domestic establishment maintained by the parent, how long he lives, whether or not predeceased by the spouse, whether he dies suddenly or after a prolonged and enfeebling illness, and so on. What responses do offspring make to this situation, and what responses should they make?

A generation ago a study based on a sample of Midwestern college students concluded: "The obligation of children to support aged and needy parents is no longer in the mores. . . . Now, the children often take into consideration the nature of their personal relations with parents in order to come to a decision as to whether or not to help them. Parents, therefore, cannot be sure of obtaining support no matter how smooth their interaction with children happens to be at a particular time."[47] The majority of the students in this study accepted the idea of caring for parents if such care involved no unusual difficulties. When confronted with the hypothetical condition that the care of parents in one's own home would involve interpersonal strife and turmoil, however, the proportion who would still feel obliged to proffer support shrank to as low as one third of those with urban background and Protestant affiliation. On the average, those students with rural backgrounds and with Catholic affiliations showed more sense of obligation to take care of

---

[44] Elaine Cumming, *et al.*, "Disengagement—A Tentative Theory of Aging," *Sociometry*, 23: 23–35 (1960).

[45] Schorr, *op. cit.*, p. 7.

[46] Townsend, *op. cit.*, p. xiii. Italics in original.

[47] R. M. Dinkel, "Attitudes of Children toward Supporting Aged Parents," *American Sociological Review*, 9: 370–379 (1944), at pp. 378–379.

parents. An earlier study reported a somewhat greater disposition to contribute to family support.[48]

There is evidence that such attitudes as those reflected in the study just cited rest on a somewhat uneasy emotional base of guilt and conflict. It is reported that American surveys "yield respectable percentages in favor of filial responsibility as long as the question is put quite simply and in ethical terms." However, when the questions are phrased so that to fulfill filial responsibility comes at a cost to one's family of procreation or to one's own advancement, support for filial responsibility drops to a minority.[49]

The impact of the reversal of roles can affect the relationship between the adult child and his parent in various ways. A recurrent theme in the clinical literature is that if the offspring has not achieved a satisfactory degree of emancipation, the spectacle of the declining powers of the once-powerful parent-figure may be emotionally upsetting. This phenomenon has been noted in the cases of veterans who return home after some years to find their fathers in a state of greatly reduced vigor.[50] On the other hand, a pattern of reversed dependence may be established relatively early in the parent-child relationship, and continue undisturbed into the period when the offspring achieves adulthood. This seems to happen particularly in cases where the mother is widowed at a relatively early age and transfers her dependence to a son. The latter pattern may complicate the son's marriage, and in some cases there is clinical evidence that the dependence of the mother prevents the son from marrying.

In the matter of dependency, as in others, there appears to be a disposition to feel that the network of obligations of a strong extended family is "right," and therefore that the offspring should be ready and willing to assist his parents. Contrary, at least in part, to this is the cultural theme that each nuclear family should be independent and self-sufficient. These appear to be two of the themes serving to engender guilt and confusion. Some Americans have felt strongly that there should be some manner of all-inclusive insurance program so that old people should have a *right* to a pension—"with no questions asked"—because they had, during their productive years, contributed to the program. Others hold that persons who are thrifty, resolute, and properly circumspect can set aside sufficient savings, insurance, and so on, so that they can take care of themselves in their old age. (In a period of long-range inflation this view must involve assumptions not only as to the adequacy of the income during the productive years and the disposition to thrift but also as to wisdom in investing in order to be able to "ride" the inflation.) An intermediate group consists of people who have been brought up with attitudes of

---

[48] H. M. Bell, *Youth Tell Their Story* (Washington, D.C.: American Council on Education, 1938), p. 26.

[49] Schorr, *op. cit.*, p. 6.

[50] Cf. various cases in R. R. Grinker and J. P. Spiegel, *Men under Stress* (New York: McGraw-Hill-Blakiston, 1945); and Therese Benedek, *Insight and Personality Adjustment* (New York: Ronald, 1946).

responsibility for members of their families, but regard the state's assumption of responsibility for the support of relatives with relief as well as with misgivings. The misgivings are related not only to whatever stigma attaches itself to a person needing and asking for help from the state, but also to the emotional conflict surrounding a seeming breakdown in relationships with the family group.

This conflict and different points of view on the subject are dramatically portrayed in Packer's novel *The Inward Voyage*. Sam Lucas, a World War II veteran, returns to his parental home and finds that his father is incurably ill and thus unemployable—a fact that has been kept from him lest it cause him undue anxiety. Instead of coming back to the comfortable home to which he has been accustomed and resuming his place as a much-loved son from whom nothing but love is expected in return, Sam is confronted with the necessity for assuming responsibility for his parents. This involves postponing marriage indefinitely, taking a job he does not want, and giving up plans for going to law school. Ill prepared emotionally to do any of these things, Sam presents a picture of frustration and acute anxiety. When another young man, Ray, suggests the idea that the state should relieve him of responsibility for his parents, Sam is driven into an angry outburst.

> Ray said, "Of course I can understand your point of view, but that doesn't mean I condone it. The trouble with you is that you're a victim of bourgeois morality."
>
> "What does that mean?" [Sam asked.]
>
> "It means that not only are you expected to be responsible for your parents' support but that you actually approve of that code. That's why human progress is so . . . slow. More than half of every new generation has this parental drag on their lives. It not only blinds you to your goal, but it's also a kind of ancestor worship—and just about as deadly."
>
> Sam said, "Well—you can't just run out on your responsibility."
>
> "It's not the children's responsibility," Ray said. "It's the state that should take care of the people who can't take care of themselves—and without any of that pauper psychology, either. In the long run the state would profit by it because it would leave the children to live more constructively."
>
> It was just about then that Sam began to get angry, seeing it as a direct affront to himself and his parents—this allusion to what he thought of as institutional charity.
>
> He gulped his drink, glared at Ray, and said, "Some of us are not the kind of callous bastards who don't give a damn what happens to their folks!"[51]

As of about 1959 Schorr estimated that around 5 to 10 percent of the aged people in the United States received cash contributions from their children.[52]

[51] Peter Packer, *The Inward Voyage* (New York: McGraw-Hill, 1948), p. 51.

[52] *Op. cit.*, p. 6. The figure would have been higher if free rent and other nonmonetary aid had been included.

He found that offspring made cash contributions least often to couples, more often to nonmarried men, and most often to nonmarried women.[53] According to the three-nation study about three fourths of America's aged were receiving government benefits, a proportion that was lower than in either Britain or Denmark.[54]

Data that give an impression of considerable familial interaction and mutual aid come from a study done in Detroit in 1955. Here the question did not concern merely cash contributions by offspring to parents but all forms of help to all sorts of relatives. With this more inclusive indicator of mutual aid it was found that about 70 percent of the families surveyed exchanged some kind of help with relatives outside the nuclear family. Of those couples having living parents it is reported that 65 percent received some help from parents and 46 percent gave help to them. The most frequently mentioned types of help *from* parents was baby-sitting, help during illness, and financial aid; the most frequently mentioned help *to* parents was assistance during illness, financial aid, and help with housework.[55]

The studies of Willmott and Young and Townsend cited above have enabled us to peer a bit more understandingly into the problem in England than we can in America. The general impression to be derived from the English studies is that the parent likes to live nearby but independently of the offspring—more often a daughter than a son—and that as the dependency of the parent becomes acute, the offspring provides appropriate aid. (Of course, Britain has a system of pensions for the aged.)

THE MOTHER-DAUGHTER DYAD IN INTERGENERATIONAL CONTACTS

The British studies have indicated that there is more continuous contact and also more mutual aid in the working class than in the middle class. One possible cause is that with greater poverty the working class has greater need for mutual aid than has the middle class. Another factor may be the traditionally greater hostility and less companionship between the sexes in the working class of England than in the middle class. The consequence for the working class of London has been to look upon the family as a sort of "woman's union" within which women defend themselves against the cruelty, neglect, uncertain and ungenerous housekeeping allowances, and desertion of their husbands.[56] Sweetser reports cross-cultural evidence that a couple tends

---

[53] *Op. cit.*, pp. 6, 19. Quotation is from p. 6.

[54] Dorothy Wedderburn, "The Financial Resources of Older People: A General Review," in Ethal Shanas *et al.*, *op. cit.*, chap. 12.

[55] Survey Research Center, *A Social Profile of Detroit: 1955* (Ann Arbor, Mich.: Institute for Social Research, 1956), Table 12, p. 19. The proportion of children giving financial aid to parents was 15 percent.

[56] Willmott and Young, *op. cit.*, p. 127. No doubt it is the competition in solidarity between the mother-daughter and husband-wife relationships that has given rise to mother-in-law jokes in this country.

to feel greater intergenerational solidarity with the wife's parents than with the husband's unless the young man inherits a farm from his father or goes into business with him, in which case there is greater solidarity with the husband's parents.[57]

Aged without Offspring: Improvisation of child-surrogates

In Table 7.1 we found that between one tenth and one fifteenth of the ever married American women of various age-categories were childless. If, to simplify our calculations, we assume all the never married are also childless, we find the proportion of childless women to be between one seventh and one eighth. What implication has this fact for taking care of the dependent aged?

In their study of Woodford, a London suburb, Willmott and Young state that "most people are not solitary," and go on to remark that "old people without children are on the whole no more isolated or neglected than those with them."[58] Noting that older people need a family, these writers report that when people in Woodford do not have children, and indeed when they have no kin at all, they work out substitute arrangements, such as these:

> Childless people treat nephews and nieces as their own children; their grandnephews and grandnieces as their grandchildren.
> Single people turn to their siblings and form a sort of nuclear family.
> Single people without relatives make quasi siblings out of single friends and thus form a kind of "family."[59]

Familism, Extroversion, and Anomia

The study of Woodford contains a tantalizing theme. It is not very well documented, but it is so important that we shall pause to consider it. If we think of familism as manifested, among other things, in a lively sense of obligations to kinsmen, both lineal and collateral, and a disposition to spend leisure in the company of relatives rather than with nonrelated friends, then the Woodford study showed middle-class people to be less familistic than lower-class people.

It appears that middle-class adults tend to spend their leisure with age-graded nonrelated people of similar background and interests—whether it be going bowling or to concerts, drinking gin or tea, discussing books or sex or

---

[57] Dorrian Apple Sweetser, "The Effect of Industrialization on Intergenerational Solidarity," *Rural Sociology*, 31: 156–170 (1966), reprinted in Robert F. Winch and Louis Wolf Goodman, *op. cit.*, pp. 397–408.
[58] *Op. cit.*, p. 57.
[59] *Ibid.*, p. 58.

diaper services. (There is some variation in the degree to which such association is also sex-segregated. At the two ends of the class spectrum there is a disposition toward all-male congeniality groups—at corner saloons and at fashionable clubs. In the middle strata there are some sex-segregated activities, but there is much more emphasis on unsegregated activities punctuated with reproaches from the hostess when the community of interests within sex groups polarizes a party into single-sex clusters.) The fact that the middle-class person does not participate in such activities by right of birth, that social acceptance is achieved and not ascribed, makes social attractiveness a reward-eliciting characteristic. For this reason incentives exist for middle-class persons to show "extraverted" behavior, to conform to their peers' expectations, and to strive to be "popular."

Willmott and Young found both the working-class residents of Bethnal Green (the East London borough) and the middle-class residents of Woodford (the London suburb) to be friendly, neighborly, and helpful, but they felt that there was a qualitative difference in the kind of friendliness. Residents of Bethnal Green were warm and easygoing and took each other for granted. The authors interpreted this as a consequence of their having known each other all their lives and of not having to make friends since their friends had been "ready-made." Residents of Woodford, on the other hand, are represented as not so easygoing, as screening each other by harsh standards of acceptance, and as having the skill of "making friends." In addition to showing the credentials of status—the right accent, good grooming, approved taste in dress, and the like—the acceptable resident of Woodford should have a "readiness to engage in conversation and . . . be rather extroverted."[60]

In the preceding chapter we mentioned the concern over popularity and being extroverted as instrumental to the achievement of career goals. Now we may add one more connecting link between the middle-class way of life and the wish to be extroverted: to acquire and maintain friends; to have engaging people with whom to carry out leisure activities. As Willmott and Young observe: "Maybe uniformity is one of the prices we have to pay for sociability in a more mobile society."[61]

We can carry the argument one step further. In a familistic setting one interacts with one's kinsmen because they are kinsmen. If in addition to being related to them, one also likes them, so much the better; if not, so much the worse; but the latter attitude does not lead to social withdrawal. The kinsmen still constitute the social field within which interaction takes place. In a non-familistic setting one has the freedom to choose his friends from those who present themselves. The opportunity exists for a much more congenial group and with highly esoteric interests. The opportunity also exists for one to be friendless or virtually so. If the negative view of familistically organized interaction is that one is obliged to interact with persons he may not especially like,

---

[60] *Op. cit.*, p. 129.
[61] *Ibid.*

the positive view is that he is provided with persons who are obliged to interact with him.

It is argued that not only does the nonfamilistic setting stimulate people to try to be socially attractive, extroverted, conforming, and filled with bonhomie; the lack of sanctions and the tentative and shifting nature of the rewards lead to a "thinness" of social relationships—to a situation where a person whom one met for the first time yesterday, and who was last night's drinking companion, is today one's friend and may be gone next week, never to be heard from again. A hypothesis—or since it will be stated informally, perhaps it should be called an idea—to emerge from these considerations is that cynicism about human nature, the opinion that social relationships are shallow, and indeed a basis for anomia are related to a shift from a familistic to a nonfamilistic social setting.

Lest the reader view the last paragraph as advocacy and lest it appear that the author is about to harness up the horse and sleigh over which he spilled scorn in the second paragraph of Chapter 1, let it be added that both familistic and nonfamilistic settings have their assets and liabilities. If the curse of familism is the obligation to spend one's time with people whose intellects are small, whose tastes are crass, and whose interest in one is manifested in snooping behavior, the coordinate curse of nonfamilism is the thinness of social relationships, the transitory nature of friendships, and the fickleness of friends. If the nonfamilistic setting demands conforming behavior to achieve acceptance, familistic settings demand conforming behavior because it is "right." If nonfamilism is good because the selection of friends with exciting talents and interests encourages one to realize his potentialities and fulfill himself, familism is good because it creates a sense of identity and of belonging and the prospect of being cared for in one's declining days.

Summary

When the offspring no longer engages in receptive or submissive behavior with respect to his parents he is showing that they need not nurture or control him and he is manifesting his independence of them. When in old age the parent behaves in a characteristically receptive and/or submissive way toward the offspring, the parent is registering dependence on the child and a situation of role-reversal prevails.

The role-system of the upper class operates to continue the dependence of the young person on the family of orientation. In the middle class the system frequently operates to transfer the young man's dependence from family of orientation to the corporation.

The relationship between grandparent and grandchild is normally good in American society because the grandparent usually carries out only the nurturant (pleasure-giving) function and not the controlling (pain-giving) function.

The Adult and His Parents 469

The average married woman can retire in her forties from her task of motherhood, although she may continue for some time thereafter to contribute (e.g., babysitting service) to the families of her offspring. Some women enter (or re-enter) the labor force as they retire from active motherhood, but there is surprisingly little variation in the proportion of wives with husbands present in the labor force; it runs from 32 percent for wives 16–19 years old to 45 percent for those 45–54 and back down to 34 percent for the 55–64 age category.[62]

A study of a working-class borough of London indicates a disposition for elderly parents to live near their offspring, especially near daughters, but not with them. During the period designated in this chapter as "early" grandparenthood there is less contact between the generations in a middle-class suburb of London than in the working-class borough; this difference tends to disappear in "late" grandparenthood. American culture is confused on the degree of responsibility that offspring should assume for the care of aged parents.

British studies of intergenerational contact, whether or not the parents are dependent, emphasize the solidarity of mother and daughter. (This may be compared with the solidarity of father and son in the traditional Chinese family and of husband and wife in the American nuclear family.) One of the English studies relates that old people without children nearby improvise young kinsmen when the elderly people are in need of family.

The chapter concludes with some speculations on the implication that situations low in familism stimulate extroversion and a particular kind of conformity.

[62] Women's Bureau Bulletin No. 294, *1969 Handbook on Women Workers* (Washington, D.C.: GPO, 1969), Table 9, p. 27.

PART SIX

Love, Mate-Selection, and the Marital Relationship:

the second phase of the affectional cycle

In the wake of urbanization and industrialization America has come to emphasize the marital relationship as a major source of emotional gratification and security and as the key relationship in the familial system. In the traditional Chinese family we saw that the relationship of the young man to his parents and especially to his father was evaluated to be much more important than his relationship to his wife. This illustrates the principle that in a strong extended family system there is less solidarity in the marital relationship than in one or more of the intergenerational relationships.

The American emphasis on the marital relationship is expressed in the form of two more or less widely held expectations: that a relationship of love will exist between a young man and a young woman before they will consider marrying each other; and that they will consider terminating the marriage if one or both feel that their relationship is no longer one of love.

Parts One, Two, and Three have discussed social functions in general and in particular the functions of the American family. In addition to noting nonaffectional elements in mate-selection, Part Four has described the roles of husband and wife in the American family. Part Five has pointed to conditions that affect the development of the individual as a member of a family from birth to adulthood. Throughout our presentation has run the thesis that extrafamilial systems affect the family's structure and functions, and that these in turn influence the experiences of the family members with implications for the development of offspring within the family. We have referred to the needs of parents as being in part intervening variables reflecting the impact of extrafamilial systems and affecting the experiences of their children and in this way influencing the development of the need-patterns of the children.

Now the offspring are growing up, are about to marry, found their own families of procreation, and begin influencing their own children. Both to understand marital interaction and to illuminate the behavior of parents it is necessary to fill in the period when the person is seeking a mate, to consider relevant cultural expectations and psychic needs, gratifications and frustrations, adolescent love affairs, courtship, and marriage—both sustained and broken. Part Six will consider dating, courtship, and engagement as mate-selective institutions, love as a mate-selective phenomenon, and the nature of the marital relationship. (It will be recalled that considerations in the mate-selective process other than love have been discussed in Chapter 10.)

18

A Need-Based Theory of Love and a Theory of Mate-Selection Based on Complementary Needs

Introduction:
The old mystery—the new problem

Love has intrigued students of Western culture for several thousand years. Men have written about it, fought about it, and committed murder and suicide over it, but its nature has remained nebulous. It seems fair to say that, so far as most men are concerned, love is something to be experienced, not something that can be defined. In other times and places it appears that love has been regarded as a topic of interest and gossip but hardly of importance. It has been remarked, however, that in the United States love has become a social problem.[1] In Parts One, Two, and Three we have described the relatively nonfunctional state of the American family and the resulting emphasis on the derived familial functions—position-conferring and especially emotional gratification. Because of this trend love has assumed transcendent importance in contemporary courtship and marital and family relations. In view of the centuries of reflection that have been accorded this topic, it requires some temerity for a writer to attempt to analyze and describe love. Such an attempt is necessary, however, if we wish to understand the modern family.

Points of Emphasis

It is the purpose of this chapter to try to account in general for the emotion of love, and to account for the kind of love-object whom the individual selects. To account for the emotion, we develop the implications of the follow-

[1] Raoul de Roussy de Sales, "Love in America'" *Atlantic Monthly*, 161: 645–651 (May 1938).

ing reasoning: Needs provide the motive power or dynamics for all behavior. As an individual becomes socialized, he learns that certain persons in his social environment have the ability to gratify his needs or to assist him in achieving gratification (recall the parental function of nurturance). Such persons in turn acquire the power to evoke needs in the individual. Early in life one learns that some persons in one's life space can be sources of gratification, that others can be agents of frustration and pain, and probably that most individuals generate in one some mixture of positive and negative effect. A consequence is that the individual develops expectations of gratification or of frustration toward persons with whom he interacts. Associated with these expectations is a set of feelings—pleasant in the case of anticipated gratification and unpleasant in the case of anticipated frustration or threat. We conceive of the pleasant type of feeling as the psychic or subjective basis of the emotion of love. And thus love is ultimately grounded in the needs of the lover. In other words, we view love as a positive emotion that one person feels in relation to another and that is based upon the former's experience of having had his needs gratified by the latter, or the expectation, or at least a hope or fantasy, that the latter will gratify needs of the former.

It is not unusual for one individual to develop expectations that a second will both gratify and frustrate the needs of the former. This is the attitudinal basis of ambivalence. Although ambivalence is present in many interpersonal relationships—especially in the intimacy of courtship and marriage—there is great variation in the degree to which positive or negative (i.e., pleasant or unpleasant) feelings predominate.

Needs in general, as well as those underlying love, may be conscious, partly conscious, or completely unconscious. The need-constellation upon which love is based is a compound of the experiences of infancy and childhood: infantile love, parental discipline, and the fear of exclusion, or "separation anxiety."

A Theory of Love

According to our theory as to the nature of love, all forms of love are based on the needs of the individual. The constellation of needs in the individual enters into that individual's choice of love-object. The theory of complementary needs in mate-selection hypothesizes that person A chooses as a love-object B, a person whose need-pattern is complementary to, rather than similar to, the need-pattern of A. The major dimensions of need whose variation appears to be relevant to mate-selection are nurturance-receptivity and control-submissiveness. These dimensions reflect the parental functions in the mate-selective process.

The writer wishes to underscore the point that not every proposition in the following theories on the nature of love and the mate-selective process is presented as a factual statement. These theories constitute a point of view or, to use a technical phrase, a conceptual scheme for the analysis of man-woman relationships in dating, courtship, engagement, and marriage. To assert that some of the theoretical remarks are not factual is not equivalent to saying that they are fantasies of a fey author; it means that to date the complete theoretical chain has not been subjected to empirical verification. Where there is relevant evidence, it will be cited.

PREVIOUS DISCUSSIONS RELEVANT TO THE PRESENT CHAPTER

Since our theorizing is cumulative, we shall begin this presentation by recalling relevant sections in preceding chapters.

In Chapter 13 we made a series of observations concerning the emergence of the infantile psyche. In view of the importance of these observations for the comprehension of love, a summary of the relevant points will be made here. It was asserted that the needs of the infant, experienced as tensions, were met by the persons who attend the infant, especially by the mother or mother-substitute; that the release of tensions was experienced as pleasure; that this pleasure was usually associated with the mother-figure; that this association was the basis of infantile love; that in the normal course of events not all tensions were immediately released; and that there was thereby created the basis for some feelings of anxiety.

The discussion in Chapter 15 took cognizance of the increasing importance of social needs, of the shift in emphasis, as the infant becomes a child, from physical to symbolic care, the emerging conception of the self, and of the internalization of parental discipline in the superego. The child normally begins to build up an ideal self by incorporating into his personality standards of skill, knowledge and morality derived from parent-figures in his experience.

Chapter 16 considered the middle-class adolescent's problems of self-validation with particular reference to sex-type and preparation for adult roles. Reference was also made to anxiety-producing and insecurity-generating situations encountered by the adolescent. For each of the three broad age groups consideration has been given to the needs characteristic of the stage.

BEHAVIOR ARISES FROM NEEDS

A postulate from which this discussion proceeds is that a person's behavior from birth to death may be conceived as the acting out of his needs. Dissatisfaction is the common attribute of all needs. For the definition of need we follow Murray: "A need is a construct . . . which stands for a force . . . which organizes perception, apperception, intellection, conation, and action in such a way as to transform in a certain direction an existing, unsatisfying situation."[2] Needs may be classified as physical or social. As contrasted with physical needs,

[2] H. A. Murray et al., *Explorations in Personality* (New York: Oxford, 1938), pp. 123–124.

social needs pertain to mental or emotional dissatisfactions; they relate to external conditions, or to images connected with external conditions.[3] The body's demands for water and food are examples of physical needs; a person's wishes for nurturance and for recognition are examples of social needs.[4] Several needs may be acted out simultaneously in behavior, so that such a simple act as studying for an examination may indicate a desire to attract favorable attention to oneself from someone the student seeks to impress (need for recognition) and simultaneously to surpass a disliked rival (need to express hostility).

The intensity and mode of expression of the social needs are apparently influenced by the structure and functions of the society and by the related culture, as well as by subsocietal structures and functions and related subcultures. It appears from the account of Margaret Mead, for example, that the typical Arapesh boy experiences relatively little need to express aggression, but that typical American boys feel this need in greater intensity.[5] In the United States the lower-class boy is reported as expressing his aggression directly in physical violence, while the middle-class boy tends to express it in the more indirect form of competitive sports. Considered by themselves, physical needs (such as those for food, elimination, and sex) are common not only to all men but to all animals. Physical needs, however, become fused with social needs and then (to continue the examples) differences with respect to eating, toilet, and sexual practices become evident among societies, among segments within a society, and among individuals within a segment of a society. In the next chapter we shall note differences in sexual practices among segments of American society; we shall base our interpretation on subcultural variation in the way in which the physical need for sexual expression is fused with various social needs.

There are other characteristics of needs that are relevant. To the extent that needs are conscious, they are commonly accompanied by anticipation of gratification. Such anticipation tends to heighten the feeling-tone so that a

---

[3] Murray divides needs into primary (viscerogenic) and secondary (psychogenic). The latter, he says, "are presumably dependent upon and derived from the primary needs." Following McDougall, Murray holds that "certain emotions are linked with certain tendencies to action." Affection, according to this theory, is related to feelings of pleasure and unpleasure and may be divided into activity pleasure, achievement pleasure, and effect pleasure.—*Ibid.*, pp. 76, 80, 90, 91.

[4] *Need for nurturance:* to give sympathy and aid to a weak, helpless, ill, or dejected person or animal. *Need for recognition:* to excite the admiration and approval of others. Other needs that the writer postulated for his study of complementary needs in mate-selection are listed in Robert F. Winch, *Mate-Selection: A Study of Complementary Needs* (New York: Harper & Row, 1958), p. 90.

[5] Margaret Mead also found Arapesh men to be mild-mannered. Cf. her *Sex and Temperament in Three Primitive Societies* in her collection of three books published as *From the South Seas* (New York: Morrow, 1939). On the other hand, another anthropologist, Reo F. Fortune, visited the Arapesh at the same time and found Arapesh men to be extremely hostile and warlike. Cf. his "Arapesh Warfare," *American Anthropologist,* 41: 22–41 (1939).

person may, for example, register considerable enthusiasm. Although the relation between intensity of need and perception is not simple and direct, there is evidence that needs organize and give direction to behavior, and may even engender distortions in perception. Examples that come to mind include the perceptual distortions of psychotics[6] and one of cartoonists' favorite subjects —the mirage of the thirsty man in the desert—while the popular saying that "love is blind" reminds us that the concept of need-based perceptual distortion is in the folk wisdom. Carefully controlled studies that have sought to relate intensity of need to perceptual processes have resulted in somewhat ambiguous findings, however, and have led one authority to offer the following judgment: ". . . there is now enough evidence . . . to suggest that not the *amount* of need but the *way* in which a person learns to handle his needs determines the manner in which motivation and cognitive selectivity will interact. . . . On the whole . . . selectivity reflects the nature of the person's mode of striving for goals rather than the amount of need which he seems to be undergoing."[7]

Because of the relation of need to infantile love and of infantile love to adult love, it is in order to consider a formulation by Theodor Reik, a somewhat heterodox Freudian. It is Reik's idea that the degree to which a person, as an adult, is capable of loving is determined by the way in which his needs were met in early childhood by his mother or mother-substitute. Reik asserts that two conditions in the person's early history have to be satisfied in order to render him capable of loving when an adult: he must have been loved by his mother or mother-substitute; but he must have felt somewhat insecure in this love, or, in other words, he must have felt that the love might be withdrawn, presumably in accordance with disciplinary practices. Translated into the language of the present discussion, Reik's thesis is that the mother must have provided a substantial measure of nurturant care and thus of gratification for the infant's and child's needs in order for him to have the experience of love. On the other hand, if the mother's level of nurturant care should be so high that the child would experience gratification of his needs before they could ever be experienced as tensions, the child would be unable to experience a need or pattern of needs which we should recognize as the desire for love.[8]

Actually, it seems doubtful that a mother could give a child such attention that he would be in a continuous state of complete gratification and hence never experience insecurity. Let us imagine, however, that a reasonable ap-

---

[6] Donald L. Burnham, "Misperception of Other Persons in Schizophrenia: A Structural View of Restitution Processes, Reality Representation, and Perceptions," *Psychiatry*, 19: 283–303 (1956).

[7] Jerome S. Bruner, "Social Psychology and Perception," in Eleanor E. Maccoby, Theodore M. Newcomb, and Eugene L. Hartley (eds.), *Readings in Social Psychology* (3d ed.; New York: Holt, Rinehart and Winston, Inc., 1958), pp. 85–94. Quotation is from p. 89.

[8] Theodor Reik, *A Psychologist Looks at Love* (New York: Holt, Rinehart and Winston, Inc., 1944), p. 174.

proximation to this extreme case were possible. Theoretically, we might expect that at maturity such a person would not expect to interact with others in terms of mutual gratification, which we understand to be the basis of reciprocal love. Rather, he (or she) might demand gratification as his right; such a person needs not a spouse but a servant.

Margaret Mead's treatise on the Samoans[9] is relevant to Reik's hypothesis. She asserts that the Samoan method of child care is such as to generate a sense of security in the child and not to create within him a sense of dependence upon any specific adult, since there is a plurality of "fathers" and "mothers" in the adult generation. Dr. Mead goes on to point out, moreover, that at the adult level, interpersonal relationships are characterized by amicability but not by any deep affect. She notes this absence of profound emotional involvement particularly in the relations between the sexes, in courtship and in marital relations, in the ease with which lovers and spouses are changed, and in the relative absence of jealousy. This is a culture that appears to approximate the ideal type of the achievement of infantile security through its child-rearing regimen. In this case, at least, a low level of infantile insecurity is correlated with a low level of affect in adult relationships. Hence we have some measure of corroboration for Reik's conditions.[10]

It would appear that in summarizing our theoretical views concerning the relationship between maternal nurturance and the subsequent capacity of the offspring for love we might invoke the type of reasoning employed in Chapter 14 to synthesize the Watsonian and Ribble-Spitz views. It will be recalled that Figure 14.3 hypothesized a curvilinear relation between nurturant care (horizontal axis) and child's independence (vertical axis) whereby it was predicted that moderate "mothering" would result in maximum independence of the child. If we were to relabel the vertical axis by substituting "capacity for love" for "independence," the same functional relationship would be hypothesized. In other words, our theory predicts that the extremes of maternal nurturance—very little or very much—inhibit the development of the child's capacity for love and that moderate amounts of nurturance maximize this capacity.

MOTIVATION MAY BE UNCONSCIOUS

The acting person may be aware, partially aware, or quite unaware of the nature of the needs underlying his behavior. To be unaware of it does not mean that the person is, or regards himself, as an automaton. As he reflects upon his own behavior, he can almost invariably discover "reasons" for it; but the person who has a sophisticated comprehension of the dynamics of behavior

[9] Margaret Mead, *Coming of Age in Samoa* in *From the South Seas*.

[10] Commenting on this type of situation, Linton observes that it would be difficult to conceive that such a culture would embody our concept of romantic love and that people so reared would feel the necessity of finding a marriage partner who would be the "one-and-only."—Ralph Linton, *The Cultural Background of Personality* (New York: Appleton, 1945), p. 143.

can frequently discern a level of motivation unknown to the person being observed. These "conscious reasons," as contrasted with "real reasons," constitute the phenomenon known as *rationalization* (i.e., the process of inventing an explanation for an unconsciously motivated event). The term is also used to designate the explanation invented.

LOVE IS BASED ON NEEDS

We have asserted that the emotion of love may be viewed as being grounded in the lover's needs. The needs involved are mostly social in nature.[11] This general point has been made by Ohmann in terms of what he calls the "psychology of attraction." He states: ". . . we fall in love with those whom we need to complete ourselves . . . whom we need to satisfy our feelings of ego deficiency."[12] He characterizes love as "a feeling of need for another personality to complete, supplement or protect our own."[13] Accordingly, Ohmann develops the general proposition that people fall in love because of the specific needs of their own unique personalities, and that they select persons with whom to fall in love in terms of the latters' capacity to fulfill the needs of the former.

In accordance with this thesis Ohmann holds that personal attractiveness is relatively unimportant in the courtship process. To the writer this seems to omit some of the need-meeting implications of beauty. In addition to the value of beauty in attracting initial attention, and in addition to the satisfaction to be derived from observing it, there is the consideration of the esteem value and the self-enhancement involved in associating with a person whose appearance is admired by one's fellows. In the writer's study of courtship it was found that with respect to females, appearance showed low but positive correlations with progress in courtship (significant at the 1 percent level), while with respect to males, the correlations were not significant.[14]

SOCIALIZATION AND THE NEED FOR ACCEPTANCE

To this point we have argued that all behavior and the emotion of love are grounded in needs, which may be conscious or unconscious. To advance the argument, it is proposed to show that the socialization process in the American middle class typically results in a need for acceptance and security and that this need in turn is experienced as a need to love and to be loved.

---

[11] In this context the terms *love* and *loving* are not identical with, nor do they necessarily connote, sexual attraction or behavior. The relation between love and sex is the subject of the next chapter.

[12] O. Ohmann, "The Psychology of Attraction," chap. 2 in H. M. Jordan (ed.), *You and Marriage* (New York: Wiley, 1942), p. 15.

[13] *Ibid.*, p. 28. This idea has been formalized as a "completeness" theory. Cf. Raymond B. Cattell and John R. Nesselroade, "Likeness and Completeness Theories Examined by Sixteen Personality Factor Measures on Stably and Unstably Married Couples," *Journal of Personality and Social Psychology*, 7: 351–361 (1967).

[14] Cf. R. F. Winch, "Courtship in College Women," *American Journal of Sociology*, 55: 269–278 (1949).

Most of the social needs are regarded by Murray as being related to achieving acceptance by one's fellows, to obtaining their esteem, and to the expression of aggression.[15] The writer regards aggression as a need largely derivative from the other two, in the sense that its degree depends in part upon the amount of gratification or frustration in the first two categories of needs. Or to phrase it differently, the amount of hostility a person feels toward his fellows tends to be inversely related to the degree to which they accept and esteem him.[16] For this reason, the following discussion will be concerned with those common experiences and their psychic correlates of American middle-class children and adolescents that bear upon their need to affiliate with others or to avoid separation, and to maintain or to improve their status. It is the writer's view that these points of departure will have explanatory value for behavior in general, and for the phenomena related to love in particular.

According to Freudian theory, the control of the child's behavior is effected by means of the actual or threatened withdrawal of the parents' love, especially of that of the mother.[17] This, Freud holds, gives the child a basic insecurity, a sense that his hold on parental love is tenuous, a fear that his behavior may be the cause of his being separated from his parents, an awareness that this affection can be preserved only at the expense of inhibiting his own impulses. Since this love is associated with the pleasure and gratification (release of tension) provided by the parents, and since its withdrawal implies pain, hunger, and accumulated tension, the significance of parental love is seen by the child as crucial for his own welfare. It is not, however, a simple matter to deny expression to those of his own impulses that he fears might result in the loss of parental love. According to Freudian theory, this conflict is normally resolved by the mechanism of repression[18] and the development of the super-ego.

---

[15] Murray, *op. cit.*, p. 150.

[16] John Dollard et al., *Frustration and Aggression* (New Haven, Conn.: Yale University Press, 1939). ". . . the original frustration-aggression hypothesis should be modified by substituting the notion of 'readiness' for the 'instigation' concept utilized by Dollard and his colleagues. Instead of saying that thwartings give rise to a drive state which automatically goads the organism into making aggressive responses (which may nevertheless be inhibited), the proposed modification lessens the inevitability of aggressive consequences; frustrations produce a predisposition to respond aggressively to certain stimuli, objects associated with the present or previous frustraters—and perhaps also with aggressive behavior generally—but aggression will be less likely to occur in the absence of these cues. . . ."—Leonard Berkowitz, "Social Motivation," in Gardner Lindzey and Elliot Aronson (eds.), *The Handbook of Social Psychology* (2d ed.; Reading, Mass.: Addison-Wesley, 1969), vol. 3, chap. 20, pp. 68–69.

[17] There is a good discussion of the subject in J. C. Flugel, *Man, Morals and Society: A Psycho-Analytical Study* (New York: International Universities Press, 1945). Cf. also Sigmund Freud, *Group Psychology and the Analysis of the Ego* (London: Hogarth, 1922), pp. 74–75. In previous sections we have noted this technique of controlling the child's behavior as being especially characteristic of the middle class.

[18] *Repression* is the rejection from consciousness of undesirable, disagreeable, shameful, or painful impulses, memories, feelings, and ideas.

Neither the undesirable impulses nor the anxiety over possible separation from the parents is destined to die, however. This is not the place to discuss the multifarious ways in which the impulses find expression. Suffice it to say that the dynamic character of these unacceptable impulses serves to perpetuate in many individuals (perhaps in all of us to some degree) a feeling carried through life that one's hold on one's relatives, friends, and associates (i.e., those with whom one has "primary" relationships) is tenuous.

> Our need for the approval of our fellow-beings, for the feeling that we are accepted by society, is indeed probably to a very large extent a continuation into adolescent and adult life of the young child's need for the approval of his parents, while the anxiety and despondency caused by the sense of being outcasts from society corresponds similarly to the infant's distress at losing their love and support.[19]

There are other circumstances that tend to stimulate the feeling that one may be cast off by his friends and rejected by strangers. Both within the family and without, the middle-class child is subject to conflicting pressures: to be a successful competitor and to be a "good brother." On the one hand, the parents transmit to the child the concept that his life goal is the realization of his potentialities (individualism), and that this realization will be evaluated in terms of the outcome of the competition between him and his peers. The reward of praise for excelling in childhood competition—from becoming toilet-trained earlier than Junior next door to winning his varsity letter—and the disapproval for failure tend to reinforce the competitive pattern of behavior. Psychic correlates of competition are hostility and envy; lectures on sportsmanship cannot remove these correlates, though they may add to them an extra load of guilt. Quite opposed to the attitudes appropriate to competition are the Christian ethic and the virtues of meekness, love, altruism, charity, and a brotherly concern not only for one's kinsmen but for all mankind.

It appears that the conflict between the competitive striving for higher status and the moral imperative to be loving and altruistic results in some degree of guilt (conscious or otherwise), and that this increases one's doubts about one's own moral worth and ultimately about one's own social acceptability. Again we have a pressure serving to augment the fear of being rejected and the need to be accepted.

The consequence of these factors is what Suttie has called "separation anxiety."[20] On the conscious level separation anxiety is experienced as a sense (or at least a fear) of loneliness, of not belonging, of not being accepted. The character of modern urban living, with its segmental interpersonal contacts, serves, of course, to intensify this feeling. It is not surprising that one who has been polling high school students since 1941 reports that their most common problem is wanting people to like them more, and that "almost three quarters of the high school students believe that the most important thing they

---

[19] Flugel, *op. cit.*, pp. 55–56.
[20] Ian Suttie, *The Origins of Love and Hate* (London: Routledge, 1935), pp. 19, 31, *passim*.

can learn in school is 'how to get along with people.'" Moreover, "the passion for popularity translates itself into an almost universal tendency to conformity among our younger generation."[21]

To be loved is obviously the specific cure for those who, as with the high school students noted above, want to be liked. And marriage offers the social and legal recognition that the person married "belongs" at least to his or her spouse. To be loved and to be married provide official certification that the person is not as repulsive and repugnant a pariah as his separation anxiety may have caused him to fear, consciously or otherwise. Moreover, marriage involves the act of "joining," as the wedding service explicitly recognizes.[22] If the desire for love is a national symptom, then perhaps it is not completely hyperbolic to speak of love as an American social problem.[23]

The foregoing analysis provides a sociopsychological basis for interpreting difficulties into which some of our middle-class marriages fall. It would appear that an important component of marital affection is the nurturant function —providing the security, reassurance, and sense of belonging that the mate is seeking. But clinical evidence indicates that the more one is seeking security, the less capable one is of giving it. If the people of our society do suffer from separation anxiety, then it would appear that our collective psychic economy is unbalanced in the sense that the demand for reassurance and security greatly exceeds the supply. To the writer, the use of the term *emotional immaturity* to explain marital incompatibility has seemed to beg the question, to replace a vague interpersonal concept with an equally vague concept from individual psychology. Perhaps this explanation will appear less vacuous if we understand *immaturity* to denote the need for security. From this line of argument it appears that we have a gross psychological deficit in nurturant personalities, i.e., personalities having the need to give sympathy, consolation, protection, comfort, and so on, to others.

LOVE DEFINED

The preceding discussion has been designed to show the conditions out of which love develops. We are now ready to consider a formal definition of love. While doing so let us take the pragmatic view that there is no single "correct" definition but that we evaluate as "good" a definition that enables us to see relationships in the field under study:

---

[21] H. H. Remmers and D. H. Radler, "Teenage Attitudes," in Jerome M. Seidman (ed.), *The Adolescent* (New York: Holt, Rinehart and Winston, Inc., 1960), pp. 597–605. Quotations are from pp. 601 and 600 respectively. See the related discussion on pages 432–433 concerning the manipulation of personalities and *Death of a Salesman*.

[22] The "real" reason why people marry, says one writer, is a deep-seated need to belong.—Cf. Rudolf Dreikurs, *The Challenge of Marriage* (New York: Duell, Sloan & Pearce—Meredith Press, 1946), p. 87. Reik expresses a similar idea in saying that the purpose of love is to be loved.—*Op. cit.*, p. 182.

[23] See the opening paragraph of this chapter.

> *Love is the positive emotion experienced by one person (the person loving, or the lover) in an interpersonal relationship in which the second person (the person loved, or love-object) either (1) meets certain important needs of the first, or (2) manifests or appears (to the first) to manifest personal attributes (beauty, skills, status) highly prized by the first, or both.*[24]

Actually, if the lover responds positively to the love-object because of beauty, skills, or the like, possessed by the latter and prized by the former, then the former is meeting certain needs in the latter (to some degree at least), and hence (1) and (2) are equivalent. The reason for including both is to suggest that the person loved, or the love-object, may be either active or passive in the relationship. From (2) it is evident that the definition does not necessarily imply a reciprocal relationship. Thus, in terms of this definition, the farm boy can love the movie star, who may be quite unaware of the farm boy's existence.

The qualifying adjective "positive" before "emotion" is necessary because both the meeting of the first person's needs and the possession of personal attributes prized by the first person can result in other emotions, shame, envy, and so on. The person loving and the person loved may be alike or unlike with respect to sex, status, or whatever. Hence the admiration of a boy for a football star and that of a stenographer for her boss (and vice versa) come within the definition. There is no qualification with respect to temporal duration, and hence an affair of a single evening and a relationship of a lifetime fall within the definition.

It will be seen that the definition might correspond to the denotations of the more mildly toned words "affection," "appreciation," and the like. The writer would be disposed to take the perhaps radical position that so far as the emotion is concerned the only difference is one of intensity. For this reason the qualifying terms—"important" needs and "highly prized" personal attributes, and so on—were incorporated into the definition. There is, however, another and more critical distinction. This involves deciding whether A and B (call either one "lover" and the other "love-object") are related only in terms of one (perhaps very narrow and segmental) role-relationship or in terms that are much broader. This brings in a distinction between a positional and a personal relationship. If A is expected to pay attention only to, and indeed be allowed only to observe, those of B's behaviors that pertain to B's position, especially to those involved in the relevant role-performance, then A's relationship to B is positional. Such is the situation where a secretary and her boss behave toward each other in terms of standard office decorum. A personal relationship involves greater intimacy, which implies that A is allowed to know

---

[24] Benedek has placed emphasis upon the passive need-meeting aspect of love: "Love is the emotional manifestation which grows out of the surplus excitation following satisfaction of the receptive needs."—Therese Benedek, *Insight and Personality Adjustment* (New York: Ronald, 1946), p. 12.

more about B's behaviors, and therefore there are fewer behaviors about which B is disposed to throw the mantle of privacy. It would seem appropriate to define "love" so that it could not apply to a positional relationship (the positive emotion here would be called something like affection or appreciation) and thus to reserve "love" for personal relationships.[25]

AMBIVALENT LOVE AND "INFATUATION"

We have defined love in terms of needs. If love is to be conceived in terms of needs, is it possible for anyone to "fall in love" against his own wishes? We may have heard of people who have fallen in love against their own better judgment; we may have had the experience ourselves. How can this happen?

The answer lies in the observation that we are capable of experiencing more than one need at a time—perhaps at different levels of consciousness—and that the techniques for satisfying these needs may be mutually contradictory. Another possibility is that over time we experience a sequence of needs, and again the means for gratifying these different needs are in conflict with each other. For example, let us say that a certain middle-class boy finds that a girl of low socioeconomic status gives him sympathy and understanding and thus gratifies his receptive or dependent needs,[26] but that another girl, who happens to be the daughter of his boss, gives promise of helping him satisfy his need for status (which may be conceptualized as a fusion of the needs for achievement and dominance).[27] Let us assume further that he decides to marry for status. He finds to his discomfiture, however, that he still "loves" the lower-class girl "against his will"; that it is not possible by a simple act of will to eliminate his need for sympathy and understanding (needs that the second girl happens not to satisfy). From the standpoint of our analysis, this boy's difficulty lies in the fact that the techniques he has hit upon to gratify two different sets of needs are incompatible. So far as his conscious resolve is concerned, there is no problem, but the "mystery of love" (that he still cares for one girl when he has already decided upon the other) lies in his lack of awareness of his own needs and of their implication. To phrase the boy's problem differently, each of these girls offers actual or potential gratification for a part of his needs but also actual or potential frustration of another part of his needs.

From our vantage point it seems clear that the boy would be in a less conflictful position if he could find a girl of high status who could give him sympathy and understanding. It seems reasonable, moreover, to presume that if he understood himself as well as we understand him from the short descrip-

---

[25] For a further analysis of the positional-personal distinction see Robert F. Winch, *Identification and Its Familial Determinants* (Indianapolis: Bobbs-Merrill, 1962), pp. 15–23.

[26] In his study of complementary needs the author followed Murray in calling this need "succorance."—*Mate-Selection*, p. 90.

[27] Murray *et al., op. cit.,* pp. 152, 164, 182.

tion, he might set about consciously and more efficiently to find a girl who would be a better match than either of the two mentioned in the story.

In the writer's judgment it is to the kind of situation obtaining in this story that the term *infatuation* is usually applied. The negative connotation of the term implies that someone is making a value-judgment of a relationship. Accordingly, infatuation may be defined as "a love relationship of which someone disapproves." In the above example the boy might well regard his relationship with the lower-status girl as "mere infatuation," which, in this case, would mean that he would be disapproving of the relationship—presumably because of her lower status. The phrase *true love* designates the opposite, or approving, kind of value-judgment. It applies to a love relationship of which the speaker is making a favorable evaluation.

DIFFERENCES AMONG GROUPS AND AMONG INDIVIDUALS IN THE CONCEPT OF LOVE

In the opening paragraph of the present chapter, note was taken of the difficulty that has confronted men in attempting to define love. It is the writer's hope that the discussion in this chapter illuminates this difficulty to some degree. It seems plausible to believe that some of the difficulty involved in analyzing love—and, indeed, the source of some of the mystery surrounding the term—may derive from differences among individuals and among groups as to just what love is. The analysis offered to this point implies that a source of variation may be in the kinds of needs involved.

Following the theory involved in Kardiner's formulation of "basic personality structure,"[28] one may say that to the degree that a group has cultural uniformity and homogeneity in child-rearing practices, there will be some corresponding uniformity in the needs of individuals. To this degree, then, there should be intragroup consensus on the nature of love. But Kardiner takes account also of the uniqueness of individuals and of cultures: the degree of uniqueness will presumably be reflected in a heterogeneity of needs.

Next we turn to a consideration of some determinants of variation in needs that become involved in the love relationship. It follows that as we consider determinants of individual differences, we are implying an answer to the question, Why is A attracted to B rather than to C? That is, we are now beginning to consider the mate-selective implications of our theory of love.

IDENTIFICATION AND THE ORGANIZATION OF NEEDS

Under the rubric of identification, Chapter 15 presented a formulation concerning the "more or less lasting influence" of parents on offspring. Of course, parents are not the only people who influence children. Let us resume that discussion by noting that it is usual for each child to have relationships

---

[28] Abram Kardiner *et al., The Psychological Frontiers of Society* (New York: Columbia University Press, 1945). This concept is basic to the whole book. Pertinent references can be located in the index.

of varying degrees of emotional importance with a number of persons. From the formulation of identification presented in Chapter 15 it follows that a relationship in childhood is emotionally important if it results in the child's being influenced (1) to become like the other, (2) to behave in a fashion that is reciprocal to the behavior of the other, or (3) to behave in a fashion dissimilar to, or contrary to, the behavior of the other. It will be recalled that these forms of influence were called, respectively, similar, reciprocal, and opposite identification.

It is proposed that the identifications of the child can be seen as a process by which the child's needs become organized. And since the influence involved in identification is "more or less lasting," we should expect to detect evidence of such organization of needs in later years. For the present argument the period of interest is that in which mates are selected. Let us imagine a boy who is favorably impressed with the energy and accomplishments of his father and with the gentleness and kindness of his mother, or another boy who is disgusted with the supine ineffectualness of his father and repelled by the whining petulance of his mother. Quite possibly the former boy would form a similar identification with his father and a reciprocal identification with his mother, whereas the latter boy might form opposite identifications with both parents. Presently we shall consider in some detail a case of mate-selection that will make this form of analysis somewhat more intelligible.

NEEDS, CULTURES, AND CONGENIALITY GROUPS

To become socialized involves learning culturalized techniques for gratifying needs. In all societies it appears that one prominent technique for gratifying needs is through association or social interaction, and, most particularly, through that kind of interpersonal relationship provided by the congeniality group.[29] Generally throughout American society and especially in the middle class we learn that one of the most gratifying (at least potentially) of congeniality groups is that dyad consisting of a man and a woman—whether married or not.[30] As this implies, Americans learn to expect much gratification from the marital relationship. For this reason Americans make heavy emotional demands upon the marital relationship. Because the American family, especially in the middle class, is relatively nonfunctional (which implies that few rewards are available except for the kind that can be obtained from congeniality groups), Americans tend to have a low threshold of frustration in marriage, and experience keen disappointment when frustrated.

HOMOGAMY AND THE FIELD OF ELIGIBLES

Chapter 10 has considered in detail the mate-selective principles of incest avoidance and of ethnocentric preference, and it has shown how in all societies

---

[29] *Congeniality group:* an informal, sympathetic association of two or more persons with common interests and habits.

[30] *Dyad:* a social group consisting of two persons.

fields of eligible spouse-candidates are created by the joint operation of these two principles. With respect to the United States it was shown

> That ethnocentric preference operated to make mate-selection more or less homogamous with respect to race, religioethnic identity, and socioeconomic status.
> That segregation in living areas and in social interaction served to create unwitting conformity to homogamy with respect to these dimensions.
> That sanctions tended to create witting conformity.
> That homogamy also prevailed with respect to age and previous marital status.
> That homogamy with respect to the last two characteristics was the result of differential association and sanctions.

The present chapter is concerned with mate-selection in a setting such as middle-class America, where the choice of mates is voluntary and on the basis of mutual attraction. It takes for granted the concept of the field of eligibles with its implication of homogamy with respect to the characteristics mentioned above. It further assumes that people with common interests are more likely to meet and select each other than those with different interests. Then it poses the question, How does mate-selection take place *within* a field of eligibles among individuals sharing interests? The theory of complementary needs in mate-selection is offered as a plausible explanation.

THE THEORY OF COMPLEMENTARY NEEDS IN MATE-SELECTION

Much of the discussion throughout this book has been relevant to the present topic. Let us now review the basic propositions underlying the theory of complementary needs in mate-selection.

I. *Propositions concerning behavior, needs, and the organization of needs*
   A. All human behavior may be viewed as activity oriented to the gratification of needs.
   B. Some human needs are innate; others are learned. We are particularly interested in those that are learned and expressed in interpersonal relationships.
   C. Certain important needs are organized by the individual's identifications.
   D. The organization of needs gives pattern to behavior and makes behavior (especially perception) selective.
   E. Needs may be experienced consciously or unconsciously. Hence a person may be completely aware, partially aware, or quite unaware of the motivation of his behavior.
II. *Propositions concerning societal determinants of gratification and changing need-patterns*
   A. In all societies social interaction in congeniality groups is an important source of gratification for social needs.
   B. In the American middle class the man-woman dyad is viewed as a singularly gratifying congeniality group.

C. In a society (like that of the United States) which has numerous cultural discontinuities and a high degree of social mobility:
1. Individuals are confronted with a succession of varied models, with the result that they tend to develop a somewhat heterogeneous set of identifications.
2. Individuals encounter shifting criteria for social approval at various ages and in various social contexts.
3. As the individual passes through the age categories new sources of gratification become accessible and some of the old ones become inaccessible, and thus the individual experiences new sources of frustration.

D. To the extent that the conditions in C are met, time brings about a disturbance in the adaptation of the individual and changes in his need-pattern.

We can now set forth the three basic propositions of the theory of complementary needs in mate-selection:

1. *In mate-selection each individual seeks within his or her field of eligibles for that person who gives the greatest promise of providing him or her with maximum need-gratification.*
2. *There is a set of needs such that if person A behaves in a manner determined by a high degree of need X, A's behavior will prove gratifying to the need Y in a second person, B.*
3. *These two needs, X and Y, in the two persons, A and B, are said to be complementary if:*
   a. Type I complementariness: X *and* Y *are the same need, and the need is present to a low degree in* B.
   b. Type II complementariness: X *and* Y *are different needs. In this case specific predictions are made about selected pairs of needs. That is, taking account of the particular X, with respect to some Y's it is predicted that B will have a high degree and with respect to others that B will have a low degree.*

An example of Type I complementariness: if one spouse, X, is high on the need to receive recognition, it would be predicted that the other spouse, Y, would be low on that need. An example of Type II complementariness: if one spouse is high on the need to be dominant, it would be predicted that the other would be high on the need to give deference. An obvious task in developing the theory is to be able to make the specific predictions involved in Type II complementariness. The types of complementary mating hypothesized in the next section constitute a bit of progress toward this goal.

From Statements II.A and II.B above it follows that the degree to which the theory of complementary needs will be operative in any culture is contingent upon the degree to which the interpersonal relationship in marriage is evaluated as an important source of need-gratification. Where such meaning is given to marriage, as in America, it is consistent that there should be individual choice of mates and a long period of dating, courtship, and engagement during which to test personalities of potential mates. By contrast, in traditional China, where the congeniality group of men was emphasized, marriages were arranged by the families—frequently between men and women who had never seen each other.

From these and previous observations it is hypothesized that mate-selection proceeds on the basis of complementary needs only under the following societal-cultural conditions:

1. The marital relationship must be culturally defined as a rich potential source of gratification.
2. The choice of mates must be voluntary (i.e., not arranged) and bilateral (i.e., both man and woman must possess at least the power of veto).
3. There must be provision for, and preferably encouragement of, premarital interaction between men and women in order to provide the opportunity for testing out personalities of a variety of potential mates.

It has been asserted that some needs are experienced unconsciously. This appears to be true of needs involved in social interaction. After some dating experience, for example, a boy will realize that with some girls he enjoys himself, can act "naturally," and so on, but that with others he feels strained or bored. It is for this reason that one needs to "test" a variety of personalities—to determine with what persons and with what types of persons one "feels comfortable" and with what persons and types one does not. Hence where the marital relationship is defined as potentially gratifying, as in this country, the practice of dating is functionally important in mate-selection.

THE STATUS OF THE THEORY

In one form or another the idea of complementary attraction can be traced back through the history of Western thought to Plato and Socrates.[31] In the present century the idea has appeared in the writings of Freudians and non-Freudians. A non-Freudian antecedent of the formulation is Durkheim, who saw attraction in friendship as based upon both similarity and complementariness of the personalities of friends. After remarking that we like those who think and feel as we do, he continues that since each of us lacks something, we are attracted to those who make up for our insufficiencies, and make us feel less incomplete and with whom for this reason the relationship results in "a true exchange of services. One urges on, another consoles; this one advises, that one follows the advice, and it is this apportionment of functions or . . . this division of labor which determines the relations of friendship."[32]

Havelock Ellis, another non-Freudian, spoke of "a harmony, not neces-

---

[31] A consideration of some of the intellectual antecedents including the distinction between *agape* and *eros* appears in *Mate-Selection*, chap. 3.

[32] Émile Durkheim, *The Division of Labor in Society* (trans. by George Simpson; New York: Free Press, 1947), p. 56.

sarily an identity, of tastes and interests" as "essential to a complete marriage union,"[33] and Ohmann states that we are attracted to "those whom we need to complete ourselves."[34]

Among the followers of Freud are Flugel, who believes that one is attracted to a person to whom one attributes elements of one's ideal self, and Benedek, who suggests that lovers exchange ideal selves.[35] And asserting that in love there is compensation for not attaining one's ideal self, Reik observes that we "jump into" rather than "fall in" love.[36]

Clinical corroboration of the principle of complementary mate-selection has been appearing in the literature for some years.[37] Of course the subjects of clinical study are not usually the most adjusted persons in the society, and for this reason the evidence might be thought of as supporting what we might call a "theory of complementary neuroses." Numerous writers of a psychoanalytic orientation have presented evidence in support of a complementary mate-selective process. For example, Mittelmann proposes five types of complementary relationship that he says he has seen in his practice:

1. A dominant and aggressive person married to a submissive and masochistic person.
2. An emotionally detached person married to one who craves affection.
3. A pair engaged in continuous rivalry for aggressive dominance.
4. A helpless and dependent person married to an endlessly supportive mate.
5. A person who vacillates between self-assertion and dependency married to one who vacillates between unsatisfied need for affection and giving support and help.[38]

In his unrestrained style Bergler tells us that "the neurosis of the woman complements the neurosis of the man she chooses, and vice versa." A masochistic woman, he says, is not conscious of her wish to be treated badly, nor is the "castrating" woman of her wish for an impotent man. Both will think of themselves as unlucky in mate-selection. "But 'luck' is not involved; unconscious choice is."[39]

---

[33] Havelock Ellis, *Psychology of Sex* (New York: New American Library, Mentor ed., 1954), p. 198.

[34] *Loc. cit.*

[35] Flugel, *op. cit.*, chap. 13; Benedek, *op. cit.*, p. 25.

[36] *Op. cit.*, p. 40.

[37] The logical status of clinical evidence is discussed in the section on "Some Studies Bearing on the Broad Conception of Nurturance" in Chapter 13 of this book and in Chapter 1 of Robert F. Winch and Louis Wolf Goodman (eds.), *Selected Studies in Marriage and the Family* (New York: Holt, Rinehart and Winston, Inc., 1968).

[38] Bela Mittelmann, "Analysis of Reciprocal Neurotic Patterns in Family Relationships," in Victor W. Eisenstein (ed.), *Neurotic Interaction in Marriage* (New York: Basic Books, 1956), pp. 81–100, esp. p. 98.

[39] Edmund Bergler and W. S. Kroger, *Kinsey's Myth of Female Sexuality: The Medical Facts* (New York: Grune & Stratton, 1954), pp. 92–93.

In 1950 the author inaugurated a study to test the theory of complementary needs in mate-selection. The subjects of the study were twenty-five young couples who had been married less than two years and an average of one year. Husbands and wives were seen separately and simultaneously. They were given two interviews and a test. One interview was designed to elicit responses that would reveal the strengths and modes of expression of various needs. In the other interview they were asked to give an account of emotionally and developmentally meaningful experiences in their lives. The test was the Thematic Apperception Test.

Research on this kind of topic is difficult. The variables pertain to motivation. In laboratory experiments on motivation it is possible to deprive rats of food for a specified period, to interpret the deprivation as hunger drive, to present the animals with some task, and then to compare such performances with those made after eating, i.e., under conditions of "high drive" and "low drive." With respect to the kinds of needs conceived to be relevant to mate-selection such experimental manipulation of human subjects is hardly feasible in a democratic society. For this reason considerable time was spent in devising interview questions for the study of complementary needs, and hundreds of man-hours were devoted to the analysis of the responses of each subject. The outcomes of this intensive analysis were stated in both verbal and quantitative terms.

The central question of the quantitative analysis was whether or not the data supported the theory. The directions of 388 correlations were predicted in accordance with the concepts of Type I and Type II complementariness as set forth above. If nothing but chance was determining the rated levels of the needs in the pairs of spouses, it would be expected that approximately half the correlations would come out in the predicted direction and half in the opposite direction; if some principle contrary to complementariness was operating, it would be expected that more than half of the correlations would take the sign opposite from that predicted. It turned out that 66 percent of the correlations showed the hypothesized sign, and the results were interpreted as supporting the theory of complementary needs in mate-selection.[40]

Having been satisfied that the evidence pointed in the direction of the hypothesis, the writer then undertook the next step in the inquiry—to discover any new ideas in the data and thereby to refine the statement of the theory.

---

[40] Of course these 388 correlations were not independent since they were all based on the same 25 couples. Hays points out that the average in a matrix of intercorrelations must be greater than or equal to $-1/(K-1)$ where $K =$ the number of variables. Cf. William L. Hays, *Statistics for Psychologists* (New York: Holt, Rinehart and Winston, Inc., 1963), pp. 576–577. Here (with some variables dichotomized and others double-dichotomized) the number of variables = 44, and $-1/(44-1) = -.023$. The minimum absolute value required of a correlation to achieve one-sided .05 significance was .34. Cf. Robert F. Winch, Thomas Ktsanes, and Virginia Ktsanes, "The Theory of Complementary Needs in Mate-Selection: An Analytic and Descriptive Study," *American Sociological Review*, 19: 241–249 (1954), esp. p. 246.

To this end the writer undertook an intensive review of all the cases in a search for processes of mate-selection. Since this was not a hypothesis-oriented procedure but a hypothesis-seeking operation, whatever was found must be presented not as fact but as hypothesis.

Two principles, or dimensions, of mate-selection seemed to be running through most, but not all, of the cases. With respect to one of these dimensions it appeared that if one of the spouses was conspicuously nurturant, the other liked to receive nurturant care or, as it came to be called, the latter was high on receptivity. With respect to the other dimension it appeared that if one spouse was highly dominant, the other was likely to be submissive. Since most of the twenty-five couples showed both of these dimensions, it was possible to cross-classify these couples in terms of the two dimensions. When this was done, a fourfold typology was derived with the following characteristics and nomenclature:

	Husband—Nurturant Wife—Receptive	Husband—Receptive Wife—Nurturant
Husband—Dominant Wife—Submissive	Ibsenian (from *A Doll's House*)	Master-and-Servant-Girl
Husband—Submissive Wife—Dominant	Thurberian	Mother-Son

Cases illustrating these four types and hypotheses concerning them appear in *Mate-Selection,* Chapters 7–11.[41]

The alert reader may have noticed something familiar about the dimensions underlying the four types of complementary mating: they are reminiscent of the parental functions—nurturance and control—that have constituted a major basis for the analysis of parent-child relations in Part Five. This suggests that the two dimensions are important not only in parent-child relations but also in marital and no doubt in other relationships that involve emotional gratification. It will also be noted that there are two types—Ibsenian and Mother-Son in which one spouse nurtures and dominates the other and thus, to use Ackerman's term,[42] "parentifies" the other. In the other two types there is not a clear-cut parent-child relationship.[43]

[41] Some thoughts on the dominance of one spouse by the other appear in Chapter 11 in *Mate-Selection* under the heading "The Pygmalion Hypothesis." It is possible that the couples who were not classifiable into one or both of the above dichotomies were near the means of the distributions along one or both dimensions.

[42] Nathan W. Ackerman, *The Psychodynamics of Family Life: Diagnosis and Treatment of Family Relationships* (New York: Basic Books, 1958).

[43] There is evidence of a convergence on nurturance and control (stated in various terms) as the two basic dimensions of interpersonal behavior and of the socially relevant elements of personality. Leary has developed a test of 16 interpersonal variables of personality and has concluded that the 16 variables can be reduced to dominance (our control) and love (our nurturance).—Timothy Leary, *Interpersonal Diagnosis of Personality:*

Immediately upon the recognition that the theory of complementary needs in mate-selection involves two dimensions whose names are similar to those of the two parental functions, there arises the question as to whether we have stumbled upon a tautology involving mate-selection and the parental functions and perhaps the function of emotional gratification as well. If we are using three different terms to refer to the same phenomenon, theoretical parsimony demands that we rid our system of the superfluous concepts. To illuminate this question let us make a few observations about mate-selection, emotional gratification, and the parental functions.

With respect to the hypothesized dimensions of mate-selection let us notice that they are presented as motives of the individual, which are subject to interindividual variation. The writer's research suggests that each individual may be seen as having some degree of need with respect to giving and/or receiving each of the parental functions. Furthermore, it has not been proposed that this formulation exhausts the motivational dimensions involved in mate-selection.

Let us turn to emotional gratification. Since in the setting under consideration mate-selection is based on love, and since love is defined as the positive emotion associated with experienced and/or anticipated gratifications coming from the behavior of the other (i.e., from the love-object), and since there is evidence that such love is based on the dimensions of complementariness, there is reason to think that nurturance-receptivity and dominance-submissiveness are dimensions relevant to the function of emotional gratification within the marital relationship. Does this mean, to use Ackerman's term, that according to the present formulation all the love involved in mate-selection—and indeed in marital interaction—implies or envisages the "parentifying" of one spouse by the other? Such is not the implication. It is true that two of the four types (Mother-Son and Ibsenian) involve parent-child relationships, but

---

A Functional Theory and Methodology for Personality Evaluation (New York: Ronald, 1957), p. 69. Couch has factor-analyzed the Leary test and agrees that the two factors just mentioned are the principal ones in that test. Couch calls them "interpersonal dominance" and "interpersonal affect," respectively, and he found these same factors to be the principal factors in the analysis of many other types of interpersonal behavioral and test data.—Arthur Stephen Couch, "Psychological Determinants of Interpersonal Behavior." Unpublished doctoral dissertation, Harvard University, 1960, pp. 235 and 554. Schaefer has used a related but different mode of analysis (the Guttman circumplex model) on several empirical studies of maternal behavior and has found two major dimensions that he has called "love vs. hostility" (our nurturance) and "autonomy vs. control" (our control). —Earl S. Schaefer, "A Circumplex Model for Maternal Behavior," *Journal of Abnormal and Social Psychology*, 59: 226–235 (1959). Cf. also Murray A. Straus, "Power and Support Structure in Relation to Socialization," *Journal of Marriage and the Family*, 26: 318–326 (1964). Cross-cultural support for these dimensions appears in Gisele J. Renson, Earl S. Schaefer, and Bernard I. Levy, "Cross-National Validity of a Spherical Conceptual Model for Parent Behavior," *Child Development*, 39: 1229–1235 (1968). This convergence of results may mean that these are two fundamental dimensions of human interaction or that they are two prevalent and pervasive ideas in the heads of contemporary social psychologists.

of course the other two do not. Moreover, the emotional gratification to be derived from the marital and from the parent-child relationships differ importantly from each other in that (1) the former includes but the latter prohibits sexual gratification, and (2) the kinds of behavior involved in nurturing and controlling vary greatly with the age of the object.

The parental functions are not, of course, individual motives but are social functions, i.e., activities and products of those activities that the family —because of its structure and its basic societal function—becomes obliged to carry out.

Tentatively, then, the answer to the question posed several paragraphs above is that the parental functions, the function of emotional gratification, and love-based mate-selection have in common the dimensions of nurturance and control. It is premature, however, to conclude that we are talking about only a single phenomenon because each of the three will undoubtedly be found to have elements not common to the others, and we are using the concepts of nurturance and control at two levels of analysis—the sociological and the psychological.

It had been hoped at the inception of the study that during the course of the research some procedure would be developed that would eliminate or reduce the requirement for clinical judgments, and which would therefore be more reliable and less time-consuming. In this effort the project was not successful. Because of the difficulty and expense of gathering and analyzing the data it seems unlikely that the study will ever be replicated—a likelihood that the writer views sadly. The theory of complementary needs in mate-selection has stimulated numerous largely irrelevant efforts at empirical verification but some useful theoretical criticism.[44] Perhaps the most important

---

[44] Just as the theory of complementary needs was coming to be known, there appeared in the literature a test with an original and attractive feature. This test, the Edwards Personal Preference Schedule, was announced as measuring fifteen needs. Its attractive feature was that it was represented as controlling for an important type of response set—"social desirability"—by means of requiring the subject to choose between paired items of presumably matched social desirability. Unfortunately for the replication of the study of complementary needs the attractiveness of a quickly administered and routinely scored test purporting to measure needs lured some investigators away from the replication of the original study. (Of course, the difficulty and cost of the original procedures might have dissuaded them from real replication.) Most of the few correlations found in these studies that were large enough to be assessed as statistically significant were interpreted as inconsistent with the theory of complementary needs. Cf. Charles E. Bowerman and Barbara R. Day, "A Test of the Theory of Complementary Needs as Applied to Couples during Courtship," *American Sociological Review*, 21: 602–605 (1956); James A. Schellenberg and Lawrence S. Bee, "A Re-examination of the Theory of Complementary Needs in Mate Selection," *Marriage and Family Living*, 22: 227–232 (1960); Irwin Katz, Sam Glucksberg, and Robert Krauss, "Need Satisfaction and Edwards PPS Scores in Married Couples," *Journal of Consulting Psychology*, 24: 205–208 (1960); John A. Blazer, "Complementary Needs and Marital Happiness," *Marriage and Family Living*, 25: 89–95 (1963). Just how valid are the scales in the PPS and what is the degree of matching of social desirability in the pairs of items with respect to the subjects taking the test are questions that remain open. Mixed evidence

contribution has come from a study by Bermann, who examined the theory of complementary needs in a context other than that of mate-selection. In a study of the stability of pairs of roommates among student-nurses, he took account of their common role as student-nurses as well as their idiosyncratic need-patterns.

> Using role theory, he reasoned that if both roommates were close to the ideal specified by the appropriate set of norms—in the case of student nurses, if both were friendly, abasing, etc.—each would serve the other as an object of identification with a resulting solidarity that would bind the two roommates into a stable relationship. From this reasoning he inferred, e.g., that if both should be low on the need to dominate, the pair should be stable (since low dominance was found to be an element in the definition of the role of student nurse). Using the theory of complementary needs, however, Bermann reasoned, as was done in Winch's study of mate-selection, that a more solidary relationship should exist where one was high and the other low on dominance (type I complementariness).

on validity appears in Vaughn J. Crandall and Anne Preston, "Verbally Expressed Needs and Overt Maternal Behaviors," *Child Development*, 32: 261–270 (1961). Evidence in support of matched social desirability appears in Allen L. Edwards, *The Social Desirability Variable in Personality Assessment and Research* (New York: Holt, Rinehart and Winston, Inc., 1957), chap. 7. A study coming to the contrary conclusion is Norman L. Corah et al., "Social Desirability as a Variable in the Edwards Personal Preference Schedule," *Journal of Consulting Psychology*, 22: 70–72 (1958). There are numerous studies that show that people view those they like as having traits similar to their own and those they dislike as being dissimilar to themselves. Cf. F. E. Fiedler, F. J. Blaisdell, and W. G. Warrington, "Unconscious Attitudes and the Dynamics of Sociometric Choice in a Social Group," *Journal of Abnormal and Social Psychology*, 47: 790–796 (1952); and for an extension to perception of persons of opposite sex, Richard M. Lundy, "Self-Perceptions and Descriptions of Opposite Sex Sociometric Choices," *Sociometry*, 19: 272–277 (1956). Unless completely neutralized, therefore, social desirability enters into research results as an artifact and by producing interspousal correlations in the opposite direction masks any effect of complementary mating.

Another study using a different procedure to measure complementariness finds no evidence of complementary matching in a set of college couples considering marriage. When the couples are segregated into those of short- and of long-term acquaintance, however, it is found that the former show evidence of matching on consensus in values and the latter on complementariness. This leads the authors of the study to believe that consensus on values is an early "filtering factor" in the mate-selective process of courtship, while complementariness is a "filtering factor" that operates at a later stage.—Alan Kerckhoff and Keith E. Davis, "Value Consensus and Need Complementarity in Mate Selection," *American Sociological Review*, 27: 295–303 (1962). A subsequent study has failed, however, to replicate the findings of Kerckhoff and Davis. Cf. George Levinger, David J. Senn, and Bruce W. Jorgensen, "Progress Toward Permanence in Courtship: A Test of the Kerckhoff-Davis Hypotheses," *Sociometry*, 33: 427–433 (1970).

Very interesting theoretical criticisms of the theory appear in: Irving Rosow, "Issues in the Concept of Need-Complementarity," *Sociometry*, 20: 216–233 (1957); and George Levinger, "Note on Need Complementarity in Marriage," *Psychological Bulletin*, 61: 153–157 (1964). Cf. also Ellen Berscheid and Elaine Hatfield Walster, *Interpersonal Attraction* (Reading, Mass.: Addison-Wesley, 1969).

More formally, Bermann hypothesized (1) that compatibility with respect to role is predictive of stability, (2) that complementariness of needs is predictive of stability, and (3) that both of these predictors considered together predict stability better than either does when taken separately. Generally, Bermann's data supported all of these propositions. Need complementarity predicted stability, but role compatibility predicted it better. Bermann's index of total compatibility, which is a combination of need complementarity and role compatibility, was the most effective predictor of stability.[45]

Bermann's study suggests that if the theory of complementary needs is worth developing further, probably the next step should be to analyze the roles of mate-selecting partners with respect to each other as well as to analyze marital roles and then to reformulate the theory so that both elements of roles and of personalities become parameters in the prediction of who will select whom in marriage.[46]

THE CASE OF BILL AND MARY CARTER

To illustrate the theory of complementary needs in mate-selection one case from the author's study is summarized below.[47]

After having spent several years in military service Bill Carter is finishing college. Mary, his wife, is out of college and is teaching school. Bill is a tall, slender chap of twenty-two. He does not appear to be very athletic. The interviewer reports him as mild, shy, and lacking in fire. Bill says that he looks tough (which hardly conforms with the interviewer's impression), but that really he isn't. He sees himself as "quiet but not withdrawn." He has few friends. In a group he likes to stand back, and he engages in no behavior that will bring him the group's spontaneous attention. On the other hand, he likes to receive recognition for any achievements. As the foregoing suggests, Bill has something of a "problem" with respect to the matter of self-expression. A clue as to why Bill has difficulty in expressing himself is seen in his statement that "I have a mild temper—too mild sometimes. I'm inclined to criticize myself and I don't assert myself enough to other people."

It appears that Bill inhibits himself in what he says to others because he fears that what he will say will be hostile, and he fears to express hostility to

---

[45] Robert F. Winch, "Another Look at the Theory of Complementary Needs in Mate-Selection," *Journal of Marriage and the Family*, 29: 756–762 (1967). Quotation is from pp. 759–760.

[46] Some relevant remarks appear in Chapters 20 and 21 below.

[47] The reader will appreciate that it is difficult to present a real case honestly and still preserve the anonymity of the subjects. For this reason names and identifying characteristics have been changed. The case record of which this is a digest runs to well over a hundred pages. Because of space limitations not all points of interpretation can be thoroughly documented. Other cases from the study are presented in chapters 7–13 of *Mate-Selection*.

other people. There is evidence, moreover, that these fears have resulted in a repression of his anger and hostility, and hence that his inhibition in expression functions at an unconscious level. Customarily such a pattern suggests that the person has learned that angry outbursts will bring upon him dire and painful consequences. In Bill's case this interpretation is supported by a story he told in the Thematic Apperception Test.[48] In this picture a young woman has her hand on the arm of a young man who seems about to leave her. Bill said: "She is trying to stop him from doing something of a violent nature. . . . She's trying to dissuade him from doing that because it would hurt him more than it would hurt the other person."

Although our information about Bill is not sufficiently comprehensive to give us a completely satisfactory explanation of how his personality developed, some light will be shed by considering his childhood and the nature of his relations with his parents.

Bill's recollection of his mother as she appeared in his childhood is that she was attractive and demonstrative. She was given to strenuous exertion and self-sacrifice on behalf of her children. (Bill has a younger sister.) Bill feels that the exertions and the self-sacrifice were somewhat exaggerated and were used by his mother as a basis for demanding the love and affection of her children. His mother was a very dominant person and apparently controlled Bill and his sister, and his father as well. Bill thinks that his mother felt "unloved," especially during menopause, and that his father did not satisfy her sexually. Although in childhood he felt closer to his mother than to his father, he has come to regard her as possessive and demanding, and now prefers his father.

Bill describes his father as intelligent, objective, quiet, considerate, deliberate, yielding, and as filled with self-pity when his mother "imposes on" him. Early in their marriage there was considerable friction between Bill's parents; they only spoke to each other for two of the first five weeks they were married. Bill admires his father's composure but changes his mind when he sees what "happens to" his father because of it. By this Bill is apparently referring to his mother's behavior in "imposing on" his father and his father's behavior in submitting and in showing self-pity.

Bill is a conformist. Like many other people, he appears to use conformity as a technique for obtaining recognition from figures in authority. At one time in his boyhood Bill's parents suggested that it would be helpful to the family if he would earn his spending money. Shortly thereafter he started selling newspapers. He built up an impressive record and worked so hard at this endeavor that his parents subsequently admonished him against overwork. When asked for his earliest memories, Bill recounted two incidents (one from

---

[48] In this test the subject is presented with a series of pictures and is asked to tell a story about each, what the people in the picture are doing, what led up to this situation, what will be the outcome, etc. The response reported here was given to card 4.

the sixth grade, and the other from the first grade), when his teachers registered marked approval of his performance in the classroom. Currently he is quite gratified when his professors compliment him on his work and ability.

Bill's consistent pattern of seeking recognition from persons of authority, plus the (for him) strongly ambivalent feelings toward his mother, suggest that in early childhood he greatly desired her approval and affection. While overtly and superficially demonstrative and affectionate, however, Bill's mother appears to have been incapable of giving him the kind of affectionate approval he sought. For this reason we may suspect that she continually frustrated him and that he tried harder and harder to earn her love.

His report that his mother felt "unloved" and that she "demanded" affection from her children suggests that she was very sensitive to any expression of criticism or hostility. To achieve her acceptance, therefore, Bill undoubtedly learned to inhibit, and indeed to repress, his expressions of hostility. As we shall see, the nature of Bill's interaction with Mary, his wife, demonstrates quite conclusively that Bill has strong unconscious feelings of hostility. It seems probable that he has possessed such feelings most of his life. Today he seldom criticizes anyone or even entertains consciously hostile thoughts. As not infrequently happens, Bill has gone to the extremity of unconsciously directing his hostility toward himself. Accordingly, he has been inhibited in his quest for recognition by a fear of competing with others and of the possibility of incurring their hostility. In high school Bill generally received good grades, but once he nearly failed a civics course; on this occasion he became very depressed and considered suicide. He tends to regard any criticism of himself as warranted and to assume the blame for anything that goes wrong.[49]

In summary form our interpretation of the developmental dynamics in Bill's case is as follows. In childhood he greatly desired his mother's approval, love, and recognition. This she did not (and probably could not) give. From these circumstances flowed two important consequences: one concerns his striving behavior, and the other, his hostility. He tried harder and harder to earn her love through his accomplishments, and subsequently generalized this drive so that it related to other figures of authority. He inhibited his tendency to express hostility, repressed it into unconsciousness, and ultimately directed

[49] If the reader is disposed to ponder on other possible outcomes for Bill, given the conditions prevailing in his childhood, he should bear two considerations in mind that point to the actual outcome as more likely than any other. In the first place, Bill's mother verges on the dominant type of "overprotective" mother of whom D. M. Levy writes in *Maternal Overprotection* (New York: Columbia University Press, 1943); and, in conformity with that author's findings, Bill shows some of the passive-dependent characteristics of the sons of such women. Neither Bill nor his mother, however, is as "abnormal" as the subjects described by Levy. In the second place, by being a quiet, submissive, yielding person, Bill's father presented Bill with a model precisely suited to Bill's problem of adjusting to his mother. It is probable that for some years he competed unconsciously with his father (and no doubt also with his sister) for his mother's favor, and it seems clear that he formed a similar identification with his father.

it toward himself. These dynamic trends resulted in the Bill we now see: earnest and hard working but noncompetitive; shy, diffident, nonhostile in thought and nonaggressive in speech and manner; self-abasing and self-blaming when "blame" is in order.

Mary, Bill's wife, is a very different sort of person. She is of medium height and weight, has dark hair, is generally attractive and very neatly groomed. She speaks energetically and vivaciously, almost dramatically. She laughs frequently and gives the impression of being secure—almost oversecure —in her beliefs. Having a quite good opinion of herself and her abilities, Mary has never been one to assume blame without due cause. She is a somewhat hostile person and generally expresses it when aroused. She is a person who "gets things off her chest."

From childhood Mary's need for recognition has been high. She studied music and greatly enjoyed performing in recitals. She was successful in dramatics in school. She enjoys working in organizations and likes positions of authority and responsibility. She has considerable need to dominate and derives gratification for this need from her work with children. Among the attractions of teaching is the obligation (as she sees it) to impart a philosophy to the children—to make them stand up and take it on the chin when they do something wrong, to teach them not to be prejudiced against each other's race and religion. For her, the role of teacher is definitely one of superordination and giving directions.

Mary describes her mother as talented, intelligent, hyperactive, dominating, and very adequate in providing for her children's physical needs. Her mother was decidedly less adequate in providing her children with sympathetic understanding. (Mary has two sisters: one older, and one younger than herself.) When Mary was a child, she liked her mother better than her father, and it is clear that Mary has formed a similar identification with her. Mary says: "When I was a kid, I just wanted to be another Mama . . . like my mother." Despite the identification there is much evidence that Mary feels quite hostile toward her mother. Her mother now "drives her to a frazzle." As in the case of Bill, it appears that her mother frustrated her affectional needs. Mary's position in the family was quite different from Bill's, however, for she was the second of three girls, and she regarded both her sisters as more talented than herself. In this situation there was undoubtedly less incentive than in Bill's case to seek the mother's approval through quiet achievement. Instead, Mary adjusted by becoming hyperactive, noisy, talkative, and generally engaging in behavior that seemed unsubtly designed to get attention.

As Mary describes the situation, her father was a relatively meaningless figure during Mary's childhood. Her father is vocationally quite successful but has been very submissive to her mother. She sees her father as easygoing, for otherwise "no one could live with Mother without being ready for an institution." Although Mary thinks of her mother as having been the preferred parent in childhood, she has shifted her preference to her father. The shift apparently began to take place as her father took more notice of her during adolescence. Mary sees herself as the most tomboyish of the three girls, regards herself as her father's son-substitute, and currently as her father's favorite. Today she seems to have quite a strong attachment to him, but still is critical of him for "allowing Mother to walk over him."

Dynamically, Mary seems somewhat less complicated than Bill. Like Bill she has a strong need for recognition, but unlike him she expresses the need much more directly. In both cases it appears that the strength of the need resulted from experiences with frustrating mothers. The differences in the attending circumstances, however, can be seen as leading to the quite different outcomes. Bill identified with his quiet, submissive father; Mary, with her hyperactive, dominating mother. Bill's younger sister apparently did not overshadow Bill with her achievements; both of Mary's sisters were more talented.

We may anticipate the discussion of cultural and psychic definitions of the ideal mate[50] by noting that both Bill and Mary had fantasies of their ideal mates that were quite different from the persons whom they actually married. Bill's early conception of the ideal mate was a girl who would be "blonde and real sweet and quiet." In early adolescence Mary conceived of her ideal as looking "like a movie star practically," but "after tussling with a few who were extremely good-looking and therefore had women falling all over them and were quite spoiled, I suddenly decided that I didn't like that at all. It dawned on me that all these years my mother had been implanting in me the real values you find in a man; he didn't have to be good-looking." From these remarks we can see that neither Bill nor Mary satisfied the other's preconception in appearance, and Mary is certainly not the "real sweet and quiet" type Bill once had in mind. Why did these two get married to each other, and how do they interact with each other? Perhaps we can answer these questions better if we tackle the latter first.

Bill started dating late in his high school career and dated a good deal while in military service. Before meeting Mary he went consistently with only one girl whom he characterized as "a very cute kid but she didn't have any brains . . . she wouldn't even consider college. I couldn't even think of life with her—I would have been miserable. I didn't think I could marry her."

Mary had dated a number of men and was engaged to two before she met Bill. The first of the two was a handsome man in a military uniform who was in a special entertainment unit. Mary remarked: "He liked me in my more glamorous moments, and I'm not glamorous that often . . . I was too natural and down to earth for him." Mary met the second man at college. He was tall and "sophisticated," although not good-looking. They were engaged after knowing each other for about two months. They planned an early wedding, but in this case the boy decided that he was not in love. One of the things that Mary liked about Bill was that he loved her as she was "naturally." This appears to have two principal meanings: with Bill she did not feel called upon to appear glamorous, and she did not have to inhibit her highly expressive nature.

[50] Cf. pages 532–536.

Mary is clearly more dominant than Bill. In contrast to his wife, who likes positions of responsibility and authority, Bill has no desire to hold office in an organization, and if he were to hold an office, he would prefer not to be president. When Bill got out of the service, he had a negative attitude toward religion and he liked to visit bars. Since meeting Mary, he has taken over her value system; he now goes to church and likes it, and he seldom drinks. She has taught him bridge and an interest in classical music. He concedes that she has had more influence on him than he has had on her.

One of the things that attracted Bill to Mary was the fact that she was outspoken, free in her criticism, and able to express hostility, whereas he could not. Since meeting his wife, however, he has learned to express a bit of his hostility, or, as he phrased it, he has "learned to roar a little." Further evidence that Bill recognizes Mary's influence on him in this regard is that he believes that she "re-created my enthusiasm." The most obvious construction on the latter remark is that she has demonstrated to his satisfaction that he need not inhibit so completely his impulses to express hostility. (From his life history, however, it seems doubtful that he has behaved very "enthusiastically" since early childhood, when he began to repress his hostility.)

In most activities it appears that Mary is the more capable. She regards herself as his superior in all intellectual areas except physics, in which she has no interest and which is his specialty. She believes that she excels him in all card games except gin rummy. They spend considerable time playing cards with each other, and she states that she gives him no quarter in these games because he is old enough to take defeat. Bill regards Mary as his superior in many ways—from card-playing to the way in which she handles people. He had an opportunity to observe her with her pupils at school one day and remarked: "We never had teachers like that when I was in school."

Mary dislikes being alone, and apparently her need of people is the need for an audience. Here Bill fits very adequately into her scheme of things. Bill expresses his admiration of her fire and enthusiasm; he is an attentive audience as she tells of her daily exploits. From time to time he gives her advice when she encounters problems in her work. She is not particularly cognizant of his function as an adviser, however, and it is his respectful attention during their daily conversations rather than his advice that provides her with gratification.

In his relationship with his wife, Bill continues his struggle for recognition. In view of her ability and dominance, he is limited in the techniques he can use to achieve recognition from her. This, however, is not a novel situation for Bill, since for most of his life he has been seeking recognition from persons whom he looks up to—his mother, his grade school teachers, his professors, and so on. There are two techniques he has hit upon with his wife. One is that of being generous and thoughtful with numerous gifts and remembrances; the other is assuming the role of attentive listener.

Now, let us analyze the couple in terms of complementary needs. Since it is clear that both spouses have a high need for recognition, it may appear at first that their needs are mutually contradictory rather than complementary. As soon as we take into account differences in modes of expression and in related needs, however, we can see that their need-patterns are complementary. Bill implements his need for recognition by means of a strong need to achieve as well as to provide Mary with attentions. Mary applauds his capacity for hard work and registers appreciation of the wide variety of attentions with which he showers her. He does not express his need for recognition in an overt, exhibitionistic fashion. If he did, he would be in competition with her dramatic style of expression. Mary implements her need for recognition by trying to dominate, by seeking deference, and by being the center of attention. Bill is self-abasing and has little need to dominate, and he gives Mary considerable deference for her many talents.

Since any normal life involves interaction with other persons besides one's spouse, we must take account of outside sources of gratification. Bill gets gratification from his work and the achievement it represents, and from professors who compliment him on the quality of his work. Through her general ability and her success in her profession Mary receives recognition from her superiors on the job, as well as from the children in her classroom.

Both Bill and Mary have a good deal of hostility. Bill's has been deeply repressed—so much so that he has not customarily even entertained hostile thoughts. Mary expresses hostility readily. Her facility in expression gives her catharsis, and appears to relieve his hostile tensions vicariously. It appears, moreover, that Bill is learning from Mary that such expressions are not always followed by dire consequences. It is this (for him) new idea that appears responsible for his "re-created enthusiasm" and for his learning to "roar a little."

Presently we shall discuss changes in need-patterns of husbands and wives. As long as Bill is unable to express his hostility, he needs as a wife someone who will express it for him. To the extent that he becomes able to express it for himself, his need for an expressive wife diminishes. It is significant, then, that Bill has come to feel that Mary is at times too "enthusiastic" and talkative. We interpreted Mary's expressive behavior as growing out of her childhood, in which she was unsuccessful in getting the amount of attention and affection she desired from her mother. From their account of their marital interaction it appears that Bill is providing her with affection and attention. It is consistent with our interpretation to learn that Mary is now able to take the blame for things more easily than she once could, and further, that Mary agrees with Bill that she is too "enthusiastic" and is cooperating in his campaign to "tone her down."

SOME IMPLICATIONS OF THE THEORY OF COMPLEMENTARY NEEDS

The theory suggests several questions useful to consider: (1) Granting that there is a demonstrable tendency for men and women to select each other as mates on this basis under certain societal-cultural conditions, does it follow that where there is opportunity for choice of associates in other types of situation, it will occur on this basis? (2) What does the theory assume or imply about changes in need-patterns of spouses? (3) What implications has the theory for marital counseling? (4) Has the theory any implications for marital happiness? In particular, is it implied that the most complementary couples are necessarily the happiest? Let us consider these questions in order.

Imagine yourself about to undertake a dangerous mission as a guerrilla soldier. From a heterogeneous platoon that includes your best friend, who is a mediocre soldier, you are permitted to select one companion to accompany you. On what basis will you choose? Will you select the person with whom you are most congenial, the one with whom you like to drink beer and shoot the breeze? Or will you choose the most skilled and trusted soldier in the platoon even though you and he have little in common? On reflection you will probably decide that you will have little opportunity for good conversation but will have much need of skilled help in detecting, avoiding, and, if necessary, destroying the enemy. More generally, this implies that to the degree that a social system is functional, its constituent positions and roles will be defined in terms of tasks to be performed and these role-specifications will have salience over congeniality, wherein the complementariness of needs is relevant. French has conducted a study that supports this theoretical argument. She found that subjects having a high degree of achievement motivation, selected for work partners competent nonfriends; those with high affiliation motivation selected the less competent friends as work partners.[51]

What does the theory assume about changes in needs? In particular does it assume that if a person loses a mate through whatever cause and remarries, he or she will seek to duplicate exactly the first spouse? The answer is not necessarily implied in the theory of complementary needs in mate-selection because the theory does not have a sufficiently developed theory of personality. The writer's view is that as people go through a variety of experiences, they learn and they adapt, with the result that their behaviors change, but still there are discernible continuities. Some theories of personality emphasize the changes; others, the continuities. It seems feasible to take note of both. Let us consider an example. At the time we saw the Carters (described earlier in this chapter) they had a Thurberian complementariness. Let us look at Bill's situation then and in the future. Bill had found security and gratification in a directive and expressive wife. What would happen in, say, twenty years? By that time it seems likely that Bill would have become a professional success; he had been working hard and had received recognition for his ability.

---

[51] Elizabeth G. French, "Motivation as a Variable in Work-Partner Selection," *Journal of Abnormal and Social Psychology*, 53: 96–99 (1956). Also relevant are E. P. Hollander and Wilse B. Webb, "Leadership, Followership, and Friendship: An Analysis of Peer Nominations," in Eleanor E. Maccoby, Theodore M. Newcomb, and Eugene L. Hartley (eds.), *Readings in Social Psychology* (3d ed.; New York: Holt, Rinehart and Winston, Inc., 1958), pp. 489–496, esp. 490, 494; Philip M. Marcus, "Expressive and Instrumental Groups: Toward a Theory of Group Structure," *American Journal of Sociology*, 66: 54–59 (1960); Theresa Turk and Herman Turk, "Group Interaction in a Formal Setting: The Case of the Triad," *Sociometry*, 25: 48–55 (1962).

It seems doubtful that twenty years later Bill would need, or indeed be able to tolerate, as much directiveness or expressiveness as was emitted by the Mary we met. (We remember that he had already begun to "quiet her down" and to "roar a bit" himself.) And so if Bill were to lose Mary, we have some notion of the probable ways in which the second Mrs. Carter would differ from the first.

Another formulation about the dynamics of the marital relationship concerns the changes in roles. We may anticipate Chapter 21 by noting that before the arrival of children and after their departure from home and budget, the marital dyad is less functional than when husband and wife are actively engaged in their parental roles. According to our theory, then, need-complementarity should prove more critical in their relationship in these less functional phases of their life cycle.[52]

What does the theory imply for marital counseling? The chief implication is that when confronted with a person or couple seeking a divorce, the theory suggests to the counselor that he check the relationship for the elements of complementariness that initially brought them together. Of course, there is no assurance that the discovery of the original elements of complementariness will prove any magic key to the restoration of connubial bliss, but it does point to what, at one time at least, was a bond between man and wife. As Martha Winch says, moreover, the theory stimulates the counselor to consider and to work with the present motivations of the spouses rather than to try to reshape them along more conventional lines.[53]

If a couple is complementarily mated, does the theory imply that they will be happy together? Very simply and despite misinterpretations to the contrary, *no!* Given some information about the needs of one person, the theory undertakes to predict the kind of mate the first person will select. It is a theory of mate-selection. It foresees that complementarily mated couples can be happy or unhappy. The grounds for unhappiness are apparent in such remarks as those of Bergler above (page 490): a very masochistic woman is likely to select a sadist for a husband. Presumably such a marriage will be quite conflictful, filled with ambivalence, and may well lead to an early break in the relationship. Accordingly there is no prediction that the more complementary the couple, the happier they will be. Yet some interpreters of the theory seem to believe that its purpose is to predict or to explain happiness.[54]

---

[52] Rosow distinguishes the following determinants of changes in a spouse's need-patterns: maturation; marital interaction; new roles both within and outside the family; and successes, shocks, and failures. Cf. *op. cit.*, esp. pp. 230–231. Cf. also *Mate-Selection*, pp. 296–302.

[53] *Mate-Selection*, chap. 16.

[54] Examples: According to Bernard's interpretation of the theory, it is only possible to determine whether or not a couple is complementarily mated by the outcome—success or failure—of the marriage; Simpson repeats Bernard's misinterpretation; and Izard explains that according to the theory of complementary needs "successful marriages are made up of people whose needs and characteristics complement each other."—Jessie Bernard, *Remar-

Supplementary Agencies of Mate-Selection: Lonely hearts clubs

As contrasted with arranged marriages, volitional mate-selection involves the presumption that men and women can meet somewhere and select each other as marriage partners. We have relatively little information about the conditions under which such meetings occur. For a working-class sample in London it is reported that initial meetings were usually "pick-ups," occurring on the street.[55] Places of employment, sporting clubs, and winter balls provide opportunities in Germany. In America the educational, occupational, and religious organizations provide opportunities for many. The existence of matrimonial advertisements, of marriage brokers, and of lonely hearts clubs, however, indicates that conventional settings function with something less than perfect efficiency as arenas for mate-selection.

Wallace, an academician who has conducted a lonely hearts club, differentiates four types of introduction services in this country:

1. Correspondence clubs, generally national in scope and operating through the mails.
2. Dating bureaus or clubs of personal contact, which are generally local in operation and "specialize in introductions made by telephone or by a third party in a club room, hotel lobby, or private home."
3. Social clubs, which arrange parties for the purpose of informal meeting.
4. Clubs that offer some combination of the above three services.[56]

According to Wallace, there are somewhat less than a quarter of a million active members of lonely hearts clubs in the country at any one time, perhaps as many as eight million Americans have been active in them at some time in their lives, and the average client is active for about a year. (Because of the absence of any nation-wide data, these estimates must be regarded as speculative and should be interpreted of course in light of the fact that his data were

---

riage: A Study of Marriage (New York: Holt, Rinehart and Winston, Inc., 1956), n., p. 340; George Simpson, *People in Families: Sociology, Psychoanalysis and the American Family* (New York: Crowell, 1960), p. 156; Carroll E. Izard, "Personality Similarity and Friendship," *Journal of Abnormal and Social Psychology*, 61: 47–51 (1960), at p. 47. An important theoretical reason for disclaiming that the theory of complementary needs in mate-selection can predict happiness is that the stability of the relationship and the happiness of the individuals would seem to be related to the degree of consistency between the need-pattern of each individual and his roles. Until role-theory and need-theory are integrated, such prediction seems impossible. Cf. "Another Look at the Theory of Complementary Needs in Mate-Selection," pp. 760–762. Citation is in n. 45 above.

[55] Eliot Slater and Moya Woodside, *Patterns of Marriage: A Study of Marriage Relationships in the Urban Working Classes* (London: Cassell, 1951), pp. 94–96.

[56] Karl Miles Wallace (with Eve Odell), *Love Is More Than Luck: An Experiment in Scientific Matchmaking* (New York: Funk, 1957), p. 33.

gathered in the 1950's.) In Wallace's experience, men outnumber women among the applicants under 38, and women outnumber men in the age group over 54.[57]

With his clients Wallace used a questionnaire to assess temperament, sociability, conformity, and interest in sex and in religion. In matching couples he sought to fit them homogamously on all these dimensions except temperament. Each client was invited to specify characteristics desired in a mate. Table 18.1 shows a percentage distribution of the results.

TABLE 18.1

Percentage Distribution of Characteristics Requested in Prospective Mates by Members of a Lonely Hearts Club, by Sex

REQUESTED BY MALES	PERCENT	REQUESTED BY FEMALES	PERCENT
Character and personality	51	Character and personality	67
Physical type	46	Economic stability	59
Age	45	Physical type	45
Love and companionship	43	Love and companionship	34
Home life; domesticity	35	Age	32
Physical attractiveness	32	Cultural background	28
Cultural background	22	Home life; domesticity	25
Religion	21	Religion	23
Sexuality	10	Physical attractiveness	20
Economic stability	3	Sexuality	4
None specified	6	None specified	5

SOURCE: From *Love Is More Than Luck: An Experiment in Scientific Match-Making* by Karl Miles Wallace and Eve Odell. Reprinted by permission of Wilfred Funk, Inc., N.Y. Since many members requested more than one characteristic (the average number requested was four), the percentages total more than 100.

For purposes of conducting research Vedder joined eleven lonely hearts clubs over an eight-year period and accepted invitations to visit over two hundred women from Florida to California. After consuming sixty-two chicken dinners in the interest of sociological research, Vedder reported that misrepresentation—among female applicants at least—was chronic: "In all instances, the women had under-estimated their age by ten to thirty years, and overestimated their social and economic position in life. Mothers had enclosed photographs of their daughters, or younger sisters. Their 'attractive homes'

---

[57] *Ibid.*, p. 115. Without documentation or reference to age group, Vedder asserts that women outnumber men three to one and because of their consequently poor competitive position are required by many clubs to pay higher fees than are asked of men.—Clyde B. Vedder, "Lonely Hearts Clubs Viewed Sociologically," *Social Forces*, 30: 219–222 (1951).

often turned out to be a backwoods shack, uncarpeted, even filthy.... The vast majority had misrepresented themselves in many particulars. Many were neurotic, possibly psychopathic, and nearly all were either physically or socially handicapped."[58]

Numerous entrepreneurs have made use of the computer to simplify the work of matching couples and of its mystique to persuade potential customers of the soundness of the principles they use in matching. Since the purveyors of these services seem generally to regard their procedures as business secrets, there is little public information as to the procedures followed by computerized dating services, but they seem to match couples on the basis of similarity of interests, tastes, and social characteristics.[59]

Summary

Love is an emotion based upon the lover's experience of having had his needs gratified by the love-object, or on the expectation or hope or fantasy that the love-object will gratify his needs. Motivation, or needs, may be conscious or unconscious. It is argued that the particular needs that enter importantly into the emotion of love are determined to some extent by the nature of the socialization the individual has undergone in childhood. Since child-rearing practices and values vary from one societal-cultural setting to another, so does the concept of the nature of love. Socialization in the American middle class seems to foster the needs for acceptance and security, and these appear to enter importantly into the middle-class concept of love.

Where love is regarded as a desirable precondition to marriage, it is theorized that mate-selection will take place on the basis of complementary needs. The central hypothesis of the theory of complementary needs states that within the field of eligibles persons whose need-patterns provide mutual gratification will tend to choose each other as marriage partners. Data supporting the theory have led to the further hypothesis that two important dimensions of complementariness are nurturance-receptivity and dominance-submissiveness. Four types of complementary mating have been constructed on these two dimensions of complementariness.

[58] *Ibid.*, p. 222. Vedder reports one advertisement presumably from a "well-to-do gentleman in early forties" that brought replies from 13,000 females, ranging in age from 11 to 103.

[59] Cf. n. 61, p. 293 above.

19

Sex, Romance, and Love

The Confusing Relation between Love and Sex

Throughout Western civilization any discussion of love seems ultimately to be confronted with the question as to the nature of the relation, if any, between love and sex. The distinction between Eve, the temptress, and Mary, the virgin mother, reminds us of the long history of a distinction between love that is profane and love that is sacred. The conception of love and sex as unitary and undifferentiated is embedded in the middle-class conception of the ideal marital relationship. With respect to other than marital relationships, however, love is given general approval whereas some condemn and others approve sexual activity. For those who are taught that premarital intercourse is wrong a cultural discontinuity exists: before marriage love is good and sex is evil, but in marriage they are expected to fuse love and sex. The purpose of this chapter is to examine some aspects of the relationship between love and sex, to examine some cultural examples, especially in the United States, and to see what principles, if any, it is possible to derive from the evidence.

Points of Emphasis

Non-Western cultures reveal considerable variation in concepts of love and sex and of the relation between them. Our official cultural heritage has tended to evaluate love positively and sex negatively. This evaluation is transmitted to *some* of each new generation, and probably *some* of this evaluation is transmitted to all of each new generation, but the proportions represented in the two uses of "some" are very difficult to estimate. To those who are taught this evaluation—or to the degree that a child is taught this—the tender

508

and the sensual components of love are conditioned apart; but in adulthood one is supposed to direct both toward the spouse. Such bifurcation of love seems reflected in the search for extramarital gratification, in frigidity, in disturbances in potency, in the attitude that sexual relations are humiliating, and in the desire for intercourse only with persons of inferior status.

Evidence concerning sexual expression in the United States leads to the tentative conclusion that the fusion of love and sex varies between the sexes and between the middle and lower classes. It is theorized that there are technological and societal conditions that produce variation in the degree of fusion of love and sex. It is argued that the American woman has tended to be more negatively oriented toward sex and more positively oriented toward marriage than the American man because of (1) the biological fact that only women get pregnant, (2) the technological fact that the control of conception is not perfect, with the consequence that unwanted pregnancies do occur, and (3) the social structural fact that in most of American society, as in many others, there is no institutionalized provision for an unmarried pregnant woman or unmarried mother and her child. With his phrase "strain of consistency," Sumner has noted a disposition for cultures to tend to evaluate positively behaviors and attitudes that are necessary or desirable because of societal structures or functions.[1] Therefore it is to be expected that as long as the conditions prevail that have been noted above, the culture will justify women in their negative attitude toward sex. Further it should be expected that as the conditions change in the direction of making sexual activity less risky for women with respect to both pregnancy and side effects, the culture will modify its negative evaluation of sex.

Love and Sex in Some Non-Western Societies

To develop a very approximate notion of the cultural and societal range of beliefs and practices concerning love and sex, it is desirable to take at least a brief note of a bit of ethnology. First, let us consider the Samoans, the Manus of the Admiralty Islands (north of New Guinea), and the Arapesh of New Guinea, all of whom have been described by Margaret Mead.[2]

Among the Samoans interpersonal relationships generally and those between lovers in particular are characterized by a somewhat casual amicability. Children and adolescents engage freely in sexual activities, and since there are no cultural sanctions against such activities, sex is not anxiety producing. Mead speaks of the Samoans as having a "sunny" and "easy" attitude toward sex and of their sexual relations as "a light and pleasant dance."[3]

[1] W. G. Sumner, *Folkways* (Boston: Ginn, 1906), pp. 5–6.

[2] Margaret Mead, *From the South Seas* (New York: Morrow, 1939).

[3] Margaret Mead, *Male and Female: A Study of the Sexes in a Changing World* (New Fork: Morrow, 1949), pp. 212–213.

Mead first visited Manus in 1928 and returned in 1953. As of 1928 she reported that the general attitude toward sex emphasized its evil side. Sex was regarded as shameful, and sexual relations were unrelieved by tenderness, good feeling, or the convention of wooing. The language contained no word for love. Premarital sexual relations were most undesirable, and the cultural sanction was implemented by sending adolescent boys away until they were ready to be married. Conjugal relationships were laden with conflict. Her report as of 1953 shows some reduction in marital hostility, but the attitude toward sex has changed little. "Sex," she says, "is still associated with anger."[4]

Although the Arapesh seem not to label sexual activity as explicitly evil, the evidence does state that sexual activity before or outside marriage is thought to be attended by evil consequences, and is therefore implicitly evil. If a betrothed couple engages in premarital relations, the girl will fail to develop to the standards of Arapesh beauty. If a young man is seduced by a strange woman, he is placing himself at the mercy of her magical practices. Within marriage, the situation is mixed. The proscription of sexual activities around the time of childbirth implies that the overtone of evil is perpetuated. On the other hand, the necessity for the continuation of intercourse for several months after conception, in order to develop the fetus properly, implies the positive notion of sex. As in the case of the Samoans, the nature of interpersonal relationships appears to be one of amicability; a felicitous marital relationship should be pleasant, agreeable, good-natured, cooperative rather than passionate.

One other instructive culture is that of traditional China. In old Chinese fiction men and women fell in love. Early in these narratives the lovers had sexual relations, but their relationships seldom eventuated in marriage. The purpose of marriage was children, and not love or sexual gratification. Marriages were arranged primarily to the satisfaction of the families rather than of the bride and groom. Accordingly, the marital relationship was sometimes a loving one, sometimes not. As we have seen, traditional China had a conception of the division of a man's emotional life similar to that of the ancient Athenians: a wife for the home and a concubine for sexual gratification. The emphasis upon concubines in the upper class and upon prostitutes in the lower class suggests that for the males, sexual gratification was not irrevocably tied to marriage. The patriarchal traditional Chinese society made no institutional arrangements for extramarital sexual gratification of wives. The degree to which there was affection in the typical relationship between a man and his concubine is difficult to ascertain. The fact that the concubine was chosen by the man himself would suggest a higher probability of an affectionate relationship with the concubine than with the wife. While it is somewhat difficult to draw a definitive conclusion about this complex society, it does seem that there was much less expectation than in American society of love and sex gratification in marriage.

[4] Margaret Mead, *New Lives for Old* (New York: Morrow, 1956), p. 405.

What may we conclude from these brief observations on love and sex in other cultures? Sex is regarded as an approved form of self-gratification in Samoa. It is regarded ambivalently among the Arapesh and the Manus, with an emphasis upon the good or positive side among the former, and upon the evil side among the latter. It is regarded as a technique of fulfilling the obligation of procreation among all of these cultures, but this emphasis is particularly strong among the Arapesh and the Chinese. Family relationships are considered as being properly amicable among the Samoans and the Arapesh, as conflictful among the Manus, and as being defined largely in terms of obligations among the Chinese. The Arapesh tend to focus love and sex in the marital relationship. Assessing marital love and sex in terms of familial obligations, the traditional Chinese see extramarital relationships as providing the male with more spontaneous affectional and sexual experiences. To a considerable extent the Manus appear to deny love and sexual gratification to both sexes. In general, the Samoans do not seem to experience love as intensely as Americans believe they themselves do; Samoans approve sexual gratification both within and outside the marital relationship.

Thus it appears that we can find non-Western instances of both the fused concept of love and sex and the concept of sex without love. Furthermore, it seems possible to distinguish two kinds of heterosexual relationship: sex for procreation and sex for recreation. Although some may object to such pigeonholing of these cultures, it does seem that a schematic categorization is more or less justified by the emphases just noted.

HETEROSEXUAL INTERCOURSE IS PRIMARILY FOR	RELATIONSHIP BETWEEN SEXUAL PARTNERS IS ONE OF	
	Love	*No (Necessary) Love*
Procreation[a]	Arapesh	Chinese
Pleasure	Samoans	Manus

[a] Because the family monopolizes the function of replacement, procreative intercourse is normatively expected to involve marital couples.

It appears, then, that love and sex are separable and that the meaning of love and of sex varies with the culture; that sexual experience may be defined as good, as evil, or as both; and that sexual expression may be permissible within broad or narrow limits. Let us turn next to a consideration of love and sex within the broad sweep of Western civilization.

Sex in Western History

There are three branches of Western culture that have especially affected contemporary American middle-class conceptions of sexual expression: early Hebrew, early Christian, and Puritan. Although the evaluation of sex among the Hebrews of Biblical times was "affirmative and robust,"[5] there were very definite limits to permissible expression: the proper setting was marriage and the purpose was procreation. Marriage might be polygynous, however; especially in the event of an infertile union it was acceptable for a man to take a second wife. Some negative regard of sex can be seen in the severe Levitical law of menstrual impurity: anything touched by a menstruating woman became "unclean."[6] Other forms of sexual expression were taboo: sodomy and pederasty were especially abhorrent. These prohibitions served to emphasize that the purpose of sex was procreation.

The high point in the denunciation of sex came in early Christianity. To the church fathers, chastity was the highest form of life. Paul's oft-quoted injunction that it was "better to marry than to be consumed with passion" seems emotionally pale when compared with a pronouncement by Clement of Alexandria that "every woman ought to be filled with shame at the thought that she is a woman."[7] Marriage was regarded as a lower form of life available to those who could not attain the heights of chastity. The Roman Church has vacillated on the question of celibacy for its clergy. It passed a rule of celibacy in the fourth century and annulled it in the seventh. There followed several centuries of conflict between the ascetic ideal and the desire of the clergy for sexual gratification, either in marriage or in concubinage. In the eleventh century the rule of celibacy was reenacted and it was confirmed by the Lateran Council in 1215. In view of the contemporary pressure to allow the Catholic clergy to marry, it seems likely that the Church will again change its policy.

In the Calvinist theology of the Puritans the desires for fleshly pleasures were manifestations of evil and their actual gratification was sinful. Of these, the desire for sexual gratification was most to be feared, denied, and controlled. Procreation was both a theological imperative and an economic necessity. Sexual intercourse for any other purpose was sinful. Therefore, although extramarital heterosexual and other forms of sexual gratification were certainly not unknown, they were officially disapproved of and on frequent occasion met with severe reprisal.[8] Although marital intercourse was presumably permis-

---

[5] Robert Wood, "Sex Life in Ancient Civilizations," in Albert Ellis and Albert Abarbanel (eds.), *The Encyclopedia of Sexual Behavior* (New York: Hawthorn, 1961), vol. 1, pp. 119–131. Quotation is from p. 126.

[6] Raphael Patai, *Sex and Family in the Bible and the Middle East* (New York: Doubleday, 1959), p. 154. After the return to Judah from the exile in Babylon around the fifth century B.C. it is reported that sex mores became more restrictive but that sex practices remained somewhat liberal. Cf. Rabbi Samuel Glasner, "Judaism and Sex," in *The Encyclopedia of Sexual Behavior*, vol. 2, pp. 575–584, esp. p. 577.

[7] Fernando Henriques, *Love in Action: The Sociology of Sex* (New York: Dutton, 1960), p. 78.

[8] A. W. Calhoun, *A Social History of the American Family* (New York: Barnes & Noble, 1945), Vol. I, chap. 7. Hunt believes that the Puritans of the seventeenth century were not as bluenosed as is generally represented: "Seventeenth-century Puritanism was tight-lipped, severe, and pious, but it was simultaneously frank, strongly sexed, and somewhat romantic . . . . The frigidity and neuroses associated with Puritanism belong to a

sible only for procreative purposes, its occasional interdiction on the Sabbath implies that perhaps some possibility of gratification was officially recognized. Holding that a birth on the Sabbath proved beyond doubt that conception had taken place also on the Sabbath, one divine refused to baptize any infants who were born on that day until his own good wife presented him with twins on a Sunday morning.

Sex in Sweden

The relatively unrestrained sexual behavior of Sweden is not totally a product of the industrial era. When Sweden was a country of peasants, there was a practice of "night courting" whereby after a young man had called on a young woman a "suitable" number of times, they entered into an enduring sexual relationship. Today Sweden is a highly industrialized country in which premarital affairs are considered perfectly normal (and it may be added that premarital sexual experience is common also in the other Scandinavian countries). According to one writer, the survival of enduring premarital relationships from the old days "has been aided by various tendencies toward sexual emancipation, including the popularity of birth control, more liberal attitudes about pre-marital relations and free love, and a greater interest in psychoanalysis." It is reported that the Swedish pattern of premarital sexual relationships results in a very large number of unplanned and undesired pregnancies as evidenced by a considerable number of abortions, legal and illegal, and by the fact that 30 percent of the first births occur within the first eight months of marriage.[9] Thus it appears that the pattern is not one of sexual promiscuity but rather of "trial marriage," wherein it seems that there is probably a relationship of affection and companionship as well as a relationship of sex.

Sex in American Society

It is very difficult to obtain credible data on sexual behavior for the population of the United States and for any meaningful segment of the population. Kinsey lists nineteen studies prior to his own.[10] None of these studies meets his

---

much later date: hellfire-and-brimstone sermons reached their zenith in the middle of the eighteenth century, and the suffocating prudishness of the Victorians came in the middle of the nineteenth."—Morton M. Hunt, *The Natural History of Love* (New York: Knopf, 1959), p. 252.

[9] Ewald Bohm and Trygve Johnstad, "Sex Life of Scandinavian Countries," in Ellis and Abarbanel (eds.), *op. cit.*, vol. 2, pp. 910–925. Bohm is the author of pieces on Denmark and Sweden; Johnstad writes on Norway. Quotation is from p. 923. Cf. also Anna-Lisa Kälvesten, "Family Policy in Sweden," *Marriage and Family Living*, 17: 250–254 (1955).

[10] A. C. Kinsey, W. B. Pomeroy, and C. E. Martin, *Sexual Behavior in the Human Male* (Philadelphia: Saunders, 1948), pp. 23–24.

standards of scientific rigor. Other writers have had similar complaints about the Kinsey study.[11] It seems appropriate, therefore, to be somewhat cautious in interpreting the findings of these studies. Not only is there the problem that these studies have been thought open to challenge on the representativeness of their samples and the honesty of their respondents, but most studies have become quite dated. Kinsey's basic data were gathered in 1938–1947, and the data for another methodologically attractive but local study (by Ehrmann) was done in 1946–1953. Although much of our information is dated and biased, the studies we shall consider are the most systematic accounts available of sexual behavior in the United States.

What are the data on sexual relations outside marriage? One study of 1300 college students in the period before World War II reports that one half of the males and one quarter of the females had had premarital sexual relations.[12] It is not clear whether there was an increase during the first half of the twentieth century in the proportion of American males experiencing premarital intercourse. On the basis of questionnaires from a set of subjects of better than average socioeconomic status Terman found a considerable increase. Kinsey, however, divided his male interviewees into an older set with median age of 43 years and a younger set with median age of 21 and found no fundamental change in overt sexual activity.[13] A study that presumably shows the relation as of the 1960's between going to college and heterosexual experience is based on a nationwide survey wherein about one third of the male freshmen and two thirds of the seniors reported having had coitus. The corresponding proportions among the women are one fifth for freshmen and a little under one half for seniors.[14] From other studies on women the available evidence points consistently to a considerable increase in the proportion experiencing premarital intercourse. (Because this statement is based on studies in which most of the observations have involved relatively well-educated women, the range of generalization is not clear.) From two studies involving as subjects women who had been born prior to 1890, it would appear that between one and two out of every fifteen (relatively well-educated?) women of that era had had intercourse before marriage.[15] Two

---

[11] Cf. among others W. A. Wallis, "Statistics of the Kinsey Report," *Journal of the American Statistical Association,* 44: 463–484 (1949); Paul Wallin, "An Appraisal of Some Methodological Aspects of the Kinsey Report," *American Sociological Review,* 14: 197–210 (1949); "Kinsey's Research Design and Statistical Methods," Sec. II in Jerome Himelhoch and Sylvia Fleis Fava (eds.), *Sexual Behavior in American Society* (New York: Norton, 1955), pp. 68–131.

[12] Dorothy Bromley and Florence Britten, *Youth and Sex* (New York: Harper & Row, 1938).

[13] Lewis M. Terman et al., *Psychological Factors in Marital Happiness* (New York: McGraw-Hill, 1938), Table 113, p. 321. Kinsey et al., *Sexual Behavior in the Human Male,* pp. 395, 415.

[14] Private communication from Donald Carns. Also: William Simon, John Gagnon, and Donald Carns, "Sexual Behavior of the College Student," unpublished manuscript (1968).

[15] Terman et al., loc. cit.; Katherine Bement Davis, *Factors in the Sex Life of Twenty-Two Hundred Women* (New York: Harper & Row, 1929), p. 20.

studies involving women born since 1910 lead to the finding that by the beginning of World War II the proportion of the better-educated women who had had premarital intercourse had risen to one half.[16]

Other findings from the Kinsey studies are as follows. Kinsey estimated that nearly 40 percent of the males but only 3 percent of the females in the United States from the onset of adolescence to the age of 16 engaged in premarital intercourse; in the 16–20 age group the proportions were three fourths and one fifth for males and females, respectively.[17] Approximately 15 percent of the total sexual outlet of married persons of both sexes derived from some source other than intercourse with their spouses; this proportion rose to over 30 percent for males and 24 percent for females over 45 years of age who had gone to college.[18] Single males who did not go beyond high school patronized prostitutes for more than 10 percent of their outlet; the proportion fell below 1 percent for the group that went to college.[19] Kinsey reported that homosexual behavior was more common among American men than women. By age 20 and with virtually no increase in the proportion at later ages 37 percent of the men had had homosexual experience to orgasm; by age 20 about 5 percent of the women were estimated to have had homosexual experience to orgasm, and this proportion rose to 13 percent at age 45.[20]

Although Kinsey did not systematically investigate the relation between love and sex, his findings have some interesting implications for this subject. He found considerable difference in the sex practices of what he called "upper-level" and "lower-level" males. These categories were defined in terms of the terminal year of education: persons in the lower level had had 0–8 years of formal schooling; middle level, 9–12 years; and upper level, 13 or more years. This means that Kinsey's "upper-level" person had had some formal schooling beyond the secondary level. This category is far too broad to be equivalent to the sociologist's conception of "upper class." It is the writer's judgment, therefore, that Kinsey's upper level should be regarded as roughly equivalent to the better-educated segments of what the sociologist would regard as the middle class.[21]

---

[16] Terman *et al.*, *loc. cit.*; Ernest W. Burgess and Paul Wallin, *Engagement and Marriage* (Philadelphia: Lippincott, 1953), p. 351.

[17] *Sexual Behavior in the Human Male*, p. 281; Alfred C. Kinsey et al., *Sexual Behavior in the Human Female* (Philadelphia: Saunders, 1953), p. 334.

[18] *Sexual Behavior in the Human Male*, p. 281 and Table 97, p. 382; *Sexual Behavior in the Human Female*, Table 173, p. 564. It does not follow that these percentages represent the proportion of marital infidelity in the usual sense since "all other outlets" include nocturnal emissions for males, and for both sexes masturbation, animal intercourse, and homosexual intercourse, as well as heterosexual intercourse with persons other than the spouse.

[19] *Sexual Behavior in the Human Male*, pp. 281, 285.

[20] *Sexual Behavior in the Human Male*, Figure 156 on p. 625, and p. 650; *Sexual Behavior in the Human Female*, Figure 82 on p. 452 and pp. 474–475.

[21] Because the middle class is vastly more numerous than the upper class in the "upper-level" educational category, it is felt that averages based on these data can be construed as applying to the middle class only.

Relevant differences between the sex behavior of the upper-level and lower-level males, according to Kinsey, were as follows: the lower-level male was typically aroused sexually only by direct contact; the upper-level male was aroused by pictures, conversation, erotic literature, and his own fantasies. In intercourse the lower-level male proceeded directly to intromission and orgasm; the upper-level male engaged in protracted sex play before actual coitus. This might include manipulation of the breasts, mouth-breast contact, and mouth-genital contacts, which the lower level was disposed to categorize as perversions.

Virginity of the female was much more highly prized in the upper level than in the lower, with the result that the lower-level male had much more premarital intercourse than the upper-level male. The technical virginity of the upper level was preserved by the substitution for coitus of frequent and prolonged petting, a practice regarded as marginally perverted by the lower level. Kissing, a commonplace in the experience of the upper-level male, was less frequent than actual intercourse in the experience of many lower-level males. If an upper-level couple had premarital intercourse, the rationalization took the form that "it is not wrong when love is involved"; in the lower level "it is human and natural to have it," and nature would triumph over morals. Finally, as they age, lower-level males became increasingly faithful to their wives, and upper-level males became increasingly unfaithful. Or, as Kinsey said: ". . . lower-level males take 35 or 40 years to arrive at the marital ideals which the upper level begins with . . . upper-level males take 35 to 40 years to arrive at the sexual freedom which the lower level accepts in its teens."[22]

With respect to the fusion of love and sex in American society the available evidence points tentatively to two conclusions. A study of sex life among college students has turned up a finding that "everybody knew" but no one else had demonstrated: that females tended to get involved in sexual relationships only when they were "going steady" and in love, but sexually active males were distinctly less confined to relationships of intimacy and love. Indeed, it is reported that whereas the girls enjoyed dating whether or not they loved the boys involved, they enjoyed sexual activities only with lovers. Boys, on the other hand, were reported to enjoy heavy petting and coitus with both lovers and nonlovers, but they enjoyed kissing more with lovers than with nonlovers.[23] Then our first tentative generalization is: In American society sex and love tend to be more closely linked for females than for males.[24]

---

[22] *Sexual Behavior in the Human Male*, pp. 363–385. Quotation is from p. 355. Kinsey asserted that masturbation was a frequent outlet among upper-level males but that among the "less-educated 85 percent" it was still regarded as abnormal and immoral. He found that masturbation accounted for between one half and two thirds of the total sexual outlet of single college males, and for about 9 percent of their total outlet after marriage.—*Ibid.*, pp. 223, 340, 375–377 and chap. 14. Another interesting finding concerns nudity in intercourse. Kinsey reported that about 90 percent of the upper-level males but only 43 percent of the lower-level males had nude coitus.

[23] Winston Ehrmann, *Premarital Dating Behavior* (New York: Holt, Rinehart and Winston, Inc., 1959), pp. 266, 269.

[24] The conclusion that women tend toward greater fusion of love and sex than do

With respect to the fusion of sex and love, moreover, there is some indication of class-linked variation for both males and females. From a study of unmarried mothers it appears that love as a precondition to premarital sexual expression may not be as widespread among girls in lower social strata as among those in college.[25] (Of course, it must still be shown that this relationship holds among nonpregnant as well as pregnant women.) So far as Kinsey's lower-level males are concerned, there is little to suggest that they conceive of sex as an expression of love. The absence of precoital play (which connotes the "tenderness" of "love" to middle-class persons), the intentness upon immediate orgasm, and the frequent insistence upon variety of sex partners are all considerations seeming to imply that sexual gratification is viewed as an end in itself, divorced from any conception of a tender and affectionate interpersonal relationship.[26] It is also reported that the lower the social status, the less is the

men is supported also by a study comparing sexual norms in Denmark and the United States and by an extensive study of correlates of the attitude of sexual permissiveness in the United States. Cf. respectively: Harold T. Christensen, "Scandinavian and American Sex Norms," *Journal of Social Issues*, 22: 60–75 (1966); and Ira L. Reiss, *The Social Context of Premarital Sexual Permissiveness* (New York: Holt, Rinehart and Winston, Inc., 1967). Further supporting evidence appears in Simon, Gagnon, and Carns, *op. cit.*

The Christensen study reports Danish respondents to be more permissive in behavior and attitude than American respondents. Another investigation finds American college students to be more conservative in sexual attitudes than their counterparts in England and Norway. Cf. Eleanore B. Luckey and Gilbert D. Nass, "A Comparison of Sexual Attitudes and Behavior in an International Sample," *Journal of Marriage and the Family*, 31: 364–379 (1969).

[25] Clark E. Vincent, "Ego Involvement in Sexual Relations: Implications for Research on Illegitimacy," *American Journal of Sociology*, 65: 287–295 (1959). In another article the same author says that it is well known to marriage counselors that there is a class difference in the way wives react to their husbands' sexual delinquencies: lower-class wives are typically concerned about the prospect of a loss of financial support, whereas middle-class wives interpret their husbands' behavior as rejection and respond with hurt pride.—"Social and Interpersonal Sources of Symptomatic Frigidity," *Marriage and Family Living*, 18: 355–360 (1956). In a psychoanalytically oriented discussion of marriage we read that the *fact* of infidelity is not important; rather, what is important is the motive of the unfaithful spouse and the interpretation placed on the behavior by both spouses.—John Levy and Ruth Munroe, *The Happy Family* (New York: Knopf, 1938), p. 92.

[26] One of Kinsey's most fascinating findings was that by the time of adolescence the sexual pattern of a vertically mobile boy would probably register the pattern typical of the social level at which he would ultimately arrive rather than that of the level in which he had been reared.—*Sexual Behavior in the Human Male*, p. 419. Kinsey found little of interest among his female subjects with respect to class-linked variation in sexual practices. He did find somewhat earlier premarital coitus among lower-level than among upper-level girls; but if the age at first coitus was related to age at marriage rather than to chronological age, the levels turned out to be quite similar.—*Sexual Behavior in the Human Female*, p. 686. For both sexes there was a correlation between sexual activity and the level of participation in church. The proportion ever engaging in certain types of sexual activities was lower among those with the higher rates of religious participation than among those with lower rates. Once the religiously active males took up disapproved sexual activities, their median frequencies were lower than those of the religiously inactive. With females, however, this relationship did not hold: when they became involved in morally disapproved types of sexual activity, their median frequencies were about the same as those of the

interest and enjoyment husbands and wives find in marital sexual relations.[27] From these observations we come to our second tentative generalization: In American society sex and love tend to be more closely linked for persons in the middle class than for persons in the lower class.

Socialization in Attitudes toward Sex in the American Middle Class

As we consider the child-rearing procedures of Western culture with particular reference to the middle class, it appears that there has been a dominant cultural theme whereby in the first decade of life sex is evil and love is good; in the second decade sex is "forbidden fruit" and love is good; and in the third decade sex is good within the prescribed condition of matrimony, and love is good. Thus in the third decade one is expected to focus on a single person, the spouse, both one's sensual and affectional desires, whereas in the formative and impressionable years of the first decade the affectional and sensual desires were conditioned apart, on the basis of the formula that love is good but sex is evil.[28]

One other aspect of this cultural theme is the idea that men are more "highly sexed" than women. In a more extreme form it is sometimes expressed that women are not "supposed" to derive gratification from the sex act, that they engage in it only to become pregnant or to gratify the "animal lust" of men. This imputation of a sort of ethereal nonsexuality to women represents a reversal of the Puritan conception in terms of which women, as the heirs of Eve, represented temptation and the downfall of man. As Horney says: "In the Victorian age it was the cultural pattern for a woman to feel sexual relations as a humiliation, a feeling that was attenuated if the relation was legalized and decently frigid."[29]

Margaret Mead says that as a corollary of the attribution of a greater sex drive to males it has been part of the "dating culture" that the boy pushes the sexual aspect of his relationship with a girl as far as the girl permits. It has been the girl's responsibility, in other words, to keep the sex impulse (both her own and that of the boy) under control. A consequence of her service as "the conscience for two," believes Mead, is a tendency toward an impaired responsiveness of the female in marriage.[30]

---

religiously inactive. The level of religious participation was more highly correlated with sexual activity for both sexes than was the broad religious grouping affiliated with (i.e., Protestant, Catholic or Jewish).—*Ibid.*, p. 687.

[27] Lee Rainwater, "Some Aspects of Lower Class Sexual Behavior," *Journal of Social Issues*, 22: 96–108 (1966).

[28] This is one of the cultural discontinuities of which Benedict speaks. Cf. page 436.

[29] Karen Horney, *The Neurotic Personality of Our Times* (New York: Norton, 1937), p. 200. Cf. also Sigmund Freud, *Group Psychology and the Analysis of the Ego* (London: Hogarth, 1922), pp. 72–73.

[30] *Male and Female*, p. 291.

The clinical literature abounds in cases of individuals who derive little gratification from intercourse with their spouses, and yet manifest sexual adequacy with other partners. Freud and his followers have remarked the disposition in some men and women to seek affectional gratification from one person and sexual gratification from another.[31] Their interpretation of this phenomenon has been largely in terms of an imperfectly resolved Oedipus complex. The reasoning is that one seeks in a spouse a person similar in certain respects to the loved parent of the opposite sex. The psychoanalytic interpretation continues that, because the Oedipus situation was imperfectly resolved, however, some individuals are unconsciously aware of the incest taboo, which inhibits complete sexual gratification in association with the spouse. Moreover, the infantile association between sex and "dirt" impels the individual to seek gratification with a person of lower status.[32]

An interpretation based upon concepts of learning and cultural impress is that the difficulty in directing both tender and sensual feelings onto the same person is a consequence of the socialization process, in terms of which the very young child has come to view sexual expression as evil and therefore sexual partners as base,[33] while the affectional role is regarded as not only laudatory but obligatory with respect to family members. In this connection Freud says: "The fact that these two streams [the tender and the sensual] do not concur, often enough results in the fact that one of the ideals of sexual life, namely, the union of all desires in one object, cannot be attained."[34]

Horney observes that a man may lack all sexual desire for a woman whom he loves and admires, but be sexually attracted to a woman of lower socioeconomic status. She then says that "for such a person sexual intercourse is inseparably coupled with humiliating tendencies. . . ."[35] The solution is that of dividing women into two groups: the "good," and the sexually accessible. Such a person, according to Horney, uses sexual relations to devaluate and humiliate his or her sex partner.

---

[31] Cf. Freud, *op. cit.*, p. 73; J. C. Flugel, *The Psycho-Analytic Study of the Family* (London: Hogarth, 1921), pp. 110–115. Cf. also R. L. Dickinson and Lura Beam, *A Thousand Marriages* (Baltimore: William & Wilkins, 1931).

[32] Associated with this conception may be the idea that persons of lower status are more "primitive," more "animal," and, accordingly, more "highly sexed." Relevant here is the conception in the white subculture of the allegedly superior sexual competence of the blacks of either sex.

[33] We have already noted the assertions of Davis and Havighurst that in the subculture of the lower class, sexual drives and behavior in children tend to be treated in a more matter-of-fact way. Cf. pages 210, 397 above; also W. F. Whyte, "A Slum Sex Code," *American Journal of Sociology*, 49: 24–31 (1943).

[34] *Three Contributions to the Theory of Sex*, in *The Basic Writings of Sigmund Freud* (New York: Modern Library, 1938), p. 599.

[35] Horney, *op. cit.*, p. 198. Another writer observes that people are taught that sex is forbidden, and upon finding themselves in marriage where it is no longer forbidden but becomes a "duty," some of them (the more neurotic) discover that sexual relations are not pleasurable.—Edmund Bergler, *Unhappy Marriage and Divorce* (New York: International Universities Press, 1946), p. 10.

The dissociation of love and sex—or the fact that some persons express love and sex in different relationships—has implications for attitudes toward extramarital sexual relations. The view that love and sex should be fused in the marital relationship has led husbands and wives to conclude that if a mate strays sexually, love must be "dead." One implication of the foregoing analysis is that, although such a conclusion may be correct, it is not necessarily so. Another implication is that such a conclusion will probably be more correct when applied to a straying wife than to a straying husband. Here we are pointing to the fact that the set of conditions noted above is favorable to the development of the double standard of sexual behavior.

Although most of the respondents in a college survey who report having had coital experience do not believe their parents are aware of that fact, yet the authors of the study are impressed with the degree of parental influence on the entire sample, which they characterize as high when the respondents began college and less but still substantial at the end of the college experience.[36]

This section on sexual socialization in the American middle class calls for a qualification in that not all Americans and indeed not all middle-class Americans subscribe to that view of sex. (One indication of the diversity of opinion on this topic is the intense conflict that has been generated in some communities over the question as to whether or not the schools should give instruction in anything pertaining to sex and on what should be the content of that instruction.[37]) A part of the "new view" presented in Chapter 14 had to do with the idea that bodily functions are "natural." Hence the middle class, especially in the upper and more literate strata, has been replacing the "sex-is-evil" theme with the "sex-is-natural" view.[38] As was pointed out in Chapter 16, however, this does not imply that adolescents are to be allowed to *do* "what comes naturally"; they *are* permitted to indicate awareness of sexual relations and of the consequences thereof. A second aspect of the "new view" and a second

---

[36] Simon, Gagnon, and Carns, *op. cit.* They also state that two thirds of the respondents said that their parents understood them. The tone of these results harmonizes with the *Life* survey reported in Chapter 16 above.

[37] During the latter 1960's various political organizations of the extreme right wing vigorously opposed public instruction about sex. It appeared that the more vocal opponents of such instruction espoused the sex-is-evil theme and saw such instruction as threatening to make sexual libertines of their children. Some comments on this topic appear in Luther G. Baker, Jr., "The Rising Furor over Sex Education," *Family Coordinator*, 18: 210–216 (1969).

[38] That the more liberal view may be age-linked is suggested by a Gallup Poll showing that the proportion of respondents saying they thought it "wrong for a man and woman to have sex relations before marriage" was 49 percent of those 21–29, 67 percent of those 30–49, and 80 percent of those 50 years of age and older. "'Generation Gap' Is Found on Sex," *The New York Times*, September 14, 1969, p. 79. A study of sexual permissiveness indicates that part of the correlation with age may result from parental responsibility for teen-age offspring. Cf. Ira L. Reiss, *The Social Context of Premarital Sexual Permissiveness* (New York: Holt, Rinehart and Winston, Inc., 1967), chap. 9.

qualification has to do with the sexual outlook of women. The kind of pronouncement so aptly phrased by Horney has presaged a new view of feminine sexuality whereby women are believed to be as able as men to enjoy intercourse and are thought to be deficient if they do not. The "fun-morality" noted above in connection with motherhood has a counterpart in sex relations, with the consequence that it becomes a responsibility of each woman—if she is to fulfill her responsibilities to the full—to "enjoy" her bed life. Expressing doubt that orgasm is as "natural" to women as to men, Mead remarks that a psychiatry based upon a masculine version of sex differences is responsible for the current view of the sophisticated that women as well as men must have a happy sex life.[39]

Some Principles concerning the Fusion of Love and Sex

At certain times and places one encounters the theme that men enjoy sex and women tolerate it. The observation that it is not always so raises the question as to such a point of view being culturally determined. A study that presents some fascinating data on questions of this type reports observations on animals, both primates and others, as well as on a selection of primitive peoples. With respect to animals the authors of this study report that in every infrahuman species there is a bilateral distribution of sexual initiative, and in most of the societies they considered they found that females were active in seeking sexual liaison with males. Their observations led them to conclude that ". . . unless specific pressures are brought to bear against such behavior (as in our society), women initiate sexual advances as often as do men." Moreover, most societies restrict the opportunities for women to have extramarital sexual relations much more than they do for men, but where women are given equal opportunity to do so, they seem to take advantage of it "as eagerly . . . as do the men."[40] Not only did these authors find cultural variation in the degree to which women exhibited the same degree of sexual initiative as men but they also concluded on the basis of their scrutiny of some two hundred societies that where the society enjoins the female to be sexually modest and retiring, she is disposed to be inactive in marital intercourse and not to experience clear-cut sexual orgasm.[41]

In American society there is the general theme that the male is more

---

[39] *Male and Female*, p. 294.

[40] Clellan S. Ford and Frank A. Beach, *Patterns of Sexual Behavior* (New York: Harper & Row, 1952), pp. 266, 101, 105, 118. The quotations are from pp. 105 and 118, respectively.

[41] *Ibid.*, p. 266. A rather intriguing sidelight on this point is their report that societies in which biting, scratching, and hair-pulling are normal concomitants of intercourse, are "inevitably . . . ones in which children and adolescents are allowed a great deal of sexual freedom."—*Ibid.*, p. 64.

aggressive sexually than the female. Consistent with this view are the reports that

> Nearly all preadolescent boys but only about one fifth of the preadolescent girls in a national study had some genital play with other children, either heterosexually or homosexually.[42]
> With age held roughly constant, males in a set of college students were sexually more experienced than the females.[43]
> Up to the time of marriage (and thus with age varying) about 80 percent of the males and less than 30 percent of the females had experienced coitus.[44]

Theories of learning suggest that if it is true that males enjoy sex more than females do, it would seem to follow that, as we have seen, males would be more aggressive than females in establishing sexual contact. Some measure of the degree to which women do not get satisfaction from sex derives from Kinsey's finding that the average married woman in his study reported that she failed to achieve orgasm in between 23 and 30 percent of her marital coitus.[45] But probably the most obvious evidence in support of the consequent in the opening sentence of this paragraph is the fact that there has been so much and such consistent demand by men that the sale of sexual access to women by men—prostitution—has been known throughout the civilized world virtually from the beginning of history. On the other hand, male prostitutes catering to women appear to have been quite rare.

Although it does not appear that enough is known to present a conclusive case in support of an anatomical-physiological cause of greater sexual gratification in males, it is not so difficult to see a set of social consequences that seem to contribute to a reduced level of pleasure in females. A crude translation of the Victorian cliché that "it is the woman who pays" would run: "It is the man who gets pleasure out of sex; it is the woman who gets pregnant." It is reasoned here that the fact that only women become pregnant and the cultural evaluation of that fact are critical in the sex difference in fusing love and sex. The prospect of pregnancy, says Thompson, affects the personality of the woman and her attitude to the man—she has a need to be loved and protected and to have one meaningful sexual relation rather than the more casual sex life of the man.[46]

If we take account only of a higher level of gratification and a stronger sex drive in males, then it follows that the relations between the sexes are asymmetrical in that women have something—sexual access—that men want. (Taking this one consideration into account, we can see the whore's price

---

[42] Kinsey et al., *Sexual Behavior in the Human Male*, p. 167.

[43] Ehrmann, *Premarital Dating Behavior*, p. 64.

[44] Kinsey et al., *Sexual Behavior in the Human Female*, p. 520.

[45] *Ibid.*, p. 375.

[46] Clara Thompson, "Cultural Pressures in the Psychology of Women," in Patrick Mullahy (ed.), *A Study of Interpersonal Relations* (New York: Hermitage House, 1949), pp. 130–146, esp. p. 139.

as restoring equilibrium to the market.) But where mate-selection is voluntary and the male is dominant—in the sense of having more discretion in choosing a wife than the woman has in choosing a husband—then the man has something the woman wants: the power to change her from a single to a married woman.

Now let us develop a theory to account for variation in the degree to which love and sex are fused. It appears that these are the relevant variables:

Technological

Contraception. What is the probability that a given act of coitus will result in an unwanted pregnancy? (For this discussion the desired pregnancy is not relevant.)[47]

Social-Structural[48]

Social positions of women. Does the society offer a choice of social positions to women, or is there only the one traditionally approved familial position, wife-mother, plus perhaps the officially disapproved position of prostitute? Is there a family pattern that does not require the presence of a husband-father?
Mate-Selection. Is it arranged or voluntary? If voluntary, does it give equal discretion to men and women?

Psychocultural

Desire for marriage. Do men and women desire it equally, or do women desire it more?
Virginity in women. Is it highly prized and regarded as essential in a bride?
Sexual gratification. Do men and women enjoy intercourse equally, or do men generally derive greater gratification?

Two observations about the questions are in order. The phrasing is slanted somewhat in the direction of the traditions of Western civilization; this is done to facilitate our using familiar examples. Also, sexual gratification is presented

[47] This does not imply that the writer believes there is no association between a wanted pregnancy and the linkage between love and sex. Since we are trying to construct an explanation for the fusing of love and sex in a situation where they are initially dissociated (not fused), it is not pertinent to consider the situation where a couple is in love and finds their love strengthened by a desired pregnancy. Generally speaking, unless one sexual partner is trying to "trap" the other, it is assumed that a pregnancy will not be desired by either member of a couple who are not in love and not married to each other. With respect to the situation where the couple is married but not in love, the situations are too varied to be considered here. For example, in traditional China the pregnancy might have brought feelings of tenderness on both sides, but in middle-class America the outcome would be more problematic.

[48] Another relevant structural variable is the form of marriage. Mead observes: "In monogamous societies, the strain on the man is seen as the monotony of sleeping always with one woman, but in polygamous [polygynous] societies, the man complains of the demands of too many wives."—*Male and Female*, p. 210.

as a psychocultural variable; on the basis of our present knowledge it is possible that some of the difference is biologically determined.

Let us employ the list of variables to look at a pair of examples. First let us consider the American middle class in Victorian times, say, at the turn of the century. By present standards contraception at that time was probably not very efficient. Accordingly, the probability that a given act of coitus would result in an unwanted pregnancy was higher than at present. The social structure offered very few choices for adult women; the "normal" woman was expected to marry and to bear children in marriage. Male dominance was a feature of Victorian society, and the virginity of the bride was highly prized. A corollary is that relatively few women experienced premarital coitus. Sex was regarded as a coarse, masculine interest. Men were thought to enjoy sex much more than did women, who were expected to be "decently frigid" and to tolerate sex only as a duty to satisfy the bestial nature of their husbands and to carry on the race. As described, this setting provided little basis for the fusion of love and sex—even less perhaps for the woman than for the man.

Let us come down to recent times and view the American middle class in the period since World War II. The techniques of contraception have been markedly improved and widely disseminated, although one cannot yet be completely certain that a given act of coitus will not result in an unwanted pregnancy. The social structure offers a woman numerous choices of social position, but the culture still values that of wife-mother as the "real" life mission of a woman. Enjoyment of sex has become culturally defined as bilateral. Virginity is much less prized or expected, and the proportion of women having premarital coitus has risen markedly. Middle-class society (unlike that of the lower class) provides no institutionalized social position for a woman who is pregnant or has a child and is not married. Accordingly, even though the proportion of acts of coitus resulting in unwanted pregnancies may be relatively low, the possibility of getting "caught" still exists, and the penalty can be severe. Herein lies the dynamic, it is theorized, that generates a strong motive on the part of women to fuse love and sex. If the intercourse is with a lover—using that word to denote a man with whom the woman has a relationship of affection as well as of sex—rather than a casual acquaintance, then the woman may feel some sense of security that if she does get "caught," she can be helped out of her predicament by a hasty marriage or perhaps through assistance in providing an abortion. From these considerations it would follow that the fusion of love and sex is, in part at least, a defensive maneuver on the part of women. It should be added immediately that these remarks do not assert or imply that the fusion is a coldly calculated maneuver—only that the culture is consistent with the facts of the social structure and the woman has been socialized into her culture.[49] From this analysis it would follow that as

---

[49] It has been proposed that American sexual practices can be summarized in terms of four standards—abstinence, permissiveness with affection, permissiveness without affection, and the double standard—and that permissiveness with affection is gaining in popu-

the efficiency of contraception increases, women will experience less need to fuse love and sex. Table 19.1 summarizes the presentations on Victorian and contemporary times and offers a projection for two generations or so in the future.[50]

To summarize the argument, if we may say that under the conditions that

> Coitus may be followed by an unwanted pregnancy.
> The society provides women with no full-time positions and roles outside the family.
> Sex affords more gratification to men than to women.
> Mate-selection is voluntary, and the male has the greater discretion.

then the "battle of the sexes" may be set forth in the following two statements:

> the man wants sexual relations with the woman without any commitment to marry her, whereas
> the woman wants marriage to the man without necessarily engaging in premarital sexual relations.[51]

Sex Practices under the Assumption of Completely Effective and Harmless Contraception: The basis of a sexual revolution

Generally speaking, although known methods of contraception are largely effective, they are not totally so. Unwanted pregnancies do occur. Moreover, oral contraceptives, which during the 1960's became so popular in the United States, have been reported to carry harmful side-effects. What would be the consequence of a completely effective, inexpensive, and readily accessible contraceptive?

The functional value of the norm proscribing extramarital (including premarital) sexual behavior is most obviously based on the fact that the society having such a proscription is ill equipped to take care of children born

---

larity. Cf. Ira L. Reiss, *Premarital Sexual Standards in America: A Sociological Investigation of the Relative Social and Cultural Integration of American Sexual Standards* (New York: Free Press, 1960). See also the same author's study of correlates of sexual permissiveness: *The Social Context of Premarital Sexual Permissiveness* (New York: Holt, Rinehart and Winston, Inc., 1967).

[50] From the data and analysis just presented it is not possible to tell whether the features of social structure have preceded or have followed the associated psychocultural factors or have developed along with them. As a sociological functionalist, the writer leans to the opinion that the cultural assessment of sex has followed the structural-functional facts of the social system and has provided a consistent and justifying "explanation." Relevant to this discussion is Hallowell Pope and Dean D. Knudsen, "Premarital Sexual Norms, the Family, and Social Change," *Journal of Marriage and the Family*, 27: 314–323 (1965).

[51] Some years ago this state of affairs was set forth in a delightful spoof by a pseudonymous author: Nina Farewell, *The Unfair Sex: An Exposé of the Human Male for Young Women of Most Ages* (New York: Simon and Schuster, 1953).

TABLE 19.1

Technological, Social Structural, and Psychocultural Factors Believed to Enter into a Disposition to Fuse or to Dissociate Love and Sex; for the American Middle Class in the Victorian and Post–World War II Periods and Projected Two Generations into the Future

ANALYTICAL CATEGORY AND SPECIFIC FACTOR		Victorian	Present	Future
			PERIOD	
Technological	Efficiency of contraception (as employed)	Relatively inefficient	More efficient but not perfect	Virtually completely efficient
Social-Structural	Social positions of women of middle class	Only traditional position of wife-mother	Many positions available but wife-mother still preferred	Probably further institutionalization of work-motherhood-work cycle
	Mate-selection	Voluntary with male dominance	Voluntary, somewhat closer to equality of choice	Probably voluntary with still more equalization of choice
Psychocultural	Desire for marriage	Probably women desired more	Probably women desire somewhat more	Probably like the present
	Virginity of women	Highly prized	Not so highly prized	Probably even less
	Proportion of women having premarital coitus	Low	Medium	Probably high
	Sexual gratification	For men chiefly	More nearly equal	Trend to equality continues
	Fusion of love and sex	Very little; perhaps a little more for men	A good deal; more for women	Probably more than in Victorian times; less than now

out of wedlock. But if extramarital sexual behavior should become totally free of the risk of unwanted pregnancy, then according to our reasoning the moral condemnation of this behavior should become less severe and ultimately cease. This is the state of affairs that makes possible and self-conscious the distinction between procreational and recreational sex. And such a change appears to be going on.

Other consequences can be expected to follow from efficient contraception. Probably the marriage rate would go down, and the median age at first marriage would rise. Such changes would result from the cessation of any need for couples to marry in order to give respectability to an unintended pregnancy and to legitimize the issue thereof. Since forced marriages would cease, only those couples would marry who feel in love and/or that they want to raise children. The elimination of unwanted pregnancies would result in some decline in the birth rate and a sharp reduction in the proportion of children rejected by their parents. Thus probably a lower proportion of the adult population would be married, but presumably the quality of relationships in nuclear families would improve.[52]

Summary

We began this chapter with a question, Are love and sex unitary, and if not, under what conditions are they dissociated and under what conditions fused? One society in the southwestern Pacific—Samoa—exemplifies the fused concept, and another, the Manus, does not. We have noted that the extolling of love and the denouncing of sex has a history as long as that of Christianity. After examining evidence concerning sexual expression in American society it was tentatively concluded that the fusion of love and sex tends to be greater among women than among men, and greater among members of the middle class than among those of the lower class.

It has been theorized that the following social-cultural conditions affect the degree to which love and sex are fused: the efficiency of contraception, the value placed upon the virginity of brides, the nonfamilial positions available to women (i.e., the careers other than that of wife-mother available to them), the institutionalized procedure of mate-selection, and the average relative level (1) of desire for marital status among men and among women, and (2) of gratification to be derived from sexual intercourse by men and by women.

[52] Cf. Robert F. Winch, "Permanence and Change in the History of the American Family and Some Speculations as to Its Future," *Journal of Marriage and the Family*, 32: 6–15 (1970). In a study of married women in the United States it is reported that one sixth of all births and nearly one third of black births were reported as unwanted by both spouses; one fifth of all births and two fifths of black births were reported as unwanted by at least one spouse. Cf. Larry Bumpass and Charles F. Westoff, "The 'Perfect Contraceptive' Population," *Science* 169: 1177–1182 (1970).

20

Dating, Courtship, and Engagement

Introduction

The terms *dating, courtship,* and *engagement* can be used to designate varying degrees of commitment. Let us use *dating* as carrying no commitment with respect to marriage, *courtship* as implying a wish on the part of the "courting" person to persuade the other to marry, and *engagement* as meaning that both parties have agreed to marry. Given these denotations, where mate-selection is voluntary rather than arranged, dating is usually a preliminary step to courtship and engagement. For this reason we shall consider dating as a stage of marriage-oriented behavior. (One way to test a cultural context for the degree to which dating is viewed as marriage-oriented behavior is to observe reactions to the dating of a couple, the members of which are not in each other's field of eligibles, e.g., when the man and woman are of different races or religions. It appears that a frequent ground for a negative reaction is that the critical person is registering disapproval at the anticipation of the marriage of the two persons who are deemed to be unsuitable for each other.) In the popular sense, courtship has generally meant that the person who is courting is in love, whereas the one being courted may or may not reciprocate the feeling. We shall use the term, however, in a more general sense that includes both dating and engagement.

Points of Emphasis

As characterized above, dating, "going steady," and engagement are stages in the process of courtship, which in American society may be viewed as (1) a form of recreation, (2) a process by which statuses are defined and achieved,

(3) a means of socializing the young into party deportment and the social graces, (4) a context in which to try out and to learn about one's own personality, (5) a setting in which spouses are selected, and (6) a form of interaction in which one undergoes anticipatory socialization into marital roles. Because of the criteria used in defining a "good date" the first of the enumerated functions tends somewhat to nullify the last: emotional immaturity and the cultural definition of the ideal love-object cause date-selection to be based on criteria that do not seem highly relevant to domestic felicity. As the individual narrows his psychic gap, that is, as he narrows the discrepancy between his aspirations and his achievements, and as he moves from emotional adolescence toward emotional maturity, he is less insecure, makes more reasonable demands of a love-object, becomes more willing to test those demands against a real love-object (as contrasted with an inaccessible love-goddess), and thereby proceeds to operate more wittingly on the basis of his psychic ideal rather than on the culturally defined ideal of the love-object. The degree to which marriage calls for adjustment is influenced by the magnitude of the cultural discontinuity between dating and marriage brought about by such considerations as the foregoing.

What Is Dating?

Hunt speaks of dating as an American social invention of the 1920's and as "the most significant new mechanism of mate selection in many centuries. In place of the church meeting, the application to father, and the chaperoned evenings in the family parlor, modern youth met at parties, made dates on the telephone, and went off alone in cars to spend their evenings at movies, juke joints, and on back roads."[1] Dating usually involves persons who are unmarried but actually or potentially marriageable to each other. It is therefore an activity characteristic of adolescents and young adults.

In some societies where marriages are, or have been, arranged, e.g., traditional China and Japan,[2] it is not unusual for the bride and groom to meet for the first time at the wedding. Of course where marriages are arranged, there is no need for dating as a mate-selective process, and dating is usually unknown. In some less exotic cultures, for example, in Western Europe, dating has not been traditional but is becoming more widely practiced as "love-marriages" become more common.[3]

---

[1] Morton M. Hunt, *The Natural History of Love* (New York: Knopf, 1959), p. 356.

[2] Cf. Chapter 2. Blood reports that among his subjects in modern Tokyo the most successful marriages occur among couples who had dated each other after they had been brought together on an arranged basis. Cf. Robert O. Blood, Jr., *Love Match and Arranged Marriage: A Tokyo-Detroit Comparison* (New York: Free Press, 1967), p. 94. In our analysis this "good" result would be expected as a consequence of the double-screening procedure.

[3] Robert F. Winch, *Mate-Selection* (New York: Harper & Row, 1958), chap. 14.

The nature of the social interaction may involve entertainment, such as movies, dances, and parties, or it may involve merely conversation and "being together." For the duration of the date, which is usually no more than a few hours, the male and female are identified as constituting a pair.[4]

The Functions of Dating

Insofar as it is related to marriage, dating is the "window-shopping" period—it carries no commitment to buy the merchandise on display. Dating in American culture has a number of functions, some of which are only remotely related to marriage. In the first place, dating is a popular form of recreation, and thereby an end in itself. In the current setting, at least where the urban ethos prevails, a date carries no future obligation on the part of either party except, perhaps, for some reciprocation in entertainment.

A second function, especially in the school situation, concerns the status-grading and status-achieving function. As Mead expresses it, ". . . the boy . . . longs for a date [but not] . . . for a girl. He is longing to be in a situation, mainly public, where he will be seen by others to have a girl, and the right kind of girl," i.e., one who pays attention to him and who dresses in the current mode.[5] In his famous article "The Rating and Dating Complex"[6] Waller made the point that in campus dating there was exploitation in two senses: each party tried to make the other fall in love "harder" and earlier, and each was interested in the other for status-considerations. So far as fraternity men and women are concerned, the latter point has been corroborated on the campus of one Midwestern university by Ray, who asserts that dating is "one of the ways of gaining, maintaining or losing prestige for the house."[7] He found this to be considerably more true of women's than of men's organizations and pointed out that while dating was one of the principal ways in which a sorority accumulated and maintained prestige, a fraternity had other avenues to prestige, such as athletics. Both in sororities and in fraternities dating was found to be quite homogamous with respect to social status, but the men's dates tended to diverge more from their own statuses than did those of the women.

A third function of the phenomenon of dating is that of socialization. It provides males and females with an opportunity to associate with each other, and thus it serves to eliminate some of the mystery that grows up about the

---

[4] This is different from the practice of group dating, evidenced especially among younger adolescents, where there is no explicit pairing of boys and girls.

[5] Margaret Mead, *Male and Female* (New York: Morrow, 1949), pp. 286–287.

[6] Willard Waller, "The Rating and Dating Complex," *American Sociological Review*, 2: 727–737 (1937).

[7] J. D. Ray, "Dating Behavior as Related to Organizational Prestige." Unpublished master's thesis, Department of Sociology, Indiana University, 1942, p. 42. Cf. also Ira L. Reiss, "Social Class and Campus Dating," *Social Problems*, 13: 193–205 (1965).

opposite sex—a mystery fostered by the small-family system in which many children have no siblings of the opposite sex near their own age.

There is a fourth function, which is a corollary of the third. The opportunity to associate with those of the opposite sex gives a person the chance to try out his own personality and to discover things about the personalities of others. In our discussion of the adolescent we noted that the social situation caused persons of both sexes to be somewhat uncertain as to how successfully they would work through their various tasks of self-validation, especially that of achieving the appropriate sex-type. The dating process is a testing ground —both in the sense of providing repeated opportunities for the adolescent to ascertain his stimulus value to persons of the opposite sex, and of providing learning situations so that he can improve his techniques of interaction. Dating allows him an opportunity to discover that potential love-objects are also insecure; thus the adolescent can universalize his insecurity and thereby reduce his own feelings of inadequacy. In the process of learning about the personalities of the opposite sex, the male, for example, ceases to react to all females as "woman" and discovers that there are "women," that females, too, are individuals and have idiosyncracies. Another way of speaking of this function is to interpret it as a means of defining the dater's identity: "To a considerable extent adolescent love is an attempt to arrive at a definition of one's identity by projecting one's diffused ego images on one another and by seeing them thus reflected and gradually clarified. This is why many a youth would rather converse, and settle matters of mutual identification, than embrace."[8]

The third and fourth functions of dating facilitate the fifth—mate-selection. Dating enables young men and women to test out a succession of relationships with persons of the opposite sex. One finds that one "gets along nicely" with some, but not so well with others; that some relationships are thrilling—at least for a time; that some are satisfying, but others are boring or laden with conflict. Through dating one can learn to interpret the behavior and thereby to diagnose the personalities of persons of the opposite sex.

By noting with which kind of person one's interaction is most gratifying one can learn something about the personality and values one would find desirable in a spouse. Armed with this experience one is in a vastly improved position to set about the task of selecting a mate. In the urban setting there is an emphasis on the need-meeting aspect of the marital relationship (in terms of affection, security, and the like), and because of the heterogeneity of the population there is considerable variation in values, life styles, and so on. The magnitude of the problem of becoming acquainted with a variety of persons of the opposite sex is compounded by the efforts of the parties involved to present themselves as different—better, more sophisticated than they are.

---

[8] Erik H. Erikson, *Childhood and Society* (New York: Norton, 1950), p. 228. Hunt quotes D. H. Lawrence as making roughly the same point.—Hunt, *op. cit.*, p. 355. Cf. also Morgan Worthy, Albert L. Gary, and Gay M. Kahn, "Self-Disclosure as an Exchange Process," *Journal of Personality and Social Psychology*, 13: 59–63 (1969).

Although there is variation among generations in emphasis on candor and spontaneity, yet the evidence of peer-induced conformity lends plausibility to the observation that "Masks are worn, in a sense, during the courtship period. In the bargaining process each party presents a phase of personality which best suits his purposes, although without conscious hypocrisy."[9] Accordingly, because of the complexity of the checks to be made and the difficulty of making them, two or three dates barely allow the testing function to get under way.

A sixth function of dating is that of intensifying the anticipatory socialization of the dating individual into marital and other adult familial roles. Such a process is begun, of course, in the person's family of orientation, for he learns a version of the content of the roles of husband and of wife, of father and of mother in his parental home. It is to be expected, however, that in a dynamic, nontraditional society such as ours each generation will believe that there are ways to improve upon their parents' conceptions of familial roles, and in the dating relationship there is opportunity for discussion of other versions. The quest for more satisfactory definitions of familial roles can be illuminated by the explorations of the dating couple into each other's values, opinions, life style and life plans, desire as to number of children, location and kind of community to live in, orthodoxy of religious orientation, occupational goals, and standard of living.

When viewing dating as a procedure for selecting a mate and for beginning the adjustment to marriage, it is important to recall the ways in which the dating relationship is *not* a rehearsal for marriage. Dating provides an opportunity to explore the personality and values of another human being in a situation of erotically tinged, fun-oriented recreation. Much of the content of marital and parental roles, on the other hand, involves the task-oriented activities of making and financing purchases; of keeping a house clean, orderly, and stocked; and of tending children. For this reason the efficiency of dating as a procedure for mate-selection and particularly as a context for anticipatory socialization into marital roles and adjustment to marriage can be only partial.

Cultural and Psychic Definitions of the Ideal Mate

What constitutes beauty is culturally defined. American culture adds that beauty is a positive value in a mate, albeit more important in a woman than in a man. To some extent all American media of mass communication participate in creating a common image or stereotype of physical beauty. Of these media, the movies, picture magazines, and "calendar art" (the visual media) are important.[10]

---

[9] Clifford Kirkpatrick, *The Family: As Process and Institution* (New York: Ronald, 1955), p. 435.

[10] The importance of the visual media is underscored by the fact that the "pin-up" seems to be as much a part of the American soldier's gear as his toothbrush.

American media of communication create a greater consciousness of the ideal female than of her male counterpart. The ideal may be broken down into its component parts: clothing, grooming, physique, and behavior. Style dictates the nature of the clothing deemed attractive, but the usual purpose of feminine clothing seems to be to display the contours of the physique rather than to shelter the body against the elements.

While clothing and grooming are thought to be the appropriate frame to the picture, beauty of face and body are generally regarded as the basic ingredients in the ideal. The previously cited study of primitive peoples by Ford and Beach demonstrates cultural variation in standards of feminine beauty. Usually, they say, a plump woman is seen as more beautiful than a slender one, and in some societies a premium is placed on tall and powerfully built women. Most cultures place a high value on a broad pelvis and wide hips, and in a few societies the size and shape of breasts are seen as important criteria of beauty with the preferences ranging "from small, upright breasts to long and pendulous ones."[11]

Standards of feminine beauty in America shift with the restless tides of fashion. One clear-cut shift in the recent history of feminine beauty concerns emphasis on parts of the female body. The beauty of the twenties was flat-chested and "boyish" as to figure, and her legs were regarded as the prime source of erotic appeal. During the later thirties the focus of manifest erotic appeal shifted to the breasts. Subsequently the advertising in women's magazines that catered to the middle- and lower-class trade was studded with offerings of merchandise that would emphasize, accentuate, uplift, and divide the breasts. Perhaps the most amusing commentary on this trend is the way in which the heroines of bygone days have been portrayed on the dust covers of historical novels with incredibly full bosoms.[12]

---

[11] Clellan S. Ford and Frank A. Beach, *Patterns of Sexual Behavior* (New York: Harper & Row, 1952), pp. 85–90. Quotation at p. 87.

[12] The cult of the bust was satirized by an edition of the *Yale Record* entitled "Happy Hollywood," which printed an "advertisement" for "Mammocreme," whose slogan was, "Put your best bust forward."—*The Yale Record*, Vol. 76, November 22, 1947. An English writer has commented: "The quasi-pornographic, semi-nude drawings known as 'pin-up girls' are distinguished by the anatomical peculiarity of slimness amounting to serious under-development, except in the region of the mammary glands, which are depicted as of phenomenal size and in a state of tension such as exists only when they are in milk. They are relatively much larger than those on the Venus de Milo, though in every other respect the figure is much slimmer."—G. Rattray Taylor, *Sex in History* (New York: Vanguard, 1954), p. 288. Demonstrating that one segment, at least, of American middle-class womanhood adopted as its ideal the "distorted image" of which Taylor wrote is a study of responses by college women showing that the ideal figure of the average respondent deviated from her actual figure by having less weight, a smaller waist and hips, and a larger bust. —Sidney M. Jourard and Paul F. Secord, "Body-Cathexis and the Ideal Female Figure," *Journal of Abnormal and Social Psychology*, 50: 243–246 (1955). As self-styled arbiter of male tastes in erotic matters the magazine *Playboy* seems to be continuing the emphases noted by Jourard and Secord. Finally, the breast appears to have become more of an erotic than a maternal symbol; Allison Davis and R. J. Havighurst suggest that the practice of

Although it is clear that the physiques of many women do not conform to the cultural definition of beauty, a number of trades have developed to provide the service of converting the less lovely into apparent beauties. The contribution of the beauticians and the clothiers, moreover, to the concept of beauty has made it necessary even for those endowed with natural physical attractiveness to become their customers in order to conform to current standards. The standards of male beauty are given vastly less publicity, but the fact that they exist is supported by commodities to tan the male customer's skin, to color and arrange his hair, to improve his figure, and even to add inches to his height.

Certain behavior attributes that enter into the cultural definition of the ideal love-object can be loosely designated by the lay term "personality," with its quantitative connotation that some fortunate persons have much of it, and the less fortunate, little. More specifically, this term seems to denote ease of conversation, a facile wit, vivacity, and gaiety. Collectively these attributes comprise the lay conception of "extroversion."

Reflection on the foregoing description of the ideal American love-object reveals that it may be summarized in the two words "beauty" and "personality." The conception of beauty is obviously external; when the contributions of the clothiers and the cosmeticians are considered, it can scarcely be said to be "skin deep." The greatest degree of emotional expression that these visual representations of the ideal achieve is the "advertising smile," which is presumed to suggest joy. The conception of "personality," as we have seen, concerns conversation and vivacity; it is seldom suggested that the ideal love-object is capable of any other feeling than that of gaiety. As in the case of beauty, the emphasis in "personality" is upon the external aspect of the love-object. We are expected to note and admire but not to "know" these love-objects.[13]

bottle-feeding threatens to make the breast a vestigial organ.—*Father of the Man* (Boston: Houghton Mifflin, 1947), p. 90.

[13] The deviations from the standardized conception of feminine joyful beauty are few but intriguing. In the absence of any known research on this subject, the writer will present his impressions. The illustrations used in advertising expensive clothing for women deviate in two respects: The delineation of the feminine figure is taller and thinner, less voluptuous. The upper-class model lacks all secondary sex characteristics; her figure is a slat topped with a coat hanger. By contrast, the lower-class "clothes horse" is shapely of leg and remarkable of bust, the latter feature being amplified, uplifted, and divided. Occasionally, the models photographed for fashion magazines deviate so greatly from the stereotype that their faces are actually ugly, while their sex is discernible only from the clothes they are advertising. In the upper-class model, the standard "advertising smile" is replaced by an absence of expression or "deadpan" look. The speculation may be made that this restraint with respect to joy and figure represents an effort to substitute upper-class "sophistication"—blasé and aloof—for lower-class vulgarity. (For some of the foregoing observations and interpretation the writer is indebted to Mrs. Grace Ambrose Stern.) A woman familiar with the merchandising of women's clothing observes: "The cheaper the dress, the more appetizing the girl; the dearer the dress, the more unappetizing the girl . . . perhaps these strange, stringy high-fashion models . . . appeal to the only customers who can afford to pay the

Why, we may ask, is the cultural definition of the love-object stated only in criteria that are external? Should we infer that the cultural definition implies an absence of popular interest in the personality of a love-object? To this writer such an interpretation seems implausible. It will be recalled that in Chapter 18 the theory of complementary needs ventured the view that the attraction of love was based upon an expectation of future need-gratification by the love-object, an expectation that might or might not have been supported in the history of the couple's relationship. To the extent that persons differ in their need-patterns it follows that they will be seeking different kinds of spouses. Let us speak of an individual's conception of an ideal love-subject stated in categories of personality (i.e., in terms of need-gratification) as a psychic definition of the love-object. It is reasoned here that the absence of personality specification in the love-object probably signifies a great diversity in the need-patterns of those who respond to culturalized love-objects and allows each seeker to supply his own specifications. In other words, through its very lack of personality specifications one culturally defined love-object can conform to, or serve as a model for, a variety of divergent and even conflicting psychic definitions.

Let us consider, for example, the brash, aggressive heroine—a not uncommon type in American media. Because of the shallowness of the usual characterization it would be quite plausible for a passive dependent male to be attracted to her in the belief that she would be the sort who could "take over" for him. And it might be equally plausible for an aggressive male to be attracted to her because she would represent a challenge and because of his underlying suspicion that in the presence of a masterful man she would reveal herself as a dependent "feminine" creature. Or a girl can project her own need-pattern by imagining that her favorite movie hero would prove to be strong and dominating and thus cause her to feel dependent and "feminine," or by imagining that he would be lonely and a trifle weak and thus stimulate her need to be needed. Qualified only by the restrictions of the actors' "types," stars of both sexes can therefore be all things to their masses of unknown lovers. In other words, the absence of detailed and intimate characterization in American media permits each reader or viewer to fill in his own characterization and thereby unwittingly to superimpose his psychic definition of a love-object on the culturally defined love-object. If the media were to offer deeper characterization, on the other hand, the opportunities for such projection of individual need-patterns would be correspondingly curtailed.

With respect to the more or less external, or objective, desiderata for a desirable love-object, it is of some interest to note one of the more apparent

prices. By the time a woman is old enough and rich enough to afford top-flight clothes, the bloom of youth is gone. She doesn't want to see how they'd look on a curvy, dewy maiden; she wants to see how they'd look on her. She can identify with these chilly, masklike, carefully created creatures whose grisly makeup has removed the bloom of youth."
—Bernice Fitz-Gibbon, "The Ghoul with the Green Face," *The New York Times Magazine*, February 12, 1961, pp. 33–34.

differences between the sexes in factors they look for in the other sex. Men are more interested than are women in the beauty and appearance of a prospective date.[14] On this point a woman psychiatrist has remarked: "Making her body sexually attractive and her personality seductive is imperative [to the woman] for purposes of security."[15] Women are more interested than are men in the ambition, industry, and financial prospects of a date. These differences obtain also in mate-selection.[16]

Cultural Definition Not Necessarily a Lifelong Ideal

Despite the fact that relatively few Americans come close to fulfilling the cultural definition of the ideal love-object, which we have seen to be largely external, most Americans do marry. Therefore, the great majority of those who marry must settle for a spouse who does not conform to the cultural definition of the ideal. There are several possible interpretations of this observation. It may be that the lover (of either sex) can fall in love so blindly that he is unaware of the imperfections of the love-object; it may be that he realizes he cannot possess the ideal love-object and hence makes a conscious compromise with his own desires; it may be that at the time of marriage he does not even subscribe to the cultural definition of the love-object.

In earlier passages we have posited a "normal" process of emotional development in American society through adolescence into maturity. Our analysis has concluded that the manner in which the American middle-class adolescent experiences societal structures and functions and his subculture leads to some degree of "storm and stress." Adolescence has been presented as the period of gross discrepancy between aspiration and reality, the period of successive self-validations and of intense insecurity. To the extent that the adolescent feels weak, insecure, and inept, it would seem reasonable for him to compensate for these unpleasant feelings through creating an imaginary "love goddess" and projecting upon her his own idiosyncratic demands for love and understanding. And since the goddess would be a creature of his own fantasies, there would be no painful process of reality-testing, which in a real relationship might well result in (1) his acceptance being qualified or denied, and/or (2) the love-object's manifesting her own "real" nature with its own idiosyncratic attributes and needs. To the extent that such "emotional

---

[14] Harold T. Christensen, *Marriage Analysis: Foundations for Successful Family Life* (2d ed.; New York: Ronald, 1958), Figs. 8 and 9, pp. 241, 260.

[15] Clara Thompson, *ibid.*, p. 139. Personal appearance has been shown to be much more important both as an interest and as a problem to female than to male high school students.—Dale B. Harris, "Sex Differences in the Life Problems and Interests of Adolescents, 1935 and 1957," in Jerome M. Seidman (ed.), *The Adolescent* (New York: Holt, Rinehart and Winston, Inc., 1960), pp. 75–84, esp. Tables 1 and 2, pp. 78, 79.

[16] Christensen, *loc. cit.*

adolescence" exists and the response to it is of the type just noted, to this extent there is a psychic demand for the love-object to be inaccessible, and as de Rougemont has remarked, inaccessibility of the love-object is an ingredient in the romantic illusion.[17]

A part of the process of passing from emotional adolescence into emotional maturity inheres in the acquisition of security and confidence. Courtship affords an opportunity for reality-testing. As an individual accumulates experience and wisdom from his successive love affairs, he begins to realize that each person of the opposite sex whom he comes to know turns out to be something other than the paragon conceived in the cultural definition of the ideal love-object. He learns that members of the other sex have their weaknesses and insecurities. It seems probable that typically the growing comprehension of the extensiveness of insecurity among others contributes to the mitigation of his own sense of insecurity as a mark of personal inferiority.

With the passage of time, moreover, another contribution to increased security and confidence comes from a narrowing of the discrepancy between aspiration and reality, a reduction of the psychic gap. Stated in the language of an earlier chapter, the discrepancy between the perceived self and the ideal self is reduced. As a sense of security develops, the person can become better acquainted with the nature of his emotional needs. We theorize that as the person comes to assess himself and his needs with increasing realism, he begins to construct a conception of an ideal love-object that reflects those emotional needs. This means that he is in the process of replacing the cultural definition of the ideal love-object stated in external (and more or less static) attributes with a personal-psychic definition of a love-object stated in attributes of personality and behavior. It is consistent with this argument, moreover, to conclude that each increment of security permits the person to deviate more from the cultural definition. Another part of this argument is the conclusion that as more and more of the person's needs are being gratified, the demands to be made in the interest of the remaining needs become more modest. In summary, then, the emotional adolescent must have a goddess to satisfy his requirements, but the emotionally mature man or woman (mature in the sense of this passage) can be satisfied with a mere human being.

This interpretation provides an explanation for a phenomenon occasionally noted in American society: that a person will subsequently marry someone whom he initially viewed with ridicule or perhaps thought too insignificant to notice. According to the present analysis such an individual is likely to make an initial response to a marriageable person of the opposite sex in terms of the cultural definition, and in such a situation as the foregoing one may surmise that the cultural definition was not satisfied. He may have been "too short," be too slight of physique, dress too garishly. She may wear glasses, have overdeveloped ankles or underdeveloped breasts. Reality-testing, how-

---

[17] Denis de Rougemont, *Love in the Western World* (New York: Harcourt, 1940), p. 269.

ever, is a concomitant of the developing acquaintanceship. It may eventuate that our individual "feels comfortable" with him or her, that he or she provides good "companionship," that they not only have common interests but enjoy engaging in them.[18] In short, it may be found that the personalities "mesh," that each satisfies important personality needs in the other. To the degree that this is true, each is implicitly employing his idiosyncratic psychic definition of the ideal, and in their relationship they are finding love.[19]

The Increasing Commitments of the Dating-Engagement Continuum

America has proliferated the number of culturally recognized gradations in the process of courtship. Folklore records that when this country was more rural than urban, a few dates—perhaps three or four—would suffice in a primary community for the neighbors to define a couple as engaged, irrespective of how the couple may have felt. With the burgeoning of the custom of dating since World War I has come the understanding that dating can be casual, oriented to recreation, and carry no commitment to marry nor to have any "serious intention" to marry. Between the uncommitted state of the casually dating individual and the serious commitment of the engaged have arisen two and possibly more gradations of commitment known by the ungrammatical phrase of "going steady." One variety of "going steady" takes account of the date as dyadically organized recreation and carries only the commitment that for the kinds of recreational occasions for which dates are appropriate each will count on the other to be the recreational partner. The second variety of "going steady" is oriented to the mate-selective function of the dating process and signifies some degree of commitment to marry or at least to consider becoming engaged to be married.

Advantages of "going steady" are that it reduces the effort required to arrange for partners for dyadically organized recreation (and in late adolescence and adulthood much recreation is organized on this basis), and it provides an opportunity to know well one person of opposite sex. With respect to the latter point the compensating disadvantage is that "going steady" deprives the individual of extensiveness of experience and the learning that goes with it.

[18] It is sometimes found that a husband or wife whose spouse has disappeared has great difficulty in providing any sort of description of the mate. This suggests that after prolonged association husbands and wives are not observant concerning the appearance of the other.

[19] Some evidence consistent with the above formulation comes from a laboratory study showing that casually dating couples show much more of the Parsonian sex-typing—instrumentally active males and expressively active females—than appears among couples who are married. Cf. Jerold S. Heiss, "Degree of Intimacy and Male-Female Interaction," *Sociometry,* 25: 197–208 (1962). Cf. also George Levinger, "Task and Social Behavior in Marriage," *Sociometry,* 27: 433–448 (1964); and Miriam L. Papanek, "Authority and Sex Roles in the Family," *Journal of Marriage and the Family,* 31: 88–96 (1969).

Dating, Courtship, and Engagement 539

The former type of "going steady" presumably indicates that the dating partners regard each other as congenial company; the latter type is taken to suggest that the members of the couple are in love with each other. From the discussion in Chapter 19, and especially from the study by Ehrmann, it appears that it is in the latter type of relationship and in engagement that middle-class girls have most of their premarital sex experiences.

Some parents and some churches condemn "going steady" at an early age because of (1) its seeming to deprive the young people of the opportunity to learn from extensive contacts, (2) the fear that it will lead to sexual intimacies with (3) the possibility of pregnancy and (4) of early marriage.[20]

A Few Data on Incidence of Broken Relationships and Reactions Thereto

Just prior to World War II Burgess and Wallin began a study of one thousand engaged couples. Among the two thousand persons involved they found that 24 percent of the men and 36 percent of the women reported that they had previously been engaged and had broken their engagements. Of course, a considerably larger proportion of each sex had "gone steady" with at least one other person than the one to whom engaged. After they took account of the fact that about one seventh of the one thousand couples subsequently broke their engagements, Burgess and Wallin concluded that "at least a third of the young men and about a half of the young women had one or more broken engagements."[21]

A study of Kirkpatrick and Caplow may be interpreted as providing evidence that the breaking up of college love affairs—at least when viewed retrospectively—is not generally traumatic to the persons involved. They obtained responses from 141 college men concerning 314 affairs, and from 258 women regarding 582 affairs. To the question, "How did you feel about the way it ended?" 50.5 percent of the men's and 45.0 percent of the women's responses fell into the categories: "indifferent," "relieved," "satisfied," and "happy." If the category "mixed regret and relief" is added, the proportions become 72.4 percent for men and 66.1 percent for women.[22]

Engagement and Its Functions

When an engagement is announced, the couple makes known to its social group that for them the dating or "window-shopping" period of courtship is ended. In any society a betrothal gives publicity to the fact that—at least for

---

[20] Early marriages will be considered in Chapter 22.
[21] Ernest W. Burgess and Paul Wallin, *Engagement and Marriage* (Philadelphia: Lippincott, 1953), p. 273.
[22] Clifford Kirkpatrick and Theodore Caplow, "Courtship in a Group of Minnesota Students," *American Journal of Sociology*, 51: 114–125 (1945).

the time being—the principals have been removed from the marriage market. Where individual choice prevails and where the culture encourages the interaction of the betrothed man and woman, the period of engagement has certain additional functions.

In the first place, it provides the couple with an opportunity to continue the process of personality-testing under the new condition of exclusiveness. It enables each person to develop a sense of "we-ness" with the prospective spouse and to determine how he reacts to it. Stated negatively, engagement permits the person to find out how he feels about cutting off love relationships with persons other than the fiancée before the commitment to the prospective spouse is made legal.

Beyond the matter of personality-testing the period of engagement provides the couple with an opportunity to continue their anticipatory socialization into, and to achieve further consensus concerning, their marital roles. These we may see as the outcomes of their settling a number of questions that will occur in marriage: the vocational plans of the husband; whether or not the wife should work, for what period and for what purpose; the number and spacing of children; the type and location of living accommodations, and so on.

Of course, as we have noted above, not all engaged couples actually marry. In their study Burgess and Wallin found, as would be expected, that the members of couples whose engagements were subsequently broken had a lower average score on the "Engagement Success Inventory" than did members of the other couples, and that for the couples who did marry the Engagement Success Inventory correlated positively with a test of "marital success."[23] From the content of the items in the Engagement Success Inventory it would appear that the couples whose engagements were broken differed from the other couples in that the former had more disagreements (for example, with respect to money matters, religion, recreation, and so on), confided less in each other, had fewer common interests, and more feelings of annoyance and regret about their engagement.[24] This evidence is consistent with the common-sense belief that couples who break their engagements tend to be pairings of less than average compatibility and thus that the mate-selective process of courtship continues through engagement in American society.

Summary and Conclusions

Where marriage has functions that are important to persons other than the spouses themselves, the relevant considerations in the selection of mates tend to be those that pertain to the interests of the families of the spouses. Such considerations are relatively overt and easily known: social status, degree

---

[23] The correlations were +.39 for men and +.36 for women.—*Op. cit.*, p. 548.
[24] *Ibid.*, pp. 306–309, for details concerning the content of these items.

of consanguinity, health, strength, property, age, and so on. It is consistent with such a conception of marriage that the mate should be chosen by a responsible member of the family rather than by the young, inexperienced person to be married. Here the arranged marriage is functional; it makes good societal sense.[25]

In American society, on the other hand, individual happiness rather than the welfare of the family of orientation is conceived as the supreme goal. Where so much of the individual's happiness is expected to come from the marital relationship, it is necessary to have some technique for testing interpersonal relationships before contracting one of such paramount importance. In this context the individual choice of mate is highly functional.[26]

In mitigation of the sharply drawn distinction of the two preceding paragraphs it should be noted that where marriages are arranged, the principals are frequently consulted, and where there is voluntary mate-selection, the parents' views frequently carry some influence. In one American study it was found (1) that over half the subjects said their parents had attempted to influence their choice of mates, (2) that parents attempted to influence mate-selection in a higher proportion of cases with daughters than with sons, and (3) that the mother sought to exert influence more often than did the father.[27] Burgess and Wallin remark that parents of American girls tend to be interested in the socioeconomic status and potential mobility of prospective sons-in-law, whereas their daughters are more likely to be interested in the personalities of their young man and in the compatibility of their interests.[28]

From these observations we may draw a conclusion as to the prime function of courtship. Where marriages are arranged, there is no reason for courtship, and courtship as we understand it is practically unknown.[29] Where individual choice of mate is the practice, a procedure for testing relationships with various potential spouses is advisable. This seems to be the prime function of courtship in American society.

---

[25] In Chapter 2 we noted the practice of the arranged marriage among the traditional Chinese.

[26] In American society marriage is the principal relationship of any importance in which choice is possible. We do have some opportunity to select our associates in a congeniality group, but we have no choice with respect to our parents, children, or other relatives, and seldom with respect to our superiors and peers at work or our neighbors at home.

[27] Alan Bates, "Parental Roles in Courtship," *Social Forces*, 20: 483–486 (1942).

[28] *Op. cit.*, p. 276.

[29] There are some societies with arranged marriages in which courtship in the form of love-making is not unknown, but, of course, in such a context courtship is not presumed to lead to marriage. Frequently such societies have cultural provisions that prevent courtship from occurring at all or else prevent it from eventuating in marriage. Examples are child-marriage, narrowness of the field of eligibles, segregation of the sexes from puberty until marriage, and close supervision (usually of the girls) by duennas or close relatives. —William J. Goode, "The Theoretical Importance of Love," *American Sociological Review*, 24: 38–47 (1959).

We have noted that the emphasis upon the affection and security aspects of the marital relationship is a characteristic of the family in an urban type of setting. A cultural fact consistent with this trend is the development of the pattern of dating, especially since World War I. Urban dwellers are amused by the fact that in bygone days in the rural regions two or three dates would suffice to mark a couple as practically engaged in the eyes of their associates.

This brings us to an important question: Do the conditions surrounding courtship in American society facilitate a "sound" choice of mate? Do they enable one to find and to regard as attractive a person with whom to share the routines, chores, and problems of housekeeping and child rearing that constitute important aspects of the domestic side of life?

To arrive at an answer let us look at two aspects of dating: the nature of the activities involved in dating, and the criteria of desirable dates (dating partners). Our culture defines dating as an activity that is an end in itself, as a form of recreation in which people participate by couples. Activities involved in dating differ considerably from the routines of marriage, such as getting in provisions, cooking, washing the dishes, bathing children, cleaning the house, making a budget and trying to keep within it, and so on. It is for this routine side of marriage that our pattern of courtship provides little preparation. Indeed, by setting up an emphasis upon exciting recreation, our courtship pattern serves to create an unrealistic set of expectations, and functions to some degree to unfit the couple for marriage.[30]

The criteria of a "good date" take the form of beauty, social graces, dancing ability, and vivacity. Generally speaking, these criteria, which constitute the cultural ideal, are set and reinforced by the single-sex peer group. These criteria, however, pertain to a date and not to a spouse.[31] Since associations with the single-sex peer group are age-graded, moreover, and tend to fade as the individual progresses into adulthood, their support is not generally available after marriage. To be concrete, let us assume that a young man brings to a fraternity dance a girl who meets most or all of the fraternity's criteria for a desirable date. The fraternity brothers register their approval; the young man is rewarded by their approbation and encouraged to develop the relationship. Let us assume, further, that on graduation the man marries the girl. In the domestic situation, success demands other criteria than the good figure, excellent grooming, and vivacity that captivated the fraternity brothers.[32] Not only have the criteria shifted, but the approval of the fra-

---

[30] One is reminded of Groucho Marx's definition of a wife as a person who doesn't think she goes dancing often enough.

[31] "The norms of courtship desirability are sometimes definitely opposed to those of marriage."—Willard Waller, *The Family: A Dynamic Interpretation* (rev. by Reuben Hill; New York: Holt, Rinehart and Winston, Inc., 1951), p. 195.

[32] Merrill observes that "much of the success of marriage depends upon the ability of both parties to accept gracefully its *unromantic* quality."—Francis E. Merrill, *Courtship and Marriage* (rev. ed.; New York: Holt, Rinehart and Winston, Inc., 1959), p. 44. Italics in original.

ternity brothers, which would presumably have made for marital solidarity, has vanished.

The degree to which our culture creates a discontinuity between the recreation, glamour, and romance of dating and the responsibility of marriage can best be seen when we contrast premarital activities in our society with those among the Arapesh. Among these mountain people of New Guinea the betrothed girl goes to live in the house of the family of her husband-to-be while she is still very young(six to eight years). During the years of her betrothal she is treated as a member of the family into which she will marry, is integrated into the family's activities, and engages in a variety of domestic duties. In contrast with our culture, that of the Arapesh creates expectations concerning premarital behavior that are consistent and continuous with those regarding marital behavior.

In America marriage brings a fairly sharp break from the previous mode of life, especially for women. American culture does not prepare people very well for marriage, which it presents as the drably monotonous anticlimax to romance. The chase is the source of fascination when boy-meets-girl, and by implication married life is too dull to warrant continuing the story after boy-gets-girl. American culture creates the stereotype of the young nubile girl as the "love goddess," of the wife as the fork-tongued, hatchet-faced battle-ax of the cartoonist's caricature. In the face of this cultural discontinuity it is not astonishing to find marital disorganization.

As with dating, engagement varies greatly in form and content. Its duration may be a few days or several years. It may be a commitment known only to the couple involved or it may receive international publicity. It may involve little or no interruption of the couple's daily routines or it may involve an extensive series of parties and celebrations. Even so, the foregoing data and analysis seem to justify the conclusion that engagement tends to be functional as a marriage-oriented relationship in the sense that it continues (1) anticipatory socialization into marital roles, (2) personality-testing with the spouse-to-be, and (3) the screening out of couples who are apparently among the less compatible.

21

Marriage

Introduction

We begin by examining the structure and functions of marriage and the roles that the functions define. As we have seen, adjustment to roles is made problematic under certain conditions, for example, cultural discontinuity. After distinguishing marital adjustment from marital success and happiness, we shall consider sources of difficulty in achieving marital adjustment and also in maintaining it. The chapter concludes with a consideration of studies that have undertaken to assess and to predict marital felicity.

The Nature and Structure of Marriage

As Burgess and Locke have pointed out, "The animal mates, but man marries."[1] The nature of the "something more" involved in marriage follows from the observation that man lives in groups, and that human groups have folkways, mores, traditions, and cultures. In every known culture marriage is in the mores. This means that although the specifications vary from culture to culture, the society decrees the form of marriage, determines who may marry whom and who is ineligible to marry whom, whether or not property is to be exchanged at marriage and from whom to whom, how many mates a man or woman may have, and lays down principles for the proper conduct of married persons and for the conditions under which marriage may be dissolved.

Some cultures permit and even encourage plural marriages. Of the possi-

[1] Ernest W. Burgess and Harvey J. Locke, *The Family: From Institution to Companionship* (2d ed.; New York: American Book, 1953), p. 6.

ble combinations, the more frequent is the marriage of one man to several women (polygyny) among, for example, the ancient Hebrews, the traditional Chinese, the Mohammedans, and the nineteenth-century Mormons. The marriage of one woman to a plurality of husbands (polyandry) has been found in Tibet and among the Todas in India. Even where polygamy (which includes polygyny and polyandry) is permitted, however, the conditions of life for the masses of the people make monogamy the most common form of marriage.

Taking account of possible variation in marital arrangements, we find that marriage is a socially approved union between one or more men and one or more women in the relationship of husband and wife.

At the time of the wedding each new spouse alters his or her societal position. In general, the more male-centered and male-dominant the culture, the greater is the significance for women of this change in societal position. In traditional China the woman was expected practically to forget her blood relatives and to move into the social orbit of her husband's kinsmen. Although American culture is less male-centered than was traditional Chinese culture, the change from unmarried to married status is still much more profound for women than for men, as is symbolized by the wedding ring and the change in name. In most societies it is assumed that any normal adult will marry. It is also usually true that the only societal position available to an adult woman is in the family.[2] Where mate-selection is voluntary and the man is dominant, it follows that the man has the power to grant the woman access to her adult societal position. From these considerations it is reasonable that the woman in American society should evince a livelier interest in *getting* married than the man.[3] Because of the fact that it is traditionally the woman who has the immediate responsibility for the welfare of young children, moreover, the woman is more dependent on the man in marriage than the man is on the woman, and for this reason she has a greater interest in *staying* married than has the man. Furthermore, the data on remarriage rates[4] suggest that it is easier for a man to remarry than it is for a woman.

For all these reasons it would seem usual for the wife to be more vulnerable than the husband to exploitation by the spouse.[5] Commenting on Amer-

---

[2] Until recently in American history the spinster had no alternative to becoming a sort of (usually unpaid) domestic in the home of a married sibling or other relative.

[3] Paul Wallin, "Marital Happiness of Parents and Their Children's Attitude to Marriage," *American Sociological Review*, 19: 20–23 (1954).

[4] See Chapter 23.

[5] Somewhat related are the following ideas: (1) Ross's "law of personal exploitation," whereby he held that the member of the dyad who cared less could exploit the one who cared more, in E. A. Ross, *Principles of Sociology* (New York: Appleton, 1921), p. 136; (2) Waller's adaptation of Ross's idea to differential involvement in courtship, which he called ungrammatically "the principle of least interest," in Willard Waller, *The Family* (revised by Reuben Hill; New York: Holt, Rinehart and Winston, 1951), pp. 190–192; and Aristotle's anticipatory application of both these ideas to his premise of male superiority, whereby he argued in the *Nicomachean Ethics* that the wife should compensate for her inferiority by loving her husband more than he loves her.

ican middle-class marriages, Burgess and Wallin remark that "marriage for the man has primarily an affectional and recreational meaning, while for the woman the career aspect of marriage, even in the companionship marriage, is of high importance."[6] And since it seems clear that in American society marriage means more to the woman than to the man, it is fitting that society pages give much more space to brides than to grooms and that women's magazines should publish articles on attracting and getting along with the opposite sex, whereas in magazines for men the major treatment of the relations between the sexes consists in picturing curvaceous females with long legs and impressive breasts.[7]

The Married and the Unmarried

Before proceeding with the analysis of marriage and the concept of marital adjustment, let us see what is known about who does marry in American society and who does not. Despite the "ball-and-chain" concept of the facetious and the cynical, most Americans do marry. By age 54 just about all are married who ever will. In the 45–54 age category about 15 out of every 16 men and women in the United States either are married or have been married.[8] When it comes to the question of just who marries and who does not, however, the picture is not very clear. It can be partially illuminated by noting differences in social characteristics between the married and the unmarried.

In the first place, it would seem reasonable that there would be psychological differences between those who marry and those who do not. The phenomenon of homosexuality comes to mind, and it might be assumed that among the unmarried would be numbered all the homosexuals. For obvious reasons there are no national statistics on the incidence of homosexuality nor on the marital status of homosexuals.[9] Clinicians report, however, that some homosexuals do marry. Farnham, for example, speaks of "married neuters," who may enter marriage either to deceive their associates about their homosexual tendencies, to deceive themselves concerning latent tendencies, or in the hope that marriage will alter their sexual orientation.[10] Although the

[6] Ernest W. Burgess and Paul Wallin, *Engagement and Marriage* (Philadelphia: Lippincott, 1953), p. 587.

[7] Imagine the response of a masculine audience to such an article as Jhan and June Robbins, "84 Ways to Make Your Marriage More Exciting," *McCall's*, October 1958, pp. 50, 147–148. In the light of the foregoing analysis it appears that American etiquette is inappropriate in directing congratulations to the groom rather than to the bride.

[8] U.S. Bureau of the Census, *Current Population Reports—Population Characteristics*, Series P-20, No. 159, January 25, 1967, Table 1, p. 7.

[9] Of course the more enduring relationships of pairs of homosexuals are sometimes referred to as marriages. For some discussion of "gay marriages" cf. Martin Hoffman, *The Gay World* (New York: Basic Books, 1968), esp. pp. 64–68, 174–179, 190.

[10] Marynia Farnham, "Married Neuters," in Hilda Holland (ed.), *Why Are You Single?* (New York: Farrar, Straus, 1949), pp. 179–198.

writer's own research has not borne directly on the differences between the married and the unmarried, these studies have shown (1) that college men who are closely attached to their mothers have a lower proportion of engagements than men not so attached and (2) that the better-looking girls and those who prefer their fathers to their mothers have a high proportion of engagements.[11] For women who go as far as high school there is a negative correlation between level of education and proportion married.[12]

From statistics on morbidity and mortality it is seen that the married are healthier—physically and mentally—than the unmarried. At all ages mortality rates are higher for the unmarried—whether single, divorced, or widowed—than for the married.[13] Rates of admissions to mental hospitals in New York State run two to three times as high for single as for married persons.[14] Married persons have a lower suicide rate than the unmarried[15] and are reported to be happier than the unmarried.[16] Married persons have lower death rates from accidents than have persons in other marital statuses. With respect to deaths in motor vehicle accidents, married men have lower rates than have men in other marital statuses; married women in the 35–69 age brackets have higher death rates from motor vehicle accidents than have single women of those ages but lower rates than have widowed or divorced women.[17]

The Functions of Marriage

Since marriage is an institutionalized relationship within the family, much of the analysis previously made of the family applies to marriage as well. Accordingly, the present discussion takes off from the analysis of functions in Parts One–Three and of familial roles, role-differentiation, role-conflict, and role-strain within the family in Chapter 12.

---

[11] Cf. R. F. Winch, "The Relation between Courtship Behavior and Attitudes towards Parents among College Men," *American Sociological Review*, 8: 164–174 (1943), and "Some Data Bearing on the Oedipus Hypothesis," *Journal of Abnormal and Social Psychology*, 45: 481–489 (1950).

[12] Paul C. Glick, *American Families* (New York: Wiley, 1957), p. 107.

[13] Metropolitan Life Insurance Company, *Statistical Bulletin*, Vol. 38, 1957, pp. 4–7.

[14] Louis Dublin, "These Are the Single," in Holland, *op. cit.*, pp. 67–85, esp. pp. 78–81. Other studies showing greater mental health among the married are Leta McKinney Adler, "The Relationship of Marital Status to Incidence of and Recovery from Mental Illness," *Social Forces*, 32: 185–194 (1953); Seymour S. Bellin and Robert H. Hardt, "Marital Status and Mental Disorders among the Aged," *American Sociological Review*, 23: 155–162 (1958); Robert M. Frumkin, "Marital Status and Mental Illness," *Sociology and Social Research*, 39: 237–239 (1955).

[15] Andrew F. Henry and James F. Short, *Suicide and Homicide* (New York: Free Press, 1954).

[16] Norman M. Bradburn and David Caplovitz, *Reports on Happiness* (Chicago: Aldine, 1965), p. 13.

[17] U.S. Public Health Service, *Accidental Injury Statistics* (Washington, D.C.: GPO, 1958).

This book has emphasized the formulation that because replacement is the family's basic societal function, the family has the derived functions of nurturance and control and of position-conferring. It has also been proposed that the family's structure brings it the derived function of emotional gratification. As we turn to the marital dyad with these functions in mind, it is immediately evident that the basic function of procreation and the derived one of emotional gratification combine to give the marital relationship a function of sexual gratification. In the present section some of these functions are considered from the special view of the marital dyad; in a later section we shall examine their implications with respect to marital roles and criteria for marital performance.[18]

In Chapters 9 and 13 it was noted that cultures that de-emphasize individualism (as in traditional China) tend also to define the purpose of marriage to be procreation and the continuation of the family line. In such a setting a childless marriage is a reason for a man to take a new wife. Some years ago a widely noted example involved the ruler of Iran. As this custom implies, such a culture values lineal solidarity over marital solidarity. On the other hand, it was noted that American culture, being more individualistic, values highly the goal of self-realization. With respect to the consequences of childlessness in the more individualistic American society, it was found that virtually every couple wanted children.[19] The *desire* for children, moreover, is positively correlated, but the *number* of children a couple has is negatively correlated, with the degree of marital adjustment.[20] To these conclusions we now add the finding that in Indianapolis marital happiness has correlated negatively with the number of living children but positively with the adequacy of control over conception and thereby with having no more than the number of children desired.[21] This finding is consistent with the results in another study restricted to a college population.[22]

---

[18] Because the parental functions refer to behavior directed to offspring and because our direct concern here is with behavior directed from one spouse to the other, we shall not pause here to consider nurturance or control.

[19] Ronald Freedman, Pascal K. Whelpton, and Arthur A. Campbell, *Family Planning, Sterility and Population Growth* (New York: McGraw-Hill, 1959), p. 47. Robert O. Blood, Jr., and Donald M. Wolfe, *Husbands and Wives* (New York: Free Press, 1960), p. 137.

[20] Burgess and Wallin, *op. cit.*, p. 722. These authors speak of "marital success" where the present writer uses "marital adjustment." Distinction between these terms is made later in the present chapter. Burgess and Wallin cite four studies showing no significant correlation between number of children and measures of "marital success" and two studies showing that the greater the number of children, the lower the "success."—*Ibid.*, pp. 714–715. Cf. also Harold T. Christensen, "Children in the Family: Relationship of Number and Spacing to Marital Success," *Journal of Marriage and the Family*, 30: 283–289 (1968), and Andrée Michel and Françoise Lautman Feyrabend, "Real Number of Children and Conjugal Interaction in French Urban Families: A Comparison with American Families," *Journal of Marriage and the Family*, 31: 359–363 (1969).

[21] Robert Reed, "The Interrelationship of Marital Adjustment, Fertility Control, and Size of Family," *Milbank Memorial Fund Quarterly*, 25: 382–425 (1947).

[22] Harold T. Christensen and Robert E. Philbrick, "Family Size as a Factor in the

Chapters 8 and 12 emphasize that the status of the married woman is usually determined by the status of her husband, which in American society is largely determined by his occupation, income, and education. It follows that the dynamic determinants of the wife's status operate outside the marital relationship—on the husband's job. It should not be overlooked that the wife's appearance and behavior have some relevance to the status of the marital couple. That relevance, however, is more in the nature of reflecting the status of the couple, or the status to which they aspire, than of the actual determination of that status. It is for this reason, as we have seen, that the man is interested in the beauty, grooming, dress, level of consumption, manners, taste, skill in entertaining, and so on, of a woman, while she is interested in his education, occupation, and "prospects." On the other hand, the wife can influence the couple's status to the extent that they find themselves in a setting of the sort described by Whyte, where the social attributes of the "company wife" are taken into account when the husband is under consideration as a prospective employe or as one to be promoted.

Marriage is the one relationship within which sex relations are permissible in every society. In Chapter 19 it was noted that there was much variation from one culture to another and among subcultures of a single society in attitudes toward sex (especially with respect to the fusion or dissociation of love and sex) and in sex practices (especially with respect to the frequency and relationships involved in pre- and extramarital sex). Such observations lead to the conclusion that the assessment of one spouse by the other with respect to the role of sex partner is everywhere qualified by the cultural context. In America perhaps the most noteworthy recent trend has been that toward the "sexual emancipation" of women as evidenced in (1) the theme that it is morally permissible for women to enjoy the sex act, (2) that there is something wrong with a woman who does not have a high rate of orgasm,[23] and (3) in the increase in the proportion of women with pre- and extramarital sexual experience.[24]

In Chapter 9 we noted that as a consequence of recent social trends the family has come to emphasize the function of emotional gratification—of providing both the joy that comes with sharing accomplishments and also the security and reassurance that provide relief from feelings of anxiety and insecurity. It is worth considering that in simpler societies the family, with its network of commitments through the extended kin, provides a sense of security; in modern society the nuclear family and especially the marital relationship fulfills this need. In this sense marital solidarity substitutes for the lineal and collateral solidarity of kinship. An important difference is that the solidarity of kin is ascribed and therefore one qualifies for the support of one's relatives through being born into the family; he must be guilty of a heinous

---

Marital Adjustments of College Couples," *American Sociological Review*, 17: 306–312 (1952).

[23] Margaret Mead, *Male and Female* (New York: Morrow, 1949), p. 294.

[24] A. C. Kinsey *et al.*, *Sexual Behavior in the Human Female* (Philadelphia: Saunders, 1953), pp. 298–302, 422–424.

crime to be disowned and ostracized and thereby to lose his rights. In modern marriage, on the other hand, the relationship is a mixture of ascription and achievement. It is ascribed in the sense that certain rights (notably the wife's claim to be supported) go with marriage as long as the marriage survives; it is achieved both in its formation—each spouse having achieved the approval of the other in order to enter the marriage—and in its survival—each spouse having to refrain from alienating the other to the point where the other feels impelled to terminate the marriage.[25]

Adjustment in Marriage

There are various kinds of evidence that Americans have to become "adjusted" to marriage. For example, one writer has studied the length of time required for 409 couples to achieve satisfactory adjustments in the following areas: sex relations, spending family income, social activities, and mutual friends.[26] The fact that his couples had been married for an average of twenty years meant that his sample was heavily weighted with marriages that were "successful" in the sense they were unbroken. He found that the majority had achieved satisfactory adjustments in all areas from the beginning, but that proportions varying from nearly one half in the case of sex relations to about one quarter in the case of mutual friends had had to work out satisfactory adjustments. He found, moreover, that those couples who were happy in marriage tended to achieve satisfactory adjustments early in marriage, and that if satisfactory adjustments were not achieved in two or more areas, the couples tended to classify their marriages as unhappy.[27]

It is desirable to distinguish marital adjustment from two other terms that are sometimes used more or less interchangeably with it: *marital success* and *marital happiness*. In the interest of clarifying the meanings of all three terms the author will propose denotations for the last two that will distinguish them from marital adjustment. In common usage success refers to the achievement of a goal. *Marital success,* then, should refer to the achievement of one or more goals of marriage. It follows that for a marriage to be pronounced successful, one or more marital goals must be either specified or implied. One frequently used criterion for marital success is sheer survival of the marriage, or, in its more familiar form, divorce is the mark of failure by this criterion. A theologically centered criterion of marital success is the production of the maximum number of human beings to worship God. Burgess and Locke propose a list of nine criteria for appraising the success of a marriage: its permanence, the happiness of the couple, their fulfilling the expectations of the community, the personality development of the spouses, the companionship

---

[25] Mead, *op. cit.,* p. 357.
[26] J. T. Landis, "Length of Time Required to Achieve Adjustment in Marriage," *American Sociological Review,* 11: 666–677 (1946).
[27] *Ibid.,* p. 677.

in their relationship, their satisfaction with their marriage, the integration of the couple (which these authors speak of as the "degree of oneness"), the "adjustment of the marriage" (by which they mean the consensus of the spouses on values and the content of the marital roles), and their sexual adjustment.[28] Hill conceives of marital success principally in terms of the emotional gratification and continuing personality development of the spouses.[29] In a previous section on "The Functions of Marriage" the author has proposed a set of goals for marriage. These goals were proposed *not* in the sense that the author was moralizing that the goals *ought* to be achieved by each married couple, but rather in the sense that societies seemed generally to look to marriages to produce these outcomes: procreation and the parental functions of nurturance and control, position-conferring, and emotional and sexual gratification.

Whereas marital success refers to a dyadic achievement, *marital happiness* is a distinctly individual phenomenon. Marital success can be assessed in the light of an onlooker's criteria; marital happiness can be determined only by the emotional response of a spouse. It is at least conceivable that one marital partner could be sublimely happy while the other might be at the nadir of despair. Marital happiness, then, refers to the tone of the subjective response of the individual spouse to his or her marriage. According to Terman, who has done considerable research on the topic, marital happiness is largely determined by one's all-around happiness of temperament.[30]

ROLE-ADJUSTMENT AND PSYCHIC ADJUSTMENT

In the discussion to follow, a distinction will be drawn between role-adjustment and psychic adjustment. An actor is said to be adjusted to a role if he knows the expectations that define the role and under the appropriate conditions can produce the behaviors expected. An actor is said to be psychically adjusted to a situation if the gratification he derives from it is commensurate with the energy he invests in it.

(To the extent that each type of adjustment is required a doubt may be raised as to the wisdom of early marriages. A section that considers problems in the role-adjustment and psychic adjustment of those who marry at young ages appears in the next chapter.)

SUBROLES AS CRITERIA OF MARITAL PERFORMANCE

The functions of marriage, which were distinguished above, suggest elements (or they might be called subroles) in terms of which to analyze marital roles and assess performance. Such a set of criteria might be these:

[28] Burgess and Locke, *The Family*, pp. 378–391.
[29] Waller, *The Family*, pp. 368–369.
[30] Lewis M. Terman and Melita H. Oden, *The Gifted Child Grows Up* (Stanford, Calif.: Stanford University Press, 1947), pp. 262–263.

Progenitor or progenitrix[31]
Parent
Position-conferrer
Emotional gratifier
Sexual partner

To these might be added others, more or less related to the specific setting. For the middle-class American, e.g.:

Host or hostess
Home manager
Companion in leisure

A person whose performance rates high on every criterion noted above would be a prize spouse. Less obvious but more generally applicable is the point that most spouses would probably perform unevenly. Before such a person is adjudged a marital failure, however, both that person and the mate would be well advised to look at the total profile of performance.

SOURCES OF DIFFICULTY IN ROLE-ADJUSTMENT

If a person knows what to expect of a recurring situation and is prepared with a repertoire of responses appropriate to the situation, he knows the role and in this sense is "adjusted" to the role involved. American men reared in civilian life are not ready for combat; they do not know what to expect, nor do they have an appropriate set of responses. The purpose of basic military training is to teach them what to expect and to respond appropriately—or, in the lay term, "instinctively." As they acquire these expectations and responses, they are learning their roles and are becoming adjusted to the situation.

For Americans there seem to be three major sources of difficulty with respect to the achievement of marital roles. The first of these sources in American life is the lack of socialization into marital roles. American society does not offer its young the kind of informal but nonetheless systematic in-service training in marital roles that, as we have seen, is routine with the Arapesh.[32] No doubt the lack of such "basic marital training" in our society stems in large part from the breakdown in the traditional ways of doing things, especially with respect to the marital division of labor and the rearing of children.[33]

---

[31] Performance would be judged in terms of fertility or sterility, and clear or tainted heredity.

[32] Indirect support for this point comes from a study of American marriages wherein couples who had experienced a relatively greater exposure to family-oriented relationships and conventional values averaged higher on a scale of marital adjustment than couples who had had relatively greater exposure to peer groups. Cf. Robert N. Whitehurst, "Premarital Reference Group Orientations and Marriage Adjustment," paper presented before the American Sociological Association at San Francisco on August 31, 1967. To the present writer it seems that one might interpret this finding as indicating that the family-oriented relationships offered more opportunity for socialization into familial, including marital, roles than did the peer-group relationships.

[33] We have already considered the breakdown of tradition with respect to familial

Our urban population has rejected to some degree the domestic division of labor of our rural ancestors, but has not created its own universally accepted, culturally sanctioned substitute set of routines. One obvious reason why universally approved routines have not arisen to replace those no longer suitable is that within our society there is such a diversity of living conditions. Let us imagine, for example, three married couples. All the husbands have comparable jobs in the same office, and two of the couples have no children. The first wife spends most of her time at her housework. The second wife has a full-time office job. The third wife is both a housewife and a mother of three children. The volume of work to be done in the three homes varies considerably, as does the amount of time available to the wives to take care of their domestic duties. In terms of the conditions stated, there is no variation in the amount of time available to the husbands to help with domestic chores; yet it is evident that the three wives have different degrees of need for the husband's help around the house. There are other conditions that cause variation in the amount of help with domestic chores a wife may expect of her husband: size of residence, ability to hire servants, amount of labor-saving equipment, degree to which such commercial services as laundries are used, her own conception of the husband's roles, the husband's conception of his roles, and so on. In the absence of culturally sanctioned routines, it is necessary for couples to improvise what we may call their own marital folkways and to develop their own private culture.

The schools in this country have undertaken to fill this instructional lacuna by offering units in the socialization into marital and other familial roles that our society has declined to provide in the more usual informal fashion within the family of orientation. Courses are offered under such titles as domestic science, home economics, and marriage and family life. The students are usually girls. When such courses depart from the purely practical (how to set a table, how to buy life insurance, and so on) into the problematic (content of the roles), the unstructured situation we are considering leaves the educators little option but to advocate "adaptability."[34]

A second source of difficulty in adjusting to American marital roles arises from cultural discontinuities. What are our adolescents taught that they must unlearn? To some extent the peer culture of adolescence emphasizes traits that attract the opposite sex—masculine daring and feminine charm—rather than domestic or other instrumental skills. Our previous analysis implies a tendency for young couples to generate expectations that their own marriages must be more exciting than the routines they observe in their parents' marriages. Such expectations create a negative set toward the routines useful in the efficient management of the home and thereby useful in defining marital roles.

---

roles in general and with respect to child rearing in particular in Chapters 12 and 14 above respectively.

[34] Ernest W. Burgess, "The Family in a Changing Society," *American Journal of Sociology*, 53: 417–422 (1948).

A third source of difficulty arises when husband and wife have learned different expectations as to the nature and content of marital roles. Such differences arise when the spouses are not from the same ethnoreligious background, or social class, or even region of the country. If the two spouses agree on the definitions of the roles of husband and of wife, on the rights and responsibilities that attend each role, they cannot suffer a lack of role-adjustment from this third source. If, in addition, they worship the same god and with the same level of devotion, have the same ideas about the optimum number of children and techniques of child rearing, have similar notions about the meaning of money, and like the same foods, they have a good deal of cultural similarity. The positive side of cultural similarity is that it provides the basis for a host of common definitions, understandings, and interests; stated negatively, there are many questions their common culture has settled for them, and hence there is small likelihood of diversity in ways of handling these questions, diversity that might otherwise lay the basis for marital conflict. Kirkpatrick cites several studies as showing "limited but strong evidence in support of ethnic homogamy and similarity of religious faith as favorable" to marital adjustment.[35]

While considering subcultural differences between the spouses, it is appropriate to digress to comment further on mixed marriages—a topic that seems to be confronting a large number of American college students. In Chapter 10 we have considered the problem quantitatively, i.e., how frequently various types of mixed marriages occur in this country. The present passage considers some consequences for the marital relationship.

We may think of a mixed marriage as a marriage wherein the husband and wife belong to different socially defined categories. Usually such categories have distinguishable subcultures. In Chapter 10 the major dimensions of such differentiation were set forth as race, ethnoreligion, and socioeconomic status.

Broadly speaking, two kinds of problem may arise: one involves the attitudes of the spouses themselves and is therefore amenable to resolution by their action; the other is generated by attitudes of people in their community, and therefore is less subject to the control of the couple involved.

In the first category arises the sort of problem that confronts a couple having different religions. If the spouses are of different Protestant faiths, say, or if one is Catholic and the other Protestant,[36] they have a problem as to whether they will or will not resolve their difference in religious commitment. The problem may arise early in their courtship, but at the latest, as we have noted above, it seems sure to come to a head at the time of beginning the religious instruction of the first child. Christensen points out that in mixed

---

[35] Clifford Kirkpatrick, *The Family* (2d ed.; New York: Ronald, 1963), pp. 388–389.

[36] This example involves the assumption that a marriage between persons of different religions will not outrage the community. For the present and in this country the assumption seems generally to be valid.

marriages there are some people who put their faith first and others who put their love first.[37] If both spouses are of the former type, the house seems destined to remain divided in religious loyalty; if one or both are of the latter, presumably religious unity is achievable. (Incidentally, another, and infrequently noted, kind of mixed marriage in one sense arises when one spouse is devout and the other is an agnostic or an atheist.)

If one spouse is black and the other white, the problem of resolving the double identity into a single identity is no longer entirely within the control of the couple. The adverb "entirely" denotes the fact that if the couple is free to move, some control is possible, for such a couple would be much more able to establish a single identity in Greenwich Village than in Jackson, Mississippi.

The level of difficulty presented by either type of problem is directly proportional to the importance placed on it by the people involved. It would appear that with respect to the first type—those involving the attitudes of the spouses—problems of religious faith are the most difficult to resolve, and that the more devout and therefore committed the spouses are to their different faiths, the more painful is the resolution. With respect to the second type, i.e., where community attitudes are involved, it seems that, at present, race is the most important category of differentiation; in communities where race is important the most obvious adjustment is for one spouse to "pass" as a member of the other's racial category, which is a manner of denying that the problem exists. In general, then, we may note the implication that the "importance" of a problem of either type to some actor is that he behaves "intolerantly" with respect to it. Having concluded our digression on mixed marriages, let us return to the consideration of role-adjustment.

At this point let us recall the discussion of "Familial Roles and Role-Strain" in Chapter 12. The enactment of a role is affected not only by the actor's knowledge of that role but also by the pressure the actor may feel to enact some other role and by the relative gratification and frustration that the actor has experienced in the two roles. Probably one of the oldest dramatic themes has to do with the dilemma of an actor facing mutually contradictory claims, e.g., love versus duty. The competition of occupation and of family for the time and energies of the husband-father is an example of role-strain remarked in Chapter 12. Of course, a parallel remark can be made concerning competing claims on the middle-class wife-mother of family versus PTA, club, civic organization, fund raising, and the life. And of course the working mother feels even more than the father the strain of competing demands. Nor are offspring immune to such problems: many undergraduates feel a "duty" to spend a holiday at home when confronted with an opportunity to engage in a more exciting activity.

It should not be thought that role-strain within the family always involves extrafamilial claims. The definitions of roles within a family can develop so

---

[37] Harold T. Christensen, *Marriage Analysis* (2d ed.; New York: Ronald, 1958), p. 296.

that two or more members find themselves in a situation of role-strain. One example would be a wife-mother whose husband and son both seek to monopolize her time and attention and who see each other as competitor for her affection. Another source of intrafamilial role-strain is dissensus as to whether marital solidarity takes precedence over filial solidarity or vice versa; this is a sociological phrasing that subsumes the "mother-in-law problem." The resolution of such problems requires a consensually supported redefinition of roles within the family.

Finally, from our belief that the functions give definition to marital roles, it should follow that the functions also point to the important problems of adjustment. Marginally supporting evidence in favor of this inference comes from a study showing that the way in which spouses evaluate their marriages correlates highly with the degree of adjustment in areas they specify as important (family expenditures, household duties, philosophy of life, and rearing children) while hardly correlating at all with adjustment in areas considered less important (for example, relations with in-laws, religious observances).[38]

PSYCHIC (OR EMOTIONAL) ADJUSTMENT

The initial studies on marital adjustment were carried out by American middle-class researchers with white American middle-class subjects. Even though some subsequent studies have used samples more representative of an entire population, and others have used such different categories of subjects as Swedes, Chinese, and black Americans, the results have usually been presented in the light of their conformity to or deviation from the previously reported findings on the white American middle class.[39]

Since the subculture of the American middle class emphasizes that the marital relationship should be a source of affectional-emotional gratifications, psychic adjustment to marriage is important in this setting. Our previous analysis has concluded that there are certain aspects of personality that are especially relevant to familial, including marital, gratifications: the dimension of dependence-independence and the needs for nurturance and control. Accordingly we shall consider psychic adjustment in marriage with respect to these variables.

---

[38] Charles E. Bowerman, "Adjustment in Marriage: Over-All and in Specific Areas," *Sociology and Social Research*, 41: 257–263 (1957).

[39] Harvey J. Locke and Georg Karlsson, "Marital Adjustment and Prediction in Sweden and the United States," *American Sociological Review*, 17: 10–17 (1952); Georg Karlsson, *Adaptability and Communication in Marriage: A Swedish Predictive Study of Marital Satisfaction* (Uppsala: Almqvist & Wiksells Boktryckeri Aktiebolag, 1951); Charles E. King, "The Burgess-Cottrell Method of Measuring Marital Adjustment Applied to a Non-White Southern Urban Population," *Marriage and Family Living*, 14: 280–285 (1952); Atlee L. Stroup, "Predicting Marital Success or Failure in an Urban Population," *American Sociological Review*, 18: 558–562. A study that uses implicitly the upper middle class of London as a standard is Eliot Slater and Moya Woodside, *Patterns of Marriage: A Study of Marriage Relationships in the Urban Working Classes* (London: Cassell, 1951).

From time to time we have considered the concept of independence and conditions presumed to favor it.[40] We may speak of a person as being dependent to the degree that his sources of gratification are controlled by the behavior of others and independent to the degree that he controls the sources of his gratification. It can be seen that the optimum level of dependence-independence is somewhere between "too dependent" and "too independent." A person who is "too dependent" would make greater demands on the love-object than a mortal other could meet. Being self-sufficient, a "too independent" individual would have little or no need for a love-object. In Chapter 18 it was noted that secondary analysis of the case materials in the study of complementary needs resulted in the hypothesis that the needs for nurturance and for control were fundamental determinants in mate-selection. Hence we shall think of these needs as providing key motivations in terms of which to assess levels of dependence and independence.

In the categories used in the study of complementary needs the most dependent husbands are those in "mother-son" marriages, and the most dependent wives are in "Ibsenian" relationships. Prototypically the independent spouse in these two types of mate-selection loves to work to provide for all the wants of the dependent spouse and also seeks to relieve the dependent spouse of all responsibility for making decisions. At the time of observation these marriages seemed to be stable. It will be recalled that they were studied soon after marriage and before the arrival of children. Instability of equilibrium might be expected with an increase in the load of dependent demands, i.e., with the advent of children and perhaps even with the initial awareness of the first pregnancy.

The degree of a person's independence—or one's invulnerability to feelings of frustration and deprivation—is apparently related not only to the total amount of one's dependent demands but also to the diversity of one's modes of gratification. A "well-rounded" person is one whose sources of gratification are diverse. The ideal-typical romantic adolescent is one who seeks all gratification in one all-consuming passion. Just as the investor with what the brokers call a "diversified portfolio" is minimally exposed to the caprices of the stock market and business conditions, so the person with diversified interests is less exposed to frustration by any one person—and hence is less dependent on that person—than is the romantic. This does not imply that one should make no emotional investment in a spouse. On the one hand, if a person projects all his emotional needs onto a single love-object, he is exposed to almost inevitable frustration because of the inability of any person to meet the needs of another so totally. But, on the other hand, if he projects no need onto the love-object, he stands to derive no gratification from that love-object.

Indeed, from our definition of love it follows that with no need directed

---

[40] See, especially, "How Scientific Have Been the Advice-Givers?" in Chapter 14, numerous sections in Chapters 16 and 17, "Behavior Arises from Needs" in Chapter 18, and "Cultural Definition Not Necessarily a Lifelong Ideal" in Chapter 20.

toward another person and hence with no expectation of gratification from that person, there can be no love and hence no love-object. To maximize the ratio of gratification to frustration within any relationship, therefore, one should project one's needs onto the love-object to the degree that the love-object gives promise of meeting those needs. Thus the optimum degree of dependence-independence vis-à-vis the love-object lies somewhere in the range of greater independence than that of our ideal-typical romantic adolescent, and of less independence than that of the person who projects no needs—makes no emotional demands—on the love-object.

In a sense we may think of the process of psychic adjustment on the part of a man to a specific woman, or on the part of a woman to a specific man, as beginning at the moment of their meeting, or perhaps even earlier if they have known each other by reputation. The process of becoming acquainted involves taking some note of the degree and nature of pleasure and/or pain in one's own responses to the behaviors of the other. We have seen that the dating-"going steady"-engagement sequence provides opportunities for each party to interact and to note the degree and nature of the gratifications and frustrations derived from their interaction. It seems clear that the better each knows the other, the better he will be able to evaluate the degree to which the other will provide for his need-gratification. On the other hand, if couples marry on short acquaintance, it follows that the knowledge each has of the other and of his own reactions to the behavior of the other is partial and fragmentary. Accordingly, they may develop what Waller calls "delusive solidarity,"[41] based upon an unreal, idealized conception of each other. It comes as no surprise, therefore, that there is empirical evidence that the marital adjustment of husbands and of wives is positively related to the duration of their premarital acquaintance.[42]

Having taken an excursion into some of the intricacies of needs and dependence-independence, we may now ask precisely what we mean by psychic adjustment in marriage. Viewed from the standpoint of either spouse, the answer may be stated in two parts. We may conceive perfect psychic adjustment to be achieved (1) when the behavior of each spouse toward the other expresses only such needs and at such intensity that the other is capable of gratifying them, and (2) when the behavior of each spouse is actually providing this gratification for the other. It is immediately evident that psychic adjustment involves the relationship between two idiosyncratic indivduals, i.e., that a person achieves psychic adjustment with a particular other who is his spouse—not with marriage in general nor with a marital role in general.

As far as can be observed, perfect psychic adjustment is never achieved. Apparently everyone frustrates his or her mate to some degree. Acknowledging the inevitability of imperfection, we may state that the achievement of psychic adjustment in marriages involves, on the part of each spouse, (1) recognizing

---

[41] *Op. cit.*, p. 296.
[42] Kirkpatrick, *op. cit.*, pp. 387–389.

and accepting that perfect psychic adjustment is illusory; (2) to the extent that he is capable, developing patterns of interactive behavior that will provide maximum gratification and minimum frustration for the other; and (3) developing interactive behavior patterns that will "handle" frustrations in the least destructive way.

Let us consider these conditions point by point. It is clear that until each spouse recognizes and accepts the proposition that his mate cannot fully meet his every emotional demand, he is doomed to frustration. A further necessary aspect of emotional realism is the recognition that one cannot meet all the needs of one's spouse and that sometimes one will frustrate her (or him).

Once the counsel of imperfection is accepted, the way is clear to follow up its implications. No matter how long or intimate the period of premarital acquaintance, it still seems that most people learn a good deal about the personalities of their spouses after marriage. As this learning goes on, one can see what things he or she can do to provide greater gratification and less frustration for the spouse.[43]

When a person is frustrated in marriage or in any other interpersonal relationship, he may react in any one of a variety of ways. He may withdraw, which means that, for a time at least, he declines to continue interacting with the frustrating person. He may sulk, which not only means that he declines to interact, but also that he registers his resentment while doing so. He may repress an aggressive reaction, which means that he is not conscious of the aggressive nature of his reaction, although he may betray its aggressive content by unwitting behavior. He may suppress an aggressive reaction, which means that although he has a lively awareness of his feelings, he succeeds in concealing them in his overt behavior. He may "explode," which means that he gives overt expression to an aggressive reaction.[44]

Each of these modes of reaction has its disadvantage. If the reaction is unconsciously inhibited, neurotic symptoms may develop. If it is consciously inhibited, resentment is harbored and "grudges" are built up. If it is overtly expressed, interpersonal conflict may be expected. Proceeding on the assumption that it is in the interest of long-range adjustment, some writers on the subject of marriage encourage their readers to "fight constructively." To this writer such advice seems about as ill-advised as prescribing castor oil for every child with a stomach-ache. If there were assurance that domestic "fights" would always drain off the animosities that initiate them, such a policy might be defensible—although painful in the short run. The obvious disadvantage

---

[43] One who overdoes in an effort to "please" the spouse, however, may develop a "martyr complex." From Ross's "law of personal exploitation" it would be expected that the "overpleasing" spouse would be the one more involved in the marriage. See note 5, page 545 above.

[44] Displacement is another way of reacting to this situation. This is a favorite subject of cartoons in the form of the man who docilely bears harassments by his wife but who is insufferably punitive with his subordinates on the job.

of such a policy is that in the heat of battle hostile remarks may be made that will leave permanent scars of resentment.

The problem of adjusting to the frustrations that do occur in marriage is one of trying to remove (or ventilate) the reaction without causing permanent damage to the relationship. Favorable conditions exist for releasing such tensions in marital interaction if each spouse is a relatively nonhostile person generally and is relatively secure and hence not easily offended. Given these conditions, the opportunity exists for each unrancorously to communicate his or her frustrations to the other, and for the latter to comprehend her or his role in frustrating the former. Here we may note the importance of joking and of a sense of humor. If the frustrated person can ventilate his frustration by means of a joke, and if the joke is not so barbed that the frustrating person is injured, then the atmosphere is cleared and neither party will nurture his resentment.[45]

Whether marital disputes are handled by serious discussion or by means of joking, it is clear that they can be dealt with most amicably when tempers are cool and when each tries earnestly to understand the behavior and feelings of the other. It is one of the ironies of interpersonal relationships that such techniques of resolving marital tension and conflict are least available to those who most need them—the hostile and insecure.

CHANGING ROLES AND NEED-PATTERNS AND THE MARITAL RELATIONSHIP

At the present state of our knowledge it is difficult, if not impossible, to try to foresee the degree and nature of the changes that will take place in each member of a couple, but it is possible to predict certain broad trends of change. For both men and women it appears that the different stages in the life cycle typically involve changes in duties and in gratifications, in roles, and in need-patterns.

Until the coming of children the marital dyad is frequently a congeniality group. The arrival of children necessitates the undertaking of the parental functions, with which we were concerned in Part Five, and the taking up of these functions, it seems, eliminates some of the opportunity for spouses to interact with each other. In their study of Detroit wives, Blood and Wolfe found what they called an "unmistakable trend" to the effect that with the coming of children husband and wife ceased to do things together and began to "grow apart" from each other.[46]

---

[45] Anthropologists speak of institutionalized "joking" relations between kinsmen in certain types of relationship. Cf., e.g., George Peter Murdock, *Social Structure* (New York: Macmillan, 1949), pp. 275 ff. A formulation relating hostility and humor appears in Sigmund Freud, *Wit and Its Relation to the Unconscious*, in *The Basic Writings of Sigmund Freud* (New York: Modern Library, 1938), pp. 631–803.

[46] *Husbands and Wives* (New York: Free Press, 1960), p. 174. Translated into Bott's language this finding might read that the coming of children results in a "segregated

After a somewhat modest start the American middle-class male typically expects that the years will bring him promotion, recognition, and increasing monetary rewards. To the extent that he is successful, he builds to a zenith of accomplishment and esteem at the point of his retirement, which comes upon him as an unwelcome and empty postlude to a full and demanding life. Because of the disappearance of the important occupational role, the wife assumes a newly discovered significance when the husband turns sixty-five or so.

For the woman the early years are busy ones if she works before the first baby and then sets about learning the trade of motherhood. As the last child enters high school, the woman enters the semiretirement resulting from the gradual termination of her important role as mother. Her retirement comes earlier than her husband's—while she is in her forties—and since employment is not categorical in the role of mother, her retirement also comes more gradually. Before she turns forty-five the life cycle of the family eliminates motherhood as an active role for the woman and thereby increases for her the residual importance of the marital role. Let us note that this event occurs some fifteen to twenty years earlier for the wife than for the husband.

Modifications in need-patterns seem to be particularly evident in people who emerge from humble origins to positions of fame and eminence. As the author has written elsewhere:

> Such seems to have been the story of the marriage of Sinclair Lewis and Grace Hegger as reported in the caustic accounts of both: his *Dodsworth*, and her *Half a Loaf* and *With Love from Gracie*. At the time of their meeting Sinclair Lewis admired Grace Hegger's cosmopolitanism. She states that in their early relationship he tended to regard her as a Princess of Faraway and himself as a sort of court jester. Her idea of a man who could sweep her off her feet had been a decorated and haughty ambassador. This sounds like an idealized version of her father, a traveled and sophisticated art dealer. Then why did she marry the awkward, homely, "penniless publisher's editor with one unaccepted novel"? "I married him because he touched my heart and delighted my brain." And at another point: ". . . no other man had ever made me feel so tenderly possessive." In her fictional account of their relationship she indicates that her wedding day was less thrilling than the day she won her major promotion at *Vogue* magazine. She points out that from *Mr. Wrenn* to *Dodsworth* Lewis's heroes "either married ladies" or made efforts to adjust themselves to the social standards of the ladies they admired. In other words both Lewis and his heroes were attracted to women of higher social status who observed social amenities rather unknown to the men. Moreover, she observes that the "resentments and personal inadequacies" of Sam Dodsworth "were really those of Sinclair Lewis."
>
> Their final parting was apparently initiated by Lewis. According to Grace Hegger his statement was to the effect that he loved her more than anyone else but that she had become "extraordinarily bullying," that

conjugal role relationship."—Elizabeth Bott, *Family and Social Network: Roles, Norms, and External Relationships in Ordinary Urban Families* (London: Tavistock, 1957), p. 55.

she had deprived him of "self-government," and that he wished no more to ask her permission, to await her plans, or to resent her orders. Lewis was perpetually animated by wanderlust, and his wife began to wish to sink roots. She feels that probably she imposed this need for security and routine on her restless husband, and that her importuning undoubtedly "made him even more restless and eager to escape." She concludes her account of their relationship by observing that through it "he experienced an interval of domestic security indispensable to his development, though in the later years he called it tyranny."[47]

No doubt Lewis was giving his side of the case when he observed that Fran Dodsworth "had a high art of deflating him [Sam Dodsworth], of enfeebling him, with one quick, innocent-sounding phrase . . . by crisply suggesting that he 'try for once to talk about *something* besides motors and stocks,' while they rode to a formidable dinner . . . she could make him feel so unintelligent that he would be silent all evening."[48]

Unfortunately no systematic study has been made of changes in need-patterns. The remarks that follow are based on clinical impressions plus more or less common-sense deductions from the obvious fact that both occupational and familial roles have life cycles. Although the Lewis case is certainly not typical, it does contain elements that are not infrequent in the middle class. A young newly married male of the middle class is typically at the beginning of his career and about to undertake the long climb to success in his vocation. The length of the road, the height of its eminence, and his doubts concerning his own capacity cause him to feel unsure and insecure. Dominant in his emotional pattern may be a need for nurturance in the form of reassurance and encouragement. If he begins gradually to achieve success, acknowledgment of his accomplishments will come to him increasingly from his business or professional associates and from others outside the home. Perhaps he will come to the conclusion that his wife does not adequately symbolize his success, that what he needs is a younger, better dressed, more glamorous wife whose appearance would be more consonant with the other luxuries now coming within his reach. If he is finding considerable gratification in the recognition that comes from outside the home, this new source of gratification may reduce the degree to which he looks to his wife for need-gratification. In terms of our need theory of love, this means a commensurate reduction in the degree of love. Whether he is or is not finding sufficient gratification in the extrafamilial recognition, nevertheless he may no longer desire a wife who will offer him encouragement in a maternal sort of way, but one who will provide recognition in the form of the you-great-big-wonderful-man adulation.

The occupational success of the husband may also stimulate the psychic maladjustment of the wife. During the early years some couples arrive at a conception of their roles that involves substantial cooperation by the wife in

[47] Robert F. Winch, *Mate-Selection* (New York: Harper & Row, 1958), pp. 302–303.
[48] Sinclair Lewis, *Dodsworth* (New York: Modern Library, 1947), pp. 23–24.

the career of the husband—perhaps through helping to pay for his professional education or through her actual participation in a business. Then as he becomes successful, it seems appropriate for her to withdraw to more traditionally feminine activities. If she is one who has been strong in the motivations to be nurturant and controlling and especially if it has been a "mother-son" marriage, she may begin to feel that his success is leaving her roleless. A further set of circumstances that can reduce the wife's adjustment consequent upon the husband's advancement occurs where a woman of somewhat unconventional ideas and tastes is called upon to do more and more entertaining of her husband's business associates and to behave generally in accordance with the conventions of the "company wife."[49]

Another way in which the need-patterns can fall out of adjustment is for the man to fail to make the expected vocational progress and to continue to look to his wife for nurturance after she has begun to bear children and is directing most or all of her nurturance upon them. The maturing of the children may present an additional emotional problem, for unless she and her husband draw back together at that time, she may find herself thwarted in the expression of her "need to be needed."

As we have seen, the theory of complementary needs asserts that in mate-selection one seeks the individual who gives the greatest promise of meeting one's needs. If we accept this idea plus the further idea that need-patterns change, then it would seem likely that after some years of marriage many couples would experience reduction in the emotional gratification being derived from the marital relationship. There are studies to support such an expectation. Pineo reports a gradual shift from the euphoria of early marriage to disenchantment in later years.[50]

Running through these observations has been the hypothesis that the more or less unforeseeable course of one's experience has its impact on one's need-pattern. As Waller observed, "Premarital agreements could perhaps be made to work if each person could be a Joshua to his own motives and arrest the processes of change within himself."[51] These observations indicate that running through the life cycle of the marriage there are changes that call for adjustment—with respect to role as well as psyche. From this it follows that an important ingredient in marital adjustment is continued self-analysis and sensitivity to the shifting needs of the spouse. These observations imply that in this day, when the decline of the traditional elements leaves the marital

---

[49] Cf. William H. Whyte, Jr., "The Wife Problem," in Robert F. Winch and Louis Wolf Goodman (eds.), *Selected Studies in Marriage and the Family* (3d ed.; New York: Holt, Rinehart and Winston, Inc., 1968), pp. 177–178. For an informal account, see "I Hate My Husband's Success," as told to Alice Lake, *McCall's*, July 1958, pp. 25, 104–105.

[50] Peter C. Pineo, "Disenchantment in the Later Years of Marriage," *Marriage and Family Living*, 23: 3–11 (1961). Cf. also Eleanore Braun Luckey, "Number of Years Married as Related to Personality Perception and Marital Satisfaction," *Journal of Marriage and the Family*, 28: 44–48 (1966).

[51] Waller, op. cit., p. 306.

relationship relatively unstructured, individual adaptability and dyadic improvisation become important in producing workable marriages.[52]

These remarks have had bearing on the course of marital love over the years, a topic to which we now turn our attention. That marriage is an intimate relationship is a truism that holds with special force in a society such as ours, which emphasizes the nuclear family and de-emphasizes the extended family, which values conjugal over filial solidarity. As a husband and wife go through many experiences together—the establishing of a home, the bearing and rearing of children, the hopes and rewards, the successes and failures of a career, the joys and tragedies of a family—there are apparently two consequences: they learn to anticipate each other's responses, and they seem to become more like each other in their responses. On the first of these points Blood and Wolfe remark: ". . . sheer living together provides the basic condition for understanding another person. The longer a man lives with a woman, the greater his accumulated store of memories of how she behaves, what upsets her, and what will make her feel better. The wisdom of experience enables him to read her facial expressions more accurately, to sense her silences, to interpret her sighs. Hearing her troubles becomes less necessary, since he can read her thoughts without words."[53]

From the romantic point of view such a state of affairs is regrettable: each spouse is ceasing to be a "mystery" to the other and is coming to take the other for granted. From a task-oriented point of view such a state of affairs is highly desirable; one of the purposes of practice for an athletic team or rehearsal for an orchestra is to enable the individual performers to mesh their performances so well that they can take each other for granted.

With respect to the second consequence of intimacy, each spouse comes to see that in some situations the other perceives some phenomena or problems a little more clearly or somehow responds a bit more effectively. Unless there are inhibiting influences, therefore, it seems inevitable that each spouse will learn from the other, and with the passage of time and the prolonging of this process they should become more and more like each other.

To pursue the relation between love and time let us consider love in three relationships: of an adult offspring for his parent, of one lover for another, and of one spouse for his or her mate.

An adult's love for a parent is perhaps best captured by the word "fondness." And so we ask, what is fondness? Normally for an adult the intense interaction with the parent is history. Then the emotional response of the adult to his parent is a reaction to past experiences—gratifications and frustrations. To the extent that one holds a parent in fond regard it would appear that one feels in the present an affect that is more positive than negative in tone—a fondness based upon a retrospective glow of appreciation over past gratifications.

---

[52] Burgess, "The Family in a Changing Society," *loc. cit.*, pp. 417–422.
[53] *Op. cit.*, p. 218.

The obvious qualitative difference between the fondness for a parent and the passionate love-hate, ecstasy-melancholy of the lover who is newly in love is generally ascribed to the absence in the former and the presence in the latter of youth and sex. The latter two nouns shed some light on the difference between the two kinds of love, it seems, but by themselves these nouns fail to provide a very complete analysis. When phrased in the language of complementary needs, the sexual element points to prospective gratifications of a high degree of intensity; and the element of youth usually implies a relationship of uncertain duration between inexperienced individuals of very limited security. The gratifications to be derived from such a relationship appear to lie largely in the future. Since those newly in love are responding largely to the anticipation of the future meeting of needs, since the young have good grounds for being unsure, since the future is always uncertain, and since the potential gratifications include some of high intensity, the prospective lover tends to be panting and passionate.

Intermediate between the placid fondness of the former relationship and the panting passion of the latter is the love of one spouse for another. To the extent that the marital relationship has proved an emotional success each has a history of having been gratified by the other and each has an expectation of a future that will continue the course of gratification. In one sense the difference between the fondness for a parent and the passion over a lover is the difference between the memory of gratification and the prospect of gratification, the difference between retrospective and prospective love. It follows that marital love should involve both fondness and passion, but also that the degree of security in marital love should mitigate the amount of panting.[54]

MEASURING AND PREDICTING MARITAL ADJUSTMENT

From the foregoing discussion it should be obvious that marital adjustment is a varied and subtle concept. Accordingly, measuring it is a difficult task. Serious work on the measurement of marital adjustment began in 1929 with the study of G. V. Hamilton,[55] and continued through the 1930's with the researches of Jessie Bernard,[56] Lewis M. Terman,[57] and Burgess and Cottrell.[58] The last of these was a pilot study for a more ambitious research

---

[54] For a somewhat related discussion see the treatment of Simone Signoret with special reference to her role in the English film *Room at the Top* in Marya Mannes, "The Age for Love," *Esquire*, May 1960, pp. 135–136, 138.

[55] G. V. Hamilton, *A Research in Marriage* (New York: Boni, 1929).

[56] Jessie Bernard, "Factors in the Distribution of Success in Marriage," *American Journal of Sociology*, 40: 49–60 (1934).

[57] Lewis M. Terman *et al.*, *Psychological Factors in Marital Happiness* (New York: McGraw-Hill, 1938).

[58] Ernest W. Burgess and Leonard S. Cottrell, Jr., *Predicting Success or Failure in Marriage* (Englewood Cliffs, N.J.: Prentice-Hall, 1939).

—larger in scale and longitudinal in method—on the prediction of marital adjustment by Burgess and Wallin.[59]

The approach of these studies has been to ask married people how happy they are in their marriages and simultaneously to ask them a number of questions that the researchers anticipate may be related to marital happiness. Usually the questions pertain to the following topics: the respondent's background, especially his recollections of his relations with his parents and his perceptions of them; such social characteristics as socioeconomic status, ethno-religious affiliation, and so on; interaction with the spouse, including areas of common interest and of disagreement; and the personality of the respondent: whether or not he is easily injured, usually cheerful, and the like. Answers to these questions were then compared with the respondents' statements as to the degree of their marital "happiness" or "adjustment," and conclusions were drawn regarding factors in the backgrounds, social characteristics, and personalities of husbands and wives that were found in successful marriages. The information on current marital interaction was used to build more elaborate measures of marital satisfaction.

Before turning to the findings of these studies, we should note that they have been criticized for methodological defects. The criticisms may be summarized under the following points:

1. Ambiguity as to the nature of the dependent variable. Is the researcher investigating marital adjustment, marital success, or marital happiness? It will be recalled that distinctions among these terms were made on pages 550–551 above. Sometimes additional terms appear to compound the confusion: marital cohesion, marital integration, and the like.

2. Measurement of the dependent variable. If adjustment is being studied, can it be assumed that the respondent has a sufficiently clear comprehension as to the term's denotation that he can give a valid answer to the direct question as to how adjusted he is? If it is happiness that is being studied, should the rating be made on the basis of the respondent's subjective feeling or on the absence of marital conflict? Moreover, the concept of happiness involves such difficulties as person-to-person differences concerning the nature of happiness, the possibility that happiness is a temperamental characteristic of the person rather than a property of the marriage, and that one's happiness may be determined to a considerable degree by factors external to the marriage. If overt conflict should be used as a negative criterion, then couples who seldom interact should rate high on adjustment. If the ratings of friends are used, another source of error enters the problem. There are great differences among people in terms of the sophistication with which they observe others, and in the degree of intimacy of friends and the extent of their knowledge of the marriages upon which they might be asked to report. To some extent these difficulties can be mitigated if we assume that a sophisticated research worker

[59] *Op. cit.*

can make his own assessments on the basis of his own observations. Even here, however, it is difficult to set up criteria with a wide range of applicability. For example, it is a matter of common observation that there is considerable variation among social classes in the expression of physical violence in domestic disputes. Should we view the dish-throwing couple as more or less "adjusted" or "happy" than the restrained couple, each member of which pours out his resentments to a psychoanalyst? To date the important studies in this area have tended to use as criteria self-ratings and friends' ratings on happiness.

3. *Ambiguity as to the unit of investigation.* (This may be related to ambiguity as to the nature of the dependent variable.) Is the unit an individual spouse or a married couple? Some studies have taken responses from one spouse in each couple and have interpreted the responses as though they reflected the attitudes and behavior of the couple. Other studies have undertaken to get testimony from both spouses but have made insufficient provision for the prevention of the contamination of responses. For example, a person filling in a questionnaire with a spouse looking on may give responses somewhat different from those he might give if responding without an interested onlooker.

4. *Disposition of respondents to slant their answers in a "respectable" direction.* The point of this criticism is the belief that some respondents give answers different from what they "really" believe, that they seek to portray themselves as respectable in terms of American middle-class values, and thus to say "nice" things about themselves, their spouses, and their relationship to each other, to portray themselves as conventional persons satisfying social expectations concerning spouses "in terms of agreement, affection, harmony, comradeship, responsibility, and stability."[60] Technically speaking, the effect of the desire to appear properly conventional creates a response set that makes test reliability spuriously high and lowers test validity.

5. *Sampling.* Some of the studies have used as respondents anyone the researchers could persuade to cooperate. An aggregate of such respondents does not entitle the researcher to generalize to any meaningful population. In such studies the respondents have generally tended to be those readily accessible to the professors doing the studies and therefore living in or near university towns and having more than the average amount of formal education. It may be surmised that such a basis of selection may result in overrepresenting two kinds of people: those who are somewhat better adjusted in their marriages than the average and thus are quite willing to talk about their marriages, and those who are hoping to obtain advice and wish to talk about their "problems." More recent studies have used more exotic aggregates of respondents—Chinese, American blacks, Swedes, and so on—and in some cases much effort has gone into improving the sampling procedure.

A summary of marriage studies done up through World War II shows a

[60] Clifford Kirkpatrick, *The Family* (1st ed.; New York: Ronald, 1955), pp. 342–343.

considerable number of factors that have been found to be related to marital adjustment, marital success, or marital happiness.[61] An analysis of the summary showed that

> Of 152 factors reported to be related to marital adjustment, success, or happiness, only one quarter had been confirmed in a second study.
> Of the 12 of these that were best supported by marriage studies it was found that
>> 1 had been confirmed in 5 out of 6 trials (i.e., had failed to be confirmed in 1 out of 6 studies).
>> 2 had been confirmed in 4 out of 5 trials.
>> 5 had been confirmed in 3 out of 3 trials.
>> 1 had been confirmed in 3 out of 4 trials.
>> 2 had been confirmed in 3 out of 5 trials.
>> 1 had been confirmed in 3 out of 6 trials.[62]

These results, says Hill, indicate "the paucity of our knowledge about the factors making marital success. . . . We are forced to conclude that the marriage texts have 'jumped the gun' in incorporating these findings centrally into the teaching content of marriage and family classes."[63]

The same sociologist who prepared the summary referred to in the previous paragraph has published in his revised family text of 1963 a more up-to-date compilation of results of studies. After an intensive review of the evidence it is his impression that the following factors have shown the strongest and most consistent association with high marital adjustment:

A. Factors operating before the marriage
  1. Happiness of parents' marriage
  2. Adequate length of acquaintance, courtship, and engagement
  3. Adequate sex information in childhood
  4. Personal happiness in childhood
  5. Approval of the marriage by parents and others
  6. Adjustment in engagement and normal motivation toward marriage
  7. Ethnic and religious similarity
  8. High social and educational status
  9. Maturity (marriage in the late twenties rather than the teens or early twenties) and similar chronological age of the spouses.
  10. Harmonious affection with parents during childhood

B. Factors operating in the marriage
  1. Early and adequate orgasm capacity, especially of the wife
  2. Confidence in spouse's affection and satisfaction with degree of affection shown
  3. Equalitarian rather than patriarchal marital relationship, with special reference to the role of husband

---

[61] Clifford Kirkpatrick, *What Science Says about Happiness in Marriage* (Minneapolis: Burgess, 1947).
[62] Waller, *op. cit.*, p. 358.
[63] *Ibid.*, pp. 357, 359.

4. Mental and physical health
5. Harmonious companionship based on common interests and accompanied by a favorable attitude toward the marriage and the spouse[64]

More or less the same kinds of items have been used to predict marital happiness or adjustment as have been used to measure it in the present. The magnitude of the correlation between the scores taken at the two times is used to gauge the accuracy of the prediction. Burgess and Wallin began their prediction study by setting up the concept of "engagement success." Their criterion for success in engagement was that the couple married. (They realized, of course, the feasibility of regarding as successful an engagement wherein a mismated couple might decide against marriage.) Their prediction index (or "engagement success" score) was a composite of items pertaining to such matters as absence of regret about and not having contemplated breaking the engagement, satisfaction with partner, degree of confiding in the partner, frequency of and satisfaction with demonstration of affection, common leisure-time interests, and agreements in several areas.[65] They found that the correlation between the prediction scores and the marital adjustment scores based on responses taken in the early years of marriage was +.39 for men and +.36 for women.[66]

When we realize that a correlation as large as .40 leaves 84 percent of the variation statistically "unexplained" $[= 100\ (1 - .40^2)]$, it can be seen that though a beginning may have been made in the predictive direction, there is a long way to go. And the significance of even this modest accomplishment may be diminished if we take account of the possibility that some of the obtained correlation may be the result of "response set," i.e., that "nice" people say "nice" things about themselves and their spouses both before and after their wedding day.

Summary

Marriage is a socially approved union of one or more men with one or more women in the relationship of husband and wife. It is usual for marriage to have the functions of position-conferring, sexual gratification, procreation, and emotional gratification. The emphasis upon one or another of these functions in the societal context gives definition to the marital roles in that setting.

---

[64] Kirkpatrick, *The Family* (2nd ed.; New York: Ronald, 1963), pp. 389, 394.
[65] Burgess and Wallin, *op. cit.*, p. 305.
[66] *Ibid.*, p. 548. For other predictive results see E. Lowell Kelly, "Concerning the Validity of Terman's Weights for Predicting Marital Happiness," *Psychological Bulletin*, 36: 202–203 (1939); Lewis M. Terman and Melita H. Oden, *The Gifted Child Grows Up: Twenty-Five Years Follow-up of a Superior Group* (Stanford, Calif.: Stanford University Press, 1947).

In the subculture of the American middle class there is special emphasis on emotional gratification.

In American society marital adjustment is thought to be a "problem." The mode of analysis of this book leads to the surmise that if a relationship frequently poses a problem of adjustment, there is considerable likelihood that it involves roles for which the actors are unprepared—either because they are untaught, mistaught, or taught differently from each other. It appears that difficulty in achieving marital role-adjustment proceeds from all three of these sources in American society. In addition there is a widespread "problem" of psychic adjustment in marriage. The life cycle of the marital relationship may bring about difficulties in both role-adjustment and psychic adjustment.

The empirical literature on marriage suffers from some ambiguity as to whether it is studying marital happiness, marital adjustment, or marital success, and it tends to blur all three into one vague concept. There are numerous studies on the factors believed to enter into marital happiness-adjustment-success. From studies based typically on urban middle-class subjects with more than average education it is reported that marital happiness-adjustment-success is positively correlated with such factors as (1) generally nonneurotic personalities of the spouses, (2) cultural homogeneity of the spouses, (3) amicable relations between each spouse and his parents, (4) the marital happiness of the spouses' parents, and (5) adequate length of the acquaintance, courtship, and engagement. Such research, however, is beset with so many pitfalls that it is impossible in the present state of the art to know whether any durable conclusions have been reached or whether those found to date will prove to be the artifactual consequences of the methods used.

PART SEVEN

Familial Disorganization and Reorganization:

concluding observations

American culture, it seems, fosters the expectation that life is and should be orderly and that families, like new automobiles, should run quietly and smoothly. Just as reflection brings the realization that jalopies, too, are part of our system of transportation, so it is important to realize that disorder is generally as natural as order, disease as natural as health, and that familial disorganization is not a recently spawned evil of the atomic age.

In Chapters 22 and 23 we consider an aspect of familial disorganization —marital dissolutions—which are a focus of American interest. Whatever the circumstances that lead up to it, marital dissolution may be viewed as a form of bereavement, and the response to bereavement, it is hypothesized, is related to the remaining spouse's previous balance of gratifications and frustrations. Just as most societies provide some relief for spouses in distressingly unhappy marriages, many societies also make provision for remarriage.

In the last chapter we return to the question as to whether or not the family in America is becoming more disorganized, and we note that the answer depends upon whether our conception of disorganization is moral, consensual, structural, or functional.

22

Marital Dissolution:
types, trends, and causes

Introduction

Death dissolves marriages everywhere, no matter what the features of the culture or the nature of the family. The *proportion* of marriages so dissolved, however, i.e., the proportion caused by death out of all marital dissolutions, is related to the culture and to the functions and structure of the family as well as to the mortality rate.

Our functional postulate leads us to expect attitudes toward the causes of marital dissolution to reveal something about the functions of the marital dyad. We saw in Chapter 2 that in the traditional Chinese family the wife had the two important tasks of bearing sons and of assisting her mother-in-law in the many categories of domestic work. In such a setting, where conjugal love is viewed as a fortuitous felicity rather than a *sine qua non* of marriage, it would seem strange if the marriage should be seriously threatened by the sexual infidelity of the husband. Rather, as we saw, the principal threats to the marriage came from the disapproval of the wife by her husband's mother and from the wife's failure to bear children.

No matter how absurd it appears to visitors from many lands, it is consistent with the importance of the function of emotional gratification in American middle-class marriage that love should be regarded as the most important criterion in mate-selection and that the disappearance of love should be viewed as ground for considering the termination of the marriage. In this context the chief significance of the sexual infidelity of a spouse is the implication of the formula: sex = love. The task of marital counseling is to train spouses not to frustrate but to gratify each other. The law, with its concept of guilt and its adversary procedure, seems curiously out of touch with the causes of marital dissolution.

Types of Marital Dissolution

Marriage can be broken by the death of one or both spouses or by the parting of the spouses. When we turn to marital dissolutions wherein both spouses survive, we find that in many societies, including our own, marriage is regarded as a civil contract and that the state specifies the conditions under which marriages may be dissolved. For this reason it is useful to distinguish between those dissolutions that are legally sanctioned and those that are not. Within the legally sanctioned dissolutions there are (1) the absolute divorce (*a vinculo matrimonii,* from the bonds of matrimony), which terminates the marriage and usually restores to at least one of the spouses the right to marry; (2) the limited divorce (*a mensa et thoro,* from bed and board), which accords legal recognition to the separate households but denies the parties the opportunity for legally sanctioned remarriage; and (3) the annulment, which asserts that owing to some condition existing at the time the couple was married no valid marriage could be contracted and therefore the parties are free to marry. (From a legalistic point of view neither limited divorce nor annulment is a legal dissolution of a marriage. In the former case the marriage remains in force; in the latter, there never was any marriage to dissolve.) Dissolutions of marriage occur in fact, whether or not legally recognized, when one party deserts the other and remains away, as well as when the two parties simply agree to live apart permanently.

The law concerning marital dissolution can be classified in the following fashion:[1]

1. In some countries marriage is completely indissoluble except by death. This is in conformity with the Canon Law of the Roman Catholic Church. Countries having this legal feature are heavily Catholic: Spain, Peru, Brazil, Colombia.[2]

2. A divorce is granted if it is shown that one party has been guilty of a grave violation of his marital obligations. Such is the situation in most states of the U.S.A., France, and many other countries.[3]

3. A divorce is granted if it is shown that the marriage is completely

---

[1] The classification is adapted from Max Rheinstein, "The Stability of the Family: A Report to the Director-General of UNESCO on the Colloquium on a Comparative Study of the Legal Means to Promote the Stability of the Family," *Annales de la Faculté de Droit d'Istanbul* (8th year; 1960), Vol. IX, No. 13, Part II, pp. 1–14.

[2] The Roman Catholic Church claims to be the one and only Church, established by Jesus Christ, and to have the "power of binding and loosing" couples in marriage. The Church teaches that it is the law of God that a consummated Christian marriage cannot be dissolved under any circumstances. For an authoritative statement of the Church's position see Patrick J. O'Mahony (ed.), *Catholics and Divorce* (Edinburgh: Nelson, 1959), esp. pp. 3, 26, 65, 75.

[3] This is spoken of as the system of *divorce sanction.*

broken in fact. In different ways this is the policy in Switzerland, the U.S.S.R., Yugoslavia, Poland, Germany, Rhode Island and Louisiana, and all the Scandinavian countries.[4]

4. Divorce by the mutual agreement of the parties. This is practiced nowhere in Europe. There is provision for it in the civil code of Belgium, but it is so hedged about with formalities that it is equivalent to (3) above. There is also provision for such divorce in Japanese law, but the practice seems to make it the equivalent to "divorce by the husband's unilateral repudiation of his wife."[5]

5. Free power of the husband to terminate his marriage by repudiation of his wife. This is still the official law of Islam and of Judaism. In most Islamic countries and in Israel there are movements to limit the husband's freedom of repudiation and to provide a possibility for the wife to bring about dissolution for cause or for factual breakdown, i.e., on the basis of (2) or (3) above.

The Legal Concept of Divorce in the United States

Generally speaking, divorce in this country can be legally granted only when it has been shown (1) that one of the marital partners has failed to fulfill or has violated his (or her) marital obligations in one or more ways specified by the law (e.g., has deserted, has committed adultery), and (2) that the other spouse is shown (or is assumed) to have conducted herself (himself) as a true and faithful spouse. In Rheinstein's phrasing, "divorce is a punishment for the guilty and a reward for the innocent."[6]

That this legal concept is vastly different from the views of many who seek divorces is evidenced in the widely remarked necessity of committing perjury and entering into collusion in order to obtain a divorce. The lack of correspondence between the law of the books and the law in action results from the apparent fact that frequently spouses seek a divorce because they find it very difficult to continue living with each other and not, or not primarily, because of any gross wrong-doing on the part of either spouse.[7] Rheinstein believes that the lack of correspondence between the written code

---

[4] This is spoken of as the system of *divorce faillité*.

[5] In many countries there are sharp differences between the "law of the books" and "the law in action." This is especially true where divorce can be obtained only with difficulty.

[6] Max Rheinstein, "Our Dual Law of Divorce: The Law in Action versus the Law of the Books," *Conference Series of the Law School of the University of Chicago*, February 29, 1952, pp. 39–47. Quotation is from p. 41.

[7] It is this fact that renders a statistical analysis of the legal causes of divorce a commentary on the law of the jurisdiction involved rather than evidence concerning the relationships of spouses seeking divorces.

and the practice results from the presence in our population of two important elements—the religiously motivated who view marriage as a sacrament, and the liberally oriented who believe in the individual's right to act without governmental restraint.[8]

In 1947 there was published a widely noted article that advocated the substitution of the best interests of society for the concept of guilt in divorce proceedings.[9] In Toledo, Ohio, an able and energetic judge of the court of common pleas, the late Paul W. Alexander, assumed leadership of this cause in the American Bar Association and succeeded in instituting in his own jurisdiction a "family court," which substitutes a therapeutic approach for the determination of guilt. Already well known and highly developed in Japan, the family court was designed to "determine the viability" of marriages coming to the court's attention and to provide the opportunity and means for counseling and reconciliation in a free, informal, and confidential atmosphere. This is to be contrasted, of course, with the atmosphere of formal contest and the effort to prove and assign guilt in the public arena of the courtroom. The procedures of Judge Alexander's court provided for a prehearing that was permissive in cases where there were no children but mandatory if there was a child under fourteen.[10] In his colorful language Judge Alexander has excoriated existing legal procedures with respect to divorce:

> . . . if there be such a thing as a truly innocent spouse, and if legal recognition that a marriage is defunct be indeed punishment, it would appear a little rough on the innocent spouse to punish him along with the guilty one. . . .
>
> Adversary procedures mean that no spouse may with impunity neglect the slightest grievance or overlook the smallest offense. He must store them up in his memory and harbor them no matter how much they may fester. . . . The minute they quit tearing at each other's throats and sit

[8] Rheinstein, "Our Dual Law of Divorce," *loc. cit.*, p. 43.

[9] Reginald Heber Smith, "Dishonest Divorce," *Atlantic*, 180: 42–45 (December 1947).

[10] Paul W. Alexander, "A Therapeutic Approach," *Conference Series of the Law School of the University of Chicago*, February 29, 1952, pp. 51–54. "In 1963, the Toledo court had 2,574 pending divorce cases and 1,721 cases active in counseling. With respect to cases in which a divorce petition had been filed, there were 717 individuals who avoided or refused counseling and 626 individuals who accepted it. Also during 1963, of 1,337 cases that were closed, reconciliation was achieved in 439, contested divorce was changed to uncontested divorce in 21, financial plans were arranged in 351, plans for visitation and companionship were arranged in 383, plans for custody were arranged in 326, and no change was noted in 162. Thus, although reconciliation was achieved in only about thirty percent of the cases, there was an overall high measure of success with the counseling service since no change was recorded in only eight percent of the cases . . . approximately forty percent of the divorce petitions are abandoned . . . [compared] with the national average of approximately thirty percent. . . ."—Henry H. Foster, Jr., "Conciliation and Counseling in the Courts in Family Law Cases," *New York University Law Review*, 41:353–381 (1966); reprinted as Appendix F in Robert J. Levy, *Uniform Marriage and Divorce Legislation: A Preliminary Analysis*, prepared for the Special Committee on Divorce of the National Conference of Commissioners on Uniform State Laws, n.d.

down to talk things over sensibly so as to settle the conflict peaceably, they risk losing out entirely through the doctrine of collusion. . . .

The instant either of them looks to the law for relief he must put aside all thought of confession, of making amends, of concession, of forgiveness. . . . The stricter the law the more he must pile accusation on accusation.[11]

One conclusion of our analysis of the family and, as we shall see, of the marital dyad in particular is that to the extent that it is functionless, its viability tends to depend upon the congeniality of the people involved. Both the family court plan and the family counseling movement are based on the premise that it is important to try to restore congeniality where possible. The family court procedure is based on the further premise that where it seems improbable that congeniality can be restored, it is desirable to allow the couple to part by means of a legal divorce without the sort of perjurous degradation required by the adversary procedure. Basic to this view is the proposition that congeniality is a characteristic of a couple rather than of an individual; hence the effort to establish the guilt of one of the parties becomes an irrelevance and a legal fiction.

Perhaps if the nuclear family were *completely* functionless, there would be little opposition to this idea. If the family were functionless, there would be no *societal* reason why divorces should not be as freely obtained as in the "drink-of-water" figure of speech from the early days of the U.S.S.R. As we have seen, however, the American nuclear family carries out not only the basic societal function of replacement but also to some extent the corollary functions of emotional gratification, position-conferring, and of nurturance and control. Since all of these have implications for children in families, the society through its political structure—the state—expresses interest in seeing that the child in a divorce case does not suffer (or suffers as little as possible) with respect to access to the benefits of these functions—loving parents, suitable models after whom to fashion himself, access to educational opportunities, and the like. Hence divorce cases are routinely concerned with the custody and support of minor children, and, as we have seen, in Judge Alexander's family court it is mandatory to have the court conduct an investigation of the case if there is a child under fourteen.

In England a group appointed by the Archbishop of Canterbury and chaired by Robert C. Mortimer, Bishop of Exeter, has proposed that the doctrine of the matrimonial offense be abandoned and that instead marriage be dissolved only on the principle of marital breakdown, i.e., if the court should rule affirmatively on the following question:

Does the evidence before the court reveal such failure in the matrimonial relationship, or such circumstances adverse to that relationship, that no

---

[11] Paul W. Alexander, "The Family Court—an Obstacle Race?" *Annales de la Faculté de Droit d'Istanbul* (8th year; 1960), Vol. IX, No. 13, Part II, pp. 164–187. Quotations are from pp. 167, 182, and 183.

reasonable probability remains of the spouses again living together as husband and wife for mutual comfort and support?[12]

The opinions of the spouses should not be enough to convince the court of marital breakdown since the law-drafting group disavowed divorce by mutual consent. This group did not adhere consistently to the principle of marital breakdown, moreover, for the report adds that if a man should treat his wife with gross cruelty, desert her, and then file a petition for a divorce, it would be against the public interest to grant a decree.[13]

In California a Governor's Commission on the Family proposed that when a petition for divorce was filed, there should be a diagnostic and exploratory interview between the parties and a counselor for the purpose of assessing the desirability of continuing the marriage. Within thirty days of filing the petition and after the interview or interviews the counselor would inform the court as to the decision of the parties, which would be either (1) that they had become reconciled, (2) that they were undertaking voluntary marital counseling in the hope of reconciliation, or (3) that they wished to proceed with the divorce. An ingenious feature of this proposal was that if the couple should elect the third option, the opportunity to have divorce counseling should be made available to them. (As we shall see in Chapter 23, Bohannan has proposed that there are six basic elements in the process of divorce, and with these in mind the proposal for divorce counseling seems to make excellent sense.)

The legislature of California paid some attention to the report of the Governor's Commission. In 1969 California passed a law that substitutes "dissolution of marriage" for "divorce," that provides that the court will dissolve a marriage when it is established that the marriage has broken down "irremediably," and that irremediable breakdown is to be demonstrated through proof that "irreconcilable differences" exist between the parties. The legislature did not incorporate the proposal for marital counseling and divorce counseling.[14]

It has been proposed that a uniform divorce law for the United States be based on the principle of marital breakdown, and as noted in point 3 on pages 574–575, this principle has been operating in some eastern European countries.[15] Rheinstein reports that Scandinavian laws view marital break-

---

[12] The Report of a Group appointed by the Archbishop of Canterbury in January 1964, *Putting Asunder: A Divorce Law for Contemporary Society* (London: S.P.C.K., 1966), pp. 38–39.

[13] *Ibid.*, p. 53.

[14] Herma Hill Kay, "A Family Court: The California Proposal," in Paul Bohannan (ed.), *Divorce and After* (New York: Doubleday, 1970).

[15] Cf., e.g., Jan Gorecki, "Divorce in Poland—A Socio-Legal Study," *Acta Sociologica*, 10: 68–80 (1966); and by the same author, "Communist Family Pattern: From Sexual Freedom to Equality of Sexes," paper presented before the American Sociological Association, San Francisco, August 1969.

down ("deep permanent discord") as the reason for terminating marriage, while mutual consent is seen as evidence of such discord.[16]

From time to time it is suggested that in this country the parties to divorce be required to have marital counseling and to attempt a reconciliation, and that a divorce decree should be granted only after the counseling has proved unsuccessful. Aside from difficulties in trying to administer such a law in cases where one spouse has disappeared, there are other objections—not only from the religious traditionalists, who view marriage as a sacrament, but also from persons of a more liberal orientation who are concerned with considerations of constitutional law. Such a procedure would tend to be more administrative than judicial in nature. As an administrative procedure, it would probably be more influenced in outcome than would a judicial decision by the moral outlook of the official in charge. Even more important is the question as to whether "a citizen who is trying to be freed from a tie of marriage [should] be compelled to submit to such a probing into his mind as a necessary condition for his petition to be considered." And what would happen if one spouse agreed but the other refused to submit to psychological diagnosis and counseling?[17]

Rheinstein has observed that in the Austro-Hungarian Empire (which crumbled in 1918) there were five different laws on marriage: for Roman Catholics, Greek Orthodox, Jews, Protestants, and Mohammedans.[18] In view of the cultural pluralism in the United States one might surmise that a good deal of distress over the divorce laws might be eliminated if couples could be classified at marriage and placed under the legal code appropriate to their classification. For example, divorce might be made impossible for Roman Catholic couples but available to members of certain Protestant denominations upon having shown the court that their marriage was broken. One difficulty, of course, is that in this country not all ascribed categorizations are lifelong—people do change their religions. A related problem is that in this country we are not nearly as identifiable by such culturally distinct classifications as are members of some other societies, and we resist the idea that we should be treated differently. A further complication would arise in the case of mixed couples. Although it, too, would have readily foreseeable problems, it is possible that some such arrangement as that of Portugal would produce less anguish. There a couple may choose to be married in a religious service with

---

[16] Max Rheinstein, "Divorce Law in Sweden," in Bohannan, *op. cit.*

[17] After advancing these objections Rheinstein concedes the state's right to try to change the personality of a criminal but asks: "Are we certain that society is better served if all men are turned into 'good' husbands and all women into 'good' wives?"—Max Rheinstein, "Marriage Stability and Laws on Divorce," *Annales de la Faculté de Droit d'Istanbul* (8th year; 1960), Vol. IX, No. 13, Part II, pp. 15–55. Quotations are from pp. 23 and 24.

[18] John S. Bradway (ed.), *Proceedings of the Institute of Family Law, April 9, 10, 11, 1959* (Durham, N.C.: Duke University, 1959), p. 220.

the prospect of no divorce or in a secular ceremony with the prospect of easy divorce.[19]

Trends in Marital Dissolution in the United States

It seems unlikely that there has ever been a society in which there was no way to get out of a marriage except to die. Some societies make the exit from an unhappy marriage sinful, illicit, and disgraceful; others make it respectable and legal. By declaring marriage to be a sacrament, the Roman Catholic Church declared it to be indissoluble. Since the Roman Church dominated the morality of Western Europe from the Middle Ages until the Reformation, it seems unlikely that there were very many legal dissolutions in the Christian world during that millennium.

From the start of the American settlements the colonists rejected the sacramental theory of marriage and placed it under civil law. As early as 1639 the colony of Massachusetts Bay provided for divorce.[20]

Figure 22.1 shows the trend in American divorces per 1000 population by five-year intervals from 1860–1864 through 1960–1964 and comparable data beginning in 1900–1904 for France and England and Wales, where divorce has been granted for cause (type 2 above); and for Switzerland and Sweden (type 3 above). The figure shows (1) that all the countries have had a phenomenal rise in the divorce rate, (2) that the countries involved in World War II (the United States, England and Wales, and France) had a peak in the years immediately following the war,[21] and (3) that despite the differences among the European countries in their divorce policies, there is relatively little difference in their curves.

From the observation that the divorce rate has increased, many people draw the conclusion that the rate of total marital dissolutions has also increased, and from this conclusion comes the moral lamentation noted on the first page of the first chapter to the effect that the modern family was thought to be riding to hell in a basket. Such a grave conclusion warrants serious scrutiny of the data. On this we offer the following observations:

1. We cannot be absolutely sure that the divorce rate[22] in the United States has risen as shown in Figure 22.1. The reason is that there has not been

[19] *Ibid.*, p. 88.

[20] Paul H. Jacobson, *American Marriage and Divorce* (New York: Holt, Rinehart and Winston, Inc., 1959), p. 89.

[21] The rate for the United States in 1946 was 4.4 divorces per 1000 population.

[22] To avoid stylistic awkwardness we use the definite article and the singular form of "rate." Actually no single rate is conventionally used. Depending upon which data are available, the rate may be divorces per 1000 marriages in the same year or in the preceding decade or per 1000 married women or married women of specified ages, or per 1000 population as in Figure 22.1.

FIGURE 22.1

Divorces per 1000 Population by Five-Year Intervals: United States, 1860–1864 to 1950–1954, and Selected European Countries, 1900–1904 to 1950–1954

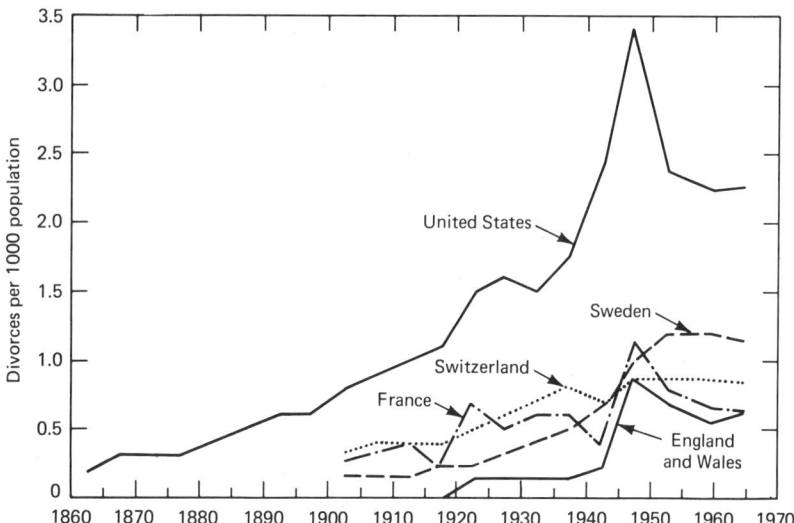

SOURCE: Data for the years 1860–1954 adapted with permission of the author from Paul H. Jacobson, *American Marriage and Divorce.* New York: Holt, Rinehart and Winston, Inc., copyright, ©, 1959, Table 42, p. 90 and Table 47, p. 98. Data for the years 1955–1964 adapted from *Demographic Yearbook 1962* (14th ed., New York: United Nations, 1963), Table 24, pp. 604–611; *Demographic Yearbook 1966* (18th ed.; New York: United Nations, 1967), Table 26, pp. 737–640.

national reporting of divorces, and it is conceivable that the rise has resulted from progressive improvement in an initially very poor system of reporting data on divorces. It is true, however, that data from other countries that have undergone industrialization and urbanization and that have better systems of vital records than do we (e.g., Sweden) show rising divorce rates. Such external evidence lends plausibility to the belief that our divorce rate is also rising.

2. Then assuming it to be true that the American divorce rate has increased more or less as shown in Figure 22.1, we are still not justified in inferring that there has been a parallel increase in this country either in

a. the rate of marital dissolutions in which the spouses survive, or
b. the rate of total marital dissolutions, including those broken by the death of a spouse.

Concerning point (a), Rheinstein argues that in bygone days, say around 1800, there were many marital dissolutions not formalized by any legal procedure. In those days, he writes: "In all layers of society, except, perhaps, the very top, the maritally dissatisfied male and, to a considerably lesser extent, the female, could avail himself of a freedom which has almost disappeared in present society, viz., the freedom of disappearance." If a man lived in rural England, he could easily lose himself in London or in Australia or in the New World; if a New Englander, he could easily migrate westward to the frontier: "The chance of punishment or other embarrassment because of bigamy was minimal for the man who had run away with or without mistress."[23]

Conditions that have brought about the loss of the "freedom of disappearance" include, in Rheinstein's judgment, the development and dissemination of the telegraph, of the airplane, of photography and fingerprinting, and of the social service agency. To this list of factors curtailing the "freedom of disappearance" should be added the tremendous improvement in record-keeping through computer-based information-retrieval systems. Because of such changes as these Rheinstein believes that an increasing proportion of cases of marital dissolution in this country and others are being handled as divorce cases. Accordingly, he says: "In the absence of statistics we simply cannot know to what extent the rise of the divorce rate indicates a rise in marriage instability or a shift from informal to formalized marriage termination due to changed social conditions and mores."[24]

It would seem likely that the increase in the proportion of marital dissolutions that are legally formalized would be related to socioeconomic status. That is, where there is wealth and the prospect of substantial inheritance, there is an incentive to have relationships legally defined. Goode has proposed a hypothesis that is consistent with this inference. "In the pre-industrial or early industrialization period of Western nations the upper classes will have higher divorce rates. Indeed, there may be almost no lower class divorces."[25] He has adduced data from Hungary and Yugoslavia to support this hypothesis.

Concerning point (b) Paul H. Jacobson has shown that because of the decline in the American death rate, the proportion of marriages broken in any year by death of a spouse has decreased more than the proportion broken by divorce has increased and that the proportion of all existing marriages that are broken in any one year by death plus divorce has decreased. For example, in the decade 1870–1879 (to avoid the war years 1860–1865) about 31 of every 1000 marriages were broken each year and less than one twelfth of these dissolutions resulted from divorce; in 1955–1964 the rate of total dissolutions was

---

[23] Rheinstein, "Marriage Stability and Laws on Divorce," loc. cit., pp. 37, 38.

[24] Ibid., p. 41. For an argument that between two fifths and four fifths of the increment of the number of divorces in 1949 over the number that would have been predicted from 1940 resulted from "an increased tendency for marriages already broken by permanent separation to end in divorce," see Calvin L. Beale, "Increased Divorce Rates among Separated Persons as a Factor in Divorce since 1940," Social Forces, 29: 72–74 (1950), at p. 74.

[25] William J. Goode, "Marital Satisfaction and Instability: A Cross-Cultural Class Analysis of Divorce Rates," International Social Science Journal, 14: 507–526 (1962). Quotation is from p. 517.

down around 27 per 1000, but divorces accounted for about one third of the total. Jacobson estimates that nearly half the dissolutions just after World War II (1946) resulted from divorces. (See Figure 22.2.)

FIGURE 22.2

Marital Dissolutions by Death (1860–1963) and Divorce (Including Annulments) (1860–1965) per 1000 Existing Marriages, United States

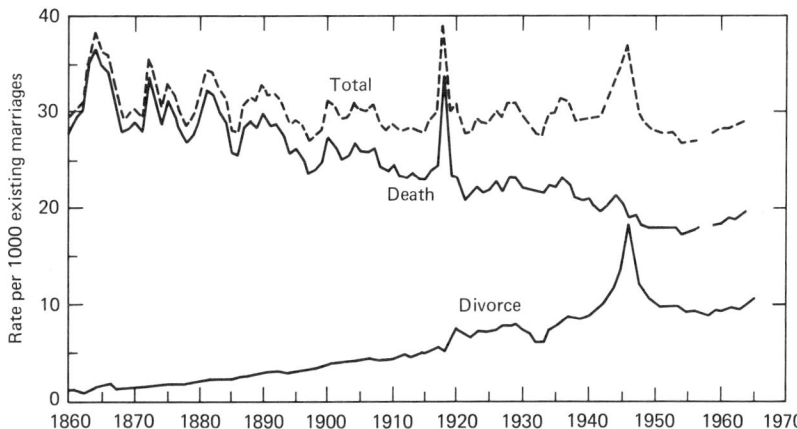

SOURCE: Divorces per 1000 existing marriages: 1860–1929: Adapted with permission of the author from Paul H. Jacobson, *American Marriage and Divorce*. New York: Holt, Rinehart and Winston, Inc., copyright, ©, 1959, Table 70, p. 142; 1930–1956: U.S. Bureau of the Census, *Historical Statistics of the United States: Colonial Times to 1957* (Washington, D.C.: U.S. Government Printing Office, 1960) Series B 178–179, p. 30; 1957–1965: *Statistical Abstract of the United States*, Table 76, p. 61.
Marital dissolutions by death: 1860–1956: Paul H. Jacobson, *loc. cit.* 1959–1963: Alexander A. Plateris, *Divorce Statistics Analysis, United States, 1963*, National Center for Health Statistics, Series 21, No. 13, October 1967, Tables A and C, pp. 1 and 4, respectively.

Causes of Marital Dissolution

When the layman is asked about the causes of divorce, he responds in terms of the incompatibility of the spouses; their lack of common interests; arguments over money, drink, and loose living.[26] The sociologist is in the practice of looking for causes of the dissolution of a social structure in its functions—especially in the decline and loss of its functions—and in the development of functions in closely related structures. Accordingly let us review some of our remarks about functions.

In our early history, when the nation was largely agricultural, the Amer-

[26] Anonymous, "The Quarter's Polls," *Public Opinion Quarterly*, 13: 350 (1949).

ican farm family came close to being a self-sufficient *economic* unit. The old and young of both sexes contributed to family production and partook of its fruits. In the absence of categorical employability there was no sharp distinction between the gainfully employed and the dependent. The economic function of the family was evident and represented a series of bonds of interdependence among family members. As the emphasis has shifted from "making a living" to "earning a living,"[27] the self-sufficiency of the family has decreased. As the major economic unit shifted from the family to the giant corporation, the family became vulnerable to the caprices of the business cycle. The substitution of earning and buying for making goods, the oscillation of the business cycle, and the premium on space in the city have made the care of economic dependents an increasing burden. Concurrently there has developed a special welfare structure (public and private) to take over the support of certain classes of dependents at the lower-income levels.

As the productive aspect of the economic function was lost from the family, the character of the economic bonds among family members was altered, and weakened. In the earlier family form, all members were economically interdependent; in the later form, they evolved into two classes—breadwinners and dependents. In purely economic terms, each member contributed to the general level of living in the earlier form; in the later form the breadwinners would be able to maintain a higher level of living if it were not for their dependents. With the loss of production, then, we see an important element in familial disorganization, including marital dissolutions. Furthermore, consensus has broken down concerning the obligations of families for the support of dependent kinsmen. Illustrative of this uncertainty are questions such as these: Should a couple with children support an aged parent who, without their support, might become eligible for old-age assistance? When the combination of both is impossible, should a girl give up marriage to support her parents? The fact that our society does not have immediate categorical answers to these questions indicates a lack of consensus.

With respect to the *political* function it was remarked in Chapter 4 that except for the feuding families of the Southern highlands the American family was not usually large enough or sufficiently well organized to be an effective political organization. There was, however, some degree of mutual protection of family members as was indicated by the practice of carrying arms on the frontier and in other sparsely settled regions. Now, of course, the carrying of arms under the ordinary conditions of urban life is illegal.

Traditionally *socialization* has been a family function and *education* has been largely so. Even before the development of the urban industrial society the school and the church were competitors for this function. Other more recent competitors are the "character building" agencies (the Boy Scouts, the YWCA, and so on), and the various media of mass communication. Removal of the father's work from the domestic arena has long since eliminated him as an effective tutor of the children. We can discern the following trends: for

---

[27] Cf. F. E. Merrill, *Courtship and Marriage* (New York: Sloane, 1949), p. 130.

more women to be employed outside the home and hence to be less available to tutor their children; for the culture to become increasingly complex so that the average parent becomes progressively less able to substitute for the school; for the school to take an increasing proportion of the child's time; for the school to assume responsibility for an increasing proportion of the total function of socialization-education; for the school to be implicitly critical of the manner in which the function is executed in the family through its establishment of such devices as parent-education groups, and the like; for the progressive relinquishment of this function not only to the school and to character-building agencies but also to mass media, especially to television.

Except for a few groups without a specialized clergy it appears that formal *religious* activity has been carried out by the nuclear family in America only under conditions of isolation. The increasing power of commerce and industry and of the state have given to these segments of American society the resources to manipulate symbols and thus to perform some of the activities subsumed under the religious function, e.g., the alleviation of anxiety and the designation of values.

For the century and a third, ending at the bottom of the depression, the birth rate and the size of the family in the United States declined sharply. We have seen that there was a considerable rise in the birth rate from the depression until just after World War II and that more recently the birth rate has been declining again. With respect to the entire period it is clear that, quantitatively speaking, the significance of the *replacement* function as a bond holding the family together has diminished.[28]

In summary, let us imagine the roles of man and woman in a maximally functional (male-dominant) nuclear family. The man would play foreman to

---

[28] Data over the 44-year period from 1922 through 1965 show that the mean number of children per divorce decree has doubled (from 0.63 to 1.32) and the proportion of children involved has nearly quadrupled (from 2.3 to 8.9 per 1000 children per year) while the absolute number is estimated to have increased nearly sevenfold (from 93,000 to 630,000).—National Center for Health Statistics, Series 21, No. 18, *Children of Divorced Couples: United States, Selected Years* (Washington, D.C.: GPO, 1970), Table 1, p. 16. Following is a chain of evidence purporting to support the proposition that the replacement function does not foster marital happiness but does foster marital stability. Locke found, as would be expected, that marital happiness scores are much lower for divorced persons than for happily married subjects. Christensen and Philbrick obtained a negative correlation between marital happiness scores and number of children. (Results of Farber and Blackman were inconclusive, however.) But, according to Jacobson, the divorce rate correlates negatively with the number of children. If functionality were not a stabilizing factor, the pattern of correlations would lead to the expectation that parents with many children would have a higher divorce rate than those with few children.—Harvey J. Locke, *Predicting Adjustment in Marriage: A Comparison of a Divorced and a Happily Married Group* (New York: Holt, Rinehart and Winston, Inc., 1951), p. 54; Harold T. Christensen and Robert E. Philbrick, "Family Size as a Factor in the Marital Adjustments of College Couples," *American Sociological Review*, 17: 306–312 (1952); Bernard Farber and Leonard S. Blackman, "Marital Role Tensions and Number and Sex of Children," *American Sociological Review*, 21: 596–601 (1956); and Jacobson, op. cit., p. 133. Cf. also the third paragraph under "The Functions of Marriage" in Chapter 21.

the woman's role of worker, official to her role of constituent, and perhaps priest to her role of parishioner. Presumably they would both assume the role of teacher with relation to their children. In this heuristic type[29] of maximum functionality, man and woman are bound together in four core relationships in addition to that of husband and wife. Because of the multiplicity of their interlocking roles each spouse is enormously important to the other. Because of their great importance to each other it is reasoned that the marital bond will be so highly durable that their liking or disliking each other becomes almost an irrelevance. As functionality diminishes, it is theorized, there is a thinning of the core relationships between the spouses and a reduction in the degree of their functional importance to each other. As this happens, congeniality becomes more important and functionality less important as a determinant of marital stability. Moreover, the functional basis of male superordination diminishes, and we begin to hear of the "equality of the sexes."

Our discussion of functions has been oriented largely to showing how the functions have varied over the history of the United States. Now let us confine our attention to American families of today and grant that with respect to the four nonfamilial basic societal functions they will cluster toward the low end of the continuum of functionality. Within this context, let us ask, which variables can we find that will explain variation in the rate of marital dissolution?

Let us proceed from the assumption that the American ethos contains an expectation that each family will carry out to the best of its ability the functions that derive from the basic societal function of replacement—position-conferring and the nurturance and control of children—and from its structure, the emotional gratification of all its members. Having these functions chiefly in mind but not excluding others, let us rephrase our question to read: Which conditions of life in American society lead to maximum functionality of the family?

First, we might note that communities vary in the degree to which they exert upon the family the expectation that it will be functional. If we assume that the family is somewhat responsive to such pressure, we next ask: under which conditions would the pressure be found to vary? We might expect to find maximum pressure on the family to be functional (or we might phrase it "community support of familial solidarity") (1) in "primary" rather than "secondary" communities and (2) in culturally homogeneous rather than heterogeneous communities.

A community is said to be primary to the degree that its members have relationships with each other that are intimate and face to face. Rural com-

---

[29] A heuristic, or ideal, type represents a voluntary distortion of empirical phenomena by positing extreme characteristics. The purpose of such distortion is to facilitate the ordering of observations and the statement of hypotheses. Thus it is possible that such a highly functional family never existed, even on the American frontier. Cf. Robert F. Winch, "Heuristic and Empirical Typologies: A Job for Factor Analysis," *American Sociological Review*, 12: 68–75 (1947).

munities and small towns come to mind as examples. To the extent that the relationships of a community tend to be anonymous and/or segmentalized we speak of the community as secondary. The usual example is the central areas of large cities.[30] If this reasoning is sound, we expect to find that rates of marital dissolution should be lower in rural areas than in urban.[31]

It is virtually definitional that a community of high cultural homogeneity is one with a single standard of behavior and one that shows strong disapproval of behavior deviating from that standard. Viewed negatively, this state of affairs constitutes the narrow-minded parochialism that eventuates in intolerance and in suspicion of the exotic. Viewed positively, this state of affairs exerts a supportive pressure on the family, as on other structures, by making demands for conformity to a consistent set of expectations. This reasoning leads to the same prediction as that made in the preceding paragraph: that rates of marital dissolution should be lower in rural areas than in urban.

For the state of Iowa in the latter 1940's Cannon has shown that rural counties do have lower divorce rates than do urban counties.[32] Perhaps the most dramatic evidence comes from Hillman's analysis of occupations of divorced males in the civilian labor force in 1950. She found that there were 14.4 divorced farm workers per 1000 ever married. In all other occupations the rate was 25.3 per 1000 ever married, i.e., more than 75 percent higher than among farm workers.[33]

Related to the foregoing is the question as to the correlation between religion and marital dissolution. In particular we might expect the nonrecognition of divorce by the Roman Catholic Church to be correlated with a low divorce rate among the adherents of that faith, but we might wonder whether or not this would carry over to the desertion rate. From an analysis of records of the Municipal Court of Philadelphia, Monahan and Kephart have concluded

---

[30] We may recall the argument in Chapter 6 to the effect that cities are not as "urban" in the sense of anonymity as such writers as Wirth were inclined to believe. But we should bear in mind that whereas Wirth's critics have shown that cities are not *absolutely* anonymous, they certainly have not shown that rural areas, small towns, and suburbs are as anonymous as central areas of large cities.

[31] The phrasing here is not intended to suggest that the writer came deductively to these predictions before having any knowledge as to the empirical facts. Rather, the purpose is to present the empirical facts in conjunction with a theory that gives meaning and scope to the facts.

[32] Kenneth L. Cannon, "Marriage and Divorce in Iowa, 1940–47," *Marriage and Family Living*, 9: 81–83, 98 (1947).

[33] Karen G. Hillman, "Marital Dissolution and Its Relation to Education, Income and Occupation," Table 12, p. 48. Unpublished master's thesis, Northwestern University, 1960. Since the marital status of a person who remarries after being divorced is "married" in the census report used by Mrs. Hillman, her rates register persons divorced and not remarried per 1000 ever married. Cf. also Karen G. Hillman, "Marital Instability and Its Relation to Education, Income, and Occupation: An Analysis Based on Census Data," in Robert F. Winch, Robert McGinnis, and Herbert R. Barringer (eds.), *Selected Studies in Marriage and the Family* (rev. ed.; New York: Holt, Rinehart and Winston, Inc., 1962), pp. 603–608.

that Catholics had the lowest divorce rate among the three major religious categories. Protestants had the highest rate, and the Jews were second. On the other hand, they also report: "The strong prohibition against divorce for Catholics . . . does not prevent the occurrence of family disorganization, as the high 'desertion' figures for Catholics indicate."[34]

In passing we may note that not only are divorce rates higher for *areas* of cultural heterogeneity but also for *couples* of diverse cultural backgrounds. The best indexes of cultural background available on large populations pertain to race and religion. A study of divorces in Iowa found that Catholics married to non-Catholics had a higher divorce rate than did couples wherein both mates were of the Catholic religion.[35] A study done in Hawaii has shown that a greater proportion of marriages of couples of different races ended in divorce than of marriages homogeneous with respect to race.[36]

It has been reasoned above that the more functional a social structure, the greater the resources it will produce and therefore the more control it will exercise over the behavior of its members.[37] The following reasoning for this hypothesis was set forth in Chapter 1: Functionality yields products or outcomes, the benefits of which can become rewards to individual members. From the proposition that resources can be used to control the behavior of individual members it follows that members of families rich in resources will have more to lose by leaving the family than will members of poor families. A rich father, for example, has more leverage with which to control the behavior of his son than has a poor father. If the theory is correct, there should be a negative correlation between measures of socioeconomic position (which we may regard as indexes of the possession of resources) and measures of

---

[34] Thomas P. Monahan and William M. Kephart, "Divorce and Desertion by Religious and Mixed-Religious Groups," *American Journal of Sociology*, 59: 454–465 (1954), at pp. 464–465. The quotation marks around "desertion" in the excerpt result from the fact that the data used were derived from desertion and nonsupport cases.

[35] Loren E. Chancellor and Thomas P. Monahan, "Religious Preference and Interreligious Mixtures in Marriages and Divorces in Iowa," *American Journal of Sociology*, 61: 233–239 (1955). On the other hand, they did not find that mixed-Protestant marriages had higher divorce rates than both-Protestant marriages.

[36] C. K. Cheng and Douglas S. Yamamura, "Interracial Marriage and Divorce in Hawaii," *Social Forces*, 36: 77–84 (1957). It is reasonable to anticipate that a culturally heterogeneous couple would have greater differences in conceptions of marital roles than would a culturally homogeneous couple. Pursuing this reasoning, we should expect more marital conflict among couples holding divergent rather than similar conceptions of marital roles. A report that divorced couples show more divergence in such role-conceptions than do couples still married appears in Alver Hilding Jacobson, "Conflict of Attitudes toward the Roles of the Husband and Wife in Marriage," *American Sociological Review*, 17: 146–150 (1952). Relevant also is a study reporting that where husbands and wives disagree in their conception of the former's role, he registers low on a scale of marital adjustment but that such a relationship did not appear where there was marital dissensus on the content of the wife's role.—Nathan Hurvitz, "The Measurement of Marital Strain," *American Journal of Sociology*, 65: 610–615 (1960).

[37] Here, as elsewhere, the phrase "other things being equal" is assumed.

marital dissolution. In other words, the proportion of marriages ending in divorce, separation, annulment, and desertion should be less in the upper strata than in the lower.[38]

Before considering the data it is necessary to point out that the prediction of the preceding paragraph does not pertain to marriages broken by death; rather, it predicts that the presence of resources creates a greater incentive for (obviously living) persons to remain in their families, especially in their marriages. Since death rates are negatively correlated with socioeconomic status and thereby contribute to the predicted differential rate of marital dissolutions, therefore, we should seek to exclude dissolutions resulting from death. Thus it would be desirable to have data that would make possible the cross-tabulation of socioeconomic level by the proportion of adults who had had their marriages broken through some cause other than death. To the writer's knowledge such data do not exist for the United States. A study by Hillman relates socioeconomic indexes to the proportion of people reported to be divorced or separated in 1950. The difficulty with her data is that all who have had a previous marriage broken and have remarried are tabulated as married, and hence their broken marriages escape notice. A study by Udry overcomes this difficulty in Hillman's data by tabulating all who have had previous marriages, but in his case the data are contaminated (for our purposes) by the fact that they include previous marriages broken by death.

Do the available data bear out the theoretical expectation that the lower the level of resources, the greater the rate of marital dissolution? Interpreting socioeconomic status (measured by occupation, income, and education) as an index of access to resources and bearing the foregoing difficulties in mind, let us see what both sets of data can tell us. Hillman's analysis shows that when divorce rates (computed on a basis that excludes remarried persons) are calculated for broad occupational categories and those categories are arranged on the generally accepted basis of their prestige, a negative correlation emerges between the prestige of the category and the divorce rate. There were approximately 17 divorced males per 1000 ever married in the upper-white-collar category, about 24 to 25 for both the lower-white-collar and the upper-blue-collar workers, and 30 to 31 for lower-blue-collar workers. (See Table 22.1.) Such results are, of course, consistent with the theoretical formulation set forth above. Also consistent is the direction of the very large difference between the divorce rates of farmers and farm managers as contrasted with those of farm laborers and foremen.

---

[38] At first it may seem that the hypothesis of a positive correlation between socioeconomic status and the divorce rate in pre-industrial and developing countries (cf. p. 582 above) is inconsistent with the prediction of a negative correlation in those countries that are industrialized, such as the United States. The point is that in both types of countries there should be a negative correlation between socioeconomic status and total rate of marital dissolutions, but in developing and undeveloped countries only the wealthy have an incentive to have their marital dissolutions legally recognized and thus to incur the expense of divorce actions.

TABLE 22.1

Number of Males 14 Years of Age and Older Who Were Ever Married and Who Were Divorced, by Occupational Categories of the United States Civilian Labor Force: 1950

OCCUPATIONAL CATEGORY	EVER MARRIED	DIVORCED	DIVORCED PER 1000 EVER MARRIED
Upper-White-Collar Workers	6,473,100	112,140	17.3
Professional, technical, and kindred workers	2,493,870	46,110	18.5
Managers, officials, and proprietors exc. farm	3,979,230	66,030	16.6
Lower-White-Collar Workers	4,065,420	101,430	24.9
Clerical and kindred workers	1,991,190	51,180	25.7
Sales workers	2,074,230	50,250	24.2
Upper-Blue-Collar Workers	6,945,840	167,610	24.1
Craftsmen, foremen, and kindred workers	6,945,840	167,610	24.1
Lower-Blue-Collar Workers	11,480,730	350,430	30.5
Operatives and kindred workers	6,859,560	179,550	26.2
Service workers including private household	1,990,830	84,600	42.5
Laborers exc. farm and mine	2,630,340	86,280	32.8
Farm Workers	4,658,220	66,990	14.4
Farmers and farm managers	3,735,150	29,370	7.9
Farm laborers and foremen	923,070	37,620	40.1

SOURCE: Adapted from Karen G. Hillman, "Marital Dissolution and Its Relation to Education, Income and Occupation," Table 12, p. 48. Unpublished master's thesis, Northwestern University, 1960.

Table 22.2 relates the rate of divorces plus separations to the incomes of men separately for whites and nonwhites. Here we find that the data for the nonwhite males conform to the pattern of a negative correlation between the magnitude of the rate and the measure of socioeconomic status. For white males, the over-all pattern is one of a negative correlation, but there is a deviation from the pattern in that males without income have a lower rate for both categories of marital dissolution than do those in the $1–$999 bracket.

Where education is the index and where, therefore, it makes sense to report data on females as well as on males, the picture becomes very mixed. If we had only the separation rates on white males, we could be categorical about

TABLE 22.2

Number of Males 14 Years of Age and Over Divorced and Separated per 1000 Ever Married, by Race and by Income Received in 1949: United States, 1950

INCOME	WHITE			NONWHITE		
	Div'd	Sep'd	D + S	Div'd	Sep'd	D + S
No Income	36.1	26.2	62.3	30.5	112.3	142.8
$1 – $999	44.4	28.3	72.7	23.2	89.5	112.7
$1000 – $1999	32.1	18.8	50.9	23.2	84.3	107.5
$2000 – $2999	30.6	15.7	46.4	24.5	71.1	95.6
$3000 – $3999	22.9	9.7	32.6	28.5	53.7	82.2
$4000 and over	2.5	0.7	3.2	3.3	3.3	6.6
Total	25.2	13.8	39.0	24.0	81.4	105.4

SOURCE: Adapted from Hillman, "Marital Dissolution and Its Relation to Education, Income and Occupation," Table 10, p. 41.

the negative correlation. If we had only the divorce rates for nonwhite females, we could insist just as categorically on a positive correlation between socio-economic status and divorce rates. And a curvilinear relationship can be demonstrated on the basis of the divorce rates of nonwhite males, the separation rates of nonwhite females, or the combined divorce plus separation rates for whites, both males and females.

Before attempting to draw any conclusion let us look at the differences between the white and nonwhite rates. Because of differential participation in occupational categories there is justification for regarding race as another index pertaining to accessibility of resources. Goode analyzed seven censuses from that of 1890 through that of 1950 and found that the first five showed distinctly higher rates of divorce for nonwhites than for whites, but the censuses of 1940 and 1950 showed virtually identical rates for the two racial categories.[39] An analysis of data based on marriages occurring in the period 1947–1954 concludes that by the end of this seven-year period the divorce rate for this relatively briefly married segment of the population was higher for nonwhites: 19.8 and 19.9 percent of the nonwhite males and females had already been divorced as contrasted with 14.1 and 16.7 for the white males and females.[40] Hillman's analysis of the 1950 census shows that whereas for females the nonwhites exceeded the whites both in rates of divorce and in rates of separation,

---

[39] Goode, op. cit., p. 49.

[40] Hugh Carter, Sarah Lewit, and William F. Pratt, "Socioeconomic Characteristics of Persons Who Married between January 1947 and June 1954: United States," *National Office of Vital Statistics—Special Reports*, Vol. 45, No. 12, September 9, 1957, p. 298.

for males the nonwhites exceeded the whites in rate of separations but the two racial categories were virtually identical in divorce rates.[41] (See Table 22.3.)

The results of Mrs. Hillman's analysis may now be summarized as follows:

1. The data do support the proposition that marital dissolutions occur more frequently among people whose positions carry relatively few resources than among those of high socioeconomic position. The clearest evidence on this point comes from the fact that rates of marital dissolution among nonwhites are shown to be between two and a half and three times as high as among whites. The rates of marital dissolution by level of income are nearly as conclusive. The divorce rates by occupational category are also consistent with this proposition.

2. The positive correlation among nonwhites of both sexes between education and the divorce rate may be interpreted as an indication that as nonwhites become more educated and presumably acquire more property, they tend to shift from informal to formal procedures for terminating marriages.

3. The presence of a mode for both white and nonwhite females at the "high school, 1–3 years" level suggests that part of these peaks in marital dissolutions may come from marriages following premarital pregnancies. (Some discussion of this topic will be presented below.)

There are other patterns in Mrs. Hillman's data that are not readily interpretable.

As previously stated, the data of Udry take remarriages into account but include dissolutions resulting from death. The negative correlation between income and marital dissolution appears in his data. (See Figure 22.3.) Somewhat less clear-cut but still discernible are the negative correlations between marital dissolutions and the indexes of socioeconomic status based on education (Figure 22.4) and occupation (Figure 22.5). To this point our functional hypothesis of a negative correlation between socioeconomic status and rate of marital dissolutions from causes other than death has been supported only by data from the United States. Goode has analyzed this relationship in several other countries with mature economies and has found the same negative correlation. These countries are: New Zealand, Australia, Sweden, Belgium,

---

[41] In interpreting these data it is relevant to know that (1) persons with annulled marriages are classified as single, (2) remarried persons are classified as married, and (3) a considerable number of divorced persons appear to falsify the report of their marital status. On the latter point cf. Paul H. Jacobson, *op. cit.*, p. 7. It is possible, moreover, to interpret the higher rate of marital dissolutions among blacks (the overwhelming majority of the nonwhites in the population of the United States) as a cultural survival of the conditions of life under slavery where it was a common practice to keep mother and children together, but no such concern was exercised to keep the father in the slave family. Another school of thought, however, places the interpretation even further back in the black's history. Cf. introduction to Part Two.

TABLE 22.3

Number of Persons 25 Years of Age and Over Divorced and Separated per 1000 Ever Married, by Sex and Race and by Level of Education: United States, 1950

EDUCATION LEVEL OF	WHITE						NONWHITE					
	Male			Female			Male			Female		
	Div'd	Sep'd	D+S	Div'd	Sep'd	D+S	Div'd	Sep'd	D+S	Div'd	Sep'd	D+S
No school	22.8	27.2	49.9	14.4	21.7	36.2	15.3	76.3	91.6	14.9	64.8	79.7
Elementary: 1-4 years	28.5	22.5	51.0	20.5	21.7	42.2	18.6	84.0	102.6	20.1	97.7	117.8
5-7 years	29.3	19.2	48.5	25.1	21.2	46.3	25.1	85.7	110.8	30.7	108.9	139.7
8 years	27.3	14.1	41.4	26.7	16.6	43.2	31.9	84.5	116.4	44.4	115.3	159.7
High school: 1-3 years	28.3	13.0	41.3	35.5	17.1	52.6	35.6	86.5	122.2	51.9	124.6	176.6
4 years	24.5	9.9	34.4	33.2	12.5	45.7	38.2	71.6	109.8	57.6	101.0	158.6
College: 1-3 years	25.9	9.3	35.2	37.1	10.0	47.0	40.5	59.2	99.7	57.9	75.9	133.8
4 years or more	17.3	6.3	23.6	35.5	8.7	44.2	30.3	39.2	69.5	64.5	57.0	121.5
Not known	42.2	35.5	77.7	36.8	23.5	60.3	32.1	107.1	139.2	37.0	116.1	153.1
Total	26.8	14.4	41.3	30.4	16.1	46.5	26.1	82.7	108.8	36.0	104.5	140.5

SOURCE: Adapted from Hillman, "Marital Dissolution and Its Relation to Education, Income and Occupation," Tables 4 and 5, pp. 25 and 27.

FIGURE 22.3

Percent of Ever-Married Males 25–34 Years of Age Who Were Separated, Divorced, or Had Been Married More Than Once at the Time of the 1960 Census, by Income and Race (Based on a 5% Sample)

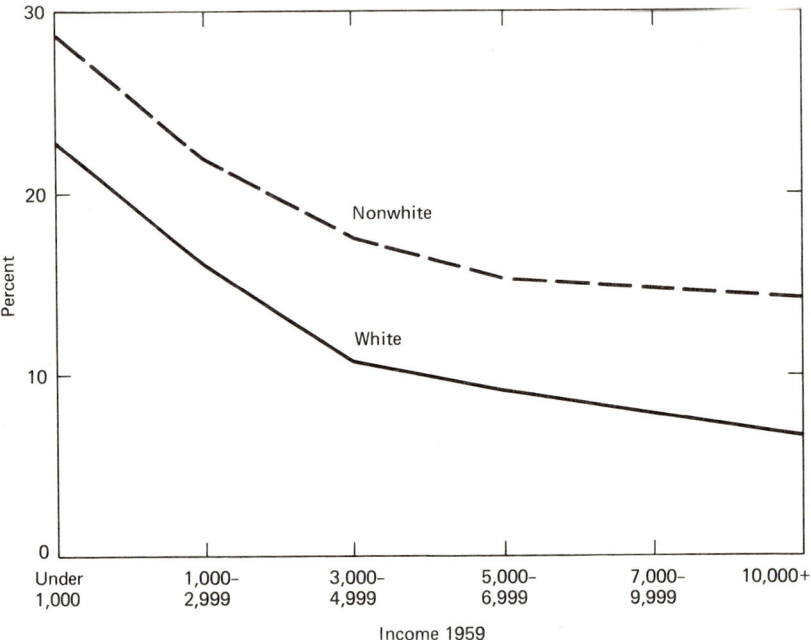

SOURCE: U.S. Bureau of the Census, *U.S. Census of Population: 1960. Subject Reports: Marital Status.* Final Report PC(2)-4E (Washington, D.C.: GPO, 1966), Table 6.

France, and the Netherlands.[42] Finally, Table 22.4 shows proportions of ever married persons who are still in first marriages with their spouses present. It is clear that this measure shows greater marital stability among whites than among nonwhites, and among farm dwellers than those who live in urban or rural nonfarm areas.

Throughout this book it has been our thesis that functionality is the most important component in the viability of a social group, including, of course, the family—both extended and nuclear—as well as the marital dyad. In consequence, it has been emphasized, where functionality is high, the members of the group tend to assess each other largely in terms of task-oriented competence. A second principle has been that in groups of relatively low functionality, the members tend to assess each other in terms of likability, i.e., in terms of the congeniality of the characteristics of their personalities. From this

---

[42] *Op. cit.*, pp. 518–521.

Marital Dissolution

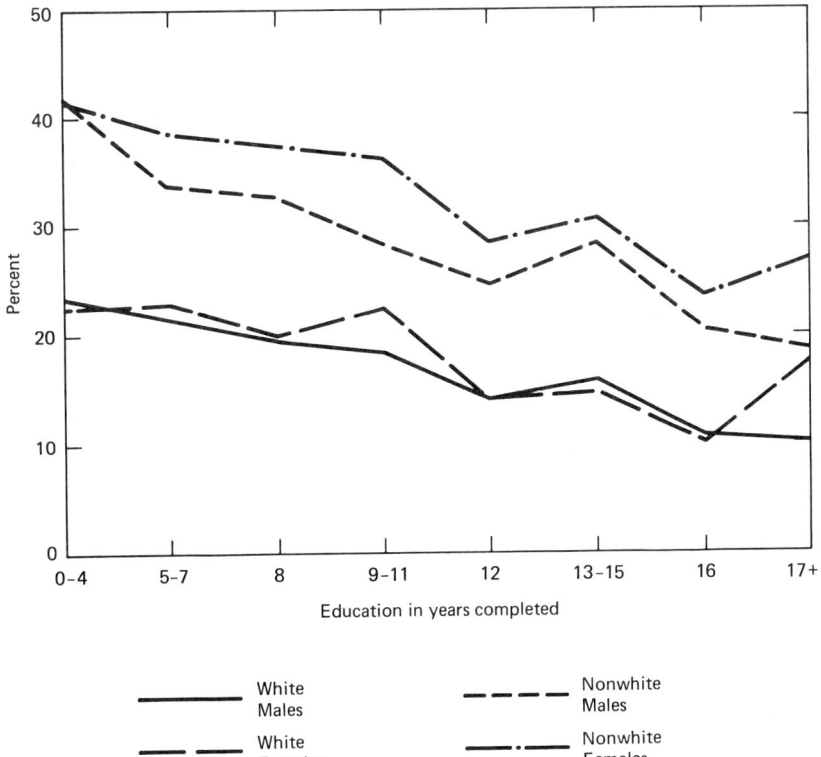

FIGURE 22.4

Percentage of Those Ever Married Who Were Divorced, Separated, or Had Been Married More Than Once at the Time of the 1960 Census, by Education (Age 14 and Over)

SOURCE: Unpublished data furnished by the Bureau of the Census.

observation we are led to examine the evidence on the relation, if any, of personality characteristics to marital dissolution.

What do we find when we turn to the research literature on the personality correlates of marital dissolution? Most studies on this general topic have related personality traits to marital happiness (as that term was defined in Chapter 21)[43] and very few have related such traits to marital dissolution. In one of the few studies to compare married and divorced subjects, Locke reported that "a person is a good marital risk if he is characterized by directorial ability, adaptability, affectionateness, and sociability."[44] After surveying the

---

[43] Cf. page 550.

[44] Harvey J. Locke, *Predicting Adjustment in Marriage: A Comparison of a Divorced and a Happily Married Group* (New York: Holt, Rinehart and Winston, Inc., 1951), p. 227.

FIGURE 22.5

Percentage of Those Ever Married Who Were Divorced, Separated, or Had Been Married More Than Once at the Time of the 1960 Census, by Occupation (Ages 25–34)[a]

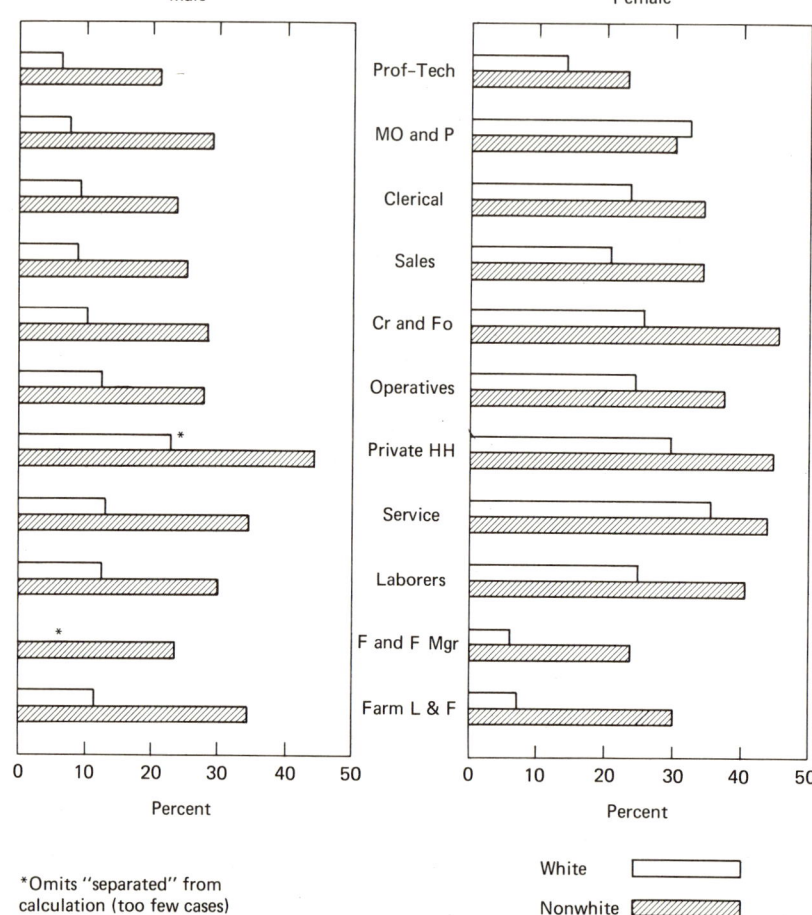

*Omits "separated" from calculation (too few cases)

SOURCE: Unpublished data furnished by the Bureau of the Census.

[a] Definitions of abbreviations in figure: Prof-Tech (Professional and Technical Workers); MO and P (Managers, Officials, and Proprietors); Clerical (Clerical Workers); Sales (Sales Workers); Cr and Fo (Craftsmen and Foremen); Operatives; Private HH (Private Household Workers); Service (Other Service Workers); Laborers (except Farm); F and F Mgr (Farm Owners and Managers); Farm L & F (Farm Laborers and Foremen).

literature on the correlates of marital happiness, Kirkpatrick concluded that there were "only low correlations . . . with measured personality traits prior to marriage," whereas within marriage happiness correlated positively with "men-

TABLE 22.4

Percentage Distribution of Ever-Married Persons Aged 14 Years and Older, by Present Marital Status, Presence or Absence of Spouse, Single or Multiple Marriages, Sex, Area of Residence, and Color: United States, 1960

PRESENCE OR ABSENCE OF SPOUSE, AND NUMBER OF MARRIAGES	ALL AREAS			URBAN			RURAL NONFARM			RURAL FARM		
	Total	White	Non-white	Total	White	Non-white	Total	White	Non-white	Total	White	Non-white
					Males							
Persons ever married	100.0	100.0	100.0		100.0	100.0		100.0	100.0		100.0	100.0
Married, spouse present												
Married once	76.1	77.9	59.3		77.4	59.0		77.6	58.1		83.5	65.9
Married more than once	11.8	11.3	16.9		11.6	16.9		11.4	16.4		7.8	18.8
Other												
Married once	9.9	8.9	18.8		9.0	19.2		9.1	20.2		7.5	11.5
Married more than once	2.2	1.9	5.0		1.9	5.0		1.9	5.3		1.1	3.7
					Females							
Persons ever married	100.0	100.0	100.0		100.0	100.0		100.0	100.0		100.0	100.0
Married, spouse present												
Married once	66.6	68.5	50.2		66.5	48.2		71.2	54.0		80.5	64.1
Married more than once	10.0	9.8	12.2		10.0	12.2		10.0	12.0		6.8	12.4
Other												
Married once	19.3	18.1	29.1		19.5	30.7		15.8	26.1		11.4	18.3
Married more than once	4.1	3.6	8.5		4.0	8.9		3.0	8.0		1.3	5.3

SOURCE: U.S. Bureau of the Census, *U.S. Census of Population: 1960. U.S. Summary, Detailed Characteristics* (Washington, D.C.: GPO, 1963), Table 176, pp. 424–435.

tal health" and "harmonious companionship based on common interests and accompanied by a favorable attitude toward the marriage and spouse."[45]

The fact that these conclusions are phrased in such general language suggests that it has proved difficult or impossible to discover any more specific personality variables that distinguish consistently between the relatively happy and the relatively unhappy, between the relatively conflict-free and those couples whose degree of conflict has already taken them to the divorce courts. It seems entirely possible that most of the correlations that have been reported have resulted from "halo effect" or "response set," which in this context would be the result of a disposition of happily married couples to speak favorably of themselves and of each other and of unhappily married and divorced couples to speak critically of their spouses and ex-spouses respectively.[46]

If we accept—tentatively, to be sure—the conclusion that very little has been found in the way of personality traits that are consistent predictors of marital felicity or stability, have we at the same time concluded that personality makes no difference in the marital relationship? Surely such a conclusion seems contrary to common sense. It may be that there is no single variable that is generally predictive in the sense that we could predict that a person high on that trait would be a good matrimonial risk irrespective of the personality of the person he marries and/or irrespective of the course of his experiences and gratifications outside the marriage. It may be that a person who is directive and makes decisions easily is a good matrimonial risk when married to someone who dislikes making decisions but also dislikes having issues left dangling and unsettled, and if, furthermore, he moves into occupational positions that not only permit but require decisiveness. But if the same man were to marry a different kind of woman and/or to have a different career line, the trait we have attributed to him might lead to frustration and conflict within and/or outside the marriage. To investigate this possibility it might be fruitful to work with detailed and intimate case histories with a view to constructing types of happy and/or stable married couples.

Our functional analysis of the family carries an implication concerning the prognostic significance of the happiness of the spouses. Generally speaking, it appears that where the nuclear family is highly functional, there will be

---

[45] Clifford Kirkpatrick, *The Family: As Process and Institution* (2d ed.; New York: Ronald, 1963), pp. 387, 393, 394.

[46] One research report that indicates a clear awareness of this problem is Georg Karlsson, *Adaptability and Communication in Marriage: A Swedish Predictive Study of Marital Satisfaction* (Uppsala: Almqvist & Wiksells Boktryckeri Aktiebolag, 1951), esp. pp. 124–125. Although studies using nonclinical samples fail to show personality traits that are consistently correlated with marital happiness, still clinical studies report otherwise. Cf., e.g., Henry V. Dicks, *Marital Tensions: Clinical Studies towards a Psychological Theory of Interaction* (New York: Basic Books, 1967). On the interpretation of findings from the clinical method, see Robert F. Winch and Louis Wolf Goodman (eds.), *Selected Studies in Marriage and the Family* (3d ed.; New York: Holt, Rinehart and Winston, Inc., 1968), chap. 1.

strong normative support for preserving marriages.[47] In this type of setting the feelings of the individual will be relatively trivial in the sense that a good citizen, no matter what his or her feelings toward a spouse may be, will be expected to remain with the spouse and to fulfill marital duties. In a minimally functional nuclear family, on the other hand, the society has relatively little interest in preserving the integrity of the marriage. In this type of setting we should expect the norms supporting marital stability to be weak and therefore the feelings of the individual spouse should be more significant in portending the stability of the marriage.[48]

We have theorized that there ought to be, and have found supporting evidence for, a correlation whereby families with greater resources would be able to offer greater rewards to members than could families with less, and that the former should therefore be more stable than the latter. An obvious next step in the theorizing is that the presence of resources should make the individual happier than he would be in their absence. To the extent that this is so we should expect to find evidence of greater marital happiness in couples of greater than of less resources. Evidence is consistent with the expectation: Williamson has found income to be positively correlated with marital happiness as that term is defined in this book (cf. page 550).[49]

It is against this theoretical backdrop that we can interpret the layman's conception of the causes of divorce—too much drink, loose living, and so on. (Cf. page 583 above.) Such "causes" are designations of and assessments of behavior of one spouse that is frustrating to the other. The probability that the resulting unhappiness leads to marital dissolution depends upon other considerations—norms and functions— that determine the stability of marriage in any societal context.[50]

Other Correlates of Divorce in the United States: Early marriages

Early marriages have been criticized because of the belief that the people involved are emotionally immature and not in position to assume the responsibilities of marriage. Supporters argue that early marriage is preferable to sex-

---

[47] It is possible for the *extended* family to be highly functional and still to have a high divorce rate as was true in traditional Japan.

[48] Because of the multitude of variables affecting any concrete case we should expect to find exceptions to this general deduction from our functional premises. Men have left their wives in the most functional of families. As before, the intent here is to designate a tendency, other things being equal.

[49] Robert C. Williamson, "Economic Factors in Marital Adjustment," *Marriage and Family Living*, 14: 298–301 (1952); and "Socio-Economic Factors and Marital Adjustment in an Urban Setting," *American Sociological Review*, 19: 213–216 (1954).

[50] Cf. Goode, *After Divorce*, chap. 10, "The Conflict Process—Themes of Complaint Made by the Wife"; and George Levinger, "Sources of Marital Dissatisfaction among Applicants for Divorce," *American Journal of Orthopsychiatry*, 36: 803–807 (1966).

ual deprivation or premarital pregnancy and that the physiological rigors of pregnancy and childbearing can be borne better in youth than later.

From an analysis of ages of women at first marriage, Glick has shown that early marriages tend to be less stable than marriages contracted at later ages. He found the median age at first marriage of women who were remarried to be about two years younger than of women who were still in their first marriage.[51] Studies have shown low age at marriage to be associated with not finishing high school,[52] low income of husband, low prestige of husband's occupation,[53] and low social class.[54]

Less obvious than the correlation between marital instability and early age at marriage is the interpretation to be placed on the correlation. One interpretation that would render the finding trivial is that by marrying early one merely increases the duration of one's risk of divorce. In a study that has controlled for exposure to this risk, however, the greater instability of early marriages is still visible.[55]

Another interpretation of the greater instability of early marriages is that it is the consequence of socioeconomic status. The reasoning runs as follows: There is evidence that divorce rates are higher in lower than in upper socioeconomic strata. It is also known that early marriage is especially frequent in the lower strata. Perhaps, then, there is nothing especially unstable in early marriages, but we are merely noting a statistical series in which the lower strata, with their high divorce rates, are overrepresented. On the other hand, one might argue in the opposite direction—that there is nothing especially unstable about marriages in the lower strata, but they appear in early marriages with their high divorce rates. As of the moment of writing no analysis has appeared that would warrant a definite conclusion on this point.[56]

---

[51] Glick, *American Families*, p. 56. Of course not all remarried women have been divorced; some have been widowed.

[52] National Office of Vital Statistics, *Vital Statistics—Special Reports*, Vol. 45, No. 12, September 9, 1957, Tables 24 and 27, pp. 339 and 348–350.

[53] Paul C. Glick and Emanuel Landau, "Age as a Factor in Marriage," *American Sociological Review*, 15: 517–529 (1950).

[54] W. Lloyd Warner and Paul S. Lunt, *The Social Life of a Modern Community* (New Haven, Conn.: Yale University Press, 1941), pp. 203, 255.

[55] To show that the data are not merely reflecting the increment of risk it is necessary to relate age at marriage to the duration of marriages ending in divorce. This has been done for some 8000 divorces in Iowa in 1945–1947.—Thomas P. Monahan, "Does Age at Marriage Matter in Divorce?" *Social Forces*, 32: 81–87 (1953), esp. Table 2.

[56] It is possible that one of the propositions in the preceding paragraph was phrased in a misleading fashion: the proposition that early marriages correlate with low socioeconomic status. The indexes of socioeconomic status used in this correlation are the size of the husband's income, the number of years of his formal schooling, and the prestige of his occupation. Because of the prospect that after marriage very young husbands might considerably increase their income and education and move into occupations of greater prestige, it is not clear to what extent these measures represent a temporary or a lasting socioeconomic status and therefore to what extent they are valid indexes. A more valid index of their ascribed socioeconomic statuses as of the time of marriage would be the

The analysis to this point leads to the conclusion that it is not known whether or not the correlation between early marriage and marital instability is "real," i.e., whether or not if marriages were classified by the prestige of fathers' occupations and if duration of marriage (and thus risk) should be held constant, there still would be a higher proportion of divorces among those who marry early. Let us assume that the correlation is in this sense real; what interpretation may we offer? One clue comes from the research of Christensen, who concludes on the basis of records in a county in Indiana (1) that there is an overrepresentation in young marriages of premarital pregnancies and (2) that premarital pregnancy tends to be associated with a higher than average divorce rate.[57] There does not appear to have been any systematic research to support our conclusion, but the analysis previously presented of the courtship-engagement sequence as a period of trials and rejections suggests that a couple experiencing enough mutual attraction to have sex relations might not still be speaking to each other if they went together long enough to get well acquainted. It seems probable, in other words, that where pregnancy forces a choice among illegal abortion, unmarried motherhood, and marriage, such marriages will contain an overrepresentation of poorly matched couples.

There is another body of evidence bearing on the interpretation that early marriages tend to be unstable because of "emotional immaturity." Adolescence in this country seems to be a period during which personality is in a state of flux. The prospect of relatively rapid change implies that the kind of mate such a person would choose might vary from one year to the next. To the extent that this is so it seems appropriate to speak of the person as being emo-

comparison of couples on the basis of the occupations and incomes of their fathers. On the other hand, the use of father's occupation would fail to reveal another relevant consideration —the possibility that early marrying males of middle-class families tend to be downwardly mobile.

[57] "Premarital pregnancy seems to be a part of the divorce-producing syndrome . . . [it] seems to intensify the conflict which a couple may already be in. . . . Not only do premarital pregnancy couples get divorced more frequently than others but they get divorced earlier after the wedding. Of the premarital pregnancy couples, those who waited until 'the last minute' to marry showed higher divorce rates than those who married soon after the condition was discovered."—Harold T. Christensen and Bette B. Rubinstein, "Premarital Pregnancy and Divorce: A Follow-up Study by the Interview Method," *Marriage and Family Living*, 18: 114–123 (1956) at p. 122. Christensen and his associates have analyzed the interval between the date of marriage and the date of birth of the first child for marriages taking place for a number of years in Tippecanoe County, Indiana. Where this interval is sufficiently short to give rise to the presumption of premarital pregnancy, these investigators find that the couples tend to have married young, to have had secular wedding ceremonies, and that the husbands tend to be classified as having laboring occupations. See also Harold T. Christensen, "Premarital Pregnancy as Measured by the Spacing of the First Birth from Marriage," *American Sociological Review*, 18: 53–59 (1953); Harold T. Christensen and Hanna H. Meissner, "Premarital Pregnancy as a Factor in Divorce," *American Sociological Review*, 18: 641–644 (1953). These articles are parts of a series published under the general title "Studies in Child Spacing." Cf. also Thomas P. Monahan, "Premarital Pregnancy in the United States," *Eugenics Quarterly*, 7: 133–147 (1960).

tionally immature. In three studies involving female subjects there are data that may be interpreted as bearing on this question. In two of the studies the data seemed to show that the girls who married early appeared less stable (and emotionally more immature?) on personality tests and had less satisfactory relationships with their parents than girls who did not marry early.[58] The third study did not find such a difference.[59]

It is not difficult to take the first step in theorizing an answer to the query as to the wisdom of early marriages: to the extent that the members of an age grade are prepared to undertake the obligations of marriage and the coordinate roles, to the extent that they wish to, to the extent that they are permitted to, and to the extent that marriage will not disadvantage them for later roles, there is no reason why the members of that age grade should not be permitted, indeed encouraged, to marry. A complete answer, as we can see, would involve analysis in terms of the several conditions just enumerated.

For middle-class Americans the most obvious part of the query pertains to the implication of early marriage for the later socioeconomic status of the couple. Since this is principally determined by the occupation of the husband, since his occupation is affected by the level of his education, and since his education may be terminated by an early marriage, the implication is that he may not be upwardly but, indeed, may be downwardly mobile. On the other hand, through his young wife's earnings, an early marriage may provide an impecunious young man with the resources to continue or to resume his education. In situations where the husband becomes educated considerably beyond the wife, he may begin to acquire the subculture of a higher stratum, discover that his wife has "low-brow" tastes, and find that he is "outgrowing" her. Thus we can see that there are two sets of conditions where early marriage would seem quite satisfactory: (1) where people are prepared at an early age to assume adult roles, which in American society is most typical of people in the lower strata with their unskilled and semiskilled occupations, and (2) where the young people are not expected to meet such demands, a situation that occurs in the upper strata where families of orientation can continue to support young people, whether singly or as married couples, and where, moreover, families of orientation can provide resources for the continuation of the education of young couples as well as for the maintenance of the latters' children. And so it appears that early marriage should prove especially disadvantageous where prolonged education is customary, where

---

[58] Floyd M. Martinson, "Ego Deficiency as a Factor in Marriage," *American Sociological Review*, 20: 161–164 (1955); J. Joel Moss and Ruby Gingles, "The Relationship of Personality to the Incidence of Early Marriage," *Marriage and Family Living*, 21: 373–377 (1959).

[59] Lee G. Burchinal, "Adolescent Role Deprivation and High School Age Marriage," *Marriage and Family Living*, 21: 378–384 (1959). This same author has summarized a good deal of literature on early marriage in "Research on Young Marriage: Implications for Family Life Education," *The Family Life Coordinator*, 9: 6–24 (1960).

young couples are expected to be economically independent at marriage, and where contraception is not practiced efficiently.

One final topic to be considered has to do with the distribution of divorces with respect to the durations of the marriages. Of course the breakup of the marriage in all senses other than the legal typically antedates the divorce by a considerable period, perhaps even several years.[60] In 1965 the median duration of marriages terminating in divorce within the twenty-two states of the divorce registration area was 7.2 years; about one seventh of all divorces were granted to couples married less than two years, about a quarter to those married less than three, and about a third to those married less than four years.[61]

Summary

Marriages are broken by death, divorce, and separation (including desertion). The sociologist looks for causes of marital dissolution—other than those resulting from death—in the functions of the family and of related structures. In the United States there appears to have been an increase in the proportion of marital dissolutions in which both parties survive, but this increase has been more than counterbalanced by a decrease in those resulting from death. Accordingly, the evidence points to a small decrease over the past century or more in the proportion of marriages dissolved each year. Although the data are not conclusive, it appears that the divorce rate in the United States rose to a peak in 1946 and since then has fallen back to a level that still exceeds the period before World War II. The increase is interpreted as resulting from a tendency for more couples to formalize their marital dissolutions.

In the United States the lack of love and of a congenial relationship is apparently a frequent cause of marital dissolution. Since this is not consistent with the legal grounds for divorce, divorce proceedings frequently involve collusion and perjured testimony. In some countries "marital breakdown" has been adopted as *a*, or *the*, ground for divorce, and the proposal has been made that it be adopted as the basis for a uniform divorce code for the United States.

Rates of marital dissolution are highest in those segments of the population having the fewest resources: the lower-blue-collar workers and the nonwhites. Furthermore, marital happiness has been shown to be positively

---

[60] In 1434 cases from the Municipal Court of Philadelphia over the period 1937–1950 the median duration between marriage and divorce was 9.7 years, whereas the median duration between marriage and actual separation was 5.1 years, a difference in the medians of 4.6 years.—William M. Kephart, "The Duration of Marriage," *American Sociological Review*, 19: 287–295 (1954).

[61] National Center for Health Statistics, *Divorce Statistics Analysis: United States, 1964 and 1965* (Washington, D.C.: GPO, October 1969), Series 21, No. 17, p. 11 and table 24, pp. 42–43.

correlated with income. Such correlations are consistent with our functional theory, which asserts that the more functional families will have more resources and thus the capacity to be more rewarding to its members than the less functional families can be, and that for this reason marriages in the more functional families should be more stable.

There is evidence that early marriages in the United States tend to be relatively unstable. There are several possible interpretations: (1) This is merely a reflection of the correlation between low socioeconomic status and marital dissolutions. (2) This is a consequence of emotional immaturity, which makes for unsound mate-selection and for childishly frustrating, rather than gratifying, marital interaction. (3) This is a consequence of there being among the early marriages a considerable proportion in which the bride is premaritally pregnant; many of these couples would reject each other if given a longer period of premarital interaction free from the pressure occasioned by pregnancy.

23

Consequences of, and Responses to, Marital Dissolution:

remarriage

Introduction

What happens when marriages are dissolved? What are the consequences for the family as a social system? How do the members respond to familial disorganization resulting from marital dissolution? Although we continue to be interested in the more general statement of the problem, our information and discussion will center on the American nuclear family.

Points of Emphasis

To an American the significance of a broken marriage seems to be, first, for the children—how they will suffer (1) from the loss of love of the absent parent, (2) from the fact that there are not two parents from whose behaviors the children can learn clear distinctions between the sex roles, (3) from the emotional difficulties the children are believed to be destined for because of the lack of the love of two parents, and (4) from the difficulty because of the financial loss resulting from the absence of a parent; and, second, for the wife-mother—(1) her difficulty in supporting her children financially and (2) emotionally, and (3) her deprivation socially and sexually. When concern is expressed for the husband-father, it frequently revolves about the financial costs of the divorce action and the maintenance of two households.

When a marriage is dissolved, the remaining spouse(s) is(are) faced with problems of readjustment, irrespective of whether the departed spouse is dead or alive. These problems of readjustment, like those of marital adjustment, may be analyzed in terms of roles and of psyches. We have concluded that the small-family system of the American middle class rates connubial solidarity over lineal solidarity and views the nuclear family as more or less detached from the extended kin, even including, to some extent at least, the families of orientation of both spouses. This small-family system, as we shall see, intensifies the problems of readjustment in both senses to marital dissolution.

A sociological analysis leads to the consideration of roles and begins by noting that there are three ways in which the nuclear family may respond to the disorganizing impact of marital dissolution: reconstituting the original organization with new personnel, reorganizing the structure with the remaining personnel, and dissolving the system. The analysis continues by examining the functions that were being carried out by the departed member.

A social psychological analysis leads to the consideration of psyches and begins by noting that in cultural contexts like that of the American middle class where mate-selection is presumed to be based on the mutual love of the spouses, both the bereaved and the divorced may be expected to feel a sense of emptiness and yearning. In the case of the bereaved this may be mixed with a sense of guilt for having done, or not having done, something, fanciful or objective, that might have prevented the death of the spouse. In the case of the divorced the reaction will probably contain a mixture of hostility over the frustrations that the ex-spouse has caused. Readjustment in both cases frequently involves the quest for a new love-object.

The Nuclear Family and Marital Dissolution

Like other social systems, the nuclear family can respond in different ways to the state of disorganization resulting from having one of its positions vacant. The disorganization inheres in the fact that the expectations defining the position are not being fulfilled. These responses are not completely mutually exclusive, and a family may first respond one way and then another.

1. The family can refill the vacant position or one of its constituent roles. This can be done with or without legal sanction.
    a. A new person may enter the family and take up the duties of spouse and of parent that were left by the departed member. If in addition the new member marries the remaining spouse and legally adopts the children, the replacement is completely legalized.
    b. A new person may enter the family to fill part or all of the role of spouse but not participate as a parent. This can happen when a deserted wife takes in a lover. The couple may marry without the man's assuming responsibility for her children.
    c. A new person may enter the familial system by filling part or all of the role of parent but not participating as a spouse. This can happen when a widowed father employs a woman to serve as housekeeper and governess to perform maternal—but not wifely—activities. It would be unusual for such a person to assume legal responsibility for the parental functions.
2. The family can reassign duties among the remaining members so that the essential responsibilities of the absent member are discharged.
    a. The remaining parent may assume the duties of the absent parent in

addition to those of his or her own role (as in the case of the widow who comes home from work, prepares her children's evening meal, bathes them, puts them to bed, and so on).
   b. The duties of the absent parent may be assigned to children, as when a son is forced at an early age into the labor force because of his father's death, or when a daughter becomes the family cook and cleaning woman because of the death of her mother.
3. The activities of the absent parent may not be continued, as when a a widowed father takes his son to live in a hotel.
4. The nuclear family ceases to exist as a more or less autonomous social system, as when a divorcee takes her brood to her parental home.

Irrespective of which response is made—maintenance of the structure with new personnel, reorganization of the structure with or without loss of function, or dissolution of the structure—there will be "problems." If the first option is followed, the remaining spouse and children must agree on the acceptability of the individual as well as upon the specification of that person's rights and duties. Reassignment is likely to entail the enlargement of each member's responsibilities and may involve duties that seem inappropriate, as when a son becomes responsible for cooking and/or dishwashing. Reduction of function will probably result in reduction of gratification; as argued throughout this book, reduction in gratification can be expected to drive the deprivation-experiencing members outside the family to seek gratification in other settings. The fourth possibility converts the previous autonomous nuclear family into a subsystem of a larger kin system with the result that members of both the nuclear family and of the extended kin system must define and accept new rights and obligations with respect to each other.

American Family Structure and Marital Dissolution

Two interrelated features of familial structure affect the significance of marital dissolution: the relative importance of the marital and the lineal relationship, and the relative importance of the nuclear and the extended families.

It seems obvious that where the marital relationship is regarded as more important than the lineal, the impact of marital dissolution will be greater. On the other hand, where—as in traditional China—the father-son relationship was transcendent, the loss of spouse becomes of secondary importance. It is also clear that the emphasis on the marital relationship is consonant with the small-family system, whereas the emphasis on lineal solidarity is consonant with some form of large-family system.

Where families are patrilocal or matrilocal, there is a built-in means of calling on the extended family in times of such crisis as the disappearance of a spouse. Even where residence is neolocal, however, there may be a strong sense of solidarity and obligation between families in time of crisis. In other words, if it is assumed that the wife-mother will take her children into her parental home, if she is welcome, and if her coming does not place a strain on the extended family, the system is organized to backstop the nuclear family. Then marital dissolution—although it may still be viewed as a crisis—is not a disaster. In sum, the capacity of the family to respond effectively to the loss of a spouse depends upon its structure and functions; its disposition to do so depends upon the culture, i.e., the sense of moral rightness and the degree of obligation to do so.

In the United States the family's capacity to respond is not uniform but varies with ethnicity. With respect to white Protestants whose ancestors migrated from Northwestern Europe, it not only appears that the American family is neolocal but carries a relatively slight sense of responsibility through the extended family. There is the expectation that once people marry, they have indicated their independence of their families of orientation and need lean no longer on their parents or other kinsmen. In this setting it is a mark of failure for the wife-mother to have to return to her parental home with her children, and the parental couple is probably not very well prepared to receive her and her brood. In this sense we have, as Goode puts it, a deficiency in the kinship system. And in this setting, where family and kinship are more woman's business than man's, it would seem that marital dissolution must tend to have a greater impact on the woman than on the man.[1]

A study of Jewish families in New York City reveals a quite different pattern. Here residence is frequently neolocal only in the narrow sense of being a separate dwelling unit, but the young couple often tries to live as close to the wife's parents as possible—perhaps in the same building and even with a private access from the apartment of the parents to that of the daughter and her nuclear family.[2] It is not surprising that there is evidence of greater

[1] Recall the observation of Burgess and Wallin to the effect that American middle-class marriages are more important to women than to men (page 546) and the remark of Margaret Mead that just as the man faces insecurity in the occupational system, the woman does in the familial system (page 550). Another writer has observed that widowed and divorced mothers face objective and subjective problems. Included in the former category are those resulting from inadequate income and limited energy to perform the augmented duties of employed worker, manager of the home, and nurturer and controller of her children. Among the subjective problems this author asserts there are frequently guilt, fear, frustration, and loneliness. She concludes that such organizations of widowed and divorced parents as Parents Without Partners can help lessen tension and relieve the subjective problems and through suggesting techniques can provide some help with the objective problems.—Marjorie P. Ilgenfritz, "Mothers on Their Own—Widows and Divorcees," *Marriage and Family Living*, 23: 38–41 (1961). Another function fulfilled by such organizations is to provide fields of eligibles for remarriage.

[2] Hope Jensen Leichter and William E. Mitchell, *Kinship and Casework* (New York: Russell Sage, 1967); and by the same authors, "Jewish Extended Familism," in Robert F. Winch and Louis Wolf Goodman (eds.), *Selected Studies in Marriage and the Family* (3d ed.; New York: Holt, Rinehart and Winston, Inc., 1968), pp. 139–148.

interaction and exchange of services among Jewish than among Protestant families.[3]

Next we shall consider the significance of the loss of a spouse-parent for the functions of the family.

THE ECONOMIC FUNCTION

Stated a bit too simply, the economic function of the American husband-father is to bring money into the family and that of the wife-mother is to exchange a portion of the money for the goods and services needed for the maintenance of the family. Of course, this assertion is not intended as a denial either that men are typically involved in large purchases—houses, automobiles, major appliances—or, indeed, that they ever go to the supermarket. Nor should it be overlooked that many married women are gainfully employed. Rather, the central point is that the wife-mother typically buys the overwhelming majority of the items purchased for consumption by the family, and thus the bulk of the day-to-day spending is central to the woman's economic function in the familial system. Accordingly, the departure of the husband-father typically means the loss of the chief source of money; the loss of the wife-mother typically results in the loss of the chief shopper.

Because the man is usually engaged in a full-time occupation, he can be adequately replaced in an economic sense only by another fully employed person, or by the equivalent in two or more part-time workers. Thus a woman whose husband has died or has deserted or divorced her may take another man into the household—either with or without marriage—to replace the missing breadwinner. Another possibility is that she may go to work—if not already working—but if she does, it is unlikely that she can bring home as much money.[4] And if she has small children, she will have to arrange either for day-nursery care or for someone else to come into her home to take care of the children during her working hours. If she has children of suitable age, one other possibility is that she may arrange for one or more of them to enter the labor force. Another recourse followed by some women is to return with their children to their parental homes.

---

[3] Robert F. Winch, Scott Greer, and Rae Lesser Blumberg, "Ethnicity and Extended Familism in an Upper-Middle-Class Suburb," *American Sociological Review*, 32: 265–272 (1967); and Robert F. Winch, "Some Observations on Extended Familism in the United States," in Winch and Goodman (eds.), *op. cit.*, pp. 127–138.

[4] Median wages and salaries are considerably higher for males than for females in every major occupational category where both sexes are represented.—U.S. Bureau of the Census, *Current Population Reports—Consumer Income*, Series P-60, No. 60, June 30, 1969, Table 9, pp. 44–45. In 1967 the median income of families with male heads was $9509 whereas the median of families with female heads was $6002.—U.S. Bureau of the Census, *Current Population Reports—Consumer Income*, Series P-60, No. 64, October 6, 1969, Table 11, p. 30.

The financial loss resulting from the absence of the major breadwinner may be mitigated by the woman's inheriting from the man or receiving the proceeds of his insurance if he has died, or through a settlement, alimony and/or child support if they are divorced. To cover the need existing where none of these possibilities is present or where none is adequate, the United States government has a program of Aid to Families with Dependent Children. Since the act leaves interpretation and administration to the individual states and other jurisdictions, the size of grant varies considerably. In 1969, when about 5.4 million children in some 1.9 million families were receiving financial assistance under this program, the range of average family grants varied from $46 per month in Puerto Rico and $47 in Mississippi to $266 in New Jersey.[5]

Initially the death of the husband-father was the most important single cause of the family's becoming dependent upon the state. This has ceased to be true largely because of the decline in the death rate and because of the increase in the proportion of the population covered by another government program, Old-Age and Survivors Insurance (with its provision for widows with minor children).

The program of Aid to Dependent Children has come under attack from some quarters as a device whereby indolent black women are given an incentive at the taxpayers' expense to migrate from the South, to engage in promiscuous sexual activity, to be continually pregnant, and to bear illegitimate children who become criminals. A very intensive study of this issue in Chicago and Cook County (Illinois) reached these conclusions:

1. The typical ADC family in Cook County consisted of a mother and three children.
2. The typical mother was between 30 and 35 years of age, was black, had been born in Mississippi, and had lived in Illinois for fifteen years or more.
3. She had been married and had had children by her husband. The children were born in Illinois.
4. The woman's husband had deserted, and she was not free to remarry.
5. She had had one illegitimate child since her husband left.
6. She expressed feelings of guilt and was aware of a stigma in the black community as well as in the general community concerning the bearing of children out of wedlock.
7. She disliked being dependent; she did not want more children; the more she had, the deeper she had had to go into debt.

By way of interpretation the authors of the study concluded:

8. Racial discrimination in employment was one of the most serious

[5] *Statistical Abstract of the United States: 1970,* Tables 453 and 455, pp. 299 and 301.

causes, both direct and indirect, of family disorganization, desertion, and illegitimacy.

9. The ADC program operated to keep the children with their mother, but because to be eligible a child had to be deprived of parental support by death, incapacity, or continuous absence of a supporting parent, the program discouraged the return of the husband-father.[6]

After recognizing that the ADC program created an incentive for the husband-father to leave home and to stay away, the authorities have modified the regulations to allow families to qualify for financial aid if (1) the husband-father is unemployed or underemployed and (2) the family is actively trying to become self-sufficient.

THE SOCIALIZING-EDUCATIONAL FUNCTION

Although Chapter 5 has noted an apparent trend in this country whereby the schools take over more and more of the socializing-educational function, there is still the expectation that the child will acquire some behaviors from his parents. One behavioral and attitudinal category that is frequently thought of in this connection pertains to sex roles. If one parent is missing, it is frequently reasoned that either (1) the children will not have an opportunity to observe the performance of activities that are characteristic of the sex of the absent parent or (2) the remaining parent will be combining both male and female activities, with the consequence that the children will be unable to distinguish between masculine and feminine sex roles. The departure of the husband-father is more frequent at lower social levels than at the higher. (See Tables 22.1–22.3.) Another aspect of deprivation with respect to the socializing-educational function widely believed to result from broken marriages is the lack of socialization of the offspring with respect to discipline and ideals; delinquency is frequently thought to follow. Conspicious in the lower strata are adolescent gangs, with their violent emphasis on masculine toughness and their rejection of femininity. These attitudes have been interpreted as consequences of the father's absence.[7]

Actually, as we saw in Chapter 15,[8] numerous propositions of the type set forth in the above paragraph have been studied with results that lead more to an agnostic view concerning the effect of the absence of either parent than seems generally to be believed.

[6] Greenleigh Associates, *Facts, Fallacies and Future: A Study of the Aid to Dependent Children Program of Cook County, Illinois* (New York: Greenleigh Associates, 1960), p. 5. Cf. also the *Addenda to Facts, Fallacies and Future,* chap. 2, esp. Table 6, p. 7.

[7] J. H. Rohrer and M. S. Edmonson, *The Eighth Generation* (New York: Harper & Row, 1960); W. B. Miller, "Lower Class Culture as a Generating Milieu of Gang Delinquency," *Journal of Social Issues,* 14: 5–19 (1958).

[8] Cf. the section on "Correlates in Children's Responses of Some Variations in Familial Structure and Functions."

OTHER BASIC SOCIETAL FUNCTIONS

In a society like ours, where the familial system tends toward minimum functionality, it would seem that although the dissolution of marriage would not have much effect on the other basic societal functions, still it should reduce the number of children born and thereby depress the degree of fulfillment of the *familial* (or *replacement*) function. According to the Bureau of the Census, however, this expectation is not borne out. Among whites the presence or absence of the husband-father seems to make no difference: where the head of the family is under forty-five years of age, both husband-wife families and families with female heads have an average of 2.1 children. Among blacks female-headed families average 3.0 children whereas husband-wife families average 2.5, or half a child less.[9]

What about the effect of marital dissolution on the derived functions? After mentioning in the next paragraph some implications for the parental functions, in following sections we shall relate the position-conferring function to role-adjustment and the emotional gratification function to psychic adjustment.

The parental functions. The departure of one parent may have one and sometimes two consequences. First, if the remaining parent works outside the home—typically true for a woman and virtually universal for a man—she, or sometimes he, will, of course, have little time to carry out the parental functions of nurturing and controlling the children. To prevent their becoming "neglected children" the remaining parent may try strenuously to find someone—typically an otherwise uncommitted female relative—to carry out the parental functions in the home. Second, if the remaining parent carries on alone, whatever nurturing and controlling the children get now comes from a single parent, whereas previously the two functions may have been more or less divided between the two parents.[10] If a parent-surrogate is brought in, it is not unusual for the children to question the legitimacy of that person's efforts to discipline them. Either case may have consequences for the children's identifications and internalization of discipline.

THE POSITION-CONFERRING FUNCTION AND ROLE-ADJUSTMENT TO MARITAL DISSOLUTION

Before beginning to consider the impact of marital dissolution on role-adjustment in families with children it is probably advisable to get some indication of the proportion and/or numbers of children involved in the United States. In 1966, 88 to 89 percent of all children were living with both parents.[11]

---

[9] U.S. Bureau of the Census, *Current Population Reports—Population Characteristics*, Series P-20, No. 191, October 20, 1969, Table 7, pp. 53–56.

[10] Cf. the discussion of the instrumental and expressive roles, pages 325, 333 above.

[11] Bureau of Labor Statistics Report No. 332 and Current Population Reports, Series

It has been estimated for 1955 that about 10 percent of all children lived with one parent only—9 percent with mothers and 1 percent with fathers.[12] As is suggested by the positive correlation between socioeconomic status and marital stability, the proportion of children living with both parents increases with family income. Of all children living in families in 1959, 59 percent of the nonwhite and 69 percent of those in white families with income under $2000 were living with both parents, whereas with income of $8000 per year and over 95 percent of nonwhite children and 99 percent of white children were with both parents.[13]

What can we say about the number of children involved in divorce actions? It is estimated that for 1965 the number of divorces and annulments in this country was 479,000 and that 132 children were involved for every 100 marriages dissolved. This means that approximately 630,000 children were affected. Since about 60 percent of the divorces and annulments involved children, the average number of children in marriages having children was over 2 (nearly 2.25) per marriage.[14] It appears that about 1 child in every 7 or 8 is being affected by divorce or annulment.[15]

Let us bear in mind that children in one-parent families are generally with their mothers and that children's positions in (at least the more urbanized parts[16] of) the society are conferred by fathers, who derive their status from the occupational system. These facts lead to the conclusion that fatherless children are deprived of a sense of societal position and integration. In homely language, they lack the answer to the locating and integrating question: "What does your father do?" Beyond this, of course, is the prospect of the stigma of illegitimacy awaiting any child who is known to have been born outside a legal marriage.

Where the dissolution results from divorce, there arises the ambiguous

P-23, No. 24, *Social and Economic Conditions of Negroes in the United States* (Washington, D.C.: GPO, 1967), p. 75.

[12] Metropolitan Life Insurance Company, *Statistical Bulletin*, Vol. 37, April 1956, Table 2, p. 3.

[13] Bureau of Labor Statistics Report No. 332 and Current Population Reports, Series P-23, No. 24, *op. cit.*, p. 76.

[14] National Center for Health Statistics, *Divorce Statistics Analysis: United States, 1964 and 1965*, Series 21, No. 17 (Washington, D.C.: GPO, 1969), Tables 29 and 30, pp. 47 and 48.

[15] Such an estimate can be made as follows for the year 1960. In that year it is estimated that 463,000 children were involved in divorces or annulments. (*Ibid.*) A proper base to calculate a rate would be the number of children in a one-year age category at about the middle of the risk group, say age 10. The number of children of age 10 in 1960 was 3,481,000.—U.S. Bureau of the Census, *Current Population Reports—Population Estimates*, Series P-25, No. 385, February 14, 1968, Table 1, p. 12. Then $463,000/3,481,000 \times 100 = 13$ percent.

[16] The argument that property is more important in rural stratification and the occupational system is more important in urban stratification is presented in Arthur L. Stinchcombe, "Agricultural Enterprise and Rural Class Relations," *American Journal of Sociology*, 67: 165–176 (1961).

relationship of the departed parent to his children. There are the correlative questions of contribution to support, custody, rights of visitation, and so on. With the remarriage of the remaining parent there is some prospect that such problems may become compounded. What are the rights, loyalties, and obligations of the older and younger generations, and can the children find their places in their tangled skeins of kinship? Will the new spouse be interested in adopting the children? Does the new spouse have children by a previous marriage, and if so, how will they feel about it? Will the children wish to be adopted by the new spouse with the implication that adoption will reduce the tie to the departed parent? And if the "real" parent and the new parent begin to procreate, how will the children of the previous marriage feel about their new half-siblings?

There are also position-conferring problems for surviving spouses (or ex-spouses). The subculture of the American majority views it appropriate that on marriage one should leave his parents and cleave to his mate. But with marital dissolution this more recent union to which he has committed his prime loyalty has ceased to exist. Now where does he belong in the kinship structure? If divorce occurs before the coming of children, he can seek to be readmitted to his family of orientation (i.e., to resume the status of child). To some extent this is possible for a divorced parent, especially if the other spouse has custody of the children.

It can be argued that the divorced or widowed man generally finds it much easier than does the women to integrate with the nonkin aspects of society. Certainly in American society the occupational system links virtually all able-bodied men into a network of task-oriented interaction. As long as he remains in the labor force, then, marital dissolution probably tends to have less impact upon the man than upon his wife.

A problem of integration with the nonkin aspects of society exists for the woman who is not in the labor force, whether because of her responsibilities to her children or because of being deterred by considerations of health or of social status. To the extent that the couple has had a social life with members of the husband's occupational group, the wife will probably find herself cut off from such interaction and tend to feel alone with her "half-orphaned" children and adrift in an indifferent society. The fact that the unit of entertainment tends to be the couple creates difficulties for her friends who try to maintain previous patterns of interaction, and since many will assume she wishes to remarry, some of her less secure married women friends will avoid her because of an assumed predatory interest in their husbands.

Where the widowed, deserted, or divorced woman seems to have an advantage over her male counterpart is in integrating with the kin group. A widowed grandmother is typically of greater use to a young couple with children than one of the grandfathers would be. Here we note again the functional bond underlying mother-daughter solidarity.

In their monumental study of societal structures Sumner and Keller commented on the problematic position of the widow. After surveying a great deal of ethnographic material, they concluded that the status of a man was usually not greatly affected by the death of his wife, but "the status of the widow is a sort of unique affair, needing definition of all sorts." Two of the more exotic practices concerning widows are the levirate and the suttee. The levirate was practiced by the ancient Hebrews and is described in the following passage from Deuteronomy, 25:5–6.

> If brethren dwell together, and one of them die, and have no son, the wife of the dead shall not marry without unto a stranger: her husband's brother shall go in unto her, and take her to him to wife, and perform the duty of an husband's brother unto her.
> And it shall be, that the firstborn which she beareth, shall succeed in the name of his brother which is dead, that his name be not put out of Israel.

By means of the levirate the ancient Hebrews provided lineal continuity to men dying without male issue and at the same time provided the widow of the deceased man with a place in the societal structure. (In colonial New England, by contrast, it was thought to be incestuous for a man to marry the sister of his deceased wife.)

In 1829 the British outlawed the Indian custom of suttee, whereby the living widow was placed on the funeral pyre of her deceased husband and entered the hereafter in his company. "Suttee" means "good wife," and it is reported that death in this fashion was claimed as an honor by the first wife of the dead man.[17]

THE FUNCTION OF EMOTIONAL GRATIFICATION AND THE EMOTIONAL RESPONSE TO MARITAL DISSOLUTION

Some writers have emphasized the common elements involved in the emotional response to the loss through death of someone close and through the rupture of the relationship by other means. The late Willard Waller has written insightfully on alienation and mourning.[18] We shall develop this point

---

[17] William Graham Sumner and Albert Galloway Keller, *The Science of Society* (New Haven, Conn.: Yale University Press, 1929), III, 1843–1844. Cf. also K. M. Kapadia, *Marriage and Family in India* (2d ed., London: Oxford, 1958), pp. 170 ff., where the practice is called "sati."

[18] Willard Waller, *The Family* (revised by Reuben Hill; New York: Holt, Rinehart and Winston, Inc., 1951), pp. 517–518. Bohannan makes the telling point, however, that there is no recognized way to mourn a divorce and that the friend of the divorcee is confronted with a dilemma as to whether the appropriate behavior is one of consolation or of congratulation.—Paul Bohannan, "The Six Stations of Divorce," in Paul Bohannan (ed.), *Divorce and After* (New York: Doubleday, 1970). The attention accorded to psychic readjustment has been largely at the level of intuitive interpretation and clinical analysis. Cf. Sigmund Freud, "Mourning and Melancholia," *Collected Papers* (London, Hogarth, 1925), Vol. IV, pp. 152–170; Waller, *op. cit.*, part 6; Thomas D. Eliot, "Bereavement: Inevitable but Not Insurmountable," in Howard Becker and Reuben Hill (eds.), *Family, Marriage and Parenthood* (2d ed.; Boston: Heath, 1955), pp. 641–668; Edmund H. Volkart, "Bereavement

of view by looking at two aspects of the family's response to the loss of a husband-father or a wife-mother in terms of the function of emotional gratification: (1) the history of gratification and/or frustration in which interaction with the departed member resulted for the remaining members, and (2) the circumstances of the departure.

With respect to the gratification-frustration history we shall offer two hypotheses, to be evaluated separately for each family member remaining:

1. Other things equal, the more the gratification provided by the departed—both absolutely and relatively—the greater should be the sense of loss. "Relatively" is intended in two senses:
   a. In terms of the remaining person's expectations; e.g., a child may have acquired the expectation that a father is not a rewarding person, and with such an expectation even a small (absolute) amount of gratification might endear the father to the child.
   b. In relation to the remaining person's perception of the gratification that the departed provided to other members of the family; e.g., a favorite child would experience a greater loss than would one of the same parent who felt he had been rejected.

It does not necessarily follow that a person who provides very little gratification is thereby providing a high degree of frustration. He may interact very little and seem more indifferent than frustrating. Accordingly, there is need of a second hypothesis:

2. Other things equal, the more the frustration provided by the departed —again both absolutely and relatively—the greater should be the sense of relief and joy.

It is thus reasoned that the amount of gratification and of frustration that the remaining person perceives as having resulted from his interaction with the departed person should influence the former's desire for the latter to remain or to leave and the degree to which the former would implement such a desire. Among such instrumental measures might have been engaging in quarrels with the departed, manifesting hostile and resentful behavior toward him, initiating divorce proceedings, failing to provide him with nursing and medical care when sick, not interfering with his disposition to drive while drunk, and so on. If we add to the considerations just noted the remaining person's perception of the departed's wish to terminate or not to terminate the marriage, it is possible to set up a schematic set of hypotheses about the remaining person's emotional response to the marital dissolution. (See Table 23.1.)

Evidence consistent with these general hypotheses comes from a study of 295 college students who were children of divorced parents. It is reported

---

and Mental Health," in Alexander H. Leighton *et al.* (eds.), *Explorations in Social Psychiatry* (New York: Basic Books, 1957), pp. 281–307. A bibliography on psychic adjustment to bereavement appears on pp. 419–422 of the last-mentioned book.

TABLE 23.1

Hypotheses about the Remaining Person's Emotional Reaction to the Other's Departure as a Consequence of the Circumstances of the Departure

		DID REMAINING PERSON WISH DEPARTED TO LEAVE?			
		Yes		No	
		Did Departed Wish to Leave?		Did Departed Wish to Leave?	
		YES	NO	YES	NO
Does Remaining Person Feel Responsible for Other's Departure?	Yes	Feelings of accomplishment and relief mixed perhaps with guilt	Maximum guilt, mixed perhaps with relief	Feelings of martyrdom	Feelings of responsibility for a tragic mistake
	No	Relief	Guilt, mixed perhaps with relief	Feeling of having been rejected; hostility	Tragedy

that the offspring who saw their homes as having been happy before the divorce experienced greater trauma in response to the divorce than did those who viewed their homes as having been unhappy.[19] It seems reasonable to assume that those who assessed their homes as having been happy had probably derived more gratification from their homes than did those who made the opposite assessment.

It is recognized, of course, that virtually any concrete case will be too complex to fit neatly into one of the eight cells in Table 23.1. With enough knowledge about a given case, however, it might become possible to classify it as belonging principally in one cell and as having something of the quality of one or more of the other cells. For example, a given case might be classified as largely a 23 (row 2 and column 3) but also something of a 21. (That is, the remaining person is ambivalent about wanting the departed to go but definitely leans in the "No" direction.) Then it would be hypothesized that the response of the remaining person would be a feeling of rejection and hostility mixed with some sense of relief.

[19] Judson T. Landis, "The Trauma of Children When Parents Divorce," *Marriage and Family Living*, 22: 7–13 (1960).

Remarriage

With or without the prefix "re-," the term "marriage" refers to only one of the relationships in the nuclear family. In view of the American emphasis on the marital relationship it is consistent that the spouses should do the selecting. Where there are children, however, they will be involved and hence can hardly avoid being interested parties in the selection. Evidence of such interest comes from the young child who says to her mother about to go out on a date, "Do you think he will like us?" and from the mother who asks her child, "Do you think he will be a good daddy?" As shown in our enumeration of ways of filling the vacant position,[20] moreover, the culture is ambiguous as to the degree to which the children and the new spouse will become involved with each other, a problem complicated by another variable—the degree to which the departed spouse, if still alive, will seek to remain in the lives of the children. It is appropriate for us to keep in mind that although "remarriage" refers only to the marital relationship, the replacement may involve the parental role as well, and some of the "problems" of remarriage result from failure to notice this elementary structural fact.

The following points describe remarriage in America in the later half of the twentieth century (actually as of 1963)[21]:

1. Nearly three out of every ten couples joined in marriage in thirty-five states and the District of Columbia during 1963 involved at least one person who had been married before.
2. Most of those who remarry—77 percent of the men and 74 percent of the women—have been divorced; of course, the rest have been widowed.
3. When they remarry, divorced persons are more likely to select mates who have been divorced than they are to choose single or widowed mates; there is similar homogamy with respect to the marriages of widowed and single persons.

A study based upon data from 1954 provides the following information about relative ages of bride and groom in remarriages:

4. Whereas in first marriages the bridegroom is on the average about 3 years older than his bride, in remarriage the bridegroom averages about 6 years older than the bride.[22]
5. The older the man at the time of his remarriage, the greater is the gap between his age and that of his bride: if he remarries at age 30, he

---

[20] Cf. the section "The Nuclear Family and Marital Dissolution," pages 606–607 above.
[21] National Center for Health Statistics, *Marriage Statistics Analysis: United States, 1963* (Washington, D.C.: GPO, 1968), Series 21, No. 16, Table 7, pp. 29–30.
[22] Paul C. Glick, *American Families* (New York: Wiley, 1957), p. 126.

averages 7 years older than his bride; if he is over 45 at the time of remarriage, he averages more than 9 years her senior.[23]

6. Conversely, the older the woman at the time of her remarriage, the less is the gap between her age and that of her bridegroom: if she remarries at age 30, she is 5 years younger on the average than her groom; if she is over 45 at the time of remarriage, she averages only 3 years younger than her groom.[24]

From still older data we learn:

7. At age 21 more than nine out of every ten unmarried men and women —whether single, widowed, or divorced—will eventually marry. At older ages, however, the probability of marriage varies considerably with sex and marital status. For example, among those unmarried at age 50 the percentages who will eventually marry or remarry (on the basis of 1948 data) are:[25]

	SINGLE	WIDOWED	DIVORCED
Males	18.2	61.6	71.0
Female	9.6	20.1	52.9

8. It is estimated that two thirds of the divorced women and three fifths of the divorced men remarry within five years, and that probably the intervals are about the same for the widowed.[26]

9. Remarriages are less likely than first marriages to be marked by honeymoon and presents and are more likely to be marked by civil rather than religious ceremonies.[27] A study done in upstate New York reports that it was 2 times as frequent for widowed and 3.5 times as frequent for divorced men as for single to have civil ceremonies; for women, civil ceremonies were 2.5 times as frequent among widowed and nearly 6 times as frequent among the divorced as among the single.[28]

Perhaps the question most frequently asked about remarriages is whether they are more or less successful than first marriages. As noted earlier, we must immediately respond that "success" is an ambiguous term. If we understand success to mean stability, we may rephrase the question by asking, Do remarriages last longer or less long, on the average, than first marriages? Even for

[23] Ibid., Table 83, p. 126.
[24] Ibid.
[25] Paul H. Jacobson, American Marriage and Divorce (New York: Holt, Rinehart and Winston, Inc., 1959). Tables 34, 36, 38, 40, pp. 78, 80, 83, 85, respectively.
[26] Ibid., pp. 69–70.
[27] August B. Hollingshead, "Marital Status and Wedding Behavior," Marriage and Family Living, 14: 308–311 (1952).
[28] J. V. DePorte, "Civil Marriage In New York State, Apart from New York City," American Sociological Review, 17: 232–235 (1952).

this phrasing it is not easy to find relevant information, and there are no data on a nation-wide basis. Moreover, as soon as we can locate relevant data, we shall be confronted with knotty problems of interpretation.

One interpretive problem arises as soon as we notice that there are two ways of becoming eligible to remarry—through divorce and through widowhood. Table 10.15 shows nine permutations of previous marital status of the two spouses, i.e., widowed-man–single-woman, and so on. (And to take account of the fact that about one eighth of the remarrying men and one sixth of the remarrying women are in third or subsequent marriages would increase considerably the number of permutations.[29]) As might be expected, some of these permutations prove more stable and others less stable than first marriages.

Basing his analysis on Iowa records for 1953 through 1955, Monahan has produced the most adequate study to date. Iowa had higher proportions of nonurban, Protestant, and white residents than the country as a whole, but its crude divorce rate (8.7 per 1000 population in 1954) was close to the national rate (9.2). Monahan concludes: "*Primary marriages* (a first marriage for both parties) show a ratio of only 16.6 divorces per 100 marriages in that category, but where both parties had been divorced *once* before, the figure doubles to 34.9, and where both parties had been divorced *twice or more* times before the ratio climbs to 79.4. . . . As to the widowed, they show abnormally low ratios: 9.9 for the both widowed *once* only, and 2.0 for the both widowed *twice or more* only."[30]

Monahan cautions his reader that these findings should be interpreted in the light of the fact that at remarriage widows and widowers average fifteen to twenty years older than divorced persons.

A final question of interpretation cannot be answered at this time. Evidence presented in Chapter 22 pointed toward the conclusion that marriages are less stable at the lower than at the higher socioeconomic strata. It does not appear that there are published data on which to conclude whether or not the socioeconomic variable "explains" the higher instability of remarriages of divorced persons than of primary marriages, i.e., whether or not the remarriages of divorced persons *within strata* are equally stable or are less stable on the average than first marriages.

Summary

Where the extended family is operative, children tend to look to it for fulfillment of all functions—the basic societal as well as the derived familial functions. In the small-family system, children typically look to their parents for fulfillment of the derived familial functions: position-conferring, emotional

---

[29] Glick, *op. cit.*, Table 96, p. 144.

[30] Thomas P. Monahan, "The Changing Nature and Instability of Remarriages," *Eugenics Quarterly*, 5: 78–85 (1958), at p. 81. Italics in original.

gratification, nurturance and control. If in the extended-family system either parent leaves the household, usually some adjustment can be improvised whereby functions are maintained. An aunt or a sister-in-law or a mother of one of the spouses can fill in for a deceased wife; an uncle or a brother for a dead or deserting husband.

In the small-family system the children look to the two parents for the fulfillment of the familial functions; when one spouse is no longer present, the maintenance of functions imposes the difficult requirement that the remaining spouse perform for both. If the wife-mother is gone, in the typical case the husband and children will suffer some loss in emotional gratification, and the children in nurturance and control. If the husband-father is gone, the children's loss in these functions may not be so great, but both for them and for the wife-mother it may be severe with respect to position-conferring.

The emotional response to both alienation and to bereavement, it is hypothesized, depends upon whether the remaining person—spouse or offspring in our context of the nuclear family—wished the departed to leave and feels responsibility for the departure, and whether the departed wished to leave.

Whether remarriages are more or less stable than first marriages seems to depend upon the previous marital status of the remarrying persons. Although these results may be altered when age at remarriage is held constant, it now appears that remarriages of the widowed are more stable and that those of the divorced, less stable, than first marriages.

24

Concluding Observations: *value positions and familial organization*

Introduction

Whether or not one concludes that the family in America is going to the dogs seems to depend in part on which evidence one heeds and in part on which interpreter one reads. Other considerations that seem relevant to one's conclusion about the American family involve the familial type—real or mythical—one uses as a model of familial organization,[1] and which familial type one thinks of as *the* American family.[2]

The trend in the divorce rate is the evidence most usually cited to support the thesis that the family is disintegrating, but contrary evidence can be seen in the fact that there has been an increase in the proportion married in the adult population—from 53.5 percent in 1890 to 65.5 percent in 1967.[3] The "population explosion" that threatens man's future can be adduced as evidence that the family's basic function of replacement is continuing, but we have seen that the crude birth rate in the United States has been declining. Some see the "generation gap" as another sign of familial disorganization, but others respond that even those most alienated from their parents establish new families of procreation in their communes and other havens from "established" society. Some see the demise of the family in the decline of sex—the "masculinizing" of women and, especially, the "feminizing" of men; others see the

---

[1] We may recall Goode's observation: "We are all guilty of loosely contrasting an undefined urban, supposedly pathological family life, with a rural, idyllic family pattern of some generations ago: the classical family of Western nostalgia is cited and praised in practically every public speech on the breakdown of the modern family and modern society."—William J. Goode, *After Divorce* (New York: Free Press, 1956), pp. 3–4.

[2] We may recall the conclusion drawn in Chapter 11 that three types of American family had been distinguished and that perhaps more could be found.

[3] *Statistical Abstract of the United States: 1968*, Table 35, p. 32.

rise of a new sexual freedom as tolling the death knell of the family—for what man would marry when he could have its "advantages" without incurring its "responsibilities"? How should we assess these facts and opinions?

Zimmerman and those who proceed from the position of Catholic doctrine have been arguing that a continuation of recent family trends would certainly bring us to the kennels. Burgess and Folsom, Hill and Foote exemplify writers who hold the contrary view. These diametrically opposite conclusions have not represented a dispute concerning the essence of the evidence but have derived from differences in value systems, and such differences are not amenable to empirical verification. Zimmerman and those who think as he does value a traditional form of the family, at least in certain salient respects. Their disapproval and alarm are evoked to the degree that the modern family diverges from the form they value. Burgess and others of his persuasion subordinate social structures—the family included—to the development and happiness of the individual. They reason that consistency in social institutions produces less pain and more happiness for the individual actor, and they see recent trends as bringing the family into progressively greater consistency with the rest of the social order. It should not be concluded that the value position of the latter writers leads them to desire the "withering away" of the family. Rather, their position is one of anticipating with satisfaction the emergence of a new family form more consistent with its change in function and with changes that have occurred in other institutions of American society. Seeing the promise of greater human happiness in the current trends, these writers do not concur that the family is going to the dogs.[4]

Purpose of This Chapter

Our purpose is to consider the value positions, the evidence, and the unknowns related to the disorganization and the reorganization of the American family.

[4] The remarks about Zimmerman's views in the paragraph above are couched in the present perfect tense because they do not register his most recently published views. Zimmerman appears to be pessimistic or optimistic about the future of the family as the trend in the birth rate is down or up. His magnum opus of 1947 was written before there was evidence of the upswing in fertility after World War II. The cover of that book was gray and green, and its pages were filled with gloom; the barbarians were at the gates. More recently he and Father Lucius Cervantes have published *Successful American Families* (New York: Pageant, 1960). This book has a bright yellow cover and notes that the birth rate has risen; the threat is over and the family has survived. What is not clear, however, is just how much of the former book Zimmerman accepted as he was writing the latter. The analysis of the earlier book is very complete, and it seemed evident that its writer was convinced as to the correctness of its morose conclusions. It would have been interesting if Zimmerman had indicated in the later book how much of his earlier analysis of the American family he would have rejected on the basis of the relatively high birth rates of the 1950's, and it would have been interesting to get a reading of his views a decade later to see whether he would have reverted to his earlier pessimism on the basis of the falling birth rates of the 1960's.

What Is Familial Disorganization?

When applied to a social system, the term "disorganization" may be used to refer to three types of change in the system. The three types are not mutually exclusive; neither are they equivalent ways of referring to the same process:

1. There is increasing disagreement among the members of the system as to their claims and obligations upon each other, i.e., there is a reduction in the degree of consensus concerning the system's constituent positions and roles.
2. There is a reduction in the number of positions in the structure.
3. There is a reduction in the number and/or range of claims and obligations made and/or honored that tie positions of the structure to each other, i.e., there is a loss of functionality.

Since each of the three types refers to a process, it implies that the state of the system is being considered at an earlier and at a later time, which we shall call time 1 and time 2, respectively. Let us consider these three types of disorganization in the context of the family.

To exemplify family disorganization of type 1 let us imagine a farmer whose son is leaving the farm to seek employment in the city. At time 1 father and son had agreed that the latter would stay on the farm, take care of the father in his declining years, and in due course take over the farm. At time 2 the father still thinks the son should follow this plan, but the son believes it is his right to go to the city.

An example of type 2 disorganization would exist when there is a shift from a joint family system to the nuclear, as would be the case if the family of the traditional Chinese peasantry should change in the direction of the American middle-class family (see Table 12.4).[5]

If the departure of the farmer's son or the transition from the stem to the nuclear family should result in a reduction in the economic functioning of the family, it would constitute an example of type 3.

Finally, "disorganization" may be used in a purely judgmental sense—as epithet or moral condemnation—to indicate that the speaker regards as bad and immoral the behaviors under consideration.

FAMILIAL DISORGANIZATION AS MORAL EVALUATION

To the extent that value positions exist among writers on the family, two major schools can be differentiated. It is relatively immaterial just what terms we use to designate these two positions. Since labeling is a convenience,

---

[5] Some might reason that reduction in the number of positions in a structure is not disorganization but simplification. In Zimmerman's view, however, the shift from trustee to domestic to atomistic forms of the family, which involves a progressive reduction in the number of positions, is disorganization.

however, let us call them "institutionalists" and "individualists." Institutionalists, such as Zimmerman[6] and Schmiedeler,[7] cherish traditional values. They would like to revive an earlier familial form as they conceive it: a family whose members are sensitive to obligations to, and control by, kinsmen, a cohesive family that fulfills its traditional functions but is not strong enough to challenge the superior authority of the church.[8] In this value system, the stability of the structure and its institutions is more important than the happiness of its members. By contrast, the individualists, such as Burgess,[9] regard individual welfare and happiness as values that transcend institutional form, and hence they are not alarmed by changes in family structure that appear to enhance human happiness.

In America the difference between the institutionalists and the individualists can be seen in their views on a variety of specific issues with respect to both the structure and the functions of the family. On the structural side two issues that are prominent are (1) some form of extended family versus the more or less detached and independent nuclear family, and (2) the acceptability of divorce. With respect to functions their differences are quite clear with reference to replacement and socialization-education and by corollary with reference to emotional gratification and the economic function. In the American context the issues are in part set up by doctrines of the Catholic Church, which has been the most conspicuous proponent of traditional views. Divorce and reproduction are topics on which the views of the Catholic Church have been categorical and hence have given rise to controversy.

In Chapter 1 and elsewhere in this book we have referred to Zimmerman's nostalgia for the type of family he has labeled "domestic," i.e., an extended system in which the family is highly functional and has much control over the behavior of its members.[10] It is with respect to divorce, however, that the division between the two views becomes dramatically clear. Since the institutionalist values the system over its constituent members, any behavior that threatens the integrity of the system is *ipso facto* reprehensible. It is consistent with this view that the traditional concept of divorce involves the idea of blame, i.e., of an innocent and a guilty party. Whereas the individualists do not

---

[6] C. C. Zimmerman, *Family and Civilization* (New York: Harper & Row, 1947).

[7] Edgar Schmiedeler, *An Introductory Study of the Family* (rev. ed.; New York: Appleton, 1947).

[8] It appears that some of the family's most violent opponents and perhaps some of its stanchest defenders may take their extreme positions because of the capacity attributed to the family to deter or to enable other structures to attain their ends. We saw, for example, that the Chinese Communists calculatedly weakened the traditional family in order to reduce resistance to the achievement of the party's goals. (See Chapter 2.) It seems conceivable that a part of the Catholic Church's support of the traditional family stems from the belief that a moderately strong family is an asset in the pursuit of the Church's goals.

[9] Ernest W. Burgess and Harvey J. Locke, *The Family* (2d ed.; New York: American Book, 1953); J. K. Folsom, *The Family and Democratic Society* (New York: Wiley, 1943); Reuben Hill, "The American Family: Problem or Solution," *American Journal of Sociology*, 53: 125–130 (1947); Nelson N. Foote, "Love," *Psychiatry*, 16: 245–251 (1953).

[10] See note 1 above.

regard divorce as a good in itself, their disposition is to regard it as a lesser evil, to eliminate the element of blame, to see divorce as an avenue of escape from an intolerable marriage, as a technique of enabling two unhappy individuals to escape further unhappiness.[11]

(Lest it be thought that a high rate of divorce is necessarily an indication of familial disorganization, it is in order to note that the traditional family among both the Arabs and the Japanese has had high rates of divorce. Where there is a strong extended family and a high rate of remarriage as has been the case in both of these systems,[12] it is more accurate to interpret divorce as reflecting a change in personnel rather than disorganization of the familial system. By analogy, a spectator at a football game does not think the game is breaking up merely because a coach substitutes one quarterback for another.)

Another sharp difference of opinion between the institutionalists and the individualists is with respect to the topic of reproduction. In the institutional view child bearing is the aim of marriage. In the individualistic view happiness is the aim of marriage; whether or not to have children, and how many, are questions to be decided in terms of the needs, desires, and resources of the individual couple. To the institutionalists a decline in the birth rate is an index of family disorganization. To the individualists it reflects the impact of extrafamilial institutions upon the family and does not necessarily imply disorganization of the family.

Institutionalists and individualists differ as to the degree of responsibility that other societal structures should assume for the function of socialization-education. The Catholic Church is committed to the idea that certain forms of instruction should be performed outside the family, but through its system of parochial schools it seeks to put such instruction under its own control. On the other hand, Father Schmiedeler holds that the family should do more than it is doing in the modern urban setting. He asserts that the school is not the place for sex instruction, which should be handled in the family, and he further avers that nursery schools are the consequence of an abandonment by the family of its rightful responsibilities.[13] Although the individualists have not been particularly explicit on these points, it is the writer's judgment that their position is in general as follows: The family should take over only as much of the function of socialization-education as it can efficiently handle.

---

[11] Or as Paul Bohannan puts it: "Divorcees are people who have not achieved a good marriage—they are also people who would not settle for a bad one."—"The Six Stations of Divorce," in Paul Bohannan (ed.), *Divorce and After* (New York: Doubleday, 1970).

[12] Cf. William J. Goode, *World Revolution and Family Patterns* (New York: Free Press, 1963), chaps. 3 and 7. The reader should note that since Goode's discussion of extended familism among the Arabs is based on data concerning the number of persons per household, it does not take account of extended families involving plural households and hence underestimates the extended familism of the Arabs.

[13] *Op. cit.*, pp. 357–364. In the light of this analysis it seems that the John Birch Society was remaining within its tradition of ultraconservatism when it turned its attention in the latter 1960's from exclusively political concerns and opposed sex-education in the public schools.

That is, there are numerous tasks that the school can carry out more efficiently, and it should be expected to do so. Under proper supervision nursery schools are desirable because they expand the social experience of the preschool child, and because they afford desirable relief for mothers.

It is understandable that the individualists, with their emphasis upon the happiness of the individual, should have shown a more marked psychological orientation than the institutionalists. The individualists have emphasized the function of emotional gratification, especially the providing of love, as central to the task of the family, and they tend to regard a family as successful when this function is going well, irrespective of what is happening in other areas of interaction. The institutionalists, who emphasize role-expectations and hence behavioral conformity, give relatively less weight to emotional gratification. To the extent that they have sensed this need, they seem to have looked to both the church and the family to fulfill it.

With respect to the economic function the differences between the two value groups are implicit rather than explicit. Both groups recognize that in the modern industrialized economy the family cannot be self-sufficient. In modern Western societies the farm family is the closest approximation to self-sufficiency. The institutionalists are disposed to hold up to urban people the farm family as exemplary in its execution of familial functions. This seems not to be due to its self-sufficiency per se, but rather to be due to the manner in which it fulfills its other functions, a manner that is consistent with relative economic self-sufficiency, and inconsistent with the manifest absence of self-sufficiency in urban life.[14] The individualists regard the farm family as well suited to rural conditions of life, but as being poorly designed for urban conditions.

FAMILIAL DISORGANIZATION AS LOSS OF CONSENSUS ABOUT ROLES

In the present section let us assume that the functions that *are* carried on in the family remain constant as do the expectations of the family's members with respect to which functions *should be* carried on within the family. A later section will take up variation in functionality.

Here we are concerned with the prescriptions defining the various roles and positions, i.e., who is expected to do what and for whom, or for the system as a whole. To the extent that there is a decrease in the level of agreement as to who does what for whom, there is evidence of familial disorganization as a loss of consensus about roles.

For example, let us imagine a family in which at time 1 all understand (1) that yard work is the responsibility of the husband-father and (2) that the preparation of breakfasts is the responsibility of the wife-mother. Let us conceive of time 2 some fifteen years later when (1) the husband-father—but only

---

[14] It is of some interest that, outside this country, the Catholic Church is strongest in areas where rural patterns predominate.

he—has come to feel that he is entitled to go golfing on weekends and that his son should assume responsibility for the yard, and (2) the wife-mother—but only she—has come to believe that she has earned the right to sleep late and that her daughter should get the breakfasts. Here there is a loss of consensus (an increase in dissensus) concerning roles within the family, which, according to our formulation, constitutes some degree of familial disorganization.

The writer is aware of no longitudinal studies on consensus and expectations concerning familial roles.[15] Related to this topic, however, was our discussion in Chapter 12 concerning the apparent decline in the differentiation of sex roles. As noted there, a traditional division of labor between the sexes seemed to have been based on the demands for strength, mobility, and continuity of effort, all of which are reduced by menstruation, pregnancy, childbearing, and motherhood. Of all familial relationships the marital is the one most explicitly based on sexual differentiation. Being the relationship out of which the complete nuclear family usually develops, the marital relationship gives orientation to the offspring, as is suggested by the phrase "family of orientation." The evidence of Chapter 12 suggests, however, that the differentiation of sex roles has been diminishing and that if the women's liberationists have their way, it will in time be replaced by unisex, and perhaps by the couvade.[16]

In view of the greater efficiency of a division of labor over an undifferentiated labor force[17]—presumably in the familial household as well as in the factory—young couples who are left without a conventionally specified sex-role differentiation will probably improvise their own division of labor on the basis of their idiosyncratic talents and incompetences. It is of course reasonable to expect that for some couples this might work entirely satisfactorily, but it does seem that all would have prolonged periods of trial and error, of adjusting and persuasion, before achieving such a satisfying accommodation. And of course such a state of affairs would render remarriage an increasingly difficult undertaking.

FAMILIAL DISORGANIZATION AS REDUCTION IN THE NUMBER OF
FAMILIAL POSITIONS

In the light of the analysis in Parts Two and Three it would be plausible to surmise that American families of bygone times may have differed from those of today in having been more differentiated, i.e., in containing more

---

[15] Blood and Wolfe have presented evidence they interpret as showing a tendency for families to increase their task-specialization as they go through the family cycle. Because of the incompleteness of their statistical analysis, however, it is difficult to assess the credibility of their results.—Robert O. Blood, Jr., and Donald M. Wolfe, *Husbands and Wives* (New York: Free Press, 1960), chap. 3.

[16] *Couvade:* a variety of customs practiced by some tribal peoples whereby the husband simulates the experience of childbearing, e.g., undergoing confinement. Cf. E. B. Tylor, *Researches into the Early History of Mankind* (3d rev. ed.; London: John Murray, 1878), pp. 291 ff.

[17] Cf. a discussion on this point in Chapter 3 above.

familial positions. The understanding of what is meant by a reduction in the number of positions is crucial for the analysis to follow. To offer an example, we should conclude that there had been a reduction in the number of positions under such circumstances as the following: Suppose that at time 1 the modal family includes the positions of husband-father, wife-mother, their children, father's father, and father's mother—five positions in all—but that at time 2 the modal family has only the three positions of the nuclear family—husband-father, wife-mother, and their children. (Of course variation in the number of children does not affect the number of familial positions.)

The only long-range evidence known to the writer as having any bearing on the number of positions in the American family is based not on the family but on the unit of the household.[18] Ogburn and Nimkoff have presented data on the size and composition of "approximate households" in 1800 and 1940. The Bureau of the Census has reported data for 1967 that seem reasonably comparable with those used by Ogburn and Nimkoff. (See Table 24.1.) It

TABLE 24.1

Composition of "Approximate Households" in the United States: 1800, 1940, and 1967

CATEGORIES OF RESIDENTS	PERSONS			CHANGES IN PERSONS			CHANGES IN PERCENT		
	1800	1940	1967	1800–1940	1940–1967	1800–1967	1800–1940	1940–1967	1800–1967
Parents and their spouses	1.77	1.77	1.72	0.00	−0.05	−0.05	0	−3	−3
Children	3.43	1.49	1.19	−1.94	−0.30	−2.24	−57	−20	−65
Others: Lodgers, servants, etc.	0.59	0.51	0.37	−0.08	−0.14	−0.22	−14	−27	−37
Total	5.79	3.77	3.28	−2.02	−0.49	−2.51	−35	−13	−43

SOURCE: Data for 1800 and 1940 were adapted from W. F. Ogburn and M. F. Nimkoff, *Technology and the Changing Family* (Boston: Houghton Mifflin, 1955), Table 18, p. 110. By permission of the publisher. These authors define the "approximate household" as the total population divided by the number of occupied residences or the number of households, including one-person households. Data for 1967 appear in U.S. Bureau of the Census, *Current Population Reports—Population Characteristics*, Series P-20, No. 173, June 25, 1968, Table 11, p. 27.

[18] "It is important to notice that household is an ecological concept, not a familistic one. A household is the set of persons sharing a dwelling unit, whether related to each other or not; a family is a set of interacting persons related to each other by blood, marriage, or adoption, whether or not living together."—Robert F. Winch, "Permanence and Change in the History of the American Family and Some Speculations as to Its Future," *Journal of Marriage and the Family*, 32: 6–15 (1970), at p. 7.

will be seen that an over-all reduction in size of household of 43 percent (2.51 persons on the average) took place between 1800 and 1967. Eighty-nine percent of the reduction in the number of persons, however (i.e., 2.24 out of 2.51) is in the single category of children. The third row of Table 24.1, which includes familial positions outside the nuclear family, also shows a marked reduction, but it includes lodgers and servants as well as relatives. From additional data it is clear that for 1940 and 1967 almost all of the "other" category (0.49 out of 0.51 in 1940, and 0.33 out of 0.37 in 1967) consists of relatives. The corresponding figure for 1800 is not available. But it follows that the maximum decrease that could have taken place in relatives (assuming that in 1800 all the "others" were relatives) is 0.22, i.e., less than one quarter of a person on the average.

As far as families in households (i.e., domestic families) are concerned, therefore, these data show that on the average there has not been any over-all reduction in the number of familial positions. Rather, the evidence suggests that on the average there has probably never been one relative per household in addition to the three-position nuclear family; it appears that in 1800 and in 1940 there was an average of about half a relative per household, and that this average had shrunk slightly to about a third by 1967.[19]

This section began on a note of apology about the inappropriateness of the data. The data cited have concerned the related members of households but have left us uninformed about families that transcend the single dwelling unit. From such studies as those of Jewish families in New York City we know that there are families that occupy two or more dwelling units. Unfortunately, we have no way of estimating the incidence of such families. In the study referred to, a typical arrangement was one whereby an older couple occupied one apartment while their daughter, her husband, and the younger couple's minor children occupied another apartment (frequently with a common wall) in the same building. A high degree of interaction between members of the two households and of exchange of goods and services (functionality) warrant our regarding residents of such a pair of dwelling units as a single familial system.[20]

Unfortunately, there are no data that can enlighten us about the number or structure of such families on a national basis.[21] Thus there is no direct basis

[19] A similar conclusion regarding the American family has been drawn by Arensberg and by Greenfield. The latter asserts that the small nuclear family was brought into New England before the Industrial Revolution by settlers from England and therefore that the small nuclear family was not a consequence of urbanization-industrialization.—Conrad M. Arensberg, "American Communities," *American Anthropologist*, 57: 1143–1162 (1957); Sidney M. Greenfield, "Industrialization and the Family in Sociological Theory," *American Journal of Sociology*, 67: 312–322 (1961).

[20] Hope Jensen Leichter and William E. Mitchell, *Kinship and Casework* (New York: Russell Sage, 1967).

[21] One of the types of American family referred to in Chapter 11 above was the "nuclear family embedded in a network of extended kin." Although we lack any estimate

for making any statement about what is happening to the structure of the American family. It is possible, however, to point to two trends leading to conflicting inferences. Studies by the author and his associates have revealed that migration is highly correlated with the absence of households of kinsmen in the community of residence. There is evidence that migration has been increasing, although not dramatically: in 1870, 77 percent of the population was reported as having been born in the state of residence; by 1950 this figure had shrunk to 74 percent, and by 1958 to 71 percent.[22] Such data probably reflect an influence toward shrinkage in the structure of the American family.[23]

The trend leading to the contrary conclusion, i.e., to the conclusion that extended familism is increasing and therefore that American familial structure should be expanding, derives from the doubling in life expectancy over the last couple of centuries from about 35 to about 70 years. Table 17.1 above shows that this fact has created the actuarial basis for three-generation (and even short-lived four-generation) familial systems where such were improbable two centuries ago.[24]

In the present state of knowledge it is not possible to determine the net result of these two conflicting effects—increasing migration and longevity—on the structure of the American family.

FAMILIAL DISORGANIZATION AS LOSS OF FUNCTIONALITY

In view of the extended treatment of functions in Parts Two and Three there is no occasion to do more than recall the conclusions of the analysis made there. With respect to the basic societal functions we may note the following high points. The shift from family farm to office and factory thins out the bonds of economic interdependence within the family. The rise of the school system reduces the degree to which the family carries out the socializing-

---

of its frequency on a national basis, it would appear to be common among Jews and Italians, and no doubt among other ethnic minorities as well.

[22] For 1870 and 1950 see *Historical Statistics of the United States*, Table C 1-14, p. 41; for 1958, U.S. Bureau of the Census, *Current Population Reports*, Series P-23, No. 25, "Lifetime Migration Histories of the American People" (Washington, D.C.: GPO, 1968), Table 3, p. 25. Unfortunately, not enough information is supplied to enable one to assess the comparability of these two series of data.

[23] Following is the chain of reasoning that justifies the inference. Since there is some evidence that the number of households of kinsmen one has in his community is related to his having been born there, an increase in the proportion of Americans who migrate from their native states should result in an increase in the proportion of individuals (and hence also of nuclear families) having no kin or few households of kin nearby. To the extent that one's kin are not in the community where one lives, it is difficult to exchange goods and services with them. Such exchange is central to our concept of functionality. The absence of functional relationships with nonnuclear kin means the familial system cannot be larger than nuclear.

[24] Cf. also Paul C. Glick and Robert Parke, Jr., "New Approaches in Studying the Life Cycle of the Family," *Demography*, 2: 187–202 (1965), reprinted in Winch and Goodman, *op. cit.*, pp. 166–177.

educational function. Replacement is still the basic function of the family and is carried out by the overwhelming majority of families; the degree of fulfillment of the function is down greatly from 1800.

Salient conclusions regarding the derived functions of position-conferring and emotional gratification are as follows: The development of a large-scale occupational system has shifted the ultimate source of position-conferring for urban people. For children and wives, status is piped from the occupational system via the husband-father through the nuclear family. There are two trends, however, that portend some reduction in this familial function. An increase in careers, rather than jobs, for women will enable them to derive status directly from the occupational system rather than from their husbands. The increase in public support of higher education may make the offspring less dependent on his father for this means of gaining access to professional and managerial positions.

It appears that emotional gratification may be a more meaningful function than in bygone days. If this is so, it may be relative to the other familial functions, which have declined in over-all significance; or it may be a consequence of the shift in the kind of society, which may tend to make the home more of an emotional haven than there was a demand for in past centuries. With respect to this function also there are two developments that command our attention: the widely heralded "generation gap" and the increasing permissiveness about sexual expression. The impression that at the close of the 1960's the generation gap had never been wider implied that the parent-offspring relationship could hardly be one of intimacy, understanding, love, and security for whatever proportions of adolescents and youth were alienated from their parents. The so-called sexual revolution is presumably leading to an increase in sexual expression outside marriage. Whether or not this will weaken the marital bond depends upon the meaning given to recreational sex. The formula "sex = love" and the view that love is exclusive lead to the conclusion that extramarital sex will have disruptive consequences. If sex comes to be treated as a more casual matter, then the effect may be slight.[25]

Societies without Families?

One final topic concerns the platitude that the family is "basic" to society, or it is sometimes phrased that it is basic to our way of life. It seems clear that our way of life would be altered if the family should disappear, but can it be argued that the family is basic to society in the sense that a society could not exist without the family?

Two societies have been proffered as teasingly problematic with respect

[25] For a somewhat fuller treatment of these points see Robert F. Winch, "Permanence and Change in the History of the American Family and Some Speculations as to Its Future," esp. p. 14.

to the question as to whether or not the family is universal. One setting in which the question is posed is the kibbutzim of Israel. According to our formulation a family is a network of two or more differentiated social positions that carries out the function of replacement. From the presentation in Chapter 3 the kibbutz described qualifies as a family.[26]

The other society, the Nayar, is viewed as having been problematic prior to the British control of India. Among the Nayars a girl acquired at, or a little before, puberty a "ritual husband." If she should be pubertal at the time, she might have sexual relations with this male. A few days later the ritual husband left and had no further obligations to his bride. This wedding was a ceremony whereby the girl became a woman and was accepted as "endowed with sexual procreative functions."[27] Thereafter the female typically had sex relations with a considerable number of men, who according to the rules were of her own or a higher caste. When she became pregnant, one among them was expected to acknowledge paternity of her child by paying the expense of her confinement. By this act he became the legal father of her child, but he did not assume responsibility either for her maintenance or for that of the child. It should be emphasized that a child was not legitimate if born of a woman who lacked either a ritual husband or a legal father for the child. The Nayars were matrilineal, and the responsibilities for the maintenance of the woman and her child were assumed by her kinsmen. As Gough says: "The Nayars . . . had a kinship system in which the elementary family of father, mother, and children was not institutionalized as a legal, productive, distributive, residential, socializing or consumption unit."[28]

Thus it took two males to perform the position-conferring function, and some of the time, at least, the actual biological father was a third. Here we see the procreative and the position-conferring functions being carried on by the woman in conjunction with males with whom she did not maintain a regular common residence or an enduring relationship. In view of the absence of any norm importuning the biological father and mother to form a lasting relationship and to assume continuing obligations to each other, it appears that the Nayars had no social structure that carried out the function of replacement. According to the formulation running through this book, therefore, they did not have a family system. That the answer depends heavily upon the definition is evident, however, in Gough's discussion, for she redefines marriage so as to include the Nayar case.

A factor that may help to explain the situation where the family does not

---

[26] Since they postulate more familial functions—the socialization of children and the stabilization of adult personalities—Parsons and Bales would not qualify the kibbutz as having a family.—Talcott Parsons and Robert F. Bales, *Family Socialization and Interaction Process* (New York: Free Press, 1955), pp. 16–17.

[27] E. Kathleen Gough, "Is the Family Universal? The Nayar Case," in Norman W. Bell and Ezra F. Vogel (eds.), *A Modern Introduction to the Family* (New York: Free Press, 1960), pp. 76–97. Quotation is from p. 80.

[28] Gough, *op. cit.*, p. 84.

exist or has only a marginal existence is the degree of emphasis on the typically masculine types of activity. Our criteria for masculine activities were physical strength, having blocks of time, and freedom to travel far from home. Levi-Strauss points out that the young Nayar men were not allowed to marry because they were needed as warriors (certainly a typically masculine occupation), and further that a similar state of affairs prevailed in Nazi Germany.[29] It might be added that after demanding total emotional commitment for blocks of time the Roman Catholic Church has forbidden its functionaries to marry, and, according to Whyte,[30] corporations seem at times to rescind the marriage contract by making heavy demands on the husband-father and by enforcing those demands with powerful sanctions. Other occupations, especially in the arts and the professions (e.g., the jazz musician), seem to make demands that render marriage, or at least marital success, highly problematic.

Thus it would appear that conditions in other societal subsystems than the family can make such heavy demands and present such intransigent sanctions that the family totters on the brink of disappearance. On the other hand, the demands and sanctions outside the family can be so slight that the family becomes the strongest subsystem and at times almost the total societal system. From these observations it does not seem necessary to conclude that the existence of a familial system, as the family has been conceived in this book, is necessary for the existence of a society.

And So?

Our purpose in this book has been to describe and to analyze the family in general and various American family forms in particular, especially that of the middle class. We have tried to be abstract enough to provide an analytical scheme for the family wherever found and yet concrete enough to have a lively sense of what has been happening to family life close to home.

The opening lines of this book took note of those who were decrying the fall of the American family, and the second paragraph suggested that the standard being employed was an idealized family of the Victorian period. The writer has just offered three criteria (or indexes) of familial disorganization—consensual, structural, and functional. There is evidence that the American family has lost functionality, and the writer conjectures that there has been some loss in consensus. Although the number of persons in the average domestic family has diminished over one and two-thirds centuries, there is no evidence of structural disorganization of the domestic family in terms of a reduction in the number of familial positions. Conflicting influences have been

---

[29] Claude Levi-Strauss, "The Family," in Harry L. Shapiro (ed.), *Man, Culture, and Society* (New York: Oxford, 1960), pp. 261–285.

[30] William H. Whyte, Jr., "The Wife Problem," in Winch and Goodman (eds.), *op. cit.*, pp. 177–188.

noted with respect to the structure of familial systems transcending the individual household, and there is insufficient information to determine the existence of a trend. These observations indicate that to date the urbanization and industrialization of America have been accompanied by some familial disorganization, but on a scale seemingly vastly less than some of the apoplectic prose would suggest.

After the British turned back the threat of a Nazi invasion, Winston Churchill spoke of Hitler's threat to wring Britain's neck. We might invoke his phrase in responding to the decriers of the family in America: "Some chicken, some neck!"

Name Index

Abarbanel, Albert, 512
Abbott, Grace, 84, 107
Aberle, David F., 262
Abrams, Ray H., 269
Ackerman, Nathan W., 492
Adams, Bert N., 305
Adams, Richard, 303–304
Adler, Leta McKinney, 547
Alberti, Leone Batista, 135
Albizu-Miranda, Carlos, 219
Albrecht, Milton C., 222
Alexander, Paul W., 576, 577
Allen, Frederick Lewis, 139, 143
Allen, Vernon L., 309
Allport, Gordon, 237
Amory, Cleveland, 212, 263
Anderson, C. Arnold, 114
Anderson, John E., 360, 381
Anderson, Nels, 404
Anderson, W. A., 222
Anshen, Ruth, 39, 47, 48, 201, 202, 265
Aoi, Kazuo, 366
Apple, Dorrian, 451
    See also Sweetser, Dorrian Apple
Arensberg, Conrad M., 165, 630
Ariès, Philippe, 311, 419
Aristotle, 545
Armer, J. Michael, 208
Aronson, Elliot, 309, 480
Atkinson, John W., 219, 395
Augustus, 247
Auld, Frank, 127
Axelrod, Morris, 323

Babchuk, Nicholas, 222
Baber, R. E., 80
Bach, George R., 405
Back, Kurt W., 144, 304
Bacon, Francis, 166
Baker, Luther G., Jr., 520
Baldwin, A. L., 112
Bales, Robert F., 4, 236, 325, 331–333, 633
Bandura, A., 408
Baratz, Gideon, 61
Baratz, Joseph, 56
Barber, Bernard, 23
Barclay, Dorothy, 111, 377, 400
Barker, R. G., 422
Barnes, Harry Elmer, 130
Barringer, Herbert R., 98, 587
Bates, Alan, 541
Bayley, Nancy, 424, 425
Beach, Frank A., 418, 521, 533
Beale, Calvin L., 582
Beam, Lura, 519
Beardsley, Richard K., 322
Beauchamp, David, 354
Becker, Howard, 110, 130, 201, 615

Becker, Wesley C., 390
Bee, Lawrence S., 494
Beem, Helen P., 204
Belknap, Ivan, 137, 150, 456
Bell, H. M., 463
Bell, Norman W., 25, 153, 633
Bell, Robert R., 323
Bell, Wendell, 133, 135, 222
Bellin, Seymour S., 547
Bendix, Reinhard, 207, 209, 212, 219, 221, 223, 224
Benedek, Therese, 253–254, 412, 463, 483, 490
Benedict, Ruth, 374, 436–437, 518
Bennett, J. W., 13
Berelson, Bernard, 179
Beresford, John C., 181
Berger, Bennett A., 138, 145, 429
Bergler, Edmund, 490, 504, 519
Berkowitz, Leonard, 480
Bermann, Eric A., 495
Bernard, Jessie, 504–505, 565
Berscheid, Ellen, 495
Bettelheim, Bruno, 60, 63, 66
Bigelow, Howard F., 83, 142
Biller, Henry B., 405
Billingsley, Andrew, 302
Birmingham, Stephen, 420
Black, Max, 5
Blackman, Leonard S., 585
Blaisdell, F. J., 495
Blake, Judith, 155, 180, 184, 195, 196, 303–304, 397
Blau, Lili R., 357
Blau, Peter M., 114, 281, 282, 309, 424
Blau, Theodore H., 357
Blazer, John A., 494
Blood, Robert O., Jr., 98, 142, 264, 335, 336, 378, 529, 548, 560, 564, 628
Blumberg, Leonard, 323
Blumberg, Rae Lesser, 23, 297, 299, 300, 609
Blumenthal, Albert, 224, 226
Boehm, Bernice R., 198
Bogue, Donald J., 156
Bohannan, Paul, 578, 579, 615, 626
Bohm, Ewald, 513
Boll, Eleanor Stoker, 410, 420
Boskoff, Alvin, 130
Bossard, J. H. S., 253, 254, 269, 410, 420
Bott, Elizabeth, 560–561
Bowerman, Charles E., 282, 494, 556
Bowlby, John, 359
Boyden, Sarah, 266
Bradburn, Norman M., 247, 547
Bradway, John S., 579
Braungart, Richard G., 220, 430
Bredemeier, Harry C., 254

637

Breese, F. H., 112
Brieland, Donald, 365
Brim, Orville G., Jr., 379, 409
Britten, Florence, 514
Brodbeck, A. J., 356
Broderick, Carlfred B., 420
Brody, Sylvia, 360–361
Bromley, Dorothy, 514
Bronfenbrenner, Urie, 333, 394, 401, 402, 408
Broom, Leonard, 204
Brown, Florence G., 199
Brown, J. S., 263
Bruner, Jerome S., 477
Bryson, Lyman, 232, 328, 442
Buchwald, Art, 329
Buck, J. L., 33
Buckley, Walter, 205
Bumpass, Larry, 181, 527
Burch, Thomas K., 33, 323
Burchinal, Lee G., 290, 293, 602
Burgess, Ernest W., 4, 95–96, 133, 255, 288, 515, 539, 540, 544, 546, 548, 550, 551, 553, 556, 564, 565, 566, 569, 608, 623, 625
Buric-Cukovic, Olivera, 331, 336
Burlingham, Dorothy, 359
Burma, John H., 270
Burnham, Donald L., 477
Burton, Roger V., 383, 387

Calderone, Mary Steichen, 185, 186
Caldwell, Bettye M., 356
Calhoun, A. W., 85, 107, 108, 109, 129, 156, 157, 161, 290, 373, 512
Campbell, Arthur A., 164, 167, 169, 176, 177, 178, 181, 248, 255–256, 548
Campbell, Donald T., 357
Campbell, John D., 383, 387
Campisi, Paul J., 304
Cannon, Kenneth L., 587
Cannon, W. B., 355
Caplovitz, David, 247, 547
Caplow, Theodore, 539
Carlsmith, Lyn, 405
Carmichael, Leonard, 104
Carniero, Robert L., 303
Carns, Donald, 514, 517, 520
Carter, Hugh, 269, 591
Cartwright, Dorwin, 98, 287, 335, 455
Cattell, Raymond B., 479
Catton, William R., Jr., 270
Cayton, Horace, 206, 271
Cervantes, Lucius, 623
Chamove, A., 398
Chancellor, Loren E., 277, 293, 588
Chen, T. H., 47
Cheng, C. K., 588
Chenkin, Alvin, 279
Chiang Kai-shek, 45
Child, I. L., 397, 409
Chow, Yung-Teh, 33
Christensen, Harold T., 194, 379–380, 517, 536, 548–549, 554–555, 585, 601
Christenson, Cornelia V., 183, 184, 185, 186
Chung, Chih-I, 40
Cicero, 250

Clague, Ewan, 90
Clark, E. L., 289
Clark, Gerald, 48
Clark, Kenneth B., 302
Clark, Ramsey, 288
Clark, Robert E., 223
Clarke, Alfred C., 222, 269, 287
Clement of Alexandria, 512
Cobliner, W. Godfrey, 354
Cole, Walton A., 47
Coleman, James S., 219, 422–423
Coleman, Rose W., 414
Conrad, H. S., 425
Cooley, Charles Horton, 236, 244, 415
Coombs, Lolagene, 172
Corah, Norman L., 495
Cottrell, Leonard S., Jr., 556, 565
Couch, Arthur Stephen, 493
Crain, Alan J., 406
Crandall, Vaughn J., 495
Creelan, Paul G., 409
Cumming, Elaine, 452, 454–455, 462
Curt, José Nine, 179

Dager, E. Z., 379
D'Andrade, Roy, 395
Daniel, Clifton, 188
Davids, Anthony, 438
Davie, M. R., 269
Davis, Allison, 206, 209–210, 211, 212, 214, 219, 240, 390, 394, 395, 397, 401, 435, 519, 533–534
Davis, Fred, 429
Davis, H. V., 356
Davis, James A., 208
Davis, Katherine Bement, 514
Davis, Keith E., 495
Davis, Kingsley, 21, 23, 55, 103, 119, 120, 121, 128, 155, 180, 184, 187, 194, 205, 254, 359
Day, Barbara R., 494
de Beauvoir, Simone, 232
deCharms, Richard, 109, 380
De Grazia, Sebastian, 125
Dennis, Wayne, 144
Dennison, C. P., 248
DePorte, J. V., 619
de Rougemont, Denis, 537
de Sales, Raoul de Roussy, 473
Deutsch, Helene, 248
DeVaughan, William L., 310
Devereux, Edward C., Jr., 5, 333
Dewey, John, 109
Dewhurst, J. Frederic, 84–85, 226
Diamond, Stanley, 65, 66
Dickinson, R. L., 519
Dicks, Henry V., 598
Dinkel, R. M., 462
Distler, Luther, 387, 406
Dobriner, William M., 139
Dole, Gertrude, 303
Dollard, John, 22, 214, 480
Donahue, Wilma, 203
Dorfman, Robert, 453, 454
Dornbusch, Sanford M., 123, 124
Dorr, Mildred, 391
Dotson, Floyd, 222

Douvan, Elizabeth, 219, 395
Drake, St. Clair, 206, 271
Dreikurs, Rudolf, 482
Driver, Edwin D., 288
Dublin, Louis, 547
Duncan, Otis Dudley, 114, 172, 207, 281, 282, 424
Durand, J. D., 87, 162–163
Durkheim, Emile, 130, 244–245, 312, 489
Duvall, E. M., 206
Dyer, Everett D., 354

Earle, A. M., 373
Easterlin, Richard A., 167
Eckler, A. Ross, 290
Edmonson, M. S., 611
Edwards, Allen L., 495
Eells, Kenneth, 206
Ehrmann, Winston, 514, 516, 522, 539
Eisenstein, Victor W., 490
Eliot, Thomas D., 615
Ellis, Albert, 512
Ellis, Havelock, 489, 490
Ellman, Mary, 330
Ellsworth, John S., Jr., 269
Empey, LaMar T., 219, 220
England, R. W., 127
Ericson, Martha C., 206
Erikson, Erik H., 436, 531
Escalona, Sibylle, 375–376

Fairchild, Roy W., 123, 124
Farber, Bernard, 585
Farewell, Nina, 525
Farnham, Marynia, 328, 329, 546
Fava, Sylvia Fleis, 397, 514
Fei, Hsiao-Tung, 39, 248
Feld, Sheila C., 330, 395
Feldman, Harold, 354
Ferguson, L. W., 424
Ferreira, Antonio, 358
Festinger, Leon, 103, 144, 287
Feuer, Lewis S., 429
Feyrabend, Françoise Lautman, 548
Fiedler, F. E., 495
Fine, Benjamin, 113, 146, 279
Finkelstein, Louis, 232, 328, 442
Fisher, S. G., 161
Fishman, Katharine Davis, 365
Fitz-Gibbon, Bernice, 535
Fitzpatrick, Rita, 290
Flacks, Richard, 126
Flugel, J. C., 411, 452, 480, 481, 490, 519
Folsom, J. K., 623, 625
Foote, Nelson N., 324, 623, 625
Force, Maryanne T., 222
Ford, Clelland Stearns, 249, 418, 521, 533
Forde, Darryl, 451
Form, William H., 144–145, 213, 323
Fortune, Reo F., 476
Foskett, John M., 222
Foster, Henry H., Jr., 576
Foster, R. G., 326
Fowler, Stanley E., 420
Fox, J. R., 262
Framptom, Merle E., 95
Franck, K., 425

Franklin, Ben, 42
Frazer, James George, 120, 187
Frazier, Alexander, 425
Frazier, E. Franklin, 74, 204, 302, 451
Freedman, Maurice, 49, 50
Freedman, Ronald, 164, 167, 171, 172, 176, 177, 178, 248, 255–256, 548
Freeman, Linton C., 18, 130–131, 262, 266, 267
French, Elizabeth G., 503
Freud, Anna, 359
Freud, Sigmund, 120, 238, 239, 251, 256, 356–357, 362, 381, 391, 392, 477, 480, 489, 490, 518, 519, 560, 615
Fried, Morton H., 47, 48
Friedenberg, Edgar Z., 105
Friedmann, Georges, 59, 65
Friedsam, H. J., 456
Fries, M. E., 414
Fromm, Erich, 125
Frumkin, Robert M., 547
Fukutake, T., 442
Furman, Bess, 199

Gagnon, John H., 105, 514, 517, 520
Gans, Herbert J., 134, 135, 138, 145
Gardner, B. B., 206, 212
Gardner, M. R., 206, 212
Garigue, Philip, 304
Gary, Albert L., 531
Gebhard, Paul H., 183, 184, 185, 186
Geiger, H. Kent, 331
Gerbner, George, 222
Gerth, H. H., 207, 234
Gibbs, Jack P., 245
Gibbs, Patricia K., 401
Gibbs, Wolcott, 139
Gilchrist, J. C., 324
Gingles, Ruby, 602
Glasner, Samuel, 512
Glazer, Nathan, 214
Glick, Paul C., 169, 181, 269, 283, 286, 290, 292, 347, 448–449, 547, 600, 618–619, 620, 631
Glucksberg, Sam, 494
Glueck, Bernard, 412
Glueck, Eleanor, 415
Glueck, Sheldon, 415
Goffman, Erving, 415, 443
Goffman, Irwin W., 207
Golden, Joseph, 270, 272
Goldfarb, William, 358–359, 414
Goldstein, Kurt, 238
Gonzalez, Nancie L. Solien, 195, 304
Goode, William J., 42, 194, 195, 336–338, 541, 582, 591, 592, 594, 599, 608, 622, 626
Goodman, Louis Wolf, 4, 262, 266, 272, 297, 299, 340, 347, 357, 377, 448–449, 451, 455, 456, 466, 490, 563, 598, 608, 609, 631, 634
Goodsell, Willystine, 79–80
Gopalaswami, R. A., 178
Gordon, C. Wayne, 222
Gordon, Michael, 366, 372
Gordon, Milton M., 207
Gorecki, Jan, 578

Gough, E. Kathleen, 25–27, 153, 633
Gouldner, Alvin W., 309
Grabill, Wilson H., 165, 174, 180
Grauman, John V., 156
Gray, Susan W., 425
Green, Arnold, 433
Greenfield, Sidney M., 630
Greenstein, Jules M., 406
Greer, Scott, 132, 133, 134, 299, 300, 609
Grinker, Roy R., 252, 463
Grønseth, Erik, 404, 427
Gross, Llewellyn, 207
Gross, Neal, 308–309
Gurin, Gerald, 330
Gusfield, Joseph R., 222

Haavio-Mannila, Elina, 331
Habenstein, Robert W., 72
Hajnal, John, 267
Hall, Calvin S., 22
Hall, John W., 322
Hall, Mary Harrington, 126
Haller, Archibald O., 208, 220, 424
Hamblin, Robert L., 335
Hamel, Harvey R., 141
Hamilton, G. V., 565
Hamilton, Walton, 255
Hammond, Barbara, 99
Hammond, J. L., 99
Hardt, Robert H., 547
Harlow, Harry F., 382, 398
Harper, G. A., 379
Harris, Dale B., 383, 425, 536
Harris, Daniel, 269, 287
Harris, Virginia, 204
Hartley, Eugene L., 206, 211, 241, 394, 395, 401, 402, 435, 477, 503
Hartley, Ruth E., 330
Hatt, Paul K., 207, 208
Hattwick, L. A., 398
Havemann, Ernest, 141, 226, 316
Havighurst, R. J., 114, 116, 206, 391, 394, 397, 401, 519, 533–534
Hays, William L., 491
Heath, Douglas H., 448
Heberle, Rudolph, 249
Heer, David M., 98, 181, 272, 335
Hegger, Grace, 561–562
Heinicke, Christoph M., 359
Heinstein, M. I., 360
Heiss, Jerold S., 333, 426, 538
Hellström, Inger, 46, 47, 50
Helper, M. M., 408
Henderson, Harry, 141, 143, 144, 149
Henley, Nancy M., 380
Henriques, Fernando M., 195, 304, 512
Henry, Andrew F., 245, 408, 547
Henry, Thomas R., 421, 424
Henry, William E., 452, 454–455
Henze, Lura F., 81
Herskovits, M. J., 74, 211
Herzog, Elizabeth, 56, 66
Hetherington, E. Mavis, 405
Hey, Richard N., 276–277
Hilgard, Ernest R., 22
Hill, Herbert, 302
Hill, Reuben, 110, 201, 269, 287, 339, 378, 379, 403, 542, 545, 551, 568, 615, 623, 625
Hillman, Christine H., 365
Hillman, Karen G., 587, 590–593
Hilton, Irma, 411
Himelhoch, Jerome, 397, 514
Himes, Norman, 185
Himmelfarb, Milton, 279
Himmelweit, Hilde, 117, 118, 119
Hitler, Adolf, 27, 154
Hobbs, Daniel F., Jr., 354
Hoffman, Lois Wladis, 331, 356, 359, 388, 389, 390, 402, 407
Hoffman, Martin, 546
Hoffman, Martin L., 219, 356, 359, 388, 389, 390
Holland, Hilda, 546, 547
Hollander, E. P., 503
Holliday, Carl, 79, 108, 160
Hollingshead, A. B., 206, 218, 219, 223, 224, 272, 277, 281, 619
Homans, George C., 13–14, 309, 324
Homer, 341
Hopkins, Harry, 93
Horney, Karen, 244, 518–519, 521
Hoult, Thomas Ford, 223
Howard, Alan, 403
Hsu, Francis L. K., 32, 33, 39, 41, 45, 50
Huang, Lucy Jen, 47
Hudson, John W., 81
Hunt, H. C., 112
Hunt, J. McV., 356, 398
Hunt, Maurice O., 196
Hunt, Morton M., 232, 512–513, 529
Hurvitz, Nathan, 221, 588
Huxley, Aldous, 27, 154, 311
Hyman, Herbert H., 219, 222

Ilgenfritz, Marjorie P., 608
Ingersoll, Hazel, 412
Inkeles, Alex, 208
Izard, Carroll E., 505

Jackson, Elton F., 243
Jaco, E. Gartly, 137, 150
Jacobson, Alver Hilding, 588
Jacobson, Paul H., 254, 291, 580, 581, 582–583, 592, 619
Jacoby, Arthur P., 354
Jaffe, A. J., 171, 315
James, William, 381, 413
Janus, 13
Jennings, Helen Hall, 324
Johnson, Benton, 120
Johnstad, Trygve, 513
Jones, Marshall B., 244, 355–356
Jones, Mary Cover, 425
Jones, Vernon, 104
Jorgensen, Bruce W., 495
Josselyn, Irene, 431, 437
Jourard, Sidney M., 533

Kahl, Joseph A., 208
Kahn, Gay M., 531
Kalhorn, J., 112
Kälvesten, Anna-Lisa, 513
Kanin, Eugene J., 177

Name Index

Kantrowitz, Nathan, 277
Kapadia, K. M., 265, 615
Kardiner, Abram, 42, 121–122, 239, 313, 485
Karlsson, Georg, 556, 598
Katz, Alvin M., 269, 287
Katz, Irwin, 494
Kay, Herma Hill, 578
Keller, Albert Galloway, 5, 201, 264, 314, 614–615
Kelley, Harold H., 309
Kelly, E. Lowell, 181, 288, 569
Kelly, George A., 393
Kemper, Warren A., 431
Kenkel, W. F., 207, 379
Kennedy, Ruby J. R., 269, 277
See also Reeves, Ruby Jo
Kenniston, Kenneth, 126, 220
Kephart, William M., 223, 587, 588, 603
Kerckhoff, Alan C., 269, 495
Kerckhoff, Richard K., 379–380
Key, William H., 134, 299
Kimball, S. T., 165
King, Charles E., 556
Kinsey, Alfred C., 114, 186, 210, 396, 420, 513–517, 518, 522, 549
Kirkpatrick, Clifford, 532, 539, 554, 558, 567, 568, 569, 595–598
Kiser, Clyde V., 165, 167, 174, 175, 178, 180
Klamm, Edward R., 431
Kleemeier, Robert W., 456
Klein, Viola, 323
Kluckhohn, Clyde, 424
Kluckhohn, Florence Rockwood, 125–126
Knudsen, Dean D., 525
Koch, Helen, 408, 409
Kohlberg, Lawrence, 388–389
Kohn, Melvin L., 401, 402, 403, 404
Koller, Marvin R., 269, 287
Kollmorgen, Walter M., 82
Komarovsky, Mirra, 80, 222, 326, 328, 426
König, René, 339, 403
Kornhauser, Ruth Rosner, 207
Kounin, J. S., 422
Koya, Yoshio, 179
Koyama, Takashi, 336
Krauss, Robert, 494
Kris, Ernst, 414
Kroger, W. S., 490
Ktsanes, Thomas, 138, 491
Ktsanes, Virginia, 491
Kuhlen, R. G., 444
Kurtz, Russell H., 196, 197, 199
Kyrk, Hazel, 86–87

LaBarre, Weston, 444
Lake, Alice, 563
Landau, Emanuel, 292, 600
Landecker, Werner S., 207
Landis, Judson T., 378, 444, 550, 617
Landy, Frank, 405
Lang, Olga, 32, 35, 43, 44
Laski, Harold J., 122
Latourette, Kenneth Scott, 41
Lawrence, D. H., 531
Lazarsfeld, P. F., 224

Leary, Timothy, 492
Lee, Shu-Ching, 40, 47, 70
Leichter, Hope Jensen, 608, 630
Leighton, Alexander H., 616
Leik, Robert K., 333, 426
LeMasters, E. E., 220, 353–354
Lenski, Gerhard, 119, 207, 208, 223, 274, 275
Leonard, Reg, 48–49
LePlay, Frederic, 32
Levi, Carlo, 183
Levin, Harry, 387, 401
Levinger, George, 495, 538, 599
Levi-Strauss, Claude, 634
Levy, Bernard I., 493
Levy, D. M., 356, 381, 414, 498
Levy, John, 517
Levy, Marion J., Jr., 13, 32, 34, 35, 36, 38, 40, 43, 44, 69, 70, 254, 342–343
Levy, Robert J., 576
Lewi, B., 414
Lewis, David M., 208
Lewis, Oscar, 209
Lewis, Sinclair, 561–562
Lewit, Sarah, 591
Lindzey, Gardner, 22, 309, 324, 393, 410, 480
Linton, Ralph, 114, 202, 445–446, 478
Lipset, Seymour Martin, 207, 209, 212, 219, 221, 223, 224
Lisonbee, Lorenzo K., 425
Locke, Harvey J., 4, 95–96, 133, 278, 544, 550, 551, 556, 585, 595, 625
Locke, John, 237, 238, 256
Loeb, M. B., 114, 116
Loomis, Charles P., 130
Loosley, Elizabeth W., 138, 139, 140, 147, 149
Lorimer, Frank, 157, 164, 166, 175, 180, 184, 187, 188, 249, 291–292
Lotka, A. J., 156, 157
Lowndes, Marion, 111
Lucas, Esther, 61
Luckey, Eleanore Braun, 517, 563
Lundy, Richard M., 495
Lunt, P. S., 206, 292, 600
Lupri, Eugen, 336
Lyle, Jack, 116, 117
Lyman, Elizabeth L., 219
Lynd, Helen M., 206, 212, 431
Lynd, Robert S., 206, 212, 431
Lynn, David B., 405, 426

McArthur, Charles, 220
McBride, Katharine, 326–327
McClelland, David C., 222, 396
McClusky, H. Y., 269
Maccoby, Eleanor E., 118, 119, 387, 394, 401, 402, 477, 503
Maccoby, Nathan, 377
McCord, Joan, 403, 405
McCord, William, 403, 405
McDonald, Margaret R., 395
McDougall, William, 476
McEachern, Alexander W., 308–309
McGinnis, Robert, 98, 587
McGregor, Douglas, 241

McGuire, Carson, 223
MacIver, Robert M., 232, 328
McKee, John P., 425
McKinley, Donald Gilbert, 403
Mack, Raymond W., 223
Maine, Henry Sumner, 130
Malinowski, Bronislaw, 14, 193, 194, 313, 410
Mandelbaum, David G., 201, 202, 265
Mann, Richard D., 415
Mannes, Marya, 565
Marches, J. R., 269
Marcus, Philip M., 503
Marquand, J. P., 212
Martin, Clyde E., 114, 183, 184; 185, 186, 396, 420, 513–517, 518, 522
Martin, Walter T., 139, 245
Martin, William E., 401
Martinson, Floyd M., 602
Marx, Groucho, 542
Marx, Karl, 42, 120
Maslow, Abraham, 244
Mason, Ward S., 308–309
Mather, Cotton, 372–373
Matza, David, 209–210, 428
Mayer, Albert J., 223
Mayer, Kurt B., 207
Mead, George H., 386
Mead, Margaret, 201, 247, 313, 366, 367, 368, 369, 374, 375, 377, 382, 410, 426–427, 434, 476, 478, 509, 510, 518, 521, 523, 530, 549, 550, 608
Meeker, Marchia, 206
Meier, Dorothy L., 133
Meier, Elizabeth G., 196, 197
Meissner, Hanna H., 601
Mencius, 37
Merrill, Francis E., 542, 583
Merton, Robert K., 144, 224
Meyerowitz, Joseph H., 354
Michel, Andrée, 335, 548
Middleton, Russell, 262
Miller, Arthur, 433, 482
Miller, H. C., 356
Miller, Helen Hill, 266
Miller, Herman P., 227
Miller, Neal E., 22, 355
Miller, S. M., 209, 211
Miller, W. B., 611
Mills, C. Wright, 121, 207, 234
Milton, G. A., 425
Mishler, Elliot G., 181
Mitchell, Donald, 269
Mitchell, G. D., 398, 411
Mitchell, William E., 608, 630
Mittelmann, Bela, 490
Moeller, Gerald H., 109, 380
Monahan, Thomas P., 277, 288–291, 408, 587, 588, 600, 601, 619–620
Monroe, W. S., 112
Moore, Barrington, Jr., 27
Moore, Wilbert E., 55, 205
Morgan, Edmund S., 128
Morley, Christopher, 212
Morse, Nancy C., 126
Mortimer, Robert C., 577–578
Moss, J. Joel, 602

Mowrer, Harriet, 110
Mowrer, O. H., 392
Moynihan, Daniel Patrick, 214
Mueller, D. D., 414
Mueller, Kate H., 327
Mulhern, James, 109
Mullahy, Patrick, 522
Muller, Herman J., 154, 187
Mumford, Lewis, 135
Munroe, Ruth, 517
Muramatsu, Minoru, 179
Murdock, George Peter, 35, 311, 314, 410, 426, 560
Murphy, Gardner, 355, 361, 422, 432
Murphy, Lois B., 361–362, 398
Murray, Henry A., 355, 424, 441, 442, 475–476, 480, 484
Mussen, Paul, 387, 406, 425
Myers, George C., 140
Myers, Jerome K., 223
Myrdal, Alva, 323

Nam, Charles B., 207
Naroll, Raoul, 131
Nass, Gilbert D., 517
Neilon, Patricia, 360
Nesselroade, John, 479
Neugarten, Bernice L., 452
Newcomb, Theodore M., 206, 211, 241, 361, 394, 395, 401, 402, 435, 477, 503
Nimkoff, M. F., 64, 82–84, 87, 194, 290, 291, 629–630
North, C. C., 208
Nottingham, Elizabeth K., 121
Nye, F. Ivan, 331, 407

Odell, Eve, 505, 506
Oden, Melita H., 551, 569
O'Faolain, Sean, 165
Ogburn, William F., 3–4, 24–25, 82–84, 87, 290, 629–630
Ohmann, O., 479, 490
Olsen, Marvin E., 335
O'Mahony, Patrick J., 574
Orni, Efraim, 52, 53
Otto, H. J., 112

Packard, Vance, 204
Packer, Peter, 464
Papanek, Miriam L., 538
Pareto, Vilfredo, 14
Park, Robert E., 130
Parke, Robert, Jr., 347, 448–449, 631
Parker, Edwin B., 116, 117
Parker, Francis, 109
Parsons, Talcott, 4, 232, 236, 325, 326, 331–333, 442, 456–457, 633
Patai, Raphael, 52, 53, 512
Patterson, John E., 181
Paul VI, Pope, 173
Peale, Norman Vincent, 127
Pedersen, Frank A., 406
Peterson, Warren, 90
Pfautz, Harold W., 207
Philbrick, Robert E., 548–549, 585
Phillips, Derek L., 247
Pineo, Peter C., 563

Name Index 643

Pinneau, S. R., 360
Pintler, Margaret H., 405
Pius XII, Pope, 173–174
Plant, J. S., 415, 423
Plateris, Alexander A., 583
Plato, 489
Pomeroy, Wardell B., 114, 183, 184, 185, 186, 396, 420, 513–517, 518, 522
Pope, Hallowell, 525
Pope, Liston, 204
Popenoe, Paul, 231
Portes, Alejandro, 424
Powell, Elwin H., 245
Powell, Kathryn S., 331
Powers, Mary G., 207
Pratt, William F., 591
Prescott, D. A., 113
Preston, Anne, 495
Pribram, Karl H., 355–356
Provence, Sally, 414

Queen, Stuart A., 72

Rabin, A. I., 65–66
Radcliffe-Brown, A. R., 14, 451
Radler, D. H., 482
Raina, B. L., 179
Rainwater, Lee, 451, 518
Ray, J. D., 530
Redfield, Robert, 130
Redlich, Frederick C., 223
Reed, Robert, 548
Reeves, Ruby Jo, 269
See also Kennedy, Ruby J. R.
Reid, Margaret, 83
Reik, Theodor, 477, 478, 482, 490
Reiss, Ira L., 26, 517, 520, 530
Reissman, Leonard, 138, 222
Remmers, H. H., 482
Renson, Gisele J., 493
Rettig, Salomon, 66
Rheinstein, Max, 574, 575, 576, 578–579, 581–582, 601
Ribble, Margaret A., 356–360, 369, 375, 381, 382, 383, 478
Richardson, Helen M., 288
Ridley, Jeanne Clare, 187
Riecken, Henry W., 103, 324
Riesman, David, 130, 139, 143, 147–148, 226, 339
Riess, Albert J., Jr., 208
Riessman, Frank, 211
Riley, John, 118
Riley, Matilda, 118
Risdon, Randall, 270
Roberts, Bertram H., 223
Roberts, Louis A., 269
Robbins, Jhan, 546
Robbins, June, 546
Robinson, John, 373
Robinson, Myra, 391
Rodgers, Robert R., 333
Rohrer, John H., 214, 611
Rommetveit, Ragnar, 308
Rose, Arnold M., 453
Rosen, Bernard C., 220, 395
Rosenberg, B. G., 405

Rosenberg, Morris, 405
Rosenfeld, Eva, 56, 145, 205
Rosenthal, Erich, 279–280
Rosenthal, Robert, 216
Rosow, Irving, 495, 504
Ross, Arthur M., 302
Ross, E. A., 335, 545, 559
Rossi, Alice, 330–331
Rossi, Peter H., 134, 208
Rousseau, Jean J., 374
Rubin, Zick, 281, 282
Rush, Gary B., 207
Russell, Bertrand, 113

Sabagh, Georges, 278
Safilios-Rothschild, Constantina, 336
St. Paul, 512
Salisbury, W. Seward, 124
Samuelson, N. M., 326
Sanford, R. Nevitt, 425, 447–448
Sarbin, Theodore R., 309, 410
Sargent, S. S., 355
Sawrey, William L., 405
Scates, Douglas E., 111
Schachtel, Ernest G., 237–238
Schachter, Stanley, 103, 144, 324
Schaefer, Earl S., 493
Schatzman, Leonard, 222
Scheinfeld, Amram, 427
Schellenberg, James A., 288, 494
Schermerhorn, Richard A., 201
Schilder, Paul, 248
Schmiedeler, Edgar, 110, 625, 626
Schneider, Louis, 123, 124
Schnepp, G. J., 269
Schnore, Leo F., 136–137, 138
Schooley, Mary, 288
Schorr, Alvin L., 457–458, 459, 462, 463, 464–465
Schramm, Wilbur, 116, 117
Schwartz, Richard D., 52, 53, 56, 57, 205
Sears, Pauline Snedden, 405, 408
Sears, Robert R., 356, 357, 382–383, 387, 388, 401, 405
Secord, Paul F., 533
Seeley, John R., 138, 139, 140, 147, 149, 325, 334
Seidman, Jerome M., 482, 536
Seltzer, C. C., 424
Senn, David J., 495
Senn, M. J. E., 410
Sewell, William H., 220, 360, 424
Shanas, Ethel, 457, 465
Shapiro, Harry L., 634
Shearer, Lloyd, 290
Sheen, Bishop Fulton J., 124, 127
Sheldon, J. H., 460
Sheldon, William H., 154
Sheps, Mindel C., 187
Sherman, Mandel, 421, 424
Sherriffs, Alex C., 425
Shirley, Mary, 414
Short, James F., 245, 547
Signoret, Simone, 565
Sills, David L., 156
Sim, R. Alexander, 138, 139, 140, 147, 149
Simey, T. S., 304

Simmons, Leo W., 203
Simon, William, 105, 514, 517, 520
Simpson, George, 130, 312, 489, 505
Simpson, Richard L., 205
Sirjamaki, John, 444
Slater, Eliot, 505, 556
Slesinger, Doris P., 171
Small, Albion W., 130
Smircich, R. J., 270
Smit, John W., 176
Smith, Adam, 161
Smith, Joel, 323
Smith, M. G., 195
Smith, M. W., 355
Smith, Raymond T., 98, 195, 304
Smith, Reginald Heber, 576
Smuts, Robert W., 85
Snyder, Clinton A., 397
Socrates, 250, 489
Sontag, L. W., 358
Spectorsky, A. C., 138, 140–141, 142, 145
Spiegel, John P., 252, 463
Spiegler, C. G., 327
Spiro, Audrey G., 54
Spiro, Melford E., 18, 25–27, 51–64, 331
Spitz, René A., 358–359, 375, 381, 382, 383, 478
Spock, Benjamin, 330, 365, 366, 384
Srole, Leo, 133, 221
Stamm, Caroline S., 406
Stanley, Julian C., 357
Stanton, F. N., 224
Steig, W., 391
Stein, Maurice R., 27
Steiner, Peter O., 453, 454
Stendler, Celia Burns, 367–369, 401
Stern, Grace Ambrose, 534
Stewart, Charles D., 315
Stinchcombe, Arthur L., 613
Stone, Abraham, 185
Stone, Gregory P., 213, 323
Stouffer, S. A., 175, 287
Straus, Murray A., 134, 220, 222, 299, 493
Streib, Gordon F., 449, 450, 456
Strodtbeck, Fred L., 125–126, 221, 395, 396, 409
Stroup, Atlee L., 556
Stycos, J. Mayone, 304
Sullivan, H. S., 355
Sumner, William Graham, 5, 201, 264, 314, 509, 614–615
Sunley, Robert, 367, 368, 375
Sussman, Marvin B., 134, 287–288, 461
Sutherland, R. L., 214
Suttie, Ian, 239, 481
Sutton-Smith, B., 405
Sweetbaum, Harvey A., 395
Sweetser, Dorrian Apple, 465–466
  See also Apple, Dorrian
Symonds, P. M., 411

Taba, Hilda, 206
Taeuber, Conrad, 156, 158, 163, 169, 194
Taeuber, Irene B., 156, 158, 163, 169, 179, 194
Talmon, Yonina, 61, 63, 64, 262
Taylor, G. Rattray, 533

Tawney, R. H., 164
Terman, Lewis M., 514, 515, 551, 565, 569
Thernstrom, Stephan, 206
Thibaut, John W., 309
Thomas, John L., 111, 173, 277–279
Thomes, Mary Margaret, 278, 406
Thompson, Clara, 522, 536
Thompson, Warren S., 187, 255
Thompson, Wayne E., 449, 456
Thoms, Herbert, 253
Thurber, Emily, 405
Thurber, James, 391
Tibbitts, Clark, 203, 449
Tietze, Christopher, 187
Tiller, Per Olav, 404, 427
Tiryakian, Edward A., 208
Toby, Jackson, 220, 221, 407–408
Tönnies, Ferdinand, 130
Townsend, Peter, 232, 233, 455, 457, 460, 461, 462, 465
Trumbull, Robert, 432
Tryon, Caroline, 422
Tseng, Sing Chu, 425
Tumin, Melvin M., 13, 205
Tunstall, Sylvia, 457
Turbeville, G., 269
Turk, Herman, 503
Turk, Theresa, 503
Tylor, E. B., 628

Udry, J. Richard, 589, 592

Vallier, Ivan, 57
Vedder, Clyde B., 506–507
Vener, Arthur M., 397
Veroff, Joseph, 330
Vidich, Arthur J., 27
Vincent, Clark E., 197, 369, 517
Vogel, Ezra F., 25, 153, 264, 442, 633
Volkart, Edmund H., 615–616

Wallace, Karl Miles, 505–506
Waller, Willard, 530, 542, 545, 551, 558, 563, 568, 615–616
Wallin, Paul, 255, 288, 328, 426, 514, 515, 539, 540, 545, 546, 548, 566, 569, 608
Wallis, W. A., 514
Walser, H. C., 253
Walster, Elaine Hatfield, 495
Walters, R. H., 408
Ward, Robert E., 322
Warner, W. Lloyd, 114, 115, 116, 205–212, 221, 292–293, 600
Warrington, W. G., 495
Washburn, R. W., 414
Watson, J. S., 361
Watson, John B., 369, 381, 382, 383, 478
Watson, Robert I., 333
Weaver, Warren, Jr., 199
Weber, Max, 42, 121, 122, 126, 207
Webb, Wilse B., 503
Wedderburn, Dorothy, 465
Weinstein, Eugene A., 310, 400
Weinstein, Karol K., 452
Weinstein, Marybeth, 199
Weiss, Robert S., 126, 326
West, Patricia Salter, 226

Name Index

Westby, David L., 220
Westoff, Charles F., 181, 527
Wharton, A. H., 107
Whelpton, Pascal K., 164, 165, 174, 175, 176, 177, 178, 180, 181, 248, 255–256, 548
White, David Manning, 27
White, R. Clyde, 222
White, Robert W., 238, 355
Whitehurst, Robert N., 552
Whiting, John W. M., 409, 410
Whyte, W. F., 519
Whyte, William H., Jr., 143–144, 148–149, 265–266, 339–340, 442, 549, 563, 634
Wicklein, John, 199
Wiley, Mary Glenn, 310
Williams, James H., 323
Williams, W. M., 202
Williamson, Robert C., 599
Willig, John, 327
Willmott, Peter, 134, 304, 460, 461, 465, 466, 467
Willoughby, R. R., 288
Wilson, Pauline, 326
Wilson, Warner, 247
Winch, Martha, 504
Winch, Robert F., 4, 18, 20, 25, 69–70, 98, 130–131, 134, 182, 262, 266, 267, 272, 289, 297, 299, 300, 304, 339, 340, 347, 357, 377, 392, 403, 448–449, 451, 455, 456, 466, 476, 479, 484, 489, 490, 491, 496, 527, 529, 547, 562, 563, 586, 587, 598, 608, 609, 629, 631, 632, 634
Winterbottom, Marian R., 395
Winthrop, John, 107, 373
Wirth, Louis, 133, 587

Wise, G. W., 357
Wolfe, Donald M., 98, 142, 335, 455, 548, 560, 564, 628
Wolfenstein, Martha, 366, 367, 368, 369–372, 374, 375, 377, 382, 410
Wood, Robert, 512
Wood, Robert C., 146
Woodside, Moya, 505, 556
Worthy, Morgan, 531
Wright, Charles R., 116, 222
Wright, H. F., 422
Wylie, Philip, 329
Wylie, Ruth C., 391
Wynn, John Charles, 123, 124

Yamamura, Douglas S., 588
Yang, C. K., 46, 48, 49
Yarrow, Leon J., 359
Yarrow, Marian Radke, 383, 387
Yinger, J. Milton, 120, 124, 127, 275
Young, Frank W., 131, 262
Young, Kimball, 223, 413
Young, Michael, 134, 304, 460, 461, 465, 466, 467
Young, Ronald, 132, 133
Young, Ruth C., 131

Zander, Alvin, 269, 287
Zborowski, Mark, 56, 66
Zecevic, Andjelka, 336
Zelditch, Morris, Jr., 236, 325, 329, 331–333
Zetterberg, Hans L., 212
Zimmer, Basil G., 222
Zimmerman, Carle, 4, 24–25, 78, 95–97, 128, 132, 137, 147, 152, 201, 247, 623, 624, 625

Subject Index

Abortions, 179, 183, 185–187
Achievement, orientation to, 219–220
Adaptability, 442
Adjustability, 442
Adolescence, 418–439
  ambiguity of, in American society, 419–422
  conflict with parents, 432–434
  defined, 418
  developmental tasks of, in the middle class, 423–427
  discrepancy between the perceived self and the ideal self, 537
  physiological criteria of, 420
  psychic conflict, 428–430
  psychic gap, reduction of the, 537
  sex-type imperative, 424–427
  "success" imperative, 423–424
  self-validation, shifting criteria for, 422–423
  "storm and stress," 423, 434–436, 536–537
Adoption, 198–200
Adult and his parents, 440–469
Adulthood, 440–469
  aged, 445–446
  middle years, 444–445
  young adults, 443–444
Advertising, as technique for mate-finding, 293
Advice to parents about rearing children, 364–384
  affection, 368
  anaclitic depression, 375
  bowel training, 369–370
  breakdown of tradition and demand for advice, 366
  character development, 367–368
  directiveness, 375
  discipline, 368
  feeding infants, 367, 370
  fun morality, 371–372
  independence, 382
  marasmus, 375
  masturbation, 370–371, 374
  "momism," 369
  moral character, 368
  "mothering," 369, 375, 381, 382
  ordering-and-forbidding techniques, 375, 376
  permissiveness, 372, 375
  personality development, 367–368
  questions parents want answered, 365
  swaddling, 374
  thumb-sucking, 371–372
  weaning, 370
Adultery, 97

Affectional-emotional gratifications in marriage, 556–560
Affinal, defined, 321
Agape, 489
Age, at marriage related to other variables, 289–293
  See also Mate-selection
Aged, 445–446
  dependency, 462–465
  desolation versus isolation, 460
  disengagement, 455, 461–462
  without offspring, 467
  retirement, 452–455
Aid to Dependent Children (ADC), 196
Aid to Families with Dependent Children (AFDC), 196
Alienation, 133, 244
Alter, as actor to whom ego relates, 5
Alternate generations, good feeling between, 451–452
Ambivalence, 474, 484–485
Anaclitic depression, 359
Analytic structure, 18
Annulment, 574
Anomia, 133, 466–467
Anomie, 133, 347–348
Anthropology, as zoo of mankind, 2
Anxiety, 475
  adaptive, 395
  alleviation of feelings of, 127, 245–246
Arranged marriage (arrangement) (*see* Mate-selection)
Artificial insemination, 183, 188
Ascribed positions and statuses, 191
Assortative mating (*see* Mate-selection, principle of ethnocentric preference in)
Attraction, psychology of, 479
Authority, familial (*see* Power, familial)
Avoidance, of complete gestation, 183, 185–187
  of conception, 183–184
  of intercourse, 182–184

Bar mitzvah, 419
Basic personality structure, 485
Basic societal function (*see* Function)
Basic societal structure (*see* Structure [social])
Bastardy, 97, 193
  See also Illegitimacy
Beauty, 532–534
Belonging, need for, 244
Bereavement, 615–616
Biophysical basis of activity, 354–355
Birth rate, 133, 153–190, 247, 256
  by birth order, 159–160
  business cycle and the, 165, 166, 167

Birth rate (*continued*)
  children, number ever born, as component of birth rate, 167
  from colonial times to the present, 156–159
  components in, 167
  differentials in, by race, 172–173
    by religion, 173–178
    by socioeconomic status, 171–172
    by urban-rural residence, 169–171
  downward trend in, 1800–1963, 162–166
  levels of explanation of, 155
  relationship to paid employment, 163
  timing of births as component of, 167
  See also Function, of replacement
Black genocide, 196
"Boys," in rural Ireland, 165, 180
"Breadwinner," 81
Bureaucratic occupations, 443

Categorical dependency, 140, 162
Categorical employability, 88–90, 91, 140, 162, 436, 452–454
Child development and rearing, absence of father, 404–406
  absence of mother, 406–407
  achievement, competitive, 394–395
  adaptability, 400
  aggression, displacement of, 403
  aggression, physical, 394
  alternation of generations, 411, 451–452
  anxiety, adaptive, 395
  behavior, striving, 395
  birth order, 410–411
  broken homes, 407–408
  child rearing, basic conceptions, 372–375
    developmental point of view, 375–376
    faddism in, 377
    new-new view, 376–377
    traditional point of view, 375–376
  conscience, development of, 388–390
  culture, subculture, and the content of learning, 393–398
  deferred gratification, 390
  delinquency, 407–408
  developmental tasks, 388
  ego-ideal, 391
  emotional warmth of parent, 387
  generations, alternation of, 411, 451–452
  goals, development of, 391
  ideal self, 391
  internalization of discipline, 388–390
  key skills of childhood, 386–388
    locomotion, 386
    manipulation, 386
    speech, 386
  maturation, 387
  moral judgment, Kohlberg's formulation of invariant developmental sequence, 388–390
  masturbation, 396
  needs, changing, and parental functions, 386–388
  ordinal position, 410–411
  parental function, control, 385–417, 418–439, 440–469
  parental function, nurturance, 351–363, 385–417, 418–439, 440–469
  permissiveness, 390
  polygyny, sororal and nonsororal, 409
  restrictiveness, 390
  self-validation, criteria for, 399–400
  sexual expression, 396–397
  social class and child rearing, 400–403
  "social self," 413
  social skills, 400
  socialization, 392
  socioeconomic status, 400–403
  subculture, 398
  working mothers, 407
Child labor, 84–85
Child, role of, 16–17, 346–469
Children, employment of, 140
  number desired, 181, 255
  reasons for wanting, 248
  value of, 161–162, 166
Childlessness, 96, 159–160, 166, 168, 173
China and the Industrial Revolution, 41–45
Cinderella fantasy, 227
"Class churches," 204
Classes (social), 73, 114–116, 205–215
  class differences in criteria of status, 191, 213
  "culture of poverty," 209
  mobility, upward, as subcultural goal of middle class, 211
  qualifications regarding the subcultures of social classes, 213–215
  subcultures of, 208–215, 390, 441–443
Collusion in divorce actions, 575
Communes, in China, 46
  religious, 127
Commuting, as a form of mobility, 316
"Company wife," 265–266, 339, 549, 563
Competitiveness, 244
Complementary needs in mate-selection, basic propositions of, 488
  changes in needs, 503
  dimensions of complementariness, 492–493
  dominance-submissiveness, 492
  happiness and, 504
  marital counseling and, 504
  nurturance-receptivity, 492
  Pygmalion hypothesis, 492
  status of the theory, 489 496
  task-oriented behavior, 503
  theory of, 487–504
  Type I and Type II complementariness, 488
Computerized dating services (*see* Dating)
Conjugal family (*see* Family)
Concrete structure, 18
Conformity and hypocrisy, 338–340, 442
Congeniality group, 486
  marital dyad as a, 560–564
Consanguineal, defined, 321
Contraception, 166, 169, 178, 182
Control, 346–469
  See also Functions, parental; Submissiveness
Concubinato, 194
Consensual union, 194

Subject Index

...elationship, 8, 16–17
...poration (*see* Mate-selection)
Couvade, 628
Cultural discontinuity, 436–437
Cultural separatism, 73
Culture as factor in birth rate, 155, 162, 166, 168, 178–179, 181–182

Dating, courtship, and engagement, 528–543
  as anticipatory socialization, 532
  computerized services, 293, 507
  contrasted with marriage, 532
  engagement continuum, 538–539
  functions of, 530–532, 539–540
  as a mate-selective process, 531
  as personality testing, 531
  as recreation, 530
  as socialization, 530–531
  as status-grading, 530
Death rate, 156–157, 163–164, 166, 173
  See also Expectation of life at birth
Debut, 420
Degania, 56
"Delusive solidarity," 558
Dependence, direction of, 455–456
  emotional, 253, 441
  independence, and interdependence (economic), 91–92
  infant's awareness of, 363
Dependents, 81, 99–100, 346
Depression, the, and the birth rate, 165, 166, 167
Desertion (*see* Marital dissolution; Divorce)
"Deterioration in belief," 125, 129
Differential association, 214–215
Differentiation, structural (*see* Structures)
Dimensions of ethnocentric preference (*see* Mate-selection)
Dissensus, 336
Division of labor, 81, 309–310
  along sex line (*see* Roles, gender-linked differences in)
Divorce, 96, 573–604
  legal concept of, in the United States, 575–580
  marital breakdown, principle of, as basis for legal action, 578–579
  See also Marital dissolution
Divorce rates, 254, 580–603
  childless couples, 254
  children in divorce, 254, 585
  duration of marriage, 603
  early marriage, 599–603
  education, 590–593
  emotional immaturity, 601–603
  extended family, 599
  familial functionality, 588, 594–595
  income, 599
  personality characteristics, 594–598
  race, 590–597
  religious affiliation, 587–588
  socioeconomic status, 588–596
  urban-rural differences, 587, 597
"Do-it-yourself," 141–142
Dog, family, 215
Domestic family (*see* Family; Familial forms, concrete)
Domestic production, decrease in, 82–83
Dominance, marital, 142–143, 335–336
Drive-reduction theory, 354–355
Dyad, 486
  nuclear, 11

Economic contribution of the modern housewife, 86–88
Economic organization of the early American farm family, 79–80
Economic self-sufficiency and interdependence of family members, 80–81, 99–100
Economics, prestige, 211
  subsistence, 211
Education, 101–119
  courses for babysitters, 111
  courses in sex, marriage, parenthood, family life, 110
  and the generation gap, 115
  median number of years of, 112
  nature of, 104–119
  nursery, 110
  school, 106–116
  shifts in educational emphasis, 108–109
  in the status system, 114–116
  and the "whole child," 109–114
  See also Function, socializing-educational
Edwards Personal Preference Schedule, 494
Egalitarianism, 54–57
Ego, as actor of reference, 5
Elderly males in the labor force, 89
Emotional deprivation, 359
Emotional gratification (*see* Function, familial derived)
Emotional immaturity, 482
Emotional life, man's, and complementary roles, 43
Emotional satisfaction from work, dilution of, 81
Employment of children and women, 83–86
Endogamy, 272
Engagement and its functions, 539–540
Entrepreneurial occupations, 443
Erogenous zones, 356
Eros, 489
Ethnic categories and ethnicity, 73, 172–177, 203–205, 214, 270–280, 302–305
Ethnocentric preference (*see* Mate-selection)
Ethnoreligious differences in social mobility, 221, 395–396
Euphoria and drive-reduction, 355
Exogamy, 272
Expectation of life at birth, 157, 163, 173
Expressive role, 325
Extended familism, 63–64, 133–134, 296, 299
Extended-familism-isolation, 11, 299–304
Extended family (*see* Family)
Extroversion, 466–467
"Exurbia," 140–141

Familial disorganization, 622–635
  as loss of consensus about roles, 627–628
  as loss of functionality, 631–632

Subject Index

Familial disorganization (*continued*)
  as moral evaluation, 624–627
  as reduction in the number of familial positions, 628–631
  and reorganization, 572–635
Familial functionality and the type of mate-selection, 264–266
Familial forms, American blacks, 73–74
  American Mormons, 73–74
  American rural, early, 75, 80–81, 129–131, 134
  American urban middle-class, 45, 75, 79, 134
  Chinese gentry, 32, 34, 35
  Chinese peasantry, 30–50
  domestic, 75, 286, 296, 298
    number of persons in, 322–323
  kibbutz, 51–70
Familial roles and role-strain, 307–343
Familial function (*see* Function)
Familial structure and composition of American families, 296–306
Familism, as defined by Burgess and Locke, 95–96
Familism, extended (*see* Extended familism)
Family, 11
  as almost functionless system, 4, 77–100
  as cause and as effect, 27–28
  conjugal, 11
  court, 576
  domestic, 11
  as economic unit, 78–94
  extended, 12
  functional and structural criteria for, 25–27
  incomplete nuclear, 12
  and job as major sources of gratification and security, 240–242
  life cycle, 347
    and adult offspring, 446–466
  loss of functions in, 257–258
  nuclear, 11
  of orientation, 12
  planning, 177–178
  of procreation, 12
  as self-sufficient economic system, 78–81
  as "woman's union," 465
  See also Function, familial; Structure, familial
Family-life education, 364–384
Father, biological, 193
  legitimator of child, 197–198
  social, 193
  See also Role, parental
Fecundity, 291
Female heads of households, 301–302
Fertility rate (*see* Birth rate)
Field of eligibles, 261–295, 486–487
Filial piety, 45
Filial responsibility, 94, 462–465
Folk-urban transition, 120–122, 138
Fondness, 564
Foster homes, 197
"Freedom of disappearance," 582
Frontier, disappearance of, 162

Frustration, reactions to in marriage, 559–560
Function, basic societal, 5, 9, 13, 14–19, 36–37, 103, 134
  core, 16–17
  as defined in this book, 9
  economic, 13, 15, 16, 34–35, 42, 58, 67, 75, 77–94, 99–100, 129, 138–142, 583–584, 609–611
  familial basic, replacement, 13, 14–15, 16, 42, 49, 153–190, 585–586, 612
  familial derived, control, 313, 385–469, 492–493, 586
    emotional gratification, 19–20, 49, 69, 236–258, 325, 356, 556–560, 586, 615–617
    nurturance, 313, 351–363, 385–469, 474, 492–493, 586
    parental, 21, 64–67, 312–313, 346–469
    position-conferring (status-conferring), 20–21, 68, 82, 111, 191–235, 325, 351, 398, 549, 586, 612–615
  family's loss of and suburbia, 132–149
  individual-oriented, 14–19
    as reward, 21–23
  as a Janus-faced concept, 13–14
  political, 13, 15, 17, 35–36, 42, 49, 58–59, 67, 94–98, 100, 129, 142–145, 584
  religious, 13, 15–16, 17, 36, 42, 49, 60–61, 67–68, 102, 103, 119–129, 148–149, 245–246, 585
  of replacement (*see* Function, familial basic)
  socializing-educational, 13, 15, 17, 36, 42, 59–60, 64–67, 101–119, 129, 146–148, 584–585, 611
  and societal complexity, 129–131
  society-oriented, 14–19
Functionality, 75
  family of great, 30–50
  family of little, 51–70
  and marital dissolution, 585–586
  and mate-selection, 264–266
Functional structure, 10
Functions, attributed to the family by Ogburn, 3–4
  of dating, 530–532, 539–540
  of engagement, 539–540
  of marriage, 547–550

"Generation gap," 250
Genitor (*see* Father, biological)
"Girls," in rural Ireland, 165
"Going steady," 538–539
"Good date," criteria used in defining, 529
Grandparent, function of, 461
  relation to offspring and grandchildren, 451–452
Grandparental generation, degree of isolation of, 456–457
Grandparenthood, 451–452
  three stages of, 455–456, 461
Gratification, emotional (*see* Function, familial derived)

Group, primary, 19–20
  social, 6
Guttman circumplex model, 493

Hedonic premise, 355
Heterogamy, 73
Home management, 326
Homosexuality, 546
Homeostasis, 354–355
Homogamy, 261, 287–288, 486–487
  See also Mate-selection, principle of ethnocentric preference in
Household, 10
  American, composition of, 629
  median size of, 298
  Bureau of the Census definition, 79
  plantation, 75
Housewifery, 413
Husband (see Role, marital)
Hypocrisy and conformity, 338–340

Ideal mate, cultural and psychic definitions of, 500, 532–538
Identification, 391–408, 485–486
  controlling function, 406
  culture, 393
  familial structure, 393, 404
  functionality, 406, 409
  influence of parents, 391–393, 437–438
  models, 391
  nurturant function, 406
  parents, as models, 399, 404
  number of, 410
Ideology of business, 126
Illegitimate birth, questions raised by, 195
Illegitimate child, conditions favoring mother's keeping, 195
Illegitimate pregnancy, penalties for, 196–197
Illegitimacy, 191
  legal, 194
  rates of, 194
  social, 194
  See also Bastardy; Legitimacy
Incest avoidance, principle of (see Mate-selection, principle of incest avoidance in)
Independence, in adulthood, 440–441
  economic, 99–100
  emotional, 478
Individualism, 96, 244–247
Individualists, 625, 626, 627
Industrial Revolution, 81, 162
Industrialization and the birth rate, 153–190
Infant, needs of, 475
Infanticide, 183, 187
Influence (see Identification; Power)
Inheritance, 200–203
  partible and impartible, 201, 202
  primogeniture and ultimogeniture, 201
Institution, 5, 10, 16, 72
  basic societal, 10
  See also Function; Structure
Institutional structure, 10
Institutionalists, 625, 626, 627
Instrumental role, 325

Interdependence, economic, 77, 99–100
Interracial marriages, percent of by race of bride and of groom, 271
"Intervening opportunities" (see Mate-selection)
"Introduction" services, 293
Isolation versus desolation, of aged, 460

Job and family as major sources of gratification and security, 240–242
Joint family (see Structure, familial)

Kibbutz, 25–27, 51–70
  family in, and social change, 62–64
  historical background of, 51–53
  joining the, 57
Kiryat Yedidim, 51–70
Kriegsvater, 153–154

Labor, division of, 77–78
  wives in, 162, 163, 166, 178
Lares and penates, 97
Lateran Council of 1215, 512
"Law of personal exploitation," 335, 545, 559
Legitimacy, 62, 192–198
  principle of, 194
  See also Illegitimacy
Levirate, 615
Lonely hearts clubs, 505–507
Looking-glass self, 244
Love, 473, 474–502, 508–527
  ambivalent, 484–485
  capacity for, 252, 478
  defined, 482–484
  infantile, 475
  "infatuation," 484–485
  parents' withdrawal of, 480
  pleasure as related to, 475
  and sex, 508–527
  theory of, 474–505
  in three relationships, 564–565
  "true," 485
Love-object, inaccessibility of, 537

Machine age, 81–83
Males, elderly, in the labor force, 89
Maintenance of dependents, 92–93
Man, assumptions concerning the nature of, 237
  as a responding machine, 237
  as self-propelling, 237
"Marasmus," 358
Marital adjustment, 550–569
  and changing roles, 560–565
  and complementary pairs, 557–558
  cultural discontinuity as source of difficult role-adjustment, 553
  dependence-independence, as personality trait in psychic adjustment, 556–560
  and desire for children, 548
  dissensus in definition of marital roles as source of difficult role-adjustment, 554
  factors operating in, before marriage, 568
  during marriage, 568–569
  measurement and prediction of, 565–569

Marital adjustment (*continued*)
  methodological defects in studies of, 566–567
  need-patterns, change in, 560–565
  nurturance, as personality trait in psychic adjustment, 556–560
  psychic adjustment, 551, 556–560
  role-adjustment, 551–556
  socialization, lack of, as source of difficult role-adjustment, 552–553
Marital dissolution, 573–604, 605–621
  alienation and mourning in, 615–616
  as legal substitute for divorce in California, 578
  causes of, 583–599
  emotional response to, 617
  ethnicity, 608–609
  familial functions, 607–618
  impact, on man, 608
    on woman, 608
  locality of resident, 607–608
  marital relationship, salience of, 607
  role-adjustment, 606–607, 612
  trends in the United States, 580–583
  types of, 574–575
  See also Divorce
Marital happiness, 550–551
Marital performance, subroles as criteria of, 551–556
Marital relations and filial obligations, 39–41
Marital roles and domestic power, 334–336
Marital status of American population 14 years old and over, 268
Marital success, 548, 550–551
Marriage, 544–570
  adjustment in, 550–569
  arranged, 44
  ascription and achievement in, 550
  broker, 293
  common-law, 194
  defined, 545
  early, 180, 292
  functions of, 547–550
  love (*see* Marriage, voluntary; Mate-selection, types of)
  Marriage Law of the People's Republic of China, 46–47
  marriage-registration area (MRA), 271
  matrilocal, 41, 231
  median age at first, 164, 165, 166, 168, 180
  neolocal, 231
  rate, 167
  teen-age, 290
  voluntary, 44, 46–47, 61–62, 69
  See also entries under Marital; Mate-selection
Married and unmarried, compared, 546–547
Mate-finding, 293
Mate-selection, 37–39, 61–62, 69, 261–295, 473–527
  age as dimension of, 282–284
  by arrangement, 264
  corporation's role in, 265–266
  criteria for, 38–39, 80–81

dimensions of ethnocentric preference in, 270–285
function in, 261–262
"intervening opportunities" in, 285–287
by mutual volition, 264
previous marital status as dimension of, 284
principle of ethnocentric preference in, 261–262, 270–289
principle of incest-avoidance in, 261–262
race as dimension of, 270–272
religioethnic identity as dimension of, 272–280
residential propinquity as dimension of, 269, 285–287
socioeconomic status as dimension of, 280–282
supplementary agencies of, 505–507
theory of complementary needs in, 487–504
"time-cost function" in, 285–287
types of, 264
  related to familial functionality, 264–266
voluntary, 46–47
Maternal role as the biosocial basis of infantile love, 361–363
Matrilocal marriage (*see* Marriage)
Median income of families by gender of head, 609
Migration, 299
  from farm to city, 82
Military structure as a position-conferring system, 227
Mixed marriage, 554
Mobility, 316
  and stability, 223–226
  in terms of consumption, 227
  upward, as subcultural goal of middle class, 211
  as a zero-sum game, 227
"Momism," 329
Monogamy, 409
"Moonlighting," 141
Moshav, 52
Moshava, 52, 66
Mother (*see* Role, parental)
Mother-child family (*see* Structure, familial)
Mother-daughter dyad, 465–466
"Mothering," 358, 478
Motivation, unconscious, 478–479
Multiple-job-holder, 141
Mutual aid, 134
Mutual volition, mate-selection by (*see* Mate-selection)

Name changing, 204
Need, defined, 475
"Need to be needed," 563
Needs, physical and social, 362–363
  in theory of love, 474
Neolocal marriage and residence, 231
Net reproduction rate, 158
"Neurotic paradox," 392
Nirvana, 237
Nonnutritional sucking, 356

Norm-senders, 309
Norms, disintegration of, 347–348
  social, subset of, 7
Nuclear dyad, 11
Nuclear family, 11
  See also Structure, familial
Nurturance, broad conception of, 356, 357–359
  narrow conception of, 356–357
  and three stages of grandparenthood, 455–456
  See also Function, parental; Receptiveness
Nurturant others, infant's belief in, 363

Occupational equality, 55
Occupational prestige, absence of differences in, 55
Office, 8
Offspring, role of, 16–17, 346–469
Old Order Amish, 82
"Oral" stage of human development, 356–357
"Organization man," 265–266, 339, 400, 442
Original nature, conceptions of, 104–106, 372–375
"Other-directed" personality, 339

Parental and childless marriages, relative gratifications of, 254–256
Parental and grandparental generations, contact between the, 457–462
Parental function (see Function)
Parental responsibility, 57, 195
Parenthood, and culture, 352–354, 413
  and emotional gratification, 246–256, 413
  penalties of, 249–250
  and personality, 250–254
  rewards of, 247–248
"Passing," 203
Pater (see Father, social)
Paternal role, 334
Pearl-Reed law of population growth, 157
Perjury, in divorce actions, 575
Personalities, manipulation of, 433
Personality, and parenthood, 250–254
  and role, 338–340
Pet as a psychic equivalent of a child, 254
Polyandry, 545
Polygamy, 545
Polygyny, 74, 545
Position (social), 5, 7, 18
  achieved and ascribed, 21, 191, 398–400
  family-oriented and society-oriented, 191–235
Position-conferring (see Function, familial derived)
"Poverty, culture of," 209
Power, 207
  familial, 23–25, 48, 98, 142–143
  of a societal structure, 23–25
Pregnancy, as occasion for marriage in Kiryat Yedidim, 62
Previous marital status (see Mate-selection)
Primary group, 236
Principle of ethnocentric preference, 261–263, 265, 270–285

Principle of incest avoidance, 261, 262, 265
Principle of least interest, 545
Principle of legitimacy, 193
Projective screen, 122–123
Property, communal and private, 200
  as influence, 203
Psychology of attraction, 473–507

Race, 73
  as ascribed characteristic, 203–205
  See also Mate-selection
Races, estimated time required for amalgamation of, 272
Rationalization, 479
Receptiveness, 441–442
Relationship, core, 8, 14–19, 36–37
  father-son, 36–37
  mother-daughter, 465–466
Religioethnic identification and familial structure, 300
Religioethnic identity (see Mate-selection)
Religion, in America, 73, 122–124
  as ascribed characteristic, 203–205
Religious function (see Function)
Remarriage, 618–620
Replacement, differentials in (see Birth rate)
  function of (see Function)
Repression, 480
Reproduction, extrafamilial, 154
  and the family, 153–154
Residential propinquity and segregation (see Mate-selection)
Resources, as rewards and potential control, 21–25, 77, 100, 391–393, 589–599
Response set, 494
Responsibility, filial, 94, 462–465
  parental, 94, 346–469
Retirement, 452–455
  and suicide, 245
Revolt of children, 96
Reward (see Resources)
Rite of passage, 420
"Robinson Crusoe" type of familial economy, 79
Role (social), 5, 6, 18
  expressive and instrumental, 325
  internalization of, 308–309
  marital, 551–556
  meanings of, 308
  parental, 346–469
  and personality, 338–340
Role-definers, 309
Role-differentiation, 307–343
Role-expectations, subset of, 7
Role-performance, 7
Role-strain, 307–343, 555–556
Roles, age-differentiated, 35, 44, 45, 79, 311–312
  gender-linked differences in, 26–27, 35, 41, 44, 48–49, 56–57, 62, 79, 311–312, 394, 397–398, 405–406
  of parent and child, reversal of, 462–465
  parental, differentiation of, 325, 329, 331–333, 404, 408
Romantic illusion, 537

Subject Index

"Rosenthal-effect," 216
Rural living, 73

Sabras, 62, 66–67
Secularization, 120–121, 244–245
 in American culture, 129
Security
 interpersonal, 241–245
 physical, 240
 psychic, 240–242, 245–246
 status, 241–244
 status and interpersonal, 242–244
 See also parallel distinction between Personality and role
Segregated conjugal role relationship, 560–561
Self-actualization, 244
Self-sufficiency, economic, 34, 99–100
Self-validation, child's task of, 251–252
"Selling oneself," 226
"Separation anxiety," 244, 481–482
Separation, marital (see Divorce; Marital dissolution)
Separation of work and home, 162
Separatism (see Cultural separatism)
Sex, 508–527
 in American society, 513–518
 differences (see Roles, gender-linked differences in)
 differentiation in occupations (see Roles, gender-linked differences in)
 dissociation from love, 520
 extramarital, 520
 fusion with love, 516–518
 premarital, 514–515, 539
 procreational and recreational, 182, 527
 romance, and love, 508–527
 in Sweden, 513
 in Western history, 511–513
Sexes, equality of (see Roles, gender-linked)
Sexual gratification, 549
Social classes (see Classes)
Social desirability, 494
Social function, 9
Social group, 6
Social mobility, 114–116
Social position, 7, 191–235
Social problem, Chinese, maintenance of aged as a new, 45
Social role, 6
Social status (see Status [social])
Social structure, 8
Social system, 6
Socialism, 54
Socialization, 101, 479–482
 for adult roles, 102
 aspects of, 102
 on basis of propinquity, 138
 on basis of social stratification, 138
 for familial roles, 101, 110
 and media of mass communication, 116–119
 for moral character, 102
 nature of, 104
 for occupations, 101
 for personality, 102
 for sex, 114
 for skills, intellectual and motor, 102
 See also Function, socializing-educational; Education
Societal complexity, 138, 152
Societal system, 6
Society, 4, 6
 folk and urban, 18
Socioeconomic status (see Status [socioeconomic])
Sociology, general, 1–29
Solidarity, "active" and "passive," 95
Spouse-candidates, field of eligible (see Field of eligibles)
Stability of family structure, 77
Station, 8
Status (social) 8, 191–235
 achieved and ascribed, 191, 398–400
 of the aged, 232–233
 of the child, 229–230
 society-oriented and family-oriented, age and sex categories, 228–233
 of women, 39–41, 230–232
 See also Position (social)
Status (socioeconomic), education, 216, 217
 as index of socioeconomic status, 207–208
 orientation to, 218
 related to income, 217–218
 income, as index of socioeconomic status, 207–208
 related to education, 217–218
 indexes of, 207–208
 occupation, 216
 as index of socioeconomic status, 207–208
 orientation to, 219
 occupational mobility, 223–226
 occupational prestige, 208
 rental value of the home, 208
Status-conferring by other structures in adulthood, 227–228
Status-inconsistency, 243
Status-orientation, of the child, 216
Sterilization, 178–179, 184
Stem family (see Structure, familial)
Stimulation, meagerness of, 359
Stratification, 55–56, 205–208
Structure, familial
 criterion for, 25–27
 domestic, 75, 286, 296, 298, 322–323
 extended, 15, 96
 incomplete nuclear, 74, 302–305
 joint, 46, 286, 296
 mother-child incomplete nuclear, 74, 302–305
 mother-child matrilineally extended, 74, 302–305
 nuclear, embedded in a network of extended kin, 302–305
 nuclear (isolated) 302–305
 nuclear (conjugal), 15, 19–21, 46, 301–305
 stem, 46
Structure, familial, categories of Zimmerman
 atomistic, 4, 95–97, 132

...ial, categories of Zimmerman (*continued*)
  domestic, 4, 95–97, 128, 132
  family, trustee, 4, 78, 95–97, 128, 132
Structure (social), 8
  analytic and concrete, 18
  basic societal, 10, 16–17
  functional, 10
  institutional, 10
Structures, differentiation of, 18
Subculture, 74, 80, 114–116
  of social classes, 208–215
Submissiveness, 441–442
Subroles as criteria of marital performance, 551–556
Subsistence-complexity, 297
Suburbia, family's response to the loss of functions, 132–149
Suburbs, conformity in, 143–145, 148
  differences among, 138
  differences between, and central cities, 136
  "dormitory," 138
  gregariousness in, 143–145, 148
  reasons for moving to, 135
  schools in, 146–148
  sex ratio of, shift in daylight and evening hours, 139
Succorance, 441
Suicide, 244–245
Suttee, 615
System, social, 4, 6
  societal, 6

Tabula rasa, 237
Television, effects of, on children, 116–119
  viewing time of children by social class, 116–117

"Tenderness taboo," 239
Tension, 475
Tension-activity-equilibrium cycle, 354–355
Tension reduction, 361
Testamentary freedom, 200, 201 (*see* Will-making)
Theology, determinants of, 121–122
  and stress, 121–122
"Time-cost function" (*see* Mate-selection)
Transvestite, 427
Trial marriage, 513

Unmarried, proportion of, 165, 180
"Unpleasure," 354
Unwanted births, 181
Urban, census definitions, 75
Urban living, 73
Urbanization, 132, 152
  and the birth rate, 153–190

Values in American culture, 125–126

Welfare programs and family stability, 93–94
White-collar jobs, 315
Wife (*see* Role, marital)
Wife-mother, subroles of in American middle class, 139
Will-making, 97, 201
Woman's dilemma, 326–333
Women, in labor force, 85–86, 133, 140, 317–319
  status of (*see* Roles, gender-linked differences in)
Women's liberation, 96, 330

Youth problems, 96

DATE DUE

DEC 10 87			
MAY 23 88			
OCT 18 88			
JA 4'91			
JA10'94			
MY20'95			
NO28'98			
12-18			
MY 5 00			

```
HQ                        104016
728
.W55     Winch, Robert F.
1971        The modern family
```

HIEBERT LIBRARY
Fresno Pacific College - M. B. Seminary
Fresno, Calif. 93702